THE ROUTLEDGE HISTORY OF CHILDHOOD IN THE WESTERN WORLD

The Routledge History of Childhood in the Western World provides an important overview of the main themes surrounding the history of childhood in the West from antiquity to the present day. By broadly incorporating the research in the field of childhood studies, the book explores the major advances that have taken place in the past few decades in this crucial field.

The volume is composed of three parts. The first part explores childhood from the Ancient World through to the Middle Ages and Early Modern Europe. The second part examines the fundamental aspects of childhood and the life of children in the West since 1500. The essays address issues such as family, work, law, sexuality, and consumption. The chapters think beyond national and continental boundaries so that readers are informed about general trends in the West, while still alert to differences in gender, class, race, and time.

The final part focuses on aspects of children's experiences in the modern world. This section explains how childhoods have developed in distinct contexts and among specific children by using the growing literature on modern childhoods in various locales and at particular historical moments.

Including essays on all the key topics and issues, *The Routledge History of Childhood in the Western World* defines how the history of children and childhood can best be understood, in the longue durée and comparatively, while still acknowledging the importance of and encouraging scholarship on specific groups, periods, places, and life course divisions. This important collection from a leading international group of scholars presents a comprehensive survey of the current state of the field. It is essential reading for all those interested in the history of childhood.

Paula S. Fass is the Margaret Byrne Professor of History at the University of California, Berkeley, USA. Her publications include *Children of a New World* (2007), *The Encyclopedia of Children and Childhood in History and Society* (2004), *Kidnapped: Child Abduction in America* (1997), and *Reinventing Childhood After World War II* (2012), edited with Michael Grossberg.

THE ROUTLEDGE HISTORIES

The Routledge Histories is a series of landmark books surveying some of the most important topics and themes in history today. Edited and written by an international team of world-renowned experts, they are the works against which all future books on their subjects will be judged.

THE ROUTLEDGE HISTORY OF WOMEN IN EUROPE SINCE 1700
Edited by Deborah Simonton

THE ROUTLEDGE HISTORY OF SLAVERY
Edited by Gad Heuman and Trevor Burnard

THE ROUTLEDGE HISTORY OF THE HOLOCAUST
Edited by Jonathan C. Friedman

Forthcoming:

THE ROUTLEDGE HISTORY OF SEX AND THE BODY
Edited by Kate Fisher and Sarah Toulalan

THE ROUTLEDGE HISTORY OF EAST CENTRAL EUROPE
Edited by Irina Livezeanu and Arpad von Klimo

THE ROUTLEDGE HISTORY OF CHILDHOOD IN THE WESTERN WORLD

Edited by Paula S. Fass

Routledge
Taylor & Francis Group

LONDON AND NEW YORK

First published 2013
by Routledge
2 Park Square, Milton Park, Abingdon, Oxon OX14 4RN

Simultaneously published in the USA and Canada
by Routledge
711 Third Avenue, New York, NY 10017

Routledge is an imprint of the Taylor & Francis Group, an informa business

British Library Cataloguing in Publication Data
A catalogue record for this book is available from the British Library

Library of Congress Cataloging in Publication Data
The Routledge history of childhood in the western world/
edited by Paula S. Fass.
p. cm. – (The Routledge histories)
Includes bibliographical references and index.
1. Children–Western countries–History.
I. Fass, Paula S.
HQ767.87.R68 2012
305.2309182'1–dc23   2012025119

ISBN: 978-0-415-78232-6 (hbk)
ISBN: 978-0-203-07571-5 (ebk)

Typeset in Sabon by
Sunrise Setting Ltd

MIX
Paper from
responsible sources
FSC   FSC® C004839
www.fsc.org

Printed and bound in Great Britain by
TJ International Ltd, Padstow, Cornwall

FOR JACK, ALWAYS

CONTENTS

CONTENTS

CONTENTS

FIGURES

CONTRIBUTORS

Beth Bailey, Professor of History at Temple University, is a social/cultural historian of the twentieth-century United States with a longstanding interest in the history of childhood and youth. She has authored or co-authored several books, including *From Front Porch to Back Seat: Courtship in Twentieth Century America, Sex in the Heartland,* and the widely assigned US history textbook, *A People and a Nation;* her most recent book is *America's Army: Making the All-Volunteer Force* (2009).

Keith Bradley is an internationally known historian of Roman society and culture. Born in England and educated at Sheffield University and Oxford University, he has held appointments at Johns Hopkins, Stanford, and the University of Victoria, British Columbia, Canada. He is currently the Eli J. and Helen Shaheen Chair in Classics and Concurrent Professor of History at the University of Notre Dame.

Daniel Thomas Cook is Associate Professor of Childhood Studies and Sociology at Rutgers University, Camden, New Jersey, and serves as an Editor for the journal *Childhood.* He is author of *The Commodification of Childhood* (Duke, 2004), editor of *Lived Experiences of Public Consumption* (Palgrave, 2008) and co-Editor (with John Wall) of *Children and Armed Conflict* (Palgrave, 2011), and author of a number of articles and book chapters on consumer society, childhood, leisure, and urban culture.

Gary Cross is Distinguished Professor of Modern History at Pennsylvania State University, author of *Kids' Stuff: Toys and the Changing World of American Childhood, The Cute and the Cool: Wondrous Innocence and Modern American Children's Culture,* and *Men to Boys: The Making of Modern Immaturity.* Currently he is completing *Packaged Pleasures: Technology and Desire in the Age of Consumerism* with Robert Proctor, and *Consuming Nostalgia in America.*

Paula S. Fass, Margaret Byrne Professor of History at the University of California, Berkeley, is the author of many books and articles, including *The Damned and the Beautiful: American Youth in the 1920s, Children of a New World: Society, Culture, and Globalization,* and *Inheriting the Holocaust: A Second Generation Memoir.* She edited *The Encyclopedia of Children and Childhood in History and*

Society, Childhood in America and most recently *Reinventing Childhood After World War II*. She is a member of the American Philosophical Society.

Joanne M. Ferraro is Professor and Chair of History at San Diego State University. Her publications include *Venice: History of the Floating City* (Cambridge University Press, 2012), *Nefarious Crimes, Contested Justice: Illicit Sex and Infanticide in the Republic of Venice 1557–1789* (Johns Hopkins University Press, 2008), *Marriage Wars in Late Renaissance Venice* (Oxford University Press, 2001), and *Family and Public Life in Brescia, 1580–1650: The Foundations of Power in the Venetian State* (Cambridge University Press, 1993).

Timothy J. Gilfoyle is Professor of History at Loyola University, Chicago, where he teaches American urban and social history. He is the author of *A Pickpocket's Tale: The Underworld of Nineteenth-Century New York* (W.W. Norton, 2006); *City of Eros: New York City, Prostitution, and the Commercialization of Sex, 1790–1920* (W.W. Norton, 1992), and *Millennium Park: Creating a Chicago Landmark* (University of Chicago Press and the Chicago History Museum, 2006). He most recently published *The Flash Press: Sporting Men's Weeklies in the 1840s*, co-authored with Patricia Cline Cohen and Helen Lefkowitz Horowitz (University of Chicago Press, 2008).

Julia Grant is Professor of History and Social Policy, and Associate Dean, at James Madison College, Michigan State University. She published *Raising Baby by the Book* (Yale, 1998), and co-edited with Barbara Beatty and Emily Cahan, *When Science Encounters the Child: Education, Parenting, and Child Welfare in Twentieth-Century America* (Teachers College, 2006). She has written essays on motherhood, childhood, gender, masculinity, and the intersections between the history of childhood and public policy. She is currently completing a book called *The Boy Problem in Urban America: 1890–1960* for Johns Hopkins University Press.

Marta Gutman teaches architectural and urban history at the Bernard and Anne Spitzer School of Architecture at the City College of the City University of New York. Her current book project starts at the Gold Rush and spans a one-hundred-year period to tell the story of California's children and show how women repurposed everyday buildings to make the world a better place for children. Gutman also co-edits *Buildings & Landscapes: The Journal of the Vernacular Architecture Forum*.

Colin Heywood is Professor of Modern French History at the University of Nottingham. His publications include *A History of Childhood in Nineteenth-Century France* (1988), *A History of Childhood* (2001), and *Growing Up in France* (2007). He is currently working on a history of childhood and youth in modern Europe.

Anne Higonnet is the Ann Whitney Olin Professor of Art History at Barnard College, Columbia University. Her books include *Pictures of Innocence: the History and Crisis of Ideal Childhood* (1998). Her many awards include Guggenheim, Getty, and Social Science Research Council fellowships, as well as grants from the Mellon, Howard, and Kress Foundations.

Anne F. Hyde is Professor of History at Colorado College. Her recent publications include "Hard Choices: Mixed Race Parents and Children in a Post-Conquest West" in *Love and Power in the American West*, edited by David Adams and Crista DeLuzio (2012) and *Empires, Nations and Families: A History of the North American West, 1800–1860* (2011), which was the winner of the Bancroft Prize and a Pulitzer Prize Finalist.

Ivan Jablonka is Associate Professor at the Université du Maine, France and Associated Scholar at the Collège de France, Paris. His recent publications include *Les Enfants de la République. L'intégration des Jeunes de 1789 à nos Jours* (Seuil, 2010), *Histoire des Grands-Parents que je n'ai pas eus* (Seuil, 2012), "Children and the State" in *The French Republic, History, Values, Debates* edited by E. Berenson, V. Duclert, and C. Prochasson (Cornell University Press, 2011).

Margaret L. King, Professor of History emerita at Brooklyn College and the Graduate Center, CUNY, researches in the fields of humanism, Renaissance Venice, women and learning, and the history of childhood. She is Editor-in-Chief of Oxford Bibliographies Renaissance/Reformation, and will publish her book *Mothers and Sons: a History* with the University of Chicago Press in 2013.

Stephen Lassonde is author of *Learning to Forget: Schooling and Family Life in New Haven's Working Class, 1870–1940* (Yale University Press, 2005). He teaches in the History Department at Brown University and is Deputy Dean of the College.

Kriste Lindenmeyer is a historian and the Dean of the Faculty of Arts and Sciences at Rutgers University, Camden. Previous to coming to Rutgers she was Professor and Chair of the History Department at the University of Maryland, Baltimore. She is the author of *The Greatest Generation Grows Up: Childhood in 1930s America* and *"A Right to Childhood": The US Children's Bureau and Child Welfare, 1912–1946.*

Dominique Marshall teaches Canadian and Quebec history at Carleton University. She researches the history of poverty and welfare, families and childhood, state formation and political economy, as well as the transnational history of humanitarian aid. She has written about the history of the Canadian welfare state, the history of children's rights and the Child Welfare Committee of the League of Nations. Her book, *Aux Origines Sociales de l'État Providence* (1998) [available in English as *The Social Origins of the Welfare State* (2006)] received the Jean-Charles Falardeau Prize from the Canadian Federation for the Humanities and Social Sciences.

James Marten is Professor of History at Marquette University. He is the author or editor of fifteen books, including *Children and War: A Historical Anthology* (2002) and *The Children's Civil War* (1998), and co-general editor of Berg's six-volume *Cultural History of Childhood and Family* (2010).

Jay Mechling is Professor Emeritus of American Studies at the University of California, Davis. He is the co-editor of *Children's Folklore: A Sourcebook* (1999) and the author of *On My Honor: Boy Scouts and the Making of American Youth* (2001).

Nara Milanich is Associate Professor of History at Barnard College. Her book, *Children of Fate: Childhood, Class and the State in Chile, 1850–1930* (Duke University

Press, 2009), received the Grace Abbott Book Prize from the Society for the History of Children and Youth. She has written about the history of children, family, law, and labor in the *Hispanic American Historical Review*, *American Historical Review*, and *Journal of Social History*.

Steven Mintz is the past president of the Society for the History of Children and Youth and editor of H-Net: Humanities and Social Sciences Online, and directs Columbia University's Graduate School of Arts & Sciences Teaching Center. His thirteen books include *Huck's Raft: A History of American Childhood* and *African American Voices: The Life Cycle of Slavery*. The creator of the Digital History website (http://www.digitalhistory.uh.edu), he moderates H-Slavery, a scholarly discussion list on slavery, the slave trade, abolition, and emancipation.

Maria Nikolajeva is Professor of Education at the University of Cambridge, UK. She is the author and editor of numerous books, the most recent *Power, Voice and Subjectivity in Literature for Young Readers* (2010). In 2005 she received the International Grimm Award for a lifetime achievement in children's literature research.

Don Romesburg is Associate Professor in the Sonoma State University Women's and Gender Studies Department and Co-Chair of the Committee on Lesbian, Gay, Bisexual, and Transgender History, an American Historical Association-affiliated society. His scholarship addresses the history of US adolescence and homosexuality.

Bengt Sandin is Professor of Child Studies, Department of Thematic Studies at the University of Linköping, Sweden. His publications include studies on early modern education and state building, child labor, street children, educational media politics, and welfare politics and the history of child psychiatry in Sweden. His recent publications include *Neither Fish nor Fowl, Educational Broadcasting in Sweden 1930–2000* with Maija Runcis (Falun 2010), and "Children and the Swedish Welfare State, from Different to Similar" in *Reinventing Childhood After World War II*, edited by Paula S. Fass and Michael Grossberg (University of Pennsylvania Press, 2011).

James D. Schmidt is Professor of History at Northern Illinois University. His most recent book is *Industrial Violence and the Origins of Child Labor* (Cambridge University Press, 2010). He is currently working on a book about corporal punishment and the legalities of school authority in the nineteenth- and twentieth-century United States.

Dirk Schumann is Professor of Modern and Contemporary History at Georg-August University, Göttingen. His most recent books include *Raising Citizens in the 'Century of the Child': The United States and German Central Europe in Comparative Perspective* (2010, edited) and *Political Violence in the Weimar Republic, 1918–1933: Fight for the Streets and Fear of Civil War* (2009).

Peter N. Stearns is Provost and University Professor at George Mason University. Stearns has authored or edited over 115 books. He has published widely in modern social history, including the history of emotions, and in world history. Representative recent works include *Satisfaction Not Guaranteed: Dilemmas of Progress in Modern Society, Doing Emotions History, Human Rights in World History*, and

Demilitarization in Modern History. He has also edited encyclopedias of world and social history, and since 1967 has served as editor-in-chief of *The Journal of Social History.*

Larry Wolff is Professor of History at New York University. His books include *Postcards from the End of the World: Child Abuse in Freud's Vienna* (1988), *Inventing Eastern Europe: The Map of Civilization on the Mind of the Enlightenment* (1994), *The Idea of Galicia: History and Fantasy in Habsburg Political Culture* (2010), and *Paolina's Innocence: Child Abuse in Casanova's Venice* (2012). He is a member of the American Academy of Arts and Sciences.

ACKNOWLEDGEMENTS

It has been a pleasure and a privilege to work with the twenty-seven authors of this extraordinary volume, which is a landmark in the new field of children's history. I am grateful for their good humor in responding to an editor's sometimes crotchety demands. I hope they feel that their willingness to join this project has been worthwhile.

There are many others whose assistance has been invaluable as I set out to organize and enlist participants for this volume. Among them, I would like to acknowledge especially Michael Grossberg, Carlos Noreña, Maria Mavroudi, Susanna Elm, Geoffrey Koziol, Nancy Sinkoff, Laura Lee Downes, and Laura Bell. At Routledge, Eve Setch has been there from the beginning and her persistence made the volume possible as she gave me the freedom to make it come together. More than anyone else, she is the mother of this volume. Laura Mothersole has been unfailingly helpful and solicitous, and Jessica Stock and Angela Yates helped to oversee the production. Finally, Alex Couglin at the Berkeley History Department and my graduate assistance, Andrea Kwon (who created the index), did excellent work as they put the final touches on what, for me (most of the time), has been a labor of love.

IS THERE A STORY IN THE HISTORY OF CHILDHOOD?

Paula S. Fass

When Philippe Ariès published *Centuries of Childhood*, a history of childhood over the course of four hundred years, in 1960 (in French, translated into English 1962),[1] he almost certainly did not know that he would begin a long history of his own, one in which his book would generate applause and outrage, and in the long term a wealth of research in a new field of history. There had been others who believed that children could be studied historically, but no one before Ariès had made the study of childhood an essential component for understanding modern western development. And no one else had provided such a good story. *Centuries of Childhood* was fertile in controversy at the time. More significantly it showed scholars that raising pointed questions about childhood in order to imagine the earliest (and least historically accessible) stage of life, and about childhood as a important element of change, could be a fascinating and fruitful, even an urgent, historical endeavor.

I begin this book with Ariès because, as the reader will shortly discover, at least one half of the authors notice him in their essays, but mostly because I hope that this volume, coming as it does fifty years after the English language edition of *Centuries of Childhood*, will firmly replace his book, both among professionals and among the more general reading public. Despite millions of words since 1960 on the subject of childhood history, Ariès's remains usually the first, and often the only, book that is read in this rich and dynamic field. And the new childhood history has itself hardly been integrated into the larger picture of western development. It is time, I am certain, to change that and to bring to a large audience the fruits of a new and vibrant scholarship that takes children and childhood seriously as historically important subjects. That scholarship is deeply sourced in many places and times in the western past. *The Routledge History of Childhood in the Western World* is intended to be read both as a culmination of an impressive scholarship incorporated into the essays that follow on a wide range of subjects relating to children, and as an introduction to the field. We now know a lot that Ariès did not know. All of the essays are original works of scholarship in themselves as well as far ranging interpretations of their specific subjects, and each provides readers with an entry into that scholarship and a set of suggested further readings to lead the reader into the much broader scholarship that lies behind it.

One of the things that Ariès did brilliantly was to tell a compelling, even a sensational, story and he made his argument both simple and vivid. That story, in its clear outlines, urged readers fifty years ago to imagine childhood as the invention of early modern Europe. How we feel about children and how we think about them – matters we often imagine to be natural – Ariès argued, began at a particular point in time as a result of changing material and intellectual circumstances. Children had once played the same games as adults, witnessed sexual activity, and as schoolchildren wandered at an early age from teacher to teacher and place to place. They were depicted as small adults. All this changed when adults began to think of children as different and to treat childhood as a special stage of life. Childhood began with a new sensibility about the young that resulted in a view of children as requiring particular and elaborate treatment. Ariès used the present as a touchstone for the past and his story is about the creation of a childhood that modern people can identify with and understand. In proclaiming childhood an invention of modern Europe, Ariès caught people by surprise and he captured their attention.

Ariès also made the specialness of childhood coincide with important historical changes and with a variety of alterations that we today define as modern in perspective and in institutions: a new attention to age ever more carefully measured; an emphasis on privacy within a closely defined and enclosed family that becomes much more oriented to matters of child rearing; the elaboration of capitalist markets and new class distinctions; and a new emphasis on literacy and the spread of schooling. In pointing out how childhood was a product of these changes and essential to them, Ariès made the new childhood both historically contingent and worthy of attention. In line with these changes, parents became much more involved with and attached to their children and began to provide them with the affection that moderns assume to be "natural" to parenting. In the process, Ariès made some harsh judgments about parents in the preceding period of time; harsh at least from our modern perspective though hardly from his own more romantic view of the pre-modern world. His was a compelling story vividly told and illustrated about a time when everything changed, so much so that something so fundamental as childhood, which we all take for granted, was just beginning to peek through the fresh historical soil. Do we now have a story good enough to replace his, and one that can garner the kind of attention that was and still is directed at Ariès?

I believe that we do. It is a story that is perhaps less surprising than the one Ariès offered, but just as compelling. The story that unfolds from the following twenty-seven essays, written by talented historians from different backgrounds, two continents, and several historical generations, is about childhood in the West as a privileged state, a status to which some children have historically had much more access than others. One of the clear conclusions that historians have come to is that modern childhoods and children's experiences are deeply affected by circumstances such as status, class, wealth, and poverty. As a result, while all children have a childhood, the kind of childhood we have come to imagine as desirable and to expect in the modern West has been available unevenly in the past, while the emphasis on this childhood has grown.

As modern Westerners have conceived and defined it, childhood as a space for development and an agent of future promise is not so much a product of a particular time as it has been a possibility that was accelerated within the conditions of the early modern period when Ariès first noticed it. The sixteenth century was fruitful in launching some of the initial conditions that turned childhood into a privilege increasingly defined as widely desirable and socially useful. But it was hardly the period that enabled the wholesale access to childhood that *Centuries of Childhood* seems to claim, not least because schooling was still only available to very few (and only rarely for girls). Indeed, it was not until the nineteenth century, at the earliest, that childhood – at least one that modern westerners can recognize – seems to have become a universal aspiration as nation states inserted it among the ideals of citizenship.

The privileges of childhood are often related to other privileges, such as race, class, wealth, and sometimes gender. But the story of childhood as a privilege is also about how western societies in the period since the nineteenth century laid out a pattern, even a paradigm, that has increasingly defined, constrained, and regulated the lives of all children as it penetrated our belief systems as not only ideal but as a requirement of proper development. By adopting various institutions that enshrined the privileges of childhood, the West has enforced these as necessary and uniquely appropriate for children. That paradigm has also spread beyond the developed West to exercise increasing influence on the nature of childhood images and children's experiences throughout the globe. It has done so through organized endeavors that Dominique Marshall examines in her essay on international child saving, but also through the products of childhood and the pictures of childhood created in the West. Some of these, as Gary Cross shows, are consumer items that appeal to children as a group apart. It is for this reason that this volume ends not in Europe or North America, which are within the traditional confines of what we usually designate as the "West," but in Latin America which is globally west but also decidedly south. Nara Milanich clearly shows how Latin American childhood has been connected to the western experience of privilege, while access to those privileges are much more exclusive and elusive in countries in the southern hemisphere.

The volume also begins well before the modern period, starting in the ancient classical world and the ancient Middle East where the dominant western religions of Judaism and Christianity were born. Ancient Greece and Rome, as well as these two religions (and later Islam), held out very particular views of childhood that have never been entirely forgotten, in part because they left a wealth of significant texts. Examining these sources, as Keith Bradley and Margaret King do in their essays, makes it clear that childhood was hardly an invention of the last four hundred years as Ariès argued. Rather, even two thousand years ago children were regarded as critical to both the future and the present; then, as now, they were objects of care and observation. In the Ancient World, as in the modern, certain aspects of childhood – especially those related to careful preparation – were a privilege only available to some. Indeed, Bradley argues that the children of the free and well-born lived in a vast sea of those deprived. In Greece and Rome, the privileges of childhood were reserved for a very few, almost all of whom were male and free. That acute delimitation of privilege has receded in the modern West, not least because Judaism and Christianity, birthed in almost the same region, introduced childhood as a positive and respected part of human experience with universal potentials.

The continuing privileges and the aspiring universalism of childhood are together the two most resonant aspects of the story that the authors of this volume tell about the period since 1500, and this story unfolds in many places and in various accents to the present. It is clear that despite Ariès's best attempts to claim that it did not exist in the medieval period, historians have recognized not only children but also the outlines of a childhood in that long period between ancient and modern times. Children then might enjoy the love and attention of parents as Joanne Ferraro demonstrates, although large portions of the population had to contend with the vicissitudes of brutal circumstances and the general unpredictability of life in Europe where marauding gangs, famine, and disease were a constant presence. Childhood for all was shorter and many children left the parental home earlier, and those who were otherwise privileged could also provide some special protections to their own children, although parenting was far more at the mercy of a decimating mortality. And while the sixteenth century introduced some changes, they hardly marked the radical revolution that Ariès suggested.

How all this affected parents' love is not easy to resolve because, like many other privileges, it is one that not all children experience equally,[2] but the historical record has rectified Ariès's error; one expressed by others during the earliest phase of investigations into the history of children when the nature of modern childhood was confused with the elaboration of expressions of family affection. The love for children cannot be said to have begun at any one point in history, while the callous treatment of children cannot be said to have ended once modern times began. Of course, certain circumstances could make the life of children brutal and their parents could do little to relieve the coarseness of their lives. This was true of slave children in the Ancient World, as Keith Bradley makes clear, and in the Americas during the modern age, as Steven Mintz shows. Unwanted children everywhere throughout the West were often disposable, killed as infants or abandoned to institutions or to the streets. The history of infanticide, as Bengt Sandin shows in the case of Sweden, is long and winding, intersecting with matters of church control, state development, as well as cultural mores and broader issues of social welfare.

A child's life in the past, like that of an adult, could be brutal but it was not brutal because it was the life of a child and therefore did not matter. Judaism and Christianity both made child life vital and important and created certain protections for childhood – so did Islam. But circumstances could make even loving parents unable to protect their children and it could make people both caring and brutal. The same nineteenth-century planter who loved and indulged his sons and daughters could create conditions that made his slaves teach their own children qualities that would make for endurance. So too, during the same period, while children's books and illustrations dwelled on the wonderful beauty and innocence of children, the West produced the factory routine which allowed, as Colin Heywood shows, terrific exploitation, long hours and dangerous working conditions for masses of working class children as young as five or six. In Latin America, middle-class people imitated European customs of the time and provided their children with overtly solicitous affection while dismissing, as refuse, the many children who resulted from illegitimate unions. Childhoods, both as ideals and as the experiences of children, change and reflect the institutional networks of a particular time and place; so too do the forms in which parents express love and caretaking. But brutality toward children is hardly the criterion by which we can judge change over time.

Childhood impinges on so many institutional realms that it is difficult, at first, to see where the story ends, or rather to separate its boundaries from the history of the West more generally. And this is part of the point; childhood, as it has developed and changed over time in the West, has not only affected the experience of almost one half of the population, but the political, economic, cultural, and social institutions created for or directed at childhood move out in widening circles of strategic influence. These circles have become much more dramatically linked in the recent West as childhood became more consciously a public concern. Some of these nests for childhood are obvious such as parenting and schooling; others require only a bit of further reflection. Such is the case with regard to the welfare institutions for orphans and delinquents that Ivan Jablonka examines, or the physical environment of buildings and objects. As childhood became a more pressing public obligation in the modern world these latter institutions evolved around the perceived needs of children. Ariès recognized that the modern world has been fertile in creating institutional and physical arrangements that are aimed specifically at children or target children in special ways, and he helped to set many historians on the path of discovering these places and material environments, as Marta Gutman shows.

Twenty-first-century readers are less inclined to see how crucial work was for childhood and indeed how integral children in the past were to the world of work, but the connection will become obvious after reading Colin Heywood's essay. Children's work has been, through most of western history including the modern period, an essential contribution to social life. During the period Ariès thought brought childhood into being, children's everyday lives were still dominated not by schooling but by labor. Most children remained deeply embedded in household regimes and routines, not so different than in the medieval period, and children continued to work even as schooling gained in significance after the middle of the nineteenth century, although they often worked outside the house. This began to vary somewhat by age by the late nineteenth century as young children were increasingly shielded from work outside the house or the farm, but work continued to define child life for older children, by which we mean those over twelve.

The same is the case for other fundamental dimensions of life and death. War and sexuality are domains from which modern Westerners have withdrawn the ideal of childhood in horror, but neither children in the past nor contemporary childhood experiences are without important connections to these arenas. Sexuality, long before Sigmund Freud made the connection, was not absent from the lives of children, as Beth Bailey shows, and the many experiences of war that James Marten examines often loomed darkly at its center. Even during the eighteenth-century Enlightenment, as Larry Wolff vividly demonstrates, the very same people who emphasized the innocence of children could find them erotically compelling. Modern Westerners have circumscribed the lives of children, marking these two arenas – sex and war – as beyond the realm of childhood, largely because they have become much more exacting about prescribing norms of development, as discussed by Stephen Lassonde. In this sense, Ariès was on target when he recognized the growing importance that the consciousness of age has played in the modern West. But as James Marten shows, even in the modern period, soldiering was often child's work simply because, until fairly recently, age simply did not matter as much; at least not as a precise measure and in many cases, it was simply unknown. Today everyone knows his or her age in the western world because the state requires various kinds of registrations.[3]

One of the great virtues of Ariès's book was to make readers aware that our modern views of children and the values we attach to childhood were subject to change. Even though he was too quick to dismiss childhood before the modern period and to ignore its variability during the modern period, he understood that we tend to see childhood through very modern lenses and have a difficult time recognizing it (as he did) when those lenses did not exist. Our lenses have been constructed, quite literally, out of images in literature for children that Maria Nikolajeva describes and the visual arts, as examined by Anne Higonnet. These have been fashioned over the last two hundred and fifty years but came to a special fruition in the second half of the nineteenth century. Indeed, Higonnet argues that childhood and photography evolved together, intimately connected in each other's sights. Perhaps the most potent source for our understanding of modern childhood as a particular form of vision was embedded in the philosophies and beliefs that came out of the European Enlightenment, as discussed by Larry Wolff. Certainly our child-rearing literature, pedagogical views, and our implicit values regarding children's innocence are deeply indebted to its insights and observations. These have been deeply engaged in the past century, as Stephen Lassonde demonstrates, as psychologies of childhood and the science of development became rich and fertile intellectual enterprises. The Enlightenment and the sciences it helped to promote accelerated the universalism that western religion had extoled, effectively defining childhood as a necessary basis for human experience.

How we as modern Westerners see children and understand childhood has been altered in important ways because we are committed to withdrawing them from certain adult spheres like war and sexuality, a messy process considering that over the past one hundred years schooling (now defined as a child's realm) has increased vastly as a time commitment that now includes adolescence under its aegis. Adolescents have been more and more exiled from the world of work where they once fitted quite closely either as apprentices or as important components of the agricultural or industrial work force. But modern adolescence, which is at once a separate life phase and deeply implicated in the social institutions of childhood, is probably at the forefront of both matters of sexuality and of modern consumerism. A moment's thought points up not just the contradictions that modern adolescence injects into childhood but its uncertain privileges. It is adolescents above all (though hardly exclusively) who have haunted society since at least the seventeenth century in the guise of the potential for disorder or delinquency, as Don Romesburg demonstrates. They also play parts, shown by Timothy Gilfoyle, that have given them an unusual agency and power when, as young criminals, they transgressed the dominant definitions of sentimental childhood as innocent, helpless, and guileless. Indeed, sex and war have often been at the very center of adolescent identity.

The first two sections of this volume aim to demonstrate how we have come to the tangled and potent place we are today with regard to children and childhood. Part I shows how children were treated in the long distant past and how they have been imagined in the most powerful currents of western thought before the nineteenth century. The reader is invited to think about the many differences between the experiences of childhood in the Ancient World, the Middle Ages, and in the modern period, but also how childhood as a form of preparation was carefully defined for those who were privileged to experience it fully. In looking toward the modern, the Enlightenment opened up childhood as a fundamental arena for human reflection and defined its contradictory currents. Part II is meant to provide readers with a wide perspective on how modern institutions, views and values with regard to childhood have evolved and changed over time since the early modern period, and the nature of the space that has been created for children by institutions as varied as the state, examined by

James Schmidt; changes in parenting practices as examined by Julia Grant; and the emotional expectations embedded in modern childrearing advice, discussed by Peter Stearns. Part II looks at the multiple means by which modern childhood has been elaborated through institutions, representations, sentiments, and ideas. Each of the authors in this section has been asked to look at the period since 1500 in the long term and to examine the many changes over time that affected children and resulted in the "modern" western view of childhood and the expectations that we have about what children's lives should be like. These essays clearly show that the "modern" perspective on children as sexually innocent, economically dependent, and emotionally fragile whose lives are supposed to be dominated by play, school, and family nurture, provides a very limited view of children's lives in the modern western past. While some children did experience this kind of childhood, for the vast majority, it is quite literally only in the twentieth century that these have been enforced as both preferred and dominant.

Since the eighteenth century, Westerners have defined, pictured, and written about childhood as a privileged ethereal realm that we all desire personally and socially. This "Age of Innocence," as Sir Joshua Reynolds helpfully named his painting, has motivated a variety of reforms both within nations in the West and across them; served as the basis for schooling; underscored the drive for good parenting advice; and stimulated global ideals of children's rights, which the West has carried to the rest of the world in the twentieth and twenty-first centuries. But as historians have discovered, these values, despite their seeming universal valence, have never been evenly experienced or applied. The West in general has been far more privileged than other parts of the globe, so over the past two centuries, it has been able to entertain these ideas and to provide more of its children with its privileges. It has also been very unevenly experienced within the West as some children could afford such a childhood while others, as Timothy Gilfoyle shows, became thieves and other criminals, roles hardly associated with innocent childhood. Some children worked early in the fields under a whiplash, while others drank sodas after school. Even in the American West, the privileges associated with childhood could be removed, as Anne Hyde demonstrates by examining the changing fate of mixed-race children. The history of childhood tells a real story, but it is not uniform and it is not fair.

These articles on sex, work, parenting, consumption, etc. are about both children and childhood and it is worth stopping briefly to talk about these two different but intertwined subjects. In its simplest form these two encompass what children do and what social norms and expectations define as appropriate to the period of life that children inhabit. But it is never quite that simple. The actual experiences of children are not only usually recorded through adult means (though we do have some evidence that is less dependent on adult observation and more direct), but expectations also define what children can do because the institutions that are created for them, such as schools, or barred to them, such as work, are fashioned through ideas and ideals regarding what childhood should be. As nineteenth-century reformers found themselves revolted by observing young children working long hours in terrible conditions and worried about them as future citizens, they began to ask for legislation that enshrined certain ages as off-limits to work and reserved for childhood. This delimiting of childhood spread by the late nineteenth century and was reinforced by school attendance requirements. As a result, more children went to school and fewer young children went to work. As Peter Stearns demonstrates, even emotions are full of expectations, with some periods viewing some emotional expressions as legitimate and others as problematic, and thus encouraging one and discouraging the other. How then do we know what children were like in the past?

This same problem can be applied to all human behavior and it is an issue that all historians face. It is not uniquely disqualifying to children's history to say that our behaviors can only be recorded and made meaningful as they are interpreted. In the case of children, historians face this issue as stoically as possible because children are more dependent on adults because their networks of caretaking make them more vulnerable to manipulation, although this dependency decreases from infancy through adolescence. Some historians, such as Maria Nikolajeva, who deals with literature created by adults and directed at children, are especially conscious of the power disparity built into this reality. This does not mean that all children are just what they are made. Timothy Gilfoyle's examination of those young people who decidedly fell outside the terrain of approved childish dependency makes this clear, and Jay Mechling addresses it squarely when he asks how we can know what children did with the institutions created to train them, such as scouting. It does mean that our access to children in the past comes usually through understanding childhood or at least requires that we understand the lens of childhood as we examine children. Some historians have been extremely successful at locating children's own voices rather than relying solely on adults' recordings of their observations. Thus Colin Heywood, Steven Mintz, and Kriste Lindenmeyer in this volume and elsewhere allow us to hear the voices of their historical subjects to an unusual degree. Studying how children preferred to play, as Gary Cross has done,[4] gives us angles on children's lives that come close to as unobstructed a view as we are likely to get. None of this should obscure how much we have learned about children by learning about childhood.

What many of these essays also demonstrate is that the dimensions of childhood have changed in the West over time and not only because more of the young were embraced by its privileges. Defining who and what a child is has deep historical consequences. By the twentieth century, in most places in the western world, childhood included not only infancy and the period between six and ten years old (when individuals are physically not yet fully formed or fully capable) as it had at earlier times, but also increasingly older children, those between ten and fourteen years old, and then also those who would be described as teenagers in the second half of the twentieth century. All of these were included as schools expanded their scope and as the labor of the vigorous young could be dispensed with. This shifting definition of who inhabits the period of childhood makes the study both much more complex and much more important. Perhaps no other historical scholars can so effectively watch as the subjects of their inquiry change before their eyes.

With these changes in definition, the privileges of childhood could also become a social disability. The possibility of protection and dependency, which had initially made childhood into a privileged state for those who could be cared for and prepared in a leisurely way by others, and was almost always denied to the most deprived (slaves, the poor, and the exploited), became a much desired status for all children because the universal drives toward child protection that took shape in the late nineteenth century were extended to larger groups of not quite adults by the twentieth century. As I have suggested above, this new expansion of childhood privilege also brought its own confusions, not least because those who were now guarded and corralled were often less than happy to be so "privileged." Thus the privileges of childhood also led to new questions regarding whether children had rights to various kinds of self-determination, and what exactly the rights of children might look like. James Schmidt addresses this matter in his examination of the relationship between children and the state. In the recent past, a revised view of children's dependence and a new appreciation of self-determination has been a critical component of the 1989 United Nations Convention on the Rights of the Child, which sees the agency of children as part of their birthright.[5] Today, the subject of childhood is fraught with new ideas and potential transformations as the model that became dominant in the nineteenth century shifts. As the essays in Part II demonstrate, by understanding the twists and turns of childhood, we are introduced to a complex and changing western landscape.

Part III is meant to make the larger picture of modern childhood developed in Part II even more complex by looking at variations, specific children, specific places, or specific times. These could have been multiplied greatly. The choices made for inclusion in this section bring out certain aspects of the complexity of modern childhoods. Many of these articles are about fairly recent childhoods, most since the nineteenth century. But whether their subjects are Nazi youth in Germany in the 1930s examined by Dirk Schumann, or African-American slaves in the American South studied by Steven Mintz, or children during the American Great Depression that Kriste Lindenmeyer focuses on, the authors of these essays look not on how western experience, viewed broadly, developed over time so we can understand how our modern understanding evolved, but on the experiences of children and childhood in one place or in a particular circumstance. Whatever the historical nature of its longer-term development, western childhood is still experienced by specific children within particular contexts, and changing historical circumstances can make an enormous difference, as Anne Hyde shows about the fate of mixed-race children in the nineteenth-century American West.

Indeed, one of the results of developments in historical research into childhood has been to demonstrate that the history of childhood can be important to all history writing in two distinct ways. First, the general development of childhood as an internal process is linked, as I have suggested, to the changes in ideas and the institutional set of developments of the state, the economy, and the culture of the West. Second, historians have been exploring how children's experiences are linked to historical events such as World War II or the Great Depression.[6] In this latter endeavor, historians have been eager to include children among the various groups that must be understood if we are to properly assess and understand particular historical events, their causes, and their consequences. Just as no understanding of the past is now complete if we leave out women, so too no real understanding of the past is possible if children are excluded as participants in the events, such as the wars that James Marten examines, the consumer society discussed by Daniel Cook, or as the victims of changing views about race.

In historicizing childhood, Ariès had also flattened the past. Ariès's provocative argument that childhood simply did not exist before the early modern period and his even more sensational claim that parents did not love or care for their children before then never could stand up to scrutiny. In order to distinguish the modern he had denied the historical complexity that preceded it.

A lack of historical sensitivity to the existence of childhood before the sixteenth century and a failure to notice the attachment of parents to their children were only two of the problems with *Centuries of Childhood*. Despite Ariès's attention to how children were represented and his use of diaries and records of schooling in various parts of Europe, his attention was strongly focused on France. As a result, he seemed to miss the multiple and tangled consequences of, among other matters, the Protestant Reformation.[7] Despite his use of graphs to bring age into focus as an increasingly significant cultural measure, Ariès shied away from the use of numbers. Most of all, he wrote as if the changes he described were applicable to everyone: rich, poor, peasant and city based. Just when social historians were starting to examine the subtle, historically situated distinctions that affected people in the past by addressing matters of class, gender, and religion, Ariès largely ignored these differences, thereby missing how modern childhood was differentially applicable and the degree to which it was both a privilege and a means to inscribe and affect intergroup relations. This was especially problematic in light of the many-layered demographic materials being gathered at just this time by the Cambridge Group for the History of Population and Social Structure. As early as 1965, Peter Laslett would bring this material to a wider audience of readers through his accessible book, *The World We Have Lost*.[8] Laslett described the complex matrix of ranks and statuses that prevailed in early modern English villages and showed that even in the seventeenth century most families were small, private, and composed exclusively of parents and their children, rather than the numerous generations often envisaged in our imagined past.

Ariès had awakened some of the interest in past family relations that Laslett and others now fed, but Ariès tended to dismiss the family as a negligible factor in children's experience in the long-ago past while romanticizing the community as a boundary-less whole in which children merged seamlessly into the larger mass. Only gradually, he argued, were they treated as a group apart and did they stop engaging in the community play of adults; only gradually did their families become their main source of socialization. Laslett's carefully defined and complex description of the differences to be found in seventeenth-century English villages made that earlier world much more understandable as one in which childhood conformed to a different set of hierarchies and was an expression of other forms of subordination and family attentiveness. In this volume, Julia Grant brings the family back to its central place as an institution of childhood while demonstrating that it is both a changing and a diverse context for child life.

Laslett showed that most families were small, as even seventeenth-century cottagers exercised forms of population control, adopting late marriage as an important strategy. Childhood was always deeply embedded in decisions about the viability of birth in a social context that could sustain it. As Bengt Sandin shows in this book, the tendency to eliminate children before they are born or immediately thereafter has been a familiar aspect of western experience and long a subject fraught with legal and moral dilemmas. Thus, a child born and allowed to develop was itself a privilege (for parents as well as children) not always or equally available to all. Ariès had largely ignored ranks as a feature of pre-capitalist society, and the very texture that the Cambridge group sought to uncover through statistical profiles of the poor and vulnerable, was absent in his book because the sources he drew on were heavily based on a literature and iconography that observed the upper ranks – the wealthy, the noble, the literate. Ariès had been examining privilege without acknowledging it.

Childhood for Ariès was a defining quality of modernity that emerged everywhere in the West at a specific time. In fact, as many of the following essays demonstrate, modern childhood with its attendant protections, its aura of innocence, its links to schooling and preparation, its sexual taboos, and its appeal to adults' sentimentality was hardly an experience common to most children even in the modern period; it was still reserved to only some in the nineteenth century, let alone the seventeenth. While the importance of the formative qualities of childhood were inscribed by Enlightenment thought in the eighteenth century, which also provided the impetus to its universalization, it was not experienced as a period set apart in its own world of play and schooling for most children until the twentieth century, after labor laws and school requirements carved it out of previous social spaces. This did not mean that childhood did not exist for those not privileged to attend school for most of the year or enjoy other aspects of childhood in its modern guise. Work could be part of childhood and living outside one's birth family could also be part of childhood. Rather, it means the childhood we validate today was not ubiquitous but coexisted with other conceptions of childhood held by people whose world was not so modern and not so privileged. These different experiences of childhood and different understandings of protection, play, preparation, and other features of children's growth from absolute infant dependency and protection to adolescent coming-of-age existed all through the modern West as part of the world of children and adults.

It also did not mean that most parents did not care for or care about their children or do what they could to protect them within the limits of their circumstances. It did mean that the unique privileges of modern childhood as a protected space sharply separated from adult forms of social life was highly dependent on state legislation that began to universalize its perspectives. Even in the United States, which by the twentieth century was the wealthiest and most universalistic of western societies and where the extension of schooling into adolescence was well under way by the 1920s, this was not taken for granted until the 1930s, as Kriste Lindenmeyer shows. Elsewhere in the West, in Germany, for example, the impulse to set children apart in institutions of preparation could become a form of absolute state control as childhood became an object of manipulation towards political goals. Dirk Schumann demonstrates that childhood could be universalized by the Nazi regime, as all Aryan children were required to become part of the *Hitler Jugend*, but distorted at the same time because it was viewed not as a privilege of development but as a province of state power. And the lack of this privilege could be literally killing to those excluded from its circles, like the Roma and the Jews. The complex role of the state was thus critical to childhood in the modern West but its particular nature was by no means predetermined. Only after World War II did those outcomes become manifest in Western Europe, United States and Canada in the context of expanded investments in schooling and child welfare. It is well for us to realize that the Europe described in this volume relies on studies highly biased toward the western and northern areas and countries. In many areas in the East and South, parts of Poland or Sicily and even in the American South, the state's penetration was uneven and thin until the end of World War II.

Modern childhood was idealized long before it was a serious reflection of child life. Childhood as an ideal of prolonged development has always been a privilege, reserved for the well-to-do and well-placed in the Ancient World as well as in nineteenth-century America. The children of Roman slaves in the Ancient World described by Keith Bradley, as well as the African-American slave children in Steven Mintz's American South, could not be protected or adequately cherished by their parents, not because they failed at love but because childhood for them was not a period of preparation for an aspirational adulthood. Defined as a period of growth – physical, emotional, and cognitive – everyone has a childhood, at least everyone who lives long enough, but as a realm of protected development, an extended time of leisured maturation, it has historically been enjoyed by few. The belief in the possibilities of childhood for all children first emerged in the eighteenth century and was then developed vigorously in the nineteenth century when it became a dominant motif in literature and visual culture.

An important dimension of this new childhood was the greater protection against disease made available to children in the late nineteenth and twentieth centuries. Most historians realize that the birth rate since the nineteenth century has declined in the West with ever greater predictability, and they are convinced that this is related to parental behavior and the elevation of childhood as a precious and carefully nurtured estate. Less often acknowledged, but fundamental to social expectations, was the rapid decline in childhood diseases that were once endemic and ravaged the population of children, diseases such as scarlet fever, diphtheria, cholera and many varieties of gastro-intestinal disorders. Most children have historically been born in a soup of infectious diseases, whose basis was bacterial, viral, and amoebic. In the West, until the twentieth century, about one-quarter of all children born would die before they reached one year old and many others would die before adolescence. Altogether about 45 percent of all children died before puberty.[9] In southern and eastern Europe, the figure was closer to 60 percent. The drastic change for children that medicine and public health measures produced, in the context of better nutrition and living standards, radically altered childhood for adults and for children. This change began in the eighteenth century, but became much more developed by the late nineteenth century and flowered in the twentieth century. Dominique Marshall points out how many international efforts in the early twentieth century on behalf of child life were organized and staffed by health professionals who were invigorated by the gospel of good health and sought to bring it first to the children of the western world and then beyond.[10] Whatever seventeenth- or eighteenth-century parents might want to do for their children, their means were limited by infection and its democratic scythe; although the conditions of the poor and of rural populations always made some even more vulnerable to the universal scourge of disease.

The decline in these diseases, as Peter Stearns notes in his essay, has had a profound effect on the expression of family emotional life. The privilege of expecting good health is a critical aspect of early twentieth-century childhood, strongly augmented after World War II by the invention of antibiotics, the conquest of polio and subsequently vaccines for other childhood diseases such as measles and whooping cough. It is suggestive that once parents began to believe they had some control, as their children's physical health became sturdier, they, together with child professionals, increasingly emphasized emotional and psychological well-being. The modern paradigm of childhood, which required that children be elaborately protected, allowed parents who were more secure in their children's physical health to become ever more alert to other forms of well-being, including child safety. Today eternal vigilance about children appears to have become the dominant western fixation.[11] None of this would have been possible without the new certainty that medicine introduced regarding the common killers of infants and children.

In the twentieth century, the privileges of the few have affected many more and become the expectations of all. While the particular form of these privileges of childhood remains far from universal even in the West, it has become a defining norm of western civilization, a norm around which we both establish our own progress and parade our superiority over other parts of the globe. Today, as the world shrinks, the pressures are not in any sense just from the West to the rest. Global competition for knowledge-based skills continues to elevate our expectations about schooling and to extend the period of dependency. These changes come at the expense of other features of child life in the West that had once been equally embraced, and force significant delays in the pay-off in a long-deferred adulthood. Play, a leisurely approach to cognitive acquisitions, and protections from commercial concerns; all these are challenged in a western world where children today are asked to respond to a newly complex context that is forcing a re-evaluation and redefinition of childhood itself. It may be well to ask whether some of the privileges of childhood, such as play, will become scarcer during the twenty-first century for many children as the dominance of commercial values force children to ever longer periods of work in school. As a product of changing history, childhood will be forced to change, and childhood as a privilege opened to many in the twentieth century may once again become less available.

Does this mean that the essays here are dated before they can be read? Yes, in some respects. As a rapidly evolving field of study, the history of childhood is constantly amplifying and revising our knowledge and understanding. But the essays in this volume cover so many of the essential issues around what we know as childhood, including its deep history millennia ago and its growing reach, that they should serve for years to come as the essential basis for everyone's knowledge of what we mean when we speak of modern childhood.

The Routledge History of Childhood in the Western World will help the reader to understand how our childhood has become the particular stage of life in which we have invested so much hope and which may today worry us as increasingly unsustainable. It will show which groups have benefitted, which have been ignored, and how as a society we have come to define ourselves so passionately according to the manner in which we value our children. It is time for the subtle, far-ranging and probing history of childhood that has grown up in the last fifty years in Ariès's wake to have its voice. This volume is the place to begin.

Notes

1 Philippe Ariès, *Centuries of Childhood: A Social History of Family Life*, trans. Robert Baldick (London, UK: Jonathan Cape, 1962; American edition, Random House, 1962).
2 The question of parental affection has generated considerable literature. Among the most significant discussions are Lawrence Stone, *The Family, Sex and Marriage In England,*

1500–1800 (New York, NY: Harper and Row, 1977); Linda Pollack, *A Lasting Relationship: Parents and Children Over Three Centuries* (London, UK: University Press of New England, 1990); Lloyd deMause, ed., *The History of Childhood* (New York, NY: Psychohistory Press, 1974). While these books were mostly concerned with whether parents loved their children and if this had changed historically, Viviana A. Zelizer's, *Pricing the Priceless Child: The Changing Social Value of Children* (New York, NY: Basic Books, 1985) switched the conversation from parental love to cultural values. In so doing, she picked up on the more consequential dimension of the matter initiated in Ariès: the changing cultural value of affectionate expression.

3 For the development of extreme age consciousness in the modern world, see Howard Chudacoff, *How Old Are You? Age Consciousness in American Culture* (Princeton, NJ: Princeton University Press, 1989).

4 Kriste Lindenmeyer, *The Greatest Generation Grows Up* (Chicago, IL: Ivan R. Dee, 2005); Steven Mintz, *Huck's Raft: A History of American Childhood*; Colin Heywood, *Childhood in Nineteenth Century France: Work, Health, and Education Among the 'Classes Populaires'* (Cambridge, UK: Cambridge University Press, 1988). See also Leslie Paris, *Children's Nature: The Rise of the American Summer Camp* (New York, NY: New York University Press, 2008); Rebecca de Schweinitz, *If We Could Change the World: Young People and America's Long Struggle for Racial Equality* (Chapel Hill, NC: University of North Carolina Press, 2011); Arianne Baggerman and Rudolf Dekker, *Child of the Enlightenment: Revolutionary Europe Reflected in a Boyhood Diary,* (Leiden, Germany: Brill Academic Publishers, 2009).

5 This is the point that is made in the *Annals of the American Academy of Political and Social Science* special issue marking the twentieth anniversary of the UN Convention, *The Child as Citizen*, ed. Felton Earls, *The Annals*, 633 (January 2011).

6 A few examples of historians who have shown the children's side of important events include: Rebecca De Schweinitz, *If We Could Change the World* (Chapel Hill, NC: University of North Caronlina Press, 2011); Kriste Lindenmeyer, *The Greatest Generation Grows Up* (Lanham, MD: Ivan R. Dee, 2005); Lisa Ossian, *The Forgotten Generation: American Children in World War II* (Columbia, MO: University of Missouri Press, 2011); Emmy E. Warner, *Through the Eyes of Innocents: Children Witness World War II* (Boulder, CO: Westview Press, 2000); James Marten, *The Children's Civil War* (Chapel Hill, NC: University of North Carolina Press, 2000).

7 Steven E. Ozment, *When Fathers Ruled: Family Life in Reformation Europe* (Cambridge, MA: Harvard University Press, 1983); Alan Macfarlane, *The Family Life of Ralph Josselin: A Seventeenth-Century Clergyman* (Cambridge, UK: Cambridge University Press, 1970); Philip J. Greven, *The Protestant Temperament: Patterns of Child Rearing, Religious Experience, and the Self in Early America* (New York, NY: Alfred A. Knopf, 1977).

8 Peter Laslett, *The World We Have Lost: England Before the Industrial Revolution* (New York, NY: Charles Scribner's Sons, 1965).

9 Richard Meckel, "Health and Science," in *A Cultural History of Childhood and Family in the Age of Empire*, ed. Colin Heywood (Oxford, UK: Berg, 2010) 168.

10 Nancy Tomes, *The Gospel of Germs: Men, Women, and the Microbe in American Life* (Cambridge, MA: Harvard University Press, 1998).

11 The articles in *Reinventing Childhood After World War II*, eds. Paula S. Fass and Michael Grossberg (Philadelphia, PA: University of Pennsylvania Press, 2011) make this clear. For childhood, education, and globalization, see Paula S. Fass, *Children of a New World: Society, Culture, and Globalization* (New York, NY: New York University Press, 2007).

Part I

CHILDHOOD IN THE ANCIENT WORLD, THE MIDDLE AGES, AND EARLY MODERN EUROPE

1

IMAGES OF CHILDHOOD IN CLASSICAL ANTIQUITY

Keith Bradley

Introduction

Augustine's spiritual autobiography, *Confessions*, composed at the turn of the fifth century AD, is a document of special significance to the social historian of antiquity because it contains specific recollections of its author's childhood. Recording the history of his relationship with God in middle age, the Bishop of Hippo begins at the beginning, from the moment of his birth, and gives an account of his childhood years full of notable details. Infancy has to be re-imagined through later observations of the very young; but Augustine knew that he had been fed at the breast, by both mother and wet nurses, and that before he could speak, imitating and memorizing sounds made by his attendants, he had first learned to express himself by tears and smiles and gestures. He knew, too, of his fits of pique towards those who had cared for him, and the bursts of jealousy towards other infants who had nursed with him. His sensitivity to the early moments of life is strong.[1]

Memory is keener once Augustine recalls the boyhood years of schooling, with teachers of elementary literacy and numeracy, and masters of literature and rhetoric. All were remembered for the ceaseless beatings they had given, against which prayers, and parents, were unavailing. Unruly and resistant to study, Augustine preferred to play with other boys, hated Greek but took to Latin more readily, and was attracted by a pagan mythology whose vanity he did not yet understand. He duly learned the great passages of Virgil by heart – the wooden horse, the fall of Troy, the shade of Creusa – and thrilled to the story of Dido and Aeneas. He also learned how to declaim, avoiding solecisms and mispronunciations (no aitches dropped), and excelled in his studies, with commendations and rewards offsetting the punishments. Yet as an adolescent, he engaged in more wayward behavior: petty thievery in the household, pursuit of vulgar entertainments, and roistering with companions, the culmination of which was a night-time raid on a nearby orchard and the theft of some pears from a pear-tree. Worse still were his frequent indulgences of rampant sexual desire: it was a matter of braggadocio to claim, and exaggerate, carnal conquests.

Augustine was born in the North African city of Thagaste in the middle of the fourth century AD into a landed family. His parents Patricius and Monica were not of the first order of wealth, but they were slave-owners and had nurses and child-minders, both male and female, to care for him through infancy and boyhood. There was also money for his schooling, first at Thagaste and then, when he was fifteen or so, in Madauros and later still at Carthage, when he was about seventeen. His parents were ambitious for him, and he received the type of education available only to the privileged, opening up the prospect of a life of civic leadership. (Comprehensive public schooling was unknown in antiquity.) Patricius, a pagan for most of his life, died when Augustine was studying in Carthage; Monica, a devout Christian much younger than her husband, was a woman of great influence. She looked carefully to Augustine's spiritual well-being, and, surprisingly, advised him in adolescence on his sexual comportment, a matter that might have been thought a father's responsibility.[2]

My purpose in this chapter is to explore some of the principal characteristics of childhood in the societies of ancient Greece and Rome, broadly defined and as I understand them; but I have begun with Augustine in the late classical world for several reasons. Augustine's account illustrates clearly how childhood was thought of in antiquity as a distinguishable phase of life that was divisible into stages – infancy, boyhood, and adolescence – and it communicates the idea that through its course, what at first was a completely formless entity, as though a piece of earth, was to be gradually shaped and molded into an adult fit to function in civic society in ways determined by those responsible for a child's upbringing. Childhood is conceptualized in purely passive terms. The account also gives evidence of the truism that it is through the eyes of adults that children in the classical world can usually be seen, which means that there are limits to what can be said about them. Any hope of understanding childhood from the vantage point of children themselves, and any possibility of uncovering a capacity children may have had to shape their own lives actively, is by definition foreclosed. It is rare, moreover, to find even personal reminiscences of childhood: Augustine's account is exceptional in this respect. For the most part, children in antiquity are known only from adults who left records of others.

Augustine's account also draws attention to the factors that must guide discussion. The experience of childhood in Greco-Roman antiquity is unlikely to have been the same for all children. An enormous expanse of time is involved, a millennium and more, a vast range of territory, and often great disparities in social standing among the children and their families at issue, whose societies were arranged in steep hierarchies quite alien to modern liberal democracies, including those in which vestiges of class structure still remain. All, crucially, were slave-owning societies, and although Augustine was as aware as anyone of the fundamental divide between free and slave, it was not important to him to speak in any detail of slaves' experiences; and in this his evidence is typical of most of the evidence that remains from antiquity. Its bias is towards the prosperous and successful, which makes it difficult ever to comprehend society in the round. A tendency to imagine that life was less harsh for the majority than I believe it to have been can result. Nevertheless, time, place, status, economic resources, gender, cultural specificity, religious identity – these are the criteria that must control any assessment. Whether a history of childhood in Greco-Roman antiquity is possible is a question to which I will return. Attention falls meantime on a collage of images, predominantly from the Roman Imperial Age with retrospective glances at earlier periods as appropriate. Augustine can be kept in mind as a guide throughout.

Formation

The stages of childhood that Augustine distinguished were widely recognized by Greeks and Romans. They were sometimes further subdivided, with childhood and adolescence split into earlier and later portions, but infancy lasted until approximately age five, boyhood until eleven or twelve, and adolescence until seventeen or eighteen. Terminology sometimes varied: the philosopher Seneca (first century AD) would sometimes use "puberty" for "adolescence."[3] But standardized ages, including ages of majority, were not the norm.

The idea that the child was in essence a malleable being also had a long history. It was the premise on which Plato based his educational regimen 800 years before Augustine, and it is the assumption that underlies the Platonist philosopher Celsus's complaint that children in his day (second century AD) were the victims of Christian proselytes.[4] It is especially evident in three works from the late first century AD. They concern elite children only, and mainly boys – Greco-Roman societies were patriarchal in character; this has to be accepted for what it is – and may be taken to represent ideals of upbringing and education among upper-class families in the Roman Imperial Age, both in the Latin west and the Greek east. Their common perspective confirms that ideals changed little over time.

Quintilian's *Oratorical Institute* is a comprehensive educational treatise that prescribes the curriculum to be followed by the upper-class Roman boy from infancy until he emerges as an orator well-trained in moral sensibility and academically equipped to participate in civic affairs: in the phrase of the elder Cato, "a good man skilled in speaking."[5] Following a tradition illustrated again by Plato, Quintilian was concerned with the formation of character as much as of the mind, with ideals of deference, obedience, and modesty uppermost in his thinking. The treatise is a testament to Quintilian's experience as an instructor of rhetoric at Rome, which included service as tutor to the grand-nephews of the Emperor Domitian. He was an astute observer of children and of their behavior. The second work is an anonymous document called *On the Education of Children*, which has survived among the moral essays of Plutarch (first century AD). While much shorter, its aim likewise is to give instruction on how the well-to-do boy is to be turned into a civic leader through literary and rhetorical learning and the inculcation of moral excellence. The acquisition of what Greeks called *paideia* and Romans *doctrina* was considered the key to all success in life.

Both works assume that the primary obligation for supervising the boy's upbringing falls on his father. Any concept of joint parental responsibility is minimal. All household decisions are those of the male head (in Latin, the *paterfamilias*; in Greek, the *kyrios*). They also assume that the child will be born into a household community where servile dependants, female nurses, and male chaperons (pedagogues) carry out the practical tasks of child-care and provide instruction in the first years. The servants are to be carefully selected, with several nurses needed in case of illness or death. Quintilian indicates that once the boy is out of the nursery he should proceed to the schools of public teachers, that of the teacher of literature (*grammaticus*) at the age of seven or so, and that of the *rhetor* at puberty, when about fourteen.[6] For both authors, however, the child is an inherently impressionable being – this is the key point – who is to be constantly shaped to a desired end with appropriate incentives towards, and rewards for, good behavior. He is also to be punished if recalcitrant or lazy, although both authors object to corporal punishment, which they regard as demeaning and suitable only for slaves.[7] In contrast, despite his own childhood experiences, which were probably far more representative, Augustine thought when he wrote the *City of God* that corporal punishment was not only uncontroversial but also ordained by

Scripture.[8] Special attention must be given to safeguarding the boy from male sexual predators. To the Greek author, male courtship of a boy of a traditional Greek kind is permissible if the intent, as in Athens and Sparta, is the pursuit of virtue, but not, as he suggests it was in other Greek city-states, for erotic purposes alone.[9] To Quintilian, obsessed with fears of effeminacy, male attentiveness is never acceptable. The Roman orator must be a real man.[10]

For the earliest stages of life, details accrue from the third item, the *Gynecology* of Soranus, a book on women's medical issues by a Greek doctor who practiced in Rome. The details are all again predicated on the assumption that strictly regulated formation of the infant, now girls as well as boys, is necessary. Here too the nurse is a significant figure. She is again to be carefully chosen because a connection is made between the quality of the care given to the nursling and the child's well-being. It was thought for example that a nurse who drank made her nursling ill.[11] Her duties are elaborately itemized – feeding, bathing, massaging, and swaddling the child – suggesting that she spent a great amount of time each day with her charge, and that her influence was consequently great. In due course, she was to help the infant to learn to sit up and walk, and, through play and storytelling, become the child's first teacher. It was best, therefore, even in Rome, for the nurse to be a Greek woman.[12] In a highly speech-conscious world, the way the child began to say words was not a trifling matter. The Emperor Hadrian was reproached for betraying his Spanish origins with a provincial accent.[13]

The ethic that prevails in these works is one of conservative conformism, and unless within controlled limits, no allowance is made for fostering individuality or independence of mind. This is especially true of Quintilian, whose educational curriculum is based on a canon of great Greek and Latin books, beginning with the *Iliad* and *Odyssey*, which must never change. The writings are prescriptive, but they must reflect something of the reality of elite children's lives in the Roman Imperial Age. Boys and girls could expect to be surrounded from their earliest moments by a cluster of adults who looked to their material needs and nurtured their development, with parents and servants skilled, ideally, in providing child-care, who together formed a household community in which children first began to learn. In time boys could expect formal schooling, as fathers engaged teachers for them, and sometimes they traveled to major cities such as Milan or Rome for the purpose, as circumstances required or warranted.[14] A regimen of literary learning and speech-making was then the norm, with much of the pupils' time devoted to memorizing and reciting passages from great books; and as they exploited what they had learned in rhetorical performance, they gradually acquired the skills of mastery that would permit them to become leaders in public life – in politics, warfare, law, and diplomacy – and to exercise authority over the complex households they would come to command as men. The triumvir Mark Antony was said consciously to have prepared himself for mastery from childhood, fitting himself into a traditional template of male leadership that served the collective interests of society in general and its leading circle of members in particular.[15] Elite Roman boys could find themselves in positions of military leadership in their late teens.

For girls education was equally normative – upper-class girls especially could be as well-educated as boys – but on the model of the well-situated Minicia Marcella, who died aged thirteen shortly before her wedding, through the agency of private tutors in the household rather than in school.[16] She was the kind of girl whose grave goods might include bronze inkwells and an ivory writing tablet as symbols of her educational accomplishments, as in a collection now visible in Berlin. But the destiny of girls was largely to become wives and mothers and to manage the households over which they presided in a society where the main purpose of marriage was to produce offspring, with almost no public roles equivalent to those of men. Distastefully to modern sensibilities, Seneca said that men were born to rule and women to obey.[17] The prescriptive works are indifferent to girls' upbringing as a result. The domestic management expected of adult women, however, required its own special training in leadership and organization: households had huge staffs, with urban and rural components, and their administration, motivated by principles of economic self-sufficiency, was multi-faceted. Altogether, for both boys and girls preparation for adult life was rigidly gendered, but there can be no thought that children of either sex were anything but valued. The future of society depended on them.

For models on which to base the formation of the child, the author of *On the Education of Children* looks especially to classical Athens (fifth–fourth century BC), a sign of a continuity of ethos in Greek attitudes towards, and practices in, childrearing across many centuries. The political developments that brought in the *longue durée* Greek subordination first to Macedon and then to Rome were not accompanied by changes in social and ideological norms.

In the classical Greek era it is about Athens that most is known. The degree of privilege and wealth separating well-to-do citizens from the majority was less pronounced than in Rome; but Athens, though constitutionally democratic, was also a male-oriented, hierarchical, and slave-owning society, with a similar ethic of citizen communality. The *kyrios* made all-important domestic decisions. Athenian women, as women in the Greek city-states at large, are sometimes said to have led more seclusive lives than their Roman counterparts, living in houses that contained separate women's quarters where young children, distanced from their fathers both physically and emotionally, spent their early years. But the extent of this difference is disputed. Nonetheless, as in Rome the purpose of marriage for Athenians was to produce children, who until adulthood were imbued with traditional values in a manner intended to preserve the social status quo.

Infancy was filled with the presence in the Greek household (*oikos*) of child-minding slaves, especially nurses who commonly swaddled infants in ways that Soranus would later have understood.[18] The practice literally involved shaping the infant physically into an attractively desirable form, but without damage to the infant's organs. It is often observable in Greek funerary art. On a memorial from the early fourth century BC, a family scene includes a nurse – unlike the family members she is significantly unnamed – holding a newborn she has wrapped in swaddling bands as the family mourns the mother who has died giving birth. She might have been a Thracian.[19]

Schooling came in time, and is well-represented by scenes of school-rooms that appear on painted vases where citizen boys can be seen engaged in the study of poetry and music. They also practiced athletics, preparing for the virtually inevitable episodes of warfare that would come in adult life. Inherently agonistic, Greeks did not always have to fight a common enemy but often fought one another. The curse of the autonomous city-state (*polis*) was the premium it placed on its sovereignty, and it caused innumerable conflicts within Hellas as a whole, proving in the long run the fatal flaw of classical Greece. Unsurprisingly, between the ages of eighteen and twenty Athenian adolescents were required, as ephebes, to undergo a period of compulsory military training.[20]

Much then in classical Athens would have seemed familiar to Quintilian and Augustine centuries later. Everything was designed to integrate the child into the citizen community and to replicate what had come before. Boys were to participate as men in civic affairs, provide soldiers for Athens' military conflicts, and manage the agricultural estates that were the mainstay of the Attic economy. The ideal was the *kalos kagathos* of Xenophon's *Oeconomicus*, a handbook on estate regulation of the early fourth century BC. One key difference was the Greek willingness to find socializing advantageous for adolescent boys in homoerotic relationships with slightly older men, which offered both sexual initiation and models of elite decorum, a pattern of culture towards which Romans felt a formal antipathy. Girls, it seems, lived relatively sheltered lives throughout their childhood, and as women were probably less independent than their Roman counterparts. They too were expected to become wives and mothers. But again domestic management demanded careful training, and according to Xenophon it was the husband, typically much older than his wife, who was to provide it. "What could she have known," his householder Ischomachus says,

> when I took her as my wife, Socrates? She was not yet fifteen, and had spent her previous years under careful supervision so that she might see and hear and speak as little as possible. Don't you think it was adequate if she came to me knowing only how to take wool and produce a cloak, and had seen how spinning tasks are to be allocated to the slaves?[21]

Plato, often thought to have been influenced by his experiences in Sparta, believed that girls and boys should receive the same education.[22] It was a radical idea that most Greeks, and most Romans, would have considered controversial.

Authors of the Roman Imperial Age were sometimes struck by what they took to be oddities in childrearing practices. Soranus thought that Gauls, Germans, and even some Greeks immersed newborns in cold water as a test of hardiness to see whether they were worth rearing.[23] Aristotle had made a similar observation about Celts much earlier.[24] Perhaps the greatest oddity, however, was the way elite citizens in archaic and classical Sparta (seventh–fourth century BC) were thought to have reared their children in the era of Soranus, which Plutarch described in his biography of the mythical founder of Sparta's distinctive social system, Lycurgus. Struck by the otherness of custom, he tells of the way decisions on whether newborns lived or died hundreds of years before were made not by their parents but by the Spartan elders in conclave; of the way nurses left infants' limbs and bodies to grow free from constraint, without swaddling; of how boys from the age of seven were separated from parents and placed in communal messes with Spartan men, training competitively to become future warriors, the bonds between fathers and sons eroded by the common living arrangements; and of the way physical rather than intellectual education was emphasized, with girls, unusually, receiving as much attention as boys in order to make them mothers of future soldiers.[25] Xenophon had also remarked on some of these features in his *Constitution of the Spartans*, noting that children's education was controlled by a public functionary called the *paidonomos*.[26] The contrast with Athens was profound, and perduring: Spartan boys were still subjected to harsh physical discipline in Plutarch's day.[27]

The remarkable feature of the historical record is the general unanimity of thought in Greco-Roman antiquity about what should happen to children during childhood and why. The theme of conforming formation for the greater social good was consistently maintained over time with only minimal variation. How children responded is difficult to tell. The stress that influential Romans and Greeks placed on the shaping of their young resembles the way they offered prescriptions for managing their slaves, who in some cases resisted both the prescriptions and their condition at large. But the evidence is too inadequate to claim a similar structural rebelliousness from children. Adolescence offers the likeliest time when it might be expected, with Augustine's theft of pears perhaps symptomatic. The author of *On the Education of Children* was sensitive to certain adolescent excesses: stealing and sexual adventures among others.[28] In a letter preserved on papyrus from Roman Egypt, a woman entreats her brother not to allow her son to wander around aimlessly and idly: "put him to work."[29]

Realities

This anonymous author also recognized that there was a category of people in his world who could be called "the poor." They are dismissed, more or less, as unfortunate and inconsequential.[30] The unfree are not considered at all. It is a typical attitude. The Spartan children discussed a moment ago were the children of the Spartiates, the Spartan elite who maintained themselves in power by exercising a warlike rule over subject dependants (Helots and Messenians); what life was like for the children of these people was not of comparable interest to observers and commentators. The same is true for the children of the slave nurses who figure so prominently in the treatises of Quintilian and Soranus. Yet the poor and the unfree always constituted the vast majority of the Greco-Roman population. How can their children's lives be understood?

Civic leadership and statecraft were the preserve in antiquity of powerful minorities who drew wealth from landownership and related commercial and manufacturing interests. Most people, in contrast, had to work for their daily bread. In towns, poor men might gather in the marketplace each morning, hoping to be hired by a rich landowner who needed laborers in his nearby vineyard.[31] It was an insecure way to make a living. Better, therefore, if not essential, to have learned a trade or craft as a child, with the promise of a more secure income to come in adulthood. Augustine thought of learning a trade as a natural alternative to the type of literary education he received, but one subject to similar tribulations.[32] The amount of formal schooling most children received was probably minimal (but strictly unknown), and the degree of literacy slight. Roman Egypt has preserved some papyrological examples of school exercises, which are tantalizing in their implications. By adolescence, however, practical learning was more important than academic learning for most, and it was a father's responsibility to secure it. The former slave Echion, a dinner guest of Trimalchio in Petronius' *Satyricon*, is pleased because his son has been well-grounded in Greek and Latin; but the boy, he says, is now to learn a trade – barbering, auctioneering, or advocacy – something, unlike poetry, with which he will be able to support himself.[33] Echion is fiction, but the sentiment expressed is realistic.

Trades and crafts were commonly handed down from generation to generation. This is one reason why upward social mobility was relatively minimal at all periods of Greco-Roman antiquity. Plato took it for granted that the sons of potters learned their fathers' craft by observation and emulation, and the Greek interpreter of dreams Artemidorus (second century AD) set down his vast knowledge in a handbook in part so that his son could learn and follow him in the same enterprise.[34] The Hippocratic oath required doctors to transmit their knowledge to their sons.[35] The feature is sometimes illustrated, quite literally, in visual evidence that depict scenes of workplaces. Sculptural reliefs from Pompeii and Aquileia show boys plausibly to be assumed the sons of the smiths portrayed at work, while in a well-known fresco from Pompeii the boy Icarus is seen at work with awl and mallet as his father, the master carpenter Daedalus, looks on. Aeneas' words to Ascanius when about to fight a duel, "Learn courage from me, my son, and true toil," encapsulate the idiom.[36] Myth and reality coincide.

The range of artisanal crafts was narrower for girls than for boys, but mothers played a comparable teaching role, traditionally and above all giving instruction to their daughters in spinning and weaving, occupations that knew no social boundaries. Celsus assumed that this was the way a woman in a poor country town would earn her living, but the Emperor Augustus was careful to have his daughter and granddaughters instructed, and no doubt knew that even Dido had made a cloak of crimson and gold for Aeneas with her own hands.[37] Lucretius thought that weaving had once been the preserve of men but had been handed over to women because men had tougher jobs to handle.[38]

Instruction was sometimes given formally through apprenticing children to master craftsmen. Contracts on papyrus from Roman Egypt illustrate arrangements for a variety of occupations, principally in textile trades but also in manufacturing (e.g. nail-making and copper-smithing), with stipulations stated on the length of the training period (one – six years), the respective responsibilities of parent and craftsman in supporting the apprentice, the length of the working day (sometimes "from sunrise to sunset"), and the number of holidays allowed. Similar arrangements are likely for children elsewhere who became cobblers, mirror-makers, bakers, barbers, jewelers, and a whole host of other trades. The Greek satirist Lucian (second century AD), originally from Syria, was apprenticed as an adolescent to an uncle to become a stonemason or sculptor. On his first day he broke a slab of stone with a chisel, was beaten, and ran home to his mother.[39] Thereafter he devoted his life to *paideia*, a rare case, I imagine, of youthful escape from the more common pattern of learning skills to be exercised over a lifetime. By Augustine's day, the de facto hereditary character of many banausic occupations had been confirmed by law, as had the agricultural occupations that consumed the great mass of small peasant freeholders and tenants of the wealthy.[40] A new Christian association between labor and sin had also been established, to what psychological effect it would be revealing to know.[41]

Long before adolescent instruction, lower-class children contributed to the household economy by performing chores. For those who grew up on farms, girls as well as boys, tending pigs, cutting down ferns, trimming vines, serving food, stirring boiling fruit syrup, and gathering firewood were just a handful of the jobs that would be done.[42] The rhythm of the seasons and the required agricultural work were assimilated as the early years of childhood passed, a pattern inferable from mosaics of the Hellenistic and Roman periods, which vividly illustrate annual rural activities. For most children work of some sort was an integral element of childhood.

What of children born into slavery? Home-born slaves are presented sometimes in elite Roman sources as favored slaves, but little of their personal experiences can be known. The poet Martial (first century AD) wrote touching memorials to favorite slave children who had died prematurely, but it would be rash to imagine that his apparent affection for them meant that the lives of the majority were enviable.[43] Slave families are attested, but they had no legal status, and many slave children must have been fathered by their mothers' owners, whose right to use (or abuse) their slave property as they wished was generally unquestioned. Slave women are said sometimes to have abandoned their children at birth because they did not want child rearing to be added to the burden of slavery.[44] On the other hand, the children of slave wet nurses were sometimes kept and nursed with the free infants of the household: Romans called them *collactanei*, infants who suckled together. (Something like this must have happened in Augustine's early life.) And a woman who had no children of her own could regard a slave girl as the daughter who would take care of her in old age.[45] When Seneca, however, met his retainer Felicio in old age on a visit to one of his country estates, he did not recognize the slave boy with whom he had played as a child and who had spent his life since laboring for the great man.[46] A Hellenistic statuette, now in Boston, of a crouching Negroid boy with face contorted and legs in shackles, and the bill of sale for the ironically named slave girl Fortunata, who was sold *c.*100 AD and transported across the Channel from Gaul to Britain, are sobering reminders of the commodified nature of every slave in antiquity, and of the permanent insecurity that governed their lives. As Ambrose, the Bishop of Milan (fourth century AD), succinctly put it: "Slavery is wretched."[47] Not that Christians saw fit to question the institution.

Cultural constants

Throughout antiquity it was thought natural that children should play. Childhood was a time of life for recreation and amusement. Plato thought play instinctual in children, and literary texts offer many allusions to childhood games – boys skimming pebbles or building sandcastles on the seashore, girls playing with dolls – and material evidence shows the toys actually used.[48] Their similarity century after century confirms the socio-cultural appreciation of childhood as a special phase of life that had its own distinctive attributes. The first toy the infant knew was the rattle, a hollow terracotta or metal container filled with pebbles or seeds, disc-shaped or in animal form (a duck, rooster, pig, dog), which was shaken to divert the child, or sometimes to induce sleep when shaken rhythmically or to stop a child from crying. It was the nurse's toy especially.[49] Then there were toys for older children: dolls, in human and animal forms (sometimes articulated), spinning tops and pull toys (chariots and carriages), hoops, walkers, dice, board games, and the ubiquitous knuckle bones that were used like modern jacks. Examples are known from all across the chronological and geographical spectrum. In Greek art the wooden roller, a stick connected to an axle supporting a box with two wheels at its sides, is a commonly shown item in representations of children, while on children's sarcophagi from the Roman era boys and girls are seen together playing leapfrog or games with nuts and balls, talking, squabbling, pulling hair, and chasing with ropes and sticks. They also chanted rhymes, as Augustine again makes clear: he once took a child's sing-song voice as a sign from God to read a sacred book.[50]

Children also kept and played with pets. Beautiful examples of funerary art from the Greek world showing children and animals include the portraits of an unnamed girl on a stele from Paros of c.450 BC, her gaze sadly fixed on two doves she holds in her arms at her chest, and of Apollonia, daughter of Aristandros and Thebageneia, a girl portrayed on a monument from Athens of c.100 BC: she looks at a dove perched on a stele to her right, touching it with her right hand as the bird turns its head towards her. The birds are the sacred birds of Aphrodite and may be symbols of the love the girls' parents felt for their daughters, heightened in their premature loss; but they are also the girls' pets, the birds the girls had played with while they were alive. Another moving example is the portrait on an Attic gravestone of the girl Melisto, perhaps six or eight years old, who holds a bird in her right hand as a little dog, a Maltese, jumps up, standing on its hind legs, while in her left hand she grasps what seems to be a doll; she smiles, happy with her toys and pets. Doves and dogs, cats, geese and roosters are standard elements of children's funerary iconography, both Greek and Roman, and represent a standard assumption that animals were a natural accompaniment of childhood. A Tanagra figurine in Vienna shows a boy riding his pet goose. Anecdotal sources add all manner of creatures: nightingales, parrots, blackbirds, jackdaws, ducks, quails, goldfinches, sheep, deer, goats, and horses. In Greek homoerotic culture, a rabbit was often a gift of courtship. Augustine remembered pet birds among his childhood toys.[51]

Play brought amusement, but it was also an aspect of the process by which learning took place and children were integrated into the adult community, according to Plato and Aristotle, to be directly tied to adult occupations (for instance farming, building, and carpentry).[52] Quintilian advocated play with ivory alphabet letters: a boy handling them would learn their names, his nurse teaching him, while in late antiquity Jerome made the same recommendation for a girl: she could sing the letters' names on the blocks, once more with her nurse.[53] Some games presumably contributed to the development of motor skills and physical coordination, and it was understood that play could contribute to good health: Soranus prescribed exercise with a pushcart for an overweight child, while later medical authorities such as Rufus of Ephesus and Oribasius approved of play all through childhood.[54] From modern analogies, pets might be expected to have helped children learn about sexual reproduction – boys might be troubled by nocturnal emissions[55] – encourage personal responsibility, and to mature emotionally, or simply to bring calm in distress. They also gave instruction in moral sensibility: dogs and horses were symbols of steadfastness and reliability, doves were maritally faithful and loved their offspring, mice were devoted to their parents, nightingales loved to learn.

Play also fostered competitiveness, perhaps preparing generations of children for adult roles of rivalry. Boys at Rome as well as at Athens and Sparta might anticipate adult experiences of warfare, and could quickly become inured by pretending to be magistrates or judges.[56] The historian Cassius Dio records that in 32 BC, a time of intense political anxiety, children at Rome divided themselves into Caesarians and Antonians and fought each other for two days.[57] The outcome was sometimes extreme. The Emperor Septimius Severus is said on his deathbed to have advised his sons Caracalla and Geta to live in harmony, enrich the troops, and despise all else; less than a year later Caracalla had his brother murdered in their mother's apartments in the imperial palace at Rome.[58] They had been at odds all their lives – brotherly strife was Romulus's legacy – and as children their contentiousness had revealed itself in quarrels over the fighting birds they kept. Cockfighting was a popular bloodsport in antiquity, exposing all who watched it to suffering and death.[59] Caracalla and Geta had been devoted to it. It was easy to draw a connection with fratricide.

At times more formal social lessons were required than those that came from play and games. One situation concerned the consumption of food. Among Greeks and Romans there was no convention like the daily family dinner of modern Western societies. Instead, whether male heads of households dined with their wives and children, or with one another, was a matter to be determined as men wished. But in respectable society there was etiquette to be learned nonetheless, instruction in which was the responsibility of the pedagogue. What was involved is conveyed in a work by the Christian author Clement of Alexandria (second century AD), aptly called the *Paedagogus*, the purpose of which is to instruct converts and the young in Christian moral decorum, with Jesus presented as the divine pedagogue from whose teaching perfection will follow. (He had taken "the form of a servant.")[60] Directions on physical comportment are duly given, with special attention to behavior at dinner. Politeness and temperance are the general themes – "We must consider the feelings of our companions at table, and avoid disgusting or nauseating them by our crude conduct, testifying to our own lack of self-control"[61] – but from Clement's detailed remarks the sorts of instruction pedagogues traditionally gave to Greek and Roman children at large become clear. Hands and chin were to be kept clean, so too the couches on which diners reclined. Small amounts of food only were to be taken from the serving tables, at appropriate moments, and they were to be eaten slowly. There were to be no facial contortions while swallowing, no talking while eating, no eating and drinking at the same time, no gulping, spitting or coughing; the head was not to be turned, the eyes were not to roll, and the nose was not to be blown while drinking. Belching and sneezes, if unavoidable, were to be quietly suppressed and so on.[62] Clement seems to have been repelled by much of what he observed around him, and he was certainly both terrified and excited when he thought of women drinking wine in mixed company: they became flirtatious and immodest.[63] His work suggests that children were not always properly trained, or else that they did not always meet the highest expectations society had of them. Romans nonetheless saw an opportunity at dinner for children to hear inspirational stories of their noble ancestors.[64]

In worlds that were full of gods, rituals marking life's passages were other childhood constants. Within a week or so of their birth, Roman infants were customarily cleansed, with nurses giving newborns their first bath before presenting the children to their mothers; children were then ritually named, boys on the ninth day after birth, girls on the eighth, and given the protective amulet called the *bulla*, a locket worn around the neck which signified free birth. It was worn until puberty when, at a formal ceremony, the boy exchanged the toga of childhood he had worn so far for the toga of manhood, with offerings of prayers to the gods of his household and a procession to the forum and the Capitol where sacrifices to the gods were performed. The ceremony was still known to Augustine. For Roman girls, the moment of transition to adulthood, often a remarkably abrupt transition, came with marriage. Elite girls typically married in their middle teens, others a few years later, with the end of childhood marked by dedications of their girlish dolls to Venus.[65] Usually their husbands were considerably older. Similar ceremonies were to be found in the classical Greek world. At Athens the child's acceptance into the family was celebrated by a private ceremony called the Amphidromia. But at the annual spring festival of the Anthesteria, held in honor of Dionysus, children aged three and four were presented with small drinking cups (*choes*) as part of the public celebration when jars of new wine were opened. Many examples survive. In turn, boys at puberty achieved adult status at the Apatouria, an annual festival for male citizens assembled in their hereditary brotherhoods (*phratries*), while girls could take part in the Arkteia, an obscure rite associated with the worship of Artemis that seems to have involved identification with female bears when the onset of menstruation was approaching. It took place at Brauron on the east coast of Attica. For Greek girls generally, marriage was again the most significant transition, occurring at relatively young ages by modern standards: typically late teens for Spartan girls – a poem tells of a Spartan girl dedicating her toys to Artemis before she marries – earlier if of high birth, as for most Athenian girls.[66] Once more husbands were considerably older: thirty was the prescribed marriage age for Athenian men.

All such rites and celebrations, maintained over the course of time, assumed that passage through childhood could be safe and successful only under the protection of superhuman forces whose approval, through appeasement, was vital for the child's incorporation into the human community and emergence into adult society. It is an assumption that reflects the fragility of life and the socializing power of traditional religious practices.

Living conditions

According to historical demographers, life expectancy at birth in antiquity was approximately twenty-five years and child mortality at all periods was high, especially in the first year of life: perhaps as many as 50 percent of all children born died by the age of ten. Virgil kept a special place for them in the Underworld.[67] Statistical sources are unavailable and no more than estimates possible, but incidental information is abundant: Quintilian lost two sons, his only children, in boyhood; Plutarch at least two sons and a daughter. The high rate of mortality was due to poor living conditions. Exceptional episodes of plague apart – at Athens during the Peloponnesian War and widely in the Roman west in the time of Marcus Aurelius – disease was rife and medicine largely ineffectual. How could it be otherwise when medical theory required that health should depend on maintaining a balance in the body among four "humors" (hot, cold, wet, dry)? Food shortages were common and diet, heavily dependent on cereals, was imbalanced and inadequate. Living standards of course varied. Conditions were more salubrious in rural communities than in large, overcrowded cities (Rome, Athens, Alexandria, Carthage), and some regions of the Mediterranean were known to be healthier than others. The privileged minority always had better food, housing, and sanitation than the unprivileged majority, but social status brought minimal advantage, and all parents knew that their children might predecease them.[68]

Death was supposed to arrive in generational sequence, but the reality was different.[69] Fathers frequently buried sons killed in battle, and mothers hated war.[70]

For children, the demographic regime meant that blended family experiences were common, as parents who had lost a spouse remarried, joined their children with those of a new partner, and produced more children together. In some respects the model of the nuclear family (father, mother and children) is important for understanding Roman family life because an enormous number of funerary epitaphs originate from immediate family members and must therefore reflect primary emotional bonds at particularly intense moments. To use the term "nuclear family," however, is to imply that the family in its day-to-day experience was a stable, two-generational domestic unit comparable to its ideal modern western counterpart. Nothing could be more misleading. As census records from Roman Egypt show, households were often complex, with free and slave members, several generations or collateral relatives, and quasi–familial relationships among the servile members. In both classical Athens and Rome, one consequence of men marrying for the first time women who were much younger was that many sons lost their fathers by the time they themselves married. At Rome this meant that sons were free from the constraints of the absolute power, peculiar to Roman culture,[71] that all fathers held over their children (*patria potestas*), which otherwise remained operative until their fathers died and prevented them from enjoying a legally independent life: they could own no property in their own right until their fathers were dead. How to judge the emotional consequences in society at large is a matter only of speculation; but Roman authors sometimes presumed that the affective bond between father and son, symbolized above all by the kiss, was especially close.[72] The Epicurean poet Lucretius thought that children were so desirable that men commonly offered sacrifices and gifts to the gods to ensure that their wives conceived.[73]

As a result, the attentions children received in many families, especially those with child-minding specialists, came from many sources, and while those who wrote about childminders knew the setbacks that they could introduce into children's lives – nurses turned to drink, pedagogues became abusive – strong affective bonds, sometimes lasting a lifetime, formed between servile attendants and their charges.[74] Chiron, the mythical pedagogue of the god Dionysus, stands as an important archetype throughout antiquity of many real-life exemplars. Children could expect to have ties with a multiplicity of people in their household universes, encountering at a minimum stepparents, stepsiblings, and half-siblings as a matter of course. The unstable, communistic character of their familial experience duly becomes observable, the complexity of their affective relationships perceptible.

Parental reactions to the early loss of children were complex. Grief could be intense, at all social levels, as the naturalistic scenes of lost children on Greek stelae and the affectionate language from bereaved parents on Roman epitaphs abundantly reveal. Quintilian's record of the deaths of his sons (and wife) is one of the most moving passages in all Latin literature, the sense of loss in Plutarch's essay consoling his wife on the loss of their daughter Timoxena palpable.[75] The notion that the ancient Persians did not see their children at all until they were well beyond infancy, so that loss could be borne more easily if the children died beforehand, whether true or not, is comprehensible.[76] Seneca, on the other hand, counseled resolution in the face of such adversity, and even Plutarch thought that there was a limit to grief. Spartan mothers were proverbial for their steadfastness in the face of their sons' deaths in war.[77] No single response, in so many times and places, is to be expected, and whether the ancients cared when their children died is not quite the right question to ask. Those who did expressed their sense of loss, but those who did not are unlikely to have engaged in acts of commemoration, and there must have been many children whose deaths were never recorded at all. It is impossible to know.

Sometimes parents were responsible for their children's deaths. Exposure of unwanted infants was a form of family limitation in antiquity motivated by several factors: poverty, physical defectiveness, illegitimacy (not necessarily a burden to the child), parental disputes, the demands of dividing estates among sons, and of dowering daughters. The practice was widespread and probably varied over time and place, but its incidence is immeasurable. Some historians think that it was common in classical Athens, and that more girls than boys were abandoned. The personal names derived from the refuse dumps where children were abandoned ("copronyms") suggest its prevalence in Hellenistic Egypt. At Rome during the Imperial Age exposure was legal, its probable ideological source residing in *patria potestas*: Augustus would not allow the child of his errant granddaughter to be reared.[78] Soranus gives a list of the criteria, by which to decide the newborn's viability, in which he focuses on health and physical form.[79] It must reflect reality. Drowning of the weak and abnormal would occur, or else strangling or smothering.[80] Those who were abandoned could be picked up and reared by anyone who chose to do so, and there were places where they could be found.[81] Many must have died, but some were claimed by slave dealers who would later sell them at a profit. The biographer Suetonius tells of two famous teachers of literature who had been exposed as infants, raised as slaves, and subsequently achieved freedom and success.[82] In Roman law, freeborn children who were exposed and reared as slaves were entitled to recover their freedom as adults, but how they proved their original status is not fully understood. The fanciful scenes of recognition in Greek and Latin comedies and romances, where tokens left with abandoned children eventually serve to identify them, are not reliable guides to historical authenticity. Exposure was formally abolished under the Emperor Valentinian, perhaps under Christian influence, but it continued regardless.[83]

The great killer diseases in antiquity were malaria, typhoid, and tuberculosis. They did not discriminate between children and adults. Some illnesses, however, were thought peculiar to childhood. They were not all life threatening, but they indicate how precarious life could be in its early stages. Commonly reported ailments that could be deadly included: thrush, sometimes contracted from nurses; dysentery, regarded as potentially fatal to children under ten; and convulsions with high temperature, deadly for children under seven. Soranus describes how bone deformities developed in infants, especially in Rome, by which he probably meant rickets.[84] The Roman encyclopedist Celsus knew that every stage of childhood brought its own problems: "Adolescence is liable to acute diseases, such as fits, especially to consumption; those who spit blood are generally youths."[85] Epilepsy could be expected to affect both boys and girls until puberty. Much is heard of bladder stones in boys, and surgical techniques were used for their removal as a last resort. The author of the Hippocratic *Prognostic* (fifth century BC) said that children between seven and fifteen were especially affected by a bladder illness that brought hardness and pain, and that it became fatal if accompanied by a fever.[86] Coughs, fevers, inflammations and sores, gastro-intestinal disorders and eye complaints are frequently mentioned. Augustine thought he had once almost died as a child from a stomach ailment.[87]

Many symptoms were observed but not understood. "Think continually," the Emperor Marcus Aurelius reflected, "how many physicians have died, after often knitting their foreheads over their patients."[88] Anatomical and physiological knowledge in antiquity was profound, or ingenious, but not medical science. Epilepsy, although regarded as hereditary, was called the "Sacred Disease" because it was thought to have been sent by the gods. Its seizures terrified children.[89] Treatments for illnesses therefore were often no more than palliatives, although some may have had restorative value. The elder Pliny (first century AD) was interested in the medicinal properties of natural substances and recommended using butter, for instance, by itself or with honey for infants who were teething, had sore gums, or ulcerated mouths.[90] Soranus offered, "poultices of the finest meal, or fenugreek or linseed and fomentations with sea sponges, especially for the gums, and... honey boiled down to the right degree."[91] Techniques such as blood-letting and clystering were practiced widely, and remedies sometime worked: Galen claimed that his program for curing epilepsy could take effect within forty days and had succeeded many times: a purgation in the spring, followed by a daily regimen of exercise, study, a carefully controlled diet, a drink made from honey and vinegar, and a medicine made from honey and the flowers called squills.[92]

Many remedies originated in folklore. Pliny reports that a gum made from the vine was good for children's sores, the wild gourd colocynthis for infants' head inflammations, basil and goose grease for their ears, rocket for soothing coughs, and glycyside for curing bladder stone.[93] But the enormous catalog of remedies he knew often seemed to combine folklore with sympathetic magic, and the distinction between the two was narrow. Parents duly responded in various non-medical ways to try to secure their children's well-being.

Praying to the gods was one strategy, and for Romans there were many children's divinities on hand.[94] Diespiter brought children into the light of day, Opis received them on the earth, Vaticanus presided over their cries, and Levana over lifting them from the ground. Cunina was the goddess of the cradle, who protected children from the Evil Eye, and the Carmentes foretold their fates. Rumina was the goddess of the breast, Potina and Educa the gods of children's drink and food, and Paventia the goddess of their fears. For adolescents there was Juventas, goddess of youth. To recognize their specialized roles in protecting all the stages of children's development was to instantiate the urgency of survival. The gods might well be called on at times of crisis in a society deeply religious, even if they did not always listen. In his monotheistic Christian zeal, however, Augustine was later, and predictably, to deride them.[95]

With prayers went magical amulets, which Greek and Roman children wore all the time. They were again a feature of children's iconography in visual sources. The Roman *bulla* was an apotropaic device as well as a symbol of free birth, as was the commonly worn phallic amulet or finger-ring, which secured the influence of the god Fascinus, the divinized penis. Some amulets were recommended as cures for certain illnesses: one of red iris for coughs, another of a dolphin's tooth for sudden anxieties; others made from exotic minerals (amber, malachite, or galaxias) gave general protection. Soranus was sceptical about their efficacy, although he understood their psychological value.[96] Galen, on the other hand, proved to his satisfaction that a peony amulet was a genuine cure for epilepsy.[97]

Parents took all precautions possible to ensure the safety of their children, and the anxieties they felt in so doing were sometimes reflected in their dreams. Augustine's mother remembered a dream caused by her concern for her son's spiritual life.[98] But other parents had more pressing concerns. To dream of a woman losing her breasts, of a small boy turning into a man, of a father having sex with a son younger than five, of fellatio with one's mother or an infant, of thunderbolts – these are some of the dreams that Artemidorus said in his handbook meant that dreamers could anticipate their children's deaths.[99] The fears they represented were widespread: Artemidorus had collected his dreams from all over the Mediterranean. It is no cause for surprise that when people wanted to know their future from popular oracles, provocative questions about children commonly came to their minds: "Shall I beget children?", "Is my wife having a child?", "Shall I rear the child?", "Is my wife going to have a miscarriage?"[100]

Historical change

Modern notions of historical progress create the expectation that change in the lives of children in antiquity was both natural and inevitable. Was this the case and, if so, how can it be shown? Change is certainly detectable in ancient political history. The transition at Athens from aristocratic government in the archaic age to the flowering of democracy in the classical era, and the growth of Roman power in Italy and the Mediterranean are developments that can be traced over time with relative ease. With social history, however, matters are different. Materials that can be compared with one another equally, for different times and places, scarcely exist.

For classical Athens, knowledge of certain social practices – adoption is one example – depends on the survival of speeches made in court by advocates when trials concerning property and inheritance took place. The speeches belong almost entirely to the fourth century BC, however, and examples are unavailable from earlier centuries. This means that the knowledge they transmit has to be set against knowledge from different types of source that are often lacking in detail or belong to literary genres whose conventions dictate different interests. The comparison that (unavoidably) has to be made – Athens of the historians Herodotus and Thucydides in the fifth century, and Athens of the orators of the fourth century – is accordingly a comparison between chalk and cheese. Moreover, the Athenocentric bias of extant classical Greek literature at large means that little can be known of life in the hundred or so city-states that constituted Hellas as a whole in the classical age, including such major centers as Thebes and Corinth. Written evidence can be supplemented by archaeology, but excavations of sites are by nature localized, and aggregate conclusions are difficult to achieve. Archaeological interpretation is often driven by whatever written evidence is left. (When there is nothing, historical conclusions can be little more than inferential: burial practices suggest that already in the Minoan and Mycenaean worlds childhood was a distinctive stage of life, but conclusions are impressionistic only.) Ceramic materials from the classical Greek city-states exist in glorious abundance, and the study of vase painting is one special sub-disciplinary field from which much about

Greek society is recoverable. Yet the vases are, once more, subject to chance discovery and unequal distribution in time and place, which renders dubious all possibility of achieving the kind of historical comparisons that historians of modern societies take as normative.

It was a distinctive feature of Roman culture to record individual achievements in prominent commemorative inscriptions, often in funerary contexts, that could be read by anyone able to read. The habit demonstrated the way men and women had triumphed over the challenges of the harsh demographic regime under which their lives were lived. From Rome itself there are tens of thousands of inscriptions, but they cluster in the first and second centuries AD. The cultural practice was not then new, but for earlier periods far fewer inscriptions remain. Whether this indicates a historical change or an intensification of the habit, or is simply due to accident, it is hard to judge. The result, however, is that because the distribution of materials is again unequal, effective comparison between an earlier and a later period is inherently difficult. Matters are complicated further once cities other than Rome are considered.

The challenges involved consequently in documenting change over time in children's lives in antiquity are formidable. But the possibility of substantial change is rendered unlikely by the fact that basic living conditions did not alter radically from one era to another, by which I mean that due to a relative absence of scientific and techno-logical knowledge, major improvements in life expectancy, patterns of mortality, and responses to disease and the hazards of nature were in broad terms unknown. Chil-dren's lives, and adults' attitudes towards and expectations of their children, cannot in all likelihood have differed significantly over time. Cultural particularism produced variations from one society to another, as with the Lycurgan system in classical Sparta or the distinctive character of Roman *patria potestas*, which maintained itself wher-ever Roman institutions established themselves. But they were no more than minor variations on a principal theme. For a thousand years and more, the prospects of all children born were, as far as I can see, essentially the same, subject only to the vari-ables to which I have drawn attention. One result is that the communal character of childrearing and family life evident in the case of Augustine had long been a cultural characteristic of Greco-Roman antiquity.

A history of childhood in antiquity, accordingly, as opposed to a description of some of the circumstances and conditions under which children lived their lives, can hardly be written in any conventional sense. Which does not mean that historians have not attempted to identify change. It is often said for instance that the realism and naturalism with which children are portrayed in Hellenistic art, in contrast to the formalism of the classical Greek period, is attributable to a greater interest in children that developed in the centuries following Alexander's conquests; and the emergence of a special interest in small children has been detected at Rome in the first century BC from what seems to be an increase in references to children in Latin literature. A further suggestion is that the rise of Christianity improved children's lives, on the assumption that it opened up spiritual possibilities that were lacking in Greek and Roman culture, and because under Christian influence children became less vulnerable to violence. I have no wish to say that any of these views is wrong. I am simply skeptical for the reasons stated.

The great shift from polytheism to monotheism in late antiquity was both real and profound. But the common inference that social improvement was a natural corollary of the rise of Christian beliefs and practices is not self-evident: as Augustine knew, corporal punishment had not disappeared from children's lives in his day, and it is indeed possible that in one important respect the conditions of childhood became more daunting, for under the new ideological regime children were now taught that their lives were governed by an all-pervasive sinfulness, as the account of Augustine's childhood with which I began, in all its anguish and guilt, clearly illustrates. The theft of pears, pagan learning, and the temptations of sex were monstrous barriers to knowledge of God, and Augustine allows something to be seen when he wrote about the burden of the Fall that Christianity imposed on the late antique world – the new climate of oppression, that is, under which many children now had to live, especially with regard to the fearful attitudes towards human sexuality that Christians opposed to conventional Greek and Roman standards. The latter had been altogether free of sinful anxiety. Contemplating a choice between a second childhood and death, Augustine chose the latter, imagining childhood as nothing but a journey through pain.[101] It was hardly a healthy outlook.

The new ideology also threatened traditional family norms in innumerable ways. In the early third century, the young Christian woman Perpetua, in her pursuit of martyrdom, abandoned her newborn child and repeatedly disobeyed and humiliated the father who tried to save her life in her trial before a Roman official in Carthage. Her behavior was aberrant. Slave children meantime were no more likely to find their condition changed than in earlier ages, and altogether a case could be made that children's lives now faced new challenges, with the issue of change over time involving the possibility of change for the worse as well as change for the better. A statue from Ostia of a Roman boy shown as an initiate of the goddess Isis leaves unanswerable questions about other forms of salvific religiosity in the early Christian era, and it may be preferable simply to recall that Roman imperial art assumed the importance of children everywhere, whether as recipients of emperors' munificence, as participants in and observers of religious rituals and public entertainments, as pitiful and despondent victims sometimes of capture in warfare, and sometimes as emperors' embodiments of dynastic succession.

Conclusions

What can be said positively is that children in the societies of Greco-Roman antiquity were never marginal beings. By definition they were powerless at birth, limited by their physical, intellectual, and emotional immaturity, but in societies demographically tilted towards the young, children were always visible and they were always drawing, or being drawn, closer and closer to full integration within their communities. Conventional texts are replete with references to them, and their images in visual sources are remarkably abundant. The centrality of children in society is assumed at all times.

The dominant theoretical view, long maintained, was that children were to be shaped into men and women who would contribute to the well-being of societies in which adult roles were governed by a gendered traditionalism that was never seriously contested. The stages of childhood were clearly demarcated, and through each stage the process of molding and nurturing was conditioned by an urgent concern to prepare children for adult life. Parents looked to their offspring to continue family traditions, while communities depended on new generations for both leaders and for their survival. Children were valuable and valued. In an unpredictable environment, however, there could never be any guarantee that the investment preparation for the adult world represented would yield a profitable dividend.

What individual children thought, as children, of the ways in which they were treated and trained, remains a subject for future research. But the patterns of acculturation and socialization to which they were exposed show relatively minimal alteration over time. One explanation of this might be that the patterns themselves were the object from time to time of serious thought and reflection. In that process children were rarely, if ever, considered outsiders.

Notes

1 Augustine, *Confessions* 1.6–8.
2 Augustine, *Confessions* 1.9–3.2.
3 Seneca, *Consolation to Marcia* 21.6; cf. *Moral Epistles* 49.3.
4 Plato, *Republic* 377b; (cf. *Laws* 789E); Origen, *Against Celsus* 55; cf. Plautus, *Mostellaria* 133–140; Pliny, *Letters* 4.19.7.
5 Quintilian, *Oratorical Institute* 12.1.1.
6 Quintilian, *Oratorical Institute* 1.2.1; 2.1.7; 2.2.3.
7 Quintilian, *Oratorical Institute* 1.3.14; *On the Education of Children* 8F.
8 Augustine, *City of God* 22.21; cf. Lactantius, *Divine Institutes* 6.19.6–8.
9 Quintilian, *On the Education of Children* 15.
10 Quintilian, *Oratorical Institute* 1.8.2; 1.8.9; 2.5.12 (for example).
11 Soranus, *Gynecology* 2.19.
12 Soranus, *Gynecology* 2.19.
13 Augustan History, *Life of Hadrian* 3.1.
14 Pliny, *Letters* 4.13; Horace, *Satires* 1.6.76–80; Ovid, *Tristia* 4.10.
15 Cassius Dio 50.17.
16 Pliny, *Letters* 5.16.
17 Seneca, *On Constancy* 1.1.
18 Cf. Plato, *Laws* 789E.
19 Cf. Pliny, *Natural History* 35.70.
20 [Aristotle], *Constitution of the Athenians* 42.2–5.
21 Xenophon, *Oeconomicus* 7.6.
22 Plato, *Republic* 377b.
23 Soranus, *Gynecology* 2.12.
24 Aristotle, *Politics* 7.17.
25 Plutarch, *Lycurgus* 14–19.
26 Xenophon, *Constitution of the Spartans* 2.2.
27 Plutarch, *Lycurgus* 18.
28 Quintilian, *On the Education of Children* 18.
29 *Oxyrhynchus Papyri* 1581.
30 Quintilian, *On the Education of Children* 11.
31 *Gospel of Matthew* 20.
32 Augustine, *City of God* 21.14.
33 Petronius, *Satyricon* 46.
34 Plato, *Republic* 467a; Artemidorus, *Dreambook* 4 pr.
35 [Hippocrates] *The Oath* 13.
36 Virgil, *Aeneid* 12. 435.
37 Origen, *Against Celsus* 1.28; Suetonius, *Augustus* 64.2; Virgil, *Aeneid* 11.72–75; cf. Xenophon, *Oeconomicus* 7.6; Virgil, *Aeneid* 8. 404–415; Apuleius, *Metamorphoses* 9.5.
38 Lucretius, *De rerum natura* 5.1354–1359.
39 Lucian, *The Dream*.

40 Cf. Lactantius, *Divine Institutes* 3.2.4.
41 Cf. Lactantius, *Divine Institutes* 2.12.9.
42 Dionysius of Halicarnassus 3.70.2; Columella, *On Agriculture* 2.2.13, 4.27.6, 12.4.3, 12.42.2; Apuleius, *Metamorphoses* 7.17–22.
43 Martial, *Epigrams* 1.88, 5.34, 7.96, 10.61, 11.91.
44 Dio Chrysostom, *On Slavery*.
45 *Oxyrhynchus Papyri* 3555.
46 Seneca, *Moral Epistles* 12.
47 Ambrose, *On Duties* 2.20.
48 Plato, *Laws* 794A; Homer, *Iliad* 15.361–366; Minucius Felix, *Octavius* 3.6; Seneca, *On Constancy* 12.2.
49 Lucretius, *De rerum natura* 5.228–230; Pollux, *Onomasticon* 9.127; Arnobius, *Against the Nations* 2.39.
50 Augustine, *Confessions* 8.6.
51 Augustine, *Confessions* 1.19.
52 Plato, *Laws* 643B–C; 797A–798E; Aristotle, *Politics* 7.17.
53 Quintilian, *Institute of Oratory* 1.1.20; Jerome, *Letters* 107.4.
54 Soranus, *Gynecology* 2.48.
55 Lucretius, *De rerum natura* 4.1030–1036.
56 Seneca, *On Constancy* 12.2.
57 Cassius Dio 50.8.
58 Cassius Dio 76.15.2; 77.2.1–6; cf. Herodian 4.4.3.
59 Cf. Plato, *Laws* 789B.
60 *Philippians* 2.7.
61 Clement, *Paedagogus* 2.60.1.
62 Clement, *Paedagogus* 2.13.1; 2.55.1; 2.13.2; 2.31.1; 2.60.1; 2.60.2–4.
63 Clement, *Paedagogus* 2.33.1.
64 Valerius Maximus 2.1.9.
65 Persius 2.70; cf. Lactantius, *Divine Institutes* 2.4.12.
66 *Greek Anthology* 6.280.
67 Virgil, *Aeneid* 6.427–9.
68 Seneca, *On Anger* 3.25.1.
69 *Digest of Justinian* 5.2.15. pr.; cf. Seneca, *Moral Epistles* 30.16; 63.14–15; 66.42; 70.4; Martial 1.114; Lactantius, *Divine Institutes* 3.17.8.
70 Herodotus 1.87; Horace, *Odes* 1.1.14–15.
71 Gaius, *Institutes* 1.55; cf. Dionysius of Halicarnassus 8.79.4.
72 Valerius Maximus 2.7.6; 4.1.5; Seneca, *Moral Epistles* 75.3; cf. Varro, *On the Latin Language* 10.4; 1059; cf. also Homer, *Iliad* 22.485–499.
73 Lucretius, *De rerum natura* 4.1236–1238.
74 Cf. Dionysius of Halicarnassus 8.51.3.
75 Quintilian, *Oratorical Institute* 6 pr.; Plutarch, *Consolation to his Wife*; cf. Pliny, *Letters* 3.7.2; 4.2.1.
76 Herodotus 1.136; Valerius Maximus 2.6.16; Strabo 733; cf. Augustine, *Confessions* 3.11.
77 Seneca, *Moral Epistles* 99; Plutarch, *Moralia* 240F, 241A, 241B, 241C, 242B.
78 Suetonius, *Augustus* 65.2.
79 Soranus, *Gynecology* 2.10.
80 Seneca, *On Anger* 1.15.2; Lactantius, *Divine Institutes* 5.9.19.
81 *Digest of Justinian* 25.3.4.
82 Suetonius, *On Grammarians* 7; 21.
83 *Code of Justinian* 8.51.2; cf. *Theodosian Code* 9.14.1.
84 Soranus, *Gynecology* 2.44.
85 Celsus, *On Medicine* 2.1.20.
86 [Hippocrates] *Prognostic* 19.11–23.
87 Augustine, *Confessions* 1.11.
88 Marcus Aurelius, *Meditations* 4.48.
89 [Hippocrates] *The Sacred Disease* 15.8–14.

90 Pliny, *Natural History* 28.257.
91 Soranus, *Gynecology* 2.49.
92 Galen, *Remedy for the epilectic child.*
93 Pliny, *Natural History* 13.67, 20.17, 20.123, 20.126, 27.87.
94 Seneca, *Moral Epistles* 60.1; Marcus Aurelius, *Meditations* 9.40; cf. 10.35; Lactantius, *Divine Institutes* 4.28.4.
95 Augustine, *City of God* 4.11; cf. Lactantius, *Divine Institutes* 1.36.
96 Soranus, *Gynecology* 3.42.
97 Galen, *On the powers of simple remedies* 6.3.
98 Augustine, *Confessions* 3.11.
99 Artemidorus, *Dreambook* 1.41, 1.50, 1.78, 1.79, 2.9.
100 *The Oracles of Astrampsychus* 24, 30, 47, 59.
101 Augustine, *City of God* 21.14.

Suggestions for further reading

The list below gives the key items on which I have relied in writing this contribution. Their titles are self-explanatory. The fundamental studies of children in antiquity are Golden (1990) and Rawson (2003). Wiedemann (1989) was pioneering. Neils and Oakley (2003) give excellent access to Greek visual sources, and the examples I cite are all to be found there. The grave goods of the upper-class Roman girl to which I refer may be seen in the Altes Museum, Staatliche Museen zu Berlin (Collection Gans 1920). Rawson (2011) provides access to a comprehensive bibliography on almost all topics, but Sallares (1991) gives additional material on living conditions. Dr Ville Vuolanto of the University of Tampere, Finland maintains an extraordinary on-line running bibliography (*Children in the Ancient World and the Early Middle Ages. A Bibliography*) which can be accessed at http://uta-fi.academia.edu/VilleVuolanto/Papers/163757 Laes (2011) extends knowledge of Roman children, and Bloomer (2011) of Roman education, although Hopkins (1978, 76–80) on structural differentiation, remains crucial for Rome in the first century BC. On Augustine, Brown (1967) has no rival. I have unashamedly pillaged material from my own studies included in the list.

Bagnall, Roger S., and Bruce. W. Frier. 1994. *The Demography of Roman Egypt.* Cambridge, UK: Cambridge University Press.

Bloomer, W. Martin. 2011. *The School of Rome.* Berkeley, CA: University of California Press.

Bradley, Keith R. 1986. "Wetnursing at Rome: A Study in Social Relations." In *The Family in Ancient Rome: New Perspectives,* edited by Beryl Rawson, 201–229. Ithaca, NY: Cornell University Press.

Bradley, Keith R. 1991. *Discovering the Roman Family.* New York, NY: Oxford University Press.

Bradley, Keith R. 1993. "Writing the History of the Roman Family." *Classical Philology* 88:237–250.

Bradley, Keith R. 1994a. *Slavery and Society at Rome.* Cambridge, UK: Cambridge University Press.

Bradley, Keith R. 1994b. "The Nurse and the Child at Rome: Duty, Affect and Socialisation." *Thamyris* 1:137–156.

Bradley, Keith R. 1998a. "The Roman Family at Dinner." In *Meals in a Social Context,* edited by Inge Nielsen, and Hanne Sigismund Nielsen, 36–55. Aarhus, Denmark: Aarhus University Press.

Bradley, Keith R. 1998b. "The Sentimental Education of the Roman Child: The Role of Pets." *Latomus* 57:523–557.

Bradley, Keith R. 1999. "Images of Childhood: The Evidence of Plutarch." In *Plutarch's Advice to the Bride and Groom and A Consolation to His Wife*, edited by Sarah. B. Pomeroy, 183–196. New York, NY: Oxford University Press.

Bradley, Keith R. 2000. "Children and Dreams." In *Childhood, Class and Kin in the Roman World*, edited by Suzanne Dixon, 43–51. London, UK: Routledge.

Bradley, Keith R. 2003. "Sacrificing the Family: Christian Martyrs and Their Kin." *Ancient Narrative* 3:150–181.

Bradley, Keith R. 2005. "The Roman Child in Sickness and in Health." In *The Roman Family in the Empire: Rome, Italy and Beyond*, edited by Michele George, 67–92. New York, NY: Oxford University Press.

Bradley, Keith R., and Paul A. Cartledge, editors. 2011. *The Cambridge World History of Slavery Volume 1: The Ancient Mediterranean World.* Cambridge, UK: Cambridge University Press.

Brown, Peter R.L. *Augustine of Hippo: A Biography.* 1967. London, UK: University Of California Press.

Cribiore, Raffaella. 2001. *Gymnastics of the Mind: Greek Education in Hellenistic and Roman Egypt.* New York, NY: Princeton University Press.

Eyben, Emiel. 1993. *Restless Youth in Ancient Rome.* London, UK: Routledge.

Golden, Mark. 1990. *Children and Childhood in Classical Athens.* Baltimore, MD: The John Hopkins University Press.

Hopkins, Keith. 1978. *Conquerors and Slaves: Sociological Studies in Roman History Volume 1.* Cambridge, UK: Cambridge University Press.

Hopkins, Keith. 1999. *A World Full of Gods: Pagans, Jews and Christians in the Roman Empire.* London, UK: Phoenix.

Huskinson, Janet. 1996. *Roman Children's Sarcophagi: Their Decoration and Significance.* Oxford, UK: Clarendon Press.

Laes, Christian. 2011. *Children in the Roman Empire: Outsiders Within.* Cambridge, UK: Cambridge University Press.

Neils, Jenifer and John H. Oakley. 2003. *Coming of Age in Ancient Greece: Images of Childhood from the Classical Past.* New Haven, CT: Yale University Press.

Parkin, Tim. G. 1992. *Demography and Roman Society.* Baltimore, MD: The John Hopkins University Press.

Rawson, Beryl. 2003. *Children and Childhood in Roman Italy.* Oxford, UK: Oxford University Press.

Rawson, Beryl, editor. 2011. *A Companion to Families in the Greek and Roman Worlds.* Malden, MA: Wiley-Blackwell.

Rowlandson, Jane, editor. 1998. *Women and Society in Greek and Roman Egypt: A Sourcebook.* Cambridge, UK: Cambridge University Press.

Sallares, Robert. 1991. *The Ecology of the Ancient Greek World.* Ithaca, NY: Cornell University Press.

Saller, Richard P. 1994. *Patriarchy, Property and Death in the Roman Family.* Cambridge, UK: Cambridge University Press.

Uzzi, Jeannine D. 2005. *Children in the Visual Arts of Imperial Rome.* New York, NY Cambridge University Press.

Wiedemann, Thomas E.J. 1989. *Adults and Children in the Roman Empire.* London, UK: Routledge.

2

CHILDREN IN JUDAISM AND CHRISTIANITY

Margaret L. King

In her *Century of the Child* first published in Swedish in 1900, Ellen Key announced that the future would be different and better. With the old baggage of religion tossed aside, modern young men and women could embrace the "holiness of generation," committing themselves to conceiving, birthing, and rearing new generations of children whose promise would be unclouded by conflict or neglect.[1] She was wrong on several counts. The twentieth century was not to be the century of the child, but rather of world war, totalitarian rule, and genocide. And the religious baggage Key gleefully scuttled was not inimical to the child, but rather a tradition uniquely characterized by pro-child attitudes and assumptions. This essay considers the biblical roots of that pro-child outlook, the development in both Judaism and Christianity of pro-child beliefs and institutions in the first five centuries of the Common Era, and the continued impact of those late-ancient models in Western Europe up to about 1500.

The Bible and the child

To believers, the Bible is the unfolding document of divine providence. It may also be read as an extended meditation on the goodness of fertility, the abundance resulting from the interlocked actions of divine creation and human reproduction. From Genesis, the first book of the Hebrew Bible, or Old Testament, through the Christian New Testament, the abundance of nature is celebrated, child-bearing is revered, and the child is exalted.

The God of the Old Testament is a Creator who rejoices in the bounty he calls into being: light and darkness, air and water and dry ground, creatures of the seas, the earth, and the sky – all these, in the first creation narrative that opens the book of Genesis, he declares "good" (Genesis 1–2:2). To complete the task of creation, he creates the human being, "in his own image" both male and female, and tells them to be creators, too: "Be fruitful and increase in number; fill the earth and subdue it" (Genesis 1:27–28).[2]

A second creation narrative follows (Genesis 2:4–3), which situates the first man and the first woman, Adam and Eve, in a glorious garden which they are invited to enjoy – except, that is, for the fruit of the Tree of the Knowledge of Good and Evil. Eve disobeys, and persuades Adam to do so as well. Enraged at this willful disobedience, God condemns male and female to their gendered destinies: Adam to tend the reluctant earth, full of thorns and thistles: "By the sweat of your brow will you eat your food" (3:19); Eve to bear children in pain: "with painful labor you will give birth to children" (3:16).

After the sheer riot of creation, amid the lush abundance of the Garden of Eden, both human production and reproduction are instituted. Henceforth, God will step aside as creator, commissioning man to create wealth by the labor of his hand, and woman to bear children by the labor of her womb: for she "would become the mother of all the living" (3:20). Henceforth, new life will be created – by God, always – but through the medium of the female body. On its capacity to do so, its fertility, rests the future of all humankind.

The great value of fertility is evidenced in God's repeated commands and promises delivered to the protagonists of the Bible narrative. In Genesis 9:7, he commands Noah to "be fruitful and increase in number; multiply on the earth and increase upon it." In Genesis 22:17, he promises Abraham: "I will surely bless you and make your descendants as numerous as the stars in the sky and as the sand on the seashore" (cf. Genesis 13:16; Genesis 15:4–6; Genesis 17:6; Genesis 24:60; Genesis 28:3; Genesis 35:1). In Genesis 26:4, he renews the promise to Abraham's son Isaac: "I will make your descendants as numerous as the stars in the sky and will give them all these lands, and through your offspring all nations on earth will be blessed . . . ."

The descendants of Isaac multiplied indeed: they numbered 70 when the family of Jacob, Isaac's son, settled in Egypt (Genesis 46:26–27) and before long, the Israelites being "exceedingly fruitful" "multiplied greatly, increased in numbers, and became so numerous that the land was filled with them" (Exodus 1:6). Forty years after he had led them out of Egypt, Moses reminds the Israelite wanderers in the desert: "The LORD your God has increased your numbers so that today you are as numerous as the stars in the sky" (Deuteronomy 1:10).

The pre-eminent value of fertility for the Israelites may explain their rejection of a custom likely once universal in human societies: that of child sacrifice. It was practiced by Neanderthals; in Minoan and Hindu civilizations; by the Maya, Aztec, and Inca; by the Celts; and by the Greeks. It was widespread in the ancient Levant where the Canaanites, a people closely related to their Israelite neighbors, regularly offered up one or more children, as did the Carthaginians, their descendants, continuing into the Roman period.

The Old Testament explicitly prohibits child sacrifice, as in Leviticus 18:21: "Do not give any of your children to be sacrificed to Molek,[3] for you must not profane the name of your God. I am the LORD." Nonetheless, the Israelites likely sacrificed children until about the time of Josiah, King of Judah (r.c.641–609 BCE). Two previous kings of Judah had notoriously offered up their own sons: Ahaz (r.c.735–715 BCE) and Manasseh (r. 693–643 BCE), each of whom "sacrificed his own son in the fire" at a time of imminent danger (2 Kings 16:3; 2 Kings 21:6; 2 Chronicles 33:6). More generally, Israelite families imitated the Canaanite custom, causing their children to "walk through the fire," as the deed is allusively characterized in scripture.

The prophets named the sacrifice of children as one of the terrible sins for which the Israelites would suffer divine punishment. Ezekiel, for example, reports God's outrage: "And you took your sons and daughters whom you bore to me and sacrificed them as food to the idols . . . You slaughtered my children and sacrificed them to the idols" (Ezekiel 16:20–21). As does Jeremiah: "The people of Judah have done evil in my eyes . . . They have built the high places of Topheth in the Valley of Ben Hinnom to burn their sons and daughters in the fire . . . ." (Jeremiah 7:30–31; see also 19:5; 32:35).

The Israelite repudiation of child sacrifice appears to be inscribed in the drama that unfolds in Genesis 22:1–18. Here Abraham is tested by God, commanded to offer up his son in sacrifice: "Take your son, your only son, whom you love – Isaac – and go to the region of Moriah. Sacrifice him there as a burnt offering on a mountain I will show you" (Genesis 22:2). Abraham obeys; but an angel stays his hand before the deed is done, and Abraham substitutes a ram as sacrificial victim. The whole future history of the Jewish people is here decided: the child's blood would not be shed, and instead, Abraham's descendants would be designated as the chosen people of God (Genesis 22:17–18).

Yet the pull of the sacrificial act remained, even after the prophets had labeled it an abomination. In the second century BCE, the Maccabean heroes who resisted Seleucid oppression were celebrated as martyrs – sacrificial victims, in effect, to the cause of Jewish survival. And two centuries later, Jesus of Nazareth suffered and died on a cross, according to Christian witnesses, for the salvation of the faithful: as written in John 3:16, "For God so loved the world that he gave his one and only Son, that whoever believes in him shall not perish but have eternal life." Child sacrifice as conventionally practiced had been prohibited; but the sacrifice of the young in a holy cause, or God's beneficial sacrifice of his own Son, were sublimations of the ancient and abominated sacrificial act, and so sanctioned.

Child killing of another sort was also central to the narrative of the survival and triumph of the chosen people. The massacres of children ordered by tyrannical kings in Exodus and Matthew (Exodus 1; Matthew 2:16–18) were horrors from which the Israelites in Egypt, in the first case, and the infant Jesus, in the second, narrowly escaped. In the Tenth Plague visited on Pharaoh, God himself ordered the death of all the Egyptian first-born – the children of the Israelites being spared when the angel of death passed over their homes (Exodus 12). The specter of the mass slaughter of children haunts both the Old and the New Testaments.

In a culture where children are valued, women are honored for their fecundity – and disgraced for their barrenness. The sadness of the infertile woman is heard in Rachel's cry to Jacob: "Give me children, or I'll die!" (Genesis 30.1); to which Jacob replies that it is God alone who gives the gift of children. And God, in fact, intervenes repeatedly in the Bible to grant that gift. Sarah and Hannah in the Old Testament were childless, but became fruitful; so did Elizabeth, the mother of John the Baptist, in the New Testament; and even Mary, a virgin, through God's deliberate action, is made fertile and conceives a son: the son of God and woman.

The whole identity of Abraham's wife Sarai, later Sarah, is summed up by her barrenness; thus she is first introduced to the Old Testament account: "Now Sarai was childless because she was not able to conceive" (Genesis 11:30). But God had a different plan: he caused Sarah to conceive and give birth to Isaac, from whom the Israelites would descend (Genesis 21:2). Burdened by her barrenness, as well, Hannah prayed to God for a child, promising to dedicate him to the Lord (1 Samuel: 1–3). In due course, she gave birth to Samuel, whom God made high priest and eventually judge over the Israelites. The woman who had been barren had become, through God's intervention, the mother of the most powerful leader of the nation.

The theme of divine intervention in the cause of maternal fertility continues without pause from Old to New Testament. The gospel of Luke opens dramatically with the miraculous conceptions of the kinswomen Elizabeth and Mary, destined to give birth to John the Baptist and Jesus, respectively. John would herald the arrival of the savior. First the angel Gabriel foretells to Elizabeth's husband the long hoped-for pregnancy of the aging and barren woman (Luke 1:13). Then Gabriel appears to Mary, whose pregnancy, as a virgin already betrothed, was equally unlikely, and makes a similar prediction: "You will conceive and give birth to a son, and you are to call him Jesus" (Luke 1:31). By the anguishing labor of their bodies and the intervention of God, Sarah, Hannah, Elizabeth, and Mary, all daughters of Eve, brought forth the men who would be "great in the sight of the Lord" (Luke 1:15) and execute God's will on earth.

For these are special children: Isaac, Samuel, John the Baptist, and Jesus, to whom could be added Moses and David, foremost among the charmed and powerful children who inhabit the pages of the Bible. Set adrift in a basket, Moses is providentially rescued by a princess, so that he may, when grown, lead his people out of Egypt and into the land of Canaan. A shepherd boy, the youngest son of seven, equipped only with a sling, David destroys the enemy of his people, the heavy-armed Goliath, champion of the Philistines: "so that all the earth may know that there is a God in Israel" (1 Samuel 17:46–47). These charismatic children are unique in the literatures of ancient civilizations: they are the saviors of their nation.

Alongside the powerful children and successful mothers in the Old Testament narrative are those who are vulnerable – and none are more vulnerable than orphaned children and their widowed mothers. The protection of widows and orphans is frequently enjoined, beginning with the command in Exodus 22:22: "Do not take advantage of a widow or an orphan," echoed, among other places, in Isaiah 1:17: "Take up the cause of the fatherless; plead the case of the widow" (cf. Deuteronomy 10:18, 24:17, 27:19; Isaiah 1:23, 10:2; Zechariah 7:10). The care of these most vulnerable members of society distinguishes Jewish society among ancient civilizations, a distinction inherited by both Christianity (see James 1:27) and Islam.

The instruction to fathers to educate their children, encountered repeatedly in the Old Testament, is also exceptional. Thus Moses commands the assembly of the Israelites: "These commandments that I give you today are to be on your hearts. Impress them on your children. Talk about them when you sit at home and when you walk along the road, when you lie down and when you get up" (Deuteronomy 6:6–7). And again: "Teach [these things] to your children, talking about them when you sit at home and when you walk along the road, when you lie down and when you get up" (Deuteronomy 11:18–19; also Deuteronomy 4:9–10; 29:29; 31:12–13; 32:46; Genesis 18:19).

The pro-childhood themes of the Old Testament continue, as has been seen, into the New. Children are surprisingly prominent in the Gospel narratives. Despairing parents bring their ailing or dead children to Jesus to be healed. Children are present in the crowds whom Jesus feeds and hail him as he makes his final procession into Jerusalem. Jesus embraces, touches, and blesses children, and elevates them as the prototype of the saved: "such as these shall enter the kingdom of God." In Acts and the Pauline and non-Pauline epistles, as well, children are present among Christian households and assemblies; and Paul and other epistolary authors greet their converts as children, urging them to progress in faith as the obedient children of God the father.

Jesus performs more than 30 miracles in the New Testament; three of these concern children – not an insignificant proportion in an age that commonly ignored the presence of children and, what appears even more poignantly in these tales, the anxieties of their parents. In the first, told at length in all three synoptic gospels (Matthew 9:18–26; Mark 5:21–43; Luke 8:40–56), one of the synagogue leaders came to Jesus and "fell at his feet. He pleaded earnestly with him, 'My little daughter is dying. Please come and put your hands on her so that she will be healed and live' " (Mark 5:22–23). Jesus follows him to his house, takes the hand of the dead girl, and recalls her to life: "Immediately the girl stood up and began to walk around (she was twelve years old)" (Mark 5:42).

In the second account, told by Matthew and Mark (Matthew 15:21–28; Mark 7:24–30), Jesus had withdrawn to the region of Tyre and Sidon, where a foreign woman, a Canaanite, approached him, crying: "Lord, Son of David, have mercy on me! My daughter is demon-possessed and suffering terribly" (Matthew 15:22). Despite her alien status, Jesus commends her: " 'Woman, you have great faith! Your request is granted.' And her daughter was healed at that moment" (Matthew 15:28).

In the third account, told in all three synoptics (Matthew 17:14–21; Mark 9:14–29; Luke 9:37–49) a man approached from within a crowd that came to greet Jesus: "Teacher, I beg you to look at my son, for he is my only child. A spirit seizes him and he suddenly screams; it throws him into convulsions so that he foams at the mouth. It scarcely ever leaves him and is destroying him" (Luke 9:38–39). Jesus expelled the demon, " . . . healed the boy and gave him back to his father. And they were all amazed at the greatness of God" (Luke 9:42–43).

In the miraculous feeding of the multitude at Galilee, in addition, a child figures prominently. Here Jesus comforts and feeds thousands of followers, described as numbering 5,000 adult males: "not counting women and children" (Matthew 14:13–21; Mark 6:30–44; Luke 9:10–17; John 6:1–15). It is a small nameless child who provides the wherewithal – five small loaves of barley bread and two small fish – to feed that multitude (John 6:8–9). Jesus blesses and distributes these meager provisions, miraculously in sufficiency to satisfy the hunger of all: "as much as they wanted" (John 6:11). Though he is not the principal player in this drama, the child's presence is not trivial: it is through him that Jesus can minister to families in need.

Similarly, children are among the crowds that line the path as Jesus, on his chosen donkey, rides into Jerusalem at the beginning of the week of his Passion; and it is children, explicitly, who hail him in the temple courts to the annoyance of the priests and scribes:

> But when the chief priests and the teachers of the law saw the wonderful things he did and the children shouting in the temple courts, "Hosanna to the Son of David," they were indignant. "Do you hear what these children are saying?" they asked him. "Yes," replied Jesus, "have you never read, " 'From the lips of children and infants you, Lord, have called forth your praise?' ".
>
> (Matthew 21:15–16; allusion to Psalm 8:2)

Elsewhere, when Jesus and his disciples are surrounded by a small crowd, Jesus makes a signal statement about the role of children. As Mark tells the story:

> People were bringing little children to Jesus for him to place his hands on them, but the disciples rebuked them. When Jesus saw this, he was indignant. He said to them, "Let the little children come to me, and do not hinder them, for the kingdom of God belongs to such as these. Truly I tell you, anyone who will not receive the kingdom of God like a little child will never enter it." And he took the children in his arms, placed his hands on them and blessed them.
> (Mark 10:13–16; also Matthew 19:13–15; Luke 18:15–18)

He touches and blesses them, and identifies the qualities that the seeker of salvation must possess: not power, not wisdom, not wealth, not experience, but the unselfconscious innocence of the child. On an earlier occasion, Jesus likewise highlights the child as paradigm:

> He called a little child to him, and placed the child among them. And he said: "Truly I tell you, unless you change and become like little children, you will never enter the kingdom of heaven. Therefore, whoever takes the lowly position of this child is the greatest in the kingdom of heaven. And whoever welcomes one such child in my name welcomes me.
> (Matthew 18:2–5; see also Mark 9:37; Luke 9:46–48)

Actual children do not appear in the Gospel of John as they do in the synoptic Gospels. But in this Gospel as well, the condition of discipleship is likened to childhood: the followers of Jesus are called "children of God," as in John 1:12–13:

> Yet to all who did receive him, to those who believed in his name, he gave the right to become children of God – children born not of natural descent, nor of human decision or a husband's will, but born of God.

And, famously, at John 3:3 is found the instruction of Jesus that he who seeks salvation must return to a state of infancy: "Very truly I tell you, no one can see the kingdom of God unless they are born again."

The emphasis on children in the Gospels is striking, and begs for explanation. The elevation of children seems to underscore the prominent Gospel theme of insurgency: the toppling of the powerful and promotion of the weak, enunciated especially in the Sermon on the Mount (Matthew 5–7) and embodied in the story of Jesus, a man of humble station, chosen by God to be born of the flesh of Mary, an ordinary woman. Common to all the Gospels, this message is especially prominent in Matthew and Luke, who preface the narrative of the career of the adult Jesus with material about his infancy in which clues to his future greatness are embedded (Matthew 1–2; Luke 1–2).

Just as the Gospels depict the primacy of children, in the Acts of the Apostles and the Pauline and non-Pauline epistles that follow, children remain thematically important – both real ones and metaphorical ones.

Real children are in the crowds and the homes of the early Christian worshipers described in Acts and the epistles. In one of these homes, the sleepy child Eutychus falls from his window perch to the ground outside – there to be either resurrected, or rescued from death by the apostle Paul himself (Acts 20:9–12). In such homes, when the householder converts along with all his dependents, children are baptized alongside the adults (Acts 10:23–48; Acts 16:14–15; Acts 16:31–34; 1 Corinthians 1:14–16.). Writing to his disciple Timothy, Paul notes that the latter had imbibed his Christian faith as a child, no doubt in their home, from his mother Eunice and his grandmother Lois (2 Timothy 1:5 and 3:14–15). And offering advice on household management in Colossians 3:20–21, Paul shows his sensitivity to children, warning fathers against excessive sternness: "Fathers, do not embitter your children, or they will become discouraged" (cf. Ephesians 6:4).

These passages describe encounters with real children. More often, children are metaphorical. In 1 Thessalonians 2:7–8, 11–12, Paul speaks of the pastorate as both mother and father to the faithful:

> Just as a nursing mother cares for her children, so we cared for you . . . For you know that we dealt with each of you as a father deals with his own children, encouraging, comforting and urging you to live lives worthy of God, who calls you into his kingdom and glory.
>
> (cf Galatians 4:19–20)

The author of John's epistle, likewise, addresses his listeners as "children" at 1 John 2:1: "My dear children, I write this to you so that you will not sin"; and at 1 John 3:7: "Dear children, do not let anyone lead you astray . . . ." Children figure in these epistles as metaphors for those who are as beloved and capable of wholesome growth; the children not merely of parents in the flesh, but also of a heavenly father.

From his joyous creation of man and woman, and their descendants through the bodies of the daughters of Eve, to his promise that all the faithful shall be children of the heavenly Father, the God of both Old and New Testament is an advocate of children and childhood. He commands the faithful to increase and multiply, cures the barrenness of women, urges compassion on the fatherless and their widowed mothers, orders fathers to instruct their children, elevates the innocence of the vulnerable child over the hypocrisy of the powerful, and promises believers that they shall be gathered up into his kingdom as children of a loving father. The high valuation of the child in the Bible is the foundation for the subsequent development of concepts of children and the treatment of actual children in both Judaism and Christianity as, in the first five centuries of the Common Era, each tradition must confront Greco–Roman societies and states.

Jews and Christians confront the Greco–Roman world

In the first five centuries of the Common Era, Jews and Christians squarely confronted the values of Greco–Roman civilization imposed by the power of the Roman state to which they were subject. Over these centuries, however, their respective positions with regard to that dominant power shifted. Numbering about four million, Jews were initially a successful and prosperous minority within the Roman Empire, constituting about one-eighth of its population in the first century CE. By the fifth century, after two disastrously failed rebellions, they had been driven from their homeland

and scattered. Christians, in contrast, were a persecuted minority for the first three centuries CE, becoming first a tolerated, then a privileged community in the fourth. Through a complex process of conversion, population increase, the advocacy of influential elites, the activity of bishops and theologians, and eventually the protection of the state, Christianity became the majority religion and most vital organism of the Roman Empire before that empire itself disintegrated.

Although their paths diverged in the late Ancient Era, still Jews and Christians shared assumptions about children deriving from the common source of their belief systems, the Bible. Both groups opposed the machinery of child slaughter, which powered Greco–Roman society. This pro-child vision was anomalous in the Greco–Roman world, where attitudes toward children ranged from indifference to hostility. This characterization holds even though individual Greeks and Romans had warm relationships with their children, as evidenced in literary texts, sepulchral inscriptions, and visual documents. These testimonials notwithstanding, Greco–Romans viewed children as irrational creatures to be trained as quickly as possible for the purposes of the adult world, and to be nourished and nurtured – or not – as patriarchal strategies required. The Greco–Roman world was, arguably, infanticidal: it was a society that ignored, exploited, or discarded children.

Among Greeks and Romans, although sons were valued, few households raised more than two or three. Of daughters, who were not necessary for the continuity of lineage and whose dowries meant a drain of family wealth, few raised more than one or two. To obtain these results, in an era when contraception was not widely practiced, some children were not reared. The decision was taken shortly after birth – in Rome, before the eighth day for males, the ninth for females – by the *paterfamilias*, the father of the household. Illegitimates, meanwhile, not born into a household were often unwanted as well. What happened to all these rejected children?

Some unwanted children were killed outright, the victims of what we know as infanticide. Most, however, were "exposed," or abandoned in a public place – a dung-heap, a public square, or the space between two columns known to demarcate such a site in the city of Rome. Although not all of those abandoned in this way died, many surely succumbed to starvation and the elements – and were thus, effectively, murdered. Others were picked up and used as servants, perhaps in the status of slave or perhaps in that of *alumnus*, a kind of foster child partially integrated into the household. Others were rounded up by slave dealers to be sold into domestic service, or to labor in farming or mining, or to staff the brothels – male and female alike. Optimists prefer to think that many abandoned children were rescued and remained free; skeptics suspect that few survived, and that those survivors were largely depressed into slavery and subjected to consequent sexual, physical, and mental abuse. We have absolutely no idea of the numbers: how many were rescued, how many allowed to die, how many disappeared into the nameless multitude of the oppressed.

Besides the murder and exposure of infants, some unwanted children met their end before they were born by abortion. Abortion was associated with women in general, and with prostitutes, adulteresses, and conniving midwives in particular: groups of women who acted outside the legitimate context of the household and without the stamp of male authority. The chorus of comment on abortion by contemporary writers and moralists suggests that abortion was widely practiced when Rome was at its height.

The Greeks and Romans should not be considered exceptionally brutal in the matter of child killing. Similar strategies were adopted for population control in ancient China and India, and among other ancient nomadic and horticultural societies. Historian Sarah Pomeroy puts it succinctly: "Infanticide is . . . a form of family planning. . . ."[4] What is striking is not that the Greeks and the Romans limited their household numbers; it is that Jews and Christians did not. Their practices at the time, not those of the pagan majority, were viewed as eccentric. It is with a tone between astonishment and censure that the Roman historian Tacitus observes of the Jews: "It is a crime among them to kill any newly-born infant."[5]

For Jews and Christians (and later Muslims, who are beyond the purview of this essay) steadily opposed the linked practices of infanticide, exposure, and abortion by which the Greeks and Romans controlled population. They believed that all children were valuable, the compelling objects of compassion and care. For Jews, children were the essential members of the family, the social group through which the covenant with God was witnessed. For Christians, children were the pattern of those whom God welcomed into his kingdom.

While infanticide and exposure for these believers were self-evidently to be repudiated as contrary to the biblical injunction to "increase and multiply," abortion was a more complicated issue. While the first-century Jewish philosopher Philo of Alexandria enunciated what would subsequently become the Christian position – that life began at conception and abortion was tantamount to homicide – some Jewish scholars hewed closer to the Roman formulation that prior to birth, the fetus was not a person. Nonetheless, Jews did not condone or practice abortion – as many Jews still do not today – except in rare cases where the mother's life was in danger. Meanwhile, Christian thinkers developed an uncompromising anti-abortion position, identifying the unborn fetus, from the moment of conception, as fully human and a child of God. That position is still held by the Roman Church today, as well as by several Protestant and post-Protestant groups.

Many modernists regret the cautious view of abortion expressed by ancient Jews, and even more the repudiation of the practice by ancient Christians – and deplore the opposition to abortion by some present-day adherents of these faiths. That controversy must be avoided here. Yet it should be emphasized that, in the context of the ancient world which routinely devalued the life of fetus, neonate, and infant – and had, moreover, no concept of the rights of women – the positions taken on abortion by Jews and Christians alike were entirely consistent with the life-affirming outlook of their scriptures and the whole pattern of their understanding of the child.

If children were not to be destroyed, what then was to be done with the children abandoned by parents or orphaned by the death of their fathers? In both Jewish and Christian communities, these children were embraced. The Jewish responsibility to care for orphans is inscribed in scripture, and again in post-biblical literature. Christians responded to the same injunctions, with each community caring for the needy in their midst. By the fourth century, bishops had taken charge of orphan care in each diocese and parish. An extensive network of institutions providing orphan care developed in Constantinople, the capital of the eastern remnant of the Roman Empire that would survive as the Byzantine Empire; and here, by the end of the fifth century, the first orphanage, the Orphanotropheion, was founded.

The education of children, like the care of orphans, was enjoined by scripture. The centrality of education for the Jews is echoed by the first-century CE Jewish author Josephus in his apologetic *Against Apion:* "Above all we pride ourselves on the education of our children, and regard as the most essential task in life the observance of our law and of the pious practices based thereon."[6] By the last centuries BCE, Jewish communities were served by synagogues as places for prayer and study; here male children received instruction in imitation of the schools that were a distinctive feature of the Hellenistic world – with the important difference that the subject of study was Torah (the first five books of the Bible), for which the necessary prerequisite was a knowledge of Hebrew, and not the literary corpus of Greco–Roman civilization.

Early Christians, in contrast, did not institute specifically Christian schools for the education of their children. For the later years of adolescence, they were content to send Christian children to Greco–Roman schools. These provided a matchless system of secular education reaching from basic grammatical instruction through the advanced studies of rhetoric and philosophy, a preparation essential for those aiming for leadership positions in church or state. Christians, at first, were wary of the moral and philosophical values conveyed in the corpus of ancient literature. But a compromise was eventually achieved, which proved to be long lasting, by which the Greco–Roman cultural legacy was adopted, though carefully filtered, by Christian civilization.

A wholly Christian education for younger students was available in monastic schools, which had begun to develop along with the evolution of monasticism itself by around the fourth century. The monasteries took in the orphans in their midst, as has been seen. In addition, they received the "offered" children, or "oblates," of generally wealthy converts, whose gift to the church was understood to favor their own salvation. Both orphans and oblates needed to be trained in Greek or Latin, depending on region, so as to participate in the chanting of the liturgy, which was the principal obligation of the monk. In addition, some children not consecrated to the monastic life received instruction within the monastery walls.

Outside the monastery, the churches developed ways to teach the rudiments of the faith both to children and to adult initiates, called catechumens, as part of the long process leading to conversion, baptism, and incorporation into the Christian community. For this purpose, not even literacy, let alone literary study, was required: instruction could be delivered orally, and scripture was regularly read aloud from the pulpit in Greek or Latin, both vernacular languages at this time. Children were also acquainted with the fundamentals of the faith through participation in child choirs, as lectors, in processions and in the celebration of the Eucharist, to which they were in this era admitted.

In Christian households, as well, parents instructed their young children. As in Greco–Roman society, Jewish and Christian children were required to show obedience to parents, and so become imbued with their beliefs and rituals. To this, early Christians introduced another expectation: the development of the moral capacity, a concern witnessing a broader concept of education than the Greco–Roman, which was more narrowly focused on academic achievement.

Accordingly, the fourth-century Greek bishop and theologian John Chrysostom (*c.*347–407) offered parents a complete guide to the rearing of children in his *Address on Vainglory and the Right Way for Parents to Bring Up their Children*, the most important pedagogical work of the first Christian centuries.[7] Children were to be brought up, he urged, "in the Lord," and prepared "as heirs of the kingdom of God."[8] In the early years, both parents are encouraged to tell Bible stories, accompanied by adult explanation and commentary, to instill moral norms. In adolescence, when the mammoth force of desire expressed itself, children are to be closely supervised, and married at an early age to an appropriate partner chosen by the family. In Chrysostom's view, parents of children are the makers of Christians:

> To each of you fathers and mothers I say, just as we see artists fashioning their paintings and statues with great precision, so we must care for these wondrous statues of ours... Like the creators of statues do you give all your leisure to fashioning these wondrous statues for God. And, as you remove what is superfluous and add what is lacking, inspect them day by day, to see what good qualities nature has supplied so that you will increase them, and what faults so that you will eradicate them.[9]

Chrysostom also gives voice to the Christian anxiety, shared by Jews, about the Greco–Roman practice of the sexual abuse of children. Among the Greeks, pederasty was widely accepted, even for freeborn youths; among the Romans, who protected freeborn male adolescents from adult male sexual predation, the abuse of juvenile slaves and prostitutes, both male and female, was widespread. Parents must protect their children from such abuse at all cost, wrote Chrysostom:

> If it were necessary to take children to a foreign land to save them from this sickness, or to the sea, or to the islands, or to an inaccessible land, or to the world beyond us, should we not do and suffer all things so as not to allow these defilements?[10]

Jews and Christians also distinguished their treatment of children from that of the pagan majority in the manner of receiving the child into the community. In Greco–Roman practice, the *paterfamilias* received – or chose not to receive – the child into his household eight or nine days after the birth. In the rituals of circumcision and baptism practiced by Jews and Christians, the family witnessed the acceptance of the child into the whole religious community.

Circumcision, the removal of the foreskin of the penis, marked the members of the Jewish community from its earliest existence. It is a requirement established by God as part of the covenant with Abraham:

> This is my covenant with you and your descendants after you, the covenant you are to keep: Every male among you shall be circumcised . . . For the generations to come every male among you who is eight days old must be circumcised . . . My covenant in your flesh is to be an everlasting covenant. Any uncircumcised male, who has not been circumcised in the flesh, will be cut off from his people; he has broken my covenant.
>
> (Genesis 17:10–14)

Thereafter, in obedience to this commandment, on the eighth day after his birth, surrounded by his family, the Jewish male infant is admitted to the Jewish community by this sign indelibly printed on his flesh. Adult converts to Judaism also submitted themselves to this painful wounding. The practice discouraged followers of the early Christians, on which account the apostle Paul persuaded the Jewish Christian elders in Jerusalem to lift the requirement for converts to the new faith (Acts 15).

Every male child and every male adult was by circumcision marked as a Jew. That identity was not contingent on family lineage, wealth, or other merit, but only on incorporation into the people who had bound themselves by a covenant with God. This focus on the person of the circumcised, who in his individual personhood acquires a unique identity, is exceptional in the ancient world, and clearly dissimilar to the Greco–Roman practice which by a paternal decision accepted the neonate into a particular family.

The Christian practice of infant baptism did not develop from the Jewish practice of circumcision – although a predisposition to the baptism of infants by Jewish converts in the early church may be explained by their familiarity with circumcision. Yet baptism resembles circumcision in its purpose. In baptism, the child is recognized as an individual loved by God, whose pilgrimage to a future relationship with the Creator begins at that moment. Baptism does not install the child in a family, a class, or a nation, but embraces him as a newcomer to the community of Christians.

Among early Christians, most of the baptized were adult converts. For them, the preparation for baptism was lengthy and closely supervised, requiring instruction and prayer. The sacrament itself, often performed on Easter Sunday, culminated a three-day liturgy. The catechumens viewed the sacrament with great seriousness. By it, all their sins were redeemed; and any sins committed subsequently threatened their salvation.

Given the importance of baptism in the preparation of adult catechumens, the eventual establishment of infant baptism, for which there could be no prior catechesis, is a bit of a puzzle. Some infant and child baptisms occurred in the earliest Christian assemblies, as when Peter or Paul baptized a householder and all the members of his family. Since the early church grew, moreover, as much by reproduction as conversion, many of the faithful by the second or third centuries – including martyrs like Saint Polycarp – had been reared in the church from childhood, and would have been baptized as infants.

But the establishment of infant baptism as the norm rested on theological arguments. In the Latin Church, Saint Augustine (though he himself was an adult convert and had written guidelines for the catechumenate) was the critical voice. His construction of the doctrine of Original Sin, elaborated as a result of his confrontation with the Pelagian heresy, necessitated the mechanism of infant baptism. If all were born laden with the burden of Adam's sin, then unbaptized children who died – and many did, given an infant mortality rate of around twenty-five percent – faced certain damnation.

To spare the young, Augustine advocated the immediate baptism of neonates. The young church in the West followed his lead, developing rituals of first communion and confirmation at middle and later childhood to ensure instruction in doctrine. The Greek Church, while it did not adopt Augustine's doctrine of Original Sin, also feared for infants dying before baptism, and so, as in the West, adopted infant baptism as a norm.

By around 500 CE, infant baptism had superseded adult baptism. Although infant baptisms were not performed on any particular day, as was the Jewish ritual of circumcision, they were performed soon after birth – immediately, when there was imminent danger of death, in which case midwives were empowered to perform an emergency baptism. Baptism was the first step on the road to salvation for all Christians, regardless of rank, sex, family lineage, ethnic origin, or any other social marker. The determination of the churches to bring the boon of baptism to every child born bespeaks a new universalism: every soul, without discrimination, is to be rescued from damnation. The value of each individual is assumed, every child possessing an eternal destiny.

The first five centuries of the Common Era are the time "when children became people," as Odd Magne Bakke entitles his indispensable book on the subject.[11] The neglect and destruction of children was deemed an abomination; their care and rearing became communal responsibilities; each individual life was valorized. The product of the first five centuries of Jewish and Christian interaction with Greco–Roman civilization was no less important than this: no child was born unwelcomed; all children were deserving of care; each child was fully human from birth and, for Christians, from conception, and was to be raised as an autonomous individual, capable of moral action, and bound not to serve prevenient generations but to create a new reality in a cosmos undetermined except by the will of God.

Medieval continuities: the legacy of the Judeo-Christian pro-child ideal, 500 to 1500 CE

As a result of the interaction of Judaism and Christianity with Greco–Roman states and society, an enhanced concept of the child and the improved care of real children were achieved in the first five centuries CE. These achievements endured over the next ten centuries, even in the bleak landscape that, in Western Europe, followed the collapse of the Roman civilization. This brief overview considers the status of children and the concept of childhood in both Jewish and Christian communities from 500 to 1500 CE.

Whereas Jews constituted a solid minority in the Roman Empire, and Christians, at first, a meager handful, their relative demographic positions reversed during the Middle Ages. Around 1000 CE, no more than a few hundred-thousand Jews lived in isolated communities in northern Europe, a number that would be further reduced by persecutions and expulsions to follow. They lived within an expanding realm of Christendom that reached, around 1300 CE, a population peak of one hundred million, at which time another ten million (at most) inhabited the Greek-speaking Byzantine Empire. The embattled Jewish communities never lost contact, however, with the network of older Jewish communities in Spain, North Africa, and the Middle East, where Jews lived freely as a tolerated minority under Islamic control.

Within this changed world, the Jews of Europe prospered in their closely-knit communities, observing the traditions they had long cherished. For Jews, the family was central; especially in the context of demographic peril, the child was precious, the talisman of future success. They proscribed the triad of child-killing actions practiced by the ancients: infanticide, exposure, and abortion (except in rare cases of thera-peutic abortion). As always, family and community embraced the male child on the eighth day of life in the ceremony of circumcision. The care and nurture of young children remained the concern of mothers, but fathers took charge of the education of their sons, whom they schooled at home or sent to teachers for Hebrew acquisition preparatory to Torah training.

From about the fourteenth century, the bar mitzvah rite took form, marking the moment, at age thirteen, that the male child becomes a "son of the commandment," an adult male capable of bearing responsibility for the continuity of the Jewish tradition. Families themselves, backed by the community at large, were responsible for the care of orphans and their widowed mothers. Although Jews accommodated in some ways the larger and dominant Christian society that enveloped them – the ceremony of circumcision was sometimes likened to baptism, for instance, and Christian servants, even as wetnurses, were admitted to Jewish homes – their reverence for ancient models of behavior did not permit assimilation.

Jews were not, sadly, left in peace in their European redoubts. They were subject not only to repeated expulsions – from France and England, most German towns, and finally from Spain and Portugal – but also to waves of anti-Semitic violence, permitted by a prevailing ideology of anti-Judaism even though the Roman Church, officially, prohibited and deplored these outbreaks. Strikingly, children are central to medieval anti-Semitism in two quite different ways: first, compelled by dire circumstances, Jews sacrificed their own children; and second, Jews were imagined to be the murderers, in the service of their ritual requirements, of Christian children.

The first pattern is observed during the pogroms of the Crusade era, and again during the Iberian expulsions of the 1490s. Attacked by Christian neighbors, before committing suicide themselves, beleaguered Jews killed their own children, sparing their offspring what they saw as the worse fate of coerced baptism and adoption into Christian society. The second pattern is seen in the intermittent sequence of blood libel accusations against Jews: an accusation that Jews had abducted and killed Christian children in order to use their blood in the preparation of matzoh for the Passover. These accusations flare up from the twelfth to sixteenth centuries, with the last noto-rious occurrence connected to the death of an Italian child, Simon of Trent, in 1475 CE. Where Jewish anxiety about their children is implicit in the first, Christian anxiety about theirs, without any visible cause, is implicit in the second.

The hysterical malice of the Christian blood libel accusations should not be mini-mized. Yet it may be recalled that this form of anti-Semitic outburst, like others, was condemned by the church – and was not so condemned, in later centuries, by modern states. It is also noteworthy that Christian anxiety about the vulnerability of children found an equally lethal expression in witch accusations, where innocent women (most often) were prosecuted for their alleged *maleficia* against children: wasting, murder, and cannibalism.

Christians themselves demonstrated their care for children in the ways developed during late antiquity. Like Jews, they opposed abortion, exposure, and infanticide. The rate of occurrence of these crimes, as all three were deemed, seems to have diminished, a perception strengthened by the rapid population growth of the period 1000–1300 CE. Such acts, nonetheless, did occur, now more often committed by women than in the past, when it was male householders who regularly dictated the exposure of newborns. Church penitentials, sermons, and moral treatises condemned the perpetrators, but showed some sympathy, expressed in the leniency of the sentences imposed for the harsh circumstances that often drove them to the deed. That indulgent outlook shifted after 1500 CE, when the prosecution of infanticide and abortion intensified, paralleling that of sodomy and witchcraft – a surge in which both Protestants and Catholics participated.

As had been the case since its establishment in late antiquity, the practice of infant baptism asserted the universal value of children: each child, regardless of social origin, nationality, or gender, but simply by virtue of being born, had access to the promise of salvation. For medieval Catholics, the baptismal rite was a central event for family and neighborhood, and was promptly performed even for paupers and illegitimates. The new Protestant churches of the sixteenth century, for the most part, reaffirmed the principle of infant baptism, although some sects, notably that of the Anabaptists, rejected it on what they saw as a sound scriptural basis. The system of godparenthood early became attached to baptism: godparents were male or female sponsors who pledged to oversee the child's growth in the faith. The ties of godparenthood were powerful, crossing class lines and providing emotional support and social solidarity – so powerful that the Church prohibited marriage with godparental kin, as they did with biological kin, within explicitly stated degrees of relationship.

The twelfth and thirteenth centuries, a period of dynamic cultural change, saw original thinking about the child. The visionary abbess Hildegard of Bingen constructed a theology centered on the Incarnation of a fleshly Jesus in the body of a virgin mother, and proposed, in her medical works, the theory of sexual mutuality in the act of conception. Also new, and almost untranslatable, is her characterization of God's creative action as *viriditas:* literally, a "greening," or life-enhancing force. Like the Old Testament, which may be read as a hymn to fertility, Hildegard celebrates the life-giving power of *viriditas* as the principal attribute of God.

Meanwhile, following upon the revived study of the corpus of Roman law, church lawyers showed remarkable enterprise in the area of what can only be called children's rights. Young persons, they ruled, are free to marry by mutual consent, even in the face of familial opposition, while at the same time, their inheritance rights are to be protected, and fathers are to be held responsible to provide protection and nurture for children and other dependents. The heavy hand of the father, which prevailed in every known civilization, is here restrained in a quite radical departure from the norm.

Around the same time, the foremost representative of the new scholastic philosophy, Saint Thomas Aquinas, identified childhood as an important stage of human life where the faculty of reason gradually unfolds. Thus children, as much as adults, when aided by divine grace, are capable of spiritual growth. Thomas's characterization of the child is revolutionary: in his view, the child is not a being who will someday become a person, but one already possessed of personhood.

Medieval Christians show a different kind of originality in their promotion of orphan care. Since antiquity, orphans as well as widows, the elderly, and the sick had found refuge in asylums of undifferentiated purpose attached to monasteries and churches. Perhaps aware of the original orphanage in Constantinople, the Orphanotropheion, which must have been observed by the many churchmen and merchants who journeyed to that eastern capital, Christian communities began in the thirteenth century to endow and construct foundling homes to nurture abandoned infants.

The most famous foundling home is the Ospedale degli Innocenti (Hospital of the Innocents) in Florence, Italy. Its magnificent colonnaded edifice was the work of Renaissance architect Filippo Brunelleschi, while the sculptor Andrea della Robbia affixed in a rondel over each column a fine relief, in a distinctive pose, of a swaddled infant. Foundling homes proliferated from their first Italian prototypes, with those in Paris, London, and St. Petersburg the most renowned of the later foundations. The instinct to found these refuges for abandoned children was surely altruistic; here is not the place to detail their high rates of mortality, and the increased rates of abandonment that were, in some cases, the perverse effect of institutionalization.

The schooling of children, as well, is a domain in which Christian Europe shone. In the turbulent early Middle Ages, monastery schools trained generations of future monks – orphans, oblates, and lay scholars – in Latin literacy. Those skills were essential both to practice the Christian liturgy, which was the prime function of monasticism, and also to cherish, copy, read, and comment upon the manuscripts stored in monastic libraries which constituted, in Latin Europe, the whole surviving written legacy of the ancient world. Such schools existed as well in Byzantium, in which context they stood alongside many other institutions devoted to education and scholarship. In the West, they were unique.

The children offered up to the monasteries as oblates were central to the success of the monastic schools. From the ranks of monastic oblates proceeded many of the leading European thinkers of the first half of the Middle Ages. From the fifth century, when the care of oblates is prescribed in the *Rule* of Saint Benedict of Nursia, through the twelfth century, when oblation largely faded away, the *schola*, or school, located within monastery walls, was the principal form of schooling available in Europe.

With the rise of towns in the twelfth century, schools attached to the cathedrals began to proliferate; and soon these gave birth to the university, a place for advanced education. Soon Christian Europe was rich in educational institutions, all evolved from church-related functions and committed primarily to the training of the clergy. The narrow purpose of these institutions meant a highly focused curriculum, to be challenged increasingly as laypersons sought an education for their children. But the medieval network of schools was the foundation on which would rest the whole European pedagogical achievement, secular as well as religious.

The most salient challenge to the ecclesiastical schools was posed by the humanists, mainly lay scholars imbued with a rich classical education. From the late fourteenth century, the humanists introduced a new pedagogy grounded in the same disciplines that had been central to the Greco–Roman system of education: grammar, literature, history, rhetoric, and philosophy. Sought after by urban and courtly elites for the advancement of their children, humanist teachers and schools became dominant by the sixteenth century, and their curriculum set the framework of secondary study into modern times.

At just this moment, the humanist educational movement encountered the Protestant, and then Catholic, Reformations. In calling for a "priesthood of all believers," the Protestant founder Martin Luther had opened the way to a new educational ideal, requiring universal literacy – an ideal expanded, a century later, by the Bohemian bishop Jan Amos Comenius, who called for the universal education of both males and females. Amid these discussions, the humanist curriculum itself became

Christianized – as in the Protestant Lutheran and Calvinist universities and the Catholic Jesuit boarding schools, which flourished from these times. The expansion of the range and purpose of educational institutions was another momentous way in which Christian Europe advanced the welfare of the child.

Conclusion

The foundations for the modern notion of the child as a human individual worthy of concern by virtue of being alive, and not because of his or her utility to family or nation, lay in the Bible – the book that is, in its different configurations, the common property of Jewish and Christian communities. During the first five centuries of the Common Era, those communities defended biblical principles with regard to the child in their momentous, yet once again divergent, confrontations with the Roman state and the Greco–Roman civilization it embodied. From that time, and through the Middle Ages, Jews in ancient Mediterranean and Western European settings, and Christians both Latin and Greek, continued to be guided by those fundamental principles, creating new customs, rituals, and institutions in which they were enshrined. When at the dawn of the twentieth century, Ellen Key welcomed a new era of the child while deprecating the Judeo-Christian religious traditions that had hitherto been the child's greatest defenders, she profoundly misconstrued their contribution to the project of child protection, nurture, and advancement. So, too, have many others since.

Notes

1 Ellen Key, *The Century of the Child*, trans. from the German by Marie Franzos (New York: G.P. Putnam's Sons, 1909), 2–3.
2 All biblical quotations are from the New International Version (NIV); available at http://www.biblegateway.com/ accessed 1/20/2012.
3 Molek, or Molech, may have been a Canaanite deity or the name assigned a sacrificial ritual.
4 Sarah B. Pomeroy, "Infanticide in Hellenistic Greece," in *Images of Women in Antiquity*, ed. Averil and Amélie Kuhrt Cameron, (Detroit, MI: Wayne State University Press, 1983), 207–219, at 207.
5 Tacitus, *History* 5.5; trans. Alfred John Church and William Jackson Brodribb; http://www.sacred-texts.com/cla/tac/h05000.htm accessed 1/17/2012.
6 Quoted by Odd Magne Bakke, *When Children Became People: The Birth of Childhood in Early Christianity* (Minneapolis, MN: Fortress Press, 2005), 176, from Josephus, *In Apionem* 1:12:60.
7 Chrysostom, *Address on Vainglory and the Right Way for Parents to Bring up their Children*, in M.L.W. Laistner, *Christianity and Pagan Culture in the Later Roman Empire* (Ithaca, NY: Cornell University Press, 1951), 85–122.
8 Quoted by Vigen Guroian, "The Ecclesial Family: John Chrysostom on Parenthood and Children," in Marcia J. Bunge, ed. *The Child in Christian Thought* (Grand Rapids, MI: W.B. Eerdmans, 2001), 61–77, at 65.
9 Chrysostom, *Address on Vainglory*, #22, at 96.
10 Quoted by Bakke, *When Children became People*, 145.
11 Bakke, *When Children Became People*.

Suggestions for further reading

The child and the Bible

The child in the Old Testament

Bergmann, Martin S. *In the Shadow of Moloch: The Sacrifice of Children and its Impact on Western Religions*. New York, NY: Columbia University Press, 1992. From a psychoanalytic perspective; identifies child sacrifice as "a ubiquitous custom that was abandoned long ago" (1), persisting in the post-religious unconscious.

Bunge, Marcia J., Terence E. Fretheim, and Beverly Roberts Gaventa, eds. *The Child in the Bible*. Grand Rapids, MI: William B. Eerdmans, 2008. Indispensable collection of 17 specialist essays dealing with both Old Testament and New Testament periods. For the former, see especially Claire R.M. McGinnis, "Exodus as a 'Text of Terror' for Children," 24–44; Esther M. Menn, "Child Characters in Biblical Narratives: the Young David (1 Samuel 16–17) and the Little Israelite Servant Girl (2 Kings 5:1–19)," 324–352; and Walter Brueggemann, "Vulnerable Children, Divine Passion, and Human Obligation," 399–422.

Chilton, Bruce. *Abraham's Curse: Child Sacrifice in the Legacies of the West*. New York, NY: Doubleday, 2008. Traces the transmutation of child sacrifice into a glorification of martyrdom, with terrible consequences for our lives today.

Finsterbusch, Karin, Armin Lange, and Diethard Römheld, eds. *Human Sacrifice in Jewish and Christian Tradition*. Boston, MA: Brill, 2006. Offers an excellent overview in 15 specialist essays. For the Old Testament period, see especially Beate Pongratz-Leisten, "Ritual Killing and Sacrifice in the Ancient Near East," 3–33; Karin Finsterbusch, "The First-Born between Sacrifice and Redemption in the Hebrew Bible," 87–108; Armin Lange, "'They Burn their Sons and Daughters. That was No Command of Mine' (Jer 7:31): Child Sacrifice in the Hebrew Bible and in the Deuteronomistic Jeremiah Redaction," 109–132; Bennie H. Reynolds, "Molek: Dead or Alive? The Meaning and Derivation of *mlk* and *mlkh* [transliteration]," 133–155.

Levenson, Jon Douglas. *The Death and Resurrection of the Beloved Son: The Transformation of Child Sacrifice in Judaism and Christianity*. New Haven, CT: Yale University Press, 1993. Explores the persistent impulse to the sacrifice of the first-born son, and the substitutions and sublimations by which it was repressed and surpassed.

Lockyer, Herbert. *All the Children of the Bible*. Grand Rapids, MI: Zondervan, 1970. Names and identifies all the children mentioned in the Old and New Testaments; a useful resource.

Stavrakopoulou, Francesca. *King Manasseh and Child Sacrifice: Biblical Distortions of Historical Realities*. New York, NY: Walter de Gruyter, 2004. Explores the Israelite practice of child sacrifice, with emphasis on the Judahite royal cult of child sacrifice up to the time of Josiah.

Voeltzel, René. *L'Enfant et son éducation dans la Bible*. Paris, France: Beauchesne, 1973. Not limited to pedagogy, explores the high valuation of the child in both Old and New Testaments.

The child in the New Testament

Balla, Peter. *The Child–Parent Relationship in the New Testament and its Environment*. Tübingen, Germany: Mohr Siebeck, 2003. Describes parent–child relationships in early Christian society in the context of Jewish and pagan family life.

Blomberg, Craig. *Jesus and the Gospels: An Introduction and Survey*. 2nd ed. Nashville, TN: B & H Academic, 2009. Places the Gospels in social historical context, and explores the birth and childhood of Jesus.

Bunge, *The Child in the Bible.* See above. For the New Testament period, see especially Judith M. Gundry, "Children in the Gospel of Mark, with Special Attention to Jesus' Blessing of the Children (Mark 10:13–16) and the Purpose of Mark," 143–176; John T. Carroll, "'What then will this Child Become?' Perspectives on Children in the Gospel of Luke," 177–194; Marianne M. Thompson, "Children in the Gospel of John," 195–214; Joel B. Green, "'Tell Me a Story.' Perspectives on Children from the Acts of the Apostles," 215–232; Beverly R. Gaventa, "Finding a Place for Children in the Letters of Paul," 233–248; Reidar Aasgaard, "Like a Child: Paul's Rhetorical Uses of Childhood," 249–277; Margaret Y. MacDonald, "A Place of Belonging: Perspectives on Children from Colossians and Ephesians," 278–304; Keith J. White, "'He Placed a Little Child in the Midst.' Jesus, the Kingdom, and Children," 353–374.

Bunge, Marcia J., ed. *The Child in Christian Thought.* Grand Rapids, MI: William B. Eerdmans, 2001. An array of 17 specialist essays ranging from New Testament to modern times. See for the New Testament period especially Judith M. Gundry-Volf, "The Least and the Greatest: Children in the New Testament," 29–60.

Francis, James M. M. *Adults as Children: Images of Childhood in the Ancient World and the New Testament.* Oxford, UK: Peter Lang, 2006. Explores the role of children as real and metaphorical actors in the Gospel narratives, Acts, and the Pauline and non-Pauline epistles.

Horn, Cornelia B., and John W. Martens. *Let the Little Children Come to Me: Childhood and Children in Early Christianity.* Washington DC: Catholic University of America Press, 2009. Illuminating study of children's daily lives in early Christian society, including family relationships, education, work, and participation in worship.

Voeltzel, *L'Enfant et son éducation dans la Bible.* See above.

Jews and Christians confront the Greco–Roman world

Bakke, Odd Magne. *When Children Became People: The Birth of Childhood in Early Christianity.* Minneapolis MN: Fortress Press, 2005. Indispensable study of children in early Christianity, surveying attitudes toward the child, the education of children, and child participation in worship. Valuable synthesis of early Christian views of infanticide, exposure, abortion, and sexual abuse at 110–152, and on the development of infant baptism at 90–103.

Balla, *The Child–Parent Relationship in the New Testament and its Environment.* See above.

Baun, Jane. "The Fate of Babies Dying before Baptism in Byzantium." In *The Church and Childhood: Papers Read at the 1993 Summer Meeting and the 1994 Winter Meeting of the Ecclesiastical History Society,* edited by Diana Wood, 115–125. Oxford-Cambridge MA: Blackwell Publishers for the Ecclesiastical History Society, 1994. Distinguishes the conception of infant baptism in the Greek Church from that in the Latin West, shaped by Augustinian theology.

Bunge, *The Child in Christian Thought.* See above. See for the early Christian period especially Vigen Guroian, "The Ecclesial Family: John Chrysostom on Parenthood and Children," 61–77; and Martha E. Stortz, "'Where or When was your Servant Innocent?' Augustine on Childhood," 78–102.

Cochrane, Charles Norris. *Christianity and Classical Culture: a Study of Thought and Action from Augustus to Augustine.* New York, NY: Oxford University Press, 1957. Classic and unsurpassed study of the intersection between Christian and classical thought.

Francis, *Adults as Children: Images of Childhood in the Ancient World and the New Testament.* See above. Offers a substantial discussion of Jewish and Christian views on infanticide, exposure, and abortion at 60–95.

Gorman, Michael J. *Abortion & the Early Church: Christian, Jewish & Pagan Attitudes in the Greco-Roman World.* Downers Grove, IL: InterVarsity Press, 1982. Thorough examination of ancient pagan, Jewish, and Christian statements on abortion, distinguishing between the positions of Jewish and Christian communities, both of which nonetheless opposed the practice.

Horn and Martens, *"Let the Little Children Come to Me."* See above. Useful for views of infanticide, exposure, abortion, and child abuse; for the development of infant baptism; and for child participation in worship, including child choirs.

Lindemann, Andreas. "'Do Not Let a Woman Destroy the Unborn Babe in Her Belly.' Abortion in Ancient Judaism and Christianity." *Studia Theologica* 49 (1995): 253–271. Updating Gorman (above), reviews Jewish and Christian arguments against abortion.

Laistner, M.L.W. *Christianity and Pagan Culture in the Later Roman Empire; Together with an English Translation of John Chrysostom's Address on Vainglory and the Right Way for Parents to Bring Up their Children.* Ithaca, NY: Cornell University Press, 1951. Examines the reception of pagan culture by early Christian thinkers, especially Chrysostom, whose unique pedagogical work is appended in Laistner's translation at 85–122.

Miller, Timothy S. *The Orphans of Byzantium: Child Welfare in the Christian Empire.* Washington DC: Catholic University of America Press, 2003. Important history of the development of philanthropic institutions in early Byzantium, foremost among them the Orphanotropheion, the world's first orphanage. Also useful for monastic schools and child choirs.

Schwartz, Daniel. "Did the Jews Practice Infant Exposure and Infanticide in Antiquity?" *Studia Philonica Annual* 16 (2004): 61–95. Powerful demonstration of the Jewish repudiation of both infanticide and exposure.

Strange, W.A. *Children in the Early Church: Children in the Ancient World, the New Testament and the Early Church.* Carlisle, PA: Paternoster Press, 1996. Concise synthesis, with important overviews of the development of infant baptism at 88–102, and of the admission of children to the Eucharist at 103–122.

Medieval continuities

Jewish life and the child

Baumgarten, Elisheva. *Mothers and Children: Jewish Family Life in Medieval Europe.* Princeton, NJ: Princeton University Press, 2004. Highlights the mother's role in the care of the young child, and the interactions of both with the surrounding Christian community.

Frojmovic, Eva. "Reframing Gender in Medieval Jewish Images of Circumcision." In *Framing the Family: Narrative and Representation in the Medieval and Early Modern Periods*, edited by Rosalynn Voaden, and Diane Wolfthal, 221–243. Tempe, AZ: Arizona Center for Medieval and Renaissance Studies, 2005. Highlights the relations of the rite to Jewish martyrdom and sacrifice on the one hand, and to Christian Baptism and Passion narratives on the other.

Goldin, Simha, "Jewish Society under Pressure: The Concept of Childhood." In *Youth in the Middle Ages*, edited by P.J.P. Goldberg, and Felicity Riddy, 25–43. Rochester, NY: Boydell & Brewer, 2004. Relates the high valuation of the child in Jewish society to anxiety about coerced baptism by Christians, the avoidance of which compelled both child sacrifice and adult martyrdom.

Hsia, R. Po-chia. *Trent 1475: Stories of a Ritual Murder Trial.* New Haven, CT: Yale University Press in cooperation with Yeshiva University Library, 1992. Close study of the blood libel episode centered on Simon of Trent.

Hsia, R. Po-chia. *The Myth of Ritual Murder: Jews and Magic in Reformation Germany.* New Haven, CT: Yale University Press, 1988. Examines the political context of a late outbreak of the ritual murder charge.

Kanarfogel, Ephraim. *Jewish Education and Society in the High Middle Ages*. Detroit, MI: Wayne State University Press, 1992. Comprehensive review of early education and Torah study among the Jews of Ashkenaz.

Kuefler, Mathew. "Anderl of Rinn, the Accusation of Jewish Ritual Murder, and the Historical Memory of Childhood." *Journal of the History of Childhood and Youth* 2.1 (2009): 9–36. Shows how the narrative sources for one alleged ritual murder illuminate our understanding of medieval childhood.

Lieberman, Julia R. "Childhood and Family among the Western Sephardim in the Seventeenth Century." In *Sephardi Family Life in the Early Modern Diaspora*, edited by Julie R. Lieberman, 129–165. Waltham, MA: Brandeis University Press; Hanover MA: University Press of New England, 2011. Discusses aspects of Jewish life in Amsterdam, Hamburg, and Livorno, including circumcision, breastfeeding, and the bar mitzvah rite.

Marcus, Ivan G. *Rituals of Childhood: Jewish Acculturation in Medieval Europe*. New Haven, CT: Yale University Press, 1996. Examines the school initiation ritual among Ashkenazi Jews, in which the father conveys his young son to the nurturing care of a male Torah teacher.

Christianity and the child

Bunge, *The Child in Christian Thought*. See above. See for the Medieval and Reformation periods especially Cristina L.H. Traina, "A Person in the Making: Thomas Aquinas on Children and Childhood," 103–133; Jane E. Strohl, "The Child in Luther's Theology: For what Purpose do we Older Folks Exist, other than to Care for... the Young?" 134–159; Barbara Pitkin, "The Heritage of the Lord: Children in the Theology of John Calvin," 160–193.

De Jong, Mayke. *In Samuel's Image: Child Oblation in the Early Medieval West*. Leiden, The Netherlands: E.J. Brill, 1996. Overview of child oblation from the fourth through twelfth centuries, stressing its importance for the development of schooling and preparation of church intellectuals.

Deller, William S. "The First Rite of Passage: Baptism in Medieval Memory." *Journal of Family History* 36.1 (2011): 3–14. Examines 10,000 jurors' testimonies that cumulatively depict the meaning and conduct of the baptismal rite in England from the thirteenth to fifteenth centuries.

Gavitt, Philip. *Charity and Children in Renaissance Florence: The Ospedale Degli Innocenti, 1410–1536*. Ann Arbor, MI: University of Michigan Press, 1990. Classic study of the famous Florentine orphanage.

Greenfield, Richard. "Children in Byzantine Monasteries: Innocent Hearts or Vessels in the Harbor of the Devil?" In *Becoming Byzantine: Children and Childhood in Byzantium*, edited by Arietta Papaconstantinou, and Alice-Mary Maffry Talbot, 253–282. Washington DC: Dumbarton Oaks-Cambridge MA: Harvard University Press, 2009,. Studies the controversy over the admission of young children to monasteries.

Kallendorf, Craig, ed. *Humanist Educational Treatises*. Cambridge, MA: Harvard University Press, 2002. Updated edition and translation of a selection of pedagogical treatises showing the integration of classical cultural ideals with Christianity.

Lynch, Joseph H. *Godparents and Kinship in Early Medieval Europe*. Princeton, NJ: Princeton University Press, 1986. Studies the early Christian origins of godparenthood as an adjunct to the ritual of baptism, and its final establishment in the Carolingian era.

Newman, Barbara. *Sister of Wisdom: St. Hildegard's Theology of the Feminine*. Berkeley, CA: University of California Press, 1987. Still the best available study of Hildegard's thought, elucidating the incarnational themes that set the child at the center of her theology.

Pullan, Brian S. *Orphans and Foundlings in Early Modern Europe.* Berkshire, UK: University of Reading, 1989. An expert and concise synthesis, not superseded.

Reid, Charles J. *Power over the Body, Equality in the Family: Rights and Domestic Relations in Medieval Canon Law.* Grand Rapids, MI: William B. Eerdmans, 2004. Studies the development of ideas of children's rights in twelfth-century Europe.

Spierling, Karen E. *Infant Baptism in Reformation Geneva: The Shaping of a Community, 1536–1564.* Aldershot UK-Burlington, VT: Ashgate, 2005. Illuminates the discussion among magistrates and people leading to a consensus on baptismal practice in the Calvinist capital.

Strauss, Gerald. *Luther's House of Learning: Indoctrination of the Young in the German Reformation.* Baltimore, MD: Johns Hopkins University Press, 1978. Traces the noble purposes, and flawed execution, of Luther's plan for the universal education of children.

Taglia, Kathryn Ann. "The Cultural Construction of Childhood: Baptism, Communion, and Confirmation." In *Women, Marriage, and Family in Medieval Christendom: Essays in Memory of Michael M. Sheehan, C.S.B.* edited by Constance M. Rousseau, and Joel T. Rosenthal, 255–287. Kalamazoo, MI: Medieval Institute Publications, 1998. Shows how these three rites developed over the Middle Ages so that they marked the phases of childhood as understood in Christianity.

3

CHILDHOOD IN MEDIEVAL AND EARLY MODERN TIMES

Joanne M. Ferraro

The history of European childhood as a field of study has virtually exploded since its inception in 1962 with the publication of Philippe Ariès's pioneering *Centuries of Childhood: A Social History of Family Life.*[1] The first to draw attention to the importance of this life stage as an area of scholarly inquiry, Ariès's work has been one of the primary influences prompting historians over the following half century to arrive at a better understanding of what childhood and parenting were like during the medieval (AD 500–1500) and early modern (AD 1500–1800) periods. His work emerged during a pivotal time for historical studies, when scholars were forging new paths of exploration. While the annals of war and treaties remained classical subjects, professional historians, particularly from the Annales School in France and the Cambridge Group for the History of Population and Social Structure in the United Kingdom, turned their attention to social history. Borrowing methods from psychology, biology, sociology, and demography they formulated new questions and crafted new narratives. Childhood as an area of historical study was a product of this moment, which was also a time of strong interest in Freudian psychoanalysis and Jean Piaget's studies of child development, areas that explored human ambivalence toward the early stages of the lifecycle.[2] The 1960s and 1970s also gave rise to the study of the so-called "forgotten people," which included the subaltern classes, women, and children. The rise of informatics and historical research based on archival and parish collections enabled scholars to reconstruct demographic patterns for nameless people by using records of birth, baptism, marriage, and death as well as tax data and notarial documents. Further, the burgeoning fields of cultural studies and art history made literary texts, diaries, poetry, ages-of-man literature, and illustrations with distinct life-cycle stages, advice books, family letters, humanist writings, catechisms, hagiography, and iconography popular sources for the exploration of social life. The confluence of all of these developments advanced childhood studies, an interdisciplinary field that would expand over the late twentieth century in multiple directions.

Economy and demography

It became apparent at the outset that there was not just one model of childhood. Several factors shaped human experience, among them broader economic and demographic cycles. The first five centuries of medieval life were ridden with invasions, famine, poverty, and high mortality, conditions that encouraged most people to organize under religious houses or warrior hierarchies supported by a mass of indentured rural laborers. Europe was a thinly populated rural sea, its peoples vulnerable to the cyclical pressures resulting from inclement weather and poor harvests. Infant mortality was high, and it was common for children to lose one or both parents. In this context, young people who survived adversity often lived with fictive kin, either under the tutelage of a secular lord; a bishop, abbot, or abbess; or a group of serfs.

After AD 1000 Europe's demographic and economic landscape changed dramatically. The invasions ceased, the birth rate steadily rose, and improved agricultural methods yielded a more plentiful and nutritious diet. Population growth in the rural sector helped break up serfdom and permitted newly freed laborers to become wage earners, thus the European economy diversified, shifting from an exclusively agrarian society to that of a rural sea now populated with significant urban nuclei. Cities and towns absorbed rural workers into guilds, and handicrafts spilled into the countryside in dispersed cottage industries. On a global level, maritime power in the Adriatic and the Mediterranean expanded, resulting in new colonies and markets in the eastern Mediterranean, North Africa, and West Asia. In northern Italy, the commercial revolution produced an international banking network, monetary exchange, maritime trade insurance, and double-entry bookkeeping. Society reorganized, with the middle ranks in urban areas growing rapidly in prosperity. The period between AD 1000 and 1300 was marked, thus, by economic expansion, a phenomenon that permitted the formation of nuclear households. Nonetheless, infant and child mortality remained high, especially among ordinary people, with as much as a quarter of all infants born failing to complete their first year of life and another quarter expiring before reaching their teens.

By AD 1300 Europe entered another cyclical downturn. The pronounced population growth of the previous three centuries stretched the limits of agrarian technology, setting off a series of famines that produced widespread malnutrition. Then the Bubonic Plague swept over Europe, decimating between a third and a half of the population between AD 1348 and 1350 and bringing the cycle of expansion to an abrupt halt. Once again the children that survived adversity had their lives disrupted, often finding themselves in truncated households.

The impact of this boom and bust activity on household structure was dramatic. In periods of slow population growth, or following catastrophic levels of mortality, there was more pressure to marry, and to marry during adolescent rather than adult years, in order to maximize the period of human reproduction and replenish the labor force. There were also generally more landed resources available as well, increasing the possibility of raising children at home. When, however, the population rose to the level where food resources and land became scarce, the situation in AD 1300, more people postponed marriage to their late twenties, producing fewer children, or did not marry at all. Poverty and malnutrition became dominant concerns, with fewer households able to support children and parents resorting to abandoning infants to foundling homes or orphanages or farming them out as domestic laborers. After the Black Death of AD 1348 trends shifted once again. Land once again became plentiful, wages rose, and couples were encouraged to wed young to compensate for demographic losses.

While Europe slowly recovered from its catastrophic losses of the fourteenth century, it witnessed yet another period of pronounced change in the balance of demographic and economic power during the sixteenth century. Once again the population reached levels that a constrained agrarian technology could not accommodate. The sixteenth century thus mirrored the period between AD 1300 and 1348, but it also witnessed high inflation, thus the problem of poverty became critical to both ecclesiastical and lay institutions. Foundling homes and orphanages multiplied, replacing family households, but there were also increasing droves of uprooted children. Poverty swept over most of the peasantry, with significant differences between Western and Eastern Europe. While the West imposed heavy taxation, it still afforded rural laborers wages and contracts or leases, however exploitative. The East, on the other hand, fell into serfdom, hardly different than slavery. In this context it is not possible to envision productive, nuclear households with fathers and mothers parenting their offspring. Rather, such adversity produced truncated households that cast children, at best, under the tutelage of institutions. In this context childhood was usually brief and most certainly a luxury reserved for the prosperous.

The eighteenth century brought new changes to the system of production that impinged on the built-in demographic structures discussed above. The guild system in urban centers was compelled to share manufacturing terrain with rural households, where all family members took part. International merchants, circulating in a global economy that reached from Europe to the Americas, Africa, and Asia, purchased both raw materials and handicrafts from these households to export to external markets. In this setting the work of both women and children was critical. Rural industrialization permitted married people to stay together and work out of the home and afforded children greater opportunity to remain with them and participate in household production.

Class and gender

Like demographic and economic trends, social class and gender were important variables that affected childhood experience. Medieval and early modern European society was distinctly hierarchical. Status was defined both by bloodline and in law, and was visually represented in dress, manners, and lifestyle. Moreover, culturally constructed rules about the norms of masculinity and femininity clearly determined peoples' roles in life. Thus children in elite households were tracked for different destinies than those of the laboring classes. The progeny of royals and nobles, or others with power and great wealth, were situated on a life-cycle trajectory that greatly depended on local inheritance practices. Roman law on the Continent and common law in England followed the principle of primogeniture, whereby one heir carried on the family name, inheriting the preponderance of the family patrimony. Likewise, one daughter was destined to marry, thus limiting the family dynasty's financial liability in expending resources for dowries. This behavioral strategy, called restricted marriage, meant that Europe's upper classes produced a significant number of unmarried and displaced men and women. Disinherited sons of feudal knights, for example, joined Crusades to foreign territories in order to net land and primary resources and to enjoy the feudal privileges they were deprived of at home. Others were constrained to join mercenary companies or to take religious vows, often against their will. Daughters of the nobility not tracked for marriage had even fewer options. They filled Catholic Europe's aristocratic convents, and, like monks, were constrained to take vows of celibacy. Similarly, non-noble elites intent on preserving the wealth of the family dynasty over time, also practiced restricted marriage. This was common practice in the oligarchic circles ruling European cities, and among the judicial and notarial elites that dominated legal life and bureaucracy. For the offspring of the wealthy and powerful, childhood under parental supervision was but a transitory moment, probably for not more than a decade, before, as adolescents, the young were placed under the supervision of surrogate adults, be it in military companies for males or in religious institutions for either sex. It is important to note that the disinherited did not necessarily remain celibate. Many produced illegitimate children who experienced stigma and marginalization.

Children from elite circles tracked for marriage remained closer to the hearth and were trained early on to be family patriarchs, astute estate managers, and military and political leaders in the case of males, or household managers and mothers in the case of females. They received home tutorial or some other form of schooling. Parents consulted late medieval advice manuals on how to care for infants and toddlers and raise and educate the young, with gender-specific instructions. Mothers in households with the financial means to betroth daughters, for example, were given books such as *How the Good Wife Taught Her Daughter* to prepare them for married life.[3] Children were also given toys and games to develop their skills. Boys undertook athletic and military training that fostered teamwork and built moral character. They also studied geography, Latin grammar, and history to prepare for their political responsibilities. Those dislodged from the natal household were also schooled in primary education and trained to serve in capacities that enhanced the status of the family dynasty, whether in military, bureaucratic, or religious service. Adolescent males were prepared for law, medicine, or government, females for domestic responsibilities. Some males boarded out, their teachers becoming their parents, while females remained at home or were enrolled in convents by age nine.

The vast majority of children were not, however, from elite circles, thus their experiences varied, largely dependent on the nature of the family household. Historical demographers have concluded that the dominant family form in Western Europe was nuclear.[4] In only a few areas, such as southern France, rural Tuscany, or among the ruling class of Venice, was the family extended. Children could only remain at home and be raised by their natal parents if the household could sustain itself economically. The financial strength of the household depended on the physical environment, the productivity of the land, and the strength of the labor market, variables that fluctuated over time. These factors helped to determine whether children attended school or worked, whether they lived with their parents at home or were farmed out to more prosperous households, whether they married young, old, or not at all. Some youngsters were apprenticed early on for rural labor, the handicrafts, or trade, depending on the opportunities their families could give them. Those in less fortunate circumstances were sent into domestic service, or deprived of any training if they came from destitute households. Many children lost one or both parents; the more fortunate among them received vocational training from an orphanage. In most of these circumstances, children were supervised by other adults, who may or may not have acted as surrogate parents. But even within the nuclear family, supervision shifted if either spouse was widowed and remarried, a common occurrence in a society ridden with war, epidemic disease, and famine. A remarried father was more likely to keep his children at home than a remarried mother.

In general, childhood was much briefer in poor or modest agrarian societies than in wealthy, urban environments. From an early age boys and girls were given tasks to assist with sustaining the family unit. Children as young as four or five might tend their infant siblings. By ages six to eight they were assigned small chores such as collecting firewood or worms on vines, herding livestock, weeding, sweeping, cleaning, carrying water, preparing food, and doing small errands. Both boys and girls might work in fields or tend farm animals. Girls also provided domestic service, helping with spinning, sewing, and lace making. Responsibilities grew exponentially between the ages of seven and twelve. By age fourteen, members of both sexes were doing the work of adult men and women, respectively. It is important to note that in medieval and early modern society the household was a center of production as well as reproduction; a place where all family members participated in some form of labor. Their activities revolved around ensuring at least subsistence level, making clothing, and constructing housing. In that context, everyone worked the land, watched the livestock, and produced the basic items critical for the survival of the household unit. Everyone engaged in the planting and harvesting of crops both for subsistence and to furnish the raw materials for manufactured products, such as flax, hemp, silk, and plants for dyes.

Some children in artisan households had the opportunity to learn the trades of their parents. This depended on the degree to which the economic activity could sustain the household. Therefore it was possible that only one or two sons became cobblers or smiths, while the others, like rural children, were forced to leave the household and seek other means to make a living. Commercialization in the cities of northern Italy, Flanders, and Germany offered greater opportunities to some than other places in Europe. Sons followed their fathers into international trade, banking, or manufacture. Moreover, where business and industry thrived there was great demand for professionals skilled in medicine, the notarial arts, and law, prosperous positions regulated by guild membership and often passed down from father to son. Often these professionals dominated civic councils, whose memberships were also hereditary.

Stages of childhood development: infancy

Within the general parameters outlined previously, historians continue to explore the specific experiences of medieval and early modern European children. Evidence for the earliest stage of the lifecycle, infancy, comes from a variety of sources, including manuals on midwifery and obstetrics, medical texts, judicial records, registers of baptisms and deaths, folk literature, the iconography of manuscript illuminations, church carvings, paintings, stained glass, printed books, and artifacts ranging from clay feeding bottles to toys.[5] The subject is also approached indirectly through studies of motherhood, unwed mothers, and infanticide. Each of these sources is open to interpretation, thus accounting for many of the controversies about childhood history. The most debated questions include whether parents were attached to their infants; whether they treated infant boys differently than girls; and whether such practices as swaddling were cruel and detached or compassionate forms of protection.

The starting point for all of these debates was the precariousness of infancy. Poor hygiene, filth, contaminated water, harmful bacteria, and limited medical expertise made infants highly vulnerable to disease. Many suffered from worms, diarrhea, and smallpox. The poor were also victims of malnutrition, which brought on a variety of deficiency diseases. As a result, infant mortality was very high, ranging between 30 and 50 percent. One in two children of the lower classes was likely to die before the age of one year. One in two of these reached their teens.

Survival depended to a large degree on how and what infants were fed.[6] Both medieval and early modern people were aware that nursing, or wetnursing, gave a baby better odds of survival than feeding through a tube or clay bottle. Today scientific studies have concluded that breast milk furnishes protection against allergy, disease, and infection because it is rich in antibodies, nutrient proteins, lipids, vitamins, and minerals. Unfortunately, some mothers of the past, especially the poor and malnourished, did not have enough milk. Others died in childbirth. Still others, in more fortunate circumstances, were accustomed to engaging wetnurses. As a result, infants were deprived of their own mothers' precious breast milk and were thus more prone to serious ailments and death.

The quantitative studies of David Herlihy and Christiane Klapisch-Zuber for medieval Tuscany show that the infants of the rich were more likely to survive than those of the poor.[7] Moreover, Klapisch-Zuber's analysis of the breast milk business, based on Florentine *ricordanze*, or family diaries, demonstrates that male and female babies were nurtured differently, with boys given preferential treatment. They were nursed for longer periods and were better supervised than girls, who were often given over to wetnurses.[8] There was not only an overall awareness that breast feeding was superior to tube feeding, but it was also believed that the character of the wetnurse would be transmitted to the child through her milk, thus fathers were careful about whom they chose to nurse their infants, particularly their male babies. Klapisch-Zuber concludes that they opted to have wetnurses for infant boys in their homes where they could be supervised. On the other hand, female babies were more likely to be given to country women, where there was greater risk of starvation if the unsupervised nurturer ran out of milk but pretended to feed the infant to prevent a loss of income. Ironically, Klapisch-Zuber also found that it was women from the wealthier classes that, with the support of their husbands, were more inclined to give their babies over to wetnurses. This stands to reason since only they could afford them. Moreover, some were under greater pressure to conceive in order to ensure the elite family dynasty, and many realized that breast feeding inhibited fertility.[9] Philip Gavitt's study of the Florentine Ospedale degli Innocenti (foundling home) suggests that male babies may have received better treatment than female ones, for female infant mortality was higher than that of males. Gavitt also reveals that the Florentine countryside was a center of wetnursing, catering to a broad clientele.[10] There are fewer records shedding light on wetnursing in medieval London, but Barbara Hanawalt finds that male infants had a better chance of survival.[11]

Most historians studying childbirth and the nourishment of infants generally conclude that parents were attached to their babies, irrespective of the high death rates. Regarding Renaissance Italy, Jacqueline Musacchio's work on *deschi da parto*, or birth trays, and other ceramics that were presented as gifts to a newborn's parents, shows their enthusiasm: they were interested in illustrating heroic themes that would influence the child's upbringing.[12] Moreover, all authorities recommended breast feeding for the health of the child. The fifteenth-century Venetian humanist writer Francesco Barbaro, for example, insisted that mothers nurse their own babies. Finally, the presence of foundling homes indicates that it was important to protect and care for infants and children. In his *Kindness of Strangers* John Boswell explains this in terms of children's value to the labor force,[13] but we can also interpret it as a sign of fundamental respect for human life. In Renaissance Italy the family was the fundamental unit of social organization, and children were critical to its survival over the long term.[14] There is a variety of visual evidence that suggests that parents treasured their offspring, dressing them in fine linens, silks, and brocades. This is particularly evident in the official family portraits of Italy's great dynasties, such as the Gonzaga of Mantua and the Pesaro of Venice, where children garbed in fine splendor were proudly displayed on canvas.

A few historians, on the other hand, have characterized specific parenting practices as evidence of cruelty. Swaddling, for example, is one of the areas where there is little agreement. Barbara Hanawalt explains that the divergence is largely due both to historians' selection of sources as well as the different ways they interpret them. Mary Martin McLaughlin, in *Survivors and Surrogates*, for example, argues that swaddling was a practice that reflected concern to provide infants with good care. She draws this conclusion from her readings of Guibert of Nogent's memoirs and the encyclopedia of Bartholomew of England. Bartholomew explained that swaddling kept the infant warm and prevented the formation of deformities. Lloyd deMause's readings, on the other hand, led him to characterize swaddling as cruel because it deprived the child of using his or her limbs.[15] Other historians have pointed out that the practice was not sanitary, with infants remaining in soiled cloth for long hours.

Surely for Europe's elite, childbirth was an important event. It represented the future of the family, the survival of a dynasty. There was indeed great ceremony surrounding childbirth, which was largely a female event up until the eighteenth century. The role of the midwife was critical, and the memoirs of these health care givers show extensive knowledge and concern for the health and welfare of infants. Midwives held important places in society, often supervised by the state and church, and were called upon to testify in judicial matters related to female sexuality, childbirth, and infant death. Likewise, godparents held a special place in the lives of Catholic children because they were pledged to care for their godchildren should the parents become ill disposed, and provided a larger network of support for the young. The birth of the child was also a fruitful occasion to renew, expand, and solidify important social and political ties through the selection of godparents.

Not all pregnancies, however, led to childbirth, but infants that were conceived in marriage had a better chance of survival than illegitimate ones. Further, the insidious presence of poverty meant that not all pregnancies were welcome. Jean-Louis Flandrin's study of sexual behavior in early modern France concludes that parents attempted to limit birth.[16] My own work for early modern Italy also reveals such practices.[17] Although the evidence is scant, priests and laymen alike in the Republic of Venice visited apothecaries and mixed the abortion potions they urged their women to drink. Birth control, abortion, miscarriage, and infanticide, however, all elude the historical record, for they usually occur in secret, thus the historical evidence is descriptive rather than quantitative.

In early modern Italy women who were single and pregnant furtively left their rural villages or tiny hamlets, at times in the company of secret partners, to give birth in the anonymity of the city, where they could avail themselves of foundling homes after their 40 days of "lying in," the term for post-natal care. They were often cared for by other women who let rooms and offered an unofficial midwifery service. In addition to providing post-natal care, these women sometimes called in priests to counsel single mothers on how to dispose of the infant in a foundling home. Such homes, first established in the thirteenth century, swelled with abandoned newborns in Italy's cities during the early modern era. Abandoned infants were in part the victims of population growth and poverty, especially during the sixteenth-century cycle of inflation when many people could not marry because of the high cost of living and the dearth of landed resources. It was not that parents did not care for their children but rather that they could not afford them. Many attached poignant notes to their infants describing how financial hardship had constrained them to relinquish their loved ones. But poverty alone does not explain infant abandonment; it was also a consequence of harsh laws regulating unmarried expectant mothers. While in Protestant territories magistrates obliged unmarried sexual partners to assume responsibility for their offspring, Catholic territories discouraged single mothers from keeping their babies. The new mother or father, or someone acting for them, felt constrained by social stigma and notions of honor to deposit the infant in a rotating cradle that pivoted between the outside and inside of a foundling home, giving over care of the infant to the nuns. Many were involved in living arrangements that, if discovered, would dishonor both them and their families. Some impoverished women, for example, had agreed to set up housekeeping with priests who reneged on their vows of celibacy or with men of high social station whose families had not tracked them for marriage. It is difficult to know how they or their partners felt about abandoning their offspring, but what is clear is that the conventions of society forbade them to raise children.

The foundling home solution in fact encouraged infant abandonment, however painful, even among legitimate parents who could not afford to feed an additional child, and the numbers of parentless babies grew exponentially through the early modern period. In fifteenth-century Florence, the Hospital of the Innocenti, a haven for the illegitimate offspring of nobles, housed about 6 percent of all baptized children, a figure that rose to 38 percent by the turn of the nineteenth century. Milan's foundling home also expanded during the late eighteenth and nineteenth centuries, taking in between 30 and 40 percent of all baptized children.[18]

The secrecy surrounding infant abandonment makes it difficult to assign agency to women alone. Men also assisted their unwed partners in discarding their infants. There were also many deceased infants that never reached a foundling home; they were instead discovered in dung heaps, ditches, sewers, and rivers, their stories remaining buried in obscurity. Despite the participation of men in the crime of infanticide, throughout Europe the culturally constructed criminal was the single woman, who either miscarried, gave birth prematurely, had a stillbirth, or was desperate enough to strangle or smother her baby. Practicing midwives were also prime suspects. In northern Europe, unmarried pregnant women were obliged to register or face punishment for infanticide should they miscarry or experience stillbirth. There was no such law in Italy, but women convicted of infanticide were potentially subject to severe punishment. It appears, however, that the penalty of death was meant to serve more as a deterrent than as an actual punishment, for authorities rarely followed through.[19] Frequently women fled before they were brought to trial and underwent a kind of self-imposed exile. Scholars disagree on what motivated judicial leniency. Some emphasize the importance of female honor, which was salvaged by discarding the infant. Others underline early modern Europeans' conception of the female sex as fragile and therefore the transgression of sexual chastity excusable. Still others hypothesize that mild discipline reflected discomfort with exempting seductive fathers from inquiry or punishment, a discomfort that may also shed light on judges' reluctance to view infanticide as homicide. Elsewhere in Europe the eighteenth century witnessed greater sympathy for women accused of infanticide. Medical research emphasized the precarious psychological condition of expectant mothers. In Enlightenment England during the 1730s and 1740s, doctors such as William Hunter called for greater understanding of emotion, arguing that the pain of labor created temporary insanity. This became part of a larger debate in the 1770s in England. In Switzerland, Johann Pestalozzi, writing in 1783, characterized infanticide as the crime of women victimized by love. German romantic literature of the eighteenth and nineteenth centuries also contained themes of sympathy for unwed mothers.

Stages of childhood development: from infant to adolescent

Once again social class, financial means, and gender played fundamental roles in determining young children's experience during medieval and early modern times. Many lived with their parents at least until the age of seven, but thereafter their lives diverged. Less is known about the first seven years of life than about other phases of the human lifecycle, but advice manuals, pictorial evidence of swaddling and playing, and artifacts such as cradles, balls, and dolls indicate that it was a period when children, under their mothers' supervision, were trained for survival but also given the leisure time to play with toys and to participate in games that shaped their fundamental socialization. Until age two they were generally swaddled to keep them secure; between two and five they freely engaged in playing; and from six or seven they were assigned some chores appropriate to their age and physical capability. Some of the evidence for this phase in the lifecycle comes from the study of accidents, others from the lives of saints. Barbara Hanawalt's *The Ties That Bound*, a study that explores when and how children were injured, finds that the mishaps occurred when they were playing ball or tag, running races, attempting to be dare devils or doing chores like drawing water, helping their mothers to cook, or in the case of boys, taking horses to be watered or running errands for their fathers at work.[20] She concludes that despite the substantial work expected, medieval people were aware of both the biological necessities and limits of the child and that they were emotionally committed. Saints' lives, of course, present problems of interpretation because the writings aim explicitly to verify miraculous acts; however, in the course of describing the saint's extraordinary feats, the authors reveal telling descriptions of ordinary children's activities that reflect an awareness of age-specific stages of childhood development. The descriptions of miracles raising the dead, moreover, disclose parental emotions of attachment and grief as well as a firm commitment to ensure the survival of their offspring.[21]

The age of seven was in many ways a turning point in attitudes about childhood, especially with the onset of the religious reformations in the sixteenth century. In Protestant households seven was the age when fathers assumed greater responsibility for childrearing and building moral character. In Catholic communities seven was the age when children were old enough to account for committing mortal sin. Children from the elite classes obtained some type of formal education beginning at age seven; others instead took on the tasks and trades associated with their future livelihoods.

There were many different kinds of educational opportunities open to the most fortunate among children.[22] Prosperous parents of the aristocracy and the wealthy business and professional classes, for example, engaged tutors to live in or visit daily to teach their children as well as accompany them on travel. Another option was to enroll sons in boarding schools that housed and fed them in addition to providing a basic education. In this case the master became the boy's surrogate father, also teaching manners and morals. Among the best examples of this are the famed Renaissance humanist schools in fourteenth- and fifteenth-century northern Italy at Ferrara and Verona, which were funded by families that wielded power and that sponsored the great innovations in art and architecture as well as urban planning. Endowed schools, that is, independent institutions run by a priest who taught Latin, were yet another option. Some towns sponsored such schools for the sons of the governing families. The boys were prepared for future lives in civic government. There were also church schools, attached to cathedrals, monasteries, and parish priests; and vernacular schools. The latter were especially popular in commercial areas. Teachers in vernacular schools offered instruction in reading and writing in the local language rather than Latin, but in addition taught commercial mathematics, elementary bookkeeping, and literature ranging from saints' lives to chivalric poems. In the Germanic regions of Europe backstreet schools were established to teach some very basic literacy and elementary education to boys and girls. Because of the high costs, schooling was reserved for the wealthy. Ordinary people could not pay for tuition or upkeep, nor could they spare the assistance of their children at work. Generally there were more urban dwellers attending school than rural inhabitants, who could ill afford to leave the fields for classes and who often lived long distances from the centers of schooling.

The most common subject taught in all of these schools was Latin, the legal language of the elite preparing for government, the professions, or the lifestyle of the great landed nobility. Only a small percentage of boys and girls attended such schools, and they generally did so between the ages of six and fifteen. The percentage of females probably reached no more than 1 percent of the population, for they were excluded from all of the professions. Girls were not entirely cut off from formal education, but they had no public outlet for what they learned. Convents taught basic reading and writing in addition to sewing and manners, but women could not teach nor enter government or the professions. Their basic options were marriage or religious life. When the Protestants closed the convents and monasteries in the sixteenth century this avenue of education was discontinued.

There was a qualitative leap in the school curriculum between the Middle Ages and the fourteenth- to sixteenth-century Italian Renaissance, when both commercialization and urbanization required more education for children. While the earlier age offered instruction in Latin via religious texts, grammars, and glosses, mainly for future clerics or secretaries and notaries that would serve secular rulers, from the fifteenth century Renaissance teachers looked to antiquity for cultural and educational models, such as the writings of Virgil and Cicero. Renaissance humanism, an aspect of late medieval and early modern high culture that developed in Italy between AD 1300 and 1500 and spread to northern Europe between AD 1500 and 1650, was an educational program that trained the oligarchs and despots of the Italian cities and the chancery officials of Europe's growing bureaucracies in grammar, rhetoric, poetry, history, and moral philosophy. The constitutional histories of ancient Greece and Rome were emphasized for their moral and historical examples; rhetoric and statecraft became new fields of study. Moreover, the humanist emphasis on critical observation as opposed to simply citing ancient authorities prepared boys for careers in law, medicine, and natural philosophy. In many ways this elite educational program in the classics perpetuated the class hierarchy and perceived gendered differences between boys and girls.

A number of important developments facilitated the education of children starting in the late fifteenth century. Among them was the invention of the printing press. Movable type made it possible to print reading primers, grammar manuals, and classical and humanist texts that could be disseminated broadly. In this context, books became very important. Another was the northern humanist movement, which spread from the Italian cities. Desiderius Erasmus (AD 1466–1536) and other northern humanists emphasized the secular program of the Italian schools but also prescribed religious training and more advanced courses in philosophy, Hebrew, mathematics, and theology. There was, for example, little agreement among theologians and laymen over whether children were inherently innocent or evil, but they concurred that childhood was the critical period when character was shaped and that education was imperative. Following northern humanism, the Protestant Reformation was a third important development influencing childhood education. Martin Luther (AD 1483–1546) advocated compulsory elementary school education for all, children were encouraged to read the Bible, and literacy levels rose. More specialized Catholic schools also arose during the mid-sixteenth and seventeenth centuries, founded by the Jesuits. They offered advanced Latin humanities, philosophy, mathematics, and physics to boys aged ten to sixteen. This was a great era for school foundation, and literacy levels among males grew significantly.

While the number of opportunities to attend schools increased during the early modern period, and civic groups, church, and state devoted greater emphasis to child rearing and education, there was also significant epistemological conflict. This was an era of religious fragmentation, with Protestants competing with Catholics to both define religious doctrine and to organize obedient, loyal followings. The issue was not simply religious difference; it was a broad conflict over how society should be organized. The Renaissance and Reformation era was also a period of growing secularism, when statecraft, beginning with the political writer Niccolò Machiavelli (AD 1469–1527), evolved into a rational science, liberated from the church and the divine, to be studied, understood, and improved. From the late sixteenth century, early modern rulers financed ever larger military and bureaucratic apparatuses and engaged scientists to improve technologies ranging from agricultural production and transoceanic navigation to the refinement of instruments of warfare and manufacture. Humanist methods of critical inquiry challenged the established reverence for the ancients advocated by more religiously inclined scholastic teachers, and the scientific debates advanced by physicians and natural philosophers fostered more skepticism. At the same time, however, the new views clashed sharply with both religious doctrine and folk wisdom and superstition. New scientific observations made the world larger, but disconcerted theologians by deposing it as the center of the universe, and ordinary people still relied on magic and spells to negotiate life's hardships and quell fears about the devil.

Approaches to child rearing existed amidst these sixteenth and seventeenth century debates. First, the Protestant split with Catholicism inculcated a different set of values. Protestants, privileging marriage and the family, refuted a thousand years of Roman Catholic tradition, which upheld the celibate ideal and religious enclosure. Instead they encouraged companionate marriage and shared parenting and admitted the possibility of divorce. Catholics, on the other hand, remained under a restricted marital regime that emphasized virginity and enclosure for unmarried women with no possibility of divorce. Protestants were highly critical of the Catholic position, which sometimes led to secret unions and illegitimate offspring. Martin Luther emphasized that the purpose of sex was procreation and that sex was a marital duty; moreover, that it was better to wed than to sin by engaging in sexual relations outside of marriage. Second, according to Steven Ozment, Protestants viewed childrearing as a "rational art"[23] that involved care of the child's physical and material needs as well as inculcating virtues and values. Spoiling was to be avoided and self-sacrifice and deference to patriarchal authority cultivated. Moreover, evangelists and radicals emphasized greater spiritual education of the young,[24] a new approach to child rearing that clashed with the emerging scientific model of empirical observation and deduction. This approach also generated conflict with secular authorities who viewed the spread of religious radicalism as subversive. There were also philosophical disagreements over the inherent nature of human beings, whether laden with original sin and naturally evil or born innocent, debates that inevitably affected ideas about child rearing in different ways. Such disagreements influenced the educated classes more than ordinary people, but ordinary people were subject to other splits as their folk wisdom came under the censorship of the Reformation churches. Religious reformers were intent on molding parent–child relationships, mandating the former to instill moral values, to invest heavily in education, and, in consequence, to separate children from adult living in order to cultivate this preparatory stage of life.[25] For the prosperous, schooling would be extended, with an emphasis on religious orthodoxy. While the minimum canonical age permitting marriage was twelve for girls and fourteen for boys, extending teens' period of study ultimately postponed marriage, a rite of passage to adulthood. Another way of viewing this is to see a prolonged adolescence associated less with street games, rites, and rituals and linked more to securing a profession, with at least secondary schooling if not university becoming mandatory. There were, of course, gendered differences: schooling for females prepared them for matrimony and domestic life rather than the professions or a trade. Both male and female youths, whose families were prosperous enough to offer them secondary education, enjoyed increasing leisure time, in contrast to working youngsters. Marriage ended childhood or adolescence for women, while emancipation or inheriting land and establishing an independent household ushered prosperous males into adulthood.

In conclusion, there were a variety of childhood experiences in medieval and early modern Europe, shaped foremost by class and gender but also by the cyclical structures of everyday life. In principle, the higher the social station and level of financial prosperity, the greater the chances of survival, the more opportunity for higher education, and the lengthier the childhood experience. Poor people were cast into the work force early on, and their lives were soon filled with responsibility and hardship. It would be fruitful to learn more about how those hardships influenced children's cognitive and psychological development. It is difficult, however, for historians to know what children felt, or how they fended for themselves in what were challenging circumstances, for they did not leave us written records. The archeology of toys, and cradles, along with songs, rhymes, and riddles offer clues of times past, but there is a lot we still do not know, especially about poor children and the desperate parents who were forced to relinquish them to the care of others or who saw them perish early.

Notes

1 Philippe Ariès, *Centuries of Childhood: A Social History of Family Life*, translated by Robert Baldick (New York, NY: Knopf, 1962).
2 On the establishment of childhood studies see: Barbara A. Hanawalt, "Medievalists and the Study of Childhood," *Speculum* 77 (2002): 440–1.
3 Hanawalt, "Medievalists and the Study of Childhood," 443–4.
4 Linda Pollock, *Forgotten Children: Parent–Child Relations from 1500 to 1900* (New York, NY: Cambridge University Press, 1983), 54; Hanawalt, "Study of Childhood," 442–3; Margaret King, "Concepts of Childhood: What We Know and Where We Might Go," *Renaissance Quarterly* 60 (2007): 373.
5 Hanawalt, "Study of Childhood," 441, 443, 445, 456–7.
6 Hanawalt, "Study of Childhood," 450–1.
7 Herlihy, David, and Christiane Klapisch-Zuber, *Tuscans and Their Families: A Study of the Florentine Catasto of 1427*, trans. David Herlihy and Christiane Klapisch-Zuber (New Haven, CT: Yale University Press, 1985), 244–6.
8 Christiane Klapisch-Zuber, *Women, Family, and Ritual in Renaissance Italy*, trans. Lydia Cochrane (Chicago, MI: Chicago University Press, 1985), 132–64.
9 Jean-Louis Flandrin, *Families in Former Times: Kinship, Household and Sexuality in Early Modern France*, trans. Richard Southern (New York, NY: Cambridge University Press, 1979), 58–59.
10 Philip Gavitt, *Charity and Children in Renaissance Florence: The Ospedale degli Innocenti, 1410–1536* (Ann Arbor, MI: University of Michigan Press, 1990), 210, 215, 227.
11 Barbara A. Hanawalt, *Growing Up in Medieval London: The Experience of Childhood in History* (Oxford, UK: Oxford University Press, 1993), 56–9.
12 Jacqueline Musacchio, *The Art and Ritual of Childbirth in Renaissance Italy* (New Haven, CT: Yale University Press, 1999).
13 John Boswell, *The Kindness of Strangers: The Abandonment of Children in Western Europe from Antiquity to the Renaissance* (New York, NY: Pantheon Books, 1988), 429; and Hanawalt, "Study of Childhood," 453.
14 Margaret King's study of *The Death of the Child Valerio Marcello* (Chicago, IL: University of Chicago Press, 1994) vividly documents a Venetian father's lifelong grief over the loss of his son.
15 Mary Martin McLaughlin, "Survivors and Surrogates: Children and Parents from the Ninth to the Thirteenth Centuries," in *The History of Childhood*, ed. Lloyd deMause (New York, NY: Psychohistory Press, 1974), 113–14, 123; Lloyd deMause, "The Evolution of Childhood," in *The History of Childhood*, ed. Lloyd deMause (New York, NY: Psychohistory Press , 1974), 37–38; and Hanawalt's analysis in "Study of Childhood," 444.
16 Flandrin, *Families in Former Times*, 153, 212–42.

17 Joanne M. Ferraro, *Nefarious Crimes, Contested Justice. Illicit Sex and Infanticide in the Republic of Venice, 1557–1789* (Baltimore, MD: Johns Hopkins University Press, 2008), 4–14, 86–7, 158–99, 161–3, 172–3, 184–9, 192–200, 205–6.

18 John Henderson and Richard Wall, *Poor Women and Children in the European Past* (New York, NY: Routledge, 1994), 10; Philip Gavitt, " 'Perchè non avea chi la ghovernasse:' Cultural Values, Family Resources and Abandonment in the Florence of Lorenzo de' Medici, 146–85," in *Poor Women and Children*, 65, 74.

19 Ferraro, *Nefarious Crimes*, 11–14.

20 Barbara A. Hanawalt, *The Ties That Bound: Peasant Families in Medieval England* (New York, NY: Oxford University Press, 1986), 271–3; *Idem*, "Study of Childhood," 449–50, 454.

21 Hanawalt discusses the hagiography literature in "Study of Childhood," 446–9.

22 On schooling, see Paul F. Grendler, *Schooling in Renaissance Italy: Literacy and Learning, 1300–1600.* (Baltimore, MD: Johns Hopkins University Press, 1989); *Idem*, "Schools and Schooling," in *The Encyclopedia of European Social History from 1350 to 2000*, ed. Peter N. Stearns (New York, NY: Charles Scribner's Sons, 2001) Vol. 5, 329–351. For convent schooling, see Sharon Strocchia, "Learning the Virtues: Convent Schools and Female Culture in Renaissance Florence," in *Women's Education in Early Modern Europe: A History, 1500–1800*, ed. Barbara J. Whitehead (New York, NY: Routledge, 1999), 5–46.

23 Steven Ozment, *When Fathers Ruled. Family Life in Reformation Europe* (Cambridge, MA: Harvard University Press, 1983), 132.

24 King, "Concepts of Childhood," 374.

25 John Sommerville emphasizes the way Puritanism was used, especially by mothers, as a means to acculturate the young in *The Discovery of Childhood in Puritan England* (Athens, GA: University of Georgia Press, 1992).

Suggestions for further reading

Abandonment and infanticide; poverty and charity

Boswell, John. *The Kindness of Strangers: The Abandonment of Children in Western Europe from Antiquity to the Renaissance.* New York, NY: Pantheon Books, 1988. A pioneering study of child abandonment.

Ferraro, Joanne. *Nefarious Crimes, Contested Justice. Illicit Sex and Infanticide in the Republic of Venice, 1557–1789.* Baltimore, MD: Johns Hopkins University Press, 2008. The detective–historian uncovers the hidden world of illicit sexual relationships and the plight of unwanted infants.

Gavitt, Philip. *Charity and Children in Renaissance Florence: The Ospedale degli Innocenti, 1410–1536.* Ann Arbor, MI: University of Michigan Press, 1990. A study of Florence's principal foundling home during the Renaissance.

Henderson, John and Richard Wall, eds. *Poor Women and Children in the European Past.* New York: Routledge, 1994. Considers the impact of poverty in households without fathers.

Terpstra, Nicholas. *Abandoned Children of the Italian Renaissance. Orphan Care in Florence and Bologna.* Baltimore, MD: John Hopkins University Press, 2005. A comparative study of foundling and orphan care in two Italian cities.

Childbirth and infancy

Fildes, Valerie. *Breasts, Bottles, and Babies. A History of Infant Feeding*. Edinburgh, UK: Edinburgh University Press, 1986. Contributes to our understanding of both infancy and motherhood.

Gelis, Jacques. *The History of Childbirth: Fertility, Pregnancy and Birth in Early Modern Europe*. Translated by Rosemary Morris. Boston, MA: Northeastern University, 1991. Focuses especially on seventeenth-century France.

Marland, Hilary, ed. *The Art of Midwifery: Early Modern Midwives in Europe*. London, UK: Routledge, 1993. Profiles the lives and work of Europe's midwives.

Childhood, general histories and historiography

Cunningham, Hugh. *Children and Childhood in Western Society since 1500*. 2nd Edition. New York, NY: Longman, 2005. A comprehensive introduction to the history of childhood, including child poverty and labor.

deMause, Lloyd. "The Evolution of Childhood." In *The History of Childhood*, edited by Lloyd deMause, 1–73. New York, NY: Psychohistory Press, 1974. A psycho-historical approach to the history of childhood.

Heywood, Colin. *A History of Childhood: Children and Childhood in the West from Medieval to Modern Times*. Cambridge, UK: Polity, 2001. A synthesis of childhood history.

King, Margaret L. "Concepts of Childhood: What We Know and Where We Might Go." *Renaissance Quarterly* 60 (2007): 371–407. An excellent historiographical essay on the literature to 2007.

Childhood, the early modern period

Ozment, Steven. *When Fathers Ruled: Family Life in Reformation Europe*. Cambridge, MA: Harvard University Press, 1983. Covers how the Reformation impacted family life and child rearing.

Pollock, Linda. *Forgotten Children: Parent–Child Relations from 1500–1900*. New York, NY: Cambridge University Press, 1983. Stresses the continuity in the treatment of children in early modern and modern England.

Sommerville, C. John. *The Discovery of Childhood in Puritan England*. Athens, GA: University of Georgia Press, 1992. Focuses on Puritanism and approaches to child rearing.

Childhood, the medieval period

Alexandre-Bidon, Danièle and Didier Lett, *Children in the Middle Ages: Fifth to Fifteenth Centuries*. Translated by Jody Gladding. Notre Dame, IN: University of Notre Dame Press, 1999. Reconstructs the lives of medieval children from various social ranks at work, school, and play.

Crawford, Sally. *Childhood in Anglo-Saxon England*. Gloucestershire, UK: Sutton, 1999. A study of childhood and family structure in medieval England.

Derevenski, Joanne Sofaer, ed. *Children and Material Culture*. London, UK: Routledge, 2000. A collection of essays that use archaeological evidence to shed light on childhood from prehistoric to Anglo-Saxon times in England.

Hanawalt, Barbara A. "Medievalists and the Study of Childhood." *Speculum* 77 (2002): 440–458. An important historiographical essay on childhood studies for the Middle Ages.

Hanawalt, Barbara A. *Growing Up in Medieval London: The Experience of Childhood in History*. New York, NY: Oxford University Press, 1993. A detailed picture of medieval life that demonstrates the continuity of the nuclear family over the long term.

Hanawalt, Barbara A. *The Ties that Bound: Peasant Families in Medieval England*. Oxford, UK: Oxford University Press, 1986. A detailed picture of everyday life.

McLaughlin, Mary Martin. "Survivors and Surrogates: Children and Parents from the Ninth to the Thirteenth Centuries." In *The History of Childhood*, edited by Lloyd deMause, 101–81. New York, NY: Psychohistory Press, 1974. Analyzes learned writings on child rearing.

Orme, Nicholas. *Medieval Children*. New Haven, CT: Yale University Press, 2001. A fascinating study of medieval children through their toys, games, songs, and work.

Childhood, the Renaissance period

King, Margaret. *The Death of the Child Valerio Marcello*. Chicago, IL: University of Chicago Press, 1994. Recounts the grief of a Renaissance father over the loss of his young son.

Klapisch-Zuber, Christiane. *Women, Family, and Ritual in Renaissance Italy*. Translated by Lydia G. Cochrane. Chicago, IL: University of Chicago Press, 1985. A study of women's roles in the Renaissance family.

Kuehn, Thomas. *Illegitimacy in Renaissance Florence*. Ann Arbor, MI: University of Michigan Press, 2002. A legal history of child illegitimacy.

Musacchio, Jacqueline. *The Art and Ritual of Childbirth in Renaissance Italy*. New Haven, CT: Yale University Press, 1999. Analyzes paintings, bowls, trays, and other material objects surrounding childbirth for their social and cultural significance.

Domestic service

Fairchilds, Cissie. *Domestic Enemies: Servants and Their Masters in Old Regime France*. Baltimore, MD: Johns Hopkins University Press, 1984. A study of master–servant relations.

Economy and demography

Cipolla, Carlo. *Before the Industrial Revolution: European Society and Economy, 1000–1700*. New York, NY: Norton, 1980. An informative survey of economic trends and their impact on living standards over seven centuries.

De Vries, Jan. "The Industrial Revolution and the Industrious Revolution." *Journal of Economic History* 54 (1994): 249–270. Discusses the importance of proto-industry and the household.

Family and household

Ariès, Philippe. *Centuries of Childhood: A Social History of Family Life*. Translated by Robert Baldick. New York, NY: Knopf, 1962. The work that pioneered childhood as an area of historical inquiry, with conclusions that initiated subsequent debates.

Flandrin, Jean-Louis. *Families in Former Times: Kinship, Household and Sexuality in Early Modern France*. Translated by Richard Southern. New York, NY: Cambridge University Press, 1979. A survey of family attitudes and behaviors, including birth control.

Goody, Jack. *The European Family: An Historico-Anthropological Essay*. Oxford: Basil Blackwell, 2000. A synthesis that traces the evolution of household structures in European history.

Goody, Jack. *The Development of the Family and Marriage in Europe*. New York, NY: Cambridge University Press, 1983. An anthropological study of family structure from medieval to modern times.

Herlihy, David and Christiane Klapisch-Zuber. *Tuscans and their Families: A Study of the Florentine Catasto of 1427*. Translated by David Herlihy and Christiane Klapisch-Zuber. New Haven, CT: Yale University Press, 1985. Provides great insight on birth, death, work, and daily life in Tuscany using the census data of 1427.

Schooling

Grendler, Paul F. "Schools and Schooling." In *The Encyclopedia of European Social History from 1350 to 2000*, edited by Peter N. Stearns, Vol. 5, 329–351. New York, NY: Charles Scribner's Sons, 2001. An overview of the European educational experience.

Grendler, Paul F. *Schooling in Renaissance Italy: Literacy and Learning*. 1300–1600. Baltimore, MD: Johns Hopkins University Press, 1989. A comprehensive study of the educational experience, differentiated in terms of social class and gender.

Strocchia, Sharon. "Learning the Virtues: Convent Schools and Female Culture in Renaissance Florence." In *Women's Education in Early Modern Europe: A History*, 1500–1800, edited by Barbara J. Whitehead, 5–46. New York, NY: Routledge, 1999. A study of convent life and female education.

4

CHILDHOOD AND THE ENLIGHTENMENT

The complications of innocence

Larry Wolff

"*On ne connait point l'enfance.*" "People know nothing about childhood," wrote Jean-Jacques Rousseau in the preface to *Emile*, published in 1762 as an enlightened program of education and quickly acknowledged as the most important and influential study of children and childhood in the age of Enlightenment. "People always look for the man in the child," Rousseau continued, "without thinking about what he was before becoming a man."[1] This prescription for learning about childhood by analytically distinguishing children from the adults they would eventually become contained within it the argument that historian Philippe Ariès would articulate two centuries later concerning the history of childhood in France: that the whole early modern revolution in thinking about children involved focusing on the childlike qualities of children rather than children as "small-scale adults."[2] The Enlightenment offered, on the one hand, a consummation of early modern historical development, looking back to the Renaissance, and at the same time, the eighteenth century marked the beginning of modern history, such that childhood in the age of the Enlightenment also pointed forward toward the social forms and concepts of modern and even contemporary childhood. Historian Lawrence Stone, considering early modern England, argued for the emergence of a "child-oriented, affectionate, and permissive mode" of family life in the eighteenth century, in the more general context of an early modern "affective individualism."[3]

While the social dimensions of the Ariès and Stone arguments have been particularly controversial – for instance, the question of whether parents loved their children more or differently after the Renaissance – the cultural landmarks of the sixteenth century have been more readily acknowledged: the new attention to children in art, as in Breughel's *Children's Games* of 1560, the new precision in organizing children's education as in the Jesuit *Ratio Studiorum* of 1599, and the new focus on children as the objects of religious attention in the catechisms of the Reformation and Counter-Reformation. The Enlightenment, however, offered a newly secular understanding of childhood, formulated with new intensity in the philosophical spirit of the century. Montaigne certainly discussed children in his essays in the sixteenth century, but in the eighteenth century Rousseau's *Emile* was a literary and philosophical work on an entirely different scale, with hundreds of pages dedicated to the subject of children. Representing a kind of culmination of early modern attentions to the subject, *Emile* also outlined a new agenda of children's issues that have remained prominent ever since. These issues include children's education – the particular subject of *Emile* – but also children's health, children's literature, the significance of gender for children, the philosophical relation of adults to their own childhoods, and the ideological meaning of children's innocence. In all these regards, *Emile* served as both a summation of early modern discoveries and the revolutionary articulation of a modern perspective in the spirit of the Enlightenment.

"To preserve children's innocence": medicine and masturbation

"One thinks only to preserve one's child [*conserver son enfant*]," wrote Rousseau. "This is not enough" (42–43). At the center of the Ariès thesis is the controversial argument that the high level of child mortality made pre-modern parents somehow sentimentally immune to becoming over-attached to their children. There is some statistical evidence to suggest that the eighteenth century witnessed a significant decrease in child mortality, correlated with the birth control revolution in France, while elsewhere, in London for instance, it has been recorded that, between 1730 and 1750, 75 percent of the population died before the age of five, but between 1770 and 1790 that percentage was reduced to 50 percent.[4] The preservation of children was thus enhanced during the age of Enlightenment, as if pivoting on the publication of *Emile* in 1762. The Ariès thesis argues that improved rates of survival permitted greater attachment to children, though the same argument could be inverted to suggest that greater concern for children led to higher rates of preservation. Rousseau not only took for granted that parents were highly attentive to preserving the lives of their children, but also seemed to imply that preservation had improved to the point that one might declare it to be "not enough."

In fact, Rousseau in *Emile* was more concerned about health than mortality, and his conception of health was as much spiritual as medical. Book One quickly proceeded to an attack on the custom of swaddling infants: "Civil man is born, lives, and dies in slavery. At his birth he is sewn into swaddling clothes, and at his death he is nailed into his coffin." Rousseau provided medical reasoning – "the inaction, the constraint to which the child's limbs are subject can only hamper the circulation of the blood and the humors" – but the unhealthfulness of swaddling was clearly in part metaphorical (43–44). In 1762, the same year as *Emile*, Rousseau's *Social Contract* declared, "Man was born free, and he is everywhere in chains."[5] In *Emile*, the Enlightenment's ideology of liberty was applied to children, beginning with the denunciation of swaddling.

Rousseau's philosophical perspective was already anticipated by the professionally medical perspective of William Cadogan, a British doctor who worked at the London Foundling Home (established in 1741 as an institutional alternative to widespread infanticide), and Cadogan published in 1748 what may be the first physician's booklet of advice on childrearing: *An Essay upon Nursing and the Management of Children from their Birth to Three Years of Age*, two hundred years before Dr Spock published the first edition of *Baby and Child Care* in 1946.

> Besides the Mischief arising from the Weight and Heat of these Swaddling-cloaths, they are put on so tight, and the Child is so cramp'd by them that its Bowels have not room, nor the Limbs any Liberty, to act and exert themselves in the free easy Manner they ought. This is a very hurtful Circumstance, for

Limbs that are not used, will never be strong, and such tender Bodies cannot bear much Pressure: The Circulation restrained by the Compression of any one Part must produce unnatural Swellings in some other.[6]

Cadogan's empirically observed medical concerns were translated into Rousseau's more metaphorical appeal for freedom. More generally, Cadogan's affirmation of the "Philosophic Knowledge of Nature" suggested an enlightened medical perspective that anticipated and probably conditioned Rousseau's "natural" prescriptions for the upbringing and education of Emile.[7] Rousseau's fat philosophical book would become the Enlightenment's definitive statement concerning childhood, but Cadogan's slim medical essay also went through ten editions in the eighteenth century.

Cadogan particularly recommended maternal nursing (as opposed to hired wet-nursing) and offered medical justification:

> When a Child sucks its own Mother, which, with a very few Exceptions, would be best for every Child, and every Mother, Nature has provided it with such wholesome and suitable Nourishment... The Mother's first Milk is purgative, and cleanses the Child of its long hoarded Excrement; no Child therefore can be deprived of it without manifest Injury.[8]

Rousseau fully agreed, but for him the principle and purpose was moral, and even political, as much as medical: "When mothers deign to nurse their children, customs will reform themselves, and the sentiments of nature will reawaken in all hearts" (47). The long-term benefits of maternal nursing to society and state were more important to Rousseau than immediate issues concerning the health of the infant.

Rousseau believed, in deference to nature, that the sickness of children was natural, and neither should nor could be medically prevented.

> Observe nature, and follow the path that she traces for you. She exercises children continually; she hardens their temperament by all sorts of tests; she teaches them early the meaning of pain and suffering. The breaking through of the teeth brings fever; sharp colics bring convulsions; long coughing suffocates them; worms torment them; disease corrupts their blood; various yeasts ferment and cause dangerous eruptions. Almost all of the first age of life is sickness and danger: half the children born die before the eighth year. Having been tested, however, the child gains strength, and as soon as he can make use of life, its principle becomes more secure. This is the rule of nature. Why would you contradict it? (49)

The statistics on childhood mortality were improving, even as Rousseau was writing, but he clearly implied that he did not regret the 50 percent mortality rate, seeing it rather as a Spartan condition for the survival of the fittest children. For Rousseau the whole issue of childhood mortality was a matter of misplaced emphasis. "I would not take charge of a sickly and feeble child ... a pupil always useless to himself and to others, who is entirely occupied with preserving himself," Rousseau declared. "As I never call a doctor for myself, I would never call one for my Emile, unless his life is in evident danger, for then the doctor can do no worse than kill him" (58–60).

Rousseau affirmed that "hygiene is the only useful part of medicine, and hygiene is rather a virtue than a science." In fact, given the state of medical knowledge in 1762, hygiene was probably the most useful health measure that could be taken as a prophylactic against severe and possibly fatal infections, but over the course of the century medicine also made available the earliest efforts at childhood inoculation and vaccination. Lady Mary Wortley Montagu, in her letters from Constantinople in 1718 as wife of the British ambassador, wrote about Turkish inoculation (using live smallpox) and decided to have her own young children inoculated. "You may believe I am well satisfied of the safety of the experiment, since I intend to try it on my dear little son," wrote Lady Mary. "I am patriot enough to take pains to bring this useful invention into fashion in England."[9] Her son Edward, born in 1713, was of the same generation as Rousseau, who was born in 1712.

The practice of inoculating children against smallpox made slow progress in Europe during the eighteenth century, and in the decade of *Emile* there occurred the celebrated voyage to Russia in 1768 of the British doctor Thomas Dimsdale, for the purpose of inoculating Catherine the Great and her son, the future Tsar Paul, who was then fourteen. Already in 1765, however, there had been proposed in the London Medical Society the less risky possibility of inoculating against smallpox by using cowpox: hence, vaccination. In 1796, Edward Jenner vaccinated an eight-year-old boy, his gardener's son, establishing not only the modern practice of vaccination but also its particular importance for preserving the lives of children. The establishment of the London Foundling Home in 1741 helped to focus Cadogan on the particular issues of children's health, and enlightened medical perspectives led, in turn, to the eventual creation of the first children's hospital, L'Hôpital des Enfants-Malades, in Paris in 1802.

Rousseau, with his suspicion of medicine, and his scarcely concealed antipathy to weak and sickly children, was by no means inclined to have Emile inoculated against smallpox. "How should we conduct ourselves with our pupil concerning the danger of smallpox?" he asked. "Shall we have him inoculated in childhood, or wait till he gets it naturally?" The word "naturally" (*naturellement*) already indicated the Rousseauist answer to the question. Rousseau knew that the practice of inoculation was growing, and chose not to endorse it any more than he actually presumed to oppose it: "I scarcely deign to deal with this question for my Emile. He will be inoculated or not according to the time, the place, the circumstances. It is almost a matter of indifference for him" (165–66). Rousseau did not live long enough to react to Jenner's successful vaccination with cowpox, but it seems doubtful that Rousseau would have considered the introduction of cowpox into human subjects as something "natural." The case of Emile thus suggests the extent to which the discussion of children's health in the Enlightenment remained ambivalent, with Rousseau almost obstinately refusing to take a strictly medical view of health and insisting rather on the rearing of a morally and spiritually healthy child.

For that reason Rousseau was entirely sympathetic to a quite different medical preoccupation of the eighteenth century, namely the profound concern about the consequences of masturbation, dating from the anonymous publication of *Onania: Or the Heinous Sin of Self-Pollution and all its Frightful Consequences in Both Sexes*, first published in London, probably around 1712. Historian Thomas Laqueur has discussed its huge impact as it went through multiple editions in the eighteenth century.

With *Onania*, masturbation ceased to be simply a religious sin and became instead a medical problem, and though the work was concerned with both sexes and all ages, it contained a particular "admonition to the youth of the nation."[10] In 1760 the well-known Swiss doctor Samuel-Auguste Tissot made masturbation a matter of medical expertise and presented the subject to the public of the French Enlightenment in his book *L'Onanisme*, also destined for multiple editions. Tissot, after reading *Emile* in 1762, sent a copy of *L'Onanisme* to Rousseau, and the two men arranged a meeting, thus bringing together the Enlightenment's Swiss expert on masturbation with the Enlightenment's Swiss expert on childhood.[11] For Rousseau the subject of masturbation belonged to the later stages of Emile's tutelage, but it was central to a concern that he developed throughout the work: the natural innocence of childhood.

"Let us assert as an incontestable maxim that the first movements of nature are always right," insisted Rousseau. "There is no original perversity in the human heart; there is not to be found in it one single vice of which we can not say how it entered there." Early education, therefore, was a negative procedure: "It consists not in teaching virtue or truth, but in preserving the heart from vice and the spirit from error" (111–13). The advent of adolescence and sexual awareness was, for Rousseau, something to be postponed, as he sought "to preserve children's innocence" (*conserver aux enfants leur innocence*) as a preservation of childhood itself. He stressed the "advantage of prolonged innocence" (282, 286). This ideology of childhood's innocence, articulated in the age of Enlightenment, would be powerfully influential in conditioning the social roles of children and the sentimental aspects of childhood in the nineteenth and twentieth centuries. Rousseau, dismissing original sin, conceived of childhood's innocence from an entirely secular perspective, and ultimately, toward the end of the fourth book of *Emile*, he connected the philosophical issue of innocence to the contemporary medical discourse concerning masturbation. He advised prospective tutors to watch closely over their wards:

> Do not leave him alone day or night; and at least sleep in his room... Challenge the instinct ... It would be very dangerous if it [the instinct] taught your pupil to abuse his senses and to seek occasions to satisfy them: once he discovers this dangerous supplement, he is lost. From then on, his body and heart will always be enervated; he will carry to his tomb the sad effects of this habit, the most fatal habit to which a young man may be subjected. (437)

The *philosophe* Rousseau and the doctor Tissot must have found much common ground for discussion in their meeting of 1762.

The vulnerability of childhood was well known, even as childhood mortality began to decline, and vaccination heralded a new age of protection, but the newly articulated innocence of childhood was conceived as dangerously precarious and was conditioned by eighteenth-century medical anxiety about masturbation. This sense of precarious innocence also meant that, even as Rousseau rejected swaddling in the name of the liberty of childhood, he also preached the strictest supervision of children: "do not leave him alone day or night." Thus, the enlightened tutelage of Emile could be, in its own way, as strictly disciplined as a Jesuit education according to the *Ratio Studiorum*. In the *Social Contract*, Rousseau argued that men were "born free," but nevertheless might have to be "forced to be free"; in *Emile* children were supposed to be free and innocent in accordance with nature, but freedom and innocence were to be closely monitored. The legacy of the Enlightenment in the centuries to follow allowed children to be cherished for their "natural" innocence, while that innocence was preserved through benevolent surveillance and systematic discipline.

"When I imagine a child": innocence and violation

Rousseau in *Emile* offered something between a philosophical treatise on education and a literary novel about the child Emile. In fact, the year in which he published *Emile* and the *Social Contract*, 1762, was just one year after the publication of his great novel *La nouvelle Eloise*, the Alpine epistolary romance that became one of the bestselling books of the century and elicited an unprecedented level of emotional response from its readers.[12] It was a work of sentiment and emotion, inaugurating an age of sentimental reading, and linking the age of the Enlightenment to that of early Romanticism. In fact, one might make the same claim for *Emile*: that, like *La nouvelle Eloise*, it too was a work of sentiment and emotion, and that the character of Emile at the center of the work was created by Rousseau with the intention of eliciting emotion from his readers. Most striking were the literary techniques of visualization that Rousseau employed to conjure Emile, to place the child protagonist before the eye of the public, seeking a sentimental response that would confirm the work's philosophical arguments. The natural innocence of childhood could be artfully evoked on the page, so as to explore "the charm that one finds in contemplating a beautiful childhood [*du charme qu'on trouve à contempler une belle enfance*], rather than the perfection of mature age" (203). This technique of visual evocation in Rousseau may be understood in the context of the artistic representation of children in the eighteenth century, and suggests that the Enlightenment's conception of childhood was not simply philosophical or pedagogical, but also fundamentally emotional and sentimental. The Enlightenment produced a modern idea of childhood by exploring and even exploiting the ways that adults looked at children.

Art history has been a crucial discipline for considering historical developments concerning childhood because there is a relatively clear record of children's increased and more varied presence in art, dating from the Renaissance.[13] Indubitably, painters of the high Renaissance, like Leonardo da Vinci, were paying greater attention to the anatomy and musculature of both children and adults, resulting in an increasingly childlike baby Jesus represented with duly observed infant proportions. By the sixteenth century, Jesus was no longer the only child appearing in European art, as the secular portraiture of children became an increasingly important subject of representation, especially at court. Bronzino painted the Medici children in sixteenth-century Florence, while Velázquez famously attended to the Habsburg children in seventeenth-century Madrid, placing the Infanta Margarita at the very heart of the court life, depicted in *Las Meninas*.

In the eighteenth century, dynastic children were already displayed with an even greater conviction of their childlike appeal. Maria Theresa brought her Habsburg heir, the infant Joseph, to the Hungarian Diet in Bratislava in 1741 to show him in the flesh to the Hungarian nobles, as she rallied their support for the War of the Austrian Succession. Art historian Michael Yonan has discussed this political moment:

In a story that became part of Habsburg legend, the young Maria Theresa appeared before an assembly of Hungarian nobles, entreating them for assistance in defending the empire from invasion. Pressing the infant Joseph to her breast she begged the Hungarians for their support, and so moved were they by this display of maternal devotion that they threw themselves at her feet and swore their eternal support. Cynics later claimed that Maria Theresa had pinched the baby Joseph during the speech, causing him to cry and thereby heightening the drama.[14]

There was an element of instant legendry here, and the eighteenth century was perhaps the first century when such an emotionally manipulative performance, exploiting the visual appeal of the child, seemed plausible.

The portrait of Maria Theresa by Martin von Meytens, painted just a few years later in the 1740s, showed her at full length in imperial grandeur, posed beneath a smaller half-length portrait of the child Joseph in formal Hungarian costume. His childlike appeal in some sense crowned his mother's splendor as his portrait hung just over her head.[15] Maria Theresa gave birth to sixteen children (though some died in infancy) and they were frequently represented in art: for instance, in the celebrated and characterful pastels of Jean-Etienne Liotard. Meytens also produced a family portrait in the 1750s to show the Empress and Emperor surrounded by all their surviving children, representing Maria Theresa with her domestic maternal charisma exercised informally through the multiple charms of her numerous offspring – probably intended in pointed contrast and challenge to her childless enemy Frederick the Great of Prussia.

In the eighteenth century, the portraiture of children, and especially of parents with children, achieved a new level of prominence in painting and diffusion in society, with such British masters as Joshua Reynolds and Thomas Gainsborough creating family portraits as one of the principal genres of representation for British elite society. Even the very grandest figures of the aristocracy, like Georgiana Cavendish, Duchess of Devonshire, famous for her beauty and her wardrobe as represented in paintings by Reynolds and Gainsborough, was also painted by Reynolds quite informally in 1784 with her baby daughter at a moment of play. The painting showed the duchess, herself one of the great charmers of her era, succumbing to what Rousseau called "the charm that one finds in contemplating a beautiful childhood," and Reynolds conveyed that charm to the viewer by representing the scene of maternal infatuation.[16]

In *Emile*, though the work was literary, Rousseau emphasized the powerfully visual aspect of appreciating childhood: "Is not the spectacle of this age a charming and sweet spectacle [*un spectacle charmant et doux*], to see a pretty child?" (207) Rousseau's valuation of childhood depended upon the "charm" that children exercised upon adults, what would later be labeled as the "cute factor." It would be associated with the appearance of children from the eighteenth century onward, reaching its culmination in the age of photography. Rousseau, however, was already fully conscious of the vividly visual impression made by children, and, in the same spirit that would motivate Reynolds and Gainsborough at their canvases, conjured Emile before the reader's eye:

When I imagine a child [*quand je me figure un enfant*] of ten to twelve years, healthy, vigorous, well-formed for his age, he inspires in me an entirely agreeable idea, whether for the present or for the future. I see him [*je le vois*] heated, alive, animated... I contemplate the child, and he pleases me. I imagine the man, and he pleases me further. I feel that I am living from his life, and his vivacity rejuvenates me. (204)

To appreciate Emile, it was necessary to visualize him, and Rousseau's writing was an exhortation to do just that. He even anticipated the reader's response to the image of the child by describing his own: the physiological response of the racing pulse, which already lay somewhere on the uncertain frontier between tender fondness and erotic excitement. The Enlightenment found the essence of the childlike quality of children in the way that the visual appearance of the child elicited a profound emotional response from the gaze of the adult.

Art historian Anne Higonnet has observed that eighteenth-century British portrait painters "created a consistent and sustained image of childhood, one which was perfectly in keeping with the latest social trends and written precepts of child-rearing." The supposed innocence of childhood was fundamental to that image as its fundamental character. Higonnet cites, for instance, Reynolds painting *The Age of Innocence* from the 1780s: a child in a white dress with hands pressed to her breast, sitting on the ground in a natural landscape, gazing in profile into the distance.[17] The identity of the child is uncertain, making her plausibly any child of the 1780s, corresponding to the ideally innocent girl Sophie whom Rousseau invented as Emile's female companion. Similarly evocative of innocence was Reynolds' portrait of Penelope Boothby in the 1780s, dressed in white and pink against a background of dark woods. She was the daughter of Sir Brooke Boothby, who also knew Rousseau and was involved in the publication of Rousseau's *Confessions*. Penelope Boothby was three when Reynolds painted her in 1788, but died at the age of five in 1791, and was subsequently painted by Henry Fuseli in 1792 – an apotheosis with an angel – and she was also represented in a marble funerary monument of 1793.[18] In such eighteenth-century images of children, a character of childlike innocence was both perceived and conceived by the artist, both faithfully recorded and imaginatively synthesized, and then ultimately deployed to captivate the viewer. Looking beyond British portraiture, one might note the famous example of Goya's *Red Boy*, that is, Don Manuel Osorio Manrique de Zuniga, at the age of three, surrounded by his pets and painted in the 1780s or 1790s.

In France, the paintings of Jean-Baptiste Greuze were particularly important for representing the Enlightenment's idea of childhood. Greuze often painted children as part of family scenes, with powerful moral and emotional messages, but he also represented children individually in a condition of emotionally charged innocence. Ariès suggested that, "the concept of childhood found its most modern expression" within the "circles of enlightened bourgeois who admired Greuze and read Rousseau."[19] The impact of Greuze on enlightened viewers may be partly appreciated from the writings of Diderot who found Greuze particularly interesting. In 1765, in the decade of *Emile*, Diderot wrote about the paintings on display at the Salon of the Louvre, and singled out for special attention Greuze's *Young Girl Crying over Her Dead Bird*. Diderot especially admired the childlike features of the subject: "One would approach this hand to kiss it, if one didn't respect this child and her suffering. Everything about her enchants." In fact, it was precisely the fact that she was an innocent, suffering child that Diderot found so enchanting. Just as Rousseau – "when I imagine a child of ten to twelve years" – became excited, so Diderot stood in front of Greuze's painting and exclaimed to himself, "Delicious! Delicious!"[20]

At the same time Diderot found himself speaking to the girl in the painting: "Come, little one, open up your heart to me, tell me truly, is it really the death of this bird that's caused you to withdraw so sadly, so completely into yourself?" He then speculated that perhaps, young as she was, she was actually weeping over having been abandoned by a man who had violated her innocence: "for having lost her bird, for having lost what you will." In other words, what he found so delicious about the image was not simply childhood's innocence, but the precariousness of that innocence, the possibility that it had already been lost, violated by a corruptive adult like himself. "I wouldn't be too displeased to have been the cause of her pain," reflected Diderot, revealing a fantasy of some sort of romantic and sexual connection between himself and the child.[21] The imagery of childhood played upon the precariousness and vulnerability of innocence: in Reynolds' portrait of Penelope Boothby, a child alone in the landscape; in Goya's *Red Boy* with two cats in the shadows closely watching a bird; and with Greuze's young girl and dead bird, which inspired one of the most famous philosophers of the Enlightenment to imagine himself as the man who might have violated the girl's sexual innocence.

Aimez l'enfance. "Love childhood," commanded Rousseau in *Emile*, and the injunction to love was especially important, because childhood was fleeting, a limited stage of joy (*jouissance*) for "these little innocents" (*ces petites innocents*). Loving childhood was not difficult, however, precisely because of childhood's "lovable instinct" (*aimable instinct*), the visually representable charm that made children irresistible in eighteenth-century art and in the photographs of the future (92).

Respectez l'enfance. "Respect childhood," Rousseau also wrote, and he particularly urged adults to let nature run its course with childhood, not to intervene to violate its natural development (131). Diderot's fantasy of intervention in the life of the girl on the painted canvas implied a readiness to violate natural innocence, and Rousseau was well aware of such fantasies because he had himself contemplated just such an intervention at an earlier moment of his life.

In the 1740s, as a young man living in Venice, Rousseau had the idea of joining with a friend in the joint purchase of a poor child from her parents; the two friends intended to prepare the child to be their specially reserved (and medically uninfected) sexual partner, that is, their sexual slave. They went as far as identifying the girl, paying off her mother, and commencing upon her education. Her name was Anzoletta, and Rousseau estimated her age to be eleven or twelve.

> I was moved to pity at the sight of this child. She was blonde and gentle as a lamb; one would never have believed she was Italian. People live on very little in Venice. We gave some money to the mother, and provided for the keeping of the girl. She had a voice: to gain her a useful talent we gave her a spinet and a music master. All that cost us scarcely two *zecchini* each per month, and we saved on other expenses. But since it was necessary to wait until she was mature, there was a lot of sowing before the harvesting. We were content,

however, to go there to pass the evenings, to chat and play very innocently with this child.[22]

Such child rearing, complete with music lessons, could be seen as a grotesque parodic anticipation of the education of Emile and Sophie, outlined by Rousseau twenty years later. In Venice in the 1740s, Rousseau was already susceptible to the charm of childhood's innocence. Though he ultimately renounced his sexual intention toward the child, and both men resolved not to become "the corruptors of her innocence," Rousseau clearly appreciated the ambivalence of her charm and understood that the visual manifestation of such innocence could actually be a provocation to violation.[23]

In the world of the late Enlightenment there was already some awareness of the provocative quality of childlike innocence. In Goethe's novel *Wilhelm Meister's Apprenticeship*, published in 1795 but in progress since the 1770s, the mysterious child Mignon, seemingly twelve or thirteen, was purchased by Wilhelm Meister from an Italian acrobatic troop to rescue her from abusive treatment. When he watched her dance, "he wanted to take this abandoned creature to his bosom as his own child, caress her and by a father's love awaken to her the joys of life." Literary critic Carolyn Steedman has studied the figure of Mignon in relation to the ambivalent vulnerability of children's innocence.[24]

In Casanova's memoirs, written during the 1780s and 1790s, this ambivalence was even more striking, as he described his attraction to girls of very young age and specified their innocence as precisely what attracted him erotically. He had sex with girls as young as eleven, but perhaps his commentary on sex with fourteen-year-old Barberina sums up best the way that childlike innocence exercised its appeal upon him:

> The celebration was new for Barberina. Her transports, her green ideas that she communicated to me with the greatest naiveté, and her compliance flavored by the charms of inexperience would not have surprised me, if I were not feeling something fresh myself. It seemed to me that I was enjoying a fruit whose sweetness I had never so fully tasted in the past ... She was not yet a big girl; the roses of her budding breasts were not yet in bloom.[25]

It was precisely her greenness, her naiveté, her inexperience, and her physical lack of development that made her erotically interesting to Casanova. In the 1740s he had sex with twelve-year-old Cecilia, part of a theatrical family, and was then approached by her eleven-year-old sister Marina. *Tu es trop enfant.* "You are too much of a child," he said dismissively – but then he changed his mind and had sex with her anyway.[26] In 1785, a sixty-year-old man in Venice (the same age as Casanova) was accused of sexually molesting an eight-year-old girl, and a Venetian tribunal – operating without any medical or legal concept of "child abuse" or "pedophilia" – heard testimony about "the sacrifice of an innocent," and wrestled with the implications for criminal justice.[27]

In 1787, Mozart and his librettist Lorenzo Da Ponte created the great seducer Don Giovanni, whose servant Leporello sang a comical aria about his master's many sexual adventures, the famous "catalogue aria" which enumerated Don Giovanni's conquests according to their nations and described their variety of physical types. There was no type in the catalog presented so emphatically as the figure of "la piccina" – the little one – a word that Mozart set to music in lewdly driven, hyperbolically elaborate repetition, as if nothing could be more archly comical than to make the audience wonder how little she might actually be. In any event there could be no doubt that some of Don Giovanni's libertine conquests were meant to be very, very little.

Ten years later, in 1797, the Marquis de Sade published his pornographic novel *L'histoire de Juliette*, the first of his fictions prominently to make use of children as victims. The opening sections of *L'histoire de Juliette* culminated in the prolonged torture, rape, and murder of a ten-year-old child, vividly described as if presuming to satisfy the pornographic fantasies of the reading public.[28] The clinical term "pedophilia" did not exist in the eighteenth century, and would await the nineteenth-century classifications of sexual psychopathology by Richard von Krafft-Ebing, but the Enlightenment's cultural construction of childhood's innocence made it possible to imagine the violation of that innocence. The emergence of child pornography at the very end of the eighteenth century, from the pen of Sade, the great philosophical pornographer of the Enlightenment, may constitute one of the most extreme responses to the enlightened agenda posed by Rousseau in *Emile*: to appreciate "the charm that one finds in contemplating a beautiful childhood."

"In aging I become a child again": memory and identity

William Cadogan based his medical advice concerning children on his experience as a doctor at the London Foundling Hospital, while Joshua Reynolds became a very experienced painter and observer of child subjects, and even Casanova could boast (and did) of considerable sexual experience with very young girls. Rousseau, however, wrote *Emile* about an imaginary child and had no great experience of children in his life. While Rousseau fathered possibly as many as five children in the late 1740s and early 1750s with his companion the seamstress Thérèse Levasseur, they were all consigned to the Paris foundling home, and he played no part in their upbringing. The relation of the tutor to Emile was thus entirely theoretical – or "philosophical" in the language of the Enlightenment – and Rousseau's notions of the natural innocence of childhood were no more empirically based than his visions of primeval human equality in the state of nature, as formulated in the *Discourse on Inequality*. Yet, Rousseau did have one resource for studying children that transcended the merely speculative, hypothetical, and imaginary: namely his memories of his own childhood. While some have seen Rousseau as the philosophical tutor of Emile, educating a new generation of enlightened children, one might do better to envision Rousseau dividing his authorial identification between the tutor and his pupil, endowing the child Emile with the character of the remembered child Jean-Jacques.

He himself frankly described the inevitable process of methodological reminiscence that underlay the writing of the book.

> There is a term of life beyond which one retrogresses in advancing. I feel that I have passed that term. I recommence, so to speak, another career. The emptiness of mature age that I feel recalls to me the sweet time of the first age. In aging I become a child again [*en vieillissant, je redeviens enfant*], and I recall more gladly what I did at ten years than at thirty. Readers, pardon me

therefore for sometimes taking my examples from myself; for to do this book well, I must do it with pleasure. (171–72)

In order to fathom Emile, Rousseau indulged in flights of remembrance in which he assumed the character of a child himself. In fact, this was one of the Enlightenment's most important contributions to modern childhood: the establishment of a meaningful relation between the child and the adult he would become, between the adult and the child he used to be. The philosophy of memory would define the relation of identity between child and adult, while a theory of education would emphasize the formative nature of childhood experience for adulthood. Rousseau would bind together the strands of memory, identity, pedagogy, and character in the related works of *Emile* and his autobiographical *Confessions*, both crucially based on personal memories of his early years.[29]

For Rousseau and his disciples, the philosophical innocence of childhood could also be formulated as nostalgic remembrance. "The child is father of the man," wrote William Wordsworth in a poem of 1802, the same year as the founding of the Paris children's hospital. He valorized the perspective of a child:

My heart leaps up when I behold

A rainbow in the sky:

So was it when my life began;

So be it now I am a man....[30]

An internal architecture of memory already integrated the Romantic personality on the threshold of the nineteenth century, and this integration was the legacy of Rousseau and the Enlightenment. While Ariès emphasized the early modern conceptual separation of childhood and adulthood and the evolution of a clear focus on the distinctiveness of childhood, the Enlightenment complicated that focus by philosophically integrating childhood and adulthood through the issues of memory and identity.

Looking back to the work of John Locke in the late seventeenth century, one discovers an emphasis on childhood in both his epistemology and his pedagogy. In the *Essay Concerning Human Understanding* in 1690, Locke noted:

He that attentively considers the state of a child, at his first coming into the world, will have little reason to think him stored with plenty of ideas, that are to be the matter of his future knowledge. It is by degrees he comes to be furnished with them.

This was consistent with Locke's celebrated view of the child as a blank slate, *tabula rasa*, or "white paper void of all characters, without any ideas."[31] This view of the child's mind would serve as the basis for Locke's highly influential pedagogical treatise of 1693, *Some Thoughts Concerning Education*. At the same time, by eliminating all trace of religious concern about original sin, Locke's neutral formulation of the *tabula rasa* was a crucial precondition for the concept of secular innocence that emerged in the eighteenth century. In the late Enlightenment of the 1790s, still under the influence of Locke, the innate intellectual qualities of children remained a subject of fascination with the serendipitous discovery of a "wild child," Victor of Aveyron, who was placed under the care of the attentive medical researcher Jean Itard.[32]

In 1739, David Hume, in his *Treatise of Human Nature*, took on directly the problems of memory and identity already suggested in Locke's *Essay*. Hume argued that memory was the imaginative force by which personal identity was constructed, the only guarantor that each person remained the same person today as yesterday; that is, he or she remembered being the same. By a chain of remembrances this became the link between adulthood and childhood, with nothing but memory to confirm that the adult was once, in fact, the child he remembers having been. "Memory not only discovers the identity," wrote Hume, "but also contributes to its production, by producing the relation of resemblance among the perceptions."[33] The relation of the present adult to the past child was thus philosophically affirmed, in spite of epistemological uncertainty, under the critical attention of the Enlightenment. Locke's prefatory statement of interest – "he that attentively considers the state of a child" – would remain relevant for the whole of the eighteenth century to follow, and the child one could consider most attentively lay within the self, accessible to memory.

The human self was understood to move forward in time, away from childhood, but Rousseau in *Emile* emphasized a nostalgia for childhood that actually reversed the directional course of development: "In aging I become a child again." Under the sign of innocence Rousseau sought to protect childhood from the encroachments of adulthood, so that children might preserve their childhood as long as possible, and he rejected any sort of education that would prematurely remove children from their naturally childlike condition: *Respectez l'enfance*. The effort to protect childhood and preserve its innocence, however, was susceptible to being undermined by the promiscuous overlapping of childhood and adulthood within the same self. Just as the adult contained within himself the memory of the child he used to be, so the child contained within himself the adult that he would eventually become. Any evidence of precocity might emphasize the uncertainty of innocence and the unstable boundary between childhood and adulthood.

The decade of *Emile*, the 1760s, was also the decade in which Mozart (born in 1756) came to the attention of the European public as a child prodigy, dazzling in his musical brilliance – but also mysterious, even disturbing, in his unchildlike precocity. When Mozart and his older sister Nannerl were brought to perform on the harpsichord and violin for Empress Maria Theresa at the Habsburg court in 1762, their father Leopold, who profited from the occasion, noted of those who heard the children play: "Mainly their amazement concerns the boy, and I've not met anyone who doesn't find it inexplicable." At the same time, while Mozart at six was inexplicable as a child, he was also commanding sentimental attention by his childlike character. As Leopold reported: "If I tell you that Wolferl jumped into the Empress's lap, threw his arms around her and covered her with kisses, people will regard it as a fairy-tale."[34]

Two years later, in England, Mozart was more attentively considered, and even tested in order to understand, in the spirit of Locke, how the child was so prodigiously "stored with plenty of ideas." Leopold commented, "My boy knows in this his eighth year what one would expect only in a man of forty." In England, King George III tested Mozart's astonishing ability to sight read, while others were more amazed at his capacity to extemporize at the keyboard. Charles Burney noted the incongruity of simultaneously precocious and childlike behaviors, as Mozart improvised an opera with nonsense words, instantly composing "an overture of 2 Movements ... all full of Taste [and] imagination, with Good Harmony, Melody & Modulation, after which he played at Marbles, in the true Childish Way of one who knows nothing."[35] Mozart would, for his whole life, sustain a childish affinity for nonsense words. In the 1760s, even as Rousseau was insisting on a distinctively childlike character to be respected in children, the child Mozart was already confounding the distinction between children and adults.

Rousseau also complicated that distinction when he regressed in memory to recover the traces of childhood contained within his adult self. In *Emile* he outlined the dynamics of this nostalgic regression, and made the innocence of childhood so alluring that no modern adult would be able to resist the temptation to try to recover it in memory. The Enlightenment's cultivation of memory, however, reached its culmination in Rousseau's pioneering autobiography, *Confessions*, which he wrote in the 1760s, though the two volumes were only published in the 1780s, after his death. In a famous passage, Rousseau described the spanking administered at the age of eight by the quasi-maternal figure of Mademoiselle Lambercier, a punishment received with a "mélange of sensuality" and which formatively shaped the character of his sexual constitution. "Who would believe," wrote Rousseau, "that this punishment of a child, received at eight years by the hand of a maid of thirty, has decided my tastes, my desires, my passions, myself, for the rest of my life?"[36] Rousseau's account of this spanking would later be cited by Krafft-Ebing and Freud as a reference point for understanding the psychology of masochism. For Rousseau himself, however, the point was not the clinical classification of his tastes, but rather the decisively formative relation of childhood to adulthood. There was a powerful current running through time and integrating human identity, but the current could move in both directions: forwards in time as formative influence, backwards in time as the memory that yielded both pleasure and self-understanding, the explanation of self.

Confessions, like *Emile*, anchored the adult self in the memory of childhood. Casanova, writing his memoirs in the 1780s and 1790s, probably after reading Rousseau's, also established his first memories as the foundation of self at the age of eight:

> Let us now come to the beginning of my existence as a thinking being. At the beginning of August in the year 1733 the organ of my memory developed. I was eight years and four months old. I remember nothing that may have happened to me before that epoch.

At that moment he was terrified because his nose would not stop bleeding, and then his grandmother took him to be cured by the even more terrifying semi-magical procedures of a folk healer on the island of Murano.[37] The details of the event itself were not as important as the fact that these were the first details of his life that he remembered, the beginning of his continuous life as a conscious human being who remembered the past stages of his self, dating back to childhood. Goethe in *Wilhelm Meister's Apprenticeship* included a fictional memoir, "Confessions of a Beautiful Soul," which again, by its title, seemed to refer to Rousseau's pioneering autobiographical example. The narrator recalled:

Up to my eighth year I was a healthy child; but I have as little memory of those years as I have of my birth. Then, when I had just turned eight, I had a hemorrhage, and from that moment on I was all feeling and memory. Every little detail of what happened then is as present to me now as if it had occurred only yesterday.[38]

As with Casanova, blood was the stimulant to childish memory to begin its lifelong work as the commemorative custodian of the self and its identity.

Rousseau, in the *Confessions*, attributed his lifelong outrage at injustice – an outrage that, philosophically, may be said to have inspired the French Revolution and the onset of modern politics and society – to a powerful sense of outraged innocence that he remembered from his childhood. He had been falsely accused of breaking the teeth of the comb of Mlle Lambercier, and as he recalled the occasion in his memoirs, he was physiologically transformed by the emotionally charged memory of childhood:

I feel as I write this that my pulse is rising again. These moments will always be present to me if I live to be a hundred thousand. This first feeling for violence and injustice has remained so profoundly engraved in my soul that every idea that relates to it restores to me my first emotion, and this feeling, relative to me in its origin, has acquired such a consistency in itself, that my heart becomes enflamed at the spectacle or the story of any injust action.[39]

Not just to understand his own adult sense of injustice, but also to feel that injustice with all its emotional force, Rousseau traveled backward through memory to childhood, where a sense of outraged innocence formed the basis of his adult character.

Conclusion: Mother Goose and *The Magic Flute*

In 1782, Goethe composed the poem *Erlkönig*, about an elf king who both seduces and terrorizes a young child riding with his father through the woods at night. The poem was intended, from the beginning, to be set to music, and a dozen different settings culminated in the definitive Schubert song of 1815. One of the hallmarks of any musical setting of the poem is that it requires the singer to perform in different voices: representing the frightened child, the reassuring father, and the sinister elf king. With the publication of the first volume of Rousseau's *Confessions* in 1782, it was just the moment for Goethe to appreciate that one poetic recitation, and one singer, could encompass the voices of adult and child, in alternation and response because every adult poet or singer contained within himself the remembered voice of the child he had once been.

The elf king was particularly interested in seducing the child by appealing to his childlike affinities:

Du liebes Kind, komm, geh mit mir!

Gar schöne Spiele spiel' ich mit dir.

You dear child, come along with me!

Beautiful games I will play with you.[40]

The language of play, however, also gave way to the language of a more brutal violation of innocence.

Ich liebe dich, mich reizt deine schöne Gestalt;

Und bist du nicht willig, so brauch ich Gewalt.

I love you, I'm excited by your beautiful form;

And if you're not willing, then I'll need to use force.[41]

The child was discovered to be dead in the final verse, his spirit presumably conquered by the compulsion of the elf king. Here again, in the age of Enlightenment, the poet was able to conjure the supreme vulnerability of innocent children.

In 1784, two years later, Immanuel Kant published the essay *What is Enlightenment?* and, without wasting a word, began to answer the question in the first sentence: "Enlightenment is the emergence of a human being from self-imposed immaturity [*Unmündigkeit*]. Immaturity is the inability to use his understanding without the guidance of another."[42] Kant thus prized adulthood over immaturity as a higher form of enlightened existence, while recognizing that the process of maturation that led from childhood to adulthood was necessarily challenging and sometimes thwarted. The pedagogical progress of the human spirit toward maturity nevertheless remained central to his definition of what it meant for a person to become enlightened. Ever since *Emile*, modern childhood has been fraught with the overlapping imperatives of innocence and play on the one hand, and education and maturity on the other. In fact, both of these concerns, education and play, were fundamental to the society of the eighteenth century.

Only one year after *Emile*, in 1763, Frederick the Great introduced compulsory primary education in Prussia by the General *Landschulreglement*. The Vatican's suppression of the Jesuit Order in 1773 left an opening in education that was met in the Habsburg Monarchy by Maria Theresa's program for universal primary education in 1775. In Poland, a Commission for National Education was created in 1773, endowed with the schools and properties of the Jesuits, and then functioned as Europe's first national ministry of education, comprehensively planning and implementing educational policy and programs. The French philosopher Pierre Samuel Du Pont de Nemours served as a representative of the French Enlightenment on the Polish commission. Meanwhile, in revolutionary France the Marquis de Condorcet devised an enlightened program of universal education before falling victim to the Terror in 1794.

If education attracted the sponsorship of the state, eighteenth-century play was sustained by a new corner of the commercial market. Rousseau wanted games for Emile and dolls for Sophie, and Lawrence Stone has described the emergence of the market for toys as part of a new "child-oriented" society in England.

Educational games that combined instruction with fun were also introduced in the mid-eighteenth century, geographical jig-saws in 1762 ... This was the time when toy-shops were springing up in provincial towns, and were doing a brisk trade selling toys that were designed merely to give pleasure to the individual child, not to gratify its parents' desire for moral or educational improvement. It was now that dolls with changeable clothing and dolls' houses were first mass produced for a commercial market.[43]

At the same time, the eighteenth century witnessed the emergence of a market for children's books, especially through the London publishing enterprises of John Newbery. Some of the books for children had earnest moral and pedagogical messages, like the *History of Little Goody Two-Shoes*, introduced in 1765, but the 1760s, the decade of *Emile*, also saw the first publication by Newbery of the whimsical, almost nonsensical, nursery rhymes of Mother Goose, presented entirely to entertain the childlike sensibility.[44] It would have been around this very time that the eight-year-old Mozart extemporaneously composed his nonsense opera to dazzle the musical experts of London.

In 1791, the last year of his life, Mozart himself was the father of a seven-year-old child, Karl Thomas, and also of an infant, Franz Xaver, born in July 1791, two months before the premiere of *The Magic Flute*, and five months before Mozart's death in December. Fatherhood did not seem to eliminate altogether what Kant might have seen as Mozart's immaturity, his fondness for childlike games and nonsense, as evident in the operatic figure of Papageno. In early July, awaiting the birth of Franz Xaver, Mozart signed a letter to his wife: "Stu! – Knaller paller – schnip – schnap – schnur – Shnepeperl – snai!" Also childish, in a different mode, was his early October prank of slipping backstage at *The Magic Flute* to play the glockenspiel himself. He played unexpected arpeggios and chords as a joke to unsettle the Papageno on stage (Mozart's librettist and collaborator Emanuel Schikaneder), and eventually "everyone laughed."[45]

The following week, on October 13, Mozart brought his son Karl from his boarding school to the performance in Vienna of *The Magic Flute*. One of Mozart's other guests at that performance was Antonio Salieri. "Karl was so delighted that I had taken him to the opera," wrote Mozart to his wife the next day. "He looks great; – he couldn't be at a better place for his health, but everything else is unfortunately pretty bad out there." Mozart then launched into a pedagogical critique of Karl's education at school, writing somewhat in the general spirit of Rousseau's *Emile*:

> I had Karl excused from school until Sunday after lunch because his serious studies (Heaven help him) will not begin until Monday ... I don't believe that his education will go down the drain if he stays out of school for a month ... Karl is neither worse nor better than he was before; he has the same bad manners, likes to get attention as always, enjoys learning *even less* than before because all he does out there is to go walking in the garden....[46]

This letter of October 14, 1791, was probably the last letter Mozart ever wrote, and in it he showed himself to be puzzling over the Enlightenment's problem of pedagogy: was it adapted to the nature of the child, and, if not, then what was he really learning? Probably Mozart had not seriously studied Rousseau's *Emile*, but by 1791, after almost thirty years, its ideas may have been generally familiar to parents. The ironic exclamation about serious studies – "Heaven help him!" (*das Gott erbarm!*) – was certainly in the spirit of Jean-Jacques.[47]

In *The Magic Flute*, Mozart composed music for a trio of boy sopranos, played on stage by real children, whose music guided Prince Tamino along the way to achieving wisdom and love. The finale of the opera began with the three boys in a garden, singing a characteristic trio:

Bald prangt, den Morgen zu verkünden,

Die Sonn' auf goldner Bahn, –

Bald soll der Aberglaube schwinden;

Bald siegt der weise Mann.

> Soon resplendent, heralding the morning,
>
> Is the sun on its golden course, –
>
> Soon shall superstition disappear;
>
> Soon the wise man will conquer.[48]

The Enlightenment had rediscovered, refashioned, and reconceptualized childhood – emphasizing its fundamental innocence. The innocence of children was medically and spiritually vulnerable; it exercised a visual charm and sentimental power, even inviting its own violation; and finally the nostalgic memory of childhood's innocence anchored the relation of identity between every adult and the child he or she had once been. From childhood each person evolved toward maturity and enlightenment, without ever forgetting or discarding the original child whose innocence marked the foundation of character. Now, in the finale of Mozart's last opera, composed and staged in the last months of his life – and even as the Enlightenment itself moved toward its conclusion with the end of the eighteenth century – the composer, who had begun his career as a child prodigy, created the music for three children, singing in the unmistakable vocal register of childhood, to celebrate in song the dawning of a new epoch. If the Enlightenment had helped to formulate and fashion a new age in the history of childhood, the voices of children now heralded what appeared to be a new stage in the history of the Enlightenment, the advent of the modern world.

Notes

1 Jean-Jacques Rousseau, *Emile, ou de l'éducation*, ed. Michel Launay (Paris, France: Garnier-Flammarion, 1966), 32; further citations from *Emile* are given in the text in parentheses, with reference to this same edition.

2 Philippe Ariès, *Centuries of Childhood: A Social History of Family Life*, trans. Robert Baldick (New York, NY: Vintage Books, 1962), 35.

3 Lawrence Stone, *The Family, Sex and Marriage in England 1500–1800* (New York, NY: Harper & Row, 1977), 405–80.

4 Jean-Louis Flandrin, *Families in Former Times: Kinship, Household and Sexuality in Early Modern France*, trans. Richard Southern (Cambridge, UK: Cambridge University Press, 1979), 199–201; C. John Sommerville, *The Rise and Fall of Childhood*, revised edition (New York, NY: Vintage Books, 1990), 183–4.

5 Rousseau, *The Social Contract*, trans. Maurice Cranston (London, UK: Penguin, 1988), 49.

6 William Cadogan, *An Essay upon Nursing and the Management of Children from their Birth to Three Years of Age* (London, UK: J. Roberts, 1748), 10.

7 Cadogan, *An Essay upon Nursing*, 3.

8 Cadogan, *An Essay upon Nursing*, 14–15.

9 Lady Mary Wortley Montagu, *The Turkish Embassy Letters*, ed. Malcolm Jack (London, UK: Virago, 1994), letter of 1 April 1718; 80–2.

10 Thomas Laqueur, *Solitary Sex: A Cultural History of Masturbation* (New York, NY: Zone Books, 2003), 14.

11 Laqueur, *Solitary Sex*, 42–3.

12 Robert Darnton, *The Great Cat Massacre and Other Episodes in French Cultural History* (New York, NY: Vintage Books, 1985), 215–256.

13 Ariès, *Centuries of Childhood*, 38–46; Sommerville, *The Rise and Fall of Childhood*, 92–3.

14 Michael Yonan, *Empress Maria Theresa and the Politics of Habsburg Imperial Art* (State College, PA: Penn State Press, 2011), 27; Derek Beales, *Joseph II: In the Shadow of Maria Theresa* (Cambridge, UK; Cambridge University Press, 1987), 27.

15 Yonan, *Empress Maria Theresa*, 25–7.

16 Stone, *The Family*, 457–8; Dorothy Johnson, "Engaging Identity: Portraits of Children in Late Eighteenth-Century European Art," in *Fashioning Childhood in the Eighteenth Century: Age and Identity*, ed. Anja Müller (Aldershot and Burlington, VT: Ashgate, 2006), 101–15; Anne Higonnet, *Pictures of Innocence: The History and Crisis of Ideal Childhood* (London, UK: Thames & Hudson, 1998), 23–30.

17 Higonnet, *Pictures of Innocence*, 23–4.

18 Higonnet, *Pictures of Innocence*, 28–30.

19 Ariès, *Centuries of Childhood*, 336.

20 Denis Diderot, *On Art, Vol. I*, trans. John Goodman (New Haven, CT: Yale University Press, 1995), 97–9.

21 Diderot, *On Art*, 97–9.

22 Rousseau, *Les Confessions, Vol. II*, ed. Michel Launary (Paris, France: Garnier-Flammarion, 1968), 66–67; Leo Damrosch, *Jean-Jacques Rousseau: Restless Genius* (Boston, MA: Houghton Mifflin, 2005), 179–80.

23 Rousseau, *Les Confessions, II*, 66–7.

24 Johann Wolfgang von Goethe, *Wilhelm Meister's Apprenticeship*, trans. Eric Blackall (New York, NY: Suhrkamp Publishers, 1989), 65; Carolyn Steedman, *Strange Dislocations: Childhood and the Idea of Human Interiority* (Cambridge, MA: Harvard University Press, 1998), 1–42.

25 Jacques Casanova de Seingalt, *Histoire de ma vie, Vol. I*, ed. Francis Lacassin (Paris, France: Robert Laffont, 1993), 843–4.

26 Casanova, *Histoire de ma vie, Vol. I*, 235.

27 Larry Wolff, "Depraved Inclinations: Libertines and Children in Casanova's Venice," *Eighteenth-Century Studies* 38(3) (2005), 417–40; see also Wolff, *Paolina's Innocence: Child Abuse in Casanova's Venice* (Stanford, CA: Stanford University Press, 2012).

28 Wolff, "Depraved Inclinations," 435–46.

29 Wolff, "'When I Imagine a Child': The Idea of Childhood and the Philosophy of Memory in the Enlightenment," *Eighteenth-Century Studies* 31(4) (1998), 377–401.

30 William Wordsworth, "My Heart Leaps Up When I Behold," in *English Romantic Writers*, ed. David Perkins (New York, NY: Harcourt, Brace & World, 1967), 279.

31 John Locke, *An Essay Concerning Human Understanding*, ed. John Yolton (London, UK: J.M. Dent, 1993), 18, 45–7.

32 Sommerville, *The Rise and Fall of Childhood*, 157–8.

33 David Hume, *A Treatise of Human Nature*, ed. Ernest C. Mossner (London, UK: Penguin Books, 1969), 306–8.

34 H.C. Robbins Landon, *Mozart and Vienna* (New York, NY: Schirmer Books, 1991), 12–13.

35 Maynard Solomon, *Mozart: A Life* (New York, NY: Harper Collins, 1995), 49.

36 Rousseau, *Les Confessions, Vol. 1*, ed. Michel Launary (Paris, France: Garnier-Flammarion, 1968), 52–3.

37 Casanova, *Histoire de ma vie, Vol. I*, 17.

38 Goethe, *Wilhelm Meister's Apprenticeship*, 216.

39 Rousseau, *Les Confessions, Vol. I*, 57.

40 Goethe, *Gedichte* (Halle, Germany: Otto Hendel Verlag, n.d.), 95.

41 Goethe, *Gedichte*, 95.

42 Immanuel Kant, *Was ist Aufklärung? Ausgewählte kleine Schriften* (Hamburg, Germany: Felix Meiner Verlag, 1999), 20.

43 Stone, *The Family, Sex and Marriage in England*, 411; J.H. Plumb, "The New World of Children in Eighteenth-Century England," *Past and Present* 67 (1975), 64–93.

44 Stone, *The Family*, 410–11.

45 Robert Spaethling, *Mozart's Letters, Mozart's Life* (New York, NY: W.W. Norton, 2000), letters of 6 July 1791 and 8/9 October 1791, 436, 441.

46 Spaethling, *Mozart's Letters, Mozart's Life*, letter of 14 October 1791, 442–3.

47 Wolfgang Amadeus Mozart, *Mozarts Briefe*, ed. Ludwig Nohl (Salzburg, Austria: Verlag der Mayrischen Buchhandlung, 1865), 472.

48 Mozart and Emanuel Schikaneder, *Die Zauberflöte, Act 2, Number 21, Finale*.

Suggestions for further reading

Important primary works relevant to childhood and the enlightenment

Locke, John. *Some Thoughts Concerning Education.* Cambridge, UK: Cambridge University Press, 1693. Influential for eighteenth-century enlightened pedagogy.

Cadogan, William. *An Essay upon Nursing and the Management of Children from their Birth to Three Years of Age.* London, UK: J Roberts, 1748. First book of medical advice specifically on childrearing.

Rousseau, Jean-Jacques. *Emile, ou de l'éducation.* Paris, France: Librairie de Firmin Didot Freres, 1762. Fundamental for the Enlightenment and for all modern thinking about children and childhood.

Anonymous. *The History of Little Goody Two-Shoes.* London, UK: John Newbery, 1765. Published in London by John Newbery as an exemplary moral story for children.

William Blake. *Songs of Innocence.* London, UK: William Blake, 1789; *Songs of Experience.* London, UK: William Blake, 1794. Many of the poems are about children or a child's perspective, in relation to innocence and experience.

Some important secondary works

Ariès, Philippe. *Centuries of Childhood: A Social History of Family Life.* Translated by Robert Baldick. New York, NY: Vintage Books, 1962. First French publication in 1960. Controversial but brilliant and deeply influential study, which did more than any other work to create the whole field of the history of childhood. Generally focused on the early modern centuries, but more concerned with the Renaissance than with the Enlightenment.

Baggerman, Arianne, and Rudolph Dekker. *Child of the Enlightenment: Revolutionary Europe Reflected in a Boyhood Diary*. Translated by Dianne Webb. Leiden, The Netherlands: Brill, 2009. Presents the diary of a Dutch boy from the 1790s.

Benzaquén, Adriana. "Childhood, Identity, and Human Science in the Enlightenment." *History Workshop Journal* 57 (2004): 35–57.

Calvert, Karin. *Children in the House: The Material Culture of Early Childhood, 1600–1900*. Boston, MA: Northeastern University Press, 1992. Includes a section on "The Natural Child" from 1750 to 1830.

Cunningham, Hugh. *The Invention of Childhood*. London, UK: BBC Books, 2006. Published to accompany a BBC radio series on the history of childhood, with the eighteenth century receiving a detailed chapter of its own.

Dekker, Rudolf. *Childhood, Memory, and Autobiography in Holland: From the Golden Age to Romanticism*. Basingstoke, UK: Palgrave Macmillan, 1999. Important study of Dutch childhood, offering valuable counterpoint to more familiar studies of England and France.

Ezell, Margaret. "John Locke's Images of Childhood." *Eighteenth-Century Studies* 17(2) (Winter 1983–1984): 139–55.

Flandrin, Jean-Louis. *Families in Former Times: Kinship, Household and Sexuality in Early Modern France*. Cambridge, UK: Cambridge University Press, 1979. Some attention to children in the context of family history.

Fletcher, Anthony. *Growing Up in England: The Experience of Childhood 1600–1914*. New Haven, CT: Yale University Press, 2008. Organized topically rather than chronologically but including much material for the eighteenth century.

Gavin, Adrienne. *The Child in British Literature: Literary Constructions of Childhood, Medieval to Contemporary*. Basingstoke, UK: Palgrave Macmillan, 2012. Includes chapter by Andrew O'Malley on *Robinson Crusoe* and the culture of childhood.

Grenby, M.O. *The Child Reader, 1700–1840*. Cambridge, UK: Cambridge University Press, 2011. Studies the readers of children's books in the eighteenth century.

Greven, Philip. *The Protestant Temperament: Patterns of Child-Rearing, Religious Experience, and the Self in Early America*. New York, NY: Knopf, 1977. Important and pioneering work for considering childhood in eighteenth-century America; addresses issues of religion in child-rearing and the variation from "authoritarian" to "affectionate" families.

Heywood, Colin. *Growing Up in France: From the Ancien Régime to the Third Republic*. Cambridge, UK: Cambridge University Press, 2007. Valuable discussion of representations of childhood and adolescence.

Higonnet, Anne. *Pictures of Innocence: The History and Crisis of Ideal Childhood*. London, UK: Thames & Hudson, 1998. Brilliant study on modern imagery of children, includes very valuable discussion of the eighteenth century.

Immel, Andrea, and Michael Witmore, eds. *Childhood and Children's Books in Early Modern Europe, 1550–1800*. New York, NY: Routledge, 2006. Collection of articles, several of which address the eighteenth century. Note Kristina Straub on servants and children in Britain; Cynthia Koepp on writing about science for children in French culture; Jill Shefrin on mothers educating daughters in Britain; Patricia Crain on *Little Goody Two-Shoes*; Jan Fergus on boys' book purchases in Britain; and William McCarthy on pedagogy.

Krupp, Anthony. *Reason's Children: Childhood in Early Modern Philosophy*. Lewisburg, PA: Bucknell University Press, 2009. Serious philosophical study of Locke, Leibniz, Wolff, and Baumgarten.

Kuchowicz, Zbigniew, and Zofia Libiszowska. "The Child in the Polish Family in the Eighteenth Century." *The Polish Review* XXVII(3–4) (1982): 70–83.

Melton, James Van Horn. *Absolutism and the Eighteenth-Century Origins of Compulsory Schooling in Prussia and Austria*. Cambridge, UK: Cambridge University Press, 1988.

Important study in the history of education and enlightened government.

Müller, Anja, ed. *Fashioning Childhood in the Eighteenth Century: Age and Identity*. Aldershot and Burlington, VT: Ashgate, 2006. Valuable collection of recent research on childhood in the eighteenth century. Note Adriana Benzaquén on medicine and children; Anna-Christina Giovanopoulos on children's legal status in Britain; Christoph Houswitschka on Locke and Rousseau; Dorothy Johnson on children's portraits; Bernadette Fort on Greuze and infant nursing; Uwe Böker on juvenile delinquency; Sonja Fielitz on Ovid for British schoolboys; Dirk Vanderbeke on *Tristram Shandy*.

Plumb, J.H. "The New World of Children in Eighteenth-Century England." *Past and Present* 67 (1975): 64–93.

Pollock, Linda. *Forgotten Children: Parent–Child Relations from 1500 to 1900*. Cambridge, UK: Cambridge University Press, 1983. Usefully gathers together a great number of sources concerning childhood, and deploys them to argue that major developments claimed for the history of childhood are not necessarily supported by the record of evidence. The eighteenth century does not emerge from this discussion as particularly distinctive.

Ransel, David. *Mothers of Misery: Child Abandonment in Russia*. Princeton, NJ: Princeton University Press, 1988. Begins with child abandonment and foundling care in the Russia of Catherine the Great.

Shorter, Edward. *The Making of the Modern Family*. New York, NY: Basic Books, 1975. Important analysis of society and demography with little attention to cultural issues. Rousseau barely makes it into the index.

Sommerville, C. John. *The Rise and Fall of Childhood*. Beverly Hills, CA: Sage Publications, 1982. Useful survey beginning with Greece and Rome. The Enlightenment is discussed in a chapter on "The Glorification of the Child."

Steedman, Carolyn. *Strange Dislocations: Childhood and the Idea of Human Interiority, 1780–1930*. Cambridge, MA: Harvard University Press, 1995. Interesting focus on the figure of Goethe's Mignon as paradigmatic for childhood in modern culture.

Stone, Lawrence. *The Family, Sex, and Marriage: In England 1500–1800*. New York, NY: Harper & Row, 1977. Huge, pioneering, and provocative study which discusses childhood in the context of family history, and argues for the emergence of a "child-oriented, affectionate and permissive mode" of family life in the eighteenth century.

Tatar, Maria. *Off with their Heads! Fairy Tales and the Culture of Childhood*. Princeton, NJ: Princeton University Press, 1993. Brilliant study of the role of fairy tales in both shaping and reflecting the evolving culture of childhood.

Wolff, Larry. *Paolina's Innocence: Child Abuse in Casanova's Venice*. Stanford, CA: Stanford University Press, 2012. Microhistorical analysis of a single case of child sexual abuse in 1785, studied in the context of eighteenth-century ideas about childhood.

Wolff, Larry. "Depraved Inclinations: Libertines and Children in Casanova's Venice." *Eighteenth-Century Studies* 38(3) (2005): 417–40.

Wolff, Larry. "'When I Imagine a Child': The Idea of Childhood and the Philosophy of Memory in the Enlightenment." *Eighteenth-Century Studies* 31(4) (1998): 377–401.

Part II

CREATING CHILDHOODS IN THE WESTERN WORLD SINCE 1500

5

PARENT–CHILD RELATIONS IN WESTERN EUROPE AND NORTH AMERICA, 1500–PRESENT

Julia Grant

There has been no more contentious debate within the history of children and youth than that regarding the relationship between parents and children. When French historian Philippe Aries's *Centuries of Childhood* first appeared in English in 1962, it catapulted social history to new levels by its sweeping historical claims, while opening the doors for decades of vociferous debates about the meaning of parenting practices, children's roles, and conceptions of childhood, or lack thereof, in different historical and societal contexts. The two key areas of contention concern whether the relationships between parents and children in the modern world have substantively differed from those in the medieval era, particularly in reference to the understanding of childhood as a specific category of human experience, and whether there has been a significant change in the quality of parent–child relationships, especially in regard to the emotional intensity of the parent–child bond.

Although these debates have subsided to a mere simmer among academics, there still remain profound misunderstandings in the public mind about parenting and childhood in the past. Historians now recognize that parent–child relationships have diverged considerably across time and space, but that nearly all cultures have had some conception of childhood as a stage of life that is distinct from adulthood, even if the boundaries between these two stages of the lifecycle have been more porous in the past. At the same time, it is impossible to make blanket statements about the humanity or inhumanity of parenting practices during any historical era, given the variations in individual human nature and gaps in our knowledge about the relationship between prescribed child-rearing strategies, what parents actually do, and the internal emotive dimensions of the parent–child bond, especially when individuals left few written accounts of these experiences. This does not mean that historians should abandon their attention to the demographic, economic, socio-political, and religious transformations that shifted the balance of power in parent–child relationships and set new cultural norms for parenting over time – quite the contrary. It does mean that humility should be our guide as we seek to dissect social norms, practices, and public writings so that we may enter more deeply into the nature of the parent–child relationship, even when it seems foreign to contemporary Western eyes.

How can we imagine a parent if we cannot see a child in a portrait of the seventeenth century? Images of little boys and girls standing stiffly, staring at the portraitist without a smile, dressed in drab adult clothing, have led some to believe that these were not really children after all. A recent account of African–American children living in a tough Chicago housing project, who, amidst typical childish antics, must endure violent threats to their health and well-being, is titled *There Are No Children Here*. But it is, in fact, Lafeyette and Pharaoh's childishness that renders their experiences endearing and makes us pay attention to the misery of their lot. Only if we understand childhood as a period of life that is similar to that of the lifestyles of contemporary middle-class families, do Lafeyette and Pharaoh cease to be children. Because children were more likely to labor and to live outside the home for a period of time prior to the nineteenth century, we have figured past children as "little adults," even though in both Western Europe and the United States, many youths were firmly ensconced in the parental home until they married during their early to mid-twenties and were afforded few, if any, legal rights until well into adulthood. Children surely engaged in more productive labor, and many shouldered what we might consider to be adult responsibilities earlier in the lifecycle than most of today's children. Even so, youths were expected to show deference to their parents, continued to receive parental counsel even when they lived outside of the home, and many maintained deep and abiding attachments to their parents as they aged, if they were lucky enough to have living and present parents.

Just as it is possible to imagine that children were children in the past, even if their experiences were vastly different than those of children today, we can also imagine a parent as someone who is primarily responsible for the upbringing of a child. During the first period of this essay, often known as the early modern era – which historians have loosely framed as lasting from around 1500 through 1800 – most parents and children occupied very different roles than they do today. Parents still bore or adopted and raised other people's children, and most, if they were able to do so, strove to ensure that their children survived and, hopefully, thrived. But perhaps the most striking difference in parenting is that children in the early modern era may have been said to serve their parents; contemporary Western parents serve their children. In contemporary Western Europe and North America, all members of the family are assumed to have their own interests and a kind of loose and relative equality reigns among family members, while early modern families were corporate and hierarchically organized. Deference and subservience to the father as the head of the household was expected from wives, children, and servants. Notwithstanding these large generalizations, complaints about "unruly" children, "disobedient" wives, runaway servants, and drastic legislation in the early Massachusetts colony that threatened stubborn male youth with the death sentence, makes it clear that not all subscribed to the cultural norm.

Prior to the mid-fifteenth century, when one can begin to see the development of an articulated interest in early childhood, medieval philosophers conceived of childhood as a period of "deficiency." The social norms in place, which including dressing young children in adult clothing and engaging them in economically productive activity as soon as possible, seem to suggest that childhood would be best thrown over for the superior status of the adult. Evidence for this view is reflected in the fact that medieval writers gave scant attention to their own early upbringings in their autobiographies. It is difficult to know the meaning behind literary conventions of this period, which relegated early childhood to the dustbin, but perhaps surviving childhood physically intact was enough of a feat to begin the celebration of one's life at a later stage.

By the nineteenth century, however, an aching nostalgia for early childhood permeated adult memoirs. Those who remembered a childhood at odds with the rosy vision of an innocent and loved child tended to describe their own experience as aberrant. Jules Vallés, author of *L'Enfant* (1879), complained: "I do not recall a caress from the time I was very small; I have not been pampered, patted, smothered in kisses; I have been beaten a lot."[1] In the imagined idyll of nineteenth-century childhood, a child was first and foremost a recipient of parental love; while his or her very childishness was meant to evoke delight for parents beyond any potential economic utility. The idea of childhood as a privileged period of life, exempt from adult responsibilities and protected from the social and political upheavals of their own time, infused children's literature in the nineteenth century, even while many real children labored in fields and factories. It is the remnants of this phenomenon that may be responsible for the sense of anxiety that many parents continue to feel when they are unable to shield their children from adult concerns. This type of childhood is a luxury purchased by affluence and is being eroded by new developments in the twenty-first century, occasioning much anxiety on the part of parents who wish to preserve at least a small niche of protected childhood for their children.

Popular misconceptions about parents and children of the past

The fact that many children of the past labored at a fairly early age meant that they were expected to be "economically useful" to their families, but that did not necessarily make them "emotionally useless."[2] Children were economic assets to families and firmly embedded in family economies. Economic interdependence forged strong bonds among family members, and facilitated deference to parents, insofar as children often had to turn over the fruits of their economic productivity to their families. Prior to the Industrial Revolution, many children worked alongside their fathers and mothers, learning the tricks of the trades that would facilitate their entry to adulthood – whether it was in farming, spinning, or blacksmithing. These activities could promote parent–child involvement, as in the case of the wife of a Danish fisherman, who instructed her children in the rudiments of literacy while she worked at her spinning wheel.[3] In the past, historians have over-emphasized the numbers of children who were placed out to work at a very young age – a phenomenon that was more common in Europe than in the United States after the first boatloads of indentured youths arrived on American shores. In eighteenth-century England, for example, between one half and three-quarters of boys and girls, aged fifteen to nineteen, lived at home with their families, and many remained there until they married.[4] Among those who were put out to learn a trade or perform domestic service during their teens, many returned home for a time before they married.

The most common response to the birth of a healthy child has always been joy, with the caveat that some had to overcome their disappointment when they failed to produce the desired son. Family members often felt the need to console parents who had delivered a girl, as in the case of English woman Mary Hatton who wrote to her brother: "Though a son would have been more welcome . . . yet I am very well assured you was glad to have a daughter" [1676].[5] Yet joy was often attenuated and not all parents, especially mothers, felt blessed by the event of giving birth. Mothers experienced fatigue and anxiety when their children were not well spaced, when they already had too many mouths to feed, or if they felt themselves ill-equipped for motherhood.

The fact that more children died at a younger age does not mean that parents were dispassionate about their deaths. Prayer, stoicism, and culturally specific emotional management strategies shaped responses to children's deaths so that these appear quite different from the responses of parents who have fewer children and for whom child death is experienced as unexpected and catastrophic. Death was a haunting specter for all early modern adults, both parents and children – a factor that no doubt impinged on all of their relationships. Among the most popular misconceptions among the public is the idea that because of high mortality rates, the recycling of the names of dead children to later siblings, and the prevalence of wet-nursing in Europe, parental attachments to young children were minimal. Injunctions for parents to steel themselves against grief as an expression of Christian belief have been interpreted as suggesting that parents did not feel grief. But can we (or should we) measure feeling without considering diverse interpretations of naming practices, or the ways in which a religious sensibility provided strategies for coping with common traumatic events, and conventional language usages in different time periods?[6] An examination of seventeenth-century German funeral sermons demonstrates that parents could be full of despair when their children died, even though cultural and religious norms attempted to constrain their grief by urging them to regard their children's death as a "gift of God." Given the ubiquity of infant death and these religious injunctions, it is not surprising that some parents did explicitly relinquish their children to God with nary an expressed regret. Yet ministers also recognized that love and loss were connected. Upon the death of his only child, Maria Elizabeth at age sixteen, her German father was visibly distraught, in a way that was out of keeping with the customs of the seventeenth century. In the funeral sermon, the minister gently chided him: "Didn't he love her too much? This commonly happens to parents who have only one child to kiss."[7] This statement suggests that parental "kisses" were common, a demonstration of love that has no utilitarian component. The sermon also warned parents against loving their children too much, lest they become unhinged when faced with their death. Even the sixteenth-century leader of the Protestant Reformation, Martin Luther, who viewed extreme grief at death as "unchristian" and encouraged Christians to be stoical in the face of it, found himself "exquisitely sick" at the death of his own eighteen-month-old child.[8]

The obsession in the historical scholarship with how parents reacted to the deaths of their children has not been matched by attention to children's sense of loss at the death of a parent, which is just as illustrative of the quality of the parent–child bond. Thomas Shephard, who was apprenticed at the age of ten in early modern England, was bereft upon losing both of his parents, "and so I was left fatherless and motherless when I was about ten years old." Shephard speaks to the sense of identity-loss that children experienced when they found that they belonged to no one for whom a child was more than an economic asset. Similarly, Adam Martindale, also from England, spoke of the "unspeakable griefe and losse of us all" for his family members after his mother died.[9] The intensity of Martindale's mourning suggests that even when parents' deaths were the norm, rather than the exception, and an extensive group of family and friends tried to step in to fill the void, parents were unique in the affection and singularity of their concern for their children.

As with differences in the processing of death, differences in parenting techniques have also led scholars astray. Evaluating parental emotions on the basis of practices we now find problematic has led some to describe parents of the past as cold and "indifferent" toward their young. Infant abandonment was widespread in parts of Europe up through the nineteenth century, but mothers were usually strategic in placing their infants in venues such as monasteries and foundling homes where they were likely to be found and cared for. Wet-nurses were less prevalent than once thought, more likely to be employed by the elite, and were often sought by women who had been advised by their doctors that their own health would suffer if they continued the practice of nursing.

Prior to the nineteenth century, whipping and what we would consider "harsh" punishments were commonplace throughout Western Europe and the United States. When children experienced physical punishments as fierce, outside of the norm of their own cultural context, and had the freedom and linguistic capacities to complain, they did. Even in early New England, however, there was more than one approach to discipline, from a stern Calvinist approach, which relied extensively on physical discipline to the more "genteel" practices of an elite group of parents, who focused on the use of affection more than discipline in the rearing of the young. But the children of stern Calvinists may have imputed different meanings to their parents' efforts to "break the wills" of children through physical punishment. Contemporary research demonstrates that when physical punishment is viewed as fair and justified by children, it is not experienced as abusive, and children's psychological well-being is not compromised. This does not mean that there are not fundamental reasons for opposing the physical punishment of children and the potential for the abusive use of it by parents, who are much more powerful than their children. Because familial rights to discipline were virtually unquestioned prior to the nineteenth century, even when parents beat their children to death, they were less likely to be charged with murder. But scholars need to be careful not to judge parents' disciplinary strategies as abusive without placing them in the proper cultural context, let alone considering the many ways in which parenting in the twenty-first century falls short of our own best ideals of child nurture. Given that inequities in power are central to the parent–child relationship, it should not be surprising that parents are capable of abusing this power, especially when other exigencies – such as poverty, a prior history of abuse and neglect, and/or a lack of familial and social support – interfere with individual capacities to be good parents.

Perhaps the most widely encompassing statement must be that widespread parental indifference, neglect, and abuse from 1500 to the present day in both Western Europe and North America has never been the norm but has exposed parents to social criticism, ostracism, and, at times, legal punishments in extreme cases, such as infanticide or severe physical abuse, maiming, and murder. Surely, the bar is higher now. Across Western Europe and North America, the majority of children are better nourished, sheltered, and schooled than they were in earlier eras, and we have less tolerance for lapses in this regard. They are more likely to live beyond infancy, and their parents are more likely to live throughout the course of their childhood. As Judith Sealander puts it, prior to the nineteenth century, "the average child was the dead child," with statistical data suggesting that the majority of children did not live beyond the age of three until the turn of the twentieth century in the United States.[10] Physical punishment, although widely practiced, is less accepted by elites, and those who beat their children to the point of causing harm resulting in trips to the doctor may be sanctioned by the state, even potentially losing the right to rear their own children. Child neglect cases sometimes turn on economic privilege, while parents whose children live in physically dangerous environments may feel that harsher disciplinary practices are necessary, even as in Western Europe and North America today, they face the power of the state in defining their practices as not only "bad" but illegal. Protecting children from the extremes of parental power in the cases of severe neglect and abuse is now a state function, and one that has been furthered by proponents of children's rights. Yet questions remain as to whether this state power is functioning effectively enough to qualitatively improve children's lives.

The matter of disciplinary strategies, and how they have been perceived by both parents and children, is a good example of the problem of taking our bearings from the perspective of only one of the parties involved. Surprisingly, few scholarly works actually investigate the parent–child *relationship* over time. This is harder to get at, of course, given that many works on parenting are based on prescriptive advice, with some speculation as to how much this advice actually percolated into parenting practices. Many scholars have gone beyond prescriptive writings to get at the practical and emotive dimensions of family life. But whether a book is about parents *or* children, most texts tend to privilege one voice over the other. This research misses the critical dynamics that are at the heart of a complicated primary relationship. Future historical research about parents and children will benefit from a consideration of the parent–child relationship as interactive, generative, and changing over time as children and parents age.

Transatlantic influences

At the level of elite discourse, many of the philosophers and theologians, as well as the pediatricians who espoused their ideas about how to properly parent a child, had a transatlantic influence, beginning with the English migrations to America in the 1600s. One can never underestimate the impact of French philosopher Emile Rousseau or English philosopher John Locke on discourses about parenting not only in the Netherlands, England, Germany, and France, but in the United States, even though it is unlikely that more than a very few people read them. Their ideas seeped into European and American homes through magazines, short treatises, and local pedagogues and ministers. Intriguingly, it may in fact have been Americans that took these discourses most to heart. The legacies of feudalism and aristocracy in Europe relegated more youth to an ordained place in the social structure. Puritans brought a legacy of intentional parenting to the American colonies, with their belief in the inherent depravity of children, writing twice as many books on parenting in English as all other religious groups.[11]

Given the wide availability of land, various professional opportunities available to male youth, universal white male suffrage after the Revolution, and the quick spread of public education and literacy in the United States in the early centuries of its development, American parents became ever more conscious of the need to prepare children to take advantage of the opportunities and choices that awaited them. Individualism, as that astute observer of American character, Alexis de Tocqueville pointed out, had rendered the American family almost unrecognizable from the perspective of French society. Paternal authority had frayed, and both male and female youth displayed an astonishing independence with nary a gap between boyhood and adolescence. With greater geographic mobility than their European counterparts as well, which lessened their proximity to traditional kinship networks, the role and influence of expert child rearing literature took on a special status in the United States, beginning in the nineteenth century and continuing to the present day.

The variability of parent–child relationships

Both the words parent and children obscure the vast differences not only between families from varying socio-economic, religious, ethnic, and racial groups but the unique and nearly universal gender differences that have shaped how women and men parent, and how boys and girls are differently parented. Definitions of parental roles for women and men have changed dramatically over time, as have expectations for the rearing of boys and girls. Norms of parenting for women and men have existed in all societies, but individual practices often depart substantially from the norm, with a large degree of variability in the emotional quality of parents' relationships to their children. Most children's testimonies from the nineteenth century suggest that fathers were more often "honored" while children's "deepest affections" were reserved for mothers in whom they were more likely to confide and from whom they expected gentle treatment.[12] But even when mothers were valorized as tender, and fathers depicted as stern, the temperaments of individual parents and children often mediated their particular roles and gender norms. Fathers tended to display their tender side to their daughters. Reformer Jane Addams, whose mother died at birth, testified to the impact of her father's "supreme affection" which afforded her access to the "moral concerns of life."[13]

The nurture of boys and girls has been sharply differentiated across the period under consideration, modern changes notwithstanding. This has been especially the case as youths enter adolescence, and girls prepare to be proper spouses and mothers, while boys engage in the task of learning to support a spouse and children. Prior to the twentieth century, the gender differences of very young children (what we would call babies and toddlers) were neutralized, with both boys and girls wearing a similar gown that was designed to assist with toilet training. Starting in the sixteenth century, a ritualized practice for boys known as breeching became widespread throughout Western Europe, when boys acquired their first trousers and were celebrated for leaving babyhood behind for boyhood. Although the age of breeching was variable, typically boys were breeched at ages of six or seven. Girls also began to wear adult-like women's clothing around this age, although there was no ceremonial significance attached to this shift because their attire had not changed as dramatically, nor was this a marker of a shift to a more privileged status in a patriarchal world. At this same age, often described as the "age of reason," both boys and girls began learning the tasks that were deemed suited to their future lives, depending on their class status – from farming and blacksmithing to embroidery, shearing sheep, and cookery. Despite the privileged status of boys, many parents took pride in sharp-witted girls, and secretly celebrated at the birth of a girl. In short, the relationships between parents and children over time are characterized by intense variability both at the level of the individual and the different cultural and social groups to which individuals belong.

Extensive, intensive, and "intentional" parenting

Historian Laurel Ulrich has documented a shift from "extensive" to "intensive" mothering in American history, tracing "intensive" mothering to the nineteenth century.[14] Extensive parenting, in which children were reared amidst a range of other daily activities and were mentored by a variety of different adults in their lives, occurred among both the poor and the rich during the medieval and early modern eras, while widespread intensive parenting – where, specifically mothers, limited much of their family labor to the rearing of children, came to characterize much middle-class parenting, beginning around the nineteenth century in both continents. Although the single generational family model was intact as early as 1600 in most of Western Europe and eventually the United States, there was no unitary composition of the family because parents often died, and re-marriages and single-parent families were common. Unlike the present day, a single-parent family was as likely to consist of a father as a mother, at least prior to the nineteenth century when mortality rates began to decline. Fathers were also more apt than mothers to send their children out to board or be apprenticed if he did not re-marry following the death of a spouse. Families might also house servants, lodgers, and kin, all of whom were presumed to be dependent and subservient to the patriarchal head of the family. Yet, in spite of what some earlier scholarship has suggested, dependency was not undifferentiated, meaning that mothers and children still occupied a unique status in the household. Fathers "ruled" the household legally, economically, and, in theory, morally, but in practice mothers often held considerable sway, particularly in the moral and emotional dimensions of family life. At the same time, children in most homes were valued beyond their economic utility, and the bonds they forged with parents were freighted with great meaning for both parties in most families.

Economically productive households, typical until the early nineteenth century, often engaged adults and children in the same chores, and sometimes housed extra relatives or apprentices, with some families sending their children out to labor and learn in other households as they approached adolescence. Children almost always maintained their deepest attachments to parents, but they were also mentored and monitored by other adults. The engagement of multiple adults in children's lives was necessitated in part by the fact that few children could expect to age into adulthood with two living parents. But beyond the facts of parental mortality, the most extreme form of parental separation, it was more common for children, whether wealthy or poor, to live for considerable stretches of time outside of the confines of the nuclear family setting. Rich or poor, it was not considered dishonorable to send your child out into the world to be socialized by other adults, but in fact most children were not apprenticed until the age of twelve or older, when their labor became more valuable. And it appears that the majority of children who left their homes to labor in other homes were poor, even during the seventeenth and eighteenth centuries.[15]

Living at home was viewed by most children as more desirable than being sent out to live with strangers or even relatives. Some of those who were able to live with their parents cherished their good fortune. Ten-year old Otto from the Netherlands, whose parents intentionally modeled their child-rearing on the Enlightenment philosophy of Jean Jacques Rousseau, wrote a diary in the 1780s, where he recognized the privilege he enjoyed in being firmly ensconced is the family home:

> Papa is afraid that I'll become an unbearable, obstinate, short-tempered, know-nothing as well as an unmannered street urchin. Oh, how little I deserve the constant care my parents take of me, and how much more pleasant it is for me to remain in their hands than to be given completely over to strangers.[16]

But living away from home did not mean that parents necessarily relinquished their responsibilities toward their children or that ties of affection did not endure. Anna Green Winslow was sent by her parents from Canada to be "schooled" in Boston by her aunt in 1771, a not uncommon practice among better-off parents who felt schooling opportunities in their own area to be limited. She kept a journal, which she shared with her parents to demonstrate her accomplishments during her sojourn. Anna complained that only her mother responded to her missives home: "Hon'd Mama, My Hon'd Papa has never signified to me by approbation of my journals, from when I infer, that [he] never reads them, or does not give himself the trouble to remember any of their contents."[17] Though Anna's deference to her parents is insinuated in her letter, her chiding tone about her father's negligence is unmistakable and was heeded. Her father responded to her to say that he approved of at least some of her accounts, suggesting that, at least in this case, her father's love for her was more conditional than that of her mother. Abigaill Levy Franks, a well-off assimilated Jew, who had migrated from London to New York in 1703, wrote regular letters to her seventeen-year-old son who had traveled to London to learn the art of business from his uncles. She spoke of the "inexpressible joy" his letters gave her, and offered advice about his manners, his use of time, and urged him to be "circumspect" in his observance of Jewish religious traditions.[18] Even a seventeen-year-old son, who had crossed the ocean to acquire a professional education, was the recipient of numerous attempts by his mother to guide his behavior, so that he would achieve social and economic success.

On the other hand, some poor children, both in Europe and in North America, were either separated from their parents because of long working hours or forced into apprenticeships because of poverty. While some youths, especially boys who were sent out to work, saw it as an escape from destitution, and even an adventure, others were bereft at the separation from parents. Forsaking home and parents could be wrenching, as in the case of John Clare, born in England in 1793, who wrote of "his dread at leaving home for an apprenticeship" because he had been "coddled up so tenderly and so long." And parents often remained involved in their children's apprenticeships, pulling them from unsuitable situations and finding more suitable placements when they could. The father of a daughter in service in New Amsterdam in 1659, instigated court action against an employer who violently abused her and immediately removed her from his employ.[19] Apprenticeship itself did not exempt parents from the responsibility to see that their children were properly cared for. Parents who sent their children off to be apprenticed, or even to foreign lands, as in the case of European families who may have dispatched their older boys to America, may have seemed uncaring, especially when they made money from the deal, as some German parents did. In most cases, parents found it inconceivable to send their children to seek their own fortunes and endure a permanent separation, unless they experienced dire poverty.

For African–American slave children, separation from parents was often a fact of existence, and choice did not factor into these arrangements. But the feeling of "belonging" to one or more parents was a luxury to be cherished. Some were forced out of their parents' care through sale, others had fathers who lived in nearby or far-off plantations (slave owners were more likely to leave children in the care of their mothers), or rarely saw their parents because of work schedules. A former slave, interviewed in 1937, complained that during slavery it seemed as if her children belonged to everyone but herself.[20] Yet when children were able to maintain parental bonds, they received enormous sustenance from these attachments, even while parents were less likely to be able to offer the kind of nurture they might have wished their children to have. Frederick Douglas remembered that when his mother managed to snatch away a piece of bread to share with him, it made him feel that he was not "just a child, but somebody's child."[21] Charles Ball recalled that his mother carried her son on her back while she worked because she could not endure the thought of his crying in her absence. African–American slave families often commonly named their eldest sons after their fathers and paternal grandfathers in order to instill a feeling of belonging. Being "somebody's child" meant that a child had a value beyond economics and an identity based on connection to a particular adult or community premised on these affectionate bonds.

Fathers as parents, mothers as care-givers

Most people have associated intensive parenting with mothers, but the first glimpses of "intentional" or mindful parenting were actually associated with fathers, well before the era of the mother in the nineteenth century. In Renaissance Italy patriarchs were encouraged to be especially mindful about the rearing of sons, no doubt in part because a blossoming mercantile economy required fathers to exercise greater guidance to ensure their son's financial success. Fifteenth-century writer Leon Battista Alberti in *The Art of Parenting* paved the way for the domesticated father by associating "manliness" with dedication to parenting. Italian advice literature enjoined fathers to practice gentle discipline, to show tenderness to their children, to take into account their children's inclinations, and to ensure that such an important enterprise as parenting was not to be left up to women.[22] It would take advancements in women's status before theologians, philosophers, and physicians devoted considerable attention to mothers as educators as well as care-givers.

When in the early 1500s, Dutch Catholic philosopher Desiderius Erasmus proclaimed that the early years of childhood were of "utmost importance," he signaled a growing consciousness of the significance of child nurture that would occupy the minds of some of the Western world's greatest philosophers in the coming centuries. During the European Reformation in the sixteenth century, more mindful parenting came to be valued as the need to produce Christian children free of sin evolved. Martin Luther, among others, urged that parenting be deemed a "rational art" rather than an "emotional venture." Otto Brunfeld, a German humanist and physician deemed parenting as a project to create not only better Christians but a better world: "If one wants to reform the world and make it Christian, one must begin with children."[23]

Because both religious and social transformations began with children, sermons, treatises, and major works of philosophy began to advise parents on proper child-rearing, with mothers being charged with care and fathers with education. The nature of the advice, which included injunctions to fathers to more firmly direct their families, sought to undermine the role of mothers, especially when it came to forming children's characters as they aged. Advice to fathers was not just about forming character for the purpose of moral probity, however, but also premised on the need to raise sons who would achieve professional success, something that took on a special urgency during the era of the emergence of the bourgeoisie.

Children's own preferences and inclinations became increasingly salient both for daughters, in the choice of a spouse, and more importantly, for boys, in the choice of a profession. According to British writer Joseph Collyer: "One must be sensible of the advantage and pleasure a boy will receive by directing his education to that particular profession, to that trade, or art, for which he appears peculiarly designed by nature."[24] [1769] Not all followed Collyer's advice but many were aware of it. American Samuel West's father, a pastor, disagreed that sons should choose their own profession, believing that youthful choices were often based on "whim and caprice."[25] Many parents also worried that girls would be subject to fleeting whims in choosing a future partner, and sought to ensure that their spouses would be not only kind but meet parental expectations in terms of class, religion, educational status, and financial wherewithal.

Reading advice literature against the grain gives us some clue as to the difference between "real" and "ideal" parenting. While the iconic wife of the founder of Methodism, Susanna Wesley, spilled considerable ink in the late seventeenth century detailing her unstinting efforts to mold her children's characters to her exacting requirements, it is clear that many parents were not so stringent. Parents were both too affectionate and too lax. An English pediatrician implied that most parents were absolutely delinquent when it came to disciplining children:

> Do not do as is now done in the world, where children are taught to rule, but not to serve . . . Children today are badly raised; not only do parents permit them every selfish wish, but they even show them how to do it.

In *When Fathers Ruled*, historian Steven Ozment finds further evidence of parental indulgence through the voice of Nuremburg pastor Veit Dietrich who warned against parents who laughed at their children's misdoings and allowed their older children to stay out "dancing until midnight."[26] Theologians urged parents to be more serious in the disciplining of children, to exert greater authority, and be less permissive. There would be no reason for advice, if authorities believed that parents were consistently rearing their children in the appropriate fashion; however, the literature does tell us much about dominant ideologies concerning the *ideal* methods of rearing children, ideals that informed parenting practices over time, especially for those who were literate and had the inclination and the time to be more intentional parents.

There is historical debate regarding whether these injunctions to fathers to exert more authority over their families during the sixteenth and seventeenth centuries actually bolstered patriarchy and strengthened parental authority over children because along with warnings about the significance of discipline, there were also calls for fathers to be more tender and considerate of their children. For instance, in the famous diary of vicar Ralph Josselin in rural England, written in the seventeenth century, he demonstrated not only grief at the death of a beloved child, but delight in her individual personality, calling his eight-year-old Mary a "pretious child, a bundle of myrrhe, a bundle of sweetness, shee was a child of ten thousand, full of wisdom . . . apt in her learning, tender hearted and loving." His concern about his children did not abet as they aged. He fretted about his older son's "debauchery" and "drunkenness," and his older daughter's choice of a marital partner. His biggest wish was that Elizabeth would make a "perfect" match before he died, choosing a partner who was economically stable, of good moral character, and with whom his daughter was pleased.[27] Although all of these reminiscences are well in keeping with his patriarchal role as guardian of the family, they also demonstrate an emotional dimension that is at odds with the dominant portrait of seventeenth-century fathers as austere and forbidding masters, imposing their wills on an entire household, all of whom were duly subservient.

The erosion of deference: mothers, fathers, daughters, sons

Among the influences of the Revolutionary War in the United States and its aftermath was an erosion of deference that filtered down to the family. European Enlightenment philosophies both sparked these events and filtered into childcare and pedagogy in the aftermath, with their emphasis on the importance of reason and the equality of man, principles that would eventually be extended to women. Apprenticeship and indentured servitude were well on their way to extinction by the early 1800s, and universal white male suffrage in the United States provided a rough equality between white men of various classes by the 1820s. Respect and consent came to be ever more critical in the marriage contract, and families increasingly cultivated independence in children. Even girls in the United States became more independent, in part because they were gaining increasing access to literacy, and because cultural norms were contributing toward less formal relations and a respect for the individuality of all family members. This informality was demonstrated by changing social conventions, whereby many children no longer were required to bow in the presence of their parents, and more likely to call their parents "papa" and "mama" than "sir" and "madam."[28]

The striking independence and "happy audacity" of the American girl was frightening to Alexis de Tocqueville, who found that girls were quite willing to express their views in conversation. He perceived that Americans girls were not sheltered or cloistered to maintain their chastity, as in the case of French aristocrats, but were educated in reason so that they could protect themselves until such time as they would find a husband.[29] Education, not only in spinning and cookery, became widespread, and many girls began to appreciate the delights of science, history, and philosophy in girls' academies and in public schools as the century wore on.

Girls' increasing literacy was matched by that of their parents, including their mothers, who were informed by the voluminous child-rearing literature, now largely directed at them. The earlier volumes, such as John Locke's *Second Treatise on Education* (1693) had stressed the cultivation of good habits and character in children through the use of reason in discipline. Rousseau's *Emile or On Education*, although not particularly influential in the United States, when it was first published in France in 1762 began to resonate with nineteenth-century writers and reformers in invoking an ideal of childhood to be cherished and protected from excessive forces of civilization. Born perfect, children were tarnished by a corrupt society. Rousseau pitied the overly civilized boy, who was forced to comply with the demands of civilized society before maturation had taken hold. His future spouse Sophie, however, was to be trained to mask her real desires in order to be appealing to men. However dreary Sophie's plight appears to be, Rousseau's ideas about the importance of honoring childhood as a stage of life where children should be sheltered from the demands of civilization would be applied to many reforms for children, both boys and girls, in the United States and Europe.

Unlike Locke, who was primarily concerned with discerning how best to prepare children for adulthood, Rousseau urged parents and educators to preserve and nurture the "natural" child by allowing for children to experience consequences for themselves rather than imposing artificial restrictions. Rousseau's ideas were so influential that some parents began to make guinea pigs out of their children by applying his theories, not always with success. Richard Edgeworth raised his son to go "about freely and do anything he liked." Although he described the boy as "bold, free, fearless, and generous," he was also undisciplined, and his father chose to send him out to sea at age fifteen to tame his wild edges. Manon Roland also aimed to be less restrictive in raising her daughter Eudora, until she was fed up with her behavior and began administering punishments. Roland was apparently not the warmest of mothers, finding her daughter to be "dull-witted," "apathetic," "cold and stupid," and eventually sent her to a convent to be schooled.[30] But it is likely that those parents who did incorporate some of Rousseau's ideas into their parenting did so selectively and in tandem with other approaches – a style of parenting that was (and is) more common than rigid adherence to any particular set of parenting ideals.

The era of the mother: intensive parenting

While extensive parenting continued to be a necessity among slave, agricultural, and working class communities, a transformation to intensive motherhood was most fully developed among the nineteenth-century literate middle classes. Family life in this era has been much romanticized, based on the many publications that sentimentalized mother love and celebrated the special qualities of childhood. Many of the actual changes in family life were due to economics and the emergence of commerce, urbanization, and the resulting differentiation between the home and the workplace. But part was also due to changing family formations occasioned in no small part by better health among parents and children and shrinking family sizes in the nineteenth century. In early New England, the average size of families was larger than in Europe due to improved nutrition, and often ranged from six to seven children; by 1900, the average American mother was having three or four children and ending her childbearing years earlier than her grandmother had.[31] This difference was not as profound in Europe, where smaller family sizes were more consistent, due to higher rates of mortality among children and of parents. And intensive and intentional parenting as an ideal stood in stark juxtaposition to the rising numbers of child laborers, institutions for juvenile delinquents, and orphanages, particularly in the latter part of the century. Intensive parenting was an exclusionary ideal that left out, and continues to leave out, very poor families, slaves, and even farm families, where maternal and child labor is central to the family's existence. Rather than singling out child rearing as a special activity, it is embedded in the day-to-day activities that families need to survive.

With increasing female literacy, smaller family sizes, and larger numbers of men leaving the home for the workplace, parenting became more of a female domain. Middle- and upper-class women experienced anxiety about the discharge of their maternal duties as their motherhood responsibilities were magnified. In a journal, *The Maternal Assistant*, designed to assist mothers in their child-rearing duties, Seba Smith (1842) observed that the intensity of the mothering role was leading to maternal anxiety:

> Everywhere we are told of the responsibility of mothers, the great and arduous duties devolving upon them; and wherever we find a mother alive to these responsibilities, and aware of these high duties, we find also an anxious, careworn, and dispirited woman.[32]

The practice of motherhood became associated with the acquisition of expert knowledge that would allow mothers to make moment-by-moment decisions about how best to develop children's moral character and intellectual development.

Anxiety accompanied mothering, especially when it was invested with such a heavy weight; however, the enormous weight given to mothering also helped to transform women's position. It was during the mid- to late-nineteenth century that women began the work of association building, of involvement in education – particularly in the kindergarten movement at the end of the century – and of eventually transforming the private interests of mothers into a kind of public motherhood, which focused on policy issues relating to children, such as juvenile justice, child labor, and mothers' pensions. Although more young women than ever remained single in the United States at the end of the nineteenth century and engaged in work, both paid or unpaid outside the home, women who chose mothering as their primary career, also found outlets in charitable and public service work for their talents.

Intentional parenting in the twentieth and twenty-first century

Perhaps the most sweeping change that affected parent–child relationships was wrought through the expansion of public schooling in the early twentieth century across Europe and the United States and the concomitant decline of child labor. Whereas much schooling in the nineteenth century was sporadic, informal, and included children of various ages in a single class, by the turn of the twentieth century, children increasingly entered the classroom at uniform ages with their peers and were schooled in ways that competed with parental socialization. This was especially the case with working-class and immigrant parents, many of whom objected to the state taking over the family function. Parents complained that schools disrupted family discipline, gave children a sense of entitlement, and failed to prepare children to earn a living. Perhaps most importantly, it was in schools that children developed strong peer cultures that would put children's cultures into tension with that of their parents.

While parents' responsibilities persisted through the centuries, and even intensified, in terms of the emphasis on parents in shaping children's characters, it is likely that children's responsibilities to their parents have diminished over time. This is not only the case with economic responsibilities, but with chores, and the more general injunctions prior to the twentieth century for children to "please" and "obey" their parents. Children's memoires and letters often refer to how hard they worked to please their parents, or how disappointed they were when they displeased them. It might not be too unrealistic to suggest that many of today's parents put more emphasis on pleasing their children than children do on pleasing their parents. Daniel Drake, a young rural American who grew up in the early 1800s, wrote about his parents in conventional fashion:

> I grew up with love and obedience to my mother, and received from her an early moral training, to which, in conjunction with that of my father, I owe, perhaps, more of my humble preparation of life to come than to any other influence.[33]

The kind of gratitude expressed by Daniel was expected to translate into the obligation to care for his aging parents. This standard was surely weakening by the beginning of the twentieth century in both Europe and the United States for a variety of reasons. Parents tended to live longer, enjoy healthier lives, and often spent their retirement in pursuit of their own individual interests. Parents' health often declines, while their adult children are raising children of their own. Women have typically been the care-givers of aging parents, but more than ever they are not only raising children but also working outside of the home. There has also been a growing emphasis on individualism that has nurtured the belief that as children age they have a "right" to lives of their own unburdened by their parents' needs. Social welfare legislation in Western Europe and North America has provided a cushion to deal with declining economic fortunes and health issues among the elderly. It is difficult to evaluate the effect of this decline of children's obligations to their aged parents or how it relates to matters of love or affection. In fact, persons from non-Western cultures frequently comment on the indifference or even contempt that Western societies show toward the aged. Yet some families continue to house aged parents, while others bring their aged parents to live close by them, if not with them, so that they can interact with and care for them on a regular basis, while its members continue to work and pursue their own nuclear family lives. Adult children often spend considerable amounts of time traveling to the family home so that they may care for their parents during periods of medical emergencies and to make care-giving arrangements. Children's obligations to their parents have undoubtedly changed, but that does not necessarily imply that they are less affectionate or more indifferent toward them.

Similarly, parents' obligations toward their children have changed significantly. Parents in earlier centuries strove to sustain their children physically, instill moral character, and ensure that their children would grow up to be responsible mothers or economically productive fathers. Since the twentieth century, parents have added to the list the need to secure children's happiness and adjustment according to the tenets of a therapeutic society. It is not that earlier parents did not wish their children to be happy but it was not the touchstone for measuring one's effectiveness as a parent. And perhaps happiness itself was differently conceived in the past as a quality that was distinct from pleasure, while in the present, happiness and pleasure seem virtually indistinguishable and are associated with the ability to provide recreation and purchasable goods for one's children. In her depiction of a New England girlhood in the early nineteenth century, Lucy Larcom made a distinction between happiness and pleasure: "We were not surfeited, in those days, with what is called pleasure; but brought up happy and healthy, learning unconsciously the useful lessons of doing without."[34] In our commodified society, parents typically think that "doing without" compromises their children's childhood, and even poor parents occasionally throw expensive birthday parties or buy trendy sneakers in the hope that these experiences and items will secure a happy childhood.

Parents also assume that children's happiness is predicated on their ability to forge social networks of peers, even though these peers may intensify the differences between parents and children. The generation gap, a term that was coined during the 1960s, was really an invention of the 1920s when many writers discussed the growing chasm between the world of youth and their parents. This was particularly true in the case of girls and immigrants, both of whom often departed from the paths their parents had travelled. Southern European immigrants to America learned that play was valued more than work as an essential part of childhood, while girls in general began to partake of the new freedoms that awaited them, as they increased their years of schooling, lived and worked outside of the home before marriage, or embarked upon professional careers. These experiences had not been possible for many of their mothers, while many of their fathers fretted about the impropriety and increasing dangers that threatened the lives of these "new women" – their daughters. Still, many daughters found their mothers to be their supporters as they forged new paths. M. Carey Thomas, who would go on to become the president of Bryn Mawr College, wrote extensively about the conflicts she had with her mother in her journal, yet when she decided to go to college, it was her mother who helped overcome her religious father's objections. She contrasted the "many and dreadful" talks she had with her father on the subject with "mother, my own splendid mother" who sided with her and helped her to achieve her goals.[35]

Young women acquired new opportunities in the world of education and work in the early twentieth century, but the emphasis on the gender of young children became more pronounced in some significant ways. In the 1920s, the clothing industry helped to inaugurate the practice of distinguishing between girl and boy babies by virtue of the color of the clothing they wore, and many parents wrote worriedly to experts about little boys who did not exhibit the behaviors of a "regular boy," who failed to stand up for themselves in a fight, who preferred to play with girls, and who were unduly sensitive. Parents worried about boys who were "effeminate," more so than girls who were too rough and tough. Lurking behind these fears was a worry that gender non-conformity, especially on the part of boys, might lead to homosexuality, contributing to a heightened gender surveillance of the behaviors of even very young children on the part of both parents and peers.

Not only childhood but also motherhood was the subject of increased scrutiny during the early twentieth century. While motherhood was sanctified in parts of Western Europe in order to advance pro-natalist policies, in the United States, where eugenics predominated, the deficiencies of motherhood were broadcast more widely. Advice directed to parents was now almost wholly secular and scientific and brought home the idea that children's health and happiness did not come naturally, but needed to be fostered through appropriate child management strategies. In 1928, when behaviorist

John Broadus Watson published his enormously influential *Psychological Care of Infant and Child*, he dedicated it to the "first mother who brings up a happy child." Ironically, however, Watson's happy child would be so only if the mother dedicated herself to a systematic approach to child rearing that put limitations on the expression of affection and regulated children's toilet training, sleeping, and eating. Similarly, the US Children's Bureau, established in 1912 by women who sought to assist mothers in matters of children's health and well-being, published pamphlets that were widely dispersed among both rural and urban mothers, most of which were in the vein of Watson's advice, including *Are You Training Your Child to be Happy?* published in 1930. This systematic approach to parenting, which was widespread in the first half of the twentieth century was displaced by the more flexible and ever-popular Dr Benjamin Spock in the 1950s, who reinforced the idea that mothers were in possession of "maternal instincts" that would guide them as they reared their children. That Spock's book of advice was so wildly popular detracted from the idea that the maternal instinct was enough to bring up a child. Instead of rigidly adhering to strict routines and systematic training, Spock suggested that if mothers gently steered their children in the right direction, there would be no need for excessive punishment. With just the right mix of affection, flexibility, and structure, Spock implied, any mother could raise a happy child.

Spock's advice probably helped some mothers, even while it clearly troubled those mothers who found mothering difficult and frustrating, and whose children did not seem to be healthy, happy, or well adjusted. Spock and other purveyors of scientific child-rearing literature have made parents, especially mothers, more accountable for the temperaments and accomplishments of their children. During the 1950s, this message was especially salient, even to the point of blaming "refrigerator mothers" for autistic children.

Unfortunately, many parents have found that they were unable themselves to secure happiness and well-being for their children and have sought expert assistance in order to achieve these elusive goals. Good parenting is now also defined by one's willingness to identify unhappiness and other signs of emotional disorder to access expert help. The medicalization of children's emotional and learning difficulties is one demonstration of this phenomenon. Parents frequently seek diagnoses and medicine for children who are sad, unhappy, and unsuccessful at school. Character has been downplayed in the quest to produce children who are not only happy, but also socially competent with their peers and academically successful.

Today, parenting continues to be mindful and children are more carefully cultivated than ever, but it is debatable whether parents have the same intensity of influence over their children as they did in the nineteenth century. It is more common than ever to have both spouses working and for children to attend school between the ages of six (or earlier) and eighteen. Here they are privy to ideas and behaviors that might be alien to their parents through the medium of educators and peers. Today as well, the range of family variations mirror in some respects an earlier period, when children might be expected to rely on only one parent, or families were composed of parents and step-parents who are biologically unrelated. This variation is due to the increase of divorce and the rise in the number of single-parent, adoptive, and same-sex families. Parents are also yielding to other influences over their children. Middle-class children, in particular, are cultivated through adult-sponsored activities, such as sports and dance classes. Their days are largely scripted, but do not necessarily revolve around family meals, prayers, and obligations to parents such as chores and labor outside of the home. The mass media is exerting a huge influence on young children, expanding the impact of peers, advertisers, and transnational products and performers, organizing a separate universe that perpetuates youthful consumerism and interactions. Children are very important in the typical middle-class family, and adults – even if not omnipresent – schedule their lives in ways that they think will make children happier and more successful. Are children less or more important, happier or not, closer to their parents, or more distrustful than in the past? The virtue of history is that it restrains us from making blanket judgments about these questions, by drawing our attention to the endless variations in the ways in which parents and children have expressed their attachments in different times and places.

Contemporary middle-class parents have much on their plates; in addition to putting bread on the table, they are responsible for providing their children with an ever-expanding array of consumer goods, enriching experiences, expert medical care – both physical and emotional – and an education that will ensure their professional success. Without these accouterments, we fear that we are somehow failing our children, that they will be doomed in the ever-more-competitive quest for success. We are no longer preoccupied with preserving childhood as a sanctified space for exploration free of adult demands. But there still remains a lingering nostalgia for the older days, when we imagine that children roamed freely in communities or urban neighborhoods, created their games from scratch, and when parent interactions were informal, common, and lacked the concerted intentionality that informs modern-day parenting. Nostalgia usually functions to deflect from our memories the elements of the past such as rampant sexism, racism, homophobia, and a greater tolerance for physical and verbal violence among children and adults that we should be glad to leave behind. Yet the romantic innocence of the nineteenth-century ideal child continues to haunt our imaginations, even in the light of all of these changes. The enormous symbolic weight of children pervades our consciousness, just as we are witnessing the weakening of the barriers between childhood and adulthood. Through our children, we mourn for what we have lost and fear for the future. Perhaps this is what defines parent–child relations in the present: we have our eyes on our children's futures, while wondering what we are sacrificing as we look backwards toward the past.

Notes

1 Cited in Colin Heywood, *Growing up in France: From the Ancien Régime to the Third Republic* (New York, NY: Cambridge University Press, 2007), 131.
2 Arianne Baggerman and Rudolf Dekker, *Child of the Enlightenment: Revolutionary Europe Reflected in a Boyhood Diary* (Boston, MA: Brill Academic Publishers, 2009), 79.
3 "Loftur Guttormsson, "Parent–Child Relations," in *The History of the European Family: Volume 2, Family Life in the Long Nineteenth Century, 1789–1913*, eds. David I. Kertzer and Marzio Barbagli, (New Haven, CT: Yale University Press), 258.
4 Deborah Simonton, "Bringing Up Girls: Work in Preindustrial Europe," in *Secret Gardens, Satanic Mills: Placing Girls in European History, 1750–1960*, eds. Mary Jo Maynes, Birgitte Søland, and Christina Benninghaus, (Bloomington, IN: Indiana University Press, 2004).
5 Linda Pollock, *A Lasting Relationship: Parents and Children Over Three Centuries* (Hanover and London: University Press of New England, 1990), 44.

6 Linda A. Pollock's *Forgotten Children: Parent–Child Relations from 1500 to 1900* (Cambridge, MA: Cambridge University Press, 1984) provides the most comprehensive coverage of this phenomenon.

7 Claudia Jarzebowski, "Loss and Emotion in Funeral Works on Children in Seventeenth-Century Germany," in *Enduring Loss in Early Modern Germany Cross Disciplinary Perspectives, Studies in Central European Histories v. 50*, ed. Lynne Tatlock, (Boston, MA: Brill Academic Publishers, 2010), 202.

8 Steven E. Ozment, *When Fathers Ruled: Family Life in Reformation Europe* (Cambridge, MA: Harvard University Press, 1983), 168.

9 Ilana Krausman Ben-Amos, *Adolescence and Youth in Early Modern England* (New Haven, CT: Yale University Press, 1994), 49, 51.

10 Judith Sealander, *The Failed Century of the Child: Governing America's Young in the Twentieth Century* (New York, CT: Cambridge University Press, 2003), 7.

11 Steven Mintz, *Huck's Raft: A History of American Childhood* (Cambridge, MA: Belknap Press of Harvard University Press, 2004), 17.

12 Stephen M. Frank, *Life with Father: Parenthood and Masculinity in the Nineteenth-Century American North* (Baltimore, MD: Johns Hopkins University Press, 1998), 133.

13 Jane Addams, *Twenty Years at Hull-House with Autobiographical Notes*, Prairie State Books (Urbana, IL: University of Illinois Press, 1990), 1.

14 Laurel Thatcher Ulrich, *Good Wives: Image and Reality in the Lives of Women in Northern New England, 1650–1750* (New York, NY: Vintage, 1991).

15 Ben-Amos, *Adolescence and Youth in Early Modern England*, 59.

16 Baggerman and Dekker, *Child of the Enlightenment*, 79.

17 Anna Morse Earle, *Diary of Anna Green Winslow: A Boston School Girl of 1771* (Boston, MA: Houghton Mifflin, 1896), 18.

18 Edith B. Gelles, *The Letters of Abigaill Levy Franks, 1733–1748* (New Haven, CT: Yale University Press, 2004), 6–7.

19 Mariah Adin, "'I Shall Beat You, So that the Devil Shall Laugh at It,'" in *Children in Colonial America*, ed. James Alan Marten, (New York, NY: New York University Press, 2007), 93.

20 James Marten, ed., *Children in Colonial America, Children and Youth in America* (New York, NY: New York University Press, 2007).

21 Wilma King, *Stolen Childhood: Slave Youth in Nineteenth-Century America* (Bloomington, IN: Indiana University Press, 1995), 1.

22 Louis Haas, *The Renaissance Man and His Children: Childbirth and Early Childhood in Florence, 1300–1600*, 1st ed. (New York, NY: St. Martin's Press, 1998).

23 Ozment, *When Fathers Ruled*, 136.

24 Joseph Collyer, *The Parent's and Guardian's Directory and the Youth's Guide in the Choice of a Profession or Trade* (London, UK, 1761).

25 Harvey J Graff, *Conflicting Paths: Growing up in America* (Cambridge, MA: Harvard University Press, 1995), 34.

26 Ozment, *When Fathers Ruled*, 133.

27 Ralph Josselin, *The Diary of the Reverend Ralph Josselin, 1616–1683* (Offices of the Society, 1908), 74, 166, 170.

28 Steven Mintz, "Parenting," in *Encyclopedia of Children and Childhood in History and Society. Volume 2*, ed. Paula S. Fass, (New York, NY: MacMillan Reference, 2004), 649.

29 Alexis deTocqueville, *Democracy in America*, book 2, chapter 9, 591–592.

30 Baggerman and Dekker, *Child of the Enlightenment*, 52–53.

31 Steven Mintz, *Domestic Revolutions: A Social History of American Family Life* (New York, NY: Free Press, 1988), 51.

32 Julia Grant, *Raising Baby by the Book: The Education of American Mothers* (New Haven, CT: Yale University Press, 1998), 2.
33 Graff, *Conflicting Paths*, 46.
34 Lucy Larcom, *A New England Girlhood: Outlined from Memory* (Boston, MA: Houghton Mifflin Company, 1889), 91.
35 Linda W. Rosenzweig, *The Anchor of My Life: Middle-Class American Mothers and Daughters, 1880–1920* (New York, NY: New York University Press, 1993) 95.

Suggestions for further reading

Apple, Rima D. *Perfect Motherhood: Science and Childrearing in America*. Camden, NJ: Rutgers University Press, 2006. Apple makes the case that scientific child-rearing in the twentieth century had a huge impact on American mothers, arguing that many of the precepts put forth by professionals actually were beneficial to mothers in their everyday practices. Unlike some other historians, she is persuaded that most mothers found scientific advice appealing.

Ariès, Philippe. *Centuries of Childhood*. London, UK: Pimlico, 1996. Ariès' important text provides the history of childhood with a central point for further exploration. Focusing mainly on medieval and early modern Europe, the book provides a wealth of information on images of children, children's games, sexuality, parenting practices, along with his provocative interpretations about the nature of family life and attitudes toward children.

Baggerman, Arianne, and Rudolf Dekker. *Child of the Enlightenment: Revolutionary Europe Reflected in a Boyhood Diary*. Leiden, The Netherlands: Brill Academic Publishers, 2009. This fascinating book opens a window into intentional parenting in the late eighteenth century, through providing for the reader a diary written by a youth in The Netherlands for the edification of his parents. The diary is buttressed by an analysis of the impact of Enlightenment philosophies on parenting by bourgeois families during this era.

Ben-Amos, Dr Ilana Krausman. *Adolescence and Youth in Early Modern England*. New Haven, CT: Yale University Press, 1994. A study of youths who lived outside of the home for part of their adolescence, this text does particularly well at capturing the voices of adolescence. Ben-Amos argues that although youths entered the workplace at earlier ages during this period, there was a long period before they achieved independence and acquired the rights of adulthood.

Classen, Albrecht. *Childhood in the Middle Ages And the Renaissance: The Results of a Paradigm Shift in the History of Mentality*. Berlin, Germany: Walter de Gruyter, 2005. In his analysis of the period of the Italian Renaissance, Classen demonstrates through prescriptive literature and other writings of men of the period that there existed an attitude of "intentional parenthood" among fathers of the middling and elite classes as early as the fifteenth century.

Cunningham, Hugh. *Children and Childhood in Western Society Since 1500*. London, UK: Longman, 1995. Cunningham addresses both Europe and North America in this volume, although greater attention is given to the European experience. The book is particularly valuable in demonstrating the significance of various ideological streams on parenting, as well as touching on the intricate variations in parenting in different parts of Europe.

Crawford, Patricia. *Parents of Poor Children in England, 1580–1800*. New York, NY: Oxford University Press, 2010. Crawford does a marvelous job of showing how class matters in terms of parent–child relationships, while showing that there are many variations within working-class parenthood. She uses numerous primary sources to demonstrate the struggles that many poor parents faced and the difficult choices they had to make during this period.

Fass, Paula S., and Michael Grossberg, eds. *Reinventing Childhood After World War II*. Philadelphia, PA: University of Pennsylvania Press, 2011. This edited volume is one of the first to address the transformation of childhood and the family in the United States after World War II. The essays build upon each other and provide extremely useful approaches for conceptualizing post-war childhood. Especially useful are Paula Fass's article, "The Child-Centered Family" and Stephen Lassonde's, "Ten is the New Fourteen".

Graff, Harvey J. *Conflicting Paths: Growing up in America*. Cambridge, MA: Harvard University Press, 1995. This innovative book examines the lives of a number of American youths from the eighteenth to the twentieth centuries, probing into the many different paths to adulthood taken by boys and girls from different ethnic, class, and regional backgrounds. He primarily relies on primary sources and seeks to provide a rather comprehensive account of the individual youth he discusses and in doing so illuminates some of the major themes in the history of youth during the periods he covers.

Greven, Philip. *The Protestant Temperament: Patterns of Child-Rearing, Religious Experience, and the Self in Early America*. Chicago, IL: University of Chicago Press, 1988. This classic text does a great job of framing the various types of child-rearing strategies present in early America. Greven demonstrates that there was no one singular approach to parenting, but that differences in religious sensibility and region contributed to differences in parenting throughout this period.

Hanawalt, Barbara A. *Growing Up in Medieval London: The Experience of Childhood in History*. New York, NY: Oxford University Press USA, 1995. Although this book is focused on the late medieval era, Hanawalt's work has been justly praised as being one of the best rebuttals of the Ariès thesis that medieval parents did not have a conception of childhood, or recognize the various stages of childhood. Using a vast array of sources in addition to published literature, including court records, guild records, and wills, Hanawalt reconstructs both social attitudes toward children and the experiences of children in families, in servant quarters, and playing with their peers.

Hiner, N. Ray, and Joseph M. Hawes, eds. *Growing Up in America: Children in Historical Perspective*. Urbana, IL: University of Illinois Press, 1985. This groundbreaking collection of essays set the framework for much of the work on the history of childhood to come in the United States. Various essays challenge previous thought about the relationship between parents and children, particularly the diversity and meaning of various parenting practices in early America. The authors also raise important questions in regard to the historiography of childhood that continue to have salience today.

Heywood, Colin. *A History of Childhood: Children and Childhood in the West from Medieval to Modern Times*. Cambridge, UK: Polity, 2002. This is a very comprehensive overview of the history of childhood primarily in Europe, with portions of the book addressing the complicated terrain of parent–child relations. The book addresses particularly well the interactional nature of parent–child relationships as well as class differences in child rearing.

Lassonde, Stephen. *Learning to Forget: Schooling and Family Life in New Haven's Working Class, 1870–1940*. New Haven, CT: Yale University Press, 2005. This eloquent text illuminates the experiences of Italian immigrant families, especially as they come into contact with public schooling in a US city. Although regional, Lassonde's study demonstrates the significance of schooling in reconstructing family life and altering the nature of the parent–child relationship.

Mintz, Steven. *Huck's Raft: A History of American Childhood*. Cambridge, MA: Belknap Press of Harvard University Press, 2004. Mintz's book is the most comprehensive account of childhood in the United States, especially in its coverage of children's lives from different class, race, and regional backgrounds. Starting with the Revolutionary War and ending with contemporary parental "panics," the book sheds important light on the meaning of the past in helping us to analyze current developments in the history of parents and children.

Ozment, Steven E. *When Fathers Ruled: Family Life in Reformation Europe*. Cambridge, MA: Harvard University Press, 1983. Ozment traces the development of intentional parenting to the reformation period and demonstrates how much importance advice writers of the period attached to fathers, both as heads of the family and as parents. The book contains numerous primary sources that prove his contention that the period was pivotal for shaping the Western European worldview in regard to families, parents, and children.

Pollock, Linda. *A Lasting Relationship: Parents and Children Over Three Centuries*. Hanover and London: University Press of New England, 1990. This is an enormously useful book providing primary sources on a number of subjects relating to the parent–child relationship from the seventeenth through the nineteenth centuries in England and the United States. Pollock is strongly associated with the "continuity" school, arguing that Philippe Aries and others have failed to recognize the many ways in which parents of the past are similar to today's parents.

Stearns, Peter N. *Anxious Parents: A History of Modern Childrearing in America*. New York, NY: New York University Press, 2003. This book covers a number of essential topics in the history of twentieth century parenting, with an emphasis on the various developments that have exacerbated parental anxiety. Stearns focuses on the role of the child sciences in creating an image of children as vulnerable and in need of careful surveillance in order to be happy, healthy, and successful.

6

CHILDREN'S WORK IN COUNTRYSIDE AND CITY

Colin Heywood

Putting children to work full time, with all the risks to their health and education it involves, is now unacceptable in the West. Childhood in the twenty-first century requires sufficient time for developing a healthy body, going through the school system, and playing among family and friends – without the burden of having to earn one's keep. Some part-time employment may be regarded as acceptable, and even beneficial, but not if it interferes with schooling.

It is therefore difficult from our present-day perspective to come to terms with the widespread employment of children in the past. This is particularly the case as most studies of child labor by historians have tended to focus on the Industrial Revolution period, taking a lead from those reformers who were outraged by the notorious conditions in its textile mills and coal mines. Some of the moral fervor of the assorted band of philanthropists, industrialists, and trade unionists who led the campaigns rubbed off on these scholars. The British historian E.P. Thompson famously described the exploitation of industrial child labor as "one of the most shameful events in our history." In the United States, Walter Trattner thought it "one of the gravest social injustices in American life."[1] Theirs was a stirring story of mill owners imposing the relentless rhythm of the machine on young children, parents expecting a wage from their offspring as soon as possible, and officials off-loading large numbers of paupers onto the mills to spare the public purse. Doubtless this remains the most common image of children's work in the public perception today. The emphasis among historians in this camp, generally on the left of the political spectrum, was very much on the need for state intervention to counter the excesses of an unregulated capitalist system. With broad support for a welfare state or some form of welfare legislation over much of the twentieth century, the time was ripe for a sympathetic treatment of pioneering efforts in this direction. Even better, it seemed that after a long struggle the reformers had won their battle against the exploitative nature of child labor: the school had replaced work for the young; however, this reassuring line of argument did not go unchallenged.

Other historians, convinced of the advantages of free markets, followed in the footsteps of those nineteenth-century industrialists who were viscerally opposed to intervention by the state on the shop floor. They cast doubt on the lurid image of working conditions in the mills put about by hostile witnesses among the reformers. They argued that child labor laws undermined the competitiveness of key industries, deprived working-class families of much-needed income, and disrupted the training of young people working beside adults. Much better than legislation, they concluded,

125

was the laissez-faire approach of allowing market forces to improve the lot for children. The growing preference for market solutions in political circles from the 1980s gave this line of argument a boost.

During the late twentieth and early twenty-first centuries, a number of developments have compelled historians to take a more pragmatic approach. They have had to take into account the remarkable persistence of child labor in developing countries, and even in wealthy countries such as the United States and Britain, where "out of school work" for a minority of children involves excessively long hours or unsuitable jobs.[2] This gives a hint that child labor may be more advantageous to the capitalist system than was once thought. Historians have also had to admit that their moral judgments on supposedly greedy and ignorant parents were often unjustified. Having followed economists in examining household budgets, they now have incontrovertible evidence regarding the poverty that blighted the existence of many families. Such studies brought out the important contribution of children (including those in their twenties or thirties still living with their parents) to the family income. The move to give children a voice in their own history, through such sources as autobiographies and oral histories, reveals how the young themselves felt about matters such as starting work or their working conditions. From this perspective, they have not necessarily looked like the passive victims of rapacious adults because they often welcomed the opportunity to take their share of work in the family.

Historians now make an effort to grasp the numerous contexts for the employment of children, including family farms, artisan workshops and employers' homes, as well as factories. They accept that some jobs taken on by children were more harmful or "exploitative" than others. They also generally agree that widespread poverty meant that many families in the West have had to rely on regular work from their children in order to survive. Even at the height of the Industrial Revolution in Britain, banning child labor outright would probably have done more harm than good. Finally, in seeking causes for the decline of child labor in the formal sector of the economy, that is to say the large factories and mines subject to official regulation, something of a consensus has emerged that an eclectic list of influences came into play. In varying degrees, historians now include technical progress in industry, rising real wages, cultural change and state intervention among these.

This chapter will therefore examine the changing social and economic context for the employment of children, the type of work they undertook in agriculture, manufacturing and the services, and the links between training and work. It will also assess the impact of child labor on the health and education of children, and investigate the reasons for the long-term shift from work to school as an essential feature of a modern childhood. The underlying assumption is that for most of the period, to quote the economist Kaushik Basu, "there are worse things that can happen to children than having to work."[3]

Changing patterns of employment for children

Working the land

Village children in the West started work at a tender age during the early modern period (*c.*1500–1800), either on a farm or in a domestic workshop. Farming families had always endured a precarious existence, vulnerable to such shocks as a spell of illness or unemployment, harvest failures, epidemics among livestock, and attacks from marauding armies. Given the abject poverty of many in the villages, and the multitude of tasks facing those employed on the land, it is hardly surprising that children were soon drawn into the world of work. The youthfulness of the population was another spur, with as much as half of the population under twenty. Moreover, villagers were convinced that the best way to learn the ways of farming was on the job, with an early start essential if the boy or girl was to acquire all the skills and the discipline they would need later in life. Hence it was not only the poor who insisted that their offspring begin work early. From around the age of six or seven, children were able to take on little tasks such as minding younger siblings, bird scaring, picking stones from fields, hoeing in the vegetable plots, collecting firewood, fetching water from a well, and minding the family's livestock. When the demand for labor on the land reached its peak during the summer, children worked in the fields beside the haymakers and reapers. At this stage, children might still play as well as work, when out herding with others of their own age in the pastures for example. The meager wages they could earn if they hired themselves out as day laborers showed that they remained dependent on their parents for their subsistence.

Once they reached their teens, the young everywhere could start more demanding work. Girls spent much of their time beside the older women on the farm, with tasks that ranged from preparing meals in the home to helping in the fields. Boys meanwhile began to bend their backs to some of the heavier work on a farm, such as leading a plough team and threshing cereals. By their mid to late teens, they would emerge as fully-fledged farm workers. A common practice in early modern Europe, particularly in the northern and western parts of the continent, was for the young of both sexes to leave home during their early teens for farm service with another family. Those from poor families might start earlier, so that there was one less mouth to feed for their parents. Charities and parish officials often boarded out pauper apprentices to local farmers and artisans from an early age. In December 1831, for example, seven-year-old Carl Degerstrom was boarded out by auction in Skellefteå, a rural parish in northern Sweden, when his family could no longer support its five dependent children.[4] As a rule, though, employers preferred to hire adolescents and young adults who were more use to them around a farm.[5] In this way, village custom was for the young to pass through a series of stages at work, graded informally according to their age and physical strength. It was a custom that gave them some protection from abuse.

With peasants making up an estimated 85 percent of the European population in 1500, it is hardly surprising that agriculture was the largest employer of children in each country until the nineteenth century at the earliest. Even in Britain, fast becoming the "workshop of the world," the category "agriculture, livestock and fisheries" still occupied more young males than any other in the 1851 census, accounting for approximately one-third of the age group ten to fourteen. Sooner or later, industrialization brought a decline in the number of children working on the land. Yet agriculture also proved stubborn in holding on to some of its child workers well into the twentieth century – and beyond for an unfortunate minority. Compulsory schooling from the late nineteenth century onwards did not stop parents on family farms in particular from expecting work from their offspring before and after class, or even from pulling them out of school whenever it suited them. Ephraïm Grenadou, born into a French peasant family near Chartres in 1897, recalled:

> Every day on returning from school I had my work to do. At midday as in the evening, I cut up two or three buckets of beets for the livestock; I mucked out the stables; and I fetched one or two barrow loads of fodder for them from a barn we had on the other side of the village.

He did not do well at school. There were complaints from all over Europe and the United States of high levels of absenteeism from schools in rural areas: for example, a survey conducted by the Ministry of Education in Spain in 1924 found that the employment of boys and girls on the land, and of girls for housework, was the main cause of non-attendance. Even during the twenty-first century, children as young as eight and nine are to be found in the United States among landless migrants from Mexico and Central America, helping with the hand harvesting of various fruits, vegetables, nuts, and flowers. Although a "small and shrinking proportion of the migrant workforce," their presence highlights the difficulty of enforcing regular schooling among this type of labor, and the peculiar reluctance of legislators in the United States, swayed by a long tradition of agrarian romanticism, to regulate child labor on the land.[6]

Conditions naturally varied according to the circumstances of the children: life in the mountains was more spartan than on the plains; arable, pastoral and mixed-farming areas all required different sets of tasks; the better-off were under less pressure to start work early than the poor; children employed on family farms were often thought to be less at risk of exploitation than those employed on large commercial farms. In the United States, for example, the family farms of New England and the Midwest, cultivated for the most part by a "sturdy middle class" of white people, produced a less oppressive working environment in the post-Civil War period than that faced by poor black sharecroppers on the industrial plantations of the South. Perhaps worst of all was the predicament of those bound into servitude. The "Runaway Slave" William Grimes, a case in point, recalled that his early introduction to life on such plantations before Emancipation was a grim regime of heavy labor, frequent floggings, and an inadequate diet. The distribution of tasks according to the age and sex of the family members might also be relaxed where labor was in short supply. On small family farms, everyone did whatever was required: Arthur Young (1741–1820) observed that smallholders in the north of England thought nothing of turning out a wife or a daughter to drive a plough in the middle of winter.

Employment in the craft economy

Children in the small workshops of the manufacturing sector also faced an early introduction to work. Like their counterparts on the farms, all but the very wealthy began by watching and listening to what was going on around them, helping their parents with little tasks at work, and taking over some of the domestic chores. From there, possibly after some time in school, the conventional route into the handicraft trades in Europe and colonial America was through an apprenticeship. From the later medieval period onwards, this was the institution responsible for transmitting the skills of a trade to adolescents, and in some cases to children. No less important, its aim was to impress upon them the moral and political values of their new milieu. The apprentices signed a contract agreeing to work for the master for a precisely-defined period, and in return the employer pledged to teach them their craft. Girls formed a substantial minority of apprentices and their job prospects at the end were inferior to those of boys. Apprentices usually started their service in their mid teens, or even later in the big cities. The only trades likely to apprentice the very young were those requiring little in the way of skill and physical strength. In the small-metal trades of the Black Country (England), such as nail making, children were often indentured between the ages of seven and thirteen. Pauper apprentices were another group likely to be placed early in a trade. In England, over 90 percent were put out between the ages of seven and nine, often into the poorer trades such as shoemaking and weaving.[7]

By the eighteenth century, the apprenticeship system was attracting a barrage of criticism, almost invariably on the grounds that it was "long, expensive, and superfluous."[8] Critics considered apprenticeship part-and-parcel of the whole regulatory regime mounted by the guilds and governments, which, they felt, was stifling economic development. Historians have often taken the same line; yet there were signs that the craft economy of the late medieval and early modern period was "dynamic, flexible, and creative,"[9] because the detailed regulations drawn up by the guilds were not necessarily reflected in practices on the shop floor. Many apprentices set up on their own before completing the full period of training. There was also evidence from southern England of apprenticeships becoming shorter and confining themselves to trade skills (at the expense of a more general education) from the mid-eighteenth century onwards. Moreover, large numbers of female artisans operated beyond the reach of guild regulations, notably in the textile trades, as did large numbers of males known in France as *faux-ouvriers* (false workers). Their origins are difficult to trace, but if some had served a formal apprenticeship, others had learned the rudiments of their trade informally "on-the-job" with their parents or an employer. In the handloom weaving industry of the Pays de Caux (France), for example, boys in their early teens often learned from their fathers by working on a second loom. In colonial America, the guild system never took hold, so informal apprenticeship was the norm. Samuel Lane, born in 1718, joined his New Hampshire family in combining farming, tanning, and shoemaking. Aged nine, he started to learn how to make shoes; at fifteen, his father moved him on to the more demanding trade of tanning.[10]

More generally, historians seeking to "rehabilitate" the guilds argue that the craft trades proved capable of responding to increases in demand well into the nineteenth century – with important implications for child workers. In place of the staid image of artisan workshops operating as isolated units of production, in the words of James R. Farr, "shops proliferated, and were interconnected in a dizzyingly complex network of credit and subcontracting relations."[11]

Looking beyond the craft economy, there was also the massive expansion of industry in the countryside from the sixteenth century onwards. Merchants in the towns sought to escape the influence of the guilds by putting out work to peasant-workers, who in their turn were eager to fill in the "dead season" in agriculture. These "proto-industrial" forms took off over much of northern and western Europe, in such trades as hand spinning, hosiery, lace making and metal working. Historians have long recognized that the grueling combination of farm and industrial work, or full-time employment in a "proto-industry," made increased demands on children and youth as well as on other members of the family.

The historian Jan de Vries argues persuasively that there was an "industrious revolution" in north-western Europe and colonial America between the mid-seventeenth and the early nineteenth centuries. This involved households reducing their leisure time, and reallocating labor from goods produced for their own consumption to marketed goods. Children would have benefited from the increase in material possessions – but at the cost of more work and little education.[12] Rather than playing or attending class, those in the handicraft trades of the towns and the villages spent their time on such tasks as hand spinning, winding bobbins for weavers, embroidering, straw plaiting, and button making. In rural Leicestershire (England), for example, an official enquiry found boys starting work from the age of six as winders in the hosiery industry, and moving on from the age of ten or so to knitting on the stocking frames in the family workshops. Some historians have asserted that this early phase of development saw the "high-water mark" of child labor during the eighteenth century in the British case. At the very least, there is plenty of evidence that child labor was "endemic" in the early industrial economy. It is also worth emphasizing that even in a family workshop, so often romanticized by critics of the factory system, the pressure on children to produce was likely to be intense. As Tessie Liu noted about the Pays de Mauges, in western France, "young children learned early on that people who loved them depended on their labor." For these handloom weavers, this meant disciplining the bodies of their offspring by constant correction to prepare them for the speed and endurance they would need to survive in the trade.[13]

The impact of industrialization

While farm children and apprentices labored quietly in the depths of the countryside or the backstreets of the towns, a new breed appeared during the nineteenth century that excited the imagination of the educated elite: the "eight-year-old worker" of the factory system. This latter group massed very publicly on the streets of the manufacturing centers before and after work, and brought the dramatic image of young children harnessed to powerful machinery. But it is now evident that this spectacle of factory children has mesmerized historians as well as contemporaries. Some qualification is necessary before proceeding further because children in factories and mines were always a minority. Recent research on national accounts reveals that in Great Britain, the outstanding leader of the Industrial Revolution of the late eighteenth and early nineteenth centuries, economic development was more gradual than once thought. In the British case, and even more so on the continent, one should really think of small islands of modern industrialization for long surrounded by a sea of pre-industrial forms.

All the same, it was industries such as textiles that provided the leading sectors for the Industrial Revolution. Among the early starters, notably Britain, Belgium, France, and the United States, industries grew rapidly, pioneered new, factory-housed, power-driven machinery, and competed fiercely with the smaller workshops in some trades. And they did take on large numbers of child workers: firstly in these pioneering areas, and later in the southern and eastern parts of Europe, and in Scandinavia. Measuring the employment of children in large-scale industry is not easy, given that the population censuses were slow to latch on to it. A clue comes from study of industrialization in the north-eastern region of the United States during the first half of the nineteenth century, based on data from the census of manufacturing in Connecticut, Massachusetts, New Hampshire, New York, and Rhode Island. It found that the proportion of the labor force composed of women and children "seems likely to have grown from about 10 percent early in the nineteenth century to roughly 40 percent by 1832; and although it began to decline soon afterward, it remained above 30 percent in 1850." Similar findings, in this case focused entirely on child workers, emerge from a study of household budgets in Britain. It revealed an "enormous growth in the employment of children in factories" during the classic Industrial Revolution period, with a near doubling of the proportion employed between the periods 1787–1816 and 1817–1839.[14] The early cotton spinneries, it is well known, relied heavily on child workers: they could handle the light, semi-skilled work on offer, and were more willing to submit to the discipline of the factory system than adults. The first mill in the United States, for example, began in a small way at Pawtucket (Rhode Island) in 1790. Ten years later, it was employing around 100 child workers on its water-powered carding machines and Arkwright water frames, plus a few adults to supervise. In a survey of water-powered cotton mills in England and Scotland during the 1780s, two-thirds of the work force were labeled "children."[15]

Conveniently, given the growing demand for child workers in the early textile mills, and a swelling tide of poor during the late eighteenth century, large numbers of pauper apprentices were on hand to provide cheap, indentured labor. Poor relief agencies adapted the well-established system of apprenticing paupers to farmers or artisans to the needs of industry by handing over batches of children to mill owners. In France, the upheavals of revolution and war during the 1790s encouraged a surge of requests from employers to the hard-pressed authorities. The owners of a cotton spinning mill offered the Minister of the Interior, Jean-Antoine Chaptal, "to employ as soon as possible some children of the Nation of both sexes: the nature of their operations lent themselves advantageously; the water-powered machines only required children for a large part of their service." In England, John Birch's Blackbarrow mill in Lancashire relied heavily on this type of labor for nearly twenty years during the late eighteenth and early nineteenth centuries, taking 256 paupers from the London parish of St Clement Danes.[16] The pathetic figure of the pauper child at the mercy of heartless adults, best known in the case of Charles Dickens's Oliver Twist, provided a potent image for child labor reformers during the nineteenth century.

Although early textile machinery could be operated independently by children, larger machinery and new generations that had grown up with the factory system meant that by the 1830s in Britain adults were becoming more prominent in the labor force. Children then worked instead as their assistants, as in mule spinning, power-loom weaving, calico printing, and hosiery. Other countries followed suit. In the spinning shop of the Sokolovskaia Cotton Mill in Vladimir province (Russia), a census of 1882 revealed the child workers to be employed in auxiliary jobs that included setting up bobbins, piecing, and cleaning machinery.[17] Similarly, in a few other industries where child workers were prominent, they worked beside adults, carrying bottles for glassblowers in the glassworks, folding and stacking paper in the paper mills, and helping to assemble boots and shoes in shoe factories. Children were also extensively employed in the mining industry, accounting for nearly half the workforce in England, opening and shutting doors in the ventilation system, hauling wagons and, on the surface, sorting coal.

Child workers therefore remained essential for the functioning of such enterprises, even as ancillary workers. They worked the same hours as everyone else, with twelve- or thirteen-hour days the norm, and often had to keep up with the pace of work of an adult. They also followed a well-worn path in learning their trades by working beside adults, and some of them would slowly work their way up the hierarchy of jobs. Some started very early, even from the age of six or seven, and children under the age of twelve or so were numerous in many workshops. Others delayed entry until their teens, particularly in trades requiring physical strength and stamina, such as basic metallurgy and machine building. It is also worth noting that mechanization was not the sole influence on the composition of the work force. Employers could choose a range of strategies, taking into account such circumstances as the labor supply available and the strength of organized labor. In Lancashire and Ghent, the boys among the piecers would become spinners on the early hand mules; in country mills around Glasgow it was the girls (on short mules). In the East Midlands of England and in the Champagne region of France, young lads learned how to operate the larger knitting machines; in Ontario, it was girls.[18]

During the latter half of the nineteenth century, child labor in industry started a long decline in the West. Isolated pockets have continued through to the present in the developed world, notably in southern Europe. In Portugal, for example, a report by Anti-Slavery International in 1992 found evidence of children working in the shoe, clothing, ceramics, and stone-breaking industries. More typical of the northern part would be the case of Norway, where a study of paid work among schoolchildren dating from 1912 found that full-time working and industrial employment had all but disappeared by then.[19] Henceforth, school rather than the shop floor was where children acquired many of the skills and the values they would need later in life, and the vast majority of young people found their jobs in the service sector rather than in manufacturing.

The service sector

Contemporary attention in the more advanced economies of the West therefore shifted from around the 1880s to "out of school" work for children: jobs taken on before and after classes, at weekends and during the holidays. This included paid work in retailing, selling newspapers, running errands, delivering milk, and minding babies. There was also an awareness that young lads who had left school were ending up in "blind alley" jobs in these areas, boding ill for youth and adult unemployment in the future. In truth, the services had always employed many young people. The streets of the big cities teemed with young people involved in such activities as hawking, sweeping crossings for pedestrians, running errands, shining shoes, performing acrobatics, and playing music. There were also the notorious chimney sweeps, who were conspicuous though hardly numerous.

More important in number than the visible street workers was the vast army of domestic servants employed by middle- and upper-class households, an occupation that became increasingly feminized from the seventeenth century onwards in northern Europe. According to the 1881 census in Britain, by that date no less than 45.3 percent of all girls listed with an occupation came under this heading. Domestic work provided an opportunity to accumulate some hard-earned savings before marriage through a grueling regime of cooking, cleaning, running errands, and helping with the laundry. It certainly declined rapidly during the twentieth century when compulsory schooling began to have a significant effect, and when young women could seek a more independent existence in shops and offices.

Historians tended to assume that child work gradually withered away in the developed economies of the world during the twentieth century. In reality, the casual work that exercised contemporaries around 1900 continued, and children in family businesses discreetly helped their parents with their workloads. During the 1970s, observers "rediscovered" child labor. They became aware that the massive expansion of the service sector during the twentieth century and the numerous part-time jobs it provided were favorable to the employment of the young. Moreover, they noted that from the 1940s, middle-class children were joining their working-class counterparts in this labor market. In some countries, notably the United States and Britain, nearly everyone now combines school with work. The Department of Labor in the former estimated in 2000 that 80 to 90 percent of high school students had entered into formal employment at some point. An investigation of schoolchildren in Baltimore at the end of the twentieth century found that approximately half those aged thirteen and fourteen worked during the school year, rising to 75 percent by the age of fifteen. Relatively high rates of child employment were also found in Denmark and The Netherlands. In the youth labor market in general, if a fortunate few have landed glamorous positions as models, musicians, and sports stars, many others have had to put up with "McJobs:" low status, low pay employment common in fast food outlets and shops.[20]

Child work and child welfare

Throughout the early modern period, governments were more concerned to find work for children than to rescue them from it. Hugh Cunningham makes the important point that the widespread employment of children in the past that has so attracted the attention of historians risks masking the large numbers of young people who were unable to find work at particular times of the year or in particular locations. That is to say many children were "unemployed," in the sense that they were not in paid work or productive labor in the home, nor were they releasing adults for such positions. The authorities in various parts of Europe and North America therefore welcomed the spread of domestic workshops and manufactures as a new source of work for children – not least for the rising tide of orphans and abandoned children that they struggled to cope with during the eighteenth century. Eventually, though, further industrialization provoked a series of reform campaigns across the nations, unleashing impassioned debates on the impact of child labor on the population.

Reformers argued that working in industrial occupations undermined the health, morality and education of children. Defenders of the factory system marshaled contradictory evidence in all of these areas; historians have since tended to line up with one side or the other. Today it is customary to distinguish the very worst forms of child labor that should be condemned out of hand, such as slavery and bonded labor, from hazardous work that may, according to circumstances, harm children, such as employment on dangerous machinery or carrying heavy loads.[21] Early reformers, taking their lead from the British, generally started by concentrating their fire on work with textile machinery and employment underground in the coal mines. They were aware of the risks of abuse to pauper apprentices, bound to long-term contracts by those responsible for poor relief, and to slaves on the southern plantations of the United States – though powerful vested interests ensured that these forms of employment persisted for a long time. Conversely, there was a general feeling that work on the land was healthy and morally invigorating for young people, except employment in agricultural gangs.

The first critics during the late eighteenth and early nineteenth centuries raised the alarm over the health of children working in the textile trades. Doctors and other reformers highlighted the threats from punishingly long hours of work in the mills, the relentless pace of the machines, brutal treatment from overseers, frequent accidents from uncovered belts, shafts, and flywheels, and the foul atmosphere produced by the stench of machine oil and dust swirling around from the raw materials. They described in vivid detail the pitiful condition of factory children they met. Dr Villermé in France suggested in 1840:

> All pale, nervous, slow in their movements, quiet at their games, they present an outward appearance of misery, of suffering, of dejection that contrasts with the rosy color, the plumpness, the petulance and all the signs of glowing health that one notices in children of the same age each time that he leaves a manufacturing to enter an agricultural canton.[22]

There was indeed much marshalling of statistics in continental Europe, where military conscription records allowed reformers to compare the state of youth in industrial and agricultural areas. The inevitable conclusion, from a careful selection of examples, was that the new manufacturing centers produced more than their fair share of puny specimens unfit for military service. Other industries accused of taking a heavy toll on child workers included the coal mines, notoriously dark, dank, and dangerous, and the glassworks, which required constant coming and going between glassblowers and the furnaces.

Defenders of the system, such as Andrew Ure in England, countered with a reassuring vision of the work as mere gymnastics, the machinery bearing the burden of manual labor and allowing children plenty of time for rest. They certainly had a strong case that some of the worst conditions for children were to be found in the smaller workshops, given the long hours and repetitive tasks evident, for example, in the silk-weaving industry of Lyon or the metal trades in Birmingham (England). Employers claimed that an early start was necessary to acquire the skills and work habits of a trade, even in the mills, and parents were keen for their children to gain a foothold in the job market.

Evidence from the children themselves on the nature of their work was as equivocal as that from adults. Some depicted their experiences on the shop floor as one long round of misery. The most famous was Robert Blincoe, a parish apprentice sent in 1799 from Saint Pancras workhouse in London to cotton mills in Nottinghamshire and Derbyshire. There he suffered from a meager diet, a fourteen-hour day, and "brutal and ferocious and merciless over lookers." By the 1820s, he was "diminutive, as to stature" and with his knees "grievously distorted." Alice Foley, employed in a large weaving shed in Lancashire during the 1900s, suffered no such brutality, and lived at home, but she too struggled with "long and exhausting hours" of monotonous work, clouds of dust and lint all around her, and degrading, unsanitary conditions.

Other reminiscences suggested a more relaxed and salubrious atmosphere in the mills. Lucy Larcom suffered the fate of many orphans, following the death of her father, in going into spinning mills at Lowell (Massachusetts) during the 1830s around the age of twelve; however, she recalled that she was pleased to feel that she was no longer a burden to anybody, and the work, changing bobbins on the spinning frames every forty-five minutes or so, was not hard. "The intervals we spent frolicking around among the spinning frames, teasing and talking to the older girls, or entertaining ourselves with games and stories in a corner." In France, Norbert Truquin found life in a woolen-spinning mill during the 1840s far superior to that in a small wool combing shop. In the mill, he enjoyed the company of other children, and when the overseers were not around, "we told stories, or discussed plays in the theatre, some jokers improvised a pulpit and amused themselves preaching; time passed cheerfully."[23] Such contradictions expose the simplistic picture presented by so many polemical works. There were signs that conditions were more dangerous and unhealthy in the early rather than the later mills; that small, barely-profitable outfits always contrasted badly with a few large, "model" enterprises; that paupers were more at risk of abuse than "free" workers with families behind them; and that some trades were inherently more pernicious for health than others.

Contemporaries took very seriously the question of the influence of child factory labor on morality. Reformers painted lurid pictures of innocent children working outside the family home and surrounded by "half-naked" adults in the steamy atmosphere of a mill. Employers countered that they supervised their workers closely and, in the larger mills separated the sexes in their workshops. They were aware of the need to reassure parents that their daughters in particular were safe in their workshops. In the Lowell mills of Massachusetts, for example, girls from the age of ten and upwards lodged in company boarding houses "under the charge of respectable women with every provision for religious worship"; in southern France, silk mill owners brought in nuns to supervise dormitories, and in some cases the workshops.[24]

The conflict between school and work was another contentious issue, among working-class parents as well as the elites. Farming families tended to see the primary school as an alien influence brought in from the towns, and made limited demands on it well after it was made compulsory. The apprenticeship system in the towns might also involve the teaching of basic literacy as well as the mysteries of a trade. There were serious questions as to whether schooling was a good investment for working class families during the early nineteenth century, before such jobs as clerk, policeman, and railway worker became available for men and (eventually) women. Legislation invariably included the stipulation that child workers spend some time in class until they had achieved basic literacy – but it usually failed. Such children were often fobbed off with makeshift classes, and in any case they were usually too tired to make much of them. Nonetheless, there was evidence of working-class demand for education in both England and France before it was made compulsory during the 1870s and 1880s – even though this often required the payment of fees. Eventually everyone in the West came round to the view that training for work should start in the schools. Indeed, it can be argued that children are useful in modern society because their schoolwork is a contribution to human capital accumulation as they prepared for their future role in production.[25]

The decline of child labor

From the middle of the nineteenth century onwards, there were signs that child labor in the formal sector of the economy, notably textile mills, factories, and mines, was beginning to decline in those countries that had started early on the path to industrialization. It continued for longer in the informal sector, in "sweatshops" in the clothing trades, for example, and on family farms. But school rather than work became established as a central feature of a modern childhood from the late nineteenth century onwards. Why this shift occurred was, as noted in the introduction, a matter of controversy among historians. The obvious answer would be that legislation gradually drove children out of the workplace. Britain led the way here, with a series of Acts during the late eighteenth and early nineteenth centuries, aimed for the most part at textile mills and coal mines. Others followed during the 1830s and 1840s, including Prussia and France, though Belgium and the United States were conspicuous in waiting much longer. During the 1880s, reformers in Italy lamented that their country was the only "civilized" nation in the world without child labor legislation: even "semi-barbaric" Russia had stolen a march on them.[26] It is indeed hard to imagine employers across the board giving up on their child workers without a struggle when the practice was so deeply embedded in the culture. Working-class parents and even the children colluded with them in resisting change. Nonetheless, this line of argument will only go so far. Clark Nardinelli made the telling point that in Britain the proportion of workers in the textile industries was already starting to fall before factory legislation began to bite during the 1830s. The laws merely encouraged the decline further by raising the costs involved in employing children. Besides, factory legislation invariably regulated rather than abolished child labor. To begin with, legislators underestimated the difficulties of enforcement, and even when they did establish more rigorous systems of inspection, cheating by employers was rife. Arguably, compulsory schooling legislation was more effective in ending child labor, as it was easier to enforce.

One should also acknowledge the moral dimension to child labor reform, with the argument that it was simply wrong, or contrary to Christian belief, to make children work. The new Enlightenment construction of childhood was at first associated with the middle classes, while working-class families held on to the older view that children were like "little animals" that needed to be knocked into shape from an early age. Viviana Zelizer has depicted a long struggle in the United States between the two classes, with the middle-class view that children were "sacred" beings eventually holding sway.[27] Such a change in ideas was indisputably part of the context for general revulsion against child labor. Finally, there is the more material influence of shifts in the workings of the labor market to consider as employers came to question the advantages of employing children, while rising real wages eased the pressure on working-class families to put them out to work.

Improvements to machinery increasingly also had the effect of reducing the demand for child workers. In the spinning mills, for example, the introduction of the self-acting mule from the 1830s meant that fewer threads broke and fewer piecers were needed. In the coal mines, innovations in underground haulage encouraged a reduction in the proportion of young children employed.

Working-class families, for their part, only gradually emerged from their dependence on children's earnings for survival. During the 1830s, for example, Dr Villermé calculated that family budgets among textile workers in France always teetered on the brink of disaster. If both parents were in regular employment, they might get by, but child-rearing responsibilities for the mother led to pressure for her to stay at home and for the older children to start work. In Philadelphia, according to the historian Claudia Goldin, "Children were a major economic resource in the nineteenth-century family, contributing income in normal times and supporting their families in especially difficult times." During the 1880s, immigrant families from Germany and Ireland were more inclined than native-born white families to send their children out to work. Irish children (including those grown up but still living at home) contributed between 38 percent and 46 percent of the family income where there were two parents and a father over fifty. Everywhere, families with a large number of children or a single parent were most inclined to send their offspring out to work rather than to school. Nonetheless, the logic is that a sustained rise in real wages at the very least made compulsory schooling palatable for working-class parents.

Conclusion

Working children were part of everyday life in the West until the late-nineteenth and early-twentieth centuries. National and local governments took it for granted that children among the mass of peasants, artisans, and laborers were better off working than remaining idle. Parents were eager to have some help in the daily struggle for existence, and so start children on some form of "apprenticeship," learning on-the-job the ways of farming, manufacturing, or housekeeping. Children were no less willing to make themselves useful. For them, poverty meant sharing beds, hand-me-down clothes and, most debilitating of all, frequently being hungry. Work would mean long hours out in the fields in all weathers, the occasional heavy-lifting task, or the monotony of sewing, hammering, turning wheels, and so forth, but it also brought a rise in status within the family and the local community, and possibly a little spending money. Custom dictated a gradual insertion into the labor force over a number of years, with parents or local authorities making some effort to protect children from exploitation. Certainly, child workers played their part in the intensification of work that came with industrialization, both in the small workshops and the factories. Yet Peter Stearns is persuasive in arguing that the biggest upheaval in the world history of childhood was the shift from an agricultural to an industrial society. Most importantly, he maintains that the "basic purpose of childhood was redefined," with the school eventually replacing work.[28] In the twenty-first century, it has become common for most young people to combine school with a little work, rather than the other way round.

Notes

1 E. P. Thompson, *The Making of the English Working Classes* (Harmondsworth, UK: Penguin, 1968), 384; Walter L. Trattner, *Crusade for the Children* (Chicago, IL: Quadrangle Books, 1970), 10–11.

2 Phil Mizen, "Child Labor in the Developed Nations Today," in *The World of Child Labor: An Historical and Regional Survey*, ed. Hugh D. Hindman, (New York, NY: M. E. Sharpe, 2009), 62–6.

3 Kaushik Basu, "Child Labor: Cause, Consequence, and Cure, with Remarks on International Labor Standards," *Journal of Economic Literature* 37 (1999): 1083–1119, (1115).

4 Elisabeth Engberg, "Boarded Out by Auction: Poor Children and their Families in Nineteenth-Century Northern Sweden," *Continuity and Change* 19 (2004): 431–57 (431).

5 Ann Kussmaul, *Servants in Husbandry in Early Modern England* (Cambridge, UK: Cambridge University Press, 1981), 72; Michael Mitterauer, "Servants and Youth," *Continuity and Change* 5 (1990): 11–38.

6 Ephraïm Grenadou and Alain Prévost, *Grenadou: paysan français* (Paris, France: Seuil, 1966), 14; José M. Borrás Llop, "Schooling and Child Labour in Spain, circa 1880–1930," *Continuity and Change* 20 (2005): 385–406 (396); Hugh D. Hindman, "Understanding the Persistence of Child Labor in United States Crop Agriculture," in *Child Labor's Global Past, 1650–2000*, eds. Kristoffel Lieten, and Elise van Nederveen Meerkerk (Bern, Switzerland: Peter Lang, 2011), 391–416.

7 Bert De Munck and Hugo Soly, "'Learning on the Shop Floor' in Historical Perspective," in *Learning on the Shop Floor* ed. Bert De Munck et al. (New York, NY: Berghahn Books, 2007), 3–32 (23); Joan Lane, *Apprenticeship in England, 1600–1914* (London, UK: Routledge, 1996), 14, 85; Deborah Simonton, "Apprenticeship: Training and Gender in Eighteenth-Century England," in *Markets and Manufacture in Early Industrial Europe*, ed. Maxine Berg (London and New York: Routledge, 1991), 227–58 (239).

8 Steven L. Kaplan, "L'Apprentissage au XVIIIe siècle: le cas de Paris," *Revue d'histoire moderne et contemporaine* 40 (1993): 436–79 (466–7).

9 James R. Farr, "On the Shop Floor: Guilds, Artisans, and the European Market Economy, 1350–1750," *Journal of Early Modern History* 1 (1997): 24–54 (25).

10 K. D. M. Snell, *Annals of the Labouring Poor* (Cambridge, UK: Cambridge University Press, 1985), chapter 5; Gay Gullickson, *Spinners and Weavers of Auffay* (Cambridge, UK: Cambridge University Press, 1986), 74; W. J. Rorabaugh, *The Craft Apprentice* (New York, NY: Oxford University Press, 1986), 9.

11 Farr, "On the Shop Floor."

12 Jan de Vries, "The Industrial Revolution and the Industrious Revolution," *Journal of Economic History* 54(2) (1994): 249–70.

13 David Levine, *Family Formation in an Age of Nascent Capitalism* (New York, NY: Academic Press, 1972) 28; Jane Humphries, *Childhood and Child Labour in the British Industrial Revolution* (Cambridge, UK: Cambridge University Press, 2010), 29, 366; Tessie P. Liu, *The Weaver's Knot* (Ithaca, NY: Cornell University Press, 1994), 224–5.

14 Claudia Goldin and Kenneth Sokoloff, "Women, Children, and Industrialization in the Early Republic: Evidence from the Manufacturing Censuses," *Journal of Economic History* 42 (1982): 741–74; Sara Horrell and Jane Humphries, "'The Exploitation of Little Children': Child Labor and the Family Economy in the Industrial Revolution," *Explorations in Economic History* 32 (1995): 485–516.

15 Caroline Ware, *The Early New England Cotton Manufacture* (Boston and New York: Houghton Mifflin, 1931), 21–3; Douglas Galbi, "Child Labor and the Division of Labor in the Early English Cotton Mills," *Journal of Population Economics* 10 (1997): 357–75 (358).

16 Serge Chassagne, *Le Coton et ses patrons: France, 1760–1840* (Paris, France: Editions de l'EHHESS, 1991), 241; Katrina Honeyman, *Child Workers in England, 1780–1820* (Aldershot, UK: Ashgate, 2007), chapter 5.

17 Boris B. Gorshkov, *Russia's Factory Children: State, Society, and Law, 1800–1917* (Pittsburgh, PA: University of Pittsburgh Press, 2009), 68–9.

18 Colin Heywood, "Age and Gender at the Workplace: The Historical Experience of Young People in Western Europe and North America," in *Working Out Gender*, ed. Margaret Walsh, (Aldershot, UK: Ashgate, 1999), 48–65 (54–5).

19 Pedro Goulart and Arjun S. Bedi, "A History of Child Labour in Portugal," in *Child Labour's Global Past*, ed. Kristoffel Lieten and Elise van Nederveen Meerkerk, (New York, NY: Peter Lang, 2011), 257–78 (273); and Ellen Schrumpf, "From Full-Time to Part-Time: Working Children in Norway from the Nineteenth to the Twentieth Century," in *Industrious Children*, ed. Ning de Coninck-Smith et al. (Odense, Denmark: University Press of Southern Denmark, 1997), 47–78 (64).

20 Mizen, "Child Labor in the Developed World," 62–6.

21 Hugh D. Hindman, "Worst Forms of Child Labor," in *World of Child Labor*, ed. Hugh D. Hindman, (Armonk, NY: ME Sharpe, 2009), 78-81; Carolyn Tuttle, *Hard at Work in Factories and Mines* (Boulder, CO: Westview Press, 1999); Marjatta Rahikainen, *Centuries of Child Labour* (Aldershot, UK: Ashgate, 2004), chapter 4.

22 Lee Shai Weissbach, *Child Labor Reform in Nineteenth-Century France* (Baton Rouge, LA: Louisiana State University Press, 1989), 49.

23 John Brown, "A Memoir of Robert Blincoe (1832)," in *The Ten Hours Movement in 1831 and 1832*, ed. Kenneth E. Carpenter, (New York, NY: Arno Press, 1972); Alice Foley, *A Bolton Childhood* (Manchester, UK: Manchester University Extra-Mural Department, 1973); Lucy Larcom, *A New England Girlhood* (Williamstown, MA: Corner House Publishers, 1985); and Norbert Truquin, *Mémoires et aventures d'un prolétaire à travers la révolution* (Paris, France: Maspero, 1977).

24 Thomas Dublin, *Women at Work* (New York, NY: Columbia University Press, 1979), chapter 3; Colin Heywood, *Childhood in Nineteenth-Century France* (Cambridge, UK: Cambridge University Press, 1988), 122–4.

25 Mizen, "Child Labor in the Developed Nations," 62-6.

26 Hugh D. Hindman, "Coming to Terms with Child Labor," in *World of Child Labor*, ed. Hugh H. Hindman, (Armonk, NY: ME Sharpe, 2009), 45–8; Carl Ipsen, *Italy in the Age of Pinocchio: Children and Danger in the Liberal Era* (New York, NY: Palgrave Macmillan, 2006), 94.

27 Viviana Zelizer, *Pricing the Priceless Child* (New York, NY: Basic Books, 1985).

28 Peter N. Stearns, *Childhood in World History* (London, UK: Routledge, 2006), 6.

Suggestions for further reading

General surveys

Cunningham, Hugh, and Pier Paolo Viazzo, eds. *Child Labour in Historical Perspective, 1800–1895: Case Studies from Europe, Japan and Colombia*. Florence, Italy: UNICEF, 1996. An eclectic but valuable collection of essays on developments during the nineteenth century.

Hindman, Hugh H., ed. *The World of Child Labor: An Historical and Regional Survey*. Armonk, NY: M.E. Sharpe, 2009. A massive collection of short articles, with coverage of key themes concerning the work of children as well as case studies from all of the main countries in the developed (and developing) world.

Lieten, Kristoffel, and Elise van Nederveen Meerkerk, eds. *Child Labour's Global Past, 1650–2000*. Bern, Switzerland: Peter Lang, 2011. A compendium of essays focusing on the international dimension to child labor, but also including a number of entries on individual countries in the West.

Nardinelli, Clark. *Child Labor and the Industrial Revolution*. Bloomington, IN: Indiana University Press, 1990. An influential work challenging an established view that child labor was necessarily exploitative, and downplaying the influence of state intervention in its decline. Mainly based on the British case but makes some international comparisons.

Rahikainen, Marjatta. *Centuries of Child Labour: European Experiences from the Seventeenth to the Twentieth Century*. Aldershot, UK: Ashgate, 2004. Provides very full account of child labor in all parts of Europe, organized around employment in the various sectors of the economy.

National and regional case studies

de Coninck Smith, Ning, Bengt Sandin, and Ellen Schrumpf, eds. *Industrious Children: Work and Childhood in the Nordic Countries, 1850–1990*. Odense, Denmark: Odense University Press, 1997. A collection of detailed essays covering aspects of child labor in northern Europe during the nineteenth century.

Gorshkov, Boris B. *Russia's Factory Children: State, Society, and Law, 1800–1917*. Pittsburgh, PA: University of Pittsburgh Press, 2009. Gives an outline of child labor practices in agriculture and industry before documenting the campaign to curb work in the factories.

Heywood, Colin. *Childhood in Nineteenth-Century France: Work, Health and Education Among the 'Classes Populaires'*. Cambridge, UK: Cambridge University Press, 1988. Emphasizes the importance of child work in agriculture as well as in industry, and the gradual move from work to school.

Hindman, Hugh H. *Child Labor: An American History*. Armonk, NY: M.E. Sharpe, 2002. A comprehensive and well-documented account of child labor in town and country.

Humphries, Jane. *Childhood and Child Labour in the British Industrial Revolution*. Cambridge, UK: Cambridge University Press, 2010. An innovative study, based on the testimony of around 600 working-class autobiographies, providing some answers to important questions arising from the Industrial Revolution period.

Kirby, Peter. *Child Labour in Britain, 1750–1870*. Basingstoke, UK: Palgrave Macmillan, 2003. A concise survey focusing on the Industrial Revolution period.

Lavalette, Michael, ed. *A Thing of the Past? Child Labour in Britain in the Nineteenth and Twentieth Centuries*. Liverpool, UK: Liverpool University Press, 1999. Draws attention to the persistence of child labor in various forms throughout the twentieth century.

Mokyr, Joel. "Accounting for the Industrial Revolution." In *The Cambridge Economic History of Modern Britain, vol. I: Industrialisation, 1700–1860*, edited by Roderick Floud and Paul Johnson, 1–27. Cambridge, UK: Cambridge University Press, 2004. Emphasizes the gradual nature of economic development in Great Britain during the so-called Industrial Revolution period.

Weissbach, Lee Shai. *Child Labor Reform in Nineteenth-Century France*. Baton Rouge, LA: Louisiana State University Press, 1989. A detailed account of the child labor reform campaign.

Some influential case studies

Bolin-Hort, Per. *Work, Family and the State: Child Labour and the Organisation of Production in the British Cotton Industry, 1780–1920*. Lund, Sweden: Lund University Press, 1989. Confronts the question of "how and why the use of children in cotton factories changed in extent and character from the early industrial capitalism in the late 1780s to the more developed and organized capitalism by 1920," focusing on the influence of the production process, the working-class family, and the state.

Cunningham, Hugh. "The Employment and Unemployment of Children in England, c.1680–1815." *Past & Present* 126 (1999): 115–50. Took an original and even counterintuitive line on child labor by drawing attention to the "large number of children for whom no work was available."

Goldin, Claudia. "Family Strategies and the Family Economy in the Late Nineteenth Century: The Role of Secondary Workers." In *Philadelphia: Work, Space, Family, and Group Experience in the Nineteenth Century*, edited by Theodore Hershberg. New York, NY: Oxford University Press, 1981. An early example of studying child labor through an analysis of family strategies.

Honeyman, Katrina. *Child Workers in England, 1780–1820: Parish Apprenticeship and the Making of the Early Industrial Labour Force*. Aldershot, UK: Ashgate, 2007. An exhaustive study of this important section of the child labor force in industry.

Horrell, Sara, and Jane Humphries. "The Exploitation of Little Children: Child Labor and the Family Economy in the Industrial Revolution." *Explorations in Economic History* 32 (1995): 485–516. Uses a data set of 1,781 working-class household budgets to investigate the work of children in the context of the family economy.

Medick, Hans. "The Proto-Industrial Family Economy: The Structural Functions of Household and Family during the Transition from Peasant Society to Industrial Capitalism." *Social History* 1 (1976): 291–315. Makes clear the increasing pressure on children to work during the period of "proto-industrialization."

Scholliers, Peter. *Wages, Manufacturers and Workers in the Nineteenth-Century Factory*. Oxford, UK: Berg, 1996. A study of an early cotton mill and its labor force in Belgium, the Voortman mill in Ghent, including an important contingent of children and young people.

Tuttle, Carolyn. *Hard at Work in Factories and Mines*, Boulder, CO: Westview Press, 1999. A forceful restatement of the view that the Industrial Revolution in Great Britain brought an increase in the employment of children in industry.

7

CHILDREN AND WAR

James Marten

Toward the end of the First World War, the American economist Irene Osgood Andrews wrote that "family life is defaced beyond recognition."[1] A more accurate observation might have been that, as in any war, it was actually childhood that had been altered almost beyond recognition by the pressures and destruction of the war. Andrews' remark transcends the Great War, of course. Since 1500, children and youths have been tightly bound up in every facet of Western warfare as observers, victims, and participants. Children and youths long to be part of the adult world around them, and wars provide an urgent opportunity to do so. The stakes are higher, of course, than in any other human enterprise. Wars can be catastrophic for children, but they can also be transformative and even liberating. Sometimes they are both.

Children and the nature of warfare

A major factor affecting the ways in which war transforms children's lives is the extent to which any given war is "limited" or "total." Limited warfare emerged in the sixteenth and seventeenth centuries and was fought largely by professional armies, maneuvering outside of heavily populated areas, without the devastating sieges that in earlier times could end in the slaughter of the population of entire cities. Under this doctrine, children and other civilians were less obviously targeted by warring nations than they were before and as they would be again in the twentieth century.

Even ostensibly "limited" wars could clearly turn into catastrophes for civilians. Any time an army passed or a battle was fought nearby, civilians suffered from dislocation, food shortages, and disease. As the historian William Beik writes, "Contact with military activity was without question the worst thing that could happen to a civilian population."[2] Peasants living near campaign routes or battlefields suffered the most, of course, but even in peacetime or between battles, civilians bore much of the cost of supporting the military, which, despite reforms during the 1600s and after, still relied on foraging and outright stealing from their unprotected countrymen. During the religious wars of the seventeenth century, for instance, the province of Burgundy was repeatedly overrun. Troops stole property, indiscriminately killed men, women, and children, and generally made life miserable for the civilians in their path. In northern France in the middle of the seventeenth century, a two-week stay by an army near Neubourg during the Fronde resulted in the destruction of two hundred buildings and, according to eyewitness reports, widespread begging and even abandonment by residents. During the War of the Spanish Succession (1701–14), Provence suffered from a typhus epidemic and actual starvation because French troops confiscated virtually all of the food in the region and the men were drafted to work on fortifications. Royal edicts and army regulations tried to control commanders and their troops and set up regular methods for obtaining supplies and requisitioning quarters, but the presence of an army for a month or a day had dire effects on all members of the population.

Sixteenth- and seventeenth-century wars relied to a great extent on domestic militias, which, combined with heavy-handed recruitment – including "pressing" young men into the navy – often drained young men and boys from communities. In England, up to 30 percent of males of military age could be mobilized at the outset of war. That left older men, women, and especially boys and girls to take the places of absent men on farms and in shops. Families were broken up at least temporarily and often permanently, as men died of disease or were killed in battle, wives and children moved away, or maimed soldiers returned, unable to support their families. Wars forced large-scale population movements and sparked increased rates of illegitimate births. Even far from the fighting, communities could be ravaged by the proximity of army units they were forced to support; diseases caused by exposure to sick soldiers and by poor diets caused more hardship and death among civilians than actual fighting. Several hundred thousand Russian civilians, including many children, died as the result of Napoleon's invasion of Russia in 1812, and civilians were also put at risk in the popular uprisings of the late 1840s throughout Europe, which often took place in cities, where it was harder to separate combatants from non-combatants. In America, residents of the Confederate states increasingly felt the "hard hand of war," in the famous words of General William T. Sherman, as US troops targeted civilian property and drove tens of thousands of women and children from their homes, especially during the Union army's 1864–5 campaigns in Georgia, the Carolinas, and Virginia.[3] But neither children nor their civilian parents were necessarily the targets of these policies, at least not as *people* – as opposed to faceless workers and occupants of farms and plantations providing sustenance to the rebels.

The transition from "limited" to "total" war – although not linear or universal – was partly the result of the politicization of cultural and social issues – religion, the effects of economic change, ethnicity – which inevitably brings communities, families, and children into harm's way. Ideology was also a major factor in wars fought after the middle of the eighteenth century. Civil wars, in particular, have always been likely to draw children and youths into harm's way. These wars are characterized by rebel armies, militias, or irregular forces fighting against standing armies of the government or one another. By necessity the former rely on the material and moral support – willing or unwilling – of the societies from which they are recruited, and the latter usually are unable or unwilling to distinguish between combatants and non-combatants. Such civil wars have traditionally found children and youths serving as soldiers or in supporting roles as cooks and camp servants, or even as spies. With their often shifting political alliances, flexible battle fronts, and extremely high rates of service by men of military age, civil wars are also most likely to disrupt local economies, leading children to take on important economic responsibilities, causing a decline in the quality of life and availability of necessities, forcing widespread displacement of populations and, in many cases, encouraging atrocities against civilians. Malnourishment is a common but difficult to measure effect of military campaigns as agricultural production is interrupted by destruction, or able-bodied men are siphoned off.

"Total" war came to the indigenous children of the Western hemisphere long before the end of the so-called Age of Limited War. Native children living in areas over which Europeans or Americans sought to project their power were directly targeted in wars of conquest from the beginning of the European exploration in North and South America through the end of the nineteenth century. They proved the point that limited war from the standpoint of the invading power, if successful, often became a "total war" for the society under attack, leading to the destruction of traditional political and economic institutions, heavy loss of life, and irrevocable intrusions into social and cultural traditions. Campaigns against native Americans by the US army were perfect examples: war consumed very few of the country's resources and posed very little risk to white society, while the tribes against whom its members fought risked everything and were exposed to the most complete of total wars. Moreover, in such wars of empire, virtually all civilian casualties and all societal disruption were endured by the indigenous peoples.

The process was repeated throughout the first three centuries of British settlement and American expansion in North America, from the Massachusetts militia's 1637 burning of the Pequot town of Mystic and the massacre of virtually all of its seven hundred men, women, and children, to the scorched earth campaigns against tribe after tribe during the quarter century after the Civil War.

Ironically, even as children were being slaughtered with their parents in the wars of conquest against the indigenous peoples in North America, Africa, and Asia, international efforts were made to establish rules of warfare that would protect not only prisoners of war but also civilians. The Brussels Conference of 1876, for instance, declared that towns without military garrisons should not be attacked and that the civilian populations of fortified towns should be given the chance to evacuate.

Such efforts failed in the face of the ability of industrialized societies to wage war at increasingly deadlier levels. The evolution of military strategy and technology since the mid-nineteenth century has inevitably blurred the line between combatants and non-combatants as the development of long-range artillery and air power led to the indiscriminate destruction of civilian as well as military targets. In addition, the location of factories and transportation hubs in densely populated cities inevitably caused massive civilian casualties when destroying those economic and military assets became a natural part of modern military strategy. An estimated 10 percent of all casualties in the First World War and 45 percent during the Second World War were civilians, many of them children and youths.

Many of the young victims of the world wars succumbed to disease and poor nutrition. As in earlier times, the ripple effects of the passing of massive armies and of compromised economies could be catastrophic. The economic conditions spawned by war directly affected the health of children and other civilians. The first conflict for which reliable statistics is available is the First World War, which came at the same time that governments and philanthropic organizations had begun to study the well-being of the youngest members of society during the first two decades of this so-called "Century of the Child." Some children were better fed and clothed and enjoyed better health during the war because of rising wages and full employment. Studies suggested a direct connection between the rising demand for labor and the real decline in pauperism during the war. A Glasgow study, for instance, showed that the number of poorly fed and clothed children attending school had dropped by three-quarters between 1915 and the end of the war. In London, Paris, and, at least early in the war, Berlin, infant mortality rates generally declined, perhaps due to government programs, a better standard of living for working-class mothers, and a reduced birth rate. Contrariwise, deaths from respiratory illnesses, including tuberculosis and influenza, rose, especially during the worldwide flu pandemic that punctuated the end of the fighting. Deaths from measles, diphtheria, and other childhood diseases also seemed to increase in Berlin. At the other end of childhood, women between the ages of fifteen and nineteen were less healthy; in London, their death rates ranged from 14 to 40 percent higher than pre-war levels, mainly due to respiratory diseases like tuberculosis caused by the migration of young women moving from the country to take jobs in cities, women who had not built up resistance to respiratory infections, as well as the decline in nutritional standards (especially in Germany), and war-related stress and work-related exhaustion. German children and other civilians saw caloric intake decline to less than 1,300 calories, with eggs and cheese disappearing almost entirely. Few people actually starved, but reduced food supplies inevitably led to epidemics that killed nearly 300,000 civilians in 1918. From a purely military point of view, these "indirect" casualties may have been unavoidable.

Children were also victims of direct attacks. They were among the victims of well-reported atrocities during the First World War, especially in German-occupied Belgium and portions of France; child-victims became notable and effective examples in British propaganda efforts. Less well-known at the time was the Turkish Government's atrocities against the Armenians, in which the destruction of specific communities of civilians stemmed from state policy rather than battlefield passion. The campaign against the Armenian population followed the Turks' draft of able-bodied men into the army or labor units; this left the elderly, as well as women and children, vulnerable to deportation and massacres. Thousands of children perished in the systematic killings in Christian villages, sometimes when churches filled with screaming women and children were burned or in the forced marches when Armenians were deported from their homes. Perhaps a million people died in the campaign now called the "Armenian genocide."

The massive air raids of the Second World War victimized millions of children and other civilians by destroying billions of dollars in property and ending hundreds of thousands of lives. Strategic bombing reflected the rising belief among military theorists that the morale and the well-being of the armed forces relied on the economic, political, and cultural health of the homefront. Perhaps a million homes in Great Britain were destroyed and 43,000 civilians killed by German air raids. British war planners believed that successful attacks on the German infrastructure – both physical and human – would render the Wehrmacht less effective. This policy resulted in the deaths of at least 420,000 German civilians, including many children, during the last two years of the war.

Some German children had more to fear from their own government than from the Allies. Nazi ideology touted pure-bred, well-politicized Aryan youth as the foundation for the thousand-year Reich, which led them to support nurturing, well-regulated, and integrated childhoods; however, that same impetus led to policies that sought to eliminate juvenile delinquents and disabled children. As the Second World War began in 1939, Hitler authorized the killing of disabled children living in German asylums. Eventually thirty "children's units" engaged in weeding out newborn infants as well as institutionalized children suffering from mental or physical handicaps. Five thousand young children were killed in the first few months of the policy, and although it is difficult to separate the number of children from the disabled adults also being murdered by the Nazis, perhaps 300,000 Germans of all ages were eventually killed.

The number of these murders paled in comparison to the campaign to eliminate Jews, the most systematic and ruthless victimization of children in the Second World War. Early manifestations of the "final solution" focused on adults, especially men who had been communists or office-holders. But in 1941, killing squads in the Ukraine and elsewhere began systematically executing dozens or even hundreds of children at a time. Despite initial resistance by a few German officers, the determined elimination of Jews by military units and in death and concentration camps did not distinguish between the old and the young. By 1945, about 1.5 million Jewish children and youths had died.

Families in wartime

Children and youths also suffer emotional casualties because perhaps the most basic experience of children in wartime has been the disruption of families. Even families that are eventually reunited at the end of conflicts are often scarred by the experiences. Little is known about the long-term effects of fathers' absences before the twentieth century, but William Tuttle suggests a number of ways in which the experience could affect a child. Even in the United States, where virtually all children lived far from harm's way, the Second World War was all-encompassing because about 1.8 million were the sons and daughters of servicemen, while millions more were the brothers and sisters of soldiers, sailors, and marines. Indeed, nearly 20 percent of American families had at least one member in the military. The absence of these family members meant different things to different children; their response often depended on the response of their mothers and the economic conditions in which their loved one's absence placed them. Children of soldiers feared that their fathers would never come home; they also feared what would happen to them if the worst did, in fact, come to pass. Thousands of children also experienced the dislocation of migration, as families followed fathers to camps and bases or sought better jobs in the burgeoning war industries. Thirty million Americans, many of them children, moved during the war, living in crowded trailer courts or apartments, and attending even more crowded schools.

Another form of family disruption occurred when wars ended and members of occupying forces who had formed relationships with women of occupied regions left their children behind. The women had often been raped or coerced, but some had formed romantic relationships or even married the fathers of their children. The products of those relationships inspired mixed emotions and policies – in many cases hatred for their mothers' fraternization and also eliciting sympathy for the children's unwitting role in the situation. A recent study of children born to German fathers and mothers in occupied European countries during the Second World War shows how the reaction of governments and people to these children once the occupation ended reflected attitudes about politics, sex, gender, and childhood. Some children watched their mothers punished physically and emotionally. German policies encouraged the integration of these "new Germans" into the Fatherland, and some were transported to Germany, and supposed safety. After the war, some children – especially girls – were unable to escape the shame attached to their mothers' indiscretions and betrayal. In France, the Vichy Government facilitated quiet, easy adoptions of children of French mothers and German-soldier fathers; in Norway, despite an effort by the War Child Committee to create a coherent policy toward these children, the most apparent result was to encourage the changing of German-sounding names to more familiar Norwegian names.

After 1945, most direct experiences of war by children and youths occurred outside of the West, although civilians suffered heavily in Cyprus during the conflict between Greece and Turkey in 1974, and tens of thousands of non-combatants, including many children, were casualties during the wars after the dissolution of Yugoslavia in the early 1990s (the largest conflict in Europe since the Second World War). On September 11, 2001, terrorists brought their form of war into the lives of thousands of American children and their parents to name just one example of the way in which war has expanded in the twenty-first century. And the scale of the exposure of children to war has continued to increase: in conflicts fought around the world between 1985 and 1995, an estimated two million children were killed and six million seriously hurt or maimed. At one point in the early 1990s, the thirty million people displaced by war included fifteen million children.

Children and youths engaging in war

Most – or at least the most immediate – effects of war on children and youths are limiting: material resources and familial stability are reduced or threatened and children's lives become increasingly circumscribed by danger, fear, and worry. But war can also provide opportunities, especially for older children, to become part of the adult world that they desperately want to join. They find opportunities to contribute to the larger good in ways impossible to imagine in peacetime.

Although it may seem counter-intuitive to modern parents who seek to protect their children from not only the reality of war but even images of war, children do not shy away from conflict and are often deeply interested in participating in war. The two world wars of the twentieth century, which came during a time when psychologists, sociologists, and educators were seeking ways of understanding children and youths, provided ample evidence for researchers investigating the effects of war on youngsters. During the First World War, Russian educators and psychologists worried that war-related literature, movies, and newspaper stories had created an unhealthy obsession and acceptance of violence among Russian youth. A generation later, Anna Freud and other researchers discovered that, far from being frightened, British children who had experienced the "Blitz" were actually drawn to the danger and excitement. Like children throughout recorded history, they integrated the situations in which they found themselves into their "normal" lives, playing in the wreckage of bombed-out neighborhoods and becoming rather heedlessly destructive themselves. But children's dark acceptance of war transcends their alarmingly natural acceptance of violence and conflict. They also clearly understand the political, religious, and economic issues over which wars are fought. Child psychologists suggest that children readily adapt to war because in their peacetime lives they are already trying to manage the traumas and conflicts inherent in growing up. For many, war becomes just another of the many trials and tribulations children experience, while enemies become just another kind of "bogeyman."

Children are easily convinced of the righteousness of a cause or country, and one way they project their commitment to a cause is through play; indeed, martial play has been a constant in children's lives throughout history. American children during the Civil War formed their own companies and learned to march, drill, and maneuver. Polish children under Nazi occupation started mimicking Gestapo interrogations and acting out executions in town squares. Until bombing raids became an all-too-real part of their lives, children in German cities played "Stuka" and prized as souvenirs the fragments of anti-aircraft shells and shards of aluminum from Allied planes that littered the streets after a raid. During "the Troubles" in Northern Ireland in the 1970s, boys played soldiers and terrorists, staged "riots" against occupying British soldiers, and emulated the Irish Republican Army martyr Bobby Sands by pretending to go on hunger strikes. In extended wars, play turns into actual service, as boys grow into manhood and become subject to conscription or volunteer for military service.

In some cases, martial play can evolve into other behaviors. Boys' companies during the Civil War, for instance, sometimes became boy gangs who robbed civilians or committed random acts of arson. German boys playing their war games during the Second World War, in fact, simply continued an old tradition when they carried those games into the constant fight for territory among working-class boys living in cities.

As in all wars, upheaval and excitement, the decline of parental supervision (due to absent fathers, or parents working long hours in war industries), the entry into the job market of many young boys, and the geographical mobility of the population led, during the First World War, to a burst of juvenile delinquency – or at least behavior that seemed delinquent to adults. Petty theft and robbery, vagrancy, and gambling seemed to occur in epidemic proportions among adolescent and even pre-adolescent boys. The British government created a new crime called "wandering" in its attempt to eliminate the aimlessness that could only lead to trouble.

A generation later, officials in Vichy France blamed a spike in juvenile delinquency on the absence of hundreds of thousands of French fathers in German prisoner of war camps; however, a recent study suggests instead that food rationing and Vichy labor policies led juveniles to steal in order to help support their families. Nevertheless, the Vichy Government pursued relatively progressive policies – continuing a trend that began before the war and which would be followed after the end of the war – that treated delinquency less as a crime and more as a condition that could be modified by active intervention by the state.

In the United States during the Second World War, the booming economy, extraordinary geographic mobility of families, and apparent lack of supervision sparked concerns about juvenile delinquency, especially in relation to declining morals among teenaged girls. The number of non-marital pregnancies and cases of venereal disease jumped, and the media closely followed the immoral activities of "V-girls," who were infamous for flirting and having sex with young servicemen. Worries about the rise of delinquency and its deleterious effects on patriotism would extend well into the post-war period, as Americans feared that the moral fiber of the nation could fail to withstand the Communist menace during the Cold War.

Although delinquency and other behaviors were a major source of concern, children and youths have also made concrete contributions to the war efforts of their countries.

Children share the material hardships and rewards experienced by their families and most wars have forced children and youths to take on economic roles out of necessity, opportunity, or patriotism. Many have willingly taken up arms.

Boys have been included in military service for thousands of years, yet the use of "boy soldiers" slowly declined after 1500. There is some evidence that armies were rather older in the early modern period than they had been before that time. During the French wars of religion in the late sixteenth century, only 10 percent of the armies were made up of teenagers – perhaps surprising given the generally shorter childhoods of the era. During the American Revolution two centuries later, American militia units called up for short terms of service and crews of privateers often included boys as young as twelve or thirteen. Sometimes they were simply accompanying fathers or uncles, while others signed up to collect the bounties awarded by some towns or states or for the chance to earn prize money by capturing British merchant ships. Up until at least the middle of the nineteenth century, armies on campaigns included large groups of camp followers – sutlers (merchants with contracts with the army to sell food and supplies to soldiers), cooks, girlfriends, washerwomen, and prostitutes, as well as wives and children. Indeed, observers noted the large numbers of children in the retinue of the European armies that fought throughout Western Europe during the wars following the French Revolution of 1789. Some of the boys accompanying the armies became paid soldiers when they were large enough to carry arms. The Austrian army put the most promising soldiers' sons into a training school for soldiers. In 1786, the French created the most thorough system for integrating children into the army with *enfants de troupe* attached to individual regiments. This carried over into the massive armies created to fight the Napoleonic wars; boys under the age of sixteen offered a tremendous source of labor as they trained to become musicians, skilled craftsman, or infantrymen. The best students and athletes among the *enfants de troupe* could even become officers and non-commissioned officers. Although the government officially forbade bringing these children of the regiment on campaign, the restrictions were frequently ignored, and untold hundreds of children died in the nightmarish retreat of the French army from Russia in 1813.

The British Navy allowed boys as young as ten or twelve to serve on warships through much of the nineteenth century. They served for about five years as apprentices, so to speak, working as servants, as "powder monkeys" carrying ammunition to gun crews during battle, and in many other roles, as they learned specific kinds of ship-board jobs and practices. At the other end of the socio-economic spectrum were the sons of elite families, sometimes as young as nine or ten, who came aboard as midshipmen and received their officer training on the job.

In the United States, thousands of boys became drummers in the Union and Confederate armies. Twelve was the official minimum age, but many younger boys actually served. Although they were supposedly forbidden to serve on the firing line – once the shooting started, they were assigned to help surgeons in the rear – hundreds ignored the rules or were suddenly thrust into danger. There were enough casualties among them that a whole genre of images, poems, and stories about "dead drummer boys" appeared in popular culture. Thousands of other boys also served. Conscription protected boys under the age of eighteen in the Union and seventeen in the Confederacy, but a younger boy could join simply by obtaining his father's permission and, especially in the South, teenagers served in home guard or "junior reserve" units.

As armies became more and more professional in the nineteenth century, the presence of children and families declined, as did the percentage of very young boys serving as orderlies, powder monkeys, and musicians. But, along with their sisters, boys became even more important contributors by helping to provide economic support on the homefront. This, too, could be seen as a liberating experience, as the suddenly in-demand young workers began to earn their own wages and became independent of their family economies at earlier ages than in peacetime.

By the mid-nineteenth century, the scale of war and its reliance on mass-produced weapons required children to participate in the production of war matériel. Of course, prior to the widespread adoption of child labor laws and the extension of mandatory education in the late nineteenth and early twentieth century, during peacetime most children were integrated into the workforce beginning around the age of twelve – or even earlier in agricultural economies – so the fact that children went to work during wartime was less jarring than the fact that they often went to work in dangerous war industries. Symbolically, when explosions ripped through arms manufactories near Richmond, Virginia, and Pittsburgh, Pennsylvania during the American Civil War, among the dead and wounded were dozens of girls and young women.

The total wars of the twentieth century pulled children and youths into the workforce in large numbers. Many children left school to go to work, partly to help families make ends meet in the absence of fathers and older brothers. Shortages in Germany forced one million students out of school; many were sent to work on farms where they could at least avoid starvation. Great Britain's laws regarding child labor were already rather byzantine, but during the war perhaps 600,000 children covered by those laws received waivers to quit school and go to work and many others no doubt went to work in violation of the law. By 1918, 133,000 children worked in the French arms industry – just over 10 percent of the total number of weapons workers.

The Second World War saw an even more complete mobilization of children. In Germany, 2 million youths (including 1.4 million girls), were sent to the country in 1942 to help bring in the harvest. Even in the United States, teenagers were pressed into war industries and other jobs, and a number of states formally relaxed their child labor laws. Between 1941 and 1945, the number of fourteen- and fifteen-year-olds in the workforce increased fourfold, resulting in the closing of hundreds of schools. The number of high-school-age children working went up by 1.9 million, while the number in school dropped by 2.25 million.

Although most Western countries relied to a greater or lesser extent on their youths to keep wartime economies going, in Germany and the Soviet Union especially, there was a quite purposeful mobilization of children for military and paramilitary duties. Hitler Youth organizations, which included girls, had been preparing for war for several years before the invasion of Poland in September 1939, to the extent that thousands of boys completed expert marksmanship training. During the war, boys as young as seventeen were put into formal military training and girls were put to work in camps for children evacuated from cities being bombed by the allies. Fifty thousand boys, some as young as seventeen, became replacements in Waffen-SS regiments. By late in the war, the SS was drafting sixteen-year-olds, and a number of younger Hitler youths were also recruited. A special tank division of seventeen- and eighteen-year-olds was organized in 1943; a year later, they were decimated during the Allied breakout from Normandy. Older Hitler youths were put in charge of construction battalions closer to home, where they built trenches and bunkers for the inevitable Allied attack. Boys as young as fifteen and men as old as sixty were part of the *Volkssturm* – "People's Storm" – that Hitler formed in September 1944 to defend the Homeland to the last man and boy. The increasingly desperate Führer and his generals organized officer training for fifteen-year-olds late in the war. Other Hitler youths were recruited to act as spies and as guerilla fighters, ambushing Allied soldiers. Thousands died on the Russian front. An estimated 5,000 Hitler Youth – some as young as eleven or twelve – defended Berlin during the last days of the Reich; only 500 survived.

According to the historian Nicholas Stargardt, the use of children as warriors and workers did not necessarily contradict the Nazis' well-publicized nurture of the future of the Thousand-Year Reich: "The measures in child welfare had suited Nazi images of an Aryan Utopia [peopled] by healthy, beautiful and happy families." But as Germany reaped the Fascist whirlwind, children were now drawn into "the competing image of the national future which was preoccupying Goebbels and Hitler: sacrifice. It was morally preferable that the whole nation should be annihilated than that it should capitulate."[4] Indeed, while earlier calls to national service by young men and boys were ostensibly voluntary, by 1944 parents faced legal action if their sons did not enlist. Few resisted the call; 70 percent of the country's sixteen-year-old boys enlisted in 1944 without coercion.

The extraordinarily difficult circumstances in which the Soviet Union found itself after the German invasion forced children to become valuable members of the war effort. Estimates of the number of children who served in the Soviet military range to as many as 300,000 boys and girls serving in a variety of capacities: in the "lads' brigades" dominated by sixteen- and seventeen-year-olds, as partisan guerillas, as nurses and laborers, as mine clearers in areas recently occupied by Germans, and as spies. Soviet ideology did not necessarily separate the capacities of adults from children, so the involvement of children and youths in the Soviet war – especially a war that, perhaps more than in any other place but Japan, resembled a "total war" in all its brutality and scope – is not particularly surprising. But the scale of their activities and the danger they posed to life and limb is nevertheless remarkable.

Since the Second World War, the recruitment of child soldiers has generally declined in the West. But they remained in widespread use in conflicts in Africa, Asia, and Latin America, especially in Columbia's four-decades-long conflict between the government and Marxist guerillas, where both sides have forcibly recruited youngsters into their military and paramilitary forces. Western governments and non-governmental organizations (NGOs) alike have worked to reduce the use of child soldiers and to rehabilitate those who have been traumatized by their often forced military service. The Western reaction to the use of child soldiers in the underdeveloped world is not surprising. Although most parents or governments in the twenty-first-century West would not admit that participating in war as a child worker or juvenile soldier is a good thing, it is clear that despite the danger and hardships, children and youths have eagerly sought ways to contribute in times of war. By doing so, they transcended the typical limitations placed on them by society.

Child welfare and war

Further evidence that wars can enhance the lives of children in certain ways is the creation of the child welfare and other social programs to help civilians cope with the demands of war. Some become permanent, some are short-lived, and still others foreshadow the agencies and programs that would later appear in twentieth-century welfare states.

In the nineteenth century, governments began to respond to the plight of children and families in wartime. During the American Civil War, for instance, local and county governments provided outdoor relief of several kinds, including, in the Confederacy, setting prices for necessities like salt and flour, establishing city markets where food was sold for little or no profit, and food and clothing drives for the children of soldiers. These also led to tentative efforts by the federal and state governments to take on the task of caring for dependent children. The United States established widow and dependent pensions for the wives and children of men who died during the war and created the Freedmen's Bureau (formally known as the Bureau of Freedmen, Refugees, and Abandoned Lands), which was charged with easing the former slaves' transition to freedom. Its most notable success was the establishment of hundreds of schools for former slaves. Finally, more than two dozen states established soldiers' orphans' schools that cared for tens of thousands of children of men who had been killed or maimed during wars or who were unable to care for children after their wives died. Most lasted only a few years, but some systems evolved into institutions caring for orphans of all kinds.

The First World War introduced or continued trends toward increasing government social welfare programs. Food shortages, for instance, encouraged the establishment of the London Sub-Committee for the Prevention and Relief of Distress, which distributed free meals to 73,000 children. Great Britain established aid programs for the dependents of servicemen, including unmarried women and their children, as long as it could be proven that they had been living as a family. Recognizing that the war had exposed the weaknesses in the country's educational system, Great Britain established a more coherent system of educational administration in the 1918 Education Bill, which abolished public elementary school fees, raised standards, required physical education, covered handicapped and nursery-school children, and raised the absolute "leaving age" to fourteen. The French Government responded to the appalling losses of young life by creating and expanding programs that provided pre- and post-natal care (including clinics and visiting nurses) to both married and unwed mothers, opened maternity hospitals, and encouraged breast feeding by mothers working in factories. German authorities rather tentatively set up programs to distribute milk and health care to children and to provide child care for working mothers. In addition, 50,000 government officials worked to instill patriotism and to mobilize German youth by creating an entire curriculum about the war, including the "Ten Commandments of War Pedagogy," which included "Thou shalt speak of battles in history class and be happy."[5]

The Second World War saw the same kinds of government interest in children. To a greater extent than in any previous war, the US Government sought to mobilize youths. A 1943 booklet titled *Your Children in Wartime* told youngsters that "you are enlisted for the duration of the war as citizen soldiers. This is a total war, nobody is left out, and that counts you in."[6] To that end, children participated in drives to collect scrap metal and other salvageable material, sold war bonds, grew "victory gardens," and knitted and sewed clothing for soldiers. American newspapers worried about "eight-hour orphans," whose mothers worked long hours in war and other industries. The 1942 Lanham Act appropriated federal funding for 2,000 child-care centers, which cared for as many as 100,000 children under the age of two at any given time. This unprecedented effort to provide day care to working mothers by the federal government incorporated just a fraction of the total number of children of working mothers. The Emergency Maternity and Infant Care program offered pre-natal and infant care to servicemen's wives and children – a foreshadowing of later social welfare programs for children in the United States.

Among the biggest government programs established for children were the evacua-tion schemes mounted to remove children to places of safety. In the 1930s, thousands of Spanish children were evacuated to Western Europe during the Spanish Civil War. The Finnish Government moved children from Eastern to Western Finland during its war with the Soviet Union on the eve of the Second World War. A little later in the decade, during the Greek Civil War, children were taken from their families and "evac-uated" to "childtowns" where they were put through anti-communist indoctrination programs.

The most elaborate evacuation plans were, not surprisingly, carried out by Germany and Great Britain during the Second World War, although in both countries the safety of the children was only one of the objectives of the evacuation schemes. Authori-ties worried that servicemen would be too distracted if their children were in harm's way, and women would be better able to work in war industries without children to care for. Moreover, children were increasingly brought into the war effort, and by the middle of the war, these evacuated English children became a major part of the food production program. Perhaps three million German children were sent to rural areas during the 1930s and the 1940s, partly as subjects of Nazi educational ideas, but, later, to protect them from Allied air raids. Indeed the overwhelming majority of evacuations took place during the war when children were sent to occupied regions of Denmark, Croatia, Hungary, and Poland. They were assigned to camps, administered and staffed by members of the Hitler Youth, where they were to be trained to become tough, loyal, enthusiastic Nazis.

The quantum leap of the scale of war in the twentieth century also led to the rise of international efforts to aid child victims that were precursors to contemporary NGOs operating in many parts of the world. The privately financed European Children's Fund fed ten million displaced and hard-pressed children after the First World War, as did the American Red Cross. Great Britain's Save the Children Fund was established in 1919, but in the 1930s expanded into Africa following Italy's invasion of Ethiopia and has since grown to cover children throughout the world suffering myriad forms of distress. Children victimized by war also became the focus of programs undertaken by the League of Nations. Guided by the five principles of the League's 1924 "Declaration of the Rights of the Child" – which included the notion that children must be the first to receive relief in times of crisis – the League established the Child Welfare Committee in the 1920s. The founding of the United Nations in 1946 led almost immediately to the establishment of the United Nation's International Children's Emergency Fund

(UNICEF), which is still the flagship organization working on behalf of child victims of war around the world.

Aftermaths: children of war in peacetime

As represented by two very different groups of survivors of the Second World War, the aftermaths of war can be deeply disturbing to children and youths.

German children had to adjust to life after the Nazis by tearing off their Hitler Youth insignia, burning pre-war propaganda items, like cigarette trading cards featuring such personalities as the anti-heroes of the "Robber State of England," and discarding other paraphernalia and weapons from their days as the personification of the Reich's future. Like children in any country at the end of a major war, they also faced difficult reunions with deeply scarred fathers, many of whom had been away for years. For many children, the reappearance of fathers intruded on routines established without them, and the frustration, defeatism, and post-traumatic stress that shaped veterans' post-war lives often made them strict disciplinarians or hopelessly distracted.

The few surviving Jews found liberation to be confusing and frequently disturbing. The chaotic liberation of concentration and work camps, the permanent disappearance of families, the loss of belongings and property, and lingering anti-Semitism meant that even those who had somehow survived the Holocaust faced extraordinary challenges. Anti-Jewish riots in Poland and other areas of Eastern Europe led many of the few remaining Polish Jews to flee. Some survivors were children, many hidden during the war from the German efforts at extermination. Twenty-five thousand unaccompanied Jewish children arrived in the American occupation zone by the end of 1946. A second diaspora followed the war, and a number of young Jews formed organizations called *kibbutzim*, whose youthful leaders advocated relocation to Palestine. For these young people, the largest war ever fought, and the worst genocide ever committed, had deprived them of childhoods and forced them into uncertain independence.

Most children and youths faced less confusing aftermaths to wars. Throughout the nineteenth and twentieth centuries, governments and schools attempted to shape the patriotism of children and youths to ensure they understood the official meanings of past wars and to prepare them to support their countries in future wars. This was particularly evident after the American and French Revolutions. Despite their dramatically different outcomes, the two major republican revolutions of the eighteenth century both led to the integration of their revolutionary ideologies into family dynamics and childrearing. Americans created the idea of "Republican motherhood," in which mothers bore the initial and primary responsibility for raising young boys and girls into responsible citizenship. In France, a similar ideology of nurturing citizenship through wise childrearing developed, along with national policies that rewarded tax breaks to fathers who sired large families and penalized bachelors over the age of thirty-six. At the height of the British Empire during the forty years prior to the First World War, English schoolbooks were filled with martial imagery and stories of martial glory. Classrooms were decorated with pictures of battles, students' physical education often consisted of military drill, and holidays and school rituals were associated with the anniversaries of important victories. The aftermaths of wars often witness determined efforts to re-orient children to new political and social realities. The ideological conflict between the Western Bloc and the Eastern Bloc after the end of the Second World War was often fought through carefully constructed schoolbooks and patriotic school lessons. East German texts and curricula sought to "de-Nazify" teachers and students by constructing an anti-fascist narrative, while West German schools strove to instill anti-Communism and democratic principles. Countries on both sides of the ideological chasm offered children and youths uncritical histories of their countries' military and foreign policies. In the United States, the Cold War and nuclear arms race led educators to make children practice "duck and cover" drills in the event of a nuclear attack and to recite the Pledge of Allegiance daily; both were intended to steel young Americans for the fight against Communism.

One last example shows the mixed effects of war on children. The invasion of the Confederacy by Union forces during the American Civil War brought devastating hardship to enslaved African–American children. Those who escaped to Union lines during the war had to endure "contraband camps" with death rates approaching 30 percent, while those remaining on plantations and farms in the Confederacy experienced shortages of food and other supplies and sometimes cruel treatment at the hands of owners and Yankee soldiers alike. Yet the abolition of slavery immediately after the war allowed four million African–American adults and children to be seen as people rather than commodities. The Civil War was to bring into power – however briefly – Republican governments that established public schools for black children that extended literacy to hundreds of thousands of former slave children and many of their parents. The constitutional amendments that provided the legal basis of racial equality – although largely ignored between the 1870s and 1950s – ensured that the great-grandchildren of the last generation of slaves would begin to enjoy the fruits of emancipation.

Few wars produce such a startling contrast between negative experiences and positive long-term effects on children as the Civil War's impact on the youngest slaves. Yet every war fought in the West since 1500 has offered, to a greater or less extent, a similarly ambiguous set of experiences and outcomes for children and youths, who must certainly endure danger and hardship, but often find ways to embrace opportunities for contributing to the societies for whom they represent the possibility of a more peaceful future.

Notes

1 Irene Osgood Andrews, *Economic Effects of the War Upon Women and Children in Great Britain* (New York, NY: Oxford University Press, 1918), 171.

2 William Beik, *A Social and Cultural History of Early Modern France* (Cambridge, UK: Cambridge University Press, 2009), 217.

3 William Tecumseh Sherman, *Memoirs of General William T. Sherman*, vol. 2 (New York, NY: Appleton, 1875), 704.

4 Nicholas Stargardt, *Witnesses of War: Children's Lives under the Nazis* (New York, NY: Alfred A. Knopf, 2006), 263–65.

5 Andrew Donson, *Youth in the Fatherless Land: War Pedagogy, Nationalism and Authority in Germany, 1914–1918* (Cambridge, MA: Harvard University Press, 2010), 244.

6 Angelo Patri, *Your Children in Wartime* (Garden City, NY: Doubleday, Doran & Co., 1943), 89.

Suggestions for further reading

General Accounts

Marten, James, ed. *Children and War: A Historical Anthology*. New York, NY: New York University Press, 2002. Nearly two dozen essays on children as actors, victims, and targets of propaganda in wars in Latin America, Asia, and among indigenous cultures from the late eighteenth through the late nineteenth centuries.

Midlarsky, Manus I. *The Killing Trap: Genocide in the Twentieth Century*. Cambridge, UK: Cambridge University Press, 2005. A comparative examination placing the genocides, politicides, and ethnic cleansings in twentieth-century Europe, Africa, Asia, and the Middle East in their political, social, and religious contexts.

Books on the experiences of children and youth in wartime

Dupuy, Kendra E., and Krijn Peters. *War and Children: A Reference Handbook*. Santa Barbara, CA: ABC–CLIO, 2010. An examination of the ways in which armed conflict and post-war efforts at reconstructions affect children and young people in modern wars.

Kucherenko, Olga. *Little Soldiers: How Soviet Children Went to War, 1941–1945*. Oxford, UK: Oxford University Press, 2011. Describes the ideological, social, and political contexts, as well as the lived experiences, of the tens of thousands of under-age youths who fought in Soviet military and paramilitary units.

Marten, James. *The Children's Civil War*. Chapel Hill, NC: University of North Carolina Press, 1998. Shows the wide spectrum of ways in which northern and southern children, black as well as white, were affected by and chose to participate in the war efforts of the Union and the Confederacy.

Stargardt, Nicholas. *Witnesses of War: Children's Lives under the Nazis*. New York, NY: Alfred A. Knopf, 2006. A comprehensive account of the experiences of German children and youths on the homefront and in the military, including politicization of Nazi youths and the persecution of the Jews.

Tuttle, William M. *Daddy's Gone to War: The Second World War in the Lives of America's Children*. New York, NY: Oxford University Press, 1995. Not only details homefront activities like scrap drives and popular culture, but also sensitively explores the way the war affected family dynamics and the ways that children and youths of different ages reacted to the war and to the absence of fathers.

Books on government policies related to children during and after wars

Donson, Andrew. *Youth in the Fatherless Land: War Pedagogy, Nationalism and Authority in Germany, 1914–1918*. Cambridge. MA: Harvard University Press, 2010. Examines wartime pedagogy and student essays to show the vast difference between the patriotic and optimistic lessons presented to children and the crushing disappointment brought by defeat.

Ericsson, Kjersti, and Eva Simonsen, eds. *Children of World War Two: The Hidden Enemy Legacy*. Oxford, UK: Berg, 2005. An anthology of original essays detailing the ways in which occupied countries in Europe dealt with the presence of large numbers of children fathered by German soldiers.

Fishman, Sarah. *The Battle for Children: Second World War, Youth Crime, and Juvenile Justice in Twentieth-Century France*. Cambridge, MA: Harvard University Press, 2002. Argues that wartime conditions led officials in the Vichy criminal justice system to see juvenile delinquents as victims rather than criminals, inspiring a change to a therapeutic rather than punitive model for dealing with youngsters.

Hermand, Jost, and Margot Bettauer Dembo. *A Hitler Youth in Poland: The Nazis' Program for Evacuating Children During Second World War*. Evanston, IL: Northwestern University Press, 1997. Describes the evacuation of millions of urban children to rural areas as part of the Nazification of German youth, including the hardships and abuse suffered by many of the children.

Starns, Penny. *The Evacuation of Children during Second World War*. Peterbrough, UK: DSM, 2004. Suggests that political considerations weighed heavier than humanitarian concerns in the decision to evacuate British children and chronicles the danger, hardships, and potential abuse to which evacuated children were exposed.

8

CHILDHOOD EMOTIONS IN MODERN WESTERN HISTORY

Peter N. Stearns

In the 1870s, it seemed very important to Americans to train children, particularly girls, in the experience and management of grief. Here was an emotion that had to be faced because, given prevailing mortality rates, it could be expected to be part of life among siblings, and it was widely believed that childhood could provide a seedbed for appropriate adult response. One result was that doll kits were available for sale, complete with mourning clothes and coffins. Fifty years later, what seemed important had changed dramatically. United States experts were now urging parents to keep children away from grief scenes, which were too intense for childhood exposure, while hoping to wean adults away from responding to death with useless, old-fashioned forms of mourning. And the doll kits were long forgotten.

Emotions, and certainly emotional recommendations, can change, and these developments form a significant part of the history of childhood. Over the past two decades historians have been working hard to learn more about this subject, with some success. There are some obvious constraints: one issue involves data. We don't know as much about children's emotions as we would like, even about today's children and certainly about children historically. Much of our information from the past features adults talking about what children's emotions should be, or about emotional problems. Getting at children's actual emotional perceptions and experience is challenging.

A second concern involves the interplay between culturally introduced change and variety on the one hand, and biological–psychological constants on the other. All historians of emotion have to grapple with the fact that some aspects of their subject are invariable – certain types of immediate fear reactions may be a case in point. Psychologists like Paul Ekman have done a great deal with cross-cultural recognition of facial expressions that denote emotion, and while there is a small amount of variance, the shared characteristics predominate. Evolutionary psychologists similarly point to standard functions that human emotions serve across time and place. Children, incompletely socialized, might demonstrate even more emotional commonalities than people in general, but even for parents, one might expect certain basic levels of affection at least in most instances. Emotions history involves exploring the tension between psychological constants and historical contingency, and this is a real challenge as well.

We can, however, suggest a framework for some real changes in children's emotional lives in Europe and North America over the past 500 years. At the outset of the modern periods in Western history, children's emotions and the expectations of those around them were being partially reshaped by changes in religion – the emergence of Protestantism – and alterations in family structure. New ideas about children, coalescing in the eighteenth century, and then the consolidation of middle-class culture, led to another set of important shifts in the late-eighteenth to mid-nineteenth centuries. Larger structural changes in childhood, including more serious commitments to schooling and the decline of child mortality, introduced significant alterations in the emotional context of Western childhood in the second quarter of the twentieth century. Pressures from consumerism and new communications technologies also encouraged adjustments into the early twenty-first century.

At the opening of modern Western history around 1500, childhood emotions were shaped by three kinds of factors. Obviously, species-inherent emotions top the list – to the extent that we can define them. An important second set of childhood emotions derives from the nature of agricultural societies. Third – not necessarily most significant, but most interesting historically – are those emotions that seem culturally specific to early modern Europe (and soon, by some extension, colonial America).

Our first question goes back to the issue of identifying emotional experiences as standard experiences, regardless of time and place, such as fear reactions in infancy. The great range of facial expressions, which children begin to express quite early in life, is another common feature of childhood – including of course the communicative role of the smile. Some analysts might add to these at least a certain element of jealousy in children's interactions with siblings – an inevitable outcropping of rivalry for parental affection, epitomized in the Biblical tensions between Cain and Abel. Western society also shared with many others a need to acknowledge some transition from simple childhood to greater sexual maturity, through ceremonies of religious confirmation – again a standard element with emotional implications. Childish anger is another common outcropping, varying with personality but always requiring some socialization response. Childhood involves some natural emotional experiences that historians ignore at their peril.

Second, Western childhood shared many characteristics with other agricultural societies, and emotional life was no exception. The frequency of infant death, in all premodern societies, obviously colored childhood emotion, and while different cultures might shape reactions distinctively, the need to deal with some grief and fear overrode cultural boundaries. Historians of Western family life once argued that the ubiquity of children's death muted emotional reactions (why grieve when the experience of child loss was so common?) but further work has highlighted how many parents noted children's passing with sorrow. The impact of sibling loss and parental distraction on children themselves is harder to pinpoint, but again the basic experience was shared among all agricultural societies. These agricultural societies also urged obedience on children, in part to prepare them for lives of work; these injunctions often excused adults from dealing with children with too much attention to emotional details. Emotional relationships among fairly large sets of siblings were another common agricultural feature. While jealousy undoubtedly entered in – and the frequent Western emphasis on inheritance distinctions among siblings could exacerbate this issue – sets of siblings also formed strong emotional bonds, often mediating between the young as a group and parents and other adults. Gender distinction was another common premodern feature, which the West shared with patriarchal societies generally. Boys might be indulged in displays of anger that were not freely permitted of girls, who were expected from an early age to learn greater emotional restraint, even in dealing with siblings. We need more work on how emotional childhood in the West nested among agricultural societies more generally, but there are clearly a number of common topics.

Within this overall context, however, childhood emotion in Western society was also conditioned by at least two more culturally specific features. Christianity was one, and the arrival of the Protestant Reformation soon after 1500 foregrounds certain aspects of Christianity that had long been relevant to children's emotion. The European-style family was the second component. By 1500 many European families – primarily below the level of the upper classes – were emphasizing relatively late marriage age, which had as one result an unusual reliance on nuclear rather than extended families. Because most people did not marry until their late twenties – presumably to limit the birth rate and prevent undue pressure on property holdings – there was relatively little overlap between even the oldest children of the family and many grandparents, given prevailing life expectancy. While kinship ties were important in villages and urban neighborhoods, key relationships occurred within the nuclear household. This unusual family pattern highlighted relationships between children and their immediate parents. Historians have also pointed out that the same system may have placed unusual work burdens on mothers as collaborators in the family economy, which might in turn have reduced the emotional energy available to women for their offspring. By the seventeenth century, for example, many peasant and artisanal families swaddled young children unusually tightly, hanging them on hooks to prevent accidents while both parents were working. This treatment surely had emotional ramifications, reducing intimacy during a crucial developmental period. Some Western families, and not just the wealthy, also sent children out to wet-nurses, again a response to the need for mothers' household labor. Although parents might visit their infants, the practice had risks for infants' physical health and clearly affected their early bonding as well. The emotional implications of the European-style family, which would be partially transplanted to the Americas, are not easy to tease out, but they deserve serious attention.

Traditional Western Christianity, and then its Protestant variant, provide the most obvious targets for analysis – though again the emotional ramifications are diverse. Christianity celebrated the emotional value of childhood, through the images of the infant Jesus. Protestant iconography played this element down somewhat, in contrast to Catholic tradition, but it surely persisted, and with it a particular valuation of the emotional bonds between mother and child. On the other hand, Christian belief in original sin, tainting infants at birth with the early sins of humanity, could have a crushing emotional effect on childhood. The notion that children were born evil, burdened by human sins since the fall of Adam and Eve, could inspire a number of hostile adult beliefs and reactions – like the widespread sense in seventeenth century Europe that infants were greedy and animal-like as they tore at their mothers' breasts. Here was a telling contrast with the warmer emotional context provided by other religions such as Islam (which opted for childhood innocence) or Hinduism (which placed strong emphasis on a positive emotional environment for early childhood prior to a later period of moral stringency). The idea that children were sinful at birth, and therefore needing correction, encouraged two related features in early modern Western childrearing. The first was a widespread use of fear to intimidate children and instill obedience. Parents might readily invoke the dire fate that awaited the uncorrected child, including death and damnation. The second – direct discipline, including physical punishments – might seem justified as well. The father of Martin Luther, the great Reformation leader, insisted on severe discipline, and his lessons surely affected the image Luther himself developed of a stern though righteous God.

Protestantism on the whole, not only in Lutheranism but in Calvinist variants as well, probably extended the disciplinary approach to childhood. Protestant fathers were given new responsibilities for the moral upbringing of (sinful) children. Physical discipline remained common. American Indians were struck by what seemed to them the harshness of European parents, who meted out spankings with considerable regularity. At an extreme, and early Methodist leaders reflected this, such techniques lasted as late as the eighteenth century. Protestant childrearing involved breaking a child's will through physical discipline or isolation or both – responding to some act of disobedience by insistence on active admission of wrongdoing and, through this, surrendering the child's will to that of the parent. This kind of discipline could, furthermore, perpetuate itself. The will-broken child would revere his parental memory and seek to replicate the approach with his own children – a pattern visible in some United States Protestant families into the nineteenth century and beyond.

We do not know how many Christian parents actually accepted all of the implications of original sin and a resultant use of fear. Many, surely, at least modified the approach with signs of more active affection and playfulness. We also know that premodern children in Western society were given a fair amount of free time for community play under the general but fairly lenient, oversight of a village community. Relations among children themselves, not only siblings but also other villagers across a fairly wide age range, had their own emotional content and might offer a considerable alternative to the emotional styles of the strictest parents. There is no reason to assume either consistency or unwavering rigidity in the emotional styles available to premodern children in Western society, despite the comparative distinctiveness of family structure and Christian doctrine.

Significant changes in this undoubtedly complex framework began to emerge by the eighteenth century, most obviously as a result of a substantial shift in intellectual orientation away from the idea of original sin. The resultant changes spread very gradually and unevenly – significant groups of Evangelical Protestants in the United States do not fully accept them even today – but the impacts were considerable over time.

Attacks on the idea of original sin flowed from the Scientific Revolution of the seventeenth century, and were translated initially by thinkers such as John Locke. They led to an intellectual redefinition of childhood, with significant emotional implications, but also, more unexpectedly, to an explicitly emotional redefinition as well.

Locke argued, essentially, that science demonstrated human capacity for reason and for educability. The species was not condemned by some primordial fault. Children in contrast should be seen as neutral "blank slates," open to bad influences to be sure, but if properly guided, capable of advances both in morality and intellectual grasp. Education, not stifling discipline, was the logical outcome of this redefinition: approaches rooted in the idea of original sin were not only incorrect but positively harmful. These ideas would play out, over the eighteenth century and beyond, on both sides of the Atlantic. Enlightenment thinkers placed growing emphasis on the importance of schooling, and some reformers even urged that schooling itself play down excessive discipline and rote learning in favor of more positive cultivation of children's creativity and positive emotions. Undue use of fear in discipline was frowned upon in this new approach. By the early nineteenth century many reformers, including authors of popular childrearing texts, went beyond the notion of the child as a blank slate to the notion of childhood innocence – an innocence that must not be corrupted by hostile adult passions or punitive discipline. Parents, according to this new argument, owed children a positively loving atmosphere, surrounded by fruitful emotions and not corrupted either by fear or anger.

The new wisdom suggested more than a greater emphasis on education for children; it also suggested, if not through strict logic at least in historical fact, a more romantic approach to childhood and family life. Protestantism, after all, placed a new importance on family life with its contention that there were no special spiritual gains from celibacy or a religious commitment apart from family. In the workings of Protestant family writers in the seventeenth and eighteenth centuries, this redefinition could extend to the idea that family life itself should become more emotionally positive and agreeable, for married couples but also for parents and children. Some historians have also argued that, amid an increasingly commercial economy, a new emphasis on the positive emotional qualities of family relationships served as a vital counterpoise to the growing competitiveness of the external environment. Whatever the pros, it became clear that more and more people looked to families for a more positive emotional experience, and while the reorientation may have begun with Protestantism, it gradually had some impact on Catholic thinking as well. In this new wisdom, motherhood gained praise as a source of positive, loving emotionality for children and for the family as a whole. Young adults, emerging from childhood, might expect to form their own family relationships on the basis of positive emotional attraction. The idea of marrying for love gained approval, as against parental arrangements for strictly economic purposes. By the eighteenth century there were even some court jurisdictions, for example in Switzerland, that might excuse a young woman from parentally arranged courtship, if she could demonstrate that she could not imagine falling in love with her fiancé.

By the eighteenth to early-nineteenth centuries, the beginnings of an alternative emotional model for childhood began to emerge, alongside the continued insistence by some communities and families on the older, disciplinary approach. Imagery in the rising middle class, widely publicized in new, partially secular childrearing manuals, emphasized the affectionate emotions that should frame family life, organized by the mother and her (hopefully innate) nurturing instincts. Children, their innocence now firmly established at least in principle, were meant to be emotionally sheltered, their loving natures encouraged. Conventional portraits of family members, often grouped around a piano, conveyed the impression of strong emotional ties between children and parents (or at least with mothers; fathers, distracted by work, were often more remote figures) and among siblings themselves. Two emotions were to be rigorously banished from the household. Fear had no constructive purpose, and by the 1820s advice manuals began to urge parents to abandon this older disciplinary tool; it would simply corrupt the innocent child. Anger, also, was not an appropriate family emotion. Parents should rein anger in while dealing with children, and hopefully children themselves would avoid the emotion as well. The innovations in advice were truly important, but obviously they won a varied reception. Many families, perhaps particularly in rural settings, maintained older beliefs and practices. As one symptom, advice about avoiding fear-based discipline continued to be repeated in all standard manuals into the 1920s, suggesting that popularizers sensed that even the predominantly middle-class audience for their own work had yet to be fully persuaded. Particular religious communities maintained older views about deploying fear for an even longer time.

The effort at innovation, however, extended beyond fear and anger. In the new emotional environment that began to be defined during the early nineteenth century, traditional uses of shame were also downplayed. Shaming children was no longer seen as emotionally beneficial, and the growing independence of nuclear families from broader communities made shame more difficult to implement in any event. Traditional communities, as in colonial New England, had offered many opportunities for shaming, for children and adults alike. Children could be identified for ridicule by siblings or by others in the larger community. Church congregations provided opportunities to identify children who had misbehaved, making them targets of group disapproval. Practices of this sort did not immediately disappear. Indeed, the expansion of schools offered new occasions: misbehaving children could be labeled in front of their classmates. But advice-givers and parents alike began to agree that guilt, rather than shame, should be an emotion of choice in disciplining children. Guilt, after all, involved a temporary withdrawal of the child from the family circle of affection, and was therefore more available than ever before. Practices that encouraged guilt, such as sending a child to his or her room, began to be preferred, at least in principle, over physical discipline itself.

A mid-nineteenth century advice book, *Home* by Catharine Sedgwick, describes the new approach. A boy pours boiling water on the family cat, to his family's horror. But the father, yielding neither to anger nor to the impulse to shame, simply and calmly says, "Go to your room," implicitly urging the family to support the child's repentance rather than applying additional blame. And, happy ending: after several days of isolation, the boy does indeed apologize and is restored without further comment to the loving family. Of course, shame was doubtless still involved in this and other modern situations, but the emphasis shifted and deliberate shaming rituals began to decline, ultimately in school settings as well.

A final revision, again beginning toward the middle of the nineteenth century and consistent in principle with the emphasis on love and innocence, affected the emotional recommendations applied to older children,. Middle-class respectability depended heavily on sexual restraint, and proper courtships (while in fact they often involved some physical contact) were meant to stop short of overt sexuality. Instead, particularly by the later nineteenth century, intense but more spiritual affection was meant to bind young couples and lead them toward matrimony. The same principle often defined friendships among teenagers and young adults, often with people of the same sex. Sexual restraint was meant to combine with opportunities for fervent emotional expression, often conveyed through abundant correspondence. In fact, of course, the balance sometimes overturned, leading to outright sexuality, but it often did not and the principles of emotional respectability were clear in any event. Expectations of romantic intensity played a particularly important role in the contemplations of teenage girls, but boys might learn some of the same vocabulary as well.

Courtship letters could easily include invocations of love reaching one's "inmost soul" or conveying an earthly version of the "divine life" that should be the "supreme end" of one's existence.

Finally, this middle-class or (in the English-speaking world) Victorian culture placed strong emphasis on more open expressions of grief. With families now tied by loving bonds, the loss of a parent or a child must be surrounded by elevated levels of emotional recognition. Funerals involved new levels of mourning, and etiquette surrounded the appropriate recognition of sorrow in others. Children were directly included in these grief rituals – the context that generated the use of mourning symbols for dolls as part of girls' play by the later nineteenth century. Children need not be protected from this kind of sadness, though family authorities urged also that the emotion was part of a larger, loving environment; and the belief that family members would be reunited in heaven helped reconcile this potentially negative experience with the larger affectionate ideology.

The emergence of a new set of emotional standards for children and for the familial environment, developing on both sides of the Atlantic although with particular vigor in Protestant circles, was an important development. It affected evaluations of family life, seen less as economic arrangements than as centers for emotional well-being – even as emotional refuges from the cold public world of work and money-making. The new culture generated novels and memoirs that stressed the special emotional qualities of childhood, and it undoubtedly cushioned the actual emotional experience of childhood and parenting for many people. The culture had, however, a number of limitations.

Primarily, it did center on middle-class values and standards, not those of the whole population. The family ethic might influence aspiring urban artisans or American farmers exposed to the same literature, but its applicability was far from universal. The fact that the childrearing literature continued to need to emphasize changes like the control of fear in discipline suggested how many families ignored the injunctions – sometimes for example continuing to invoke "bogeymen" to scare misbehaving offspring. Other divisions complicated the picture as well. In the United States, Evangelical Protestants maintained older views about children's sinfulness, even as the mainstream Protestant denominations, after vigorous debate in the 1820s and 1830s, began to adopt the newer themes of innocence. Among American Catholics, as well, strongly influenced by immigrant Irish leadership, invocations of fear remained an important part of discipline, right up to the 1950s when wider accommodation with the larger middle-class culture at last gained ground. Even amid innovation in emotional standards and experience, older patterns and a variety of mixtures added obvious complications.

Various settings might also challenge the most widely publicized values. Schools, for example, did not quickly keep pace with the dominant imagery. Teachers often expressed anger against unruly pupils. Shaming continued, as in the identification of "dunces" with special caps and positioning at the front of the class. Only in a few experimental settings was any real effort made to make schools an affectionate environment. The disparities affected most school students, of course, and not just the middle class, but for many middle-class students the emotional contrast between school and home must have required some real flexibility.

Even in willing middle-class families, a number of nuances applied. In the first place, the new emotionology was strongly gendered. Young children, in their innocence, might be seen as relatively undifferentiated emotionally, but not so older girls and boys. Girls, in principle, must be socialized for their later family. They must be taught to express love and (where appropriate) grief, but they must also learn restraint of anger, seen as unladylike and counterproductive. Boys were held to a different regimen. It was important to restrain anger within the family, but many authorities and novelists urged that boys must not lose the capacity to be angry, which would serve them in later life as manly crusaders against injustice or as competitive businessmen. One of the values of the sports urged on middle-class boys in the last decades of the nineteenth century was their ability to help boys channel anger without losing the emotion. A number of experts recommended boxing for this purpose, as well as team sports. Boys must also learn to master fear – a value to which girls, the gentler sex, need not be exposed. Boys' stories abounded in examples of courage, from brothers who faced down bullies to soldiers who withstood great odds to expand the national empires or (in the United States) defend one side or the other in the Civil War. There was more to all this than simple reading matter. Many boys socialized outside the home, and their standards of play often drove home the importance of being able to respond to provocation with anger and to demonstrate courage. In the United States, a new word, "sissy," initially applied to sisters, came by the 1870s to designate boys who were not able to measure up to the appropriate emotional standards.

Adolescence was another concept vital to accommodate the emotional standards generated within the nineteenth-century middle class. The intensity of the belief that children should be affectionate, and sexually restrained, complicated the advent of sexual maturity and potential emotional rebelliousness. The idea of adolescence as a (hopefully bounded and temporary) period in which children's adherence to respectable standards might be challenged was an important bow to reality. Parents still hoped to retain control over their children and receive affection in return (particularly where girls were involved), but the idea of adolescence might facilitate adjustment to a less tractable reality. First discussed in Europe in the 1830s, research on the special emotional and physical features of adolescence gained ground in the United States by the 1880s, and the word itself began to pass into the general vocabulary.

Finally, it is important to recognize that the new emotional culture applied to childhood was in many ways quite restrictive – one reason that boys or adolescents might seek some independent means of expression. Attacks on the use of fear and traditional forms of discipline might be well and good, but the new standards were hardly invitations to emotional freedom. Children were expected not only to be obedient but also to be actively affectionate, and to learn to put a lid on open expressions of emotions like anger. Much of their approved reading was directed to literature that sought to clearly illustrate and instill appropriate emotional discipline. This could be heavy handed. Guilt itself was a powerful new weapon of emotional discipline, perhaps harder to shake off than shame. The new importance given to education, as well as to the standards of respectability, meant the parental supervision of children in some ways increased. Playtime, for instance, should be directed toward constructive learning, not to random activity. Some children clearly found this emotional environment stifling. Certain new diseases began to be identified that arguably resulted from the needs of some children to protest the family environment indirectly so as not to challenge its unassailably affectionate intentions. Most notably, by the later nineteenth century, a certain number of girls began to manifest eating disorders, in the form of anorexia nervosa, as a symptom of their need to differentiate themselves from family expectations without declaring open emotional rebellion. Modern medical identification of anorexia, emerging from the mid-nineteenth century onward, initially had far more to do with familial emotional patterns than with a social idealization of slenderness, which would fully develop only somewhat later.

Elements of the powerful emotional culture of the nineteenth-century middle class proved quite durable, helping to frame family imagery even in the present day. Some of these complications such as anorexia nervosa, and diversity of reactions have survived as well. But the early twentieth century brought a number of changes to the structure of childhood that would in turn have important emotional consequences. The result would be something of a new amalgam, but with an emphasis on another round of innovations in emotional standards and experiences.

Three structural changes were particularly influential. First, between 1880 and 1920, throughout the Western world, child and infant mortality began to plummet. From about 20 percent of all children born in 1880, young child mortality dropped to 5 percent or so by 1920, and would continue to fall thereafter. Here was a huge change: for the first time, families no longer had to expect that a child would die; siblings no longer had to face death as a standard experience. Added to this was the fact that death of all sorts moved out of the home, to hospitals and funeral parlors: emotional confrontation with death was no longer an inescapable part of growing up.

Second, capping a longer trend, the birth rate began to drop to an average of only about two children per family, with only a bit of variation by social class (with middle-class families still the smallest). This meant that children now grew up with few siblings. Combined with the increasingly common experience of schooling, this meant that many of their ties would be formed with other children of their same age, rather than siblings. It might also mean, within the family and particularly before school years, that contacts with parents would become more intense because of the absence of sibling intermediaries. Here was another change with interesting, though complex emotional implications.

Finally, the world into which children were being socialized was changing. Increasingly, Western economies were dominated not by the early stages of industrialization, but by a more complicated managerial and service-sector economy. For many, this meant that the importance of schooling increased, and most social groups began to devote longer and longer periods of childhood to schooling, rather than just the primary school years. Schooling itself became more demanding, with new forms of examination (in Europe) or more rigorous grading systems (in the United States). Adult economic success arguably depended on new kinds of emotional restraint – successful salesmen or middle-level managers needed the abilities to seem friendly at all times, and to keep any anger under wraps. This too might call on new types of socialization for children in advance of economic maturity.

Symptomatic of these various changes in structure, a new breed of childrearing expert began to emerge, with particular intensity in the United States. Instead of religious and moral guidance, parents now began to seek out apparently scientific expertise, in the form of psychologists and pediatricians and childrearing literature expanded rapidly. New periodicals, like *Parents' Magazine* in the United States, showed the desire of experts to reach a wider public, to convince them that their own impulses or traditional values were no longer adequate for the complex task of raising a child; and it expressed the felt need of many parents, particularly but not exclusively in the middle classes, to gain access to new kinds of advice as well. Revealingly, it was in the 1920s that many grandparents began to move out of the homes of their younger kin; easy sharing of intergenerational knowledge became more difficult, and many young parents and experts alike agreed that this was a good thing, that emotional success depended on considerable innovation. American childrearing literature became particularly bountiful, adding whole sections to popular bookstores, but Europeans picked up similar advice, as the global popularity of a post-World War II guru, Dr Benjamin Spock, clearly expressed. Government agents got in on the act. In the United States the widely distributed government pamphlet, *Infant Care*, initially devoted to physical health, began in the 1920s to expand into urgent emotional recommendations. By the 1950s, White House conferences on childhood began to address children's happiness, not the more conventional health issues. On both sides of the Atlantic social workers began to translate some of the new emotional standards into their work with the poor and into evaluations of parental adequacy – though often with a certain degree of flexibility. Here was another set of external sources pressing for emotional change.

Under the spur of substantial structural changes – never before had families been so small, death so remote – and the pressing recommendations of outside experts, many parents began to take on new responsibilities for the emotional health and development of their children. Psychiatrists, like the redoubtable Sigmund Freud, were urging that dysfunctional adults were the result of parental bungling. It became more important than ever before for responsible parents to recognize that they needed to guide their children actively and appropriately. As children's physical health became more reliable, with better living standards and medical care, parents almost consciously took on new burdens in the emotional sphere.

Several significant readjustments in emotional values resulted from this new framework. These began to emerge in the United States by the 1920s – though their actual adoption was a gradual process – and affected Europe a bit later, from the 1950s onward. Some regional, as well as personal and social class, variance continued, but there were some important general trends.

Two changes reduced adult strictures on children, in principle and also in fact, in ways that affected emotional life. Beginning in the early twentieth century, and with the United States probably in the lead, efforts to insist on elaborate etiquette for children began to decline. Children no longer had to follow extensive protocols in dealing with adult friends of the family. Clothing became more relaxed, and so did posture. A Dutch sociologist has aptly termed the overall trend one of "informalization." Emotions were not directly involved but more informal habits did include allowing children to discuss emotions more openly and widely – though emotional experience might not loosen to the same degree. A bit later, and with Europe ultimately in the lead, concerns about controlling sexuality eased as well – a second change in adult standards. A more permissive sexual public culture, and by 1960, more reliable and available birth control devices, helped parents and other adult authorities realize that sex was not as dangerous as it had seemed to respectable families in the nineteenth century. Repression of masturbation loosened, and formal and informal attempts to prevent premarital intercourse relaxed as well – and by the 1950s, the actual age of first intercourse dropped. One result of these often fairly self-conscious attempts to ease nineteenth-century repressions was increasing and positive interactions between parents and children. As early as the 1920s in the United States (Europe followed later), fathers often began to stress a more friendly style with offspring, even seeking, as the vernacular put it, to become "pals." Mothers in fact took on the burdens of discipline more directly, but by the early twenty-first century, older children were often citing parents, particularly mothers, as best friends, and maintaining high levels of communication and emotional contact.

These developments were important, but in some ways they masked the more direct trends in emotional socialization, where parents took on greater responsibilities for guidance of children at least at the younger ages. Key trends here, pushed by experts and popularizers but increasingly assimilated by many parents, involved a growing sense that children were emotionally vulnerable, incapable of dealing with almost inevitable emotional issues without adult assistance. By the 1920s, many American childrearing manuals were defining problems that bore both on childhood and later adult behavior. Children not properly assisted with their emotional development would have troubled childhoods, at an extreme, actually endangering others, while also failing to develop full functionality in later work or family life. "Festering" was a revealing word in the advice literature. Children left to their own devices would develop emotional sores that could not heal, affecting them directly, but even more important, impeding their adult success. Parents, who were not only guided but also actively assisted by experts if necessary, must step in.

Several emotions were defined in this new context, and entirely novel emotional problems were uncovered. Jealousy was an intriguing case in point. Dominant family imagery from the nineteenth century had largely ignored jealousy, doubtless in the hope or expectation that family affection would trump occasional sibling tensions. In the 1920s, however, family experts and popularizers began to highlight the problem of what was now called sibling rivalry – the intense hostility that a toddler would experience on the arrival of a new-born brother or sister. Some authorities claimed that the emotion was inevitable. Many termed it extremely dangerous, threatening the physical safety of the baby and, if untended, leaving the toddler emotionally crippled into adulthood. Active parental intervention was held to be essential. Parents should carefully tend to the toddler, giving it new and clearly identified possessions to distract from any sense of threat from the new arrival. Intractable cases might be referred to a therapist. Although the problem was defined by psychologists and social workers, many parents, now that they felt responsible for emotional development and aware that, in a small family, tensions between children over parental affection might be more acute than in a larger sibling cohort, quickly joined in. Polls in the United States by the 1930s listed the control of sibling rivalry as one of the top two or three problems parents normally faced.

But jealousy was not the only new target. Approaches to fear were recast. Psychologists now claimed that children were victims of a host of fears, again virtually inevitably, that required parental intervention. Assuming that children could handle these emotions by themselves was a mistake, as was falling back on a more traditional approach that would simply urge greater courage. Indeed, fear could be so unmanageable that injunctions to courage might actually make matters worse. So parents should carefully reassure while actively limiting the fear situations to which children were exposed. New remedies included night lights for children afraid of the dark. In the same spirit, many traditional children's stories were recast, to reduce the fear element.

Experts also reconsidered grief. As children's death rates declined, it was understandable that many parents and family experts sought to keep young people away from grief situations – which might now be bypassed for the first time in history. Grief was too unpleasant and intense for children, the new expertise contended. Even funerals might be too much, and for several decades many authorities urged that children be kept away. Euphemisms urged the use of substitutes for stark words like death or dying – terms like "passing" were less likely to rouse fear or other intense reactions.

In the same vein, some authorities began to argue that even guilt was too intense an emotion for children to handle, and urged parents to use more emotionally neutral forms of discipline.

And finally anger came in for review. By the late 1930s, most childrearing manuals began substituting the term aggression for anger, a clear sign that this emotion was encountering new levels of concern and condemnation. In contrast to Victorian emotionology, which was sought to channel anger into useful purposes (at least for boys), the new wisdom saw no virtue in anger at all. Again, parents should step in to help children understand how important it was to keep anger under control and to realize that it had no useful purpose. Teenagers were reminded that displays of anger would reduce their popularity, while in the 1950s popularizers warned parents of the links between adolescents' lack of self-control and juvenile delinquency.

These various revisions, all calling on parental oversight, were of course diversely received, depending on social class, religious culture, and even parental personality. Mothers, according to most reports, were more open to concerns about children's fears than fathers who were more prone to insist on childish courage. Some strictures faded a bit with time. The most intense attacks on sibling rivalry yielded somewhat by the later twentieth century, partly because parents and authorities realized that the problem was not as severe or ubiquitous as had previously been thought, but partly because many parents simply internalized the standard advice and kept a watchful eye on this aspect of emotional development. Some revisions also entered into the approach to grief, and the effort to insist on limiting children's access to funerals softened by the 1960s and 1970s.

Still, the dominant sense of the child's fragility and the need for adult oversight persisted strongly. New problems were identified, although within the same basic framework, by the final decades of the twentieth century – and new therapies were also introduced as well.

In the first place, the same childrearing culture that stressed the importance of emotional oversight and, through this, childish control of emotions, now seen as unrelievedly negative, also called upon children to be openly cheerful. The association of childhood with happiness had gained headway in the nineteenth century, in places like England and the United States, as part of the new celebration of childish innocence. By the 1890s, vague ideas were increasingly focused into claims that children should be urged to be cheerful as part of a pleasant emotional demeanor that would make family life more rewarding – after all, children were now economic liabilities, as their work declined, so they might be expected to provide emotional rewards – and as part of the personality that would encourage adult success. By the 1920s, parents were drawn further into this process as childrearing manuals devoted long sections to the importance of happiness among children. Hopefully, the literature suggested, many children might be naturally happy, but here too it was clear that parents should step in when needed to ensure a positive emotional environment. The new adult responsibility to assure happy childhoods was a close companion to the modern responsibilities for emotional oversight. It could add significantly to parental activities and concerns, but it could also press on children directly because they were increasingly expected to present smiling faces on most occasions and were often carefully interrogated about what was wrong when the smile was absent.

New emotional problems followed in part from the increasing rigors of schooling. As early as the 1850s, some German authorities had identified children, particularly boys, who fidgeted and had problems concentrating during school sessions. The issue received more concerted scientific attention during the early twentieth century, when it was finally given the label of Attention Deficit Disorder. Here was a new way that both parents and teachers could call attention to an emotional issue among some children, and the understanding facilitated an increasing number of diagnoses, throughout the Western world although particularly in the United States. By the 1950s, drug treatments were available, notably through the use of Ritalin, and thousands of children began to submit to treatment. Here was an important entering wedge to the growing impulse to seek not only counseling therapy but also outright medication to deal with children who could not measure up to current emotional norms.

More serious still was the advent of emotional depression as a common diagnosis for children and adults alike, again a new marker that developed from the early twentieth century onward. Among children, depression might be associated with school pressures or social tensions among peers, or as a result of divorce or other growing manifestations of family instability. It was also noted that the new expectation that normal children should be actively cheerful complicated the experience of sadness, making it harder for children to manifest this milder emotion without risking a depression diagnosis. Again, a variety of medications increasingly intervened. By the twenty-first century, a significant minority of older children, those, for example, entering college, were taking one or more prescription drugs to deal with emotional issues. This was another important sign of the theme of overt emotional control in the framework of contemporary childhood in the Western world.

The strictures of parents and adults were not, of course, the only shaping force in the actual emotional life of children in the most recent historical period. Two other frameworks, though harder to define, were also involved. First, thanks to systematic schooling, children began to interact widely with same-age peers after a fairly brief few years either at home or in daycare settings. Indeed, one of the pressures on parents to attend to children's emotional socialization, even by the toddler stage, resulted from the brevity of their primary control: if children were not partially shaped by age six, the game might be lost.

Peer culture was not a new experience for children, particularly boys, but its importance undoubtedly increased. The culture was not necessarily in harmony with recommended emotional standards. Challenges to overcome fear or deal with bullying surfaced frequently, even though adult authorities tried to counteract some of the pressures (bullying, for example, was first singled out in the 1920s when so many efforts to protect children against emotional intensity were taking shape). Peer contacts might also allow some children to share sadness or anger more freely than parental standards allowed at home, sometimes providing welcome outlets for a richer emotional life, but who create difficult tensions with approved standards. By the early twenty-first century "social networks," such as Facebook, facilitated peer contacts, and they were often used to share (sometimes seemingly trivial) emotional experiences, another sign of the importance and dynamism of peer contacts as emotional outlets.

Finally, and again with increasing intensity through the twentieth century and beyond, children's emotional life was also shaped by a consumer culture now directed explicitly at children themselves rather than through parental intermediaries. This consumer culture might, of course, be shared with peers for the boundaries were quite porous.

The forms that were dominant in children's consumer culture changed over time. In the late nineteenth century, cheap, exciting novels, dubbed "penny dreadfuls" were one of the first commercial products to reach children directly. Soon there were movies, comic books, then radio shows, and then after World War II, children's television programs. The twentieth century produced a growing array of motion pictures specifically directed at child or teenage audiences. In the 1980s and 1990s, new technologies brought popular video games. After 1990, growing productions stemmed from the Internet.

Some children's consumer products meshed with the recommended emotional standards fairly well. Disney productions, launched in the 1920s and increasingly gaining a global audience, sought above all to make children happy. Disney movies might include careful doses of fear, but rarely toward any extreme. They often reflected affectionate family values. Some of the entertainments, including Disney or Disney-like theme parks, might indeed provide family leisure opportunities and a chance for emotional sharing between children and adults.

Other products, however, were not so easily compatible with recommended standards. From the late nineteenth century onward, juvenile authorities and alert parents worried openly that much commercial children's fare involved excessive amounts of violence, aggression, and sexuality – precisely some of the emotional areas that were supposed to be kept under control. Many groups sought to ban or censor some of the commercial fare, and some producers (for example, in Hollywood) periodically accepted some limitations on children's exposure, while in Europe, government control of some media for a time limited options as well. But there was no question that many children, particularly but not exclusively in the more independent teenage years (a designation which began to push into younger ages), did find opportunities to experience a variety of emotions through entertainment or games that challenged approved standards. Indeed, the availability of emotional alternatives was surely one of the key appeals of the various new media. Efforts at censorship almost invariably fell short, partly because of legal valuation of free speech, partly because media technologies became increasing sophisticated in their ability to reach children directly, partly because adults themselves were divided about whether protection or entertainment best expressed their obligations to the youngest generation.

Authorities recurrently contended that exposure to commercial emotional culture stirred emotions in children directly, making some, at least, more angry and violent, or fearful and violent, than would otherwise have been the case. These were accusations leveled at comic books in the mid-twentieth century, just as they were levied at "exploitation" movies aimed at a teenage audience in the 1970s or the Internet fare and video games of the early twenty-first century. Evidence was at best mixed. Most children took media emotionality in their stride – or avoided it on their own if they found it uncomfortable. The vicarious emotions simply offered a diversion in the broader patterns of emotionality. But some individual children, probably troubled in other respects, might confuse emotional representations and reality, and act out accordingly.

Many aspects of children's emotional history over the past five centuries remain to be probed. The complexity of the contemporary emotional framework, with its emphasis on control combined with virtually unfettered media alternatives and the clear importance of peer emotional contacts, reminds us that, even today, it is hard to generalize about children's emotional life. Over the modern periods, religion has receded, save for a minority in the Western world, as a shaping emotional force. It has been replaced by new expertise and related parental standards, both of which altered considerably under the impact of the Enlightenment. It has been shaped as well by huge, objective changes in child life: the reduction of the birth rate, the limitation of death, and the requirements of schooling over work. It has also been affected by changes in technology and commerce, particularly recently. Various forces have competed for roles in shaping children's emotional life, and children themselves have actively contributed. The process continues in the present day.

Suggestions for further reading

On premodern childhood

See Linda A. Pollock, "Honor, Gender and Reconciliation in Elite Culture, 1570–1700," *Journal of British Studies* 46 (2007): 3–29; Linda A. Pollock, "Parent–Child Relations in Europe 1500–1800," in *Family Life in Early Modern Times*, eds. Marzio Barbagli and David Kertzer, (New Haven, CT: Yale University Press, 2001), 191–220; Albrecht Classen, ed., *Childhood in the Middle Ages and the Renaissance: the Results of a Paradigm Shift in the History of Mentality* (Berlin, Germany: deGruyter, 2005); Erik Erikson, *Young Man Luther: A Study in Psychoanalysis and History, revised edition* (New York and London: W.W. Norton & Company, Inc. 1993); Barbara A. Hanawalt, "Medievalists and the Study of Childhood," *Speculum* 77 (2002): 440–60; Steven Ozment, *When Fathers Ruled: Family Life in Reformation Europe* (Cambridge, MA: Harvard University Press, 1983); and Pauline Stafford, "Parents and Children in the Early Middle Ages," *Early Medieval Europe* 10 (2001): 257–71.

Relevant surveys of the history of childhood

Hugh Cunningham, *Children and Childhood in Western Society Since 1500* (London, UK: Longman, 2005); Paula Fass, *Encyclopedia of Children and Childhood: In History and Society* 3 VOL Set (New York, NY: Macmillan Reference USA/Thomson-Gale, 2004); Jens Qvortrup, William A. Corsaro, and Michael-Sebastian Honig. *The Palgrave Handbook of*

Childhood Studies (New York and United Kingdom: Palgrave Macmillan, 2009); and Peter N. Stearns, *Childhood in World History*, 2/e (New York, NY: Routledge, 2011). See also Viviana Bowman, *Scholarly Resources for Children and Childhood Studies: A Research Guide and Annotated Bibliography* (Lanham, MD: Scarecrow Press, 2007); and Colin Heywood, ed. *A History of Childhood: Children and Childhood in the West from Medieval to Modern Times* (Malden, MA: Blackwell Publishing, 2004).

On developments in the eighteenth–nineteenth centuries

Refer to Marilyn R. Brown, ed. *Picturing Children: Constructions of Childhood Between Rousseau and Freud* (Surrey, UK: Ashgate, 2002); Peter Gay, *Schnitzler's Century: Love, Hate and Privacy in the Victorian Bourgeoisie* (London: Penguin Books, 2002); Phillip Greven, *The Protestant Temperament: Patterns of Child-Rearing, Religious Experience, and the Self in Early America* (New York: Knopf, 1977); Jan Lewis and Peter N. Stearns, *An Emotional History of the United States* (New York, NY: New York University Press, 1998); and Anja Müller, ed. *Fashioning Childhood in the Eighteenth Century: Age and Identity* (Burlington, VT: Ashgate, 2006). See also Linda A. Pollock, *Forgotten Children: Parent–Child Relations from 1500 to 1900* (Cambridge, UK: Cambridge University Press, 1983); Anthony Rotundo, *American Manhood: Transformations in Masculinity from the Revolution to the Modern Era* (New York, NY: Basic Books, 1994); and Catharine Marie Sedgwick, *Home*, 20th ed. (Boston, MA, James Munroe and Company, 1850).

Useful studies of emotion and emotion history

Paul Eckman, *Emotions Revealed, 2nd ed: Recognizing Faces and Feelings to Improve Communication and Emotional Life* (New York, NY: Henry Holt and Company, 2003); Nicole Eustace, "Emotional Life," in *Encyclopedia of Children and Childhood: In History and Society, 3 vol*, ed. Paula S. Fass (New York, NY: Macmillan Reference USA/Thomson-Gale, 2004); Barbara H. Rosenwein, "Worrying about Emotions in History," *The American Historical Review* 107 (2002): 821–845; Melvin Konner, *The Evolution of Childhood: Relationships, Emotion, Mind* (Cambridge, MA: Harvard University Press, 2010); and Peter N. Stearns, *American Cool: Constructing a Twentieth-Century Emotional Style* (New York, NY: New York University Press, 1994).

On developments in the nineteenth–twentieth centuries

See Joan Brumberg, *Fasting Girls: The History of Anorexia Nervosa* (New York, NY: Random House, Inc., 2000); Peter N. Stearns, *Anxious Parents: A History of Modern Childrearing in America* (New York and London: New York University Press, 2004); and Cas Wouters, *Informalization: Manners and Emotions Since 1890* (Thousand Oaks, CA: Sage Publications Ltd. 2007).

9

CHILDREN AND THE STATE

James Schmidt

The relationship between young people and the state in the modern period has been filled with paradoxes. As modern liberal polities developed in the West, their histories were inextricably bound up with questions of inclusion and exclusion, what one historian has called "the borders of belonging." The product of the eighteenth-century Enlightenment and the Age of Revolutions, the modern state originally was an exclusive fraternity of brothers: white, male, and adult. Over the last two centuries, much of the history of the modern West chronicles efforts by excluded groups to win inclusion in the polity. Ironically, the trajectory of young people in that story has been the opposite, ever-increasing exclusion from the daily life of adults with which the polity is concerned. Children, though not youths, have been the objects of the state rather than actors within it.[1]

Indeed, the modern state, especially in its administrative functions, has been critical in the creation of modern childhood, and concomitantly, adulthood. In between, the state has outlined a borderland of belonging, variously called youth, adolescence, and in darker corners, juvenile. At the start of the modern period, the legal walls between childhood and adulthood were not as fortified as they would become over the two to three centuries between the eighteenth-century Enlightenment and postmodernity. To be sure, young people suffered many legal disabilities, especially those regarding participation in formal acts of government such as suffrage, but many areas of life simply lay outside the purview of the state. While apprenticeship structured the work relations of young people, especially boys, no restrictive child labor laws prevented young people under a certain age from working outside the household. The children of the elite or even the middling sort might attend school, but nothing compelled all of the bodies of all the young people in a polity to be in any one place at one time. Marriage and sexuality came under the purview of the church and, in the Anglophone world, the common law. Unions between young people, while not common or encouraged, were nonetheless possible. As the modern state developed, it erected ever-stronger barriers between the world of children and adults, barriers that created separate experiences for younger people in commonplace human activities such as work, marriage, and learning. At the boundaries of belonging, a juvenile criminal system marked some young people as beyond both the legitimate realm of adult activities and acceptable limits of youthful ones. In no small measure, then, age-segregated modern society is a child of the state.

At the same time, however, children, in the language of liberalism, were always citizens in waiting, and this central paradox – of exclusion before inclusion – has troubled adult thinkers from the eighteenth century onward. The problem was a simple one: children do not stay children. In a pre-modern Europe, where membership in the polity was based on inherited status, such a truism meant little, but the rise of the modern state in the Age of Revolutions that began with the American Revolution of the 1770s and extended into the French Revolution of the 1790s and beyond, changed all of that. The children of a republic occupied a quite different place than did those of a monarchy. Republics, and the nominally democratic states that followed them, especially in France and the United States, drew their legitimacy from the consent of the governed, which rested in turn on the capacity of the citizen to deploy reason. In Enlightenment thought, such politics placed young people outside the state. In the aftermath, however, political elites faced the question of how unreasonable children were supposed to become reasonable adults. In the early nineteenth century, that quandary had limits, for the state was still confined by other lines of exclusion: race, gender, and religion. As other excluded groups fought for and won admission to the formal processes of the state, every young person became an incipient citizen. The answer to the puzzle was compulsory education: young people would be trained to be the citizens of the future. Universal consent would rest on universal coercion.

One final paradox developed in the twentieth century, especially after World War II. The restrictions on the actions of young people that the state established over the course of the nineteenth and early twentieth centuries became redefined as the rights of childhood. The notion of children's rights presents an ironic counterpoint to the core of possessive individualism in all other rights movements of the modern period. Liberal polities have been largely loathe to admit group rights in the first place. "Rights" has normally meant a statement about the position of the individual vis-à-vis the state. Yet the social movements of the nineteenth and twentieth centuries have made a powerful statement for the rights of groups: workers, women, blacks, Jews, immigrants, prisoners, lesbians, gays, transgendered, and disabled. In almost all cases, such movements have been undertaken by the group, for the group, and their claim has been on greater inclusion in the polity. In contrast, movements for children's rights have usually, though not always, been fostered by people outside the group, and the claim has been for greater exclusion from the polity, or more colloquially, from adulthood. The consistent rallying cry has been to give young people "a childhood," which can be defined as a lived experience that differs significantly from adult daily life. Substantive participation by young people in a normal activity of daily adult life such as wage work signals the loss of the rights inherent to children and childhood.

The result of the paradox of children's rights has been a refocusing of substantial branches of the state on the lives of young people. In particular, state-based plans for attention to infant and child mortality and health have undergirded much of the development of the bureaucratic state in the West. The same can be said for child poverty. In the long history of provision for the poor in Europe and America, youths have always had a more legitimate claim on public assistance than adults. Although such claims came under siege in the late twentieth and early twenty-first centuries, central government programs to alleviate poverty and provide health care services for children lay at the heart of the state itself as well as the interactions young people have with it.

Another result has been an ever-growing body of modern law focused on young people. Modern youth suffrage movements lowered the voting age to eighteen, an age often equivalent to the age of military service for young men. At the same time, youthful free speech movements tested the application of such liberal concepts when applied to non-citizens. While seemingly dramatic, suffrage or high constitutional law was not the center of the discussion of children and the state. Such debates more often focused on day-to-day concerns such as custodial rights in divorce or procedural due process in juvenile court. As before, the paradoxical position of young people colored these debates as dependence, both biological and psychological, hovered over the proceedings.

Citizenship emerged as a central conception in modern polities in the Age of Revolutions. In the monarchial systems that preceded the rise of bourgeois states, status in fixed social groups had marked membership in the state, but in the wake of the American and French revolutions, national constitutions proclaimed birthright citizenship in the state as a whole. At first limited by gender, race, property ownership, and the like, these expansive definitions of citizenship became more inclusive over the two centuries that followed, but one limitation remained: age. The French constitution of 1791, for instance, limited citizenship to males over twenty-five, while the radical document of 1793 dropped the age to twenty-one. In France and elsewhere, citizenship and concomitant suffrage rights did not equate with political power. In the most obvious case, the US Constitution of 1789 ensconced age-graded limits on federal office holding, while the French Constitution of 1795 limited membership in the Directory to those over age forty. At the same time, however, another central marker of male citizenship – military service – settled at a considerably younger age, often in the middle teens, leaving a tension that would only be partially resolved in the later twentieth century.[2]

Suffrage and military service outlined key relationships between young men and the state in the West, but for much of the nineteenth century and good parts of the twentieth, race and gender limited their meaning. Consequently, young people encountered the state in places mostly outside of the formal halls of politics and diplomacy. Chief among these was in the field of work. For a very long time in European history, young people had started to help out at home at a fairly early age, and many of them had worked outside the home in bound relationships, either in service or apprenticeships. Before the nineteenth century, the state had been involved in these activities in a variety of ways. Legal systems dating back to the late medieval era regulated the terms of apprenticeships, and parish and town authorities in the Anglophone world regularly placed poor children in bound relationships to provide for their support. Starting in the seventeenth century, the servant stream that fed plantation agriculture in British North America drew upon these antecedents, sending thousands of young people to work and die in the tobacco fields of the Chesapeake Bay region. With the urban poor growing in the eighteenth century, some areas of Europe began to hear calls for compulsory labor for young people lest "they be abandoned to the wildness of their own nature and let run loose savage in the street," as British reformer Isaac Watts had put it.[3]

The early modern relationship between the state and youthful labor had revolved around compulsion to work, but the nineteenth century brought a monumental reversal. Influenced by the Romantic understanding of childhood innocence, reformers in the industrializing states of Europe and then America confronted the new problem of factory-wage work for children. Starting with the Factory Act agitation in Britain in 1802, central governments slowly redefined the relationship between the state and youthful labor towards state compulsion *not* to work. In France, for instance, a key turning point was the 1874 child labor law, which built on an 1841 statute to limit industrial work for children and for female minors under age twenty-one. Drawing on the experience of the British, the statute set up a system of inspectors, a common feature of child labor restriction. Child labor reform, as these movements came to be called, represented both a statement of what should be and an increasing creation of what was. Children should not be at work; they should be at school. Such an assertion of social authority ran squarely into older and emergent working-class understandings of a productive childhood, but the violence of modern industrial life slowly adjusted young workers and their families to this new legal reality.[4]

Child labor reform actually proceeded in two ways, and both left a legacy of an age-segmented relationship between young workers and the state. One involved abolition or absolute prohibition. In Europe as well as in the United States, prohibitionists started at age ten, worked their way to twelve, and eventually ended up somewhere between fourteen and sixteen. In Britain, the original Factory Act of 1802 simply limited working hours: eight for children aged nine to thirteen, twelve for those fourteen to eighteen. By 1901, all work was prohibited for young people below age twelve; by 1933 that age had risen to fourteen, and fifteen for heavy work. Similar points eventually obtained in France (fifteen) and Germany (sixteen) as well. Notwithstanding exceptions in such areas as agriculture and domestic service, such divisions aimed to mark the absolute line between childhood and what followed, but lawmakers also structured the period after prohibition. Such regulations left less dangerous jobs open to middle teenagers, while reserving others for older teens and adults. This outcome drew upon developed notions in the law regarding youthful incapacity, ideas voiced pointedly by US jurist Thomas McIntyre Cooley in 1884: "Children, wherever they go, must be expected to act upon childish instincts and impulses." Child labor regulation both recognized and created this sense of childish incapacity. As young people became increasingly cut off from the world of work, they knew less about it. At the same time, most child labor law allowed youthful employment after a certain age and under certain conditions. In short, one came of age as a worker slowly – under the protective umbrella of the state.[5]

As the state came to control work, so too did it come to oversee marriage and sexuality, another central facet of human experience that became explicitly and implicitly linked to citizenship across the modern era. For much of European history, marriage and sexuality had been regulated by the local community in conjunction with the church after the spread of Christendom. By the eighteenth century, that began to change, most notably with Lord Hardwicke's Marriage Act of 1753 in Britain. As marriage shifted to state control, so, too, did divorce and custody proceedings. As numerous historians have shown, a dramatic shift occurred in parental rights to children. The eighteenth century had left a legacy of patriarchal rights. Men had a property right in their progeny, one that the courts usually honored in the relatively rare divorce proceedings and in the relatively more common chancery courts for orphans. Across the course of the nineteenth and into the twentieth centuries, divorce slowly shifted to a much simpler and easier judicial process and, along with these changes, courts in the United States fashioned what became known as the "best interests of the child" doctrine. The result was that mothers increasingly gained custodial rights to their offspring.

In the Anglophone world, marriage had also been regulated by common law, and these notions outlived the transition to state-based marriage. For instance, the Massachusetts Supreme Court of Judicature still clung to the common law age of consent to marry when it decided a case under that state's marriage statute nearly one hundred years later. In sanctioning the marriage of a thirteen-year-old girl to an older youth, the court acknowledged that common law rules might "seem to disregard the protection and restraint, with which the law seeks to surround and guard the inexperience and imprudence of infancy," but the critical matter was the sanctity of marriage itself. A low age of marriage would "guard against the manifold evils which would result from illicit cohabitation." The court's reasoning was explicitly naturalistic: common law ages for marriage represented "that period in life, when the sexual passions are usually first developed."[6]

While courts might have been satisfied with settled precedent, others were not, and beginning in the late nineteenth century, reformers across the Atlantic world sought to raise the age of consent, both to marry and to engage in sexual activity. Central to these changes in the relation of the state to young people were groups outside of its ken, especially the various Societies for the Prevention of Cruelty to Children. Both consciously and ironically related to similar societies for animal cruelty, these groups of usually middle-class reformers sought and won dramatic increases in the age of consent, in the process creating modern statutory rape law. While often seen as something entirely new, this legal regime actually built upon another previous set of rules about youthful sexuality lodged in such civil actions as seduction and breach of promise to marry. But as is so often the case, reform called for the creation of a mythical past, and reform groups at the local level set about to combat the evil of precocious sexual experience. Such efforts were often aimed at the growing working class in industrializing and urbanizing areas, but historians have shown that working people did not simply react to these changes. Instead, they frequently used the state for their own ends, deploying the judicial process to police youthful sexuality in ways aligned with their own customs and traditions. In the teeming communities of progressive era New York City, as Stephen Robertson has shown, working-class families deployed the "shadow of the law" to compel marriage in cases of premarital intercourse, even rape. In one such instance, Peter Waldenstein, a twenty-six-year-old Russian salesman, had apparently drugged and then raped Susan Russell, seventeen. Seeking marriage, Susan's brothers confronted Waldenstein and then carried the case to the authorities. Under threat of a rape charge, Waldenstein eventually relented and married Russell. Even in less dramatic cases of consensual premarital activity, families could still use emerging statutory rape laws to encourage marriage with a "ruined girl."[7]

The regulation of youthful sexuality was intimately intertwined with general youthful disorder, patterns of behavior that began to be called "juvenile delinquency" by the late eighteenth century. In Britain, for instance, elite commentators became concerned about Sabbath-breaking, gambling, and especially property crimes such as petty theft. Related to the rise of compulsory schools, which we shall address in a moment, fears about juvenile delinquency also captured growing concerns about youthful crime and general urban disorder. Young people became both cause and symptom of all that was wrong with the modern urban-industrial city; the response by reformers had momentous implications for the relationship between young people, citizenship, and the state. Responding to "child vagrancy" as it was often called, state and non-state actors across the West mounted a massive campaign of intervention into the lives of children and youth, particularly those of the working class. Again, such campaigns were not entirely novel, for they drew upon practices such as placing out that had been used by poor law authorities for centuries. Still, the level of intervention practiced by such groups as the Children's Aid Society in the United States reached new levels as middle-class men and women removed children from their homes and placed them in new households, often in the supposedly purifying air of the countryside. Such actions represented the rise of a new domestic ideal, one that saw motherhood and the new romantic childhood as the center of respectable family life.[8]

The apparatus of the state expanded even more with the advent of reform schools and similar institutions. The impetus for special institutions for "troubled" children and youths came from at least two quarters. On one side, educational advocates wondered what to do with truant children or those who were too difficult to manage in the schools themselves. More important, prison reformers strove to remove young people from "adult" prisons. This motivation was tied to a larger change in the criminal culpability of young people. In most of the early modern West, young people had been tried, convicted, and punished in ways similar to adults. The records from Britain's Old Bailey in the eighteenth century show the widespread use of capital punishment for young people. Indeed, the solicitor general claimed in 1785, probably extravagantly, that youths under twenty-one comprised nine-tenths of those hanged. If that figure was exaggerated, it nonetheless indicated the ways in which the law did not shield young people from criminal responsibility. Similarly, children and youths were usually incarcerated along with other offenders in the haphazard gaols of the early modern city. With the rise of sentimental and domestic notions of childhood in the Romantic period, prison, or worse the gallows, no longer seemed an age-appropriate spot for innocent cherubs. Yet young people continued to refuse to conform to the images laid out for them in ladies magazines. The modern prison, with its emphasis on the reformation of the soul, transferred with relative ease to the modern school, and its more disciplinary counterpart, the juvenile reformatory. Here, young people would be taught to be subordinate to authority, be it at work, at school, or in the street. In this sense, as state power over young people expanded, they found themselves increasingly segregated in the legal process itself. As childhood expanded, their legal personhood shrank.[9]

At the same time, however, the process of juvenile reform pointed in a paradoxical direction towards the beginning of a very long process that would lead to the re-inclusion of young people as legal actors by the latter part of the twentieth century. Such broad shifts are normally hard to pin down, but in this case, historians and other scholars generally recognize a singular starting point: Chicago in the late nineteenth and early twentieth centuries. There a group of reform-minded men and women, mostly women, waged a successful campaign that resulted in the establishment of the first Juvenile Court in 1899. Their goal was to separate juvenile justice in both form and substance from adult criminal law. In Illinois itself, this effort explicitly rejected an 1870 court decision that had granted procedural rights to young people. In place of the panoply of constitutional safeguards that had arisen over the nineteenth century, child savers hoped to transform juvenile justice into something different than the adversarial process of the legal system. Judges, assisted by reformers themselves, would become kindly fathers, applying the gentle hand of the state to the bottoms of misguided youth. As David Tanenhaus has shown, the juvenile court did not arrive fully developed at the turn of the century. Rather its defining features – summary decisions, indeterminate sentencing, and the like – emerged in a political struggle that took decades. Indeed, it was a long road that would end only with the re-emergence of civil rights for youthful offenders after World War II.[10]

The juvenile court movement both reflected and spawned another important shift in how the state related to young people: the rise of a therapeutic ethos in treating "juvenile delinquency." By the early twentieth century, reformers across the West had begun to understand youthful problems in medical terms. Drawing upon the work of psychology pioneer G. Stanley Hall, whose 1904 tome *Adolescence* defined a field and a folkway, William Healy and others in the juvenile courts began the systematic search for environmental causes for wayward youths. Though starting with nineteenth century assumptions about "character," Healy and his associates elsewhere soon turned to environmental factors such as poverty to explain juvenile crime. As with many scientific discourses of the twentieth century, these notions lost their narrow institutional moorings to lay the basis for the modern child guidance movement. At such institutions as the Judge Baker Clinic in Boston, children and youths found themselves treated for their deficiencies, at first at the assignation of the courts and later at the behest of their troubled parents.[11]

While the modern state in Europe developed along both similar and divergent lines, its relationship to troubled children and youths often paralleled what occurred in the United States. Often drawing explicitly upon developments in the United States, European reformers also slowly moved toward a therapeutic approach to underage criminality. In France, a 1912 law decriminalized all transgressions for children under age thirteen and signaled a movement towards a more therapeutic approach. Decades later, a 1942 law under the wartime Vichy regime and a 1945 statute in the post-war era both pointed toward penal irresponsibility for young people, even if that did not always occur in practice. Still, the French system often mirrored US juvenile courts by, for example, closing hearings to the public. To the east, the therapeutic ethos had limited influence in Russia under the late Tsarist governments, but the Revolution marked a significant departure in Russian thinking and lawmaking about youthful criminality. A Decree on Commissions by Minors in 1918 ended court trials and prison sentences, turning over juvenile crime to three-person commissions that included a medical practitioner. During the middle-Stalinist period, policy swung back to a hard line. As in other parts of Europe, fears about a juvenile "crime wave" led to the Decree of 7 April 1935 that extended adult penalties to juvenile offenders. In the post-Stalinist period, however, the rehabilitationist approach returned, and by 1967, the Soviet government enacted a law that created "public educators," court-appointed volunteers who would supervise troubled youths. In brief, across governments, liberal and conservative, democratic and totalitarian, a common approach to youthful crime emerged. Young people were increasingly seen as wards of the state whose indiscretions should be treated instead of punished.[12]

Incarceration and therapy represented, and continue to represent, one extremity of the relationship of the state to childhood and youth. They rested upon and reinforced the exclusion of people before a certain age from full citizenship. Certain young people in the modern West increasingly found themselves treated as wards of the state, subject to long-term restriction without the procedural rights granted to adults by liberal constitutional polities. But at the same time, the modernizing state depended upon the creation of a model citizen who would give consent willingly to the political process, obey the dictates of that process, and generally act in a "responsible" manner. If the modern state depended upon a political culture constituted as an opposite to the supposedly carefree notions of modern childhood, still the inhabitants of that happy land must one day don the mantle of citizenship. The solution to this puzzle came in the form of modern compulsory schooling, the taken-for-granted institutional form that became the hegemonic model of experience for young people by the early twentieth century in the West, and eventually across the planet. Ensuring compliance with the regime of compulsion occupied the time of state authorities across the twentieth century, but in the end, school, not the penal system, would be the center of the interaction between young people and the state. It is hard to avoid overstatement in considering this massive change in the human past, but no other experience has so dominated the daily life of one group of humans.

While compulsory schooling became a commonplace, and then a right, by the latter part of the twentieth century, it arrived in piecemeal fashion, and the aims and intentions of its architects pointed in multiple directions. One direction was amelioration; another was social control. Churches across the western world had offered religious instruction to poor children for centuries, but by the eighteenth century, secular charity schools began to spring up in Britain and elsewhere. Hermann August Francke's charity school near Halle became a showpiece of continental efforts, while in Britain a lively debate spurred by Bernard de Mandeville's 1723 attack on charity schools led the way to the growth of the movement there. In Britain's North American colonies, charity school instruction took off with the religious awakening of the middle eighteenth century. In general, these early efforts combined training in piety and labor, aiming to make the poor "industrious in their stations."[13]

School building in the eighteenth century took place in monarchical polities, where the very nature of the state relied upon obedient subjecthood, something schools could supply, both in their results and in the daily culture of their classrooms. The schoolmaster represented father, monarch, and state. The American, French, and other revolutions of the late eighteenth century and beyond altered the political culture of the modern state and, concomitantly, the place of schools to and within it. Tied into a broader Atlantic discussion, debates about education among elites led in many directions. In early nineteenth-century Britain, for instance, Joseph Lancaster experimented with "monitorial schools," a system whereby a headmaster taught advanced students who taught the rest. In the United States, efforts by such luminaries as Benjamin Rush and Judith Sargeant Murray led to the rapid growth of female academies, as elites began to believe that educated sons of the republic required educated mothers. If Rush and others sponsored reforms that pointed in ways modern eyes would see as progressive, he and many others also plainly laid out the motives for widespread schooling in the republic. Calling for "absolute authority" on the part of schoolmasters in a 1786 essay, Rush believed that schools must "prepare our youth for the subordination of laws and thereby qualify them for becoming good citizens of the republic."

Authority in the schoolroom could "convert men into republican machines," something that "must be done if we expect them to perform their parts properly in the great machine of the state," Rush concluded. Such notions crossed the Atlantic, appearing in a similar form in France. "Children belong to the Republic before they belong to their parents," declared French revolutionary Georges-Jacques Danton. French law would take more than a century to catch up with these republican sensibilities, but the impetus for universal education provided by the Revolution's claims on citizenship outlasted the revolutionary governments of the eighteenth century.[14]

Such sentiments led to the rapid growth of various kinds of public schools in the early nineteenth century, but the mere existence of the schoolhouse did not mean incipient citizens sat at its desks. Later in the century, local and national governments began to enact compulsory attendance laws. In Britain, the 1870 Elementary Education Act began the process of making attendance compulsory there. In the German provinces, some localities began enforcing compulsory attendance laws in the early nineteenth century, and by the turn of the twentieth century, they had achieved some measure of success in fastening young children in school. By 1908, German educational reformer Wilhelm Polligkeit could outline "the right of the child to education," a right that would foster "activity as a citizen of the state" as well as "insight into the legal order of the state." In France, attendance policy remained much more relaxed through the vagaries of various governments. Starting with the 1833 Loi Guizot, the French government tried to reach out to peasants in the countryside, but encountered much resistance. The 1874 child labor law and subsequent educational legislation in 1882 advanced these efforts and prompted a wave of school building, but working people in city and country continued to attend sporadically. On the other side of the Atlantic, a healthy enforcement apparatus for school attendance started to appear sporadically in various states by the 1820s, and within a century, the truant officer was known to every child in the country.[15]

In the United States, the "state simplification" of compulsory schooling also prompted conflict. A careful study of Italian immigrants and schools in New Haven, Connecticut, found that school officials continually worried about an "army" of truant boys in the late nineteenth and early twentieth centuries. Immigrant families saw schooling as an imposition on the family economy and existing modes of socialization. As one put it, "School is a kind of castor oil America forces the younger generation to swallow, but it will not influence their lives in the least." *Padroni* labor recruiters, parents, and young workers themselves placed factory above school, but such resistance did not last. By the 1930s, youths in New Haven had begun to adopt a different attitude about schooling, seizing upon the social and economic opportunities it provided.[16]

In the southern United States, a different kind of resistance arose in the mid-twentieth century: resistance to integrated public education. The educational system in the United States grew up with racial division at its core, but the Jim Crow system cemented segregation as a central facet of American schooling in southern states. When African-Americans used the legal process to challenge and then dismantle that system, some southern localities famously responded with "massive resistance," simply closing their public schools, sometimes for years. But such extreme responses represented the last ditch stand of a lost cause. The fact that the civil rights movement in the United States focused much of its efforts on schools dramatically altered the terms of modern schooling by making rights-based arguments for inclusion against a state system bent upon exclusion under the guise of "separate but equal." By that time, much of the resistance to compulsory schooling had abated, with the notable exception of religious minorities who won exemptions. What had begun as an openly expressed means of controlling the unruly poor had become the primary vehicle for social and economic aspiration. Under the modern regime of schooling in the United States, no child could be left behind.[17]

The rise of compulsory schooling in the West paralleled and drew upon the state's commitment to child welfare in the late nineteenth century and it grew exponentially in the twentieth. When Swedish child advocate Ellen Key foresaw the coming era to be the "century of the child" in 1900, her declaration was predictive. At the dawn of the twentieth century, the state directed little attention to the welfare of children, but that would change dramatically in the decades after 1900. As we have seen, juvenile courts and schools grew apace, but the most high-profile development came in central bureaucracies directed to the needs of mothers and infants. Drawing upon the new sociology and the gritty experience of the settlement house movement in Britain and the United States, reform-minded individuals, often women, pushed policy elites to develop programs for the needs of children and youths. In the United States, such social welfare luminaries as Grace Abbot and Julia Lathrop and organizations such as the National Child Labor Committee prompted the Theodore Roosevelt administration to act. A White House conference in 1909, devoted to child welfare, led to legislation that established the US Children's Bureau in 1912. Operating from a vision that encompassed the "whole child," Bureau leaders Lathrop and Abbott made the agency a clearinghouse for information and action on a wide variety of fronts: birth registration, pure milk, child labor reform, education, and the host of issues raised by the world wars. The Bureau helped to enact and administer the 1921 Sheppard–Towner Act, the first piece of federal legislation aimed squarely at the medical and economic needs of mothers, infants, and children. The law supplemented expanding state-based mothers' pension acts, and while it died in 1929, it laid the foundation for later federal intervention through the New Deal's Aid to Dependent Children, and the Great Society's Aid to Families with Dependent Children programs.[18]

As in the United States, the involvement of the state in child welfare in Europe took an increasingly interventionist tack from the late nineteenth century onward, but reactions to that general approach in the later twentieth century illustrate the limits of the state's hold on young people. French authorities had moved towards a more active role for the state in family life across the course of the nineteenth century, but the 1889 law on *abandon moral* opened up vast new powers to remove children from families. Such actions paralleled developments in Germany, where reformers tried to move towards a more "scientific-managerial" approach, even in the face of opposition from more conservatively minded religious authorities. In particular, the 1922 German National Child Welfare Act drew on earlier progressive efforts to make child welfare more scientific, preventative, and therapeutic. In Britain, welfare officials deployed the 1908 Child Welfare Act and numerous pieces of follow-up bills to move towards a more therapeutic regime that increasingly stressed preventative social work in families as the way to provide for young people as well as to prevent juvenile crime. In Britain, however, interventionist goals were tempered, particularly in the immediate post-World War II era. A statement from the Home Office in 1948 made this theme explicit: "To keep the family together must be the first aim, and the separation of the child from its parents can only be justified when there is no possibility of securing adequate care for the child in his own home."[19]

Child welfare programs had both expanded the power of the central state and, at the same time, configured childhood in a way that suggested a broader notion of "rights" for young people. The child welfare programs promoted, if not created, by such agencies as the US Children's Bureau would eventually find their way into international statements about the fundamental rights of the child, but in a narrower sense of "rights," the juvenile court system took center stage. Since its inception, the juvenile court system in the United States had been a pristine symbol and an actual embodiment of the fraught relationship between young people, the state, and citizenship in liberal polities. It both shielded young people from the harsh criminal laws and adversarial court procedures of the western legal system *and* denied them the basic rights of citizenship outlined in the Bill of Rights and other foundational documents of liberal democracy. The utility of the former goal was poignantly illustrated by US Supreme Court Justice Potter Stewart in his dissenting opinion for *In re Gault* (1967), the case that dramatically altered procedural rights for young people in US law. Recalling a time before the juvenile courts, Stewart told a chilling story about an 1828 case: "So it was that a 12-year-old boy named James Guild was tried in New Jersey for killing Catharine Beakes," Stewart wrote. "A jury found him guilty of murder, and he was sentenced to death by hanging. The sentence was executed. It was all very constitutional."[20]

Stewart's brethren saw the matter differently, and *Gault* heralded a new era of thinking about the legal personhood of young people. Arising in the remote mining town of Globe, Arizona, the case involved fifteen-year-old Gerald Francis Gault. Accused of making an obscene phone call to a neighbor, Jerry Gault was committed to the Arizona Industrial School for Boys, better known as Fort Grant. With none of the procedural or appeals protections of an adult offender, it was a six-year sentence to an institution already notorious for ill treatment of its inmates. Gault's parents fought back, and with the assistance of the American Civil Liberties Union, the case made its way to the Supreme Court where, in an 8:1 opinion, the court applied Fourteenth and Sixth Amendment jurisprudence to juvenile court cases, stipulating that they must include such due process protections as proper notification of charges and the right to counsel. Drawing upon a wide array of sociological data as well as his own experience in previous cases involving young people, Justice Abraham Fortas, writing for the majority, cut away the veil of paternalism surrounding the juvenile courts and the facilities to which they sent their charges. Such places were not schools but prisons, Fortas reasoned, places where young people were confined for "anything from waywardness to rape and homicide." In light of this reality, Fortas continued, "it would be extraordinary if our Constitution did not require the procedural regularity and the exercise of care implied in the phrase 'due process.' Under our Constitution, the condition of being a boy does not justify a kangaroo court."[21]

Denounced by critics and honored more in the breach, *Gault* signaled the arrival of a newer understanding of children's rights, one that departed significantly from what had come before. For much of the twentieth century, notions of children's rights had echoed US child labor reformer Alexander McKelway's famous "Declaration of Dependence." This progressive era document asserted the right of young people to be "helpless and dependent," to be free from "daily toil," to have an education, and "to play and to dream." His colleague in the National Child Labor Committee, Edgar Gardner Murphy, had put it more pithily: the child had "the divine right to do nothing." Reformers across the Atlantic World had generally understood such sentiments to be at the heart of what was meant by "children's rights." Indeed, by 1989, these ideas had become sacralized in the United Nations Convention on the Rights of the Child. Along with an enumeration of rights regarding health, education, and labor, the UN Convention affirmed that: "children have the right to relax and play, and to join in a wide range of cultural, artistic and other recreational activities."[22]

Stated in this fashion, "children's rights" imagined young people as non-citizens, non-participants in the state. At the same time, however, a newer understanding of children's rights was emerging, one that drew upon earlier developments but which also pointed toward debates that would resonate into the twenty-first century. By the time of the UN Convention, a commitment to freedom of thought and expression had become commonplace. In its somewhat conflicted Article 12, the Convention affirmed: "When adults are making decisions that affect children, children have the right to say what they think should happen and have their opinions taken into account." Lest such bold declarations indicate a substantial change in power, the authors immediately clarified: "This does not mean that children can now tell their parents what to do." Applied to the state, such a position viewed children and youths not simply as objects of state action or as potential citizens, but as vital participants. In fact, the late twentieth century was not the first time such ideas had surfaced. The early Soviet period in Russia witnessed increasingly dramatic assertions of children's rights as citizens of the state, and as actors independent of their parents. At various levels of Soviet society and particularly in the schools during the 1920s, "self-government" came to the fore in the form of children's soviets – councils that were intended to provide a place for young people's participation in political discussion and decision making. More radical groups went further, asserting a right of children to leave their parents if they wished. "The hour of the children's rebellion against their parents in every family has come," declared radical Fedor Orlov-Skomorovsky in 1921. "And it is not a frightful time: it is a wonderful, long-awaited time." While such extreme sentiments rarely found their way into daily practice in Soviet society, the communist revolution in Russia pointed towards a dramatically different way of seeing children's rights.[23]

Not surprisingly the Soviet view did not catch hold in the modern West, but ironically, in the heart of the Cold War, a group of "child liberationists" in the United States articulated a vision of children's rights that went far beyond anything imagined by radicals in socialist Russia. In a 1974 book appropriately titled *Birthrights*, Richard Farson explicitly tied children's rights to other liberationist movements at the time, noting that children's "oppression" was now visible in ways previously unseen. Through the new lens of civil rights, young people appeared "powerless, dominated, ignored, invisible." Writing in the same year, another American author, John Holt, outlined what new children's rights would look like. Holt would give children such rights as "equal treatment at the hands of the law," "the right to vote, and take full part in political affairs," and "the right to work, for money." In brief, Holt believed, children should have "the right to do, in general, what any adult may legally do." Farson and Holt clearly occupied radical, even shaky, cultural, social, and legal ground, but their ideas connected with the wave of youth activism that swept the western world in the 1960s and 1970s. Those movements had not secured adult rights for children, nor had they intended to. But in response to restive youths, the United States had lowered the voting age to eighteen in 1971. In the youth-saturated culture of the post-war period, it was possible to envisage a very different relationship between children and the state.[24]

Perhaps the most remarkable example of children's citizenship emerged in Sweden. As Bengt Sandin has shown, the post-World War II Swedish state outlined a new definition of childhood, one that understood children as vital individuals whose voices counted in broader political discussions. This new view had many sources, but one came from a new emphasis on the "physical integrity" of young people via bans on corporal punishment, first in schools in 1957 and then inside the family in 1979. These laws essentially recognized children as having the same rights as adults, and the Swedish welfare state built upon that notion through such practices as child allowances, which, by the 1970s, were seen as primarily belonging to children themselves, at least older ones. Throughout the 1970s and 1980s, a broad program of early childhood development and education programs increasingly created spaces for young people to develop identities separate from their parents, while the state instructed parents that such fostering of independence was their proper role. Even in the conservative environment from the 1990s onward, the Swedish state actively pursued a "best interests" approach, drawn upon the UN Convention. A national children's ombudsman attended to children's affairs, and young people in general were expected to voice their concerns about schooling, health, and other matters of interest to them.[25]

The Swedish case, however, was both divergent from much of the rest of the West, and at the same time, in line with broader traditions. After all, the Swedish *state* decided that children needed to be heard; the *state* – a coterie of professional and political elites – was in the driver's seat, not young people themselves. The power of the state in the lives of children and youths had built upon two centuries of social and political development in the West. By the early twenty-first century, that relationship continued to display remarkable continuities with ideas first outlined in the late eighteenth and early nineteenth centuries. Certainly, young people had gained procedural rights in the courts in both criminal proceedings, and sometimes in civil cases involving divorce, custody, and the like. Court rulings, statutes, and even the UN Convention had asserted a right to free speech for young people. Against these individual rights, however, a state apparatus controlled the bodies of young people in ways antithetical to the experience of adults, save prisoners. In order to foster civic participation in the future, the modern state prevented remunerative labor, punished crime, oversaw family life, ensured health, and, most important, compelled education. In most cases, it did so without the participation of its wards. Radicals occasionally pointed out the paradoxes inherent in this social, cultural, and political outcome, but in the main, children and youths remained outside the borders of belonging, as both the vessel of perfect citizenship and the ultimate expression of its absence.

Notes

1 "Borders of belonging" is Barbara Young Welke's phrase in *Law and the Borders of Belonging in the Long Nineteenth Century United States* (New York, NY: Cambridge University Press, 2010). My understanding of citizenship and the politics of inclusion also draws upon,

among others, Mae M. Ngai, *Impossible Subjects: Illegal Aliens and the Making of Modern America* (Princeton, NJ: Princeton University Press, 2003); Nancy MacLean, *Freedom Is Not Enough: The Opening of the American Workplace* (Cambridge, MA: Harvard University Press, 2006); and Margot Canaday, *The Straight State: Sexuality and Citizenship in Twentieth-Century America* (Princeton, NJ: Princeton University Press, 2009).

2 Holly Brewer, *By Birth or Consent: Children, Law, and the Anglo–American Revolution in Authority* (Chapel Hill, NC: University of North Carolina Press, 2005), 40–44.

3 Quoted in Sharon Braslaw Sundue, *Industrious in Their Stations: Young People at Work in Urban America, 1720–1810* (Charlottesville, VA: University of Virginia Press, 2009), 127.

4 Colin Heywood, *Childhood in Nineteenth Century France: Work, Health, and Education among the "Classes Populaires,"* (New York, NY: Cambridge University Press, 1988), 260–289.

5 *Powers v. Ware*, 53 Mich. 507 (1884), 515.

6 *Parton v. Hervey*, 67 Mass. 119 (1854).

7 Stephen Robertson, *Crimes against Children: Sexual Violence and Legal Culture in New York City, 1880–1960* (Chapel Hill, NC: University of North Carolina Press, 2005), 102–107.

8 Peter King, "The Rise of Juvenile Delinquency in England 1780–1840: Changing Patterns of Perception and Prosecution," *Past & Present* 160 (1998): 122; Christine Stansell, "Women, Children, and the Uses of the Streets: Class and Gender Conflict in New York City, 1850–1860," *Feminist Studies* 8 (1982): 309–335.

9 Brewer, *By Birth or Consent*, 212.

10 David S. Tanenhaus, *Juvenile Justice in the Making* (New York, NY: Oxford University Press, 2005).

11 Kathleen W. Jones, *Taming the Troublesome Child: American Families, Child Guidance, and the Limits of Psychiatric Authority* (Cambridge, MA: Harvard University Press, 1999).

12 Sarah Fishman, *The Battle for Children: WWII, Youth Crime, and Juvenile Justice in Twentieth-Century France* (Cambridge, MA: Harvard University Press, 2002), 26–27, 200–204; Catriona Kelly, *Children's World: Growing Up in Russia 1890–1991* (New Haven, CT: Yale University Press, 2007), 213, 230, 271.

13 Sundue, *Industrious in Their Stations*, 130–133.

14 Sundue, *Industrious in Their Stations*, 127–161; Carl F. Kaestle, *Pillars of the Republic: Common Schools and American Society, 1780–1860* (New York, NY: Hill and Wang, 1983), 7; Sylvia Schafer, *Children in Moral Danger and the Problem of Government in Third Republic France.* (Princeton, NJ: Princeton, University Press, 1997), 43.

15 Harry D. Hendrick, *Child Welfare: England 1872–1989* (London, UK: Routledge, 1994), 29–30; Edward Ross Dickinson, *The Politics of German Child Welfare from the Empire to the Federal Republic* (Cambridge, MA: Harvard University Press, 1996), 74–75; Heywood, *Childhood in Nineteenth Century France*, 62, 260–289.

16 Stephen Lassonde, *Learning to Forget: Schooling and Family Life in New Haven's Working Class, 1870–1940* (New Haven, CT: Yale University Press, 2005), quotation on 53.

17 Jennifer Ritterhouse, *Growing Up Jim Crow: How Black And White Southern Children Learned Race* (Chapel Hill, NC: University of North Carolina Press, 2006).

18 Kriste Lindenmeyer, *"A Right to Childhood": The US Children's Bureau and Child Welfare, 1912–1946* (Urbana and Chicago, IL: University of Illinois Press, 1997).

19 Schafer, *Children in Moral Danger and the Problem of Government in Third Republic France*, 43–44, 66; Dickinson, *Politics of German Child Welfare*, 154; Hendrick, *Child Welfare*, 220.

20 *In re Gault*, 387 US 1 (1967), 80.

21 Ibid., 28–29; David S. Tanenhaus, *The Constitutional Rights of Children: In re Gault and Juvenile Justice* (Lawrence, KS: University Press of Kansas, 2011), especially 3–23, 86–87.

22 McKelway quoted in Hugh D. Hindman, *Child Labor: An American History* (Armonk, NJ: M.E. Sharp 2002), 44; Edgar Gardner Murphy, *The Case Against Child Labor*, Alabama Child Labor Committee pamphlet 1902, Rare Books Room, Wilson Library, University of North Carolina-Chapel Hill, 6; United Nations Convention on the Rights of the Child, preamble, Article 31.

23 UN Convention, Article 12; Kelly, *Children's World*, 62–65.

24 Joseph M. Hawes, *The Children's Rights Movement: A History of Advocacy and Protection*, (New York, NY: Twayne Publishers, 1991), 115–116.

25 Bengt Sandin, "Children and the Swedish Welfare State: From Different to Similar" in *Reinventing Childhood After World War II*, ed. Paula S. Fass and Michael Grossberg (Philadelphia, PA: University of Pennsylvania Press, 2012), 110–138.

Suggestions for further reading

Many thanks to my Northern Illinois University colleagues Andy Bruno, Sandra Dawson, Heide Fehrenbach, and Emma Kuby who provided bibliographic suggestions.

General accounts

Hendrick, Harry D. *Child Welfare: England 1872–1989*. London, UK: Routledge, 1994. Valuable survey of many issues involving children and the state, including welfare, labor, crime, and education.

Heywood, Colin. *Childhood in Nineteenth Century France: Work, Health, and Education among the "Classes Populaires."* New York, NY: Cambridge University Press, 1988. The starting point for understanding numerous issues regarding children and the state in nineteenth-century France, with particular attention to child labor.

Kelly, Catriona. *Children's World: Growing Up in Russia 1890–1991*. New Haven, CT: Yale University Press, 2007. Comprehensive and highly readable account of Russian childhood including valuable sections on education and juvenile crime, especially in the Stalinist period.

Citizenship, rights, and the state

Brewer, Holly. *By Birth or Consent: Children, Law, and the Anglo–American Revolution in Authority*. Chapel Hill, NC: University of North Carolina Press, 2005. Essential to understanding legal personhood of children and youths before the rise of the modern state.

Fehrenbach, Heide. *Race after Hitler: Black Occupation Children in Postwar Germany and America*. Princeton, NJ: Princeton University Press, 2007. A close look at how the state in post-Nazi Germany dealt with issues of race and youth.

Grossberg, Michael. *Governing the Hearth: Law and the Family in Nineteenth-Century America*. Chapel Hill, NC: University of North Carolina Press, 1985. Still the most important starting point for law and the family in nineteenth-century America.

Grossman, Joanna L. and Lawrence M. Friedman. *Inside the Castle: Law and the Family in 20th Century America*. Princeton, NJ: Princeton University Press, 2011. Synthetic treatment of family law in the modern United States with attention to many of the subjects covered in this essay.

Hawes, Joseph M. *The Children's Rights Movement: A History of Advocacy and Protection*. New York, NY: Twayne Publishers, 1991. The standard account of the modern children's rights movement.

Lindenmeyer, Kriste. *"A Right to Childhood": The US Children's Bureau and Child Welfare, 1912–1946*. Urbana and Chicago, IL: University of Illinois Press, 1997. The definitive account of the first federal agency devoted to child welfare in US history.

Pearson, Susan J. *The Rights of the Defenseless: Protecting Animals and Children in Gilded Age America*. Chicago, IL: University of Chicago Press, 2011. Ties the child-saving movement to a broader "sentimental liberalism" of the late nineteenth century.

Schumann, Dirk, ed., *Raising Citizens in the "Century of the Child": The United States and German Central Europe in Comparative Perspective*. New York, NY: Berghahn Books, 2010. Excellent collection of essays that speaks directly to children and citizenship, particularly in the introduction to the volume.

Skocpol, Theda. *Protecting Soldiers and Mothers: The Political Origins of Social Policy in the United States*. Cambridge, MA: Belknap Press, 1992. Highly influential work on the modern state that stresses child welfare programs as part of the "maternalist" thesis.

Crime

Fishman, Sarah. *The Battle for Children: WWII, Youth Crime, and Juvenile Justice in Twentieth-Century France*. Cambridge, MA: Harvard University Press, 2002. Stresses the continuities of juvenile justice across the war period with a valuable look at later developments.

Robertson, Stephen. *Crimes against Children: Sexual Violence and Legal Culture in New York City, 1880–1960*. Chapel Hill, NC: University of North Carolina Press, 2005. An important account of young people and sexuality at the local level.

Tanenhaus, David S. *The Constitutional Rights of Children: In re Gault and Juvenile Justice*. Lawrence, KS: University of Press of Kansas, 2011. Brief but vivid account of the *Gault* case and related issues regarding the legal rights of young people.

Tanenhaus, David S. *Juvenile Justice in the Making*. New York, NY: Oxford University Press, 2005. Important work on the juvenile court system that emphasizes the lengthy process of its creation.

Education

Donson, Andrew. *Youth in the Fatherless Land: War Pedagogy, Nationalism, and Authority in Germany, 1914–1918*. Cambridge, MA: Harvard University Press, 2010. Explores the ways in which World War I changed German educational systems.

Kaestle, Carl F. *Pillars of the Republic: Common Schools and American Society, 1780–1860*. New York:, NY Hill and Wang, 1993. The standard account of the common school movement in the United States and its relationship with republican thought.

Ritterhouse, Jennifer. *Growing Up Jim Crow: How Black And White Southern Children Learned Race*. Chapel Hill, NC: University of North Carolina Press, 2006. Includes a look at the daily realities of segregated schools in the US South.

Lassonde, Stephen. *Learning to Forget: Schooling and Family Life in New Haven's Working Class, 1870–1940*. New Haven, CT: Yale University Press, 2005. An invaluable study of the results of compulsory education on the immigrant community in one US city.

Labor

Schmidt, James. D. *Industrial Violence and the Legal Origins of Child Labor*. New York, NY: Cambridge University Press, 2010. Investigates the power of law in the creation of child labor as a cultural construct.

Sundue, Sharon Braslaw. *Industrious in Their Stations: Young People at Work in Urban America, 1720–1810*. Charlottesville, VA: University of Virginia Press, 2009. Looks at changes in the youth labor market and the rise of charity schools across the eighteenth and early nineteenth centuries.
See also works by Brewer, Hendrick, Heywood, and Kelly noted above.

Welfare

Dickinson, Edward Ross. *The Politics of German Child Welfare from the Empire to the Federal Republic*. Cambridge, MA: Harvard University Press, 1996. Critical book on German history outlining two long-standing approaches to child welfare: conservative and "social-managerial."
Jones, Kathleen W. *Taming the Troublesome Child: American Families, Child Guidance, and the Limits of Psychiatric Authority*. Cambridge, MA: Harvard University Press, 1999. Explores the medicalization of delinquency in the early twentieth century.
Ladd-Taylor, Molly. *Mother–Work: Women, Child Welfare, and the State, 1890–1930*. Urbana and Chicago, IL: University of Illinois Press, 1994. Places child welfare at the center of the modern state.
Schafer, Sylvia. *Children in Moral Danger and the Problem of Government in Third Republic France*. Princeton, NJ: Princeton, University Press, 1997. Examines a critical piece of legislation in French history regarding parental versus state authority.

10

THE VEXED HISTORY OF CHILDREN AND SEX

Beth Bailey

How does one write a history of children and sex? The editors of a scholarly collection on the topic subtitled their introductory essay "Here There Be Dragons," and perhaps no truer words appear in that volume. In the modern western world, the union of children and sex, of childhood and sex, has been perilous ground.[1] Historical actors mapped this territory much as early explorers charted the world, with uncertain knowledge and fearful certainty, while scholars of the topic have, in a variety of ways, found their explorations fraught with danger: to their own deeply held beliefs, to theoretical consistency, to methodological clarity.

Moreover, the topic shares the challenges faced by any scholar writing about children, especially when looking back at recent decades. We lack access to children's own voices; those that exist are almost without exception recorded, to purpose, by adults. Thus we have access to adult perceptions of childhood sexuality, to adult attempts to manage or control the relation of children to sex (in its many forms), as well as to records of sexual misconduct or abuse, but to few, if any, unmediated sources of children's experience. Joining children's history to the history of sexuality simply compounds the problem. It is easy to locate discourses about sex: legal discourses, regulatory discourses, discourses of surveillance or advice, of fantasy or control. "Sex" itself, is hard to find. Thus in the end, those difficulties push my essay toward a study of the contested meanings of childhood and a discussion of the cultural constructions of children, childhood, and sex.

So let me begin with a proposition. Sex, in the modern western world, defines the boundary between childhood and adulthood.[2] It is sex, more than anything else, that divides childhood from what comes after, whether that later state is adulthood or youth or adolescence or some other historically defined category. Sex in physiological terms sets the boundary between childhood and puberty or sexual maturity. Sex in terms of experience defines the boundary between forms of acceptable childhood sexuality and adult sexual acts. Sex in terms of knowledge delimits the boundary between innocence and knowledge, precocity and depravity.

These boundaries are not clear and transparent; they are instead contested and historically contingent. Thus it is in struggles over those boundaries, in the conflicts between competing definitions and the tensions within each, that we can most clearly see the construction of what seems natural. Furthermore, it is the very separation of childhood and adult sexuality that so closely links childhood to sexuality in modern cultures as societies attempt to enforce that separation through elaborate systems of law, institutions, and ideologies. A whole constellation of social practices has been created as modern societies attempted to protect children from sex and adult sexuality.

Over time, a series of often co-existing and contested understandings of the nature of childhood combined with shifts in the role of the family, the state, and the organization of the economy to yield an understanding that is now dominant, if not universalized and naturalized. In ways that were gradual, uneven, and contested, the prevailing definition of the meaning of childhood in European and then American culture shifted from assumptions grounded in a belief in original sin to a sentimentalized notion that innocence – most particularly sexual innocence – was the fundamental defining quality of childhood. That understanding fits uneasily with an industrializing world, where the children of the poor, highly visible and often less than angelic in appearance and behavior, seemed to put to lie a belief in childhood innocence that lay at the heart of the Victorian family. That belief in childhood innocence, however, was a key impetus to reform. Rather than divide children into two camps, the innocent and the corrupt, ours and theirs, Victorian reformers claimed childhood innocence as universal and sought to protect that natural innocence from corrupting forces that included exposure, experience, knowledge, and exploitation.

Twentieth-century recognitions of infant and childhood sexuality raised new questions about definitions and boundaries as the newly defined uncorrupted nature of childhood eroticism now seemed to demand protection from the corrupting effects of guilt and repression, while movements for sexual liberation and struggles for rights led some to assert that hard-gained protections were instead denying children the right to sexual pleasure. In contrast, late twentieth-century cultures of childhood sexuality were marked by tensions between an increasingly sexualized culture combined with increasingly early average age at puberty and media-driven concerns about child sexual abuse and abduction that led parents to constrain children's freedom and independence in ways that extend, to a remarkable extent, across class, race, and gender.

The universalizing impulse, seen most clearly in nineteenth-century reform, reveals the growing power of a bureaucratizing state as standard definitions based on chronological age trumped differences in individual maturity, physical development, culture, and circumstance. The move toward universalization both obscured and highlighted the fact that childhood is not easily universalized. Childhood (like youth, adulthood, or old age) is gendered, raced, and classed, and while the larger impulse may have been protection, the results were uneven and often punitive. As in so many reform movements, there has been a tension between protection and rights. And in the fundamental insistence that innocence is what defines childhood, the actions taken by parents, reformers, and the state to protect children in their innocence may well deny them necessary knowledge, sexual agency, and the right of consent.

Just as most people in premodern or preindustrial societies had a more immediate acquaintance with the processes of birth and death than do we, so, too, were they more directly exposed to the process of sex. Children shared that knowledge. Privacy was scarce when a one- or two-room hut housed parents, children, livestock, and quite possibly some unrelated adults, and in any case standards of privacy were often quite different than those of current American and European societies. People were accustomed to sharing beds with members of their households and even, when traveling, with strangers. Children commonly slept in the same room as their parents unless the family had uncommon wealth; when families were poor or winters were cold enough, the whole family might share one bed. There was no privacy for marital relations; children heard and saw adults having sex. Animals, too, were a source of sexual knowledge. Children saw animals copulating and giving birth; few adults saw any need to protect children from such observations.

That is not to say that because young children had knowledge of sex that they were not protected from adult sexuality and adult sexual contact. British common law, for example, set the age of consent for girls at ten. On the other hand, it is difficult to know whether children in isolated communities were especially vulnerable to incest or sex, in various forms, with older children or even adults.[3] Colin Heywood, writing about isolated communities in France even following industrialization, argues that while it is possible that in small communities of people tied by land and family such behavior was closely monitored and discouraged, it is also possible that such ties made people reluctant to intervene in family affairs or to strain relationships within the community.[4]

In general, it seems, no one paid much attention to childhood sexuality on its own terms before the late eighteenth century. There are few, if any, records of children's sexuality or experiences with sex. One notable – and certainly not representative – exception is the records kept by Jean Héroard, doctor to the infant prince who would become Louis XIII. Writing in 1602, when the Dauphin was barely one year old, Héroard described the visit of a young girl: "he pulled up his gown and showed her his 'cheater' with such enthusiasm he was beside himself." Héroard also noted when the Dauphin's nurse or other ladies of the court took the child to bed with them to "fondle his 'cheater'." This, of course, is not an ordinary child. The Dauphin was betrothed at birth to the Infanta of Spain and even before his first birthday, was told stories about going to bed with his wife to be. Héroard records approvingly that when asked, "Where is the Infanta's darling?" the one-year-old Dauphin put his hand on his "cheater" – to the great amusement of all present. While such stories are striking in their rarity rather than their representativeness, they do suggest a greater openness to both ribald humor and to children's genital play in the seventeenth century than in those that follow, and not only for French royalty. Shortly after 1800, in another example, an English father bragged of his son's precociousness: "George is a noble fellow ... he is even at this age a very naughty boy. I am afraid he is often found in bed with little Penelope's nurse."[5]

Neither medical nor religious authorities paid much attention to childhood sexuality during this era. Masturbation, the form of sexual expression most closely related to prepubescent children, drew relatively little attention through the seventeenth century. Masturbation posed no concern to physicians, whether about the health of the individual or of the broader society. One tract, *The Haven of Health*, published in 1596, endorsed masturbation for young males: orgasm, wrote Thomas Cogan, "maketh the body more light and nimble; it opens the pores and conduits ... quickeneth the mind, stirreth up the wit."[6] The Catholic church, in contrast, treated masturbation as a sin, though most frequently defined as venial or lesser. While a few church authorities did define "improper thoughts, and the sins of impurity" as mortal sins, widespread among young people, Saint Ignatius Loyola's *Spiritual Exercises*, composed during the early sixteenth century, does not even include masturbation in its careful delineation of venial and mortal sins. Calvinists, likewise focused on boys, worried less about masturbation than other childhood sins. Historian Lawrence Stone argues that during the seventeenth and eighteenth centuries, "even the most Calvinistic of children, brought up in fear of hell-fire, nevertheless were not too deeply disturbed by the problem of handling their early impulse."[7]

At the same time, it is critical to understand (in historian Roger Cox's words) "the depth of belief in heaven and hell, in the sinfulness of human beings and in the boundless grace of God that could be felt by a Puritan parent." Cotton Mather, writing in the American colonies in 1689, argued that children "go astray as soon as they are born. They no sooner *step* than they *stray*, they no sooner lisp than they *ly*. Satan gets them to be proud, profane, reviling and revengeful as *young* as they are." Those parents who believed most seriously in doctrines of original sin and the profound need for salvation saw childhood misconduct as a matter of very high stakes; they took extraordinary measures to instill discipline and self-denial and to make the child obedient to his or her parents. Such understandings may well have shaped parents' responses to children's sexual experimentation or masturbation, and without question they emphasized the role of parents – mothers, in particular – in an increasingly emotionally intense nuclear family.[8]

In the sixteenth through the eighteenth centuries, most children lived in a rural and fairly isolated world. They had short childhoods, gradually taking on greater and greater levels of responsibility. Children engaged in what we would understand as adult work quite young while at the same time delaying the move to adult life – marriage, setting up households, having children – until ages that were relatively late by comparison. Parents of such children, in a world where close to half of all urban children and close to a third of rural ones died before the age of six, worried more about sickness, health, and salvation than about emerging philosophical debates over the nature of children; the doctrines of the church and the teachings of their priests; or ministers combined with folklore and community standards to shape the framework for their governance of the very young.[9] But among the educated classes, conversations had begun that would radically reshape not only definitions of childhood but the experiences of children ranging well beyond the boundaries of the economically secure.

During the eighteenth century, theologians and philosophers – though perhaps to different ends – increasingly devoted themselves to discussions of the nature of childhood. Some historians, such as Colin Heywood, argue that concern with the nature of children and their place in society originated with the Puritans, who – though some of their members were willing to describe children as "filthy bundles of original sin" – sought to draw young people into the reform movement that characterized the church. Others, including Pat Thane, credit the rise of capitalism in western Europe during the fifteenth through eighteenth centuries for the increased interest in child rearing. Parents of the middling ranks had an interest in preparing children for success in that world; it was newly necessary to educate male children to competency in commerce or a profession and to insure that members of the following generation did not lose or dissipate an inheritance that did not take the tangible form of land.[10]

During the late seventeenth century, the writings of John Locke began to influence understandings of the nature of childhood in ways that would profoundly affect adult approaches to childhood sexual experience and sexual knowledge. In his 1689 work, *An Essay Concerning Human Understanding*, Locke took his first steps toward a new concept of human nature that focused attention on children's experiences as the origin of the adult self.

> Let us then suppose the mind to be, as we say, white paper, void of all characters, without any ideas; how comes it to be furnished? Whence comes that vast store, which the busy and boundless fancy of man has painted on it with an almost endless variety? Whence has it all the materials of reason and knowledge? To this I answer in one word, from experience: in that all our knowledge is founded, and from that it ultimately derives itself.[11]

Locke, in proposing that the child's mind was *tabula rasa*, that children must be educated to the practice of reason, did not imagine the child as innocent; he had no sense that childhood offered "an Elysian paradise of goodness and reciprocity." Nonetheless, he moved away from the firmly held concept of original sin to acknowledge the "incompatible disposition" of children's acts and children's nature.[12] Locke's understandings circulated widely, not only through his own writings but in simplified forms such as the children's book, *A Little Pretty Pocket-Book*, published in 1744. This volume was available in North America during the 1750s and then circulated again, in a pirated form adapted for the American audience, after the American War of Independence.[13] By that point in time, perhaps the greatest influence on western understandings of the nature of childhood – and thus on the shape of institutions meant to structure the lives of children – was an emerging belief that childhood was defined by innocence. Jean-Jacques Rousseau, the strongest proponent of such understandings, began his controversial and widely read work, *Émile, or on Education*, with these words: "Everything is good as it leaves the hands of the Author of things; everything degenerates in the hands of man." By the early nineteenth century, sentimentalized notions of childhood innocence were powerful and widespread; it was not uncommon to encounter claims that children possessed, in their original innocence, a "sense of wonder, an intensity of experience and a spiritual wisdom lacking in the adult."[14] That innocence – and sexual innocence was critical here – became the fundamental definition of childhood, and its protection the task of both the family and the state.

In both Western Europe and America, questions of children's nature and of proper modes of child rearing had become by the mid-eighteenth century critically important topics for the urban middle classes and for the philosophers, scholars, educators, and theologians upon whom they relied. Such shifting understandings would influence adult attitudes toward children and sexuality, shaping law, practices, and institutions, and thus our understandings of childhood and of children's lives over much of the following centuries. As authorities increasingly defined childhood as a state of innocence, those children who betrayed some lack of innocence – whether through behavior, experience, or precocious knowledge – were defined as abnormal, pathological, or degenerate. At the same time, reformers, parents, and, ever more frequently, the state worked to protect the innocence of children, attempting to set universal norms for appropriate acts, creating institutions to manage behavior, passing legislation, and turning to a variety of mechanisms to guarantee that children were not exposed to forms of knowledge that might corrupt an essential innocence that, as much as anything else, was believed to define childhood.

While notions of childhood innocence were first clearly articulated in the 1760s and did not reach their sentimental apogee until the early nineteenth century, by the mid-eighteenth century, historians can already find a "new feeling for childhood," most particularly in relation to sexual crimes. During this period, cases of "cruelty to children" first began to appear in the French court system, the actual number of such cases inflated in the public sphere by false rumors of children abducted and sent to the Americas, captured and bled for the royal bath, killed in mysterious circumstance, or taken and held for some form of sexualized "secret pleasure." While these unfounded rumors tell us little about the experiences of children, the fact that such rumors circulated shows a shift in public sensibility and a new concern about the fragility and vulnerability of children.[15]

Statistics on cases of rape brought before the Parlement of Paris in the seventeenth and eighteenth centuries, analyzed by Georges Vigarello, illustrate this changing sensibility, as well as the increasing role of the courts in public life. During the seventeenth century, an average of three rape charges were brought before the Parlement of Paris each decade. By the late eighteenth century, an average of twenty-five cases were filed each year, and by far the greatest percentage of those were accusations of child rape. These cases overwhelmingly focused on prepubescent girls. Significantly, charges of incest were almost non-existent, as were allegations that boys had been sexually assaulted.

Perhaps an even more powerful indication that adults had begun to view children's vulnerability to sexual assault more seriously are accounts of ordinary people acting to prevent or punish the sexual assault of a child. In 1759, for example, "a troop of peasants of both sexes" in Franconville seized a man in the act of raping a five-and-a-half-year-old girl "in the redcurrant bushes" and handed him over to the bailiff, and in 1764 a group of people in a café in the rue de la Boucherie in Paris joined together to summon the Watch because they were so "overcome with horror" by the story told by a thirteen-year-old shopgirl. Surgeons and midwives also showed new initiative: the Paris surgeon who examined three-year-old Jeanne Dore, who had been raped and beaten by a casual laborer, went immediately to the police, and in 1769 another surgeon himself took the accused rapist of a five-year-old girl he had examined into custody.[16] An article in the *Gazette des tribunaux* indicates the seriousness with which child rape was regarded, describing "rape committed on a pre-pubescent child" as a "type of assassination."

While charges of child rape appeared in greater numbers over this period, judgments did not suggest a widespread assumption of childhood innocence or of adult culpability. In more than 70 percent of the cases, or 36 of the 51 recorded between 1760 and 1785, the accused was found innocent. While such charges provoked much stronger outrage than in the past, and a greater willingness to take action, that did not change the courts' unwillingness to convict productive adults for such crimes.[17] In part this was due to the sort of evidence presented. Thus in one case, the surgeons reported that the child had "bruised and crushed" private parts and evinced "the discharge of whitish humors," but nonetheless concluded that "there had not been intromission" – and thus no rape. Perhaps more significantly, judges were suspicious about victims' conduct, even those of very tender years. In one 1777 case, the judge noted that the child, aged six or seven, was said to be a prostitute, soliciting soldiers, and had been seen "copulating with a young man." And even the prosecutor who worked to imprison a scrap-metal dealer to three years in prison for raping a ten-year-old girl worried that the child was "too well-informed for her age" and guilty of "libertine" behavior toward the defendant. In such cases, the "perversion" of the child diminished the culpability of the rapist, even as the crime of child rape was taken more seriously than in the past.[18]

By the late eighteenth century, major changes in the social and economic organization of western nations had begun to transform children's lives. Economic class, here, was the great divide: industrialization shaped the lives of poor children and their economic betters in diametrically opposite directions. As the rural poor moved to cities, seeking work and sustenance in a rapidly transforming world, children as young as three were put to work in factories, sent out to scavenge on the streets, to carry messages, sell papers, or pick pockets to earn their keep in whatever way they could. With large numbers of children living on the streets – referred to as "Street Arabs" – many turned to prostitution or other forms of sexual activity for survival.

At the same time, middle-class children in North America and western Europe were treasured and protected in new ways. As children became more of an economic liability than an asset for middle-class families, parents chose to have fewer children and to invest more resources in their upbringing and education. In the United States, the birth rate dropped by almost half during the nineteenth century, and that change was most dramatic in urban middle-class and professional families, who devoted more care to each individual child, working to foster discipline and self control and shape their moral development. Girls, in particular, were held to high standards of moral purity, which was seen as fundamental to their future roles as wives and mothers.

By 1821, four out of ten people living in western Europe were under the age of fifteen. These young people were more visible than ever, the children of the poor forming unruly gangs on city streets, loitering and carousing, mixing with adults and forming a marked contrast to growing understandings of the proper nature of childhood. Peter Gaskell, in his 1833 *The Manufacturing Population of England*, describes the sexes "mingling in wild carouse" in circumstances in which "crimes of all shades are perpetuated, blasphemy, fornication, adultery, incest, child-murder," while the mid-nineteenth century exposé, *New York by Gaslight*, told of drunken revelry in dirty saloons and streets.[19] Organized efforts to protect such children developed from a combination of fear of the broader chaos engendered by rapid urbanization and industrialization, as it seemed that such children posed a threat to the social order, and the broader reform impulse that emerged in tandem with the visible evidence of the harsh effects of economic development.

During the late nineteenth century, reformers created various organizations devoted to the protection of children, and, while motivated by the sight of "waifs and strays" sleeping on the street, starving, without sufficient clothes to withstand the cold, they were also concerned about children's vulnerability to sexual exploitation and attack and about their exposure to the sexualized world of the streets and the knowledge of degenerate companions. Perhaps ironically, the first child protection organization, the New York Society for the Prevention of Cruelty to Children, founded in 1874, developed from the founder of the American Society for the Prevention of Cruelty to Animals. In 1874, tenement visitor Etta Wheeler discovered a child named Mary Ellen who was being horrifically abused. Finding no agency that would rescue the child she finally turned, in desperation, to Henry Bergh, the founder of the Society for the Prevention of Cruelty to Animals. He immediately declared, in the apochryphal version of the story: "The child is an animal. If there is no justice for it as a human being, it shall at least have the right of a cur in the street." Bergh was, in fact, quite reluctant to intervene and made clear that he was acting as a "humane citizen" and not in his capacity as president of the animal protection society. Nonetheless, the publicity surrounding Mary Ellen's case fostered broader reform.[20] Child protection organizations spread through industrialized nations, not only offering aid and refuge to poor and orphaned children, but also working to force the respective states to recognize the rights of children and to take legal actions to protect them from exploitation, neglect, and harm, even from their own parents. The Church of England's Waifs and Strays Society (named after the medieval term "wayves and steyves" or pieces of ownerless property) went "waif hunting" in the early morning hours to find and rescue children sleeping on the streets; in 1911 it noted that "the greatest urgency ... [is] on behalf of those whose lives are in the midst of moral temptation, and where the danger is literally a soul-danger."[21] The language of "purity" and "innocence" used by these reformers had powerful sexual connotations, even when children's sexual vulnerability was not described. But during the 1880s and on through the early twentieth century, in both England and the United States, the sexual abuse and sexual knowledge of children was a matter of great public concern.[22]

In both England and the United States, efforts to protect children from sexual experience were tied to social purity movements that worked to suppress the widespread practice of prostitution. Although some historians argue that reports emphasizing the large numbers of child prostitutes in European cities may instead have been a way to discuss all forms of sexual activity or abuse, and that the sensationalized tales of forced prostitution fueled a broad moral panic that worked to "attack the sexual behavior and moral standards" of those who lived outside the world of Victorian middle-class values, they were nonetheless central to efforts to change the legal age of consent – the age at which a person is considered legally competent to consent to sexual activities.

In 1885, journalist and editor W.T. Stead published a series of articles in the *Pall Mall Gazette*. "The Maiden Tribute of Modern Babylon" was a sensationalist tale of child sexual exploitation. Although the British Parliament had raised the age of consent from ten to twelve in 1861 (making "carnal knowledge" of a girl aged between ten and twelve a misdemeanor) and then again to thirteen in 1875, legislation to raise the age further had stalled before Parliament in the mid-1880s. Stead, drawn into the struggle through connections with the founder of the National Society for the Prevention of Cruelty to Children, wrote a first-person journalistic exposé about the purchase of a thirteen-year-old girl for the purposes of prostitution. The child, Eliza Armstrong, was examined by a midwife/abortionist to verify her virginity, taken to a brothel, and chloroformed before Stead himself entered the room. Although Stead was jailed for abduction and aiding indecent assault, in the wake of his exposé Parliament raised the age of consent to sixteen.[23]

Building on the British campaigns, America's largest women's organization, the Woman's Christian Temperance Union (WCTU), began campaigning to raise the age of consent in the United States. State law rather than federal statute governed age of consent, and in the mid-1880s, the median legal age of consent for American states was ten. Over the following decade, reformers succeeded in their campaigns, passing legislation state by state that raised the median legal age to fourteen, with twenty-two states establishing consent at sixteen or older. The federal government, in turn, raised the age of consent in places of federal jurisdiction to twenty-one in 1899.

These campaigns to raise the age of consent were not without opposition. In Britain, some members of Parliament, with public support, argued for an early age of consent; ten was widely proposed. British arguments rested on the differences of class. Some girls, it was argued, were sexually aware and experienced from an early age; legislation to protect their innocence was misguided at best. And many girls appeared physically mature well before the age of thirteen, much less sixteen; why should a young woman who was physically capable of childbearing be treated as a child? Gender mattered as well; as same-sex contact was legally prohibited, boys who had sex with adult men under any circumstances were viewed as double victims while girls, even those below the age of thirteen, were often questioned in court about their sexual knowledge and charged with precocity.[24] In the United States, by contrast, the issue of race provided the strongest grounds for opposition to higher ages of consent. Raising the age of consent, southern opponents argued, might "enable negro girls to sue white men." Proposed legislation in southern states sought to exempt girls who were not of "previously chaste character," with the understanding that few white male juries would presume that black girls and young women were "previously chaste." The state of Georgia, in fact, did not raise the age of consent from ten to fourteen until 1918, during the First World War.

It is critical to recognize the struggle, here, over definitions of childhood and their implications. The WCTU waged its US campaign in the language of childhood innocence, calling for the protection of "baby girls," "girl children," and "infants," while attempting to raise the age of consent to the late teens. By legislating "innocence," states denied young women, even up to the age of eighteen or twenty-one, the right of consent. And court records reveal that some parents used these laws to control rebellious daughters by charging their boyfriends with statutory rape.

Arguments over the proper age of consent, as they took place in both England and the United States during the 1880s, centered on boundaries. What was the difference between a girl and a woman? What marked that boundary? Was it physical development? Mental capacity? Moral development? Was it, in fact, determined by the child's relative innocence, her lack of exposure to the corrupting forces of sexual knowledge and experience?

Such reasoning would create a fundamental paradox. While the rape of an innocent young girl was held to be the worst of crimes, that rape, according to this set of beliefs, also corrupted her innocence, by giving her a precocious sexual knowledge. Thus the child victims of rape or incest – no matter how powerfully the crime was decried – were put outside the full protections of childhood, placed in a different category. Those with sexual knowledge were seen as a threat to the innocence of other children, requiring separation from them, most often in institutions devoted to redemption and reform.

Thus the notion of the innocent child was twinned with its opposite: the corrupted child, the degenerate child, the delinquent child. For those who believed so completely in the doctrine of childhood innocence, the inconvertible evidence of childhood misconduct and even traces of evil raised difficult questions. If children were by nature innocent, from whence came depravity? The answer seemed obvious: they had been corrupted by their environment.

Through the nineteenth century, as belief in the fundamental innocence of children was crafted and reinforced by the writings of educators, advisors, and philosophers, portrayed by poets and painters, woven into the fabric of the middle-class family, children were the subject of powerful campaigns to protect them from their own sexuality and from sexual knowledge and experience. Significantly, reformers did not distinguish between the children of the middle classes and those of the poor; however, as they universalized childhood, holding middle-class expectations for children whose environment offered little in the way of middle-class protections, they offered new protections for the most vulnerable children and condemned those who failed to meet the expectations of innocence and purity that surrounded Victorian childhood.[25]

Between 1880 and 1930, in attempts to "guard the boundaries of knowledge," social reformers and government officials attempted to control children's access to the night-time city. Campaigns to keep all children safe from premature exposure to adult sexual knowledge – the "dark wisdom" to be found in the public spaces of night-time cities – led to the creation of supervised recreation centers, to juvenile curfews, and to regulation of child street labor. As Florence Kelley explained of her work in Chicago, "there is a tradition among the boys themselves that in order to be a 'wise guy' he must know the greatest possible amount of evil ... and he must tell the last newcomer everything he knows or can invent." Reformers believed that access to the night-time streets gave boys and girls precocious knowledge, corrupting them and then other children with whom they came into contact; however, despite curfews and other such legislation passed in many American cities, such attempts to control the sexual knowledge and the physical freedom of working-class and poor children had little effect.[26]

Other campaigns to protect the sexual innocence of children centered on sensational literature. Once again, reformers meant to protect children's natural innocence. By the mid-1870s, the Beadle and Adams publishing firm had realized that the dime novels it published for working-class adults were also read by children, and launched a new series of adventures stories aimed at children – "Half-Dime Series" – for half the price. Faced with the difficulty of explaining why innocent children were drawn to tales of violence (which were believed to arouse sexual impulses), reformers argued that such publications seduced and corrupted otherwise innocent children. The most outspoken and effective opponent of dime novels and their half-dime companions was Anthony Comstock, founder of the New York Society for the Suppression of Vice (incorporated in 1873) and author of the 1883 *Traps for the Young*. Comstock, making his case against such publications, tells of a boy arrested for selling pornography who pointed to a stack of dime novels in his room, confessing: "There, there's the cause of my ruin – that has cursed me and brought me to this!" Most crime committed by the young, argued Comstock, was "the direct result of evil reading."

In another attempt to protect children's innocence, a growing advice literature combined medical and moral messages to warn about the dangers of masturbation. It is not surprising that attempts to instill self-discipline and purity in the offspring of the nineteenth-century middle class would focus on sexuality, but such warnings reached back to a series of pamphlets published in the early eighteenth century, all of which suggest the emergence of new attitudes toward childhood sexuality. The first of these (whose title is worth quoting in full) was "Onania or the Heinous Sin of Self-Pollution and All Its Frightful Consequences, in both sexes, considered with Spiritual and Physical Advice to Those who have already Injur'd themselves by this abominable Practice." Full of descriptions of the moral and physiological consequences of such acts – "cessation of growth, phimosis, paraphimosis, strangurious, priapism, fainting fits, epilepsy, impotence, and in woman, fluor albus, hysteric fits, consumption, and barrenness," it sold surprisingly well, and was issued in nineteen English-language editions by 1760, as well as in French and German. By the early nineteenth century, a practice that had earlier prompted only mild censure had become the focus for fears about childhood sexuality.[27]

To combat the evils of masturbation, English public schools turned to games such as rugby and cricket, which provided boys with non-sexual outlets. Health reformers such as the American Sylvester Graham offered dietary regimens designed to inhibit masturbation and nocturnal emissions. Inventors created mechanical devices to the same end. One such device, intended to discourage sexual arousal in boys and young men, encircled the penis with a ring of spikes. Another restrained the hands and covered the genital area with a girdle of cold, wet cloths. In 1894, eleven boys in a mental institution in Kansas were castrated in an attempt to cure them of the habit of masturbation. The local press condemned this action, but the *Kansas Medical Journal* wrote, in its defense, that the boys "were confirmed masturbators... This abuse weakened the already imbecile mind and destroyed the body. The practice is loathsome, disgusting, humiliating and destructive of all self-respect and decency, and had a bad moral effect on the whole school."[28]

While castration (and clitoridectomy) were radical responses, scholars have argued that the routine circumcision of infants, normalized during the 1870s in Britain, was largely due to concern about masturbation. If children were sexually innocent, if childhood was, in William Acton's words, a period of "absolute sexual quiescence," how to explain children's masturbation or fondling of their genitals? Such acts, if not attributed to bad influences or to servants' practice of tickling the child's genitals to calm him, were explained as the result of irritation caused by a tight foreskin or uncleanness, both of which could be prevented or ameliorated by infant or early childhood circumcision.[29] J.H. Kellogg, who in the 1880s published a list of thirty-nine signs through which one could recognize a masturbator, offered circumcision to be done – "without administering an anesthetic, as the brief pain attending the operation will have a salutary effect upon the mind, especially if it be connected with the idea of punishment" – as a possible solution should all other proposed remedies fail.[30]

Some scholars, such as James Russell Kincaid, see in Victorian constructions of the innocent child, a parallel eroticization that persists to the present day: "The child is constructed," Kincaid writes, "so as to make its eroticism necessary and the image of the erotic child central and not marginal to our culture." Following this logic, the editor of *Children and Sexuality: From the Greeks to the Great War* approvingly describes Lewis Carroll's photographs of "his little girl friends" as "some of the most sensitive yet latently sexual images ever seen in art."[31]

While social reform efforts based on notions of childhood innocence played critical roles in early twentieth-century culture, they were accompanied by rapid changes in North American and western European definitions of childhood and sexuality. Sigmund Freud's writings on infant and childhood sexuality were enormously influential, even though they were sometimes altered almost beyond recognition as they passed into public discussion. Freud argued that sexuality did not first emerge at puberty, but instead developed in stages from infancy to the age of six or so, at which point the child passed into a period of latency that lasted until puberty. According to Freud, the manner in which each child passed through the stages of sexuality (oral, anal, and phallic) would in large part shape their adult lives. Other contemporaries of Freud, such as psychiatrist Albert Moll, focused on the development of "healthy" individuals rather than the "pathological" subjects who engaged Freud's psychoanalytic focus, and described sexuality as an active force in children from infancy onward.[32] Such understandings lessened the moral opprobrium against childhood masturbation, especially as they were later translated into "common sense" child-rearing advice by popular advisors such as Dr Spock, whose *Baby and Child Care* sold more copies between the mid-1940s and the mid-1970s than any book other than the Bible.

Twentieth-century western Europeans and North Americans also saw a marked shift from respect for the knowledge of parents, extended families, and communities in raising children toward a new emphasis on expert knowledge and scientific child raising. During the 1920s and 1930s, behaviorists, (who argued that behavior is shaped by conditioning) such as John B. Watson, neither condemned nor praised childhood sexuality, but advised parents to limit physical contact with their children. "Treat them as though they were young adults," Watson advised parents in his 1928 work, *Psychological Care of Infant and Child*. "Dress them, bathe them with care and circumspection. Let your behavior always be objective and kindly firm. Never hug and kiss them, never let them sit on your lap … Shake hands with them in the morning."[33]

Such approaches shifted dramatically during the last six decades of the twentieth century. In 1943, Margaret A. Ribble described the erotic sexuality of the infant as good and necessary to the developing child, writing that:

> Nature seems to have a purpose in this earliest biological endowment of pleasure, for it gives the child a sense of the goodness of his physical self. It puts the first stamp on the rightness of physical pleasure, which is one of the basic roads to happiness. The child's body is the tool which introduces him to life, and he must feel that it is a good tool. His mental self and his awareness develop hand in hand with the physical … Erotic feeling is diffuse in a baby, but it is not misplaced and does not imply something evil which must be weeded out.[34]

Likewise Dr Spock emphasized the importance of physical affection for the developing infant: "Every baby needs to be smiled at, talked to, played with, fondled – gently and lovingly – just as much as he needs vitamins and calories, and the baby who doesn't get any loving will grow up cold and unresponsive." Parents, in this universe of advice, were urged to treat children's sexuality as natural and good and to avoid doing anything that might introduce feelings of guilt or otherwise compromise the child's continuing development of a satisfying sexual nature. Writing of children's fascination with their own feces during the "anal phase" in his 1965 *Between Parent and Child*, Haim Ginott explained to potentially disturbed parents that:

> Special care must be taken not to infect [the child] with disgust towards his body and its products. Harsh and hasty measures may make the child feel that his body and all of its functions are something to dread, rather than to

enjoy ... Though not in an adult way, the infant's enjoyment of his body and its functions is sexual in nature ... He handles his limbs and delights in being touched, tickled, and cuddled. These early touchings and strokings are part of his sex education. Through them he learns to receive love.[35]

In many ways, this emerging emphasis on the natural – and good – erotic nature of the infant and young child continued belief in childhood innocence. Unlike Victorian notions of innocence, which tightly bound childhood to sexuality by so powerfully denying the connection, this twentieth-century construction rejected notions of asexual innocence for belief in the natural and uncorrupted erotic nature of the child – a different form of innocence that demanded protection from the corrupting influences of guilt, repression, or inappropriate knowledge.

Twentieth-century reformers also continued to grapple with the problem of the sexual abuse of children. Historian Carol Smart, examining these struggles in Britain between 1910 and 1960, argues that such efforts centered around the notion of harm to the child, a harm first defined as moral, then physical, and finally, as primarily psychological. Relying on accounts in medical literature about outbreaks of venereal disease in children's homes, most of these transmissions (sometimes rendered as "innocent"), as was the case of an outbreak of gonorrheal vulvo-vaginitis in seventeen girls between the ages of six and ten years in "an exceptionally well-administered home," were attributed to "fomite." As the account explained: "Many little girls are carriers of gonorrhea as a result of infection by towels, w.c.'s [sic], and lavatories." While physicians would not have believed such tales about adult infection with gonorrhea, they were willing to accept such "far fetched theories" of "innocent transmission" when it came to children. It was not until the 1980s that venereal disease was regularly treated as an indication of sexual abuse. Likewise, historian Roger Davidson demonstrates that legal and medical authorities in Scotland during the early twentieth century often cited the superstition of the "virgin cure" – described as "a common belief among the lower classes that connection with a virgin will cure a venereal disease" – as a way to desexualize the sexual assault of children, even though few of those charged offered such an explanation.[36]

While some historians have argued that it was the turn to psychoanalysis that allowed authorities to dismiss evidence of the sexual abuse of children as fantasy, it is clear that nineteenth-century debates about the boundaries between child and consenting adult, the medical profession's adoption of "innocent" transmission models, and the public claims about the "virgin cure" all worked to hide evidence of sexual abuse and adult exploitation of children even as society emphasized the need to protect childhood innocence.

Perhaps it is not surprising, given the growing emphasis on the sexual and erotic nature of children, that prominent anthropologists and sex researchers began to argue that intergenerational sex was not necessarily, in and of itself, harmful to children. In *Sexual Behavior in the Human Female* (1953), Alfred Kinsey and his co-authors noted that it is "difficult to understand why a child, except for its cultural conditioning, should be disturbed at having its genitalia touched, or disturbed at seeing the genitalia of other persons, or disturbed at even more specific sexual contacts."[37]

The liberation movements of the late 1960s and 1970s – most particularly the sexual revolution, women's movement, and gay liberation movement – had a strong, though surprisingly short-lived impact on North American and western European understandings of child sexuality. Combining belief in the unspoiled erotic nature of infant and child with a broader set of claims that new approaches to love and sex could somehow re-make the world, some reformers sought an end to "repressive strictures" that, they believed, created sexual perversion and misery in later years. Hal M. Wells argued in *The Sensuous Child* that children have a "right to sexual pleasure" and joined a small but vocal cohort of adults who either promoted adult–child sex or argued that it need not be traumatic. Psychiatrist Alayne Yates proposed that "non-coercive father–daughter incest" could produce "sexually competent and notably erotic young women," while various groups in western Europe, Great Britain, and the United States campaigned against ages of consent and championed intergenerational sex. As the spokesperson for a coalition of groups campaigning to end the prohibition of adult–child sex argued in 1979:

> We are engaged in a war between the forces of sexual liberation on the one hand and the forces of sexual repression on the other. Man/Boy love and cross generational sex have become the cutting edge of that war. Repeal all age of consent laws! Freedom of sexual expression for all![38]

Such claims were far on the margins during the 1970s (though one might also note that the claims of radical feminism and gay liberation were also well outside the mainstream), and although they gained significant attention, they never came anywhere close to common-sense status or legislative initiatives. Most citizens of modern democratic nations were ambivalent about the new claims for children's rights that emerged during the 1970s, even when not related to such emotionally explosive issues as sex, and in any case, arguments for "Man/Boy Love" sounded to most more like a case for legalizing pedophilia than for an expansion of the rights of children.

Nonetheless, public attitudes toward children's sexuality and sexual curiosity shifted dramatically during the 1980s. Discussions about whether children's "natural" sexual curiosity should determine the boundaries of experience were supplanted by an extraordinary suspicion of adult–child contact.[39] In the United States, at least, the shift was quite plausibly driven by the women's movement and reactions to it. From the early 1970s on, many feminists insisted that claims or signs of incest must be taken seriously, and their claims brought about significant changes (parallel, perhaps, to changes in legal and medical approaches to accusations of rape).[40] Some feminists also joined more conservative Americans to question the benefits of the sexual revolution, finding little liberation in what they saw as a patriarchal definition of sexual freedom. And as more women claimed equality in the public sphere or were pressured into the workplace by a changing economy, angry public discussions about the impact of such decisions on children – a debate that would eventually develop, among the upper-middle classes, into "the mommy wars" – heightened sensitivity to claims about harm to children.

It is difficult to reject scholarly claims that a "moral panic" about children's vulnerability to sexual abuse made the US public and legal system receptive to a bizarre set of claims about sexual abuse and Satanic rituals that originated in 1983 with a two-and-a-half-year-old boy and eventually expanded to a claim that 360 pre-school-age children had been sexually abused in the McMartin Daycare Center in Manhattansville, California.[41] Yet at the same time, from 1983 through 1987, charges of past or present sexual abuse of children by priests surfaced, on average, once a week; such revelations have been largely substantiated despite cover-ups by some members of the church hierarchy and Vatican pressure that undermined the provisions of the United States Conference of Catholic Bishops' 2002 *Charter for the Protection of Children and Young People*.[42]

And while children run a much greater risk of sexual abuse by a family member or someone else who occupies a legitimate place in his or her community, fear of child abduction, rape, and murder have driven school curricula, community standards, and parental decisions. A 2004 survey in Britain found that ten- and eleven-year-old children rarely ventured outside, whether to play or even walk to school because both they and their parents feared that they would be kidnapped by a stranger or sexually abused by a pedophile.[43] Adults' fears about sexual predators has fundamentally altered the experience of childhood, restricting children's freedom of movement and delaying the development of independence and autonomy in realms that have little or nothing to do with sex.

Just as the relationship between children and sex or sexuality has proved both difficult and contested through history, it has presented scholars with uncommon difficulties as well. As the economically developed nations of the West have sought to extend the protections they offer their own children to the children of other nations and cultures (as in the 2000 Optional Protocols to the United Nations Convention on the Rights of the Child, which specified increased protection for children at risk of sexual exploitation), anthropologists and other scholars have struggled with the implications of such acts. In some ways, such reform attempts return us to a version of the question over which so many historians of progressive era social reform movements struggled during the 1970s and early 1980s: does a universal notion of childhood extend, however incompletely, the protection enjoyed by the relatively privileged to their less advantaged peers? Or does such universalization deny the material, social, and cultural realities of children in less-privileged or less-dominant cultures?

As western notions of children's sexual innocence are increasingly promoted as a global ideal, anthropologists such as Heather Montgomery have argued that we must pay attention to other cultures' own definitions of appropriate behavior and abuse. Focusing on the difficult case of child prostitutes in Thailand's sex tourism trade, she offers evidence that these children and their parents understand child prostitution as appropriate filial obligation. Neither their own sexuality nor sex with foreign adult men is the focus of these children's identity; they see themselves as dutiful sons or daughters, acting in ways that cement their place in their families and societies. Noting that mothers don't seem to worry about the impact of such experiences, even with evidence that adult penetration has caused physical harm – "It's just for one hour. What harm can happen to him in one hour?" – Montgomery concludes: "Even owning my own feelings of revulsion and condemnation at this, it was clear that the children and their parents had a radically different understanding of sexuality and their bodies from my own."[44]

Montgomery's conflicted response brings us to a fundamental methodological issue, one in which theoretical commitments may well conflict with moral instincts or gut-level certainties. Writing about social construction theory, sociologist Chris Jenks offers a clear and succinct definition for scholars of childhood. "All contemporary approaches to the history of childhood," he writes, "are clearly committed to the view that childhood is not a natural phenomenon … [but instead] childhood is a social construct." His claim is accurate and rarely contested. But what does it mean to apply such understandings to the emotionally charged topic of children and sex, most particularly when boundaries are not clear? What of consensual sex between an adult and a willing youth? A pubescent child? A six year old? A toddler or an infant? All of these are constructed categories, changing over time and across culture and place. But – for me at least – there is some point at which the boundary between childhood and age starts to feel absolute; some point at which the constructed nature of the meaning of childhood and of sex begins to seem less negotiable. My faith in social–historical construction isn't shaken, but I still find a need to draw lines.

Responding to Jenks's carefully stated definition, historian Louise Jackson quite compellingly points to the tensions at the boundaries of such theoretical positioning when it comes to the topic of children and sex. As Jackson writes:

> The historian's task is to delineate how decisions on this question were reached in the past and how they impacted on the lives of ordinary children. Yet most historians who look at child sexual abuse have to deal with intense personal beliefs that childhood does mean something different from adulthood and that sexual acts between adults and children are wrong.

In the end, she asks, "If childhood, the body, sexuality, morality are cultural constructs, what are we to do with our own sense of ethical judgement?"[45] In other words: here there be dragons.

Notes

1 Larry L. Constantine and Floyd M. Martinson, eds., *Children and Sex: New Findings, New Perspectives* (Boston, MA: Brown and Company, 1981), 3.
2 Quote from Kerry Robinson and Cristyn Davies, "Docile Bodies and Hetero normative Moral Subjects: Constructing the Child and Sexual Knowledge in Schooling," *Sexuality and Culture* (2008), 224.
3 Sterling Fishman, "The History of Childhood Sexuality," *Journal of Contemporary History* (1982), 273–74.
4 Colin Heywood, *Growing Up In France: from the Ancien Régime to the Third Republic* (Cambridge, MA: Cambridge University Press, 2007), 276.
5 Anthony Fletcher, *Growing Up in England: The Experience of Childhood, 1600–1914* (New Haven, CT: Yale University Press, 2008), 13.
6 Fletcher, *Growing Up*, 12; quote taken from Thomas Cogan, *The Haven of Health* (1596).
7 Fishman, "Childhood Sexuality," 271–272; Stone, *The Family, Sex, and Marriage in England 1500–1800* (1977) quoted in Fishman.
8 Roger Cox, *Shaping Childhood: Themes of Uncertainty in the History of Adult–Child Relationships* (London, UK: Routledge, 1996), 11–13, 45.
9 Estimates of childhood mortality rates vary. The estimate here, for seventeenth-century Europe, comes from Bernd Hermann, "City and Nature and Nature in the City," in *Historians and Nature: Comparative Approaches to Environmental History*, eds. Ursula Lehmkuhl and Hermann Wellenreuther (New York, NY: Oxford University Press, 2007); non-urban death rates are 25 to 30 percent. See also Louis Hass, "Childhood," in Peter N. Stearns, *Encyclopedia of Social History* (New York, NY: Taylor & Francis, 1994), 146–49, and the estimates offered for pre-industrial America in Janet Golden, Richard Meckel, and Heather

Monro Prescott, *Children and Youth in Sickness and Health: A Historical Handbook and Guide* (Westport, CT: Greenwood Press, 2004), 3.

10 Heywood, *History of Childhood*, 22–23. On capitalism, Heywood relies on Pat Thane, "Childhood in History," in Michael King, ed., *Childhood, Welfare and Justice: a Critical Examination of Children in the Legal and Childcare Systems* (London, UK: Batsford Academic and Educational Limited, 1981) 10.

11 John Locke, *An Essay Concerning Human Understanding*; quoted in Heywood, *History of Childhood*, 22.

12 Heywood, *History of Childhood*, 22–23; Cox, *Shaping Childhood*, 47, 75, 125.

13 Mark I. West, *Children, Culture, and Controversy* (Hamden, CT: Archon Books, 1988), 1–7.

14 Heywood, *History of Childhood*, 59

15 Georges Vigarello, *A History of Rape: Sexual Violence in France From the 16th to the 20th Century*, 76–77.

16 Vigarello, *Rape*, 78–80.

17 For the continued power of such understandings, see Stephen Robertson, *Crimes Against Children: Sexual Violence and Legal Culture in New York City, 1880–1960* (Chapel Hill, NC: University of North Carolina Press, 2005).

18 Vigarello, *Rape*, 84–85.

19 Eric Hopkins, *Childhood Transformed: Working-Class Children in Nineteenth Century England*, 6; 118 (Gaskell quote); Roger Cox, *Shaping Childhood*, 78 (population statistics); Peter C. Baldwin, "Nocturnal Habits and Dark Wisdom," *Journal of Social History*, Spring 2002, 594; Hugh Cunningham, *The Children of the Poor: Representations of Childhood since the Seventeenth Century* (Cambridge, MA: Blackwell, 1992), 22–24, 47.

20 Lela B. Costin, Howard Jacob Karger, and David Stoesz, *The Politics of Child Abuse in America* (New York, NY: Oxford University Press, 1996), 52–57.

21 Alyson Brown and David Barrett, *Knowledge of Evil: Child Prostitution and Child Sexual Abuse in Twentieth-Century England* (Devon, UK: Willan Publishing, 2002), 31–39.

22 Cunningham, *Children of the Poor*, 145

23 George Rousseau, "Introduction," in *Children and Sexuality: From the Greeks to the Great War*, ed. George Rousseau, (New York, NY: Palgrave Macmillan, 2007), 12; Brown and Barrett, *Knowledge of Evil*, 13–17; Cox, *Shaping Childhood*, 148–153.

24 Katherine D. Watson, "Katherine D. Watson responds," in *Children and Sexuality*, ed. Rousseau, 200–202.

25 For a discussion of the sexually corrupting child, see Danielle Egan and Gail Hawkes, *Theorizing the Sexual Child in Modernity* (New York, NY: Palgrave Macmillan, 2010), 47–49.

26 Baldwin, "Natural Habits," pp. 593–4; 601; boundaries of knowledge quote from p. 606.

27 Fishman, "Childhood Sexuality," 274–75.

28 Robert Darby, "The Masturbation Taboo and the Rise of Routine Male Circumcision: A Review of the Historiography," *Journal of Social History* (2003), 742.

29 Darby, "Masturbation Taboo," 742.

30 Darby, "Masturbation Taboo," 744.

31 James Russell Kincaid, *Child Loving: The Erotic Child and Victorian Culture* (London, UK: Routledge, 1992); Rousseau, "Introduction," 4–10; see also the wide range of critical book reviews of Kincaid's work.

32 Danielle Egan and Gail L. Hawkes, "Imperiled and Perilous: Exploring the History of Childhood Sexuality," *Journal of Historical Sociology*, (2008), 358–59.

33 Henry Jenkins, "The Sensuous Child," in *The Children's Culture Reader*, ed. Henry Jenkins (New York, NY: New York University Press, 1998), 213; Jenkins quotes from John B. Watson, *Psychological Care of Infant and Child* (New York, NY: Norton, 1928), 81–82.

34 Jenkins, "The Sensuous Child," 216; he quotes from Margaret A. Ribble, *The Rights of Infants* (New York, NY: Columbia University Press, 1943), 11.

35 Jenkins, "Sensuous Child," 217–18; Haim G. Ginott, *Between Parent and Child: New Solutions to Old Problems* (New York, NY: Macmillan Press, 1965), 178, 180.

36 Carol Smart, "Reconsidering the Recent History of Child Sexual Abuse, 1910–1960," *Journal of Social Policy* 29 (2000): 55–71; Roger Davidson, "'This Pernicious Delusion': Law, Medicine, and Child Sexual Abuse in Early-Twentieth-Century Scotland," *Journal of the History of Sexuality*, 10(1) (2001): 62–77.

37 Alfred C. Kinsey, Wardell B. Pomeroy, and Clyde E. Martin, *Sexual Behavior in the Human Female* (Philadelphia, PA: Saunders, 1953), 121.

38 For discussion of 1970s notions of child sexuality, see Steven Angelides, "Feminism, Child Sexual Abuse, and the Erasure of Child Sexuality," *GLQ* 10(2) (2004): 145–146.

39 For an interesting discussion of childhood sexual curiosity and shifting cultural boundaries, see Henry Jenkins, "The Sensuous Child," who begins his discussion with Sue Miller's 1994 novel *The Good Mother*.

40 See Linda Gordon, "The Politics of Child Sexual Abuse: Notes from American History," *Feminist Review* (1988): 56–64; and critique offered by Angelides in "The Erasure of Child Sexuality."

41 For material on this case and the subsequent trial see Prof Douglas O. Linder, University of Missouri-Kansas City School of Law, website on Famous Trials: http://law2.umkc.edu/faculty/projects/ftrials/mcmartin/mcmartin.html accessed July 2011.

42 Mary Gail Frawley-O'Dea, "The History and Consequences of the Sexual-Abuse Crisis in the Catholic Church," *Studies in Gender and Sexuality*, 5(1) (2004): 14, 17.

43 Amelia Hill, "'Stranger Danger' Drive Harms Kids," *The Observer*, May 23, 2004, online, retrieved 12 July 2011.

44 Heather Montgomery, *An Introduction to Childhood: Anthropological Perspectives on Children's Lives* (Malden, MA: Wiley–Blackwell, 2008), 181–200; quote from p. 199. See "Children and Globalization" in Paula S. Fass, *Children of a New World: Society, Culture, and Globalization* (New York, NY: New York University Press, 2007).

45 Louise A. Jackson, *Child Sexual Abuse in Victorian England* (London, UK: Routledge, 2000), 11. Jackson quotes Jenks; original source is Chris Jenks, *Childhood* (London, UK: Routledge), 6.

Suggestions for further reading

Overviews and Theoretical Claims

Cox, Roger. *Shaping Childhood: Themes of Uncertainty in the History of Adult–Child Relationships*. London, UK: Routledge, 1996. Thoughtful overview of historical understandings of the nature of childhood in western history; especially interesting is Cox's analysis of parents' attempts, in changing historical contexts, to handle (or deny) the physical, sensual, and even erotic nature of their relationships with their children.

Fishman, Sterling. "The History of Childhood Sexuality." *Journal of Contemporary History* 17 (1982): 269–283. Focused on adult attitudes toward children's masturbation, this article traces changing moral climate, sources of authority, and institutional control of child sexuality in western culture from the seventeenth through twentieth centuries.

Montgomery, Heather. *An Introduction to Childhood: Anthropological Perspectives on Children's Lives*. Malden, MA: Wiley–Blackwell, 2008. Montgomery, an anthropologist, argues here (and in other published work) that cross-cultural comparisons demonstrate that notions of childhood innocence, often treated as universal and biological, are not western nations' attempts to make the protection of children's sexual innocence a global ideal, but are instead based on western ideas of sexual identity and western definitions of childhood.

Montgomery, Heather. "Child Sexual Abuse – An Anthropological Perspective." In *Children and Sexuality: From the Greeks to the Great War*, edited by George Rousseau, 319–347. New York, NY: Palgrave Macmillan, 2007. Montgomery argues that we need to "distinguish between indigenous cultural practices, which may appear abusive to outsiders, but are not considered so internally to a community, and those which are acknowledged as aberrant."

Children's experience

Heywood, Colin. *Growing Up In France: from the Ancien Régime to the Third Republic.* Cambridge, MA: Cambridge University Press, 2007. A rare effort to describe children's experiences, with careful attention to differences of gender, class, region, and family structure. Discussions of sexuality are fairly brief but worthwhile.

Sexual abuse and child protection

Brown, Alyson, and David Barrett. *Knowledge of Evil: Child Prostitution and Child Sexual Abuse in Twentieth-Century England.* Portland, OR: Willan Publishing, 2002. The authors trace the efforts of voluntary and state organizations to control child prostitution, placing those efforts and the young prostitutes themselves in broader social, economic, and political context. If innocence is held to define childhood, what does it mean when children are tainted by experience, by knowledge of evil?

Hopkins, Eric. *Childhood Transformed: Working-Class Children in Nineteenth-Century England.* Manchester, UK: Manchester University Press, 1994. Hopkins argues that working-class childhood was transformed (a change that included both greater sexual protection and increased control over children's sexuality) during the nineteenth century as rising philanthropic or compassionate motives joined a growing desire for social control during a time of "unprecedented social change."

Jackson, Louise A. *Child Sexual Abuse in Victorian England.* London, UK: Routledge, 2000. Jackson analyzes debates over age of consent in Victorian England through her study of the treatment of child sexual abuse cases, emphasizing the clouded status of girls who were seen as both victim and (because corrupted by sexual activities or abuse) as a danger to other children.

Robertson, Stephen. *Crimes Against Children: Sexual Violence and Legal Culture in New York City, 1880–1960.* Chapel Hill, NC: University of North Carolina Press, 2005. This deeply researched work uses records from the Office of the District Attorney for New York City to show how medical, popular, and psychological ideas about childhood shaped legal definitions of sexual violence against children.

Vigarello, Georges. *A History of Rape: Sexual Violence in France From the 16th to the 20th Century.* Translated by Jean Birrell. Malden, MA: Polity Press, 2001. This study, translated from the 1998 publication in French, includes a chapter on the emergence of child rape in the nineteenth century.

Children as sexual agents

Egan, R. Danielle, and Gail L. Hawkes. "Imperiled and Perilous: Exploring the History of Childhood Sexuality." *Journal of Historical Sociology* 21 (2008): 357–59. Focusing on the nineteenth and twentieth century in the Anglophone West, the authors examine the "social and political implications" of child protection, arguing that the "discourses of protection foreclose the possibility of the sexual agency of children."

Jenkins, Henry, ed., *The Children's Culture Reader*. New York, NY: New York University Press, 1998. A US-focused cultural studies collection that emphasizes the agency of children. Part I considers ideas of childhood innocence; Part II childhood sexuality. See especially Jenkins's piece, "The Sensuous Child," on children's sexual curiosity and shifting boundaries of acceptability.

11

AGE, SCHOOLING, AND DEVELOPMENT

Stephen Lassonde

Philippe Ariès observed in *Centuries of Childhood* that there were two concepts of childhood by the end of the seventeenth century that signaled a fundamental shift in attitudes toward children in Western societies. The first was the idea that children should be "coddled" by family members; that is, that they had come to be regarded as objects of affection and attention – sources of pleasure and "charming toys" in Ariès's words. The second was the idea that children were "fragile creatures of God who needed to be safeguarded and reformed." The latter notion, he says, came from outside the family – from "churchmen and moralists" – but this attitude came to reside within the family as well. In the eighteenth century, Ariès argues, a new element joined the first two: "concern about hygiene and physical health." These three attitudes culminated during the nineteenth century in the "sacralization" of children among the urban middle classes in Europe and North America, in the creation of mass schooling, and by the end of that century, in a permanent reversal of infant and child mortality.[1]

Most of the debate arising from *Centuries of Childhood* settled upon the degree to which children's needs were recognized as distinct from those of adults, before the modern era. Critics fixed upon Ariès's tendency to downplay or even deny what distinctions existed between adults and children and his apparent disregard of evidence that the "concept of childhood" had a long (if less pervasive and culturally resonant) tradition in Western societies before its purported "discovery" in the seventeenth century. Much more work, then, has been devoted to the "first concept" identified by Ariès – the sentimentalization of childhood and the increasing centrality of children to the meaning of family life.

Overlooked by most critics has been the role of education in defining and institutionalizing childhood, a topic to which he devoted almost half of his book. Also rarely addressed was Ariès's discussion of the gradual adoption of age as a mechanism for creating cohorts of learners that would later take on deeper significance in the way that children's unfolding capacities came to be understood. The beginning of the twentieth century on both sides of the Atlantic witnessed the convergence of interest in the systematic study of human growth, of children's physical health, and of children's cognitive, emotional, and sexual development. The co-occurrence of these areas of scientific inquiry was made possible, to a large extent, by the creation of mass schooling in Europe and North America, which contributed to the delineation of the "normal child," and forged increasingly precise links between the identification of children's development and the notion of "age exactitude."[2]

Heightened sensitivity to the significance of age, the creation of behavioral norms surrounding each age, and the increased tendency of individuals (children especially) to internalize the importance of minute discontinuities between social, biological, and chronological age, distinguish the experience of children in the West since the end of the nineteenth century. Indeed, age has become such an important framework for assessing the capacities, rights, and obligations of children that it is difficult for contemporary societies to comprehend a time when this was not so. Still, the most profound changes in the regard for age in the West have come only in the latter half of the modern era, after the seventeenth century. And what might be called the 'cultural consolidation of childhood' – the drawing together of institutions and resources devoted to children to produce a coherent, more or less uniform social experience for growing up – wasn't realized until after the nineteenth century. These developments belong to Ariès's second concept – the desire to protect and reform children.

Age and the transformation of political authority in the "age of reason"

The desire to "reform" children has ancient roots, but until the modern era, only children of the most elevated members of any society received systematic instruction, usually in preparation for future positions of power. In pre-modern Europe, the aristocracy and the Church controlled most forms of education. Literacy – facility in both reading and writing, but primarily the former – was stimulated by the introduction of the printing press and the rise of capitalism, which made the ability to read, write, and cipher advantageous in commerce. However, the perceived necessity for mass schooling had a very long gestation period because the impetus to shape all children's development depended first upon a fundamental reorientation of the individual to the state.

Under feudalism, the individual's status was determined by primogeniture and patriarchy. Patriarchal political theory supported the hereditary authority of the monarch and compared the power of the father over his children with that of the monarch over his subjects. The authority of the monarch arose from his or her purported exclusive link to God; and the principle of primogeniture asserted that the source of the authority of the first-born was also based on a traceable connection to the deity. The Protestant Reformation upheld and emphasized the authority of the patriarch but rejected the connection of the monarch to God. Parent–child relations were crucial in this formulation because they embodied, in miniature, the prerogatives of ruler–subject in the father's authority over his children and of children's obedience to all social superiors. In "this vision," comments Holly Brewer, "most adults had the status of perpetual children ... in relation to those above them in the social hierarchy," in the sense of being dependent on, or subject to, the power of their social superiors. But an important parallel shift occurred at the same time. According to Brewer, it was during the sixteenth century that "children became a metaphor for obedience to church and kingdom." That is, children were symbolically relegated to an inferior – if special – status.[3]

Protestantism asserted that the power to consent to earthly authority belongs to a community of believers whose membership represents the exercise of free will by each community member and depends on the possession of reason by the individual. During the seventeenth century the understanding of reason shifted from the "recognition of the correct ordering of the universe to reason as a process, as conscious actions," which make consent possible. With the rise of consent-based political ideology, says Brewer, children became the "antithesis of those people who have the capacity to reason." Especially in John Locke's formulation during the seventeenth century, she observes, children occupied a categorical if temporary station as those *who could not*, by definition, exercise consent. In parallel, the validity of the scientific method as the foundation for discovering and explaining the operations of natural phenomena advanced "analytical reasoning rooted in experience"; and the convergence of these views placed the development of reason in children under great scrutiny.[4]

The emerging "age of reason" in children (which had been acknowledged in Western medieval societies) was located at around the age of six or seven, and included the ability to distinguish between right and wrong. However, the newer formulation featured a recognition of the ability to perform abstract reasoning and the capacity to understand the consequences of, and therefore to be held accountable for, one's actions. In a moral order so weighted by the responsibility to choose church member-ship – to exercise consent – this had profound political implications. The distinction between children (who lack reason) and those with "sufficient years of understand-ing," established the border between those who did or didn't qualify for a whole range of privileges and responsibilities in Anglo-American common law after the seventeenth century. Over the course of the eighteenth century in England and North America (and particularly in the United States after the Revolutionary War), specific ages of eligi-bility became increasingly standard and in general, were raised. Oath-taking and the capacity to serve as a witness, for instance, had been permitted among children as young as six but were increased to fourteen. Fourteen became the "age of discretion": the ability to "know the law," to "know the difference between right and wrong, good and evil," and to "understand the actions of one's behavior."[5]

Culpability moved beyond the young person's ability to distinguish between good and evil, so that a child could not be found guilty of a crime "but only of criminal potential." Norms for the ages at which a young person could be prosecuted for criminal offenses, own property, serve on a jury, join the military, vote in elections, and enter into marriage were all, legally, brought into rough conformity during the late eighteenth century. Innovations in penal, social welfare, and educational institutions were implemented to deal with the dislocations caused by industrialization during the nineteenth and twentieth centuries, and they similarly reflected heightened distinctions among children, older children ("adolescents"), and adults that were being advanced in common law of the era. By the early nineteenth century, the child's environment was seen as overriding its ability to exercise reason until he or she reached fourteen.

By contrast, the bases of political authority were slower to change in Catholic Europe. The Counter-Reformation attempted to redress at least one retrograde aspect of Catholicism's disregard for the development of reason and its role in consent: the sacrament of confirmation. Before the Reformation, the sacrament of confirmation usually followed on the heels of baptism, but the timing of this rite was delayed by the Catholic Church in response to Protestantism's new emphases on reason and consent.[6] Whereas baptism defeated the stain of original sin and acknowledged the infant's acceptance into the church community, confirmation signaled the growing child's acceptance, in return, of the responsibilities of church membership. However, among Catholics, until the Counter-Reformation there was little controversy over whether the child, to be confirmed, should be at "the age of reason" (seven), or merely old enough to recite vows (about three), or whether it mattered at all. The Reformation had greatly elevated the role of confirmation and all that implied about the individual's relationship to God and membership in the community of believers. Other reforms, similarly, might be construed as increased concern with children's ability to understand the tenets of Catholicism, such as efforts to catechize children during the Counter-Reformation through the creation of Sunday schools, the indoctrination of children to improve church attendance, or to spur the practice of confession. Yet, each of these initiatives flowed not from a new appreciation of the role of consent in Catholicism in reply to the Reformation but from an effort to bolster the power of the Church over kin and clan. The Council of Trent, argues John Bossy in his classic essay, "The Counter-Reformation and the People of Catholic Europe," campaigned to expand the power of the parish over family and clan. Promoting the interests of the Counter-Reformation church and fidelity to the principle of parochial worship, the impetus was to empower an existing but dormant *local* authority with ties to the centralized, trans-factional power of the Church at the expense of a popular piety held hostage to feuding clans, which had for centuries ignored the parish as an inconvenient entity.

Catechizing children exemplified the Counter-Reformation's effort to turn "collective Christians into individual ones," he says.[7] A new stress on the relationship of the *individual* to the Church, however, facilitated the future cultivation of citizenship and the authority of the state among the faithful by projecting the child as a future adult-member of the Church and by analogy, as a citizen of the state. Through the mechanism of catechism, then, the Church realized the utility of schooling as a tool to shape the popular mind. This would become crucial later on in the sponsorship of mass education in European societies, even if during the expansion of state-sponsored popular schooling in the eighteenth and nineteenth centuries the church often attempted to block or circumvent the spread of secular schooling.

Popular schooling and the rise of age grading

Popular schooling drew upon the broadening belief in human – and especially children's – malleability as Enlightenment thought spread its influence across the West.[8] This new view of children contained elements of hope and fear: children were capable, given the proper environment, to grow into exemplary members of society, but they also had the capacity to incline to sin and idleness. The "hopeful" side of children's potential blossomed into the Romantic view of children as naturally innocent and even god-like in their goodness and purity. They held out the promise of redemption for humankind and therefore required protection from the corrupting influence of adults. The "fearful" side of the belief in children's malleability spoke to the need to inculcate a sense of right and wrong in children – what would come to be known as "moral education" among nineteenth-century Anglo-American reformers, educators, and moralists. Popular schooling took root for other reasons as well, such as the necessity to create a loyal and informed citizenry during the rise of modern European states, the desire to reduce crime by equipping young people with the means to make a living, and to fashion future workers to the needs of rapidly changing local, regional, and national economies.

Social control was a fundamental justification for popular schooling wherever it was introduced, and later, as compulsory schooling was contemplated, politicians and statesmen appealed to property owners' sense of self-interest in exacting support of education for other people's children. As Mary Jo Maynes showed in her comparison of the rise of popular schooling in southern France and southwestern Germany during the eighteenth and nineteenth centuries, the desire to exercise control of "the people" found a variety of forms and was rarely successful to the degree that historians have believed, or elites at the time, had hoped.[9] It emerged sporadically across Europe after 1500 and in colonial British North America beginning in the seventeenth century. According to Maynes, the most significant factor in the presence of literacy and schooling was the penetration of markets and spread of commerce. The geography of popular schooling, then, corresponded with the degree of affluence, locally and regionally. In general, rural areas had the lowest rates of literacy (especially among females) and the fewest schools; and while urban areas were more likely to have higher rates of literacy, within cities, literacy rates and the accessibility of schooling reflected the relative wealth of each city's neighborhoods.

"Popular" education meant that school *might* be attended by anyone, not that every child was free to enroll. A number of restrictions prevented schools from being popular in the sense of *mass*, universal education, which was not widespread in the West until the twentieth century. Europe had (and continued to maintain) single-sex schools and favored schooling boys over girls long after school attendance became compulsory in the late nineteenth century. Co-education in Europe went in and out of vogue in the modern era depending on what "reform" was being advanced and whether the Catholic Church or the state held the reins. Therefore, even in areas where it was once popular, it was by the eighteenth century banned in the same places in the belief that girls should not have male instructors or that male pupils might molest or corrupt their female classmates.[10] In the United States, where co-education became customary by the end of the eighteenth century, African-, Native-, and later Mexican-American children were only rarely schooled until the late-nineteenth century and even then, what schooling they received was patently inferior to that offered European Americans. Poor children were less likely to be schooled than children of better means, whether in the United States or Europe until school attendance became compulsory.

Universal compulsory education had distinct origins in Europe and North America. In explaining the emergence of mass schooling in the West, some historians have emphasized the role education came to play in preparing young people for the industrial workplace, acting as a "sorter" of people with widely divergent aptitudes into a variegated occupational structure, and, increasingly, as a conveyor of credentials in a system that feeds economies reliant on workers with certified training. Over time, success in school came to serve as a proxy for the capacity to learn the skills workers would need in whatever occupations they aspired to. Other historians have stressed the importance of schooling in socializing children, competing with the family and religion in transferring habits, dispositions, and aptitudes generationally. Still others, such as Francisco O. Ramirez and John Boli, argue that what mass schooling did most effectively was create citizens. And the project of citizen-creation, they say, best explains the over-arching drive to adopt compulsory school attendance throughout the West. At bottom, it was the success of emerging nation-states to endow individuals as the "building blocks" of society that enabled nation-states to undercut the importance of corporate collectivities, such as the kinship group, the village, region, or church. This realignment was predicated upon a shift of "sovereignty" (the bases of all value and authority) as emanating from God, to one in which humanity is seen as its rightful repository. The "transformation of the Western cultural framework," observed Ramirez and Boli, revealed two new purposes:

> The construction of economic progress expressed in material terms as the expansion of markets ... and the increasing efficacy of technology ... [and] the comprehensive development of the individual as a moral, economic, political, social, and cultural being. Hence, the glorification of God was replaced by the glorification of the autonomous human project, while the salvation of the soul was replaced by the expansion of the capacities and personality of the individual.[11]

The literature on compulsory school attendance illustrates just how difficult it is to generalize about the causes and timing of its rise in Europe and North America. Its implementation varied dramatically even within national borders. In the future Germany, this effort began as early as 1619 in Weimar, but was not adopted by the federal government until 1920. In Spain, the first proclamation on the necessity of universal, public, and free schooling was issued in 1812, but as late as 1922, only half of all twelve-year-olds attended school. In the United States, Massachusetts passed the first state compulsory school attendance law in 1852, Mississippi passed the last one in 1918. Nations across the European continent ranged from early adopters like Denmark (1855) to Italy, which didn't enforce schooling to the age of fourteen for all children until 1962. Ideological impulses, political stakes, economic causes, and sociocultural beliefs combined with enormous variability on both sides of the Atlantic[12] and its story is fascinating for this reason. However, its significance lies in the transformations it wrought, such as the complete association of literacy with schooling, the insistence upon the adoption of a national language and suppression of regional dialects, and of the written over the spoken word. These changes would be critical to citizen-making and mass political participation. The concept of the child as the object of development, both as a site of investment by the state *and* as a future resource to itself, to society, to the economy, and to the national polity has roots in Christianity's conception of the individual's relationship to God, but its increasing importance illustrates the shift described by Ramirez and Boli. Finally, the creation of mass schooling, Maynes says, opened a temporal space – a "universal phase in the individual life course" – for the collective socialization of children in every society that adopted it.[13]

As these goals came to dominate arguments justifying the universality of schooling and more stress was placed on standardizing what teachers taught and students learned, eventually children's chronological age came to be viewed as inextricably linked with their cognitive growth and later, social development. Until the advent of compulsory school attendance, however, grouping children by age had little role in shaping considerations such as pedagogy, modes of discipline, the length of the school day or number of days in a school year, whether both reading and writing were to be taught, or whether girls and boys should be taught together or kept apart. There was nothing axiomatic about the segregation of children by age and ability. As each nation implemented compulsory school attendance, it grappled, ultimately, with the problem of aligning children's "chronological" ages with some notion of "mental" or "developmental" age, derived from the pervading use of IQ testing in Europe and the United States after World War One.[14] But before this happened in colonial North America and early modern Europe, schoolrooms were filled with young people of all ages, and each progressed at various rates and with a variety of aims. Pupils were drilled at the teacher's desk in the front of the class, one-by-one, or in small groups. In preparation for their daily recitations with their teacher, who, in the earlier era of popular schooling might have mastered no more than reading and writing, pupils would memorize passages of the Bible or whatever printed book their family happened to own. This was a laborious and time-consuming mode of instruction, however. Once urban schools began to form and school attendance became compulsory, teaching the largest number of students at the least expense and greatest effectiveness became a priority. "Grading" the schools was hit upon as the solution, and it fueled a seemingly insatiable demand for free, public schooling, especially in the United States during the latter half of the nineteenth century.

Compulsory mass education brought all children under the supervision of one institution, with three consequences:

(1) It provided, for the first time, a basis for comparing children to one another systematically and across the social spectrum.
(2) It had the force of the state behind educators' decisions to differentiate children by age and (perceived) intellectual endowment, which meant that it could create a mechanism for administering tests systematically to determine the placement of children in courses of study with other children of like ability.
(3) The meaning of the categories created to distinguish children in aptitude and maturity were reified in the culture beyond the schools.

This took place "within" children themselves (internally, psychologically), *among* children (socially), between children and their parents, and between families and every institution that supported (or even exploited) their children. But it is important to remember that graded schooling was designed, originally, to "grade" the curriculum and the teacher, *not* students. Students, at first, were merely "classified" in the sense of being grouped by the material they had mastered. Age was not, initially, a consideration. Grading became a way of standardizing what was being taught. It was a way of dividing the labor of teachers into manageable slices of knowledge that could be transmitted to a "class" of students who could move through a curriculum that was sequenced and led to student mastery of a specific body of knowledge. As schooling became normative and then compulsory, the classification of students by their "degree of attainment" corresponded increasingly with students' ages. The youngest pupils were novices. They hadn't the tools or aptitudes they would gradually attain by progressing through the curriculum. Because it was mandated that they begin school at the same age, however, as each cohort moved through graded schools, their ages became, *de facto*, more uniform over time. In so doing, they established age-grade norms.

Public schooling in the United States was notoriously fractious and intensely local in orientation. Standardization in all respects was the trend in the long-term, but there were, across the American continent, more exceptions to the rule than the push for grading would suggest. Maris Vinovkis, *et al.*, estimated that age-grading took a full century to implement – from 1840 to 1940. Nonetheless, the triumph of graded schools not only enforced greater conformity among children's ages; it also established a way of measuring the relative success or failure of any school to educate its pupils. Children's promotion or "retardation" (the term used for the ratio of pupils forced to repeat a grade and who, therefore, fell out of synch with their "age-grade") became the index of an individual school's or an entire school system's effectiveness in comparison with others. In the United States, continuing children for as long as possible into secondary school became a goal of educators in the industrial Midwest and in the Northeast as early as the late nineteenth century. By 1900, the use of promotion rates as a way of rating the success of each school eventually created pressures to promote children for social reasons: that is, to keep them in step with their age cohort so that they could avoid the social stigma of falling behind – the effects of which were purportedly discouragement, underperformance, erratic attendance, behavior problems, and premature school-leaving.[15]

In Europe, class and gender have obscured the salience of age as a metric of children's development to a greater degree than in the United States, where it came to be so closely intertwined with schooling.[16] Despite the earlier and more rapid spread of state-mandated compulsory school attendance laws in much of Europe, school-leaving, which, in many nations was age nine, eleven, or twelve rather than fourteen, remained the most significant age marker for many children well into the twentieth century. Wage-earning, even though undertaken to support the household economy in working-class families, signaled meaningful independence for the budding adolescent and was, thus, more important than the minute articulation of children's ages so characteristic of childhood in the United States. Whether you were a boy or a girl and whether you were more likely to make a living with your head or your hands were the key factors in the degree to how you experienced autonomy as a young person.

In England, for example, compulsory education laws raised the proportion of ten-year-olds in school full-time from 40 percent of the population to 100 percent between 1870 to 1900, and yet a mere 9 percent of fourteen-year-olds were still in school at the beginning of the twentieth century. Within the English working class, increasingly there were two tracks of employment by the First World War. Less than a third of school-leavers in London at the turn of the century went into apprenticeships, while the other two-thirds went into unskilled, "dead-end" jobs. For those fortunate enough to gain apprenticeships, until they turned eighteen their wages were dampened by their status as learners; but apprenticeship yielded to the higher wages of an adult worker once they graduated to a skilled trade. The unskilled laborer earned higher wages than his apprenticing counterpart initially, but "this situation was reversed," according to John Gillis, once he reached eighteen or nineteen when he was "compelled to ask for adult wages." While a small proportion of the unskilled received something approximating a "man's" wage, the great majority were rebuffed, forced to compete against younger, cheaper, and therefore, more employable workers.[17] As a result, one contemporary observer remarked that there were two "turning points" for young workers: from the ages of twelve to fourteen, when school-leaving marked their "second birth," and from seventeen to eighteen years of age, when the unskilled settled at the bottom of the social scale for the remainder of their lives, as skilled males entered manhood. Anything approaching "adolescence" was the privilege of the middle class in England, no less than France and Germany.[18] Although secondary schooling grew steadily after 1900, it wasn't until after World War Two that it enjoyed the kind of expansion in Western Europe that had occurred in the United States between 1900 and 1940, when half of all seventeen-year-olds completed high school.

Age exactitude and the developmental paradigm

"It is as if," remarked Ariès, "to every period of history, there corresponded a privileged age and a particular division of human life: 'youth' is the privileged age of the seventeenth century, childhood of the nineteenth, adolescence of the twentieth." These characterizations, he proposed, are the product of popular interpretations of a society's demographic structure.[19] Lengthening life expectancy in the West has inspired scholars during the last two decades to nominate two more phases to take a place among the "ages of man." Peter Laslett, who observed that life expectancy at birth had risen by 73 percent in England and the United States during the twentieth century, mused upon the emergence of a "third age" in Western societies: "the crown of life ... [a] time of personal self-realization and fulfillment ... after our children have left us and after we have given up our jobs." And a century after G. Stanley Hall identified adolescence as a critical interlude between childhood and adulthood, another life stage had been inserted between adolescence and adulthood – "emerging adulthood." Emerging adulthood encompasses the span from age eighteen through the twenties, "in cultures that allow young people a prolonged period of role exploration." Whether in the future the "third age" commands popular or scholarly attention, the identification of this stage and of "emerging adulthood" lends credence to Ariès's observation about the inclination of societies to privilege one phase of life over another depending on the meaning they see in their relationship to the demographic structure.[20]

What is indisputable is that the "discovery" of adolescence by Hall heightened awareness of the importance of an intervening stage of life between childhood and adulthood, which, in turn, paved the way for a refined delineation of the stages of life in general and of children's development in particular. The signposts of children's journeys from infancy to maturity multiplied as the twentieth century progressed. Now childhood is parsed into sub-stages so numerous that current standard college textbooks on child development note that adulthood is preceded by early infancy, infancy, late infancy, early childhood, middle childhood, and pre-, early-, middle-, and late adolescence. In Europe and the United States, the push to understand children's individual physiological, cognitive, and emotional growth by the latter half of the nineteenth century eventually evolved into a second end: to devise universal standards of development for children from birth to adulthood. One of the most striking aspects of the mounting interest in children's development, as historian Howard Chudacoff has shown, is the variety and number of groups who concerned themselves with children. The emerging medical specialty of pediatrics illustrates this phenomenon during the late nineteenth century in the United States and was joined by the spreading interest in "child study," the rise of child psychology, the child-guidance movement, the anti-child labor movement, the playground movement, and the accelerating demand for child-rearing expertise. The result was to underscore a new consciousness about age, the articulation of life stages, such as adolescence, and the construction of the developmental paradigm by the mid-twentieth century.[21]

The developmental paradigm has two components. The first, which might be thought of as the scaffolding that supports all other study of children and adolescents, is devoted to documenting the physiological growth of children. It has a comparatively straightforward ancestry and persists today as a field of study known as "auxology." The second component seeks to comprehend children's cognitive, social, moral, sexual, and emotional development and is much more eclectic and complex in origin. It has had a briefer lifespan, but has exerted enormous influence over the study of children's passage from infancy to adulthood and the perception of the significance of age. Almost every major figure in psychology in the West has had something to say about the nature and organization of children's development, so what follows will be an overview meant only to sketch out its implications for the increased significance in the modern world of the concept of age.

While the first studies of human proportion are found in antiquity and originate in artistic rather than scientific inquiry, it wasn't until the eighteenth century that anyone sought to document children's changing physical proportions from birth to adulthood, when Johann Georg Bergmüller produced a geometrically derived height curve in 1723. Although a significant achievement, according to biologist–physician–historian James Tanner, Bergmüller neglected the pubertal growth spurt and therefore his study "lacked naturalistic accuracy." This task wouldn't be accomplished for another century, when the first systematic recording of a child's growth was made by the Count de Montbeillard of his son from birth to age eighteen (1759–1777). Montbeillard, according to Tanner "established the existence of the pubertal growth spurt, and seasonal changes in growth-rate, and confirmed the occurrence of [anatomical] shrinkage during the day." In the first third of the nineteenth century, Adolphe Quetelet famously explored the form of the human growth curve and "fitted ... a mathematical curve to empirical values."[22] In his rendering, however, the pubertal growth spurt was "lost" again until Henry Bowditch, whose studies of Boston school children during the last quarter of the nineteenth century produced the first practical growth chart with boys' and girls' growth percentiles indexed according to age, re-established it. Bowditch's standards of growth made it possible to locate the physical characteristics of any child along the axis of age and growth within an entire population of children. In "rediscovering" the pubertal growth spurt, Bowditch implicitly defined the border between childhood and adolescence. This insight became the basis for Tanner's creation, during the third quarter of the twentieth century, of a scale to identify the onset of adolescence and of "functional maturity," which was marked by the emergence of secondary sexual characteristics during adolescence. Tanner's contribution, moreover, reveals developmental psychology's "early and enduring alliance with the biological sciences" and the use of the longitudinal study, which was the methodological backbone of auxology as a field and the favored assessment tool of psychologists who had pioneered intelligence testing at the turn of the twentieth century.[23]

"Tanner Scaling," which is widely used today by developmentalists of every persuasion, offered a world standard for assessing skeletal growth and reinforced the Western appetite for age exactitude. While Tanner's contribution was to emphasize "variability among individuals and groups as an indicator of the environments in which growth is expressed," André Turmel showed how the creation of standardized ways of measuring, recording, and displaying all aspects of children's development from the mid-nineteenth to the mid-twentieth century resulted in the invention of the "normal child." This effect was amplified by the innovation of intelligence testing during the early twentieth century. Alfred Binet and Théodore Simon in France, Cyril Burt in England, and Lewis M. Terman, Edward L. Thorndike, and Henry H. Goddard in the United States, and Wilhelm Stern in Germany at the turn of the twentieth century established methods of measuring children's unfolding cognitive capacities and introduced the idea of "mental age." Charts, graphs, and other modes of visualizing growth according to measured distributions across populations of children were used, ultimately, to enact social change by depicting children's development as following a script. A model of the "normal child" was, thus, increasingly shared across groups variously concerned with children's well-being – by educators, child-welfare professionals, pediatricians, human biologists, child psychologists, the producers and consumers of popular child-rearing literature, and more recently by media watchdogs. The collective effect was to transform statistical averages into developmental targets for all children. These targets produced the notion of "developmentally appropriate" behaviors for children, and prescribed "developmentally appropriate practices" to guide parents, educators, and policy makers.[24]

While the history of developmental science is tangled and fraught with tensions – between theory and practice, between the relative importance of the child's innate endowment and its environment, between insistence on observation in the laboratory or clinic versus "naturalistic" settings such as the home, community, and school, and the on-going discourse between child-development experts and the consumers of information that popularizes their research – one effect has been to enhance the perceived significance of age in Western societies. Beginning in the 1920s in the United States, state- and foundation-funding sponsored child-development research, emphasizing measurement, methodology, and experimentation. Over time, in academic psychology, the more self-consciously scientific developmental psychologists established hegemony and exercised immense influence over the subfield, even though the relationship of developmental psychology to general psychology waxed and waned over the course of the century.

Although the developmental paradigm rose on a framework created by the research of developmental science, its success during the twentieth century is owed to changing social and demographic conditions and to the critical role of some entrepreneurial child-rearing experts, as well as the "silent partner" in developmental research – parents.[25] Culturally, the ground had been prepared by the transformation of the "sturdy" Victorian child to the "fragile" child of the twentieth century. According to historian Peter Stearns, the disappearance of grandparents from the middle-class household left a vacuum of wisdom and experience to deal with children's everyday problems and parents bereft of child-rearing know-how. Compounding the impact of their absence, the trend toward fewer children in the middle class meant that parents had more time to observe and worry over each child. A former belief in the emotional resilience of children, says Stearns, was replaced by nagging doubts about their capacity to confront and overcome fears.[26]

By the 1920s, child-rearing advice aimed at a mass audience filled the growing gap between the new sense of children's vulnerability and parents' seeming incapacity to protect them. At the core of expert advice was the conviction that careful monitoring of the child could positively affect its future. The obverse of this belief was the fear that irreparable damage could be done to a child by an inattentive parent. In the same decade, psychologist John B. Watson declared that children's emotional dispositions were "set" by the time they were three years old. Watson fed the fear of children's innate vulnerability and pointed to the need for further scientific study, which in the United States was to be fulfilled by the creation of the Society for Research in Child Development in 1933.

Fears about the child's fragility, meanwhile, were temporarily countered during the 1930s by Arnold Gesell, who created a systematic database to document the "normal" sequence of children's physical, cognitive, and psychological growth. Gesell's *An Atlas of Infant Behavior* (1934) and *The First Five Years of Life* (1940), posited his theory of maturation, or "development schedules," which asserted the importance of the biological aging process in children, offering a counterpoint to Watson's behaviorist orthodoxy a decade earlier. Gesell's insistence on the acceptance of children's "bad behavior" as natural and resistant to correction, urged parents to relax their vigilance around discipline. His development schedules effectively shifted the focus from nurture to nature and this would be his lasting legacy.

Gesell was tempered, in turn, by pediatrician Benjamin Spock, whose *Common Sense Book of Baby and Child Care* sold nearly four-million copies within a decade after its release in 1946. Spock's "pocket-size" paperback guide to child-rearing hit the market at a moment of unprecedented opportunity. Never before had there been so many well-educated women entering motherhood for the first time and thus, never were so many women capable of, and interested in utilizing child-rearing literature on such a vast scale. Spock stressed the importance of relaxing standards that had been rigidly applied by Watson's disciples, and directed readers to a parenting style that regarded itself as "child-centered," but was less permissive than Gesell's laissez-faire parenting. Child-centered parenting moved the popular prescriptive literature on middle-class parenting away from regimentation and emotional detachment to an attitude that both parent and child are creatures of nature endowed with untapped and under-appreciated instinctual wisdom.

In charting a middle way between Watson and Gesell, Spock drew significantly on the work of Sigmund Freud who viewed the first few years of the child's life as critical to its future development and capacity for happiness. Freud's theory of infant sexuality (1905) outlined the child's passage through three libidinal stages early in life as necessary to achieving emotional and sexual health in adulthood. While Freud described the child's early years as fraught with dangerous pitfalls, he also advocated an ongoing and vigilant compromise between rigidity and laxness in the rearing of children, which was to become Spock's guiding principle. Meanwhile, Spock's contemporary, German-émigré and Vienna-trained psychoanalyst, Erik H. Erikson, popularized and extended Freud's theory of early child development by sequencing a series of "psychosocial" tasks to be accomplished and integrated from infancy through childhood, adolescence, and maturity. The unifying thread, reaching back to Freud at the beginning of the twentieth century and extending through Gesell, Spock, and Erikson at mid-century, was that children's development followed a predictable biological script. This set the stage for renewed interest in the work of Swiss psychologist, Jean Piaget, whose work in the 1920s and 1930s was primarily concerned with mapping the child's increasing, step-wise aptitude for organizing knowledge. Piaget's resurrection further intensified belief in a linear conception of maturation at a time when both social and parental intervention in children's development was on the rise.

By the mid-twentieth century, four major influences had converged to establish the developmental paradigm as the new creed for those who thought about childhood and parenthood into the foreseeable future:

(1) The abandonment of faith in children's innate resiliency for one in which children were seen as fragile and requiring constant attention.
(2) A growing body of research that mapped out the development of children by stages that built one upon the other with consequential outcomes, and which reinforced the importance of intervention at earlier ages.
(3) The emergence of a corps of professionals – academic psychologists, psychiatrists, social welfare workers, pediatricians, and educators – who stressed the need for parental vigilance.
(4) An expanded, well-educated cadre of middle-class mothers eager to apply the lessons of the most up-to-date parenting techniques.

Piaget's conception of discrete, ordered stages reached its apogee among developmental scientists between the early 1960s and late 1980s. His ascendance in the United States, which has been described as the "cognitive revolution," was touched off in part by the "space race and competitive tensions between the superpowers." "In general psychology," psychologists Carol Magai and Susan McFadden explain:

> ... cybernetic science and the emerging availability of computers as fast-paced thinking devices played a role in the shift from questions of learning to questions of cognition and artificial intelligence, and resulted in a focus on problems of memory and information processing.[27]

The appearance of Thelen and Smith's ground-breaking, *A Dynamic Systems Approach to the Development of Cognition and Action* (1994), signaled the eclipse of Piaget, but the notion of linear development and "developmentally appropriate practice," with its highly articulated understanding of the significance of age continued to be endorsed by early childhood professionals and parents alike. Therefore, even while doubts about Piaget's scheme began to creep into the theoretical and empirical work of developmentalists as early as the mid-1970s, it appeared that parents in the United States increasingly engaged their children in cognitive activities aimed at accelerating their developmental progression between 1950 and 2000.[28]

The picture in Europe is equivocal and so variegated that generalization remains difficult. Certainly there has been an acceleration of the use of age to orient judgments about children's aptitude and "readiness" for secondary schooling in Europe since World War Two. While the "streaming" (or its equivalent, "tracking," in the United States) of school children into secondary schools based on measured aptitude occurs between ten and thirteen years of age for children in most countries, schooling lasts longer on average across the European continent than it had before the war. Moreover, the bases for diverting children into more or less academically inclined secondary schools seems to have shifted from intelligence testing earlier in the century toward the principles of "progressive" education. Indeed, the UK's Plowden Report of 1967 placed Piaget's theory of developmental sequencing squarely at the center of its rationale for a "child-centered" primary education system in England. Somewhat mitigating evidence that developmental thinking and age-consciousness had saturated European attitudes toward child rearing, however, is the fact that academic organizations, devoted to the study of child development, were relative latecomers: the European Society for Developmental Psychology, for instance, wasn't launched until 1994, having existed for twenty-five years as a subcommittee of the International Society for the Study of Behavioural Development, which wasn't established until 1969. This remains perplexing considering that Piaget himself was Swiss and developmental psychology was so deeply rooted in experimental psychology as it emerged in late-nineteenth-century Europe.

During the twentieth century, the *social* meaning of chronological age was joined with the concepts of physiological, cognitive, and emotional development through an intensified pursuit of a scientific basis for understanding human growth. This served as the foundation for the construction of the developmental paradigm and by the latter half of the twentieth century, *age itself* became the critical signifier of children's comparative cognitive development and socialization, of norms governing the expression of affection toward and by children, and as indices of children's physical health and psychological–emotional well-being.

Parents, the silent partners in the construction of the developmental paradigm, have been, at times, skeptical of the motives of child-development experts and reluctant, at points, to apply theories at odds with their own experiences with children. For much of the second half of the twentieth century, however, many American middle-class parents have construed the dogma of linear development, not as a sign to let their children "be," but as an invitation to worry that their children were not entering and exiting each developmental stage with sufficient alacrity. As a consequence, parents looked to child-rearing experts to tell them whether they were raising their children in a developmentally appropriate manner, and educators looked to early childhood experts to guide them in implementing developmentally appropriate practices, in part, to reign-in overanxious parents who pushed their children too hard. To what degree parents in Europe experienced similar pressures is unclear; however, we might speculate that they have been more resistant to such concerns, for after all, it was Piaget who referred to US researchers concerned with ways to accelerate child development as the "American question."[29]

Notes

1 Philippe Ariès, *Centuries of Childhood: A Social History of Family Life*; trans. R. Baldick (New York, NY: Vintage Books, 1962), 132–33; and see Viviana Zelizer, *Pricing the Priceless Child: The Changing Social Value of Children* (New York, NY: Basic Books, 1985) on the spread of children's "sentimentalization."

2 I have borrowed the phrase "age exactitude" from Judith Treas, "Age in Standards and Standards for Age," in *Standards and Their Stories; How Quantifying, Classifying, and Formalizing Practices Shape Everyday Life*, ed. Martha Lampland and Susan Leigh Star (Ithaca, NY: Cornell University Press, 2009), 75.

3 Holly Brewer, *By Birth or Consent: Children, Law & the Anglo-American Revolution in Authority* (Chapel Hill, NC: University of North Carolina Press, 2005).

4 Brewer, *By Birth or Consent*, 6; 45; 75; 103.

5 Brewer, *By Birth or Consent*, 6; 45; 228.

6 Brewer, *By Birth or Consent*, 66; 228.

7 John Bossy, "The Counter-Reformation and the People of Catholic Europe," *Past and Present* 47 (1970): 62–63.

8 Hugh Cunningham, *Children and Childhood in Western Society since 1500*. 2nd Edition. New York, NY: Longman, 2005.

9 See Francisco O. Ramirez and John Boli, "The Political Institutionalization of Compulsory Education: The Rise of Compulsory Schooling in the Western Cultural Context," in *A Significant Social Revolution: Cross-Cultural Aspects of the Evolution of Compulsory Education*, ed. J.A. Mangan (London, UK: The Woburn Press, 1994), 10–11; Mary Jo Maynes, *Schooling for the People: Comparative Local Studies of Schooling History in France and Germany, 1750–1850* (New York, NY: Holmes and Meier, 1985), 8.

10 See Maynes, *Schooling for the People*, 130–33.

11 Francisco O. Ramirez and John Boli, "The Political Institutionalization of Compulsory Education," 5.

12 See Mangan, *A Significant Social Revolution*; Maynes, *Schooling the People*; and Maynes, *Schooling in Western Europe: A Social History* (Albany, NY: SUNY Press, 1985).

13 Maynes, *Schooling for the People*, 3; 185; 187–88.

14 Clyde Chitty, *Eugenics, Race, and Intelligence in Education* (London, UK: Continuum, 2007), chapter 4.

15 Maris A. Vinovskis, David L. Angus, and Jeffrey E. Mirel, "Historical Development of Age Stratification in Schooling," in *Education, Society, and Economic Opportunity: A Historical Perspective on Persistent Issues*, ed. M.A. Vinovskis (New Haven, CT: Yale University Press), 171–93.

16 This is my reading of the historiography on childhood and education and Europe, an assessment confirmed by communication with Maynes by email, January 14, 2012.

17 John Gillis, *Youth and History: Tradition and Change in European Age Relations, 1770–Present* (New York, NY: Academic Press, 1974), 126–27.

18 John Gillis, *Youth and History*, 127, quoting Arnold Freeman, *Boy Life and Labour* (London, UK, 1914), 127; Gillis, *Youth and History*, chapter 4; see Linda Clark, "France," chapter 11; and Mary Jo Maynes and Thomas Taylor, "Germany," in *Children in Historical and Comparative Perspective*, ed. Joseph M. Hawes and N. Ray Hiner (New York, NY: Greenwood Press, 1991), chapter 12.

19 Ariès, *Centuries of Childhood*, 32.

20 Peter Laslett, *A Fresh Map of Life: The Emergence of the Third Age*, Cambridge, MA: Harvard University Press, 1991. Laslett, *A Fresh Map of Life*, vii, 3, 69; Jeffery Jensen Arnett, "Emerging Adulthood: A Theory of Development from the Late Teens through the Twenties," *American Psychologist* 55 (2000): 469.

21 André Turmel, *A Historical Sociology of Childhood: Developmental Thinking, Categorization and Graphic Visualization* (New York, NY: Cambridge University Press, 2008), chapters 2–4; Howard F. Chudacoff, *How Old Are You? Age Consciousness in American Culture* (Princeton, NJ: Princeton University Press, 1989).

22 James M. Tanner, *A History of the Study of Human Growth* (Cambridge, UK: Cambridge University Press, 1981); S.J. Ulijaszek, F.E. Johnston and A. Preece, eds., *The Cambridge Encyclopedia of Human Growth and Development* (Cambridge, UK: Cambridge University Press, 1998) 4–5, 102, chapter 3; Tanner, "A Brief History," 5.

23 Carol Magai and Susan H. McFadden, "Historical Background," in *The Role of Emotions in Social and Personality Development: History, Theory, and Research*, ed. C. Magai and S.H. McFadden (New York, NY: Plenum Press, 1995), 10.

24 Turmel, *A Historical Sociology of Childhood*, 66, 116, 182–83; Tanner, *A History of the Study of Human Growth*, 125–25; 146–55; Jo Anne Brown, *The Definition of a Profession: The Authority of Metaphor in the History of Intelligence Testing, 1890–1930* (Princeton, NJ: Princeton University Press, 1992).

25 See Gerrit Breeuwsma, "The Nephew of an Experimentalist: Ambivalences in Developmental Thinking," on the "ambivalent" relation between parents and developmental psychologists, in *Beyond the Century of the Child: Cultural History and Developmental Psychology*, eds. Willem Koops and Michael Zuckerman (Philadelphia, PA: University of Pennsylvania Press, 2003), 183–203.

26 Peter N. Stearns, *Anxious Parents: A History of Modern Childrearing in America* (New York, NY: New York University Press, 2003), chapter 2. On the disappearance of grandparents from twentieth-century households, see Steven Ruggles, "The Transformation of American Family Structure," *American Historical Review* 99 (1994): 103–28.

27 Magai and McFadden, "Historical Background"11.

28 Maryellen Schaub, "Parenting for Cognitive Development from 1950 to 2000: The Institutionalization of Mass Education and the Social Construction of Parenting in the United States," *Sociology of Education* 83 (2010): 46–66. On Piaget's impact on developmental psychology, see Erica Burman, *Deconstructing Developmental Psychology* (London, UK: Routledge, 1994), esp. chapter 11. On emerging challenges to Piaget, see, for example, Klaus F. Riegel, "The Dialectics of Human Development," *American Psychologist* 31 (1976): 689–700.

29 See Erica Burman's lucid essay on the influence of Piaget on developmental psychology in chapter 11 of her book, *Deconstructing Developmental Psychology*; the quote is from page 156.

Suggestions for further reading

General

Fass, Paula S. and Grossberg, Michael, eds. *Reinventing Childhood after Post-World War II*. Philadelphia, PA: University of Pennsylvania Press, 2011.

Hawes, Joseph M. and Hiner, N. Ray, eds. *Children in Historical and Comparative Perspective*. New York, NY: Greenwood Press, 1991.

Debate on Ariès

Hareven, Tamara, ed. "Symposium Marking the Twenty-Fifth Anniversary of Philippe Ariès', *Centuries of Childhood*." *Journal of Family History* 12(4) (1987).

Hendrick, Harry. "Children and Childhood." *ReFresh: Recent Findings of Research in Economic and Social History*, 15 (1992): 1–4, http://www.ehs.org.uk/ehs/refresh/default.asp.

Pollock, Linda. *Forgotten Children: Parent–Child Relations From 1500 to 1900*. Cambridge, UK: Cambridge University Press, 1983.

Shahar, Shulamith. *Childhood in the Middle Ages*. New York, NY: Routledge, 1990.

Education

Bredekamp, Sue, and Carol Copple, eds. *Developmentally Appropriate Practice in Early Childhood Programs*, rev. ed. Washington, DC: NAEYC, 1997.

Gillard, Derek. "Plowden and the Primary Curriculum: Twenty Years On," (March 1987) http://www.educationengland.org.uk/articles/04plowden.html.

Gillard, Derek. "*Us and Them: A History of Pupil Grouping Policies in England's Schools* (December 2008) http://www.educationengland.org.uk/ articles/27grouping.html.

Hogan, David. "From Contest Mobility to Stratified Credentialing: Merit and Graded Schooling in Philadelphia, 1836–1920." *History of Education Review*, 16 (1987): 21–42.

Labaree, David F. *How to Succeed in School without Really Trying: The Credentials Race in American Education*. New Haven, CT: Yale University Press, 1997.

Lassonde, Stephen. *Learning to Forget: Schooling and Family Life in New Haven's Working Class, 1870–1940*, chapter 1. New Haven, CT: Yale University Press, 2005.

Mangan, J. A., ed. *A Significant Social Revolution: Cross-Cultural Aspects of the Evolution of Compulsory Education*. London, UK: The Woburn Press, 1994.

Tyack, David. *The One Best System: A History of American Urban Education*. Cambridge, MA: Harvard University Press 1974.

Vinovskis, Maris A. *Education, Society, and Economic Opportunity: A Historical Perspective on Persistent Issues*. New Haven, CT: Yale University Press, 1995.

Child rearing

Grant, Julia. *Raising Baby by the Book: The Education of American Mothers*. New Haven, CT: Yale University Press, 1995.

Hulbert, Ann. *Raising America: Experts, Parents, and a Century of Advice About Children*. New York, NY: Knopf, 2003.

"Measuring" children

Beatty, Barbara. "From Laws of Learning to a Science of Values: Efficiency and Morality in Edward L. Thorndike's Educational Psychology." *The American Psychologist* 53 (1998): 1145–52.

Chapman, Paul Davis. *Schools as Sorters: Lewis M. Terman, Applied Psychology, and the Intelligence Testing Movement*. New York, NY: New York University Press, 1988.

Fass, Paula S. *Outside In: Minorities and the Transformation of American Education*. New York, NY: Oxford University Press, 1989.

Developmental psychology and its history

Cahan, Emily D. "Toward a Socially Relevant Science: Notes on the History of Child Development Research." In *When Science Encounters the Child: Education, Parenting, and Child-Welfare in Twentieth Century America*, edited by Barbara Beatty, Emily D. Cahan, and Julia Grant. New York, NY: Teachers College Press, 2006.

Cairns, Robert. "The Emergence of Developmental Psychology." In *Handbook of Child Psychology* 4th ed., edited by Paul Mussen, 41–102. New York, NY: Wiley, 1983.

Erickson, Erik H. *Childhood and Society*. New York, NY: W.W. Norton & Co., 1950.

Koops, Willem, and Michael Zuckerman, eds. *Beyond the Century of the Child: Cultural History and Developmental Psychology.* Philadelphia, PA: University of Pennsylvania Press, 2003.

Pillemer, Davis, and Sheldon H. White, eds. *Developmental Psychology and Social Change.* Cambridge, UK: Cambridge University Press, 2005.

Sears, Robert R. *Your Ancients Revisited: A History of Child Development.* Chicago, IL: University of Chicago Press, 1975.

12

MAKING ADOLESCENCE MORE OR LESS MODERN

Don Romesburg

For at least the last five hundred years, adolescence has been a historically and culturally contingent transition between childhood and adulthood. For the past half-century, historians have explored the social construction of *adolescence*, how *adolescents* have adapted to and influenced its changing contours, and the *youth cultures* produced in the tensions between them. Families, institutions, laws, and developmental stages have saddled adolescents with a compulsory futurity that insists they will always be headed elsewhere. Boys' and girls' success or failure in becoming men and women has been measured through their capacities to grow up in the right ways, on the right schedules. Young people have acted on a continuum between conforming to and transgressing age roles designed to harness them. In the process, they have transformed expectations regarding identity, work, school, family, morality, nationalism, and the market.

This essay builds upon what some historians have characterized as the rise and fall of modern adolescence in Western Europe and North America. Let me clarify what I mean by "modern" because so many scholars mean such different things by it. The project of modernity operates through a faith in societal improvement based in a capitalist marketplace and the rational ordering and management of people. To some extent, modernity recognizes the individual's capacity for free will and self-determination, although this has always been highly racialized, gendered, and conditioned on social standing. Modern people are expected to reproduce and expand the productive, moral, and orderly nation-state.

With oversight by families, employers, teachers, and institutions, modern adolescents are supposed to self-regulate development toward maturity and social norms. State investment in modern adolescence makes it a key conduit of broader social and civic transformation. A heightened appreciation for adolescence means expanded resources devoted to young people's development. This pressures boys and girls to realize societies' aspirations through their own maturation. When given such importance, adolescents on the whole, through the sheer diversity of lives they lead, can only disappoint. When modernity fails the young, societies tend to blame adolescents.

In brief, I argue that adolescence became initially more modern, and subsequently, something else that I am describing as "more or less modern." Societies first increasingly invested in what adolescence could do for civilization and the nation. Then, as the promise of modern adolescence lost its allure, societies retained much of its structure but pursued a more cynical management of adolescents. This occurred in uneven, sedimentary ways rather than in discrete stages. Young people navigated older expectations and practices along with newer systems, institutions, and ideologies.

More specifically, I trace this process from the early modern period to the turn of our present century. In the sixteenth through eighteenth centuries, boys and girls with varying social standing and mobility navigated through unevenly applied patriarchal demands. These devalued youths in relation to their elders, but accommodated distinct positions for them. From the mid-eighteenth through early twentieth centuries, the elaboration of modern adolescence had growing value and purpose. Massive state investment in its successful production promised to reproduce national power and advance civilization. Youths who "failed" this project or fell outside of its aspirations, as many invariably did, faced distinct burdens, but also pushed its boundaries. In the mid-twentieth century, the intensity of this project began to lessen. Still, domesticating adolescents was one way to address post-war uncertainties and anxieties amidst the growing complexity of consumer culture, youth cultures, and social justice movements. "Teenagers" embodied a normalization of young sexualities and consumption. Teens often complied with but sometimes strained against their domestication. Since then, wariness toward adolescents has largely overtaken the modern vision of adolescence as producing order and hope, even as young people have advocated for a right to determine their own developments within an increasingly interconnected global context. Both adolescents and adolescence face an uncertain future.

Early modern youth: navigating patriarchy (1500s–1700s)

From the 1500s through the 1700s in Western Europe and colonial North America, young people navigated strong patriarchal systems under brutal conditions. It was an accomplishment simply to reach adolescence. Childhood mortality rates were high throughout the era. In England, for example, approximately 140 infants out of every 1,000 died in their first year, with another 30 percent of children dying of diseases before they reached fifteen. Many others were killed in accidents or orphaned by their parents' death.[1]

Ostensibly, fathers and masters, naturally and legally, headed households. Wives, children, and servants were subordinated. This mirrored the Great Chain of Being, a medieval and early modern Christian conceptual hierarchy that placed God at the top followed in succession by kings, aristocrats, and peasants. Adolescence was already thought of as a semi-dependent transition between childhood and maturity. Gender and status influenced deeply the ways in which young people lived and worked. Some boys and girls found opportunities that, over time, loosened patriarchal order.

For girls and boys from aristocratic and wealthy backgrounds, adolescence was often a time of preparation for their most valuable task of maturation – marriage. Older traditions of dowry were, by the sixteenth century, joined by widespread Western European adoption of primogeniture, which privileged a family's oldest son in the transfer of name and property. Dowry and primogeniture delayed marriage, extending youth and promoting considerable parental power over young people's choice of spouse. Rising marriage ages in Western Europe required the social management of an extended sexual delay after the onset of puberty. For those who would not marry, it imposed deep sexual frustrations, for women who were sometimes sent to convents as well as for younger sons who could not reproduce legitimate offspring.

Families carefully oversaw girls' sexualities and reputations to make them as desirable for marriage as possible. Many continued to live at home into their twenties, only leaving when a husband was secured. While constrained by these circumstances, some wealthy girls had extra-familial social possibilities. When formal education occurred, it was principally in sex-segregated, cloistered religious orders. By the 1700s, early consumer society provided another degree of personal expression. Through dress, some wealthier girls could fashion feminine selves. In deciding how to adorn themselves, however, they most often consulted with parents with an eye toward displaying the taste and cultivation that would enhance their status in the marriage market. Marriage remained a basic expectation. Its circumstances were seldom wholly a result of girls' choice.

Boys from families of stature and wealth also faced the burdens of patriarchy and primogeniture, but had routes to maturity beyond marriage. They joined professions, trades, or the priesthood. From the 1600s through the mid-1700s, civic-run education expanded, especially in Protestant countries. As with more widespread Catholic schooling, most was directed toward boys. By the 1700s, this encouraged a sense of self and society beyond older models of patriarchy. In French boarding and day schools, for example, boys trained to become mature social participants and forged bonds with classmates and teachers. Some, particularly sons not first-born, sought opportunity through the military and New World exploits. Over time, such associations and distance from fathers loosened paternal authority, promoting homosocial bonds between young men. They also created intergenerational masculine allegiances outside of the family that reaffirmed patriarchy more generally. English patriarchy weakened as land scarcity and the early Industrial Revolution resulted in declines in primogeniture and apprenticeships. In colonial New England, a stronger patriarchy continued well into the 1700s, due in part to wealthy fathers' ability to grant all sons (rather than just the eldest) land inheritances.

Among peasants across many parts of Europe, nascent youth cultures flourished. In rural France and elsewhere, youth-abbeys and other groups of unmarried young men gathered to compete, brawl, and revel during festivals. They also enforced moral codes regarding gender, age, and association. Communities granted gangs license, because, as Natalie Zemon Davis argues, their censuring activities often fitted into larger systems of patriarchal order.[2] In particular, they policed sexual behaviors and reputations. Girls, having no such authority, faced harassment and were trafficked in territorial "honor" brawls. In France and Germany, civic leaders alternately armed and struggled to contain formal and informal associations of misrule. In North America, Chesapeake colonists tolerated youthful carousing as male prerogatives, but socializing was more loosely structured than in Western Europe. In New England, patriarchs' tight control dampened young men's camaraderie.

Youths from poor families had to contribute to household labor as soon as they were able. Boys and girls from modest or middling backgrounds worked as they entered their teens. Most stayed close to home. Age limits and gender restrictions inhibited entry into trade apprenticeships, and so many labored within their families or as unskilled servants for nearby masters. Families sought fair work arrangements for their children. Through collective oversight and appeals to masters' paternalist responsibility for servants, communities attempted to mitigate abuse, neglect, or exploitation. Servants could not marry and could be severely punished for out of wedlock sexual practices or pregnancies.

In times of overpopulation and famine, boys' and girls' migration increased. This put pressure on hierarchical order and youths exercised some agency. In English towns, few stayed more than a year on one job as they looked for better pay or more favorable conditions. Yet servant girls, in particular, faced greater sexual exploitation as the labor force became mobile. England set the first modern age of consent law in 1576, for girls, at ten; similar Italian and German statutes set the age at twelve. American colonies also chose ten or twelve. Even at this low age, trial juries often took the girls' morality into account when deciding whom to blame.

Lower-status boys and girls also entered expanding empires. In 1635, over half of the English who headed to the Americas were between sixteen and twenty-three. Some were as young as ten. Spain, Portugal, England, and Holland funneled destitute boys into seafaring and promised dowries to girls who relocated overseas. English orphans, runaways, and vagrants transported to the Chesapeake faced skewed sex ratios, indenture, and high rates of mortality. Seventeenth-century English colonial girls there capitalized on their scarcity, marrying younger than in Western Europe or New England. In their mid-to-late teens they chose to wed older suitors of greater means and status. Across the colonies, African–Americans who survived enslavement into their teens faced the greatest likelihood among all slaves of sale, forced transportation from birth families, sexual abuse, and unwanted pregnancies.

Throughout the eighteenth century, lower-status girls and boys took advantage of weakening patriarchal structures created by economic and cultural shifts. In Western Europe, nascent industrialization drew on unmarried girls, as the traditionally female activity of spinning was transformed into capitalist labor. By the latter part of the century, officials at state-sponsored German, French, and English industrial schools for girls sought to frame them as factories of feminine virtue. These places also provided young women collectivity through which to begin to conceive of themselves as members of a distinct age cohort and culture. In British North America, the Great Awakening (1730s–1740s) attracted young people, especially among the rural poor. Through its promises of immediatism in conversion and spiritual revival, peer cultures challenged patriarchal deference. The American Revolution further eroded intergenerational hierarchy and provided youthful colonists with a sense of shared identity through participation. After the war, the poor boys that had done much of the soldiering sought pensions and/or release from indenture.

By the second half of the eighteenth century, early modern patriarchy gave way to more liberal emphases on the market, selfhood, and individual rights. European and American adolescent practices and prerogatives matched up unevenly with the developing concept of modern adolescence. Some young people, particularly of higher status, were able to approximate some of the expectations of a gradual adolescence filled with education and cultivation leading toward autonomy, citizenship, and moral family life. Many others, however, found new opportunities for work, culture, and consumption that exceeded this design.

Making adolescence modern (1750s–1904)

Within liberal humanism childhood was refigured as an innocent blank slate. Puberty supposedly brought a radical second birth of fundamental moral, biological, and mental transformations through which a child grew from neediness into rational, productive, civilized, and gendered citizenship. In *Émile* (1762), Jean-Jacques Rousseau espoused adolescence as the development of girls and boys into mature complementarity that subordinated women to men. He believed that desire induced by pubescent sexuality, if delayed and nurtured, cultivated virtuous gendered interdependence. As Joel Schwartz explains, Rousseau claimed that boys were first to sublimate desire into male friendship, then balance yearnings for girls with a developing masculine "advantage of reason."[3] In the following decades, German writers in the *Sturm and Drang* movement emphasized that torment spurred young people toward irrationality, destructiveness, and eroticism. Taken together, Rousseau's call for development toward rational maturity and *Sturm and Drang*'s characterization of youth as a period of passionate, impulsive desire to be weathered and overcome would typify modern adolescence.

By the late eighteenth and early nineteenth centuries, among wealthy and middle-class boys, opportunities abounded to achieve a liberal maturity. These boys built upon, rather than overturned, their fathers' manhood ideals. Even as they embraced intergenerational obligations required by older patriarchal structures, they sought intimate male peer friendships. When courting girls, boys were expected to strive for a personal balance of reason and sentiment. This perspective rejected the idea of parentally arranged marriage and drew upon cosmopolitan emphases on emotional intimacy and romance.

Such boys grew into active public lives of letters, commerce, and politics. European and American states relied upon religious or quasi-religious organizations to steer these young men toward virtuous manhood. In the early nineteenth century, English and American counselors encouraged urban middle-class boys to wall themselves, in Joseph Kett's words, "within the fortress of character" to avoid the temptations of urban and peer life far from parental oversight.[4] In the second half of the century, muscular Christianity spread from Anglican efforts to prepare young men for imperial service to broader attempts to cultivate moral restraint, masculine athleticism, and courageous camaraderie in the bodies, hearts, and souls of young men. Through organizations such as the YMCA (spreading from London in 1844 to the United States and Europe), it reasserted a vigorous role for Protestant masculinity.

School growth expanded and recentered modern adolescence. By the 1850s, northeastern and midwestern US towns commonly had public high schools. By the end of the century, American public secondary education was overwhelmingly co-educational, with girls dominating enrolment and graduation numbers. Europeans criticized the American system and sex-segregated day schools increased in France (*lycée* and *collège*) and Germany (*gymnasium*). While Scandinavian countries went co-educational late in the century, sex segregation continued to dominate in Europe.

Adults managed school structures, but youths asserted their own cultures. In Western Europe and the United States, peer hazing and crushes addressed anxieties and affections as students policed one another for transgressions of gender, sexual propriety, and hierarchy. Young people forged intense homosocial peer bonds and worked out ideas and identities within dormitories as well as secret societies, fraternities, and other associations. Organized sport was one adult attempt to manage this semi-autonomy.

Eighteenth- and early nineteenth-century middle-class girlhood, too, took on liberal forms. In Protestant Germany, England, and the United States, parents, pedagogues, and physicians believed education should develop girls' taste, modesty, cheerfulness, and household management along with basic literacy and mathematics. The German figure of the giggling, diary-writing *backfishe* emerged, a mid-teen girl who internalized the social order in her transition from carefree innocence into maturity. Protestant girls generally learned to balance what Martha Vicinus calls "distance and desire" through the cultivation of independence and duty.[5] They were encouraged to enact sexual restraint and social norms as they engaged in broadening mixed-sex social activities. By contrast, French Catholic convent schools were transformed after the revolution into sex-segregated state and private boarding institutions. French girls faced, as they had before, strict surveillance and were kept in ignorance about sexuality prior to marriage. They cultivated relational identities, collaborating to negotiate institutions, evade authoritative control, and fan cross-sex flames through subtle flirtations. Both Protestant expectations of self-regulation and Catholic tension between surveillance, sexuality, and innocence would become central to modern female adolescence.

As modern adolescence coalesced, it bifurcated youth into those who, to some degree, approximated its ideals and inhabited its aspirational institutions, and those seen as needing other forms of management and discipline. In the 1810s, New York founded the House of Refuge to shelter and sequester homeless, destitute, and vagrant children and youths. By the mid-century, major Western European and American cities had state-run reform schools. These promoted gendered discourses of domesticity, regimentation, and industry, but were often like prisons. French, British, German, and American administrators imitated each other's institutions. Reform schools became laboratories through which a scientific approach to adolescence emerged through the study of crime, poverty, and age. This led to psychological and sociological approaches to delinquency, institutionalized first in Chicago's juvenile court (1899).

Juvenile justice underpinnings also came from the middle-class reform movements' approaches to youth racialized as nonwhite. Mid-nineteenth-century US evangelical women carried scientific racism and expectations of gradual post-pubertal development into missionary work, as did Englishwomen with London's "ragged children" and African "mission children." Through late-nineteenth-century US orphan trains, Native American boarding schools, and similar programs in the British Empire, the mass redistribution and "uplift" of indigenous, poor, and immigrant populations served imperial needs. Older forms of apprenticeship disappeared across Europe and North America, but after the US Civil War (1861–1865), the Freedman's Bureau and southern state authorities forced tens of thousands of newly emancipated African–American teenaged boys and girls into agricultural "apprenticeship" to former slave holders. Free black adolescence meant navigating the humiliation and vulnerability of structural and interpersonal indifference, segregation, and violence. The growing black middle class provided some avenues for youth possibility, including schooling, reform, and club activities.

Working-class young people at play stimulated many observers' fears. Reformers worried over new "low" forms of mass consumption that working-class youths embraced, such as British "penny dreadfuls" and American "dime novels," and sought to legislate bans or replace them with prescriptive literature. The nineteenth-century French archetype of the simultaneously sweet and debauched garment factory girl had her counterpart in the apprentice, now conceptualized as a mobile boy ready for riotous assembly. Across Europe and North America, links between poor boys' recreations and delinquency raised the greatest concern, although late in the century attention was also paid to girls' sexual delinquency.

At the turn of the twentieth century, working-class youths pioneered heterosocial "treating." This blended commercialized leisure, informal sexual barter and affection. Girls gained some freedom from parental oversight but lost intergenerational homosocial protection. Boys assumed greater economic burdens but also, as chaperonage declined, enjoyed more interpersonal power. Collectively, boys' gangs and gatherings dominated urban youth cultures. As with early modern youth-abbeys, girls were vulnerable to boys' advances and censure. Still, girls were able to assert some agency through making boys accountable to peers and families. Wage-earning girls also had a new, if still limited, voice within their families. If finances permitted, they also made their own consumer choices.

Governments legislated modern adolescence as an extended pubertal period of sexual delay. Age of consent laws rose from as low as ten to between thirteen (France 1863) and sixteen (England and Wales 1885). Sweeping European and North American mandates encouraged the view of teenage women as little girls victimized by lecherous men. Jurors continued to adjudicate based on their perceptions of girls' sexual knowledge and experience. Gender, class, and race biases led to uneven policing of girls as well as prosecution of men of color, working-class men, and immigrants. New laws often extended age of consent and sexual crime coverage to boys.

By the century's end, doctors and other experts were turning to social evolutionary theory to divide youths along tracks of care that intersected with institutions developed to manage them. American psychologist G. Stanley Hall wove all this together into his *Adolescence: Its Psychology and Its Relations to Physiology, Anthropology, Sociology, Sex, Crime, Religion, and Education* (1904). Hall suggested that each individual's life course recapitulated humanity's evolution from savagery to civilization. This marked adolescence as a universal life stage of storm and stress, vulnerable yet uniquely rich with potential. It imagined that advanced societies could harness the lag between one's pubertal, moral, and mental maturities to personal, social, and national advantage. During a prolonged adolescence, youths could carry forward strengths of the primitive past, sublimated into ever-advancing progress through clear gender differentiation and a gradual sexual path to marital procreation. While modern adolescence was supposedly available to all, Hall believed that so-called "primitive peoples" rushed into an early reproduction that short-circuited proper socialization. Moreover, as David Macleod writes, "Staying on Hall's schedule was distinctly a class privilege."[6] Boys were at the center of Hall's vision. He viewed girls as beholden to "periodicity" and criticized those who lost what he perceived as proper femininity while pursuing educational ambitions.

Hall charted a path to the future for Germans alarmed by a perceived rash of schoolboy suicides, Britians concerned with the industrial and imperial impact of boys' poor health, and Americans grappling with a diversifying, mobile population. *Adolescence* drew on European and US scholarship and its first printing sold over 25,000 copies worldwide. It inspired major works in France (G. Compayré's *L'Adolescence* [1909]), England (J. W. Slaughter's *The Adolescent* [1911]), and Germany (C. Bühler's *Das Seelenleben des Jugendlichen* [1922]) and attracted an international following of reformers, youth organization leaders and educators. Adolescence had become modern: a nationalist and humanist accomplishment of individual will and feeling, peer affinity, family nurturance, institutional administration, legislation, and expert guidance.

Modern adolescence and the great state (1900s–1940s)

Throughout the first half of the twentieth century, adolescence held the state's interest as a core nationalist project. It promised to strengthen empires, foster social stability, and build robust societies. Many across Western Europe and North America were optimistic about the capacity of social engineering to solve dilemmas of girls' expanding prospects, women's political rights, declining middle-class birthrates, sexual and social pathology, and growing immigrant, imperial, and nonwhite populations.

Social scientists responded to the complexity of urban, industrial, and consumer societies. They gradually transitioned away from a clear-cut celebration of middle-class adolescence that pathologized others as inherently inferior. Instead, they sought to incorporate diverse youth into universalized adolescent developmental processes, social activities, and gender/sexual adjustments. From the 1910s through the 1930s, experts standardized stages of physical and psychosexual development. Sigmund Freud and psychoanalytically influenced psychologists such as Albert Moll, Phyllis Blanchard, and Wilhelm Stekel argued that pubertal sex forces tested childhood "tendencies" that by adulthood were resolved or resulted in a fixation. Sociologists and anthropologists from the 1910s through the 1940s added environmental explanations, delimiting adolescence as culturally specific within a global range of pubertal youth experiences. This encouraged toleration of a wide array of adolescent expressions. Still, experts criticized those who transgressed norms too much or too persistently for a supposed incapacity to adjust to their society.

Heterosexuality became defined as a fusion of cross-sex desire with an idealized model of middle-class, monogamous, gender normative, companionate marriage. Experts claimed heterosexuality was psychologically mature, socially normal, and biologically natural. At the same time, it was understood to be not inevitable but a developmentally vital accomplishment. In this context, adolescents had to walk a "tightrope of normalcy" between self-expression and maladjustment. They were expected to be heterosexual (but not too sexual), gender normative (but not overcompensating), and well-adjusted heterosocially (but not promiscuous).[7]

Across Europe and North America, proponents of social hygiene, which combined scientific research and public education in an attempt to manage the sexuality of the masses, translated this ideology into practice. In England during and after World War I, they mounted campaigns to provide working girls with programs in nutrition and social purity. These linked future motherhood to other programs to produce healthy, orderly citizens. French and German leftists and feminists hoped social hygiene would dismantle the sexual double standard and help girls avoid unwanted sexual advances, venereal disease, and pregnancy. American mass secondary school gave educators a captive audience for sex education. Its trajectory arched from "birds and bees" nature study through the advancing history of civilization. This culminated in linking students' personal fulfillment to their adjustment to modern heterosexuality. Most explicitly in Nazi Germany, the school curriculum wedded patriotic triumphalism, eugenic science, and pronatalism. This became part of the state's effort to press adolescents into national service. Social hygiene sought to replace the sexual cultures adolescents interacted with at home, with peers, or on the street with a modern approach that standardized development of love, family, and society for the state.

Expert discourses and social hygiene efforts were part of the broader institutionalization of adolescence. American cities and the British government established juvenile courts and guidance clinics that assessed the causes of delinquency and directed wayward youths through education and varied services. Unlike the Anglo–American models, German juvenile justice continued to emphasize penal sentencing even as, by the 1920s, it incorporated some welfare-oriented approaches. Across Western Europe and North America, authorities largely brought in boys for property crimes and status offenses. Experts characterized them as immature. Girls, most often targeted for sexual offenses, were seen as dangerously precocious. Boys' sexual offenses rarely received the same attention as either boys' property crimes or girls' sexual activities. Homosexual offenses, however, could lead to institutionalization, indefinite treatment, and eugenic sterilization. Sterilization was either voluntary, as implemented in much of Europe, or compulsory, as in the United States and Germany. Eugenics found its most extreme outcomes under the Nazi regime. The Nazis killed, abused, and sent to concentration camps youths diagnosed with mental and physical disabilities together with Jewish girls and boys. Those who survived faced generational ruptures, hard labor, sexual violence, malnutrition, and trauma.

The American democratization of co-educational secondary schooling attracted first girls, and then boys, from across class and ethnic backgrounds. It also justified massive governmental, philanthropic, and social scientific investment seeking to discipline diverse populations into a cohesive industrialized nation-state. This contrasted with Europe, where most working-class adolescents continued to labor until after World War II. By 1930, the majority of US youths attended high school.

Adolescents in school expressed themselves within and beyond state aspirations for orderly development. The massive influx of diverse youths overtook adult capacities to manage them. Academically, many rejected gendered and class-based curricular tracks, opting instead for courses they hoped would propel them into white-collar careers. Some left school to work. Within youth cultures, students became literate in social hierarchies of leaders versus followers, heroes versus fans, and national collectivity versus ethnic subcultural identity. As with past generations, peers policed one another in regard to civic, social, and sexual norms. They also created systems of dating, rating, and belonging.

In Europe and the United States, youth programming sought to fill adolescent social lives and temper urban and industrial unrest. In the 1900s and 1910s, adult-led British and American organizations such as the Boy Scouts and Girl Scouts emphasized athletics, nature worship, intergenerational mentoring, clear gender roles, courage, and teamwork. Mostly popular among pre-adolescents, such organizations often struggled to hold the interest of the young as they reached their teens. The youth-led

German Wandervogel shared values of athleticism and training with Anglo–American organizations. Unlike those groups, it could be sympathetic to socialism, emphasized more free expression of ideas, and encouraged direct political engagement. It also had far more appeal to older adolescents than the scouts. Ethnic and religious groups also created organizations to cultivate character alongside community solidarity.

Following World War I, interwar political parties and governments sought to channel youths as symbols of an eternally regenerative nation and as loyal male and female counterparts. The UK Labour Party's League for Youth (1926) and French Catholic, fascist, and leftist student organizations sought to channel young men's street life into political engagement. In the New Deal, the US Civilian Conservation Corps harnessed unemployed young men during the 1930s to develop natural resources and personal character, while the National Youth Administration employed young men and women to build infrastructure. As the Nazis centralized power, they made participation in their youth organizations compulsory. Hitler Youth were to strive toward military excellence and physical perfection while the League of German Girls was famed as heroines on the "birth front" of the National Socialist struggle. By the early 1940s, the numbers brought in through compulsory participation overwhelmed Nazi state infrastructure. Many adolescents became disenchanted with the promises that participation would produce greatness.

As even the extreme example of Nazi programming suggests, social control was, at best, incomplete. Despite the array of discourses and institutions developed to manage adolescence, adolescents exercised new prerogatives in the marketplace. Working-class American and English girls composed a heterosocial mix of low-wage workers engaged in retail, waitressing, and factory work. Adolescent working-class and poor boys frequently took unskilled, poorly paid, and sporadic employment. British boys underutilized job placement services and day continuation schools, in part because they were resistant to their mandates. Urban work and play provided many social and sexual opportunities. In 1920s Chicago, for example, the Juvenile Protective Association worried over the complex urban economy of desires in which newsboys, in addition to selling papers, sometimes ran johns to prostitutes or sold their own bodies to men to earn money to take gals out on the town.

In the United States, laboring sons and daughters of European immigrants continued to participate in expanding cultures of commercialized amusements and peer-driven heterosocial mixing. They frequently clashed with families over autonomy and expressivity. By the interwar period, working-class European girls and boys followed suit. By the 1920s and 1930s, American middle-class girls and boys embraced "dating" as a rite of adolescence. Over time, parents, reformers, and social scientists gradually accepted limited heterosexual expression ("petting") as useful to normal development.

Across class lines, girls found ways to express themselves through consumerism. This was often accompanied by modern femininity's disciplinary expectations. These included what Joan Brumberg calls the "body projects" of mass personal hygiene and beauty cultures. Some contemporary commentators saw flappers and other "modern girls around the world" as excessive consumers, dupes of popular culture, or promiscuously expressive. Others, however, saw them as emblems of healthy nationalism and reflecting a robust youth. Girls themselves used consumer culture to express themselves beyond the dictates of families, ethnic communities, or institutions. Vicki Ruiz describes how some Mexican–American girls, for example, crafted hybrid adolescent identities by painting their faces with widely available cosmetics, donning affordable fashions, and taking cues from the movies. Middle-class and African–American girls, according to Kelly Schrum, also appropriated adult cosmetics and Hollywood models to adolescent norms and practices.[8]

Jon Savage viewed early twentieth-century adolescent dancing as an informal, disorganized resistance from below to state control. Bringing together peer-based heterosocial mixing, commercialized amusements, and youth-driven cultures, boys and girls took up transnational rhythms in collective activities in which they presumed a right to pursue their own pleasures. During World War II, middle-class bobby soxers and sexually active "victory girls" on both sides of the Atlantic, working-class and nonwhite American zoot suiters, French zazous, and German swing kids all helped build visible expressive youth cultures.[9] Their moves complicated state maneuvers to reproduce patriotic, orderly, and participatory nationalism through adolescent development.

By the mid-1940s, the vision that massive investment in and management of modern adolescence could lead to an eternally youthful, powerful state seemed less viable. Marketplaces and youth cultures facilitated adolescent expressivity beyond state design. Post-war efforts shifted to cultivating adolescent dependence that served families, communities, and nations through well-adjusted sexualities, consumption, and education.

Teenagers as more or less adolescent (1945–1970s)

In the mid-twentieth century across North America and Western Europe, American norms, including heterosexuality, consumerism, and mass education, helped redefine the modern adolescent as the teenager. This played out differently in various contexts but led toward greater transnational youth affinities. Young people assumed teenage roles in learning, leisure, and love, and many embraced their domestication even as they remade it on their own terms. Other teens actively engaged with political and cultural movements toward social transformation.

During the late 1940s through the 1960s, social scientists viewed the successful teenager as one who experimented with self-expression yet internalized social norms on schedule as they adjusted to adult identity. Experts domesticated teenage rebellion and generational conflict as typical. Longitudinal developmental studies, first in North America in the 1930s and then proliferating across Europe in the post-war era, quantified normative adolescence. British-based Anna Freud and US-based Peter Blos and Erik Erikson gained transatlantic audiences through their assertion that the solutions to teen problems rested in individual and familial adjustments. Healthy personality development, the central psycho-social task of adolescence, was achieved by the attainment of mature, normative identity.

Key to this process was heteronormativity, the internalization of white, middle-class ideals of sexually fulfilling nuclear family domesticity as aligned with the security and success of the post-war democratic capitalist state. "Family life education" furthered "heterosexual consciousness," as Susan K. Freeman writes.[10] Sweden led the European push for rational adolescent sex education that emphasized the virtues of healthy, well-adjusted heterosexuality for the individual and society. American sex education, building on curricula developed since the 1920s, emphasized successful preparation for heterosexual marriage and extolled narrow gender roles. Together, these promoted dominant sexual norms while encouraging awareness of bodies and psychological perspectives.

Compulsory heteronormativity also produced pathologizing and punitive measures for those who failed to comply. Schools participated in a transnational Lavender Scare that encouraged the persecution of gay people as "sexual psychopaths." In the United States, school districts screened teachers for homosexual "tendencies" and fired those arrested on moral charges. Counselors monitored students for gender transgression or sexual perversion. Related persecutions occurred in Canada and Great Britain. West Germany and France retained explicitly anti-gay World War II laws on the grounds that they protected youths.

Juvenile justice blamed working-class girls' sex delinquencies and out-of-wedlock pregnancies on family psychodynamics, such as confusion or anger over neglectful fathers. By the 1960s in the United States, during a time of expanding civil rights demands, familiar attacks on black urban culture and the black family got rewritten through psychoanalytic narratives. As exemplified by the US Department of Labor's 1965 Moynihan Report, these expressed alarm over masculinized, smothering-yet-neglectful mothers and absent, emasculated fathers that supposedly resulted in overly precocious "children" having children.

During the 1950s and 1960s, American teenagers shifted from social dating toward the more monogamous dedication of "going steady." This initially alarmed parents, but came to be understood as appropriate rehearsal for married life. In the post-war era, Americans married younger and in higher percentages than ever before; by 1959, nearly half of US girls were married by age nineteen. Soaring US teenage pregnancy rates peaked for the century in 1957. This did not cause great alarm, in part because many teenage girls married prior to becoming pregnant, while many other girls, after becoming pregnant, left school or work to opt for early marriage. In West Germany, alternately, premarital coitus faced greater stigma in the 1950s than it had under the Nazis, but still occurred at higher levels than in most of Europe. Throughout Western Europe, patterns similar to those in the United States took hold after the mid-1950s economic recovery and lasted into the late 1960s. As marriage became nearly universal, couples had children when they were younger.

Hopes and concerns about teenagers were also bound into consumerism. In the United States, Grace Palladino argues, teenagers had by 1957 become "the nation's most exciting new consumer market," albeit decades in the development.[11] Girls, for example, were initiated into mass-produced menstruation products and "junior figure" clothing sizes and styles. These put bodily functions and diverse shapes at odds with the streamlined, attractive, sexually aware but innocent teenage body. Advertisers and experts exhorted boys and girls to protect their emotional and social health by investing in clear skin.

State efforts to domesticate teenage consumerism met limited success, as with the 1953–1955 US and British attempts to censor comic books by linking them to delinquency and sexual deviancy. While European and Canadian media and politicians regularly lamented the "Americanization" of their teens, they also saw healthy consumption as developing individual expression and commitment to the capitalist state. British media portrayed its teenagers as classless while opposing more visibly working-class youth cultures. This led New Left critics such as Theodor Adorno and Herbert Marcuse to attack youth consumerism as working against liberation by interpellating the individual into a depoliticized relationship with corporate consumer capitalism. More recently, Axel Shildt and Detlef Siegfried argue that even 1960s counter cultural European youths navigated this tension not through anti-materialism but through a differentiation of consumption through subcultural expression and local adaptation.[12]

Teenagers were assertive, active interpreters of the products and media targeting them. Rock'n'roll gave middle-class audiences diverse working-class messages of rebellion, consumer yearning, generational conflict, sex, and love. This soundtrack also underscored "girl-crazy" boyhood and boy-obsessed girlhood. By the 1964 musical "British Invasion," influence increasingly flowed in both directions across the Atlantic. That year, twenty-two million American teens made up a $12 billion consumer market, spending another $13 billion of their parents money. In Europe, too, growing disposable teenage income, a more prosperous working class and expanding middle class, and advanced communication and transportation connection led to youth tourism to hot spots such as London, Amsterdam, Berlin, Copenhagen, New York, and California. Consumerism and, later, social protest generated transnational youth-driven cultures and countercultures.

States hoped to manage teenage adjustments though various institutions. In the 1950s and early 1960s, youth commissions addressed juvenile delinquency, channeled teenage consumerism, and fostered adolescent social adjustment and civic involvement. In the three decades after World War II, a near majority of British, French, German, Dutch, and Nordic teenagers stayed in school. US graduation rates peaked around 80 percent in the late 1960s and early 1970s. Across Europe and North America, state investment made post-secondary education increasingly accessible. While European and Canadian efforts to integrate working-class and nonwhite youth into secondary and post-secondary schooling were not without controversy, they were not as intense as US struggles with racial desegregation. After the Supreme Court's *Brown v. Board of Education* ruling (1954), implementation battles were fought over the next two decades.

Many youths, far from being domesticated by institutionalization, consumerism, and heteronormativity, became political and countercultural activists. In the United States, African–American teenagers occupied the front lines of what Wilma King calls the "Emmett Till generation," mobilizing as "tender warriors" who pushed for access to schools, public accommodations, and broader justice.[13] Their actions inspired some white students to stand with them and provoked others to oppose their cause. In the 1968 "Blow Outs," Mexican–American students walked out of East Los Angeles high schools to protest overcrowding, teacher and administrative discrimination against Chicano students, a high dropout rate, and a lack of inclusive curricula. By the end of the sixties in Europe and North America, young people sought to transform society and confronted the state over militarism and empire, students' rights and civil liberties, sexual and gender liberation, environmentalism, and social justice. Increasingly, though, many members of Western societies viewed adolescents with alarm and pessimism.

Youth less adolescence? (1970s–2000s)

Adolescents, it turns out, are neither mere vessels of modern state intention nor domesticated teenagers. Contemporary girls and boys still navigate the structures of earlier times, but often without the romance once attached to them. In the late twentieth century, policymakers across the political spectrum fought over what to do with adolescents. Young people's diverse lives continued to challenge narrow concepts of what adolescence should be.

Even Western European and North American teens best equipped to follow normative developmental trajectories have struggled with transitions toward adulthood. Extended dependency and high expectations of educational achievement have become central to adolescence even as secondary and post-secondary schooling have lost their value as guarantors of career opportunity. These have intensified adolescents' personal burdens to realize economic, psychological, and social success.

Since the 1970s, many young people have created lives beyond the orderly futurities desired by the state and corporate marketplace. In the United Kingdom and to a smaller extent elsewhere, punk aesthetics have reflected a working-class, sometimes xenophobic disenchantment with society. Other antisocial groups have included Sweden's *raggare* and more recent neo-Nazi youth in Germany, France, the United States and elsewhere in the West. In the 1990s and early 2000s, American school shootings by white, middle-class boys led to renewed discussions about media violence, gun access, bullying, and alienation.

Societies have pathologized low-income, nonwhite, and immigrant girls and boys for academic under performance, unemployment, criminality, drug abuse, sexual irresponsibility, and, more recently, terrorism. Nordic countries have attempted to address alienation related to social diversity through broad educational access, high gender equality, and universal social assistance. In the United States, official school racial desegregation was largely dismantled by the 1990s. Since then, poor youths of color have assumed a disproportionate burden of what some call a "school-to-prison pipeline."[14]

Extensions of young people's rights were followed by restrictions. In 1970 the United Kingdom lowered the voting age to eighteen, and Canada, West Germany, the United States, the Netherlands, Finland, Sweden, Ireland, and France followed suit. In the United States, years of youth activism led to greater educational access for poor, minority, and female students. But since the 1980s, the Supreme Court has restricted student expression and privacy. American juvenile justice reform established due process rights in the 1960s and 1970s. Court cases began to underwrite the notion of other rights for the young. But in the 1980s and 1990s, prosecution of minors as adults increased. The United Kingdom has paralleled the American approach, but Germany's Juvenile Justice Act of 1990 implemented a more generous welfare model.

Youths have also been viewed as victims and perpetrators of transgressive sexualities. In the mid-1970s, two decades after the peak in US teen pregnancy, policymakers broadcast a "crisis" about out-of-wedlock teen births that focused on African–American girls. Religious conservatives urged abstinence-based education, blaming feminism, welfare, contraceptive and abortion access, and comprehensive sex education. A 1996 federal law withdrew support from teenage mothers while expanding abstinence-until-marriage education. In 2009, the United States shifted course, funding evidence-based teen pregnancy prevention, which effectively ended the federal abstinence-only subsidy. In 2010, US rates of teen pregnancy and birth, the lowest in seventy years, continued to be far higher than in Western Europe. While Western European programs vary, all give teenagers consistent, evidence-based information and access to contraception and condoms. Public education there encourages personal decision making, respect for young people's choices, and a shared responsibility between adolescents and society. Across North America and Europe, median ages of marriage have substantially risen and more young people cohabit. This diminishes marriage and parenthood as markers of maturity.

The emergence of lesbian, gay, bisexual, and transgender (LGBT) youth activism especially underscores adolescent sexual agency that exceeds the constraints of modern adolescence. As early as 1966, for example, Vanguard, a San Francisco activist group of homeless LGBT youth, demanded an end to police harassment and access to social services. In the 1970s, American, Canadian, French, British, and German gay liberationist and lesbian feminist youth groups mounted critiques of heteronormative institutions, experts, and state power. By the late 1970s, social service and legal discourses characterized LGBT youth as vulnerable subpopulations in need of intervention. Since the 1990s, though, LGBT youth have engaged in renewed activism confronting state and social limitations on their right to safety, identity, sexual activity, and participatory citizenship. It has sparked controversy with those who see them as yet another manifestation of an indulgent world spinning away from proper life course development.

Anxieties about adolescent sexuality resonate with broader concerns about youths as particularly susceptible to "disorders of consumption."[15] One manifestation of this has been the rise in recreational drug use, which peaked in the early 1980s in the United States and in the 1990s in Western Europe. In the United Kingdom and United States, young people have faced heightened drug prosecutions. Another marker is the rise in eating disorders since the 1970s, which first hit girls and, more recently, boys. Related, many youths, particularly girls, have added pressures of fitness and dieting to their body projects, while at the same time in the United States (and increasingly across the western world) childhood and adolescent obesity is often framed as an epidemic. Many cultural critics have lamented the late 1990s "girl power" commodification of feminism that emphasized personal sexual empowerment over structural transformation.

New media has also inspired new fears. The UK Video Recordings Act of 1984 sought to prevent teens from viewing violent, sexually demeaning films at home. A year later, US Senate hearings on rock music led to parental advisory warnings on music albums. Gangsta rap faced mid-1990s calls for censorship and the video games industry instituted ratings. Primed by late 1970s and 1980s transnational child pornography and abduction panics, the Internet's rise brought sensationalist media coverage of online youth predators. New media makes youth cultures more transnational and immediate in ways that exceed easy oversight. Adolescents continue to adapt global media to local contexts.

Conclusion: contempt or collaboration?

In a recent essay, historian Michael Zuckerman argues that despite the changing meanings of American adolescence, a "regime of rejection" from the colonial era to the present has established a continuity, of sorts, in adult animosity toward the young.[16] Yet the modern project of adolescence was distinct from the eras preceding and following its ascendance. Today, modern adolescence has been largely abandoned as a project of possibility. The homogenizing lenses through which we have attempted to see young people keep failing. Contemporary sociopolitical regimes have distaste for the long-term investment that believing in a more expansive and generous vision of adolescence requires. Better, we assume, to blame the young for their failure to get with whatever program still has funding.

Perhaps we need to grieve not the loss of adolescence, but maturity. As increasing numbers of adolescents and adults opt out of marriage and face unstable employment, we chastise our collective failure to grow up. Perhaps young people could teach us all a thing or two about thriving outside "maturity." When more adults are finding it less desirable or possible to attain markers of adulthood, why expect adolescents to strive for it?

To recapitulate: early modern youths negotiated multiple forms of local patriarchal control and expanded the possibilities for adolescence in the process. Modern adolescence as a life stage was consolidated through expert discourses and structural, ideological, and institutional forces. As centralized state management failed to reproduce patriotic, orderly, and eugenic nationalism, the teenager emerged, promising well-adjusted normativity and consumption. This, too, failed to capture youth. Adolescents now face both structures of modern adolescence and a generalized disillusionment with its promises.

A hundred years after G. Stanley Hall defined adolescence, psychologist Jeffrey Arnett has gained international recognition for his concept of "emerging adulthood" as the new century's next universalizing developmental life stage, squeezed in between adolescence and maturity.[17] But in a neoliberal world of tough love and austerity measures, aren't most of us ceaselessly emerging? As we chart a course through our precarious present, our challenge is to find new ways to appreciate young people, not as victims, projects, or threats, but as collaborators.

Notes

1 Lynda Payne, "Health in England (16th–18th c.)," in *Children and Youth in History*, Item #166, http://chnm.gmu.edu/cyh/teaching-modules/166 (accessed October 12, 2011).

2 Natalie Zemon Davis, *Society and Culture in Early Modern France* (Palo Alto, CA: Stanford University Press, 1975).

3 Joel Schwartz, *The Sexual Politics of Jean-Jacques Rousseau* (Chicago, IL: University of Chicago Press, 1984), 81.

4 Joseph Kett, *Rites of Passage: Adolescence in America 1790 to Present* (New York, NY: Basic Books, 1977), 108.

5 Martha Vicinus, "Distance and Desire: English Boarding School Friendships, 1870–1920," in *Hidden From History: Reclaiming the Gay and Lesbian Past*, ed. Martin Duberman, Martha Vicinus, and George Chauncey Jr. (New York, NY: Meridian, 1989), 212–229.

6 David I. Macleod, *The Age of the Child: Children in America, 1890–1920* (New York, NY: Twayne Publishers, 1998), 25.

7 Don Romesburg, "The Tightrope of Normalcy: Homosexuality, Developmental Citizenship, and American Adolescence," *Historical Sociology* 21(4) (2008), 417–442.

8 Joan J. Brumberg, *The Body Project: An Intimate History of American Girls* (New York, NY: Random House, 1997); Modern Girl Around the World Working Group, *The Modern Girl Around the World: Consumption, Modernity, and Globalization* (Durham, NC: Duke University Press, 2008); Vicki Ruiz, "'Star Struck': Acculturation, Adolescence, and Mexican American Women, 1920–1950," in *Unequal Sisters: An Inclusive Reader in U.S. Women's History*, 4th edn., ed. Vicki Ruiz and Ellen Carol Dubois (New York, NY: Routledge, 2008), 346–361; Kelly Schrum, *Some Wore Bobby Sox: The Emergence of Teenage Girls' Culture, 1920–1945* (New York, NY: Palgrave Macmillan, 2004).

9 Jon Savage, *Teenage: The Prehistory of Youth Culture, 1875–1945* (New York, NY: Penguin Books, 2007).

10 Susan K. Freeman, *Sex Goes to School: Girls and Sex Education before the 1960s* (Urbana, IL: University of Illinois Press, 2008), i.

11 Grace Palladino, *Teenagers: An American History* (New York, NY: Basic Books, 1996), 175.

12 Axel Shildt and Detlef Siegfried, "Introduction: Youth, Consumption, and Politics in the Age of Radical Change," in *Between Marx and Coca-Cola: Youth Cultures in Changing European Societies, 1960–1980*, ed. Axel Shildt and Detlef Siegfried (New York, NY: Berghahn Books, 2006), 1–35.

13 Wilma King, *African American Childhoods: Historical Perspectives from Slavery to Civil Rights* (New York, NY: Palgrave Macmillan, 2005), 155–168; Rebecca de Schweinitz, *If We Could Change the World: Young People and America's Long Struggle for Racial Equality* (Chapel Hill, NC: University of North Carolina Press, 2009).

14 Catherine Kim, Daniel Losen, Damon Hewitt , *The School-to-Prison Pipeline* (New York, NY: New York University Press, 2010).

15 Christine Griffin, "Troubled Teens: Managing Disorders of Transition and Consumption," *Feminist Review* 55 (1997), 4–21.

16 Michael Zuckerman, "The Paradox of American Adolescence," *Journal of the History of Childhood and Youth* 4(1) (2011), 13–25.

17 Jeffrey Arnett, "Emerging Adulthood: A Theory of Development from the Late Teens Through the Twenties," *American Psychologist* 55(5) (2000), 469–480.

Suggestions for further reading

Anthologies

Austin, Joe, and Michael Nevin Willard, eds. *Generations of Youth: Youth Cultures and History in Twentieth-Century America*. New York, NY: New York University Press, 1998. An excellent historiographic introduction sets up a strong essay collection attentive to gender, race, class, and sexuality.

Levi, Giovanni, and Jean-Claude Schmitt, eds. *A History of Young People in the West*, 2 vols. Cambridge, MA: Belknap Press, 1997. Essays address European youth from Ancient Greece through the mid-twentieth century, touching on family, religion, politics, culture, society, and art.

Martin, James, ed. *Children and Youth in a New Nation*. New York, NY: New York University Press, 2009. This collection presents rich primary sources for interpretation and essays that underscore how changes in childhood and adolescence brought on by republican and democratic ideals and practices shaped young people.

Maynes, Mary Jo, Birgitte Søland, and Christina Benninghaus, eds. *Secret Gardens, Satanic Mills: Placing Girls in European History, 1750–1960*. Bloomington, IN: Indiana University

Press, 2005. An outstanding introduction leads into eighteen essays focusing on Northern and Western Europe that detail the social construction of girlhood and girls' roles in labor, consumerism, education, sexuality, society, and culture.

Sauerteig, Lutz D. H., and Robert Davidson, eds. *Shaping Sexual Knowledge: A Cultural History of Sex Education in Twentieth-Century Europe*. London, UK: Routledge, 2009. Explores links between sex education, citizenship projects, medicine, religion, family, the state, and shifting representations of gendered and sexualized youth.

Schildt, Axel, and Detlef Siegfried, eds. *Between Marx and Coca-Cola: Youth Cultures in Changing European Societies, 1960–1980*. New York, NY: Berghahn Books, 2006. A collection that seeks to understand the recent past through links between consumerism, leisure, activism, sexuality, and subculture.

Surveys

Gillis, John. *Youth and History: Tradition and Change in European Age Relations, 1770–Present*. New York, NY: Academic Press, 1981[1974]. This trailblazing social history draws on demographic and economic indicators to assert that modern adolescence involved youths – principally male – as active agents influenced by and transforming their circumstances.

Kett, Joseph. *Rites of Passage: Adolescence in America 1790 to Present*. New York, NY: Basic Books, 1977. Marking four epochs of transition, this social and cultural history asserts that major structural shifts for youths during the nineteenth century led to the elaboration of the "age of adolescence" throughout the twentieth.

Mintz, Steven. *Huck's Raft: A History of American Childhood*. Cambridge, MA: Belknap Press, 2004. Broken into pre-modern, modern, and post-modern eras, this survey covers diverse male and female childhoods and youths through ideologies, institutions, cultures, and experiences from early colonial encounters through the recent past.

Mitterauer, Michael. *A History of Youth*. Translated by Graeme Dunphy. Oxford, UK: Blackwell, 1992. This cultural and social European history spans five hundred years and is arranged thematically, addressing puberty and adolescence, transitional milestones, positions of youth within social institutions, youth cultures, and contemporary adolescence.

Monographs

Adams, Mary Louise. *The Trouble with Normal: Postwar Youth and the Making of Heterosexuality*. Toronto, Canada: University of Toronto Press, 1997. Through a reading of Canadian discourses about youth in sex-education materials, court and school records, and media, this work asserts that modern adolescence was transformed by the elaboration of heterosexuality and companionate marriage as oppositional to homosexuality.

Ben-Amos, Ilana Krausman. *Adolescence and Youth in Early Modern England*. New Haven, CT: Yale University Press, 1994. Describes how experiences of growing up from 1500–1700 varied widely by gender and social group, and concludes that early modern adolescence was a prolonged, dynamic life phase involving separation from parents, entry/exit from service, establishing of marriage, and other rites of passage.

Bailey, Beth. *From Front Porch to Back Seat: Courtship in Twentieth-Century America*. Baltimore, MD: The Johns Hopkins University Press, 1988. Describes the demise of the nineteenth-century model of "courtship" and subsequent evolution of "dating," linking this to the democratization of education, urbanization, and developments in mass communication, transportation, popular culture, and economy.

Comacchio, Cynthia. *The Dominion of Youth: Adolescence and the Making of Modern Canada*. Waterloo, Canada: Wilfrid Laurier University Press, 2006. Comparing boys and girls across ethnic and class backgrounds from World War I through the mid-century, this book argues that modern adolescence became a market force, cultural phenomenon, peer-based identity, nationalist project, pedagogical directive, and social scientific concern.

Deluzio, Crista. *Female Adolescence in American Scientific Thought, 1830–1930*. Baltimore, MD: Johns Hopkins University Press, 2007. This book analyses biological, medical, psychological, and anthropological writing about girlhood to show how a century of expert discourse reworked the meaning of femininity and adolescence.

Dyhouse, Carol. *Girls Growing Up in Late Victorian and Edwardian England*. London, UK: Routledge & Kegan Paul, 1981. During this crucial era for the development of modern adolescence, the family and broader social contexts played a larger role than the school in the socialization of girls into modern femininity.

Fass, Paula S. *Outside In: Minorities and the Transformation of American Education*. New York, NY: Oxford University Press, 1989. Asserts that throughout the twentieth century, schooling's promise to bring racially, ethnically, socioeconomically, and gender-diverse youths into a national experience transformed adolescence and drove the push for universal, pluralistic education; youth also made institutions from within.

Jobs, Richard I. *Riding the New Wave: Youth and the Rejuvenation of France after the Second World War*. Stanford, CA: Stanford University Press, 2007. Foregrounding age and gender as analytical categories, this cultural history asserts that as France became decolonized, Americanized, and industrialized, youth consumerism and dynamism symbolized a promising, if troubling, national future and transformed young people.

Lombard, Anne. *Making Manhood: Growing Up Male in Colonial New England*. Cambridge, MA: Harvard University Press, 2003. In early New England, young men viewed patrilineal, rather than peer or heterosocial relationships as principal, but over the eighteenth century a loss of paternal power and a greater recognition of emotional experience led to new ideals for boys in which women and peers assumed central roles.

Moran, Jeffrey. *Teaching Sex: The Shaping of Adolescence in the Twentieth Century*. Cambridge, MA: Harvard University Press, 2000. American emphases on cultivating adolescent sexual self-control as a form of social control and intervening into youth malleability to prevent adult sexual "disorder" reverberated throughout twentieth-century sex education, even as pedagogical models changed.

Neubauer, John. *The Fin-de-Siècle Culture of Adolescence*. New Haven, CT: Yale University Press, 1992. This book draws expansively from European and US sources to assert that modern adolescence was discursively consolidated in the decades around 1900 because it was taken up in intertwined ways by psychology, criminal justice, pedagogy, sociology, and literature, and that these shaped young people's lives and identities.

Odem, Mary. *Delinquent Daughters: Protecting and Policing Adolescent Female Sexuality in United States, 1885–1920*. Chapel Hill, NC: University of North Carolina Press, 1995. Focusing on reformers' and officials' discipline of working-class girls, this work highlights how moral campaigns fueled by race, class, and gender tensions led to uneven sexual regulation in which even parents utilized laws and courts to reassert authority over daughters' autonomy.

Pollack, Linda A. *Forgotten Children: Parent–Child Relations from 1500–1900*. Cambridge, UK: Cambridge University Press, 1983. Countering a prevailing thesis about a lack of parental regard of early modern children, this work underscores historical continuity in parental empathy for adolescent sons and daughters, including advocacy for them once they left home.

Redding, Kimberly A. *Growing Up in Hitler's Shadow: Remembering Youth in Postwar Berlin*. Westport, CT: Praeger, 2004. Drawing from oral histories and archival sources, this work covers the radical shift from Nazis' enforced inclusion of adolescents in the vision of an eternally youthful state to a post-war state mistrust of boys and, especially girls, as a "youth problem"; youths, however, were remarkably resilient.

Schlossman, Steven. *Love and the American Delinquent: The Theory and Practice of "Progressive" Juvenile Justice, 1825–1920*. Chicago, IL: University of Chicago Press, 1977. An early important juvenile justice history that asserts that an evolving vision of benevolence led to greater intervention into young people's lives resulting in fewer rights, more diagnosis and prevention of "delinquency," and heightened distrust of adolescents and their families.

Springhall, John. *Coming of Age: Adolescence in Britain, 1860–1960*. Dublin, Ireland: Gill and Macmillan, 1986. This work traces modern adolescence in expert discourses, play, work, and juvenile justice that converged in the late nineteenth and early twentieth centuries to address shifting class conditions; in mid-twentieth century consumer society, these led to tensions drawn between the disruptive teddy boy and the redemptive teenager.

Todd, Selina. *Young Women, Work and Family, 1918–1950*. New York, NY: Oxford, 2005. This social and economic history shows how, despite poverty and struggle, working-class girls created new possibilities within the work practices and cultures central to their lives through which they became more mobile, gained new stature within families, assertively demanded better laboring conditions, and created new ways to play and relate.

13

THE PHYSICAL SPACES OF CHILDHOOD

Marta Gutman

Physical spaces are a measure of any society's attitude toward children. To picture the ways in which childhood has changed in the West, we need to imagine this society without the physical spaces for children that began to proliferate during the early modern period, multiplied during industrialization, and spread across the world during imperial expansion. In the historical past, children used houses, streets, yards, shops, and other places made by adults as spaces in which to live, play, learn, and work. They continue to do so. But, in 1500 it would have not been possible to find a house with a child's bedroom, a neighborhood with a playground, or a city with a public high school. Special rooms for children appeared in houses as settings purposefully made for children became part of modern society (and pivotal to the construction of modernity in global society). Schools, orphanages, kindergartens, day care centers, hospitals, reform schools, and special prisons were built, as were playgrounds, summer camps, children's museums, and libraries. These physical spaces and a special material culture – cribs, high chairs, strollers, clothes, toys, books, and food – became means by which adults set out and put into effect their objectives for modern children and their childhoods.

Materiality matters in the history of childhood. In the last decade, interest in the physical spaces of childhood has escalated even though historians, geographers, ethnographers, and other scholars have recognized for some time that children, as social actors, use, appropriate, and interpret space on their own terms. This new attention is due to the explosion of interest in childhood studies generally, but physical space also offers a unique and useful lens to grasp childhood as an ideal imagined by adults, as an arena shaped by social relationships, and as an experience of children. Because space is where childhood is lived, the material world offers a treasure trove of historical evidence of how children use, interpret, shape, and imagine their everyday lives. Physical spaces, the architectural historian Abigail Van Slyck has noted, allow us to grasp "the historical experience of being young."[1] Objects and spaces of the material world are also ripe for studying transnational cultural exchange and assessing adult actions, fantasies, and beliefs about children, including whether or not adults use space to exercise ethically adequate goals for children and their childhoods.

In this essay, I call for the most part on examples from the United States to show that physical space is not a backdrop for childhood but rather the two, space and childhood, are mutually constitutive. An informed observer would no longer suppose a child to be the blank slate proposed by John Locke – an empty vessel that a parent or teacher fills up with social norms and cultural ideals. A child is also no longer imagined to be a "passive receptor" of any sort.[2] Similarly, regardless of its visual or aesthetic qualities, to consider a building or place in isolation, an entity unto itself, strips the physical world of its personal meaning and political importance. My argument calls on points about space made by the political philosopher Henri Lefebvre. For any person, including a child, there is a dynamic rather than a static relationship between a physical place, its social make-up, and childhood as an ideal or imagined condition because space is at once a tangible, social, and discursive construction. We may shape our buildings and thereafter they may shape us, to paraphrase Winston Churchill, but human actions also mold the built environment.[3] Historically adults, especially reformers like the child savers of the late nineteenth century, appreciated the first point more than the second, when they counted on material culture to construct childhood.

In the long run, adults invested considerable cultural, social, and economic capital in spaces for children because they imagined an object, a building, or a landscape would put into effect their goals for childhood not simply mirror them. The history of modern childhood is also full of stories of stingy school boards, penny-pinching philanthropists, and parsimonious public agencies that refused to invest in children's spaces. These groups were just as likely to rent a room or repurpose a building as build a new structure from the ground up. The few men and many women who were determined to make a better world for children often relied on these less formal ways to establish schools, orphanages, hospitals, kindergartens, and other institutions, given the often less than generous contributions to their capital campaigns. For that and other reasons, children did not benefit equally from adult largesse, and physical spaces made for children worked to ingrain social inequalities and prejudices as well as to endow them with a special, idealized world.

The architectural history of modern childhood is relatively new in the United States, and its inventors are indebted to others for insights, even for framing questions. One debt is to Philippe Ariès who, with the publication of *Centuries of Childhood: A Social History of Family Life*, invited his colleagues to think about childhood as a new field of study in the early 1960s. Although historians were quick to contest (and discard) his claim that "in medieval society the idea of childhood did not exist," they took note of other important contributions. One was to insist that childhood be historicized, even if as a consequence Ariès downplayed the similarities that exist among all children, "the immutability of the special needs of children" regardless of the historical moment or geographical location of their lives.[4] Another important insight, almost always ignored by critics, was Ariès's view of the mutual dependence of childhood, physical spaces, and material culture in the modernizing West.

In early modern Europe, the modern understanding of childhood began to emerge among the privileged classes: a sentimental ideal that emphasized a child's innocence and underscored the child's difference from adults. Since the beginning of this construction of childhood intersected with the development of the modern concept of public and private, special objects and places were created for children in these realms. As Ariès insisted, adherence to a new model for childhood obliged adult members of well-born families to alter the material world to ensure their children had a good childhood, one that was protected, happy, and playful. Invented for privileged children, the new value placed on childhood diffused to the middle class, entered into and aided the expansion of colonial empires, and came to dominate the goals for all children in theory, if not always in practice, during the twentieth century. The explosive expansion of consumer culture in contemporary society, with children as avid participants, may raise questions about their innate innocence, but the continued effect of this ideal on the material world is obvious. Even though some critics hypothesize the end of childhood and others highlight the deleterious effects of physical segregation on family life, these manifestations of the ideal childhood are a commonplace. Children are believed to need special spaces, including access to nature, toys, clothes, and other special objects. All of this, "the stuff of childhood," as one historian puts it, is necessary to sustain the good childhood in lived experience.[5]

At home

The spread of this ideal, imbued with the desire to protect children, is one reason that the long childhood, an extended period of economic, legal, social, and emotional dependence, came to characterize family life in the modern West. It is also one reason that distinct physical spaces for children began to appear in houses. Before the Industrial Revolution, in the sixteenth and seventeenth centuries, a child did not expect to sleep in a separate bed, to say nothing of a separate room, whether living in a farmhouse in a North American colony or in a townhouse in a German city. For the most part, children lived in a generationally integrated world, working, eating, sleeping, and playing with diverse members of the household. This physical proximity answered social expectations for childhood: it allowed children to learn from adults, by modeling their practices on family members and to move expeditiously through this stage of life, by taking on new duties perhaps at age seven, certainly by ten or eleven. When defined as a time of innate moral depravity rather than asexual innocence, childhood was a period in life to get through, not to prolong.[6]

Houses started to change when new ideals of childhood began to intersect with other revolutionary changes in society – the separation of home and work, the modern concept of public and private life, and the rise of consumer society. In the face of such modernizing changes, and as they became convinced of a child's innate innocence, parents counted on domestic space and all sorts of "stuff" to protect children from adult sexual desire, to display children as valuable objects, and to insulate themselves from childish behavior and activities (mess, clutter, and noise). The crib, stroller, and highchair are perfect examples. Together, changing ideals and changing places worked to define and prolong childhood as a time of dependency. The condition of dependence, implicitly tied to "powerlessness, submission, bodily inferiority or weakness," Carolyn Steedman has argued, set parameters for childhood before it was described in terms of specific biological age.[7]

The nursery, the first room for children to appear in houses was initially patched together from available space and furniture, then made on purpose in houses for the elite. By displaying and confining children, this physical space offered bourgeois parents the precise kind of cultural capital needed to secure class distinction in an industrializing society. In this room, a child did not engage in any kind of productive activity that contributed to the family economy. Rather privileged boys and girls were expected to eat, to sleep (eventually in separate beds), and especially to play in a space that was described as a "play paradise" in Germany.[8] The location upstairs (in the United States, the attic was a traditional site for play) or toward the back of the house underscored separation as the ideal condition for children and privacy as essential to bourgeois respectability.

In short order, special objects changed a child's experience of this and other rooms that came to constitute a purpose-made cultural landscape for childhood inside a middle-class house. If willing to use cast-off furniture to begin with, parents looked with increasing favor on new child-size furniture, designed and marketed to appeal to middle-class taste, and used it to furnish nurseries, bedrooms, and playrooms; they also decorated these rooms to ensure a "visual code of childishness" prevailed in them. A similar visual culture prevailed in illustrated children's books and in clothes worn by privileged children. By the end of the century in the United States, the nursery was assigned to infants, the playroom to older children, and separate bedrooms provided for boys and girls. The historian Karin Calvert ascribes this further specialization of domestic space to fascination with age grading in all aspects of life and a new understanding of sexuality in infants and young children.[9]

Middle-class parents counted on those kinds of domestic spaces to display, protect, and isolate children; they also used them to educate, socialize, and in due course discipline them. The command, "go to your room" became a means to segregate children from adult society. In 1750, boys and girls used every room in most houses; after 1900, they slept and played in different rooms that were furnished to express age and sex. If new behaviorist theories of child development mandated that kind of environmental specificity to ensure a happy childhood and successful transition to adulthood, the material manifestation directed boys and girls toward class-specific, gendered social futures. The demand for "precise calibration" between material culture, gender, and stage of life in a child's room persists, as do anxieties about outcomes.[10] Parents succumb to the obligation to buy more stuff, not only to ensure a good childhood but also because they hope that boys and girls absorb bourgeois norms (including about sexuality) as they grow up.

In the nineteenth century, working-class boys and girls did not expect to play in a nursery, sleep in separate bedrooms, or wear clothes purposefully made for them. A separate bed was an unthinkable luxury in a tenement apartment as was a room designed specifically for play, as much as a mother may have wanted to offer either amenity to her child. Interiority was hardly a sign of exalted social status if a boy had to scramble to find a place to sleep each night (after working all day in a factory) or his sister could not attend school because she did not own a pair of shoes or was expected to mind younger siblings at home. Working-class children were more than willing to play outdoors and appropriated stoops, yards, streets, and other places not made for the purpose of play. Some resisted attempts to direct them to the outdoor analogue of the playroom – the urban playground introduced by reformers starting in the late 1880s and intended to direct play in gendered and class-specific ways. Many urban children did not welcome this or other adult interventions into their public lives, preferring spaces and practices of their own invention. Other children (and their parents) welcomed new public play places, defining this signature space of modern childhood as democratizing, even if it was intended to contain, organize, and direct play.[11]

Adults thus introduced more than one dynamic into children's spaces. They counted on physical separation to embody the sentimental ideal of childhood; they also used children's spaces to put into effect other goals by linking physical forms with different social and political objectives for children. The value of middle-class children began to rise in the late nineteenth century as children became treasured for their emotional contribution to family life rather than for the market value of their wage labor. Because children, prized for sentimental reasons, could not be replaced, their value increased, and laws, policies, institutions, and places emerged to protect them as "priceless" children in Viviana Zelizer's words.[12] Examining domestic space shows that middle-class and upper-class children still had lots of work to do, even if they were no longer expected to contribute to the family economy. In Canada, children helped care for sick siblings at home; their diaries, drawings, and surviving buildings show how children (and parents) used each other and domestic spaces to cope with the tension and crises of illness. The wealthiest Americans went so far as to erect separate buildings for their children. The Vanderbilts built a full-scale cottage in the upper-class summer resort in Newport, Rhode Island. The cottage may have evoked middle-class domesticity, but this building, like the grand estate of which it was part, enhanced the family's upper-class status. So, too did the Vanderbilt children when they used it to play.[13]

In school

The proliferation of primary schools, noted by Ariès in early modern France, demarcated the beginning of what would become an architecturally specialized and differentiated educational landscape for children. His analysis may have ignored the medieval schoolroom, the institutional space that framed boys' education in Europe (girls learned at home), but it pointed to this incontrovertible fact: schooling would become the central experience of modern children and school buildings the central site where childhood was lived.[14] That transformation came with another equally profound revolution – the spread of the printed word. This democratization of knowledge (and its acquisition) altered human culture, first by making texts available to read, without mediation by a preacher or a king; and second by making books and all sorts of other printed matter affordable to a mass reading public that included children.

In all industrial nations and most of their colonies, public schools, coupled with compulsory education, fulfilled the state's interest in teaching children to read, write, and calculate. Massive, multi-story, masonry buildings were expensive to erect, teachers had to be paid, and authorities justified the cost to taxpayers by insisting that public schools ensured a stable future for nation and empire. Attending school would make all children, especially working-class children, more or less literate and produce healthy, respectful, and industrious adult citizens, workers, and parents. Working-class children understood the blunt, even brutal attempt to socialize them through mandatory education, and they and their parents contested egregious expressions of authority.[15] Albeit bitterly disputed, the assertion of state authority prevailed: education, centered on intellectual, social, emotional, and physical development came to be the work of all children. As built, public schools delineated contradictory aspirations for children, accentuating the right to education and the place of privilege, power, and prejudice in its execution.

The United States is a good example. This nation invested in constructing an architecturally differentiated landscape for public education after the turn of the twentieth century, but the process began earlier in fits and starts in the new republic. Tutors taught wealthier children at home while poor children studied in charity schools – grim buildings that contained the rigid monitorial system proposed in England by the Quaker reformer Joseph Lancaster and adopted all over the world. In the United States the economic advantage of this system was obvious to municipal governments, mindful of scarce tax revenues: a single master taught hundreds of children in a large ungraded classroom and counted on older students, called monitors, to supervise group recitations.[16] Whether gathered under a window or a motivational text posted on the wall, the arrangement alluded to a principle subsequently embraced by other reformers, into the twentieth century. As Loris Malaguzzi, leader of the Italian Reggio Emilia movement, pointed out, children learned from three teachers: the instructor, their peers, and the classroom space.[17]

In the United States before the Civil War, school committees experimented with other pedagogical methods, relied on rented rooms and repurposed buildings, and looked to women to teach (less expensive to hire than men). In Boston, mixing educational and other civic uses in government buildings made sense because the school committee wanted to demonstrate citizenship as well as to instill in students respect for the law. Quite literally a boy moved from schoolroom to wardroom, as he grew up.[18] Overall, while both boys and girls attended co-educational primary schools, more boys than girls advanced through single-sex grammar schools. In any city, attending high school was unlikely for all but the most privileged until the turn of the twentieth century. In northern cities, public schools were racially segregated as a matter of course; and in southern states, legislatures criminalized the education of slaves. Some enslaved children learned to read and write but not in a public building deliberately made or set side for the purpose. The necessarily secret space that defined this aspect of their childhood, could have been the bedroom of a sympathetic mistress or the backroom of a church.

Smaller towns used refurbished materials to build one-room, ungraded schools. Placed at the edge of settlement, where inexpensive parcels of land were easily acquired, location, construction material, and building type worked together to shape childhood. From the outside, the small building, with a central entry framed by the pitch of a gable roof, recalled a house or a chapel, especially when a town's budget was flush enough to permit construction of a steeple-like belfry. Otherwise, a teacher rang a hand-held bell to start the school day. Inside, the space evoked the feel of meetinghouses: students sat on backless benches set against exterior walls; the teacher used the only desk in the room, reminiscent of a minister's lectern.[19] That arrangement fell out of favor, as disaffection with shoddy construction, poor lighting and ventilation, ineffective heat, uncomfortable furniture (cast-off pews or other furniture made without consideration for a child's body), and foul sanitary conditions (an outhouse was a luxury) prompted demands for reform. The call for universal free public education, issued by Horace Mann in the 1830s, and new handbooks by Henry Barnard, published in the 1840s with architectural designs for common schools, set the stage for change in cities and towns, but not necessarily in the countryside where most children lived. The one-room, single-teacher schoolhouse, sometimes but not always painted red, remained ubiquitous until the consolidation of rural school districts after the turn of the twentieth century. In the racially segregated South, black children were more likely to attend a crowded, run-down, one-room school than a new, enlarged, improved country school. Reserved for whites only, these buildings enunciated race privilege and thus white supremacy until the civil rights revolution of the 1950s.[20]

In cities, the implementation of free, centralized, age-graded instruction required new buildings, public agencies, and tax dollars to support it. When the Quincy Grammar School (1847–1848) opened in Boston, the design set a new paradigm for public school architecture in the United States including identical, separate, age-graded classrooms, relatively generous windows, central heating, indoor sinks, and a shared assembly hall. From the street, the school may have looked more like a large house than a factory, but inside students learned habits of mind, eye, and hand that prepared them for life in a class-stratified society. Seating literally fixed children in place: their desks, sized to fit a young body, were bolted to the floor in straight lines. The calibration of space between writing surface and the attached seat allowed a student to stand up when asked to recite. The teacher continued to use a separate desk, usually set on a platform at the front of the classroom, with blackboard and clock mounted on the wall behind her. Together, architectural design, furniture, pedagogy, discipline, and routine answered the call for attention, timeliness, standards, and hierarchy in public education.

Design continued to matter as immigrants from all over the world and migrants from the countryside poured into American cities. School boards not only built more primary schools, but also began to differentiate the educational landscape with high schools and eventually vocational schools and junior high schools. Authorities counted on buildings to keep rambunctious children off city streets, while the recognition of the vulnerability of children forced a redefinition of parental roles that stressed their duties rather than their rights. Faced with the ingrained tradition of parental control (and repeated crises in public health), reformers hoped to challenge immigrant authority and contain the menace to the future by revamping childhood in schools.[21]

Architects, working in concert with school boards, discarded the old-fashioned, monolithic, masonry structures in favor of large, multi-story, steel-frame buildings organized symmetrically around schoolyards. The crenellated massing delivered light and air to classrooms and corridors, and especially in high schools accommodated auditoriums, gymnasiums, cafeterias, science laboratories and even swimming pools. These specialized teaching spaces made it possible to execute reforms, including the organization of curriculum around academic departments.[22] Because floor plans looked like letters (usually E, H, or U; sometimes L or T) the schools would be called alphabet schools and the availability of light and air, from very large windows (one side of the room only) and up-to-date building systems, touted as evidence of progressive design in education. So too would the "wider use of the school plant," for afterschool activities that included adult education, political meetings, and Americanization programs.[23]

Not every student benefitted. In 1914, a young African–American boy, Thurgood Marshall, enrolled in his neighborhood school – the racially segregated P.S. 103 in West Baltimore. Built in 1877 on the then fashionable "cells and bells" model, the two-story, red brick school had not changed much in the intervening forty years. This building, an "object lesson" in racial inequality, offered a tangible example of the point that this illustrious graduate would make to the US Supreme Court in 1954. Separate but equal in American public education was unconstitutional because separate could never be equal, including in physical space. Other habits also died hard. In new schools, the standard classroom (with uniform windows and space for about forty students), remained pervasive until the middle of the twentieth century, as did fixed desks set in straight rows.

Kindergartens were the exception. Invented by the German reformer Friedrich Froebel during the 1830s and subsequently exported all over the world, including to the United States, a kindergarten formalized for boys and girls between three and six the step between home and school. By insisting that education follow in logical sequence a child's mental, physical, and spiritual development, Froebel translated into a practical program the Romantic argument that adults were obliged to help children discover their inner natures. The goal was to act on the "soul of the child through the experiences of the body," one historian wrote.[24] Songs, dances, gymnastics, and games with toys offered as gifts, developed manual dexterity, stimulated the intellect, and helped a child feel the universal spirit (the moral reason behind things). Children also explored nature – a goal in synch with the Romantic definition of childhood as innocent, natural, and free. In gardens attached to German schools, children tended plots, where they grew flowers and vegetables and were encouraged to give surplus to needy families.[25]

In the United States, kindergarten teachers made Froebel's radical assertion their own: that all children, not only privileged children, deserved the right to childhood. Whether attending a fee-for-service or free (charity) school, a child's learning began with the same gift: a soft, brightly colored yarn ball dangling from a string that represented the self and unity. The balance, nineteen more gifts, continued to engage the senses of touch, sight, sound, and smell and make play and movement part of the school day. By 1869, Milton Bradley found a ready market for the special toys that he manufactured for use in kindergartens.[26] Middle-class families had also begun to accept the concept that children could be taught through how to play, and educators agreed play could be orchestrated, or choreographed, to achieve pedagogical goals.

Kindergarten teachers also experimented with design, even when they rented room. In the first free kindergarten west of the Rocky Mountains, set up by Kate Douglas Wiggin in a former public school classroom, children found moveable red tables and matching chairs with red cushions, plants, a canary, a fish bowl, pictures, and closets stuffed with toys. "The kindergarten provides a room, more or less attractive," Wiggin wrote in *The Relationship of the Kindergarten to Social Reform*. "It is a pretty, pleasant, domestic interior, charming and grateful to the senses."[27] This charity was cost effective, the teacher insisted, because it was preventive and it was also democratizing because it welcomed all children, regardless of race, ethnicity, or religion. Why build reform schools, penitentiaries, and poorhouses when investing in inclusive spaces for early childhood education offered a surer, less expensive route to citizenship? Her point still holds.

Like houses, schools offer examples of insights gained from taking a spatial perspective on the history of childhood. The usual account of the progressive revolution in American education stresses the difference of twentieth-century experiments from nineteenth-century practices. The kindergarten is held to be a paradigm of old-fashioned rigidity. Thinking physically brings to light the ties of the pragmatic, hands-on, child-centered approach to education, almost always ascribed to John Dewey's influence, to innovations of the kindergarten movement. Boys and girls played together with blocks, water, and sand; teachers demanded moveable furniture and made nature study, outdoor play, and other group activities including music and dance part of the school day. This history also points out that it is misguided to assess the practice of repurposing buildings merely as an indicator of adult parsimony. Since low-rent spaces in older buildings facilitated innovation, this method of urban institution building for children is a telling example of the point, underscored by Jane Jacobs throughout *The Death and Life of Great American Cities*, that new ideas come from experimenting with older things and practices.

Other experiments, also dependent on transnational exchange and improvising with makeshift and repurposed buildings, carried into the twentieth century the use of the physical space of a school to reform childhood. To take one example: knowing that fresh air and sunshine cured tuberculosis in the early stages of the disease, reformers decided to test the effects on impoverished, malnourished children during the summer. In an early experiment in Germany, sick children lived and studied in prefabricated, industrial sheds, open to the air, and played outside several times a day. Furniture had to be moveable, because classes were held outdoors. The astonishing improvement, in both physical health and intellectual achievement, fueled the call to recalibrate the authoritarian relationship between teacher and student in classroom space.[28] Advocates of child-centered education insisted that light, air, sunshine, and flexibly arranged furniture fill the classrooms of all children, as a right of childhood.

The revolution in design began modestly. To begin with, open-air classrooms were added to public schools and libraries – in the United States often built on roof tops and placed near outdoor space, set aside for play. Purpose-built examples followed and included, after the First World War, innovative one-story public elementary schools in California. In suburban schools, organized around large courtyards, operable glass partitions ensured fresh air and access to the collective space of the school community. For rural communities, the state department of education developed a less costly model – a prefabricated, one-room, open-air school for children of migrant farm workers.[29] Avant-garde architects also experimented with open-air schools and offered sleek designs that became signature examples of modern architecture in France, Germany, Holland, and most other countries in Europe. Whether a multi-story urban block or a one-story suburban school made up of attached, individual pavilions, fully glazed exterior walls delivered light, air and sun to classrooms and retractable partitions opened onto gardens and courtyards. After the Second World War, low-slung, modernist, pavilion-style, public elementary schools, modeled on one built in Crow Island, Michigan, became ubiquitous in American suburbs. To nurture creativity in children, a popular goal during the Cold War, educators imported tools from the kindergarten, open-air, and playground movements: boys and girls played with blocks, water, and sand in light-filled classrooms that opened onto courtyards, designed for play.[30]

The choreography of education and play in post-war schools underscores the symbolic importance of children's spaces (and their activities), an importance heightened in times of political and cultural crisis. During the Cold War, controversy dogged the proposition that elementary school children should learn through unstructured play in pavilion style schools as some called for more basic and structured learning.[31] The debate continues in New York City where the contemporary "Back to the Basics" movement limits playtime in kindergartens and elementary schools. Just about one hundred years after Caroline Pratt introduced wooden unit blocks to enable open-ended, imaginative play in her Greenwich Village classroom, many young children are no longer offered this key component of child-centered education.[32]

At play

Like schools, physical spaces made for play proliferated as concerns about the deleterious effects of industrialization and urbanization on children exploded in the late nineteenth and early twentieth centuries. Child savers, men and women eager to prevent juvenile delinquency among the working-class youth, joined other reformers to insist that all boys and girls deserve to play. The architectural outcome, many and different places for organized recreation, invited the use of play and play spaces as tools for socialization and enculturation. In the United States, one well-known preoccupation was to use play to reinforce racial privilege in gender-specific ways.

Summer camps can serve as an example. By the end of the nineteenth century, adults had come to believe that organized, regular contact with nature in the summer would save children from the problems of the industrial city. In the United States, proprietors opened up shop, starting in the 1880s for boys and soon extended the offer to girls. Explicitly couched in associations with the "natural child" and Native American culture, the manufactured experience of the wilderness included persuading boys and girls to adopt "Indian" ways. The focus on gendered readings of this camp experience, especially around the campfire downplayed the racist implications of a practice that left intact stereotyped interpretations of Native American culture.[33] However sobering the use of play to reinforce race privilege, the movement to organize recreation also had democratizing effects. This was the case in the grand public swimming pools opened in New York City during the New Deal. With these pools, children enunciated their right to public space and even racially integrated some of these settings, despite the widespread proscription against race mixing in swimming pools at this time in American history.[34]

For another example, we need to take a closer look at the playground movement. As the sheltered-model of childhood took hold among the urban middle classes, child savers inserted themselves into the play culture of working-class children, determined to direct, control, contain, and draw a physical boundary around play as they drew a social boundary around childhood. Although heralded as innovators, recreation reformers called on concepts that had been in place since at least the kindergarten revolution, calling on these notions: that play is the work of childhood, that children need to learn to play with age-appropriate toys and activities, and that contact with nature is needed for a good childhood. In the Progressive Era Luther H. Gulick Jr, who began his career at the YMCA, Henry S. Curtis, a psychologist trained by G. Stanley Hall, and Joseph Lee, a wealthy Boston lawyer and philanthropist, added new ingredients to the Froebelian mix – the intent to age-grade play and circumscribe it in specific places. These objectives, coupled with child saving and child study, escalated the use of play as a tool for socialization and education among working-class children.[35]

The inventors of the child-study movement, Gulick and his mentor Hall, forged a provocative link between physical education and child development and emphasized the fundamental human impulse to play. It had been confounded in the industrial age, which, because it denied access to outdoor activity, deprived children of the ability to develop motor skills and moral capacity. Both, they argued, developed from natural instinct, and Gulick targeted specific muscles for the development of specific moral faculties.[36] Adult guidance was critical, especially through the tortuous stage of adolescence to which Hall had called special attention. Boys and girls also needed different physical challenges because their biological (and thus ethical) make-up differed.[37] Gulick, who became director of physical education for New York City public schools, formed, with Lee and Curtis, the Playground Association of the America in 1906. The municipalization of recreation was a stated goal as was the determination to reorganize the play of immigrant children.[38]

As these ideas took hold in the United States, women organized to win public space for children to play in cities. All citizens had reason to be concerned about the geography of play, but women were especially vocal. It was common, especially for boys, to play on open lots, but that kind of ground was disappearing as cities modernized. It was also problematic for recreation – unhealthy, ungraded, informal, and unsuited for play in a child-centered society. Reformers also demanded that children be able to play off city streets, out of mud, manure, and vehicular traffic. Their special concern was boys, as a moral panic about male street culture, especially of working-class youth, swept through cities at the end of the century.[39]

In Oakland, California, clubwomen made the case for playgrounds as a right of childhood during a dispute about land use that rocked the city in 1899. "Do not rob the children," the Oakland Club insisted, its members deploring "anything that looks like robbing the children of rights that are only just becoming recognized."[40] The Club proposed the city build a new playground that accommodated older pastoral visions of park, with open space, trees, and a bandstand and newer ones of active recreation, with separate areas for girls and boys to play. A fan of G. Stanley Hall would have questioned the assertion that a public space, planned by women, offered the best route to manhood, but those concerns did not matter to women who fought for land and equipment.

And fight they did. The request for public money fell on deaf ears, and a few years later, the Club equipped, at its own expense, a playground adjacent to Tompkins Grammar School, a public school in the working-class district of West Oakland. The club also hired supervisors, with the goal being to teach children "to play healthfully, enjoyably and with unselfish fairness toward others" and deter "juvenile delinquency and youthful mischief." Children voted with their feet: in the summer of 1907, hundreds came every day for six weeks to use the slide, sandbox, seesaw, and swings; and the next year, boys and girls "stood in line waiting for their allotted time."[41] The implication of success was clear, although the terms depend on point of view. A clubwoman saw at-risk children who elected to come to a space designated for organized play rather than spend time at the nickelodeon, hang out the street, or just plain do nothing. From the point of view of children – here was one more place to play, with the street continuing to appeal to at least some of them.

Looking back on the experiment at Tompkins Grammar School, the Recreation Department credited the "progressive organization of women," the Oakland Club for the early success. It estimated "more than a thousand children were kept off the streets, taught the gospel of fair play and team work, and given a wholesome leisure hour interest."[42] The hope was that directed play in a dedicated place would teach boys and girls the social skills necessary for citizenship in a democratic society. "The sandpile for the small child, the playground for the middle-sized child, the athletic field for the boy and the girl in the teens – these are fundamental conditions without which democracy cannot continue," Gulick wrote in *Lippincott's Magazine*. "Upon them rests the development of that self-control which is related to appreciation of the needs of the rest of the group and of the corporate conscience that is rendered necessary by the complex interdependence of modern life."[43]

The playground in West Oakland shows that space and childhood have bearing on democracy but not in the terms put forth by Gulick. The physical and social construction of space at this playground differed from the model espoused by recreation reformers. Strict grading by age and sex did not apply in this place, even though monitors supervised children at play. A sand box and slides were placed in the same space, boys and girls of different ages played on the same equipment, and the site was racially integrated – all counter to the explicit advice of recreation reformers. The suggestion is that this is a public place for working-class boys and girls in the neighborhood – one where children know they have a right to childhood because they have a public space to play.

In public

Children learned to live with other public places made expressly for them: the orphanages, asylums, prisons, reform schools, hospitals, and other structures that came to constitute what I call the charitable landscape for children. The carving out of a special public realm for children – a defining aspect of modern childhood – began when cities opened institutions for children in need of the care and assistance of the public. Municipalities sought to take care of foundlings and orphans in orphanages and asylums long before either private families or schools turned their attention to special spaces for children. The Ospedale degli Innocenti in Florence, sometimes called the first orphanage, was given a central role in the city early in the modern era.

In 1419, the city hired Filippo Brunelleschi, a leading architect in the Italian Renaissance, to design the new orphanage, a church-run charity, at the edge of town. A fellow member of the Silkweaver's Guild generously endowed the building fund, making it possible for Brunelleschi to add a large U-shaped building to a medieval complex that was composed of a church, courtyard, and dormitory. Calling this addition, with a grand loggia, the first orphanage is a bit of an exaggeration because children had been abandoned at this site for decades. Nonetheless, the new building, by virtue of its purpose, made manifest the municipality's newfound interest in taking care of abandoned children. Terracotta medallions, designed by the sculptor, Lucca della Robbia and prominently displayed on the loggia, associated foundlings with the Christ Child and celebrated the idealization of children and sanctity of childhood that was part of Renaissance culture. The loggia also served a practical purpose, subsequently answered in other institutions by a small revolving door – to shelter a newborn baby from inclement weather and render anonymous the person who delivered the child to the charity's front door.

The architectural history of modern childhood continued to be full of examples of charitable institutions built not only to house boys and girls but also to make clear their condition and their needs to the charitable public. These instititions, which came to include special prisons, industrial schools, and reform schools, also spelled out discipline and reproduced class and other social differences including those presumed to stem from disability, delinquency, gender, or race. One consequence is the astonishing range of structures that dotted the charitable landscape for children. Early in the twentieth century, for example, the state government ran a home for blind boys and girls in Berkeley, California; on the outskirts of nearby Oakland, women built orphanages for older and younger white children; in town, they did the same but included Chinese girls and boys. Each establishment began in a repurposed house, intended to address the special needs of each group. Whether purpose-built or not, these institutions recorded human differences among children. Like the girl's bedroom in an upper-middle-class house, the effect was intended to be long lasting, to endure – not only to shape childhood within each institutional home but also through instruction to direct children to gender-, race-, and class-specific futures in the adult world.[44]

Taking note of the fact that cities, churches, charities, and other organizations have had to provide for children for a long time and to meet all kinds of misfortunes of childhood demonstrates this fact about modern childhood. Cities now care about all children not just those who have no parents or who are outcasts. In the early twentieth century, women, rather than men, became the vehicles for this activism, making sure that children had, in addition to playgrounds and orphanages, special hospitals, libraries, and museums. These places may have precipitated the isolation of children from adults, but they also endowed children with public spaces – spaces that demonstrate not only their right to childhood, but also became sites where children make decisions about their public life.

I close with one ancedote. Faced with demands for safety (and pressure from litigious parents), see-saws, slides, swings, and jungle gyms have disappeared from most of the playgrounds in New York City. Only a few pieces of this equipment remain in use. Recently, one young girl watched another climb the bars of a jungle gym in northern Manhattan. "It's fun," she said. "I'd like to see it in our playground. Why not? It's kind of dangerous, I know, but if you just think about danger, you're never going to get ahead in life."[45] Like other examples discussed in this essay, this place shows that thinking about the spaces of childhood enriches the history of childhood; thinking about the spaces of childhood also helps us imagine different futures for children and helps us to understand the worlds children make for themselves.

Notes

1 Abigail A. Van Slyck, "Review of 'Kid Size: The Material World of Childhood'," *Winterthur Portfolio* 39(1) (2004): 71.

2 Karen Sánchez-Eppler, *Dependent States: The Child's Part in Nineteenth-Century American Culture* (Chicago, IL: University of Chicago Press, 2005), xv.

3 The Churchill quote is cited by James Borchert, "Alley Landscapes of Washington," in *Common Places: Readings in American Vernacular Architecture*, ed. Dell Upton and John Michael Vlach (Athens, GA: University of Georgia Press, 1986), 281–82.

4 Philippe Ariès, *Centuries of Childhood: A Social History of Family Life*, trans. Robert Baldick (New York, NY: Vintage Books, 1962), 128; Harry Hendrick, "Children and Childhood," *ReFresh* 15 (1992): 1.

5 Gary Cross, *Kid's Stuff: Toys and the Changing World of American Childhood* (Cambridge, MA: Harvard University Press, 1997).

6 Karin Calvert, "Children in the House, 1890 to 1930," in *American Home Life, 1880–1930: A Social History of Spaces and Services*, ed. Jessica H. Foy and Thomas J. Schlereth (Knoxville, TN: University of Tennessee Press, 1992), 76–93.

7 Carolyn Steedman, *Strange Dislocations: Childhood and the Idea of Human Interiority* (Cambridge, MA: Harvard University Press, 1995), 7.

8 Ingeborg Weber-Kellerman, "Die Kinderstube: A Cultural History of the Children's Room," in *Kid Size: The Material World of Childhood*, ed. Alexander von Vegesak, Jutta Oldiges, and Lucy Bullivant (Milan and Weil am Rhein, Germany: Skira, editore and Vitra Design Museum, 1997), 31.

9 Calvert, "Children in the House," 86 (quote), 87.

10 Calvert, "Children in the House," 90.

11 Elizabeth A. Gagen, "Play the Part: Performing Gender in America's Playgrounds," in *Children's Geographies: Playing, Living, Learning*, ed. Sarah L. Holloway and Gill Valentine (London, UK: Routledge, 2000), 213-29; Sarah Jo Peterson, "Voting for Play: The Democratic Potential of Progressive Era Playgrounds," *Journal of the Society of Gilded Age and Progressive Era* 3(2) (2004): 145–75.

12 Viviana A. Zelizer, *Pricing the Priceless Child: The Changing Social Value of Children* (New York, NY: Basic Books, 1985).

13 Annmarie Adams and Peter Gossage, "Sick Children and the Thresholds of Domesticity: The Dawson–Harrington Families at Home," in *Designing Modern Childhoods*, ed. Marta Gutman and Ning de Coninck-Smith, 61–81; Abigail A. Van Slyck, "The Spatial Practices of Privilege," *Journal of the Society of Architectural Historians* 70(2) (2011): 210–39.

14 Nicholas Orme, *Medieval Schools: From Roman Britain to Tudor England* (New Haven, CT: Yale University Press, 2006): 12–62.

15 Anna Davin, *Growing Up Poor: Home, School, and Street in London, 1870–1914* (London, UK: Rivers Oram Press, 1996), 99–101.

16 Dell Upton, "Lancasterian Schools, Republican Citizenship, and the Spatial Imagination in Early Nineteenth-Century America," *Journal of the Society of Architectural Historians* 55(3) (1996): 238–41.

17 Thomas Müller and Romana Schneider, *Das Klassenzimmer/The Classroom* (Tubingen, Germany: Wasmuth, 2011), 8.

18 Rachel Remmel, "The Origins of the American School Building: Boston Public School Architecture, 1800–1860" (Doctoral dissertation, University of Chicago, 2006).

19 Jessica Collier, "The Transcendental Schoolroom: Childhood Education and Literary Culture in Antebellum America" (PhD diss., University of California, 2012).

20 Jonathan Zimmerman, *Small Wonder: The Little Red Schoolhouse in History and Memory* (New Haven, CT: Yale University Press, 2009), 49; Jennifer V.O. Baughn, "A Modern School Plant: Rural Consolidated Schools in Mississippi, 1910–1955," *Buildings & Landscapes* 19(1) (2012): 43–73.

21 Michael Grossberg, "'A Protected Childhood': The Emergence of Child Protection in America," in *American Public Life and the Historical Imagination*, ed. Wendy Gamber, Michael Grossberg, and Hendrik Hartog (Notre Dame, IN: University of Indiana Press, 2003), 216.

22 Dale Allen Gyure, *The Chicago Schoolhouse: High School Architecture and Educational Reform, 1865–2006* (Chicago, IL: Center for American Places at Columbia College Chicago, 2011), 81–83.

23 Clarence Arthur Perry, *Wider Use of the School Plant* (New York, NY: Dept. of Child Hygiene, Russell Sage Foundation, 1910).

24 Nikolas Rose, *Governing the Soul: The Shaping of the Private Self*, 2nd ed. (New York, NY: Free Association Books, 1999), 183–84.

25 Susan Herrington, "The Garden in Froebel's Kindergarten: Beyond the Metaphor," *Studies in the History of Gardens and Designed Landscapes* 18 (1998): 329–30.

26 Michael S. Shapiro, *Child's Garden: The Kindergarten Movement from Froebel to Dewey* (University Park, PA: Pennsylvania State University Press, 1983): 68–69.

27 Kate Douglas Wiggin, "The Relation of the Kindergarten to Social Reform," (San Francisco, CA: California Froebel Society, 1884), 2.

28 Anne-Marie Châtelet, "A Breath of Fresh Air: Open Air Schools in Europe," in *Designing Modern Childhoods*, ed. Marta Gutman and Ning de Coninck-Smith, 108–11.

29 Marta Gutman, "Entre moyens de fortune et constructions spécifiques: Les écoles de plein air aux États-Unis á l'époque progressiste (1900–1920)," *Histoire de l'éducation*, 102 (2004): 157–80.

30 Amy F. Ogata, "Building for Learning in Postwar American Elementary Schools," *Journal of the Society of Architectural Historians* 67(4) (2008): 562–91.

31 Roy Kozlovsky, "Adventure Playgrounds and Postwar Reconstruction," in *Designing Modern Childhoods*, ed. Marta Gutman and Ning de Coninck-Smith, 171–90.

32 Kyle Spencer, "With Blocks, Educators Go Back to Basics," *New York Times*, November 28, 2011, A-18.

33 Abigail A. Van Slyck, "Connecting with the Landscape: Campfires and Youth Culture at American Summer Camps, 1890–1950," in *Designing Modern Childhoods*, ed. Marta Gutman and Ning de Coninck-Smith, 32–33.

34 Marta Gutman, "Race, Place, and Play: Robert Moses and the WPA Swimming Pools in New York City," *Journal of the Society of Architectural Historians* 67(4) (2008): 532–61.

35 Howard P. Chudacoff, *Children at Play: An American History* (New York, NY: New York University Press, 2007), 99, 107–16; Abigail A. Van Slyck, *A Manufactured Wilderness: Summer Camps and the Shaping of American Youth, 1890–1960* (Minneapolis, MN: University of Minnesota Press, 2006), 43–48.

36 Benjamin G. Rader, "The Recapitulation Theory of Play: Motor Behaviour, Moral Reflexes, and Manly Attitudes in Urban America, 1880–1920," in *Manliness and Morality: Middle-Class Masculinity in Britain and America, 1800–1940*, ed. J.A. Mangan and James Walvin (New York, NY: St. Martin's Press, 1987), 123–34.

37 Howard P. Chudacoff, *How Old Are You? Age Consciousness in American Culture* (Princeton, NJ: Princeton University Press, 1989), 72–78; Donald Mrozek, "The Natural Limits of Unstructured Play, 1880–1914," in *Hard at Play: Leisure in America, 1840–1940*, ed. Kathryn Grover (Amherst, MA: University of Massachusetts Press, 1992), 210–26.

38 Joseph Lee, *Constructive and Preventive Philanthropy* (New York, NY: Macmillan Company, 1902), 235.

39 Ning de Coninck-Smith, "Where Should Children Play? City Planning Seen from Knee-Height: Copenhagen, 1870–1920," *Children's Environments Quarterly* 7(4) (1990): 54–61.

40 "Do Not Rob the Little Children, Miss Mary McClees Makes a Strong Plea for a Proper Playground," *Oakland Tribune*, Sept. 17, 1899; "Ladies at the Library Meeting," *Oakland Tribune*, Sept. 18, 1899.

41 Dewitt Jones, ed. *Oakland Parks and Playgrounds* (Oakland, CA: Oakland Parks and Recreation Departments and the State Emergency Relief Corporation, 1936), 206.

42 "History of the Oakland Recreation Department" (Typed mss, Oakland History Room, Oakland Public Library, c. 1920), 1–2; George E. Dickie, "Report of the Playground Commission," in *The Park System of Oakland, California* (Oakland, CA: City of Oakland, 1910), 125.

43 Luther H. Gulick Jr, "Athletics for School Children," *Lippincott's Monthly Magazine* 68 (August 1911): 201, cited in Rader, "Recapitulation Theory of Play," 131.

44 For this point, see Nina E. Lerman, "'Preparing for the Duties and Practical Business of Life': Technological Knowledge and Social Structure in Mid-19th-Century Philadelphia," *Technology and Culture* 38(1) (1997): 31–59.

45 John Tierney, "Grasping Risk in Life's Classroom," *New York Times*, July 18, 2012: D-1. The headline in the digital edition reads, "Can a Playground Be Too Safe?"

Suggestions for further reading

My thanks to Rachel Remmel and Jennifer Collier for sharing unpublished research, Marci Clark for assistance in preparing the annotated bibliography, and to Gene Sparling and Paula Fass for comments.

General accounts and bibliographies

de Coninck-Smith, Ning, and Jens Bygholm. *Barndom Og Arkitektur: Rom Til Danske Børn Igennem 300 År*. Århus, Denmark: Forlaget Klim, 2011. The book documents spaces designed for children by Danish architects and urban planners. The focus is on how the scale of the child has been interpreted in social housing, nurseries, schools, hospitals, sanatoria, playgrounds, orphanages, and museums, primarily during the twentieth century.

Gutman, Marta, and Ning de Coninck-Smith, eds. *Designing Modern Childhoods: History, Space, and the Material Culture of Children*. New Brunswick, NJ: Rutgers University Press, 2008. This anthology shows how spaces made for children are critical to the construction of modernity in global society by examining the history and design of places and objects made for children.

Gutman, Marta. "Children and Space." Oxford Bibliographies Online (OBO): Childhood Studies, http://oxfordbibliographiesonline.com/Annotated bibliography A comprehensive annotated bibliography of works analyzing the history, design, and use of children's spaces.

At home

Adams, Annmarie. "The Eichler Home: Intention and Experience in Postwar Suburbia." In *Gender, Class, and Shelter: Perspectives on Vernacular Architecture, V*, edited by Elizabeth C. Cromley and Carter L. Hudgins, 164–78. Knoxville, TN: University of Tennessee Press, 1995. This essay analyzes the dynamic relationship of architectural intention to human experiences of domestic spaces, including of children and teenagers.

Calvert, Karin. *Children in the House: The Material Culture of Early Childhood, 1600–1900*. Boston, MA: Northeastern University Press, 1992. In this study, material culture is used to analyze changing constructions of childhood in the United States. By examining furniture, toys, and other objects used in raising children, the book shows that parents tried to mold their children into prevailing notions of childhood.

Ogata, Amy F. "Building Imagination in Postwar American Children's Rooms." *Studies in the Decorative Arts* 16 (2008–2009): 126–42. This article analyzes children's spaces in post-war suburban houses in the United States and shows that during the Cold War the child's playroom and bedroom offered a new focus to the household.

Weber-Kellermann, Ingeborg. *Die Kindheit: Kleidung und Wohnen, Arbeit und Spiel; Eine Kulturgeschichte [Childhood: A Cultural History of Clothing and Housing, Work and Play]*. Frankfurt, Germany: Insel Verlag, 1979. This text analyzes the socialization of German children in the nineteenth and twentieth centuries through clothing and housing, work and play.

In school

Brosterman, Norman. *Inventing Kindergarten*. New York, NY: Harry N. Abrams, 1997. This book, generously illustrated, reconstructs the origins and development of the kindergarten system of education.

Burke, Catherine and Ian Grosvenor. *School*. London, UK: Reaktion Books, 2008. The authors survey the architectural history of schools, using examples from Great Britain to illustrate how school buildings help organize time and space for teachers and students. Different points of view are addressed, from students, teachers, and parents to architects and administrators.

Châtelet, Anne-Marie. *La naissance de l'architecture scolaire: Les écoles élémentaires Parisiennes de 1870 à 1914.* Paris, France: Honore Champion, editeur, 1999. This is a comprenhensive history of school building in France during the Third Republic. The focus is Paris, where some three hundred schools were built after new laws were passed, making schooling free, secular, and compulsory, and regulating design and construction.

Châtelet, Anne-Marie, Dominique Lerch, and Jean-Noël Luc, eds. *Open-Air Schools: An Educational and Architectural Venture in Twentieth-Century Europe.* Paris, France: Éditions Recherches, 2003. This bi-lingual anthology documents open-air schools in ten European countries to show that they were a focus for educational experiment, for furthering preventive medicine, and for architectural innovation.

Lawn, Martin, and Ian Grosvenor, eds. *Materialities of Schooling: Design, Technology, Objects, Routines.* London, UK: Symposium Books, 2005. The anthology explores the materiality of schooling, meaning the objects, technologies, and routines used in the education of children. Design is given its due but emphasis is placed on how objects are given meaning, used, and linked into socially active human networks.

Saint, Andrew. *Towards a Social Architecture: The Role of School-Building in Post-War England.* New Haven, CT: Yale University Press, 1987. A prize-winning account of school building in post-war England that assesses the impact of social goals and mid-century modernism on architectural design.

At play

Cavallo, Dominick. *Muscles and Morals: Organized Playgrounds and Urban Reform.* Philadelphia, PA: University of Pennsylvania Press, 1981. This study of the movement to organize urban recreation between 1880 and 1920 argues reformers, who formed the Playground Association of America, wanted to remove children from city streets and supervise play in purpose-made environments to control crime, Americanize immigrants, and socialize children.

Downs, Laura. *Childhood in the Promised Land: Working-Class Movements and the Colonies De Vacances in France, 1880–1960* Durham, NC: Duke University Press, 2002. This is the first history of France's *colonies de vacances,* an extensive network of summer camps created for working-class children in the late nineteenth century. The focus on the creation of and participation in these summer camps offers insights into the location and significance of childhood in French working-class cities and within modern France.

In public

Adams, Annmarie, and David Theodore. "Designing for 'the Little Convalescents': Children's Hospitals in Toronto and Montreal, 1875–2006." *Canadian Bulletin of Medical History* 19(1) (2002): 201–43. The essay explores more than a century of changing ideas about the health of Canadian children through the architecture of pediatric hospitals in Montreal and Toronto.

Cmiel, Kenneth. *A Home of Another Kind: One Chicago Orphanage and the Tangle of Child Welfare.* Chicago, IL: University of Chicago Press, 1995. This book offers a comprehensive, even-handed account of the American orphanage, using the history of the Chicago Nursery and Half-Orphan Asylum to expose changing attitudes toward child welfare and to shatter popular myths about orphanages. Special attention is given to architecture and planning.

Gavitt, Philip. *Charity and Children in Renaissance Florence:The Ospedale degli Innocenti, 1410–1536.* Ann Arbor, MI: University of Michigan Press, 1991. This book analyzes the

Ospedale degli Innocenti (Hospital of the Innocents), designed and built between 1419 and 1445 by Filippo Brunelleschi. Through a close reading of archival material it describes parental concerns, tracks the lives of abandoned children and shows that hospital officials replicated the structure and values of the Florentine family within the orphanage.

Murdoch, Lydia. *Imagined Orphans: Poor Families, Child Welfare, and Contested Citizenship in London*. New Brunswick, NJ: Rutgers University Press, 2006. The author challenges melodramatic narratives of child abandonment to show poor families sought places for children in state-run and charitable institutions in London.

Van Slyck, Abigail A. "Reading: The Experiences of Children as Library Users." In *Free to All: Carnegie Libraries and American Culture, 1890–1920*, edited by Abigail A. Van Slyck, 201–5. Chicago, IL: University of Chicago Press, 1995. In this chapter, the author discusses the rise of the children's reading room in Carnegie libraries and gives attention to children's experiences, including the special rooms set aside for them to use.

14

PLAY, GAMES, AND TOYS

Gary Cross

Until modern times, play was a periodic catharsis, associated with fairs and festivals rather than with childhood. Games, whether on boards or grassy fields, were the periodic indulgences of youths or adults, not primarily – or even often – of children. Playthings and toys often originated in adult ceremonies and in their play, and children found limited time and resources to either play with or make their own toys. Among the many changes that came with the modern world of industry, professionalization, and schooling was the identification of play, games, and toys with childhood. This transformation was closely related to broad economic and social changes. They shifted playtimes, places, and activities to children; created conflicts over and debates about children's play and playthings that engaged parents and educators; and affected merchandisers and, more subtly, children themselves. These transformations culminated in the twentieth century as play and toys came to serve both as tools for training children to assume adult roles and as venues and tools for children's fantasy. They also came to ambiguously express children's autonomy while serving commercial interests in ways that frequently led to "moral panics" – intense cycles of anxiety – by parents and other adults.

Play and playthings in the premodern West

To simplify a very complex reality and to focus on mostly European and colonial American sources, pre-industrial play (for most before 1850) took place in the context of a subsistence agricultural/craft economy, where narrow aristocratic elites controlled access to a limited and largely stagnant surplus of goods and where time free from labor was severely restricted for all but the rich. For the vast majority of the population, the household was the location of most work, and all members, except for infants, were expected to contribute to its well-being. Of course, children found time and place for their own play when busy parents were not supervising them, but those times and places were rare. Play was confined to intermittent breaks in long workdays. The workgroup was also the site of most play. It was in that group that traditions of play were passed down from one generation to the next. This was the case for even the wild and rebellious customs of youth – like drinking, mumming (group begging for food and drink with an implied threat if not provided), and holiday mischief. Because homes were mostly small and largely devoted to work, play took place almost exclusively outside the home – on the street or rural clearings. As was the case with

267

adults, children often played rough games that tested courage and loyalty to the group, especially among boys.

Another site and time of play was the festival, a community celebration, rather than child-focused activity. Seasonal feast days took place when weather and market changes increased consumption or reduced production or the demand for manufactured goods. For example, seasonal surges in the availability of food at harvests, together with the inability to preserve excess, led to festivals in the late autumn and early winter. Many holidays, though nominally religious, coincided with hiring fairs and lulls in farm work. Whatever their origins, they were opportunities for games, spectacles, and chaotic rule-defying play. The most famous is Carnival (still practiced in many predominantly Catholic countries and regions), the pre-Lenten festival that invited celebrants to indulge in food and drink, but also sex (weddings and pre-nuptial conceptions were common). Revelers insulted elites, threw food and even stones at each other, and even cross-dressed and otherwise reversed roles – practices often called Saturnalia. Children were often allowed to join in this bawdy and chaotic "play," though adults, especially young men, dominated the festivities. Typical was the Shrove Tuesday celebration in Derby, England, where men and boys participated in the free-for-all "football" match: Throngs gathered around a ball, pushing, kicking, and, in general, fighting to drive the ball toward goals on either side of town. These rough, sometimes brutal contests were hardly distinguishable from riots. Philippe Ariés's famous *Centuries of Childhood* (1962) claimed that, until modern times, children and adults intermingled in play. In this context, adults played more like kids and children were exposed precociously to adult vices like drinking, promiscuous sex, gambling, and violent and boisterous games.

Aristocrats, the landed gentry, and wealthy merchants of course, enjoyed a different play culture, one that became increasingly separate from the plebeian world of festivals starting in the seventeenth century as the rich withdrew support from these often rowdy public pleasures. While they participated in their own exclusive sports (like hunting, horse racing, tennis, and golf), these elites, with access to time and domestic space, also developed their private forms of play, such as refined dance, chamber music, and card and board games, in which children had only marginal roles. The European (and American) aristocracy also created pleasure gardens. In the eighteenth century, a ring of private entry-by-fee gardens surrounded London. Even the opening of royal parks to the public (such as occurred in London as early as 1661 and Vienna in 1766) and grand urban green spaces such as New York's Central Park (completed in 1873), were not designed particularly for children's play and exercise.

In contrast to the festival calendar, European elites had the time for extended travel to resorts first located near "healing wells" and later at seashores. While vacations were the norm for the rich and their offspring at schools, few wage earners had enough savings to forgo work for more than a few days. "Vacations" for them were without pay and usually during seasonal downturns of business activity or during machine renewals (that coincided with the English custom of "wakes week" when churches were refurbished). These aristocratic sites and times set the stage for the modern vacation and tourist destination. Probably most characteristic of pre-industrial play and games was that they were centered more on the desires and needs of adults than children, a pattern that was brought to North America and into the early American republic.

It is no surprise that toys and other playthings were rare for children of the poor and were often miniatures of parental possessions, activities, and obsessions for children of the rich. Of course, even peasant children made balls, whistles, and miniature animals and figures from cast-off wood, stone, and animal parts. And simple types of toys were passed down through many generations. Common toys like hoops, hobby horses, toy animals, jointed dolls, and knucklebones (precursors of the modern "ball and jacks") were common in the ancient Mediterranean as they were in medieval and early modern Europe. Few have survived. "Fashion babies" served in the late fourteenth century to display and advertise Paris fashion, but thereafter were passed down to children as dolls. Soldier miniatures, designed first for kings and nobles to plan wars, gradually were given to their sons for play. Dollhouses, containing miniature furniture, date from sixteenth-century Saxon Germany. They too were made for wealthy women to display their status and for their amusement. Only at the end of the eighteenth century were dollhouses built specifically to instruct girls in the arts of housekeeping (so-called Nuremberg Kitchens from the famous toy center in the German world). The same was true of balloons that began as fads for eighteenth century French women of fashion before they were passed down to children. The carousel has its origins in an aristocratic game of adult men riding wooden horses (presumably to train for the ancient sport of jousting). Other children's toys had their origins in festival displays with effigies of saints or Biblical stories being miniaturized and passed down to children as play sets. Beginning in the sixteenth century, Germans carved "Noah's Ark" play sets to edify and amuse children for use especially on Sundays. These trends coincided with the birth of a toy industry in southern Germany, centered at Nuremberg, which from the late 1400s drew upon wood from nearby forests to employ numerous craftspeople from surrounding villages to carve dolls, play sets, and toy weapons and musical instruments for distribution throughout Europe and eventually the world.

From colonization until the Civil War era, most American male children had relatively few playthings, especially after the toddler years. The pressures of work on farms and in trades limited playtime. During settlement, a period of relative scarcity, parents seldom thought of toys as tools of learning or character building. The young learned their gender roles and job skills by assisting in their father's or a master's daily work. And religious strictures against idleness, especially in Puritan New England, made children's games suspect. In many families, adults brought out toys only on special holidays (like Noah's Ark on Sundays). Most important, however, was simply the relative paucity of manufactured luxury goods of any kind. Many manufactured toys were expensive, and were often imported from Germany until the end of the nineteenth century.

Of course in more wealthy, free, and settled families, infants and toddlers received teething toys, rattles, hobby horses, jumping jacks, and building blocks. These playthings grew more elaborate in the nineteenth century with the availability of mechanical push toys that rang bells or toy instruments (horns, drums, and pianos). These "child quieters" were intended to divert those too young to work. Even if older boys were given few toys, they found time to play and often made their own toys. They improvised, creating fantasy worlds with whittled sticks, castaway bits of cloth, stones, gourds, wheel rims, and mother's clothespins. More often, however, they played their own, often rough, games in unsupervised groups. The press of parents' work and the availability of open space (especially in rural areas and small towns) gave boys ample opportunity to form into small gangs where they tested each other's courage and displayed loyalty at play, without necessarily requiring toys. Finally, toys were probably more available for boys than girls. Sixty-six percent of boys in American portraits between 1830 and 1870 are shown with toys whereas only 20 percent of girls were depicted with any plaything, and these were mostly dolls.

Industrialization and the shift of play to children

In a long and still continuing process that took off first in the 1770s in England, industrialization brought machines and specialized workplaces to the manufacturing of goods. The resulting intensification of work gradually drove out play from labor (as work became closely supervised and punctuality enforced). Industrialization also sharply reduced the seasonal ebbs in the flow of work so characteristic of artisan and agricultural life and the community festival culture. Still, industrialization made possible new forms of leisure time, including the modern notions of free evenings, the weekend, and paid summer vacations. This process also liberated people from work at the beginning and end of life, leading to the rise of opportunities for childhood play as well as retirement. In the short run, however, the "industrious revolution" seems to have increased the annual hours of work by eliminating numerous holidays and daily work breaks (both of which occurred in England from the 1790s to 1850). This meant both the expansion of children's factory labor and the number of working hours for children and adults. Although working hours in factories were gradually lowered and the age of entry into work was raised in the nineteenth century, children's labor remained a necessity for many working-class families into the early twentieth century in Europe and the United States.

Industrialization allowed children, especially from the emerging propertied middle class, to withdraw early from the labor market to attend school but also to enjoy significant times for vacation and daily play. The expansion of factories, offices, and other specialized workplaces meant also the gradual removal of work from the home. This made the affluent home a place of family leisure by the mid-nineteenth century, in Christopher Lasch's words, a "haven from a heartless world" of increasingly impersonal labor and economic competition. It also created new spaces for children's play. Prosperous Victorian families tried to isolate themselves from the boisterous public and make the home an effective alternative to the unwelcome crowd. One of the principle motivations for modern suburbanization was to separate middle-class families and especially their children from the "dangers" of the busy city and the street play of the working-class youth. These suburban homes set many precedents: situated on large private lots, they could have gardens and, as a later American variant, extensive front and back lawns, providing opportunities for family games. Parlors became settings not only of the performance of amateur singing and piano playing (as music training of children became a mark of family refinement) but also of demonstrations of "magic lanterns" and other scientific toys, and the playing of "uplifting" parlor games (educational card and board games often with religious or business themes). On the second floor, the nursery (really a playroom), not only isolated the very young from their parents, but also provided a special site for toys and play.

In the broadest sense, industrialization and related cultural changes both expanded opportunities for children to play and made the times and places of play far more child-focused. This was especially true in the US. Boisterous community festivals gradually were bowdlerized, domesticated, and organized around children. The best example is Christmas. Beginning in the 1820s, Christmas became a holiday for giving to children in the American Northeast; in fact, this became the principle time for receiving toys. Similarly, birthdays became child-focused in the nineteenth century and later (starting in the 1930s) so did Hallowe'en. These transformations of festivals reflected both a middle-class rejection of the old traditions of Saturnalian celebrations (and fears of the sometimes threatening crowds that they engendered) and a growing attraction to the "wondrous innocence" of the child – a desire to awaken delight in the as-yet unjaded young and perhaps to recall through children some of the pleasures that adults once enjoyed in Saturnalia.

Somewhat slower to emerge was the child-centered vacation and tourist site. Vacations were rare for most Americans and Europeans until well into the twentieth century and, until the 1950s, they were seldom organized around children. This is no surprise because few couples with children could afford an extended holiday, and those that could usually sought separate diversions for the children rather than time with them. Middle- and upper-class parents in the eastern United States sent their offspring away to summer camp as early as the 1880s. This was in contrast to European camping and hiking groups that catered to adults. American clergymen, seeking a wholesome alternative to the slum's dirty hot streets for poor children, organized primitive camps. Other children's camps were organized by private school headmasters to provide their pupils with a retreat into nature and with "character" training during the summer recess. Children's camps reached down the social scale by the 1920s under the auspices of the Scouts, YMCA, religious, and ethnic groups. These camps, first organized on military principles and designed to teach discipline and gender roles for older children, gradually shifted after 1930 to serving younger children, providing age-segmented activities and camp sites and replacing the work and "roughing it" values of early camps with comfortable cabins, sports and swimming facilities, and organized play. Summer camps represented recognition of the needs of children during summer vacations from school and offered at least the middle-class child an alternative to idleness and the presumed dangers of street and gang play. It still allowed them to be separated from parents.

That began to change in the 1930s and 1940s as parenting magazines in the United States especially encouraged adults to bring children along and share in their discoveries on vacations. The 1950s saw the widespread use of the station wagon for inexpensive and informal tours of national parks and heritage sites. The increasingly roomy family car was to provide family togetherness on long automobile trips to the Grand Canyon or Old Faithful. The holiday increasingly was meant for family bonding and renewal and for celebrating children's desire.

The shift to child-centered playtime was paralleled by the transformation of leisure places toward the end of the nineteenth century. While civic elites fostered large showy parks, sometimes associated with zoos or museums, social reformers advocated smaller neighborhood parks to make green space accessible to the poor and especially their children in their own neighborhoods. The American playground movement was a natural outgrowth of these trends. Beginning modestly, in 1885, when Boston's public schools began providing sandboxes for poor children, soon

271

playground advocates sponsored neighborhood parks throughout the immigrant districts of American cities. Kansas City introduced the park commission and a network of public playgrounds in 1893 and was soon followed by most American cities. In 1906, Luther Gulick and others founded the Playground Association that later become the National Recreation Association with the goal of providing alternatives to the street for mostly poor children. The focus on the poor reflected concerns that immigrant and working-class children were endangered by the hazards of street play and by gangs. Early playgrounds were fenced off and strictly supervised by trained recreation staff. Gradually, however, the recreation movement reached out to children of all social classes. The same pattern was followed by the swimming pool movement. Public pools first were built to provide hygienic diversion for mostly working-class boys and men, but by the 1920s pools were being constructed in all types of communities for wholesome children's play (though also increasingly racially segregated as they served both sexes). The movement to provide special places for children's play was extended in the 1870s when members of small-town churches participated in the Fresh Air Fund by opening their homes to slum-dwelling children from New York City during summer vacations. Even the campaign for public libraries of the late nineteenth century extended to providing children's book rooms by 1900.

European children experienced a similar, but less developed movement to organize children's play. Middle-class British reformers were early proponents of urban public parks and recreational centers funded often by the philanthropy of local merchants and manufacturers. Out of the Sunday School movement of the early nineteenth century (at first intended to foster literacy as well as religion among working children) emerged adult-sponsored sports and recreation activities, including notable football (or soccer) teams, several of which became early professional clubs in the 1880s. English philanthropy similarly focused on the "training" of youths through patronage of sports clubs, and playground centers. There were a few summer camps dedicated to poor children from Leeds, Bradford, and other industrial towns, but, in the 1890s, the British camping movement was organized for young adults (often members of religious or political communities) rather than for children. In 1937, the Butlin holiday camp introduced a provided-service and entertainment-centered camp experience to mostly young people and families. Similar to the non-profit holiday camps was the Youth Hostel Association, founded in 1929 and offering 281 hostel lodgings for youths and teens cycling and hiking across Britain. The Holiday Fellowship, with roots in the 1890s, offered 90 guesthouses to nature-loving ramblers (by no means exclusive to children) by the end of the 1930s. In France, beginning in 1883, both church and secular educators organized children's camps (a division that was repeated with sports teams from the 1890s and youth hostels from 1929). Catholics recognized that sport was an excellent vehicle for preserving the flock – an insight not lost on their secular opponents at the village public school. In this same period, trade unions and left-wing parties in France, Germany, and elsewhere in Europe also organized youth camps, excursions, and sports activities as alternatives to commercialized leisure, and, of course, to inculcate working-class political and social values. In the interwar years, Italian and German fascists organized camps, holiday excursions and other recreations to instill political loyalty through party youth organizations and family leisure organizations, the Dopo Lavaro and the Kraft durch Freude. Similarly the Soviet Union developed an extensive network of summer camps for children under the Communist Party's Young Pioneers that emphasized non-commercial recreation and political training.

A similar shift of leisure sites toward children is revealed in the history of amusement parks and seaside resorts. Like traditional festivals, New York's Coney Island and other outdoor resorts at the seashore, lakes, and other similar sites often provided occasions for outbreaks of Saturnalian disorder and "dangerous" delights that deeply offended middle-class taste and morality. At Coney Island's three amusement parks (built between 1897 and 1904) and their many imitators elsewhere, one found an array of freak shows, music halls, bars, stall games, thrill rides, and spectacles. At first, relatively few children attended these sites of excitement and sensuality designed mostly for young adults and couples. Grown-ups may have acted like children, but they seldom burdened themselves with kids when they went to such parks. Gradually, however, amusement parks themselves became child-centered when they introduced miniature carousels and Ferris wheels and built amusement centers in middle-class, child-friendly settings like Playland on Rye Beach (on New York's Long Island) in the mid-1920s. This was part of the broader trend toward the child-focused vacation site, but it was also a way of making "dangerous" crowds into "playful" crowds, thus creating a new middle-class culture that featured the wondrous innocence of childhood. Disneyland (1955) built on these trends, by providing a constant evocation of childhood wonder and the nostalgic longings of the "child within" with its rides themed on Disney cartoon and movie productions. Appealing to children as a form of freshly discovered delight and to adults as nostalgia for Disney memories during their own childhood, Disney attractions like the Dumbo Flying Elephants, Mad Tea Party, and Tom Sawyer's Island have survived for a half century at Disneyland and Walt Disney World, and similar rides prevail at Disneyland Paris (opened in 1992). Europe saw a parallel development of amusement park and seaside resorts such as Blackpool, England, but were late in adapting them to children.

Emerging patterns of play: adult control and indulgence

Times and sites of play became child focused in the nineteenth and twentieth centuries, but questions remain regarding how this play was affected by adults. This matter is not easy to address because of the ambiguous attitudes of adults about the value of play and the purposes of games and playthings. The difficulty is also related to the constraints historians experience documenting children's motives.

Trying to make play productive in the form of personal exercise and physical games is an ancient practice, but in the nineteenth century, this quest gained new life in the athletic training offered in clubs and especially schools. "Athleticism" based on gymnastics had been popularized in the "Turner movement" in Prussia by the famous teacher and nationalist, Father Friedrich Ludwig Jahn early in the century. By the 1840s, his exercises on poles, bars, ladders, ropes, and competitive gymnastic matches had been introduced to many German schools. But, despite the encouragement of American disciples in Boston as early as 1826, few schools built gymnasia until much later. German immigrants brought gymnastics with them when they entered American cities in large numbers after 1848. And athleticism was promoted by the YMCA, which, beginning in 1869, built gymnasia in addition to libraries in major towns in the United States and Britain.

It was team games that attracted more players and ultimately mass audiences. And these games emerged in elite schools rather than in sports clubs. Central to this change was the emergence between 1840 and 1860 of the muscular Christian doctrine in the English public (private boarding) school. The ideology of the "healthy mind in a healthy body" was widely promoted by headmasters at England's elite boarding schools, who from about 1845 outlawed disorderly unsupervised games and blood sports and replaced them with rule-based team games like cricket, rugby, and English football (with its modern code of rules established in 1863). The British clergy, with public school upbringing and imbued with the philosophy of muscular Christianity, taught football to poor parish boys on Saturday afternoons. Other working-class children learned the game in YMCAs, boy's clubs, or schools. Soccer was easily learned with its simple rules and was widely popular because of its premium on quickness and agility rather than on brute strength or unusual size.

Amateur athleticism led to the invention of basketball in 1891 by the American YMCA's James Naismith. Basketball was designed to provide exercise and competition without the threat of injury, which was so common in other ball games. The key was the raised goal or basket, which obliged the player to throw it softly in an arc to succeed. Other sports also shaped the play of American children, especially boys: baseball, a team game played by middle-class urban men trickled down to the working classes and eventually to children in the years after the Civil War. In 1939, Little League baseball was organized to provide age-graded teams and competition for American boys, assuring children opportunity to play and develop skills in competition with others of the same age and eliminating the multi-aged street play that sometimes degenerated into gangs dominated by older children. American football, with origins in northeastern colleges in 1869 became a major sport and spectator activity in the collegiate extra-curriculum by 1900 and soon thereafter passed into high schools. Beginning in 1929, men organized football teams for boys. This became the "Pop Warner" program in 1934. In the 1930s, most players were teenagers, but gradually the game was introduced to younger ages. Today it reaches down to five year olds. Adults, who tried to turn the sometimes rough games of children into organized team sports, were also often trying to train the young to succeed in a competitive but rule-based enterprise economy. These efforts inevitably came up short, both in suppressing undirected play and in training youths for bourgeois virtue.

Even more, the changing role of toys reflected adult efforts to shape children's play. We can see this in the American example. Only after 1865 did American manufacturers produce toys in large numbers, and then often as a sideline to other activities. Makers of wood, metal, mechanical, and print and paper goods produced miniatures of their "adult" products or used waste materials to make batches of cheap children's playthings for Christmas sales. After the Civil War, cheap cast iron molds and clockwork mechanism increased the variety of toys. Dolls became both cheaper and more elaborate in the nineteenth century. Around 1820, bisque and china molds offered realistic faces on dolls while rubber (1850), celluloid (1881), and composition of wood fiber and glue (1895) lowered prices and increased the durability of dolls. Most of these toys were still too expensive for any but the affluent (a clockwork figure cost from one to about three dollars when daily wages were scarcely that high). But even the poor could afford cheap "penny toys" (wooden tops, tiny toy swords, crude animal figures, and rag dolls, for example).

Because parents purchased almost all toys, at least until the 1930s, their tastes and attitudes determined the market. Victorian-era toys, such as moralizing board games like "Mansion of Happiness" were often didactic. Parlor toys like magic lanterns (early slide projectors) and zoetropes (devices that created the illusion of a moving object) taught children the love of science and technology. The mechanical savings bank of the 1870s and 80s (featuring a figure that shot a bear or danced when a coin was deposited) taught the parent-approving lesson of thrift, even as it was a source of amusement. Many were imitations of adult activities and tools, and invited boys to anticipate adult roles. Toy catalogs featured toy hammers, saws, and even garden tool sets for boys, and dolls and miniature houseware sets for girls. With some notable exceptions, these toys were not designed to encourage fantasy (there were no masks or cowboy hats, nor figures made in the image of boy heroes). They also served as tools for more solitary play, reflecting parents' desires to isolate their sons from the influence of unsupervised gangs.

In the nineteenth century, girls received relatively few dolls during their childhoods and these were often repaired rather than replaced. Mothers often sewed their daughter's dolls' clothes and many girls used plain "sewing" dolls as mannequins to learn the craft of the seamstress. Children were not allowed to play with their fragile "lady" dolls except on special occasions. And Victorian girls took their cues from storybooks and their parents to re-enact social rituals including tea parties and even funerals with their dolls. Baby dolls were rare until late in the century because girls in large Victorian families usually had a real baby sibling to care for. Many dolls looked like adults with whom the child was to identify.

The training function of toys persisted into the twentieth century, even providing a role as a substitute for work training for older middle-class boys who earlier might have been apprentices. Many boys' toys were supposed to prepare boys for an optimistic world of mechanical gadgetry and business success. The electric train, invented in 1906 by Joshua Lionel Cowen, remained, until the 1960s, the most important boys' toy. Model train makers stressed realistic details and up-to-date equipment and promised to bring fathers and sons together in play. Many construction toys first appeared between 1901 and 1914, including Meccano and Erector sets, the Tinker toy spool and stick, and Lincoln Logs. Automobile replicas by Tootsietoy, Buddy "L," and Arcade showed a similar fascination with "the latest thing." Working toy replicas of batteries, cameras, and factory machinery introduced boys to technological progress. Many boys' toys in the fifty years after 1900 closely reflected dramatic changes in transportation, science, communications, and construction. The introduction of toy cars and airplanes closely followed the real things. Chemistry and other science sets introduced boys to the secret processes of nature. All of these toys attempted to minimize the barrier between the plaything and the real thing. The percentage of American males between the ages of fourteen and nineteen years old at work had decreased from 61 to 40 percent between 1890 and 1930. Middle-class boys of ten or even sixteen years of age could look to sophisticated construction sets as fun, but also as practical, training for modern careers in engineering and science.

By contrast, almost all girls' toys of this period had domestic themes (dollhouse furnishings and appliances) and were not career-oriented. Parents bought companion and baby dolls that were to teach girls to care and nurture. For younger children, a new wave of child-development experts, especially advocates of Kindergarten, promoted

building blocks, crafts, and other educational playthings. The didactic and often austere character of educational toys limited their appeal to children (and to indulgent
parents) and thus their ability to shape modern childhood.

In fact, by the end of the nineteenth century, the direction of children's toy development began to shift to playful and fantasy toys and stories. Early signs of this
appeared in a new literature for children (Lewis Carroll's *Alice in Wonderland* of
1865, for example) and in middle-class parents' attempts to relieve their offspring
from their own austere upbringings and to display their new wealth. As early as the
1870s, middle-class children found the opportunity to purchase their own toys and
gadgets offered as premiums for young readers who bought magazine subscriptions.

By 1900, a rising generation of American toy and doll makers created a rapidly
changing series of fantasy toys. In 1903, Albert Schoenhut, a German-born maker of
toy musical instruments, introduced whimsical and topical Humpty Dumpty Circus
play sets (some of which featured Teddy Roosevelt's Safaris). These toys appealed
to adult nostalgia for circus wagons from their childhood but also to the new and
novel. Others were drawn from folk literature, but more often from the ever-changing
stories and characters of comics and movies. Storybook and comic characters like the
Brownies (1890s) and Baby Snookums (1909) were made into dolls, games, and play
sets. The 1900s also produced fad dolls that appealed both to adults and children. The
Billiken doll featured an Oriental boy's face with a monkey's body and was first sold
to adults as a good luck novelty during the recession of 1907–1908. The next year, E.I.
Horsman sold it as a child's doll. Similarly the Kewpie doll, a small chubby girl with
a topknot, began as a character in a woman's magazine story and in 1911 became
a popular child's doll. Character dolls were also used to sell new mass consumer
goods. In 1905, Aunt Jemima pancake flour packages included coupons to be mailed
in for printed cloth dolls of a black "Mammy" figure. The teddy bear, based on a
story of the American President Teddy Roosevelt sparing a baby bear on a hunt,
became an international craze in 1906. In addition to the soft figure of a bear stuffed
with upholstery material, Teddy appeared also in songs and storybooks. This cuddly
toy provided children with a sense of security and protection; it also attracted adults
as a fad, as a way of making children seem innocent and charming, and later as a
reminder of their own childhoods. In their continuous transformation, toys reconciled
contradictory longings – representing the timeless and the timely, the emotional needs
of young children and the whimsy and nostalgia of adults.

After 1900, (copying German innovations) E.I. Horsman and Effanbee produced
distinctive "character" or "New Kid" dolls in the United States. Appearing in the
form of children with short legs, big and sparkling eyes, often slightly askance, and
dimples and rosy cheeks, these character dolls exuded a cheerfulness that reflected a
more tolerant view of children and served as companions of youngsters in an expectation of carefree play. Doll makers used soft and washable materials and flexible joints
as an inducement for cuddling and play. Raggedy Ann and Andy of the 1920s commercialized the traditional rag doll by giving Ann and Andy distinct personalities. The
most successful of these companion dolls was Patsy by Effanbee (1924), who along
with her "sisters" formed a "family" of composition dolls that came with numerous fashionable clothes for dress-up play. Movie and storybook characters became
subjects of doll makers too. The most famous of these dolls was made by Ideal Toys
in the image of the children's movie star Shirley Temple in 1934. The Bye-lo Baby

of Grace Storey Putnam (1923), modeled after a three-day-old infant, was part of a trend toward infant dolls. This culminated in the 1930s with the Dy-Dee Baby and Betsy Wetsy baby dolls that needed a diaper after "mother" fed them. In the smaller families of the twentieth century, baby dolls served as a substitute for the child's care for real babies and, along with the companion dolls, taught girls to be nurturing. But they also celebrated the innocence and naiveté of the child. Although research found that boys also played with dolls, these playthings became increasingly associated with girls only. In the early twentieth century, doll play was transformed from practical training in sewing and social etiquette to the enjoyment of childhood and keeping up with fashion trends.

All this coincides with an important change in attitudes about childrearing in the United States, a shift away from utilitarian concerns about the economic value of the child and her future and toward the "priceless child," valuable to adults as a delightful innocent who should be kept out of the adult world (especially the labor market) as long as possible. A new more permissive image of the child (what I call the "cute") made children's wants or imagined wants something to be indulged rather than rejected.

In some ways, these trends in playthings and the shifts in attitudes toward children were shared on both sides of the Atlantic. German producers of children's goods anticipated the "cute" that was so evident in American commercial culture after 1900. The Steiff company of Dresden was an innovator in producing whimsical stuffed animals. German doll designers encouraged children's play and identification with dolls that looked like children. Even early German comic strips featured active (even naughty) children. However, German toys lost their dominance in the United States during World War I and after Hitler came to power in Germany in 1933, as military priorities further weakened the German playthings industry. More broadly, the "cute" theme did not develop nearly so far in Europe as in the United States, partially because of the persistence of rationalist and utilitarian views of training children. Toys, for example, remained mostly miniatures of adult activities (dollhouses, vehicles, battle ships and war planes, for example) rather than fantasy-based toys. Though Disney and his licensed images of Mickey Mouse and Donald Duck were very popular in Europe in the 1930s, Europeans were late in developing Disney's cultivation of the cute.

In early twentieth-century United States, advertisers, but also producers of everything from comic strips and movies to new holiday rituals, made the "wondrous innocence" of the child part of a parent-to-child gifting culture that challenged old notions of cross-generational reciprocity (where all members of the family were expected to contribute to its material well-being). At the root of this romantic, but also materialistic, understanding of children was a complex parental reaction to the changing world of adults. Parents projected a longing for escape from the rigors, responsibilities, or at least boredom of office jobs onto children and their "never lands" and "secret gardens." Giving gifts to children let adults recover, in the (hopefully) delighted child, their own lost wondrous innocence, often now fallen victim to satiation in the consumer age.

Modern toys: commercialization, autonomy, and panic

While some toys continue to reflect parental aspirations for their children and their quest for "wondrous innocence," especially in America starting in the 1930s toys increasingly appealed to children's separate world of fantasy and to their aspiration for autonomy and sometimes their rebellion against parents. Perhaps because of the political upheavals of the 1930s and preparation for war (especially in Germany and Italy where the Nazis and Fascists had little tolerance for such fantasy), the American experience was unique in the West. Japanese toymakers adopted these trends as early as the 1920s and became innovators in fantasy/fad playthings from the 1950s. Over the long run, these patterns of commercialized childhood shaped global patterns of children's play and playthings. As a result, in the following pages, American social and cultural trends will be emphasized.

Facilitating and profiting from these trends were increasingly integrated toy, media, and advertising industries. Ironically, during the Great Depression, as parents found it harder to purchase expensive play sets (like those of Schoenhut who went bankrupt), toymakers offered cheaper single toy figures, especially soldiers, that boys could buy one by one and collect on their own. Toy guns, formerly rare, became more common, as they became cheaper, and sometimes sold directly to children. This trend was part of a broader American departure from adult-controlled fantasy culture as children found commercial venues for their "own" stories and heroes. This coincided with the emergence in the early 1930s of afterschool radio fiction and Saturday afternoon movie serials for children and, by 1937, comic books.

These stories, often derived from working-class pulp magazines, featured science fiction, jungle, and crime themes that deviated sharply from parent-pleasing themes of earlier children's stories and heroes. The result was a series of moral panics as American parents reacted to increasingly violent "blood and thunder" radio programs and, even more, to comic books that became sexualized and even sadistic after World War II, leading to a Comic Book Code (1954) that eliminated themes objectionable to many parents.

In the 1930s, radio, movie, and comic-book heroes shaped American children's play by being featured as toys. Images of the cowboy star, the tough detective, the boxer, the space man, and the superhero were licensed to toy makers. Tom Mix, Dick Tracy, Popeye, Buck Rogers, and Superman offered boys a wide variety of toys (guns and wind-up figures, especially). Buck Roger's space pistols (1934) let boys act out the science fiction stories heard on children's radio and the real world of adults was abandoned. Girls had their own celebrity toys in Shirley Temple dolls (from popular movies) as well as play sets and kitchenware embossed with images of Little Orphan Annie (who was heard on radio as well as seen in the comic strips), but these were more conventional and far less threatening to parents.

In the 1930s, the hero began to replace the machine as the central prop of play in the United States. While the construction set of the 1910s and 1920s called the boy to imitate practical men and to imagine his future role in an orderly world of economic and technological progress, the new male fantasy toy beckoned the youth to a faraway realm dominated by conflict. No longer did technology seem to offer a future of progress and prosperity. Rather than invite a boy to identify with his father (often unemployed in the Depression), the new toys evoked an image of strong men, free from the bonds of family. These playthings shared a common penchant for fighting and subduing enemies, not construction or achievement.

Not all of these licensed toys challenged adult values and memories, of course. Mickey Mouse and other Disney cartoon personalities drew upon the tradition of the "cute," the Teddy Bear, and character doll. In 1930, Walt Disney licensed the likeness of Mickey Mouse for dolls and other toys and Mickey's look was quickly cutsified and spread. In 1938, he allowed toys based on "Snow White" to be introduced along with the movie – originating a now common marketing practice.

Following World War II, American toys returned to the themes dominant before 1930. In a period of new scientific advances and perhaps closer bonds between fathers and sons, many new playthings were miniatures of contemporary technology, especially those that celebrated the space program and missile development in the late 1950s. War toys allowed sons of veterans to rehearse the "heroics" of their fathers, but most boy's toys celebrated more prosaic deeds and technology – model farm equipment, bulldozers, trucks, and service stations offered by companies like Tonka.

The post-war period also produced a craze for cowboy toys in the United States. This went well beyond the well-established traditions of cowboy suits, holster sets, and Lincoln Logs. Cheaply made miniature frontier towns, ranches, and especially forts let boys re-enact cowboy and Indian dramas seen at the movies. Television in the 1950s built on the children's programming of the 1930s to create popular celebrities whose persons and stories were easily transferred to playthings. Radio and movie cowboys, including Hopalong Cassidy, Roy Rogers, the Cisco Kid, Davy Crockett, and the Lone Ranger graced the toy shelves of the late 1940s and early 1950s. But the rise of prime-time Westerns that swept the nation in the five years after 1955 created an even greater swelling of Western toys. These Westerns were designed for the whole family, at least all the males. Romantic settings of space travel in the future and Western heroes in the past were imaginative worlds shared by fathers and sons.

The tradition of companion and baby dolls returned with the Betsy McCall doll (promoted by a fashion magazine). The Ginny Doll also emphasized clothing, accessories, and cosmetics in miniature. Nevertheless, these dolls still looked like children and the dolls that mothers played with and thus were not a break from the past.

While the 1950s seemed to be a throwback to an earlier era, it did mark the rise of toy advertising on children's TV programs that strongly promoted a separate world of children's fantasy and playthings. The "Mickey Mouse Club," Disney's afterschool TV show (1955–1959), ushered in year-round toy advertising directly to children (there was none on radio), designed to appeal to the child's imagination rather than the parent's values. Mattel displaced earlier toy companies with advertising toy guns and later the Barbie doll.

Appearing first in 1959, Barbie revolutionized doll play. Designed to resemble a teenage girl fashion model with an exaggerated womanly shape, Barbie let girls imitate the preening and shopping rituals of adult women and allowed them to identify with an adult female body. Despite resistance from mothers who continued to favor the companion dolls (like the early 1950s Ginny or the 1920s Patsy), girls found in Barbie a symbol of a hoped-for future of teenage freedom from the constraints of childhood and the duties of their mothers. Owning a Barbie has become a rite-of-passage for girls across the globe, having been introduced in England as early as 1961 (though Barbie competed with Sindy there until the 1990s) and became very popular in Eastern

Europe shortly after the collapse of communism in 1989 and thereafter in Asia. Barbie was selling in about 140 countries by 1997.

Over time, Barbies lost their adult-defying aura. Even though mothers and feminists repeatedly opposed Barbie for her exaggerated sexuality and identification with consumerism and viewed her as a poor role model for young girls, within a generation Barbie became more "innocent" in her facial features and increasingly seen by children as a "fairy princess." In 2001, the Bratz doll line emerged as a challenge to Barbie. With a vaguely "ethnic" look with big, almond-shaped eyes with heavy shadow and lips painted with red gloss, Bratz dolls offered the same array of fashion and consumer themes as Barbie had done for decades. Though invented by a former Mattel employee, which after a lawsuit led to Mattel's ownership of the brand, Bratz has inherited the role that Mattel's Barbie once played and has raised parental concerns about the premature introduction of sexuality (and "street culture") to the innocent play of little girls. Critics complain that profit-hungry doll and toy makers have no qualms about advertising these parent-displeasing dolls and other products directly to children through new media. In turn, children win their way over their parents' objections through "pester power."

The American toy company, Hasbro, introduced GI Joe in 1964, a boy's dress-up doll, realistically representing the average soldier. Unlike the cheap and impersonal plastic soldiers of the 1950s or the expensive sets of toy soldiers that their fathers might have known, GI Joe had moveable limbs and was a foot tall; thus, he could be posed and equipped with the latest military clothing and weaponry. While GI Joe invited boys to play war the way their fathers might have fought in World War II or in Korea, it was still a break from father's play and would be even more so in the 1970s.

The 1930s link of toys to media fantasy was extended with the Star Wars movies (1977–1981) when American boys were first inundated with toy figures, vehicles, and play sets built around re-enacting the rivalry of Darth Vader and Luke Skywalker on the screen. Unlike cowboy play, for example, Star Wars toys were largely divorced from the memories and expectations of parents. This led to a wave of toy lines called action figures built on the adventure/fantasy movies and TV cartoons in the 1980s and 90s (for example, He Man, Dino-Riders, Teenage Mutant Ninja Turtles, Power Rangers, and Pokémon as well as cartoon/toy line products like Strawberry Shortcake and Care Bears). The action figure craze even transformed GI Joe. While Joe became an adventurer rather than a fighter in 1970 (largely in response to parental discomfort with war play during the Vietnam conflict), he returned in 1976 as Super Joe, a standard action figure (smaller and no longer dressable) and in the guise of a futuristic warrior with paired enemy figures. This version of GI Joe was no longer identified with the military experience of fathers. Following the trend, he even got his own cartoon show in the 1980s to help push his toy line. The conflicting feelings of adults toward the military were avoided and most parents ignored the war play of their young. At the same time, war play was detached from whatever historical or moral purpose military toys had earlier embodied.

Beginning in 1972, toys competed with and often paralleled video games. Simple games like electronic ping-pong played in arcades were quickly supplemented with graphic video action available on home-game consoles for TV and hand-held electronic toys. While this craze died in the early 80s, the much-improved graphics and action of Nintendo and other video systems from 1988 brought the video game back. These interactive electronic adventures heavily emphasized fantasy violence and brought criticism for their increasing intensity, addictive attraction, and tendency to isolate boys from others. Middle-class parents had long feared that their children were adopting minority or working-class pleasures (as they sometimes were). Many so-called "moral panics" were eventually resolved when adults embraced at least part of the innovation (for example, Barbie and even video games).

When action figures, video games, Barbie and other consumption dolls, and similar toy fads sparked repeated concern among parents and educators, traditional toys like marbles, yo-yos, and even often imaginative construction toys like Lego found it difficult to compete. By the end of the twentieth century, American toys were primarily drawn from a never-ending and always changing world of media fantasy.

This was a culmination of a trend that began with silent adventure movies after 1905, was advanced with Saturday matinee showings of cartoons and serials as well as after-school radio programs for kids in the 1930s, and furthered by Saturday morning kids' programming on TV from the 1950s. By the 1970s, all this led to children's movies on tape and disc and to video games. Indoor media entertainment has displaced street games and informal playgroups, reducing children's opportunity for exercise and social interaction.

Of course, European children had a somewhat different experience in the second half of the twentieth century. Mattel and Hasbro did not displace European toy makers. British Meccano and Hornby electric trains enjoyed a revival after 1950 and the Lesney "Matchbox" cars updated a tradition of play based on realistic miniatures of adult life. The Swedish Brio company perpetuated high-quality non-representational wooden toys (simple trains, cars, animals, and blocks) and promoted them as an educational alternative to licensed character toys. The German Playmobil company (founded in 1974) thrived by offering sturdy plastic updates of traditional wooden play sets. Few European toys were based on licensed media characters. And the relatively small role of TV advertising to children impeded European development of the fad and fantasy toys that thrived in the United States.

Still, this did not mean that European children were not subject to American influences. European toy companies survived by imitating or becoming subsidiaries of American toymakers. In 1962, the Lines Brothers of Britain made an obvious "knock off" or copy of Mattel's Barbie doll called Sindy. Lego of Denmark, which in the 1960s built a loyal clientele with its plain interlocking plastic blocks, in the 1980s, introduced kits to models based on space, pirate, and other fantasy themes; by 1999, Lego offered licensed models from the Star Wars movies. In 1966, Britain's Palitoy became the distributor for Hasbro's GI Joe (called Action Man in Europe). Even Brio distributed Mattel and Hasbro toys in the 1950s and 1960s. By 1985, the American warehouse retailer, Toys "R" Us, arrived in England and soon thereafter on the continent, promoting mostly American-originated toys and dolls.

Of course, European educators and cultural critics continue to resist the Americanization of childhood and call for restrictions on TV advertising of toys (ads directed to children under twelve were banned in Sweden in 1991). But with globalization of media and retail, European and American childhood has become much alike. This has meant the eclipse of games, play, and playthings with roots before the media-based and rapidly changing commercialization developed by American (and increasingly east Asian) corporations.

Suggestions for further reading

Preindustrial Play

Ariès, Philippe. *Centuries of Childhood: A Social History of Family Life*. New York, NY: Vintage, 1962.

Grober, Karl. *Children's Toys of Bygone Days*. Translated by Josephine Nicoll. London, UK: Badsford, 1928.

King, Constance. *Antique Toys and Dolls*. New York, NY: Rizzoli, 1978.

American play and playthings

Adams, Judith. *The American Amusement Park Industry: A History of Technology and Thrills*. Boston, MA: Twayne Publishers, 1991.

Chudacoff, Howard P. *Children at Play: An American History*. New York, NY: New York University Press, 2007.

Cross, Gary. *Kids' Stuff: Toys and the Changing World of American Childhood*. Cambridge, MA: Harvard University Press, 1997.

Cross, Gary. *The Cute and the Cool: Wondrous Innocence and the Commercialization of Modern American Childhood*. New York, NY: Oxford University Press, 2004.

Forman-Brunell, Miriam. *Made to Play House: Dolls and the Commercialization of American Girlhood, 1830–1930*. New Haven, CT: Yale University Press, 1993.

Jenkins, Henry. *Children's Culture Reader*. New York, NY: New York University Press, 1998.

Kasson, John. *Amusing the Million: Coney Island at the Turn of the Century*. New York, NY: Hill and Wang, 1978.

Kline, Steven. *Out of the Garden: Toys, TV, and Children's Culture in the Age of Marketing*. New York, NY: Verso, 1993.

Kline, Steven, Nick Dyer-Witheford, and Grieg De Peuter. *Digital Play: The Interaction of Technology, Culture, and Marketing*. Montreal and Ontario, Canada: McGill-Queen's University Press, 2003.

Register, Woody. *The Kid of Coney Island: Fred Thompson and the Rise of American Amusements*. New York, NY: Oxford University Press, 2001.

Van Slyck, Abigail. *A Manufactured Wilderness Summer Camps and the Shaping of American Youth, 1890–1960*. Minneapolis, MN: University of Minnesota Press.

European and global play and playthings

Baranowski, Shelley. *Strength through Joy: Consumerism and Mass Tourism in the Third Reich*. New York, NY: Cambridge University Press, 2004.

Cross, Gary and Greg Smits. "Japan, the U.S. and the Globalization of Children's Consumer Culture," *Journal of Social History* 38(4) (2005): 273–91.

Cross, Gary and John Walton. The *Playful Crowd: Pleasure Places in the Twentieth Century*. New York, NY: Columbia University Press, 2005.

Downs, Laura Lee. *Childhood in the Promised Land: Working-Class Movements and the Colonies de Vacances in France, 1880–1960*. Durham, NC: Duke University Press, 2002.

De Grazia, Victoria. *The Culture of Consent: Mass Organization of Leisure in Fascist Italy*. New York, NY: Cambridge University Press, 1981.

Sutton-Smith, Brian. A *History of Children's Play*. Philadelphia, PA: University of Pennsylvania Press, 1981.

15

CHILDREN AS CONSUMERS

History and historiography

Daniel Thomas Cook

Sparse, disjointed, and at times myopic, histories of children as consumers in the Western world nevertheless constitute a substantive area of scholarly inquiry. Historical interest in the child consumer did not arise until the 1980s and did not take hold until the 1990s despite the clear evidence that children had been thought of, acted upon, and behaved as consumers at least a century earlier in the US context. The lag between the onset of historical practice and the beginning of historical scholarship speaks not simply to the legacy of the marginalization of children in historical and social research generally. The peripheral position accorded children's consumption in historical research also indicates some conceptual difficulties that come to the fore when attempting to account for children's consumer practices.

The core, pressing problem in the historiography of children as consumers centers on determining what constitutes "children's consumption," i.e. which practices, goods, and social actors are to be included in this category. Historians face the confounding problem of the inescapable ubiquity of children's financial and resource dependence on parents, or on adults generally. Children of the middle classes of the late nineteenth and early twentieth centuries in particular – many of whom had been liberated from direct, wage-earning production – had scarcely any disposable money of their own, particularly in the case of infants and the very young. Hence, virtually all children's consumption is and has been mediated in some manner, thereby implicating adults/parents rather directly in their experience as consumers.

Child dependency in this sense operates as a structural dynamic that challenges the researcher to think past economistic conceptions, both of a "consumer" as one who makes purchases independently of others and also of "consumption" as an individualized act undertaken by and for oneself. Karen Sánchez-Eppler, writing of the necessity of recognizing children's "dependent state," considers how it "embodies a mode of identity of relation to family, institution, or nation, that may indeed offer a more accurate and productive model for social interaction than the ideal autonomous individual... ."[1] Consumption and consumer activity render the dependent state of children readily apparent while complicating the outlines of inquiry. What makes something a "child's" good? When a child possesses it? When it is purchased by another for a child? When a productive apparatus designs and makes it with a child in mind? And, when is something particularly a *consumer* good, as opposed to an artifact of material culture? These questions remain only half addressed in the history of children's consumption.

Children's dependent state in this manner contributes to the relative historical silence about the goods, practices and contexts of their past consumer worlds. Children's consumption finds itself either ignored in general histories of childhood or relegated to a side commentary, such as in the otherwise fine studies by Steven Mintz and Hugh Cunningham. Similarly, general histories of consumption and advertising have not recognized the child consumer or the place of children in consumer culture to any significant extent except where children's goods or spaces are noted as something of an aside to or a special instance of a legitimate or "real" (i.e. adult) world of commercial goods, spaces and meanings.[2] The quasi-derivative nature of children's commercial participation, perhaps coupled with the fluidity of ability and knowledge associated with different ages of childhood, has enabled a kind of historical blindness – or, at least, a civil disinterest – to the consumer worlds of childhood generally. It is unsurprising, then, that little attention would be paid to examining the history of such non-effective, derivative social actors engaging in a somewhat inconsequential social activity.

The kinds of resources related to "children's consumption" also render the definition of the subject problematic. Goods known, or presumed, to be made for children – particularly prior to the mid-twentieth century – were not, on the whole, thought worthy of preservation by adults, who regularly exercised the prerogative of disposal, or were unable to be preserved to any great extent. As "trivial" things of a passing age, children's garments and toys for children often were made of cheap material, with relatively few of these goods surviving for posterity. What survived often were items of the middling or well-to-do classes, especially in the case of garments, which, for the lower classes, were usually handed down until they became rags.[3] Children's everyday practices and involvement with materials and goods remain hidden from or unavailable to the historian to a far greater extent than with "adult" objects. Indeed, some of the most readily available records of products made for children's use are to be found in the promotions, advertisements, and chronicles produced by market actors i.e. manufacturers, advertisers, merchants, and trade publications. Hence, scholars who write on the history of children's consumption find themselves confronted with ever-present, if subtly posed, questions regarding its historical veracity and social relevance. With the boundaries and content of the commercial worlds of childhood rarely clear, and the social import of children's goods and commercial activity often opaque to many, it becomes incumbent on the researcher to demonstrate the existence and significance of such worlds in ways not expected of those who study "adult" worlds or consumption.

Another problem relates to how children themselves made meaning out of commercial goods. Children's expressions about goods can be ephemeral, not recorded or not deemed worthy of being recorded, and preserved by strategically situated adults. Notions or expressions of "desire," when not available directly from children themselves, have to be read from measures like sales and popularity of goods, or found in the recounting of childhood experiences in memoirs often by famous people.

Given these issues, it is understandable that there exists no coherent historical narrative, cohesive body of knowledge, or tradition of thought about children as consumers in the Western world. Rather, this field of inquiry may best be conceptualized as a number of different histories undertaken for particular reasons, within specific fields and crafted in response to a variety of questions and problems. In the following discussion, I examine historical studies of children's consumption with the idea of laying bare some of the conceptual differences and difficulties encountered by the different authors so as to make the problem of the "child consumer" explicit and, hopefully, informative. I have chosen authors who have focused on goods understood primarily as consumer items, rather than as mainly artifacts of material culture. The distinction here is fine and may not readily hold up under strict scrutiny; I make it guide the discussion toward discerning the specifically commercial import of goods and products in relation to the childhoods under consideration.

Eighteenth century

Published in 1982, J.H. Plumb's chapter on "The New World of Children in Eighteenth Century England" represents perhaps the earliest historical treatment of consumption in relation to children. Plumb sets his sights on discerning the impact on the home of increased availability of money due to rapid industrialization. In the wake of John Locke's assertions in *Some Thoughts Concerning Education*, first published in 1693, Plumb argues that children's inevitable "fall from grace" (i.e. loss of innocence) gradually came to be understood not as an original evil inherent in the child – as in Calvinist thought – but as something acquired with experience in the world. Education, he asserts, became social rather than religious to the extent that the child's "nature" came to be seen not as something fixed but as malleable.[4]

During the eighteenth century, the emerging money-based economy of an industrializing productive apparatus allowed for greater class fluidity and social movement than ever before. The confluence of a new conception of children as malleable beings with a class structure in the process of opening up made education a particularly significant node of intergenerational procurement of status. In short, the social futures of children become a market to be honed and exploited: "Few desires will empty a pocket quicker than social aspiration – and the main route was, then as now, through education, which combined social adornment with the opportunity of a more financially rewarding career for children." In this vein, Plumb documents the rise and popularity of secular, liberal education and the commercial market for textbooks as evidence that parents sought to "invest" in children in various ways as suggested by, among other things, advertisements for small private academies.[5]

Commercial interest in education extended to amusements, toys, literary books, and leisure travel for the rising English bourgeoisie. These objects and activities, according to Plumb, often tended to have a didactic thread woven through them and were not seen as promoting pleasure for pleasure's sake. He notes as well the increasing specialization in children's clothing and the manufacture of other objects intended for practical use, like cradles and diapers. Despite admonitions to the contrary by some, objects for children's amusement also began to proliferate. The child's world had become "more emotionally and intellectually exciting" than it was for past generations, even if this excitement did not extend into all classes of children or to all aspects of the new childhood.[6]

In Plumb's view, children and their lives became enmeshed in the world of goods and commerce through the class aspirations of adults of a newly expanding capitalist economy. Children were not implicated as direct purchasers of many of these goods but as vehicles for vicarious consumption and vicarious display. Children had indeed become objects for Plumb, implying both that they had been "subjects" at some time prior, and that the commercial world had a hand in their objectification.

Nineteenth century

Plumb's work indicates that children's inability or lack of opportunity to participate directly as consumers in an emerging commercial world did not preclude commerce from structuring key aspects of their lives. Many who have written on the consumer aspects of nineteenth-century childhoods similarly sought evidence of commercial presence by focusing on everyday artifacts that would be attractive to middle-class parents' emergent sensibilities regarding desired identities of or abilities for children. A few endeavored to capture children's involvement with goods so as to demonstrate their active engagement with the materials of an emerging commercial culture.

Mary Lynn Stevens Heininger offers a sweeping discussion of a "century of childhood" that covers 1820–1920 in the United States. Examining popular images of children in magazines, some toys, children's furniture, and household objects like napkin rings adorned with images of children, she discusses how the material culture of childhood reflects – oftentimes quite simply and directly – a changing adult view of children and childhood. Heininger finds, like Plumb, a movement away from a severe, Puritan view of children as originally evil and toward an increasing sense of innocence and purity in children. The children depicted in these artifacts, likely purchased, owned, and displayed by the middle class, are portrayed as extensions of "nature's bounty" associated positively with animals, young animals in particular, shown with somewhat uniform "cherub"-like round features in their faces.[7]

Heininger suggests that the commercial world is implicated in childhood history in several ways. For one, the changing economy over this century removed many men from the household, who left to work for wages outside the home on a daily basis, effectively producing a separate domestic sphere of women and children. The separation of spheres was moral as well as economic to the extent that the market values favored in the work world contrasted starkly with the ideology of sentiment in the home, where children increasingly embodied and symbolized the antithesis of pecuniary value. So too, children's worlds became increasingly separate from that of adults, as indicated by increasing specialization in the manufacture of their dress, furniture, playthings, and publications.

The irony, not emphasized by the author, is the contradictory way in which children – or more precisely, the "child" as a figure – came to represent purity and non-market values in and through the marketplace. Heininger unfortunately does not delve into the relationship between depictions of children on material objects, the increasing availability of goods made specifically with children in mind, and the desire for these things by children themselves, thereby collapsing several kinds of production and use into a single category or perspective. The extent to which the middle classes became consumers and the extent to which the "child," as symbol and concept, becomes an object of and for commercial value – and the relation between these – remains unexamined by Heininger. Hence, the particularly commercial status of goods and of social relations likewise remains opaque.

Material goods serve for Heininger as visible and somewhat shared touchstones of changing notions of childhood. Literary sources enable insights not always readily available in public, material culture like furniture or dress, and not easily located in oft-consulted historical documents found in municipal, church, or business records. Taken together, literary resources can offer glimpses of the breadth, reach, and texture of commercial values and meanings otherwise perhaps unattainable through standard means. In particular, fiction, magazines, and memoirs present opportunities for capturing description, meaning, and sentiment of consumer lives that were not systematically or contemporaneously documented but nonetheless found expression. Such treatments may help illuminate, as Dennis Denisoff puts it, the "small-scale acts of identity formation"[8] that helped create consumer culture in the nineteenth century.

In nineteenth-century Britain, as Lorraine Janzen Kooistra shows, the tie between children, Christmas, and consumerism was regularly dramatized in periodical publications, newspapers, and gift books like *Home Thoughts and Home Scenes* (1864). Images of warm, sentimental domestic life mixed easily with scenes of gift giving at the holiday time that served in many ways as models for enacting a proper, festive Christmas. Echoing Heininger's point, the tableaux on these pages depicted and thereby reinforced ideologies of home as a female sphere often by encapsulating and isolating children within that sphere, giving a sense of protection from the outside (market) world, making children "particularly desirable objects for adult Christmas consumption."[9]

Scholars generally concur that in significant, but not always clear and direct ways, toys and other amusements implicated children in commercialization. Examining these things helps to establish the presence of consumer goods in the lives of children and their families. Drawing mainly from the fiction and advice books of Maria Edgeworth, Teresa Michals notes that the child's toy in the nineteenth-century British context supported notions of an innocent, separate childhood for the middle class by focusing on training. Manufactured toys also exposed anxieties about the "relation between middle-class identity and commercial consumption"[10] to the extent that parents worried that possession and ownership could lead to desires for excess on the part of children, distracting from their training function.

In studying the miniature world of toy theaters, Liz Farr speculates about the relationship between consumer playthings, fantasy, and imagination. Combing through the remembrances of key British literary figures such as Charles Dickens and Robert Louis Stevenson, among others, Farr finds that play with these theaters provided the basis for later literary efforts. They also allow for insights about the effect of drama on the juvenile imagination through which can be seen "a growing culture of spectacle" that "reached deep into childhood." The children, as "capitalist subjects," Farr contends, thereby learned to "structure their relations to the world through mass-produced fantasies of financial success and fantasy fulfillment" while at the same time this became a means to test reality against its representations."[11] In these treatments, the "child" again arises as a socially negotiable object for adult deployment and symbolic exchange as children's life worlds and experiences are not – with the exception of famous personages – readily available.

In his discussion of toys in the US context, Gary Cross, a historian of twentieth-century childhoods, supports the narrative thread that runs from Plumb to Heininger to those found in British childhoods by Michals and Kooistra. In *Kids' Stuff: Toys and the Changing World of Childhood*, Cross identifies changing attitudes toward children, particularly those of parents, as the underlying impetus for the design and function of toys. Originally cast-off adult objects, toys gradually became associated with children and children's play even though, as amusements, they remained suspect in terms of "distracting" children from serious endeavors. Hence, they were rare and brought out only on special occasions before the American Civil War (1861–1865).

After the war, American manufacturers began to mass-produce toys as a sideline to other commercial activities. Significantly, as Cross argues, manufacturers produced and sold toys according to standards they thought were important, such as durability and educational value. Some toys, especially those meant for boys, were miniatures of adult objects e.g. garden tools, firearms, and shovels, while dolls and domestic devices like small irons were made for girls. These and other toys, for Cross, indicated a conservative view of children that "respected the past" while delivering what parents of the middle class "expected." Cross contends that toys did not, in the context of nineteenth-century American life, seek to infuse any "personality" into the dolls or spark the fantasy or imagination of children. American parents, apparently, were content with things as they were.[12]

Either in depictions of children or parents in everyday materials and print cultures or in the specialization of children's goods, particularly toys, researchers who chose to look found commercial goods and values to have been present in the lives of nineteenth-century children and parents. Without evidence that apparently speaks to children acting as direct consumer-purchasers, some researchers nonetheless have attempted to uncover ways that children engaged with the materials and meanings of a nascent, emerging commercial culture. Surviving manufactured materials, apparently used and altered by children, offer a few clues to their involvement.

Trade-card scrapbooks of the 1870s and 1880s provide Ellen Gruber Garvey with evidence of children's engagement with consumer culture. On the pages of these books, pieces of promotional trade cards and print advertisements were arranged by children, likely girls, into narratives and themes that often comment either on the child's life or on the advertisements themselves. Combined with an analysis of marginalia, Garvey finds an active child making use of the materials of commercial culture in ways not intended by the producers, even as some manufacturers became aware of children's scrapbooking of them and began to produce cards for that purpose. Part personal expression, part gender training, the existence of trade-card scrapbooking demonstrates in some measure that children in the late nineteenth century attended to and involved themselves with specifically commercial images and meanings not necessarily directed at parents.[13]

Through an examination of fiction, autobiographies, and surviving dolls themselves, Miriam Formanek-Brunell's study of the doll industry similarly finds that girls (and boys, to a different extent) used dolls in ways that most likely would not have been prescribed by adults. Thus girls sometimes abused them and demonstrated aggression toward these supposed objects of care. Formanek-Brunell presents some evidence that girls in the early twentieth century demonstrated a keen consumer acumen when it came to acquiring dolls as in, for instance, becoming knowledgeable about the different prices for the different dolls and engaging in sometimes labor-intensive comparison shopping.[14]

Twentieth century

Historical treatments examining some aspect of children and commercial life of the nineteenth century sought, in large part, to document the existence, reach, and perhaps growth of commercial activity around children. Researchers pursued evidence of how such activity reflected or represented changing cultural notions of childhood, changing middle-class parental attitudes toward children, and some sought to catch a glimpse of how children understood or interacted with aspects of commercial culture. Aside from the confidence that "consumption," in some sense of the term, increasingly mattered to parents and children over the course of this century, these studies, taken together, strain attempts to offer a general or overarching narrative about children and consumer life.

Histories which deal with twentieth-century children's consumption, in contrast, examine an array of sites and a plurality of modes through which the "child" becomes constructed as "consumer," and most concentrate on the period from 1890 to 1940 in the United States. Some focus on specific industries, others attend to how different and new forms of media addressed both children and mothers, and served as new vehicles for the presentation of goods and consumer lifestyles. These studies on the whole seek to explain the rise, proliferation and perhaps contemporary dominance of a children's consumer culture, often by detailing how various entities – mainly commercial enterprises – constructed the "child" to be compatible with particular notions of "consumer."

Curiously, few have attempted to discern how children themselves understood and handled commercial meanings and consumer goods, even as children's "agency" has arisen as a primary focus of social and culturally oriented consumer behavior research. An important exception is David Nasaw's study of working-class children in New York in the early 1900s. Children, mostly boys, patronized the new Nickelodeon movie houses, finding in their darkened rooms some space for privacy as well as often salacious entertainment from the moving pictures. Nasaw argues that children – who earned money often by selling newspapers or shining shoes – were active in their attempts to seek entertainment and pleasure from the new commercial culture available in cities. These boys were significant to the success of the early movie houses not simply due to their patronage, but also due to their collusion with local owners against the moral reformers who were trying to close down these establishments.[15]

Nasaw's work, by attempting to glean the child's perspective, marks an intervention into the interpretation of children's place within an emergent consumer culture. His emphasis on children's direct engagement with the pleasures of consuming entertainment complicates views like those of the contemporaneous reformer, Jane Addams, who saw such establishments as only exploitative. Kathy Peiss, in her research on adolescent girls and young adult women in New York during this same time, likewise finds that commercial entertainment provided the means through which aspects of personal identity and the exercise of power can be realized.[16]

Lisa Jacobson, in examining the 1890–1930s period, concentrates on representations of middle-class children, showing various ways in which the children were "imagined and socialized as consumers" and how the "child" as icon served as a barometer of anxieties about social change. She seeks to explain how a "positive re-evaluation of children's consumer identities in the 1920s and 1930s came about" at a time when consumer culture was struggling for dominance with a culture of thrift in the United States.[17]

Her research illustrates that advertising goods to young people and portraying children as consumers increasingly became standard fare in consumer magazines in the 1920s and 1930s, with the "child" serving both as target audience and rhetorical figure for promotions to adults. Jacobson details various efforts by schools, banks, and civic organizations that offered consumer education with the ideas of instilling values of thrift and restraint.[18] These, together, give evidence not only of the existence of a children's market for promoters, but also of the growing presence and problem of children as spenders, an important enough development to spur efforts to curtail their consumption.

For Jacobson, a key figure in the re-evaluation of children's consumer identities resides in the boy consumer of 1930s advertisements. As the "hero" of advertisers' dreams, the boy consumer combined authorial male power – as in the role of knowing about or recommending products to adults in advertising scenes – with an emphasis on desiring and attending to consumer goods, usually considered a feminine preoccupation. This "reassuring figure," according to the author, mediated the contradiction between hedonism and control, helping to "soften" and "contain" the dichotomy between a consumer ethos and a producer ethos. Emerging expertise in child development combined with progressive notions of play, according to Jacobson, also responded to and attempted to counteract the perceived injurious environment arising from an increasingly commercialized middle-class childhood in the 1930s. Efforts to create the ideal playroom went hand-in-hand with a re-evaluation of play as simple and unconstrained, yet purposeful and contained within the ideological and physical space of the companionate home.[19]

In a series of books, Gary Cross defined play and toys as sites that demonstrate tensions generated by the commercial involvement of children and parents. In the early 1900s, the US toy industry faced cultural headwinds that considered children's play a form of excess. Character and fantasy toys appealed to parents, according to Cross, because they reflected a new ethos regarding children who became objects of love, innocence, and parental nostalgia. Echoing Viviana Zelizer's thesis, Cross argues that children, no longer thought of as laborers and sources of income, could be allowed to indulge their fantasies and imaginations. Toys permitted such indulgence while giving parents the opportunity to recover their own lost childhoods in their children's play. Toys that reinforced gender norms, those that promised educational benefits, or that built children's "character" further made consumption palatable for an aspiring middle class.[20]

Cross has elaborated his view that parents and adult nostalgia served as the primary engines for children's consumption in the *Cute and the Cool*. He finds in the goods, advertisements, and print culture of early twentieth century both a longing for the past – represented in the "cute," wondrous child – and a foreboding figure – symbolized by the "cool," transgressive child. The cute child represents parental retreat into nostalgia by evoking a sense of "wondrous innocence" – of delight – often through gifts. The cool child arose from early comic books, migrated to television shows in the 1960s and can be seen in the characters of videogames today. This child embodies the negation of the "cute" as it enacts unabashed consumer desire stripped of its sentimental pretensions: "Kids now had their own desires, and parents' only role was to be sure that they lit up when given a gift."[21] Cross believes that the last twenty years has seen a proliferation of children's fantasy through products directly aimed at children that has helped to release children's consumption from parental controls and oversight.

Cross and Jacobson cast their nets widely in an effort to capture and explain some of the broad sweep of the rising children's culture of consumption in the twentieth century by examining many industries and practices. In my own work, I investigate the development of a particular industry – children's clothing in the United States, 1917–1962 – and the ways in which the "child consumer," as a commercial-conceptual figure, arose and changed over time. Trade publications of the newly forming industry suggest that early departments for juvenile clothing in urban department stores were structured around the presumed perspective, motivations, and foibles of the mother consumer. Beginning in the late 1920s, the goods, merchandising, spatial layout, and philosophy guiding retail departments shifted to orient themselves increasingly around the presumed perspective of the "child."[22]

This fundamental change in outlook, enacted by commercial actors, drew upon their insights about changing relations between middle-class mothers and their children. The change in commercial perspective from mother to child indicates a broad transformation toward the imputation of "personhood" status to the child through consumer desire and participation. Newly minted "commercial personae,"[23] like the notion of the "toddler" in the 1930s, at once functioned as a merchandising category, an age and size range, and as new designation of the life course.[24] The confluence of market and social designations or categories arose not only from industry, but also from changes in educational practices, popular culture and new, middle-class attitudes toward parenting. Children thus cannot be conceptualized outside of the changing commercial-market context and children's involvements in consumer activities and contexts must be made part and parcel of childhood history and not a sideline or appendage to that history.

The history of child consumers takes the changing discourses and conceptualizations of children (and parents) as its central focus and problem. As noted previously, the impetus for this approach derives from the historically ancillary position of children in social relations generally and to the consumer-market economy in particular. Twentieth-century historians, however, tend to seek explanations regarding how children became legitimate consumers and childhood as a site for commercial exploitation and exploration. In *Babes in Tomorrowland*, Nicholas Sammond takes direct aim at the rhetorical–discursive construction of the "American Child." Examining the intertwined histories of Walt Disney, the man, Disney the corporation, and developmental psychologists' views of the "child" in the 1930–1960 era, Sammond argues that Disney and his productions entered into an existing "discursive matrix" that had constructed a universal, generic child. During a time of increasing public concerns about the effects of "bad media" (i.e. movies) on the (generic) child, Disney entered the scene with the idea that "good" media could produce "good" children. For Sammond, Walt Disney branded himself as the embodiment of the corporation's benevolent intentions, which then carried this message into theme parks, television, and through several generations.[25]

Concluding discussion

The erratic historiography of children as consumers speaks both to the marginality of the subject and to the quality and types of sources. The difficulty with plotting something that resembles a coherent historical narrative of children as consumers arises from the conceptual and historical ambiguity of the subject itself – that is, the social definition and status of a "child" and, further, of a "child consumer" in relation to understandings of economic action. Without many resources of their own, children have had little ability to act as the independent economic actors that animate economists' formulations. Children, rather, cannot be disentangled from relations of economic dependency with parents, particularly mothers, even as the precise meaning and nature of this dependency clearly varies according to historical and social circumstance.

Hence, the ability to delineate what constitutes consumption *by* children as opposed to consumption *for* children in any given context or period remains elusive. Few scholars discussed here have ventured such an attempt. Most have put their efforts into illuminating and describing the ways in which "consumption" or "capitalism" have become insinuated in definitions of childhood over an uneven historical and social landscape. Attention thereby has been trained on investigating how the notion of the "child," as a conceptual figure, has become variously implicated in consumer-market arrangements as a symbol of a commercializing domestic sphere, as the focus for advertising and marketing efforts, and as the object of, and for, monetary and emotional parental expenditure. It is mainly in this latter sense that children's dependency with adults, particularly parents, comes into relief and has the potential to help redefine the economic, consumer activity of historical children as relational, rather than only individual.

It is interesting to note that those who attempted to address the child's active participation in the world of consumption write on nineteenth-century childhoods, while historians of twentieth-century children's consumption tend to concentrate on commercial enterprises and commercial discourses about children and childhood. I suspect this division has taken place in part due to the dominance of commercial enterprise in the 1900s, both economically and in the moral imagination, particularly since the 1990s when these histories were written. At that time, the problem of the "child consumer" gained newfound attention as both a social problem in public culture and media *and* as legitimate market actors in ways unconsidered in previous times, no doubt prompting efforts to account for present-day concerns with historical context and explanation. Hence, much of the history of children's consumption, it seems, garners its impetus from recent, contemporary attention paid to children and their increasing entanglements in commercial life as consumers.

Scholars generally concur in a few areas, including key turning points in this history. For the nineteenth century, it is the 1870s, after the American Civil War, when both commercial and social attentions turn toward children and their goods. The other turning point is in the 1930s when, in multiple industries, the market actors such as retailers and manufacturers begin recognizing and accounting for the child's perspective and addressing the child as a consumer. However, besides these general conclusions and apart from the broad sweep of observations that confirm an ever-increasing market for children's goods since the eighteenth century, little can be said more generally about the material.

This state of affairs poses a number of opportunities. For one, historians of childhood would do well to attend to the consumer-popular culture aspects of the childhoods they examine on par with other areas of concern. How different children occupying different childhoods, with regard to race, ethnicity, social class, and geography, experienced or were implicated in commercial life stands as glaring exclusions of history that must be rectified. The point here is not about forcing a false or unrepresentative sense of the place and importance of consumption in and to all childhoods, but to make this realm of life activity a necessary component of analysis and scholarship. As opposed to being relegated as ephemeral or merely illustrative, conceiving of consumer culture and consumer life as integral to childhoods contributes to the aim of representing experience in context. So too, all histories are guilty of looking "where the light is," that is to say that they focus mainly on the experiences and lives of the middle class and exclusively those of the dominant, white racial majority. It will take some effort and ingenuity to break through the epistemological, conceptual, and practical barriers that have made the history of children as consumers an interesting, but exceedingly limited, stream of the history of childhood.

Notes

1 Karen Sánchez-Eppler, *Dependent States* (Chicago, IL: University of Chicago Press, 2005), 125.
2 See Jackson Lears, *Fable of Abundance: A Cultural History of Advertising in America* (New York, NY: Basic Books, 1994); Roland Marchand, *Advertising the American Dream: 1920–1940* (Berkeley, CA: University of California Press, 1985); Rosalind Williams, *Dream Worlds, Mass Consumption in Late Nineteenth-Century France* (Berkeley, CA: University of California Press, 1982); Steven Mintz, *Huck's Raft: A History of American Childhood* (Cambridge, MA: Harvard University Press, 2004); Hugh Cunningham, *Children and Childhood in Western Society Since 1500* (Harlow, UK: Pearson Longman, 2002).
3 Doris Langley Moore, *The Child in Fashion* (London, UK: Batsford, 1953), 18.
4 Neil McKendrick, John Brewer, and J.H. Plumb, *The Birth of a Consumer Society* (Bloomington, IN: Indiana University Press, 1982), 69.
5 Ibid, 71, 71–80.
6 Ibid, 90, 91–93.
7 Mary Lynn Stevens Heininger, "Children, Childhood, and Change in America 1820–1920" in *A Century of Childhood, 1820–1920*, ed. Mary L.S. Heininger (Rochester, NY: Margaret Woodbury Strong Museum, 1984), 14, 15, 23, 19.
8 Dennis Denisoff, *The Nineteenth-Century Child and Consumer Culture* (Aldershot, UK: Ashgate, 2008), 1.
9 Lorraine Janzen Kooistra, "Home Thoughts and Home Scenes: Packaging Middle-Class Childhood for Christmas Consumption," in *The Nineteenth Century Child and Consumer Culture*, ed. Dennis Denisoff (Aldershot, UK: Ashgate, 2008), 157.
10 Teresa Michals, "Playthings: Toys and Theater: Experiments Before Breakfast and Toys, Education and Middle Class Childhood," in *The Nineteenth Century Child and Consumer Culture*, ed. Dennis Denisoff (Aldershot, UK: Ashgate, 2008), 33.
11 Liz Farr, "Paper Dreams and Romantic Projections: The Nineteenth-Century Toy Theater, Boyhood and Aesthetic Play," in *The Nineteenth Century Child and Consumer Culture*, ed. Dennis Denisoff (Aldershot, UK: Ashgate, 2008), 53.
12 Gary Cross, *Kids' Stuff* (Cambridge, MA: Harvard University Press, 1998), 21, 23, 25–26.

13 Ellen Gruber Garvey, *The Adman in the Parlor: Magazines and the Gendering of Consumer Culture, 1880s to 1910s* (Oxford, UK: Oxford University Press, 1996), 51–67.

14 Formanek-Brunell, Miriam, *Made to Play House: Dolls and the Commercialization of American Girlhood, 1830–1930* (Baltimore, MD: Johns Hopkins University Press, 1993), 23–29, 163–165.

15 David Nasaw, "Children and Commercial Culture," in *Small Worlds: Children and Adolescents in America, 1850–1950*, ed. Elliot West, and Paula Petrik, (Lawrence, KS: University of Kansas Press, 1992), 17.

16 Kathy Peiss, *Cheap Amusements* (Philadelphia, PA: Temple University Press, 1986).

17 Lisa Jacobson, *Raising Consumers* (New York, NY: Columbia University Press, 2004), 1, 3.

18 Ibid, 16–54, 56–92.

19 Ibid, 96, 160–182.

20 Cross, *Kids' Stuff*, 82–146.

21 Gary Cross, *The Cute and the Cool* (Cambridge, MA: Harvard University Press, 2004), 151.

22 Daniel Thomas Cook, *The Commodification of Childhood: The Children's Clothing Industry and the Rise of the Child Consumer* (Durham, NC: Duke University Press, 2004), 17–21.

23 Ibid, 66–95.

24 Ibid, 85–94.

25 Nicholas Sammond, *Babes in Tomorrowland: Walt Disney and the Making of the American Child, 1930–1960* (Durham, NC: Duke University Press, 2005). See, for instance, David Buckingham, *The Material Child* (London, UK: Polity, 2011); Daniel Thomas Cook, "The Missing Child in Consumption Theory," *Journal of Consumer Culture* 8(2) (2008): 219–243.

Suggestions for further reading

Calvert, Karin. *Children in the House: The Material Culture of Early Childhood, 1600–1900.* Boston, MA: Northeastern University Press, 1992. A material culture analysis mainly of clothing, furniture, and toys for children over a four-century period, covering North American and European contexts, that addresses how these materials reflected changing notions of childhood.

Denisoff, Dennis, ed. *The Nineteenth-Century Child and Consumer Culture.* Hampshire, UK: Ashgate, 2008. With a focus on the British experience in the nineteenth century, the themes of play, nationhood, desire, and domesticity are explored in various chapters by way of literary and historical analysis.

Jacobson, Lisa, ed. *Children and Consumer Culture in American Society: A Historical Handbook and Guide.* Westport, CT: Praeger, 2008. In essays, bibliographies, and primary resources, this handbook serves as a guide to studying the history of the consumer lives and contexts of US children.

Kline, Stephen. *Out of the Garden: Toys and Children's Television in the Age of TV Marketing.* London, UK: Verso, 1993. At once in-depth and far-ranging, Kline examines the interplay between children's literary and popular culture with the rise of consumer culture and television, examining in particular adverting and the rise of character toys.

Korsvold, Tora. "Proper Toys for Proper Children: A Case Study of the Norwegian Company A/S Riktige Leker (Proper Toys)." In *Childhood and Consumer Culture*, edited by David Buckingham, and Vebjørg Tingstad, 31–45. Houndsmills, UK: Palgrave, 2010. An examination of the changing notions of and tensions between "proper" versus "improper" toys of a Norwegian toy company, Riktige Leker, in response to market forces and changing definitions of children and of child–adult relations in Norway.

Leach, William. "Child-World in the Promised Land." In *The Mythmaking Frame of Mind*, edited by James Gilbert, Amy Gilman, Donald M. Scott, and Joan M. Scott, 209–38. Belmont, CA: Wadsworth, 1993. A discussion of how various "institutional collaborators," such as retailers, social workers, and politicians, together helped build a child-world of goods and spaces in urban department stores, mainly New York, during the Progressive Era.

Nasaw, David. *Children of the City*. New York, NY: Oxford University Press, 1985. A significant historical account of city life, seen often from the perspective and practices of children at the turn of the twentieth century, with particular attention paid to children as workers and consumers, and to struggles with parents over money.

Seiter, Ellen. *Sold Separately: Parents and Children in Consumer Culture*. New Brunswick, Canada: Rutgers University Press, 1993. Seiter combines historical analysis of advice to US mothers and of toy advertising to parents and children in the twentieth century to make a case for incorporating children's understandings of marketing and products in the study of the commercial lives of children and parents.

Smith, Jacob. "Books that Sing: The Marketing of Children's Phonographic Records, 1890–1930." In *Childhood and Consumer Culture*, edited by David Buckingham, and Vebjørg Tingstad, 46–60. Houndsmills, UK: Palgrave, 2010. An historical case study of the ways in which the Victor phonograph record company (United States) sought to create and engage a child audience and market for specifically "children's" records with entertainment appeals to children and educational appeals to parents.

Stonely, Peter. *Consumerism and American Girls' Literature, 1860–1940*, Cambridge, UK: Cambridge University Press, 2003. An examination of how women fiction writers deployed the figure of the girl in contexts of consumption as potential ways of realizing certain forms of social power and of addressing various cultural tensions thereby addressed.

16

PICTURING CHILDHOOD IN THE MODERN WEST

Anne Higonnet

Pictures imagine the Child. At every stage in its modern history, visual representations have made childhood look natural. From the eighteenth century onward, each successively dominant image technique has persuaded us in its particular formal way. Oil portrait painting, mass-reproduced prints, analogue photography, digital photography, and now ultrasound medical imaging have each produced a vision of what it means to start human life.

The Child with a capital C is an idea, embodied for us by art, by the "image" part of the word imagination. In 2012, a political, legal, and ethical debate storms around the latest of those image ideas. Yet the pictures at the heart of the debate have scarcely been examined, let alone considered as representations of the Child. So it has been during the entire modern history of childhood. What we take for granted in the present allows us to understand how much we took for granted in the past. Today's blindness reveals yesterday's.

Will pictures decide when life begins? Campaigns to mandate ultrasounds before abortions have been waged throughout the United States, since about 2005. Abortion opponents believe women who are forced to see an ultrasound of their fetus will recognize its right to life. The picture is supposed to prove the existence of a person. No other sort of evidence seems equally capable of producing the same effect, and not just on pregnant women. The national debate around ultrasounds may be more about reaching a general public than about preventing abortions. The larger purpose of demanding mandatory ultrasounds is to redefine when life begins, or, in other words, to redefine the fetus as a Child.

And yet, in simple but powerful ways, the fetal images in question artificially construct their subject. In ways that echo the persuasive powers of all images of children, ultrasound pictures rely on both representational choices, and on social context.

Fetal ultrasounds eliminate the body of the pregnant woman. The space around the fetus is represented by a flat black fan shape, which bears no resemblance to a uterus. The penetration of the pregnant body by ultrasound machinery leaves no trace in the picture, whether it happened through the wall of the abdomen or (controversially) along the passage of the vagina. Fetal imagery does not show the complete biological dependence of the fetus on the maternal placenta, let alone the nourishment of the placenta by the rest of the mother's body, which itself depends on the mother's access to food, water, and shelter. Mandatory ultrasound laws, furthermore, require doctors to describe the physical features of the fetus, not of anything else.

The frame of the ultrasound picture acts as a boundary between the fetus and the pregnant body. As if by magic, the ultrasound image makes maternal flesh vanish, and allows us to imagine we share the same space with the fetus. An internal enclosed space has been opened to our gaze, like a dollhouse with a fourth wall missing. The minuscule uterine interior loses any real dimensions as it passes into the scale-free world of the photographic, and so does the fetus. We are free to imagine the fetus on any scale, including the size of a baby who has been born. The fictions of the ultrasound picture make it possible to imagine the fetus as an independent individual we are encountering.

Yet fictions are ultimately signs, and so we should pause to consider what exactly those signs are. All we have at the center of controversial first-trimester ultrasounds are grainy black and white sketches of a primitive human form. Over the past twenty years, developments in ultrasound technology have made the signs of the fetus increasingly detailed. Nonetheless, the image of the fetus remains a ghostly shadow, one that has to be decoded and deciphered because it is so abstract. Even highly trained doctors can have trouble interpreting the visual information of first-trimester ultrasounds.

However difficult to decipher, fetal ultrasounds have become pictures people want to see. Behind mandatory ultrasound law lies a whole new visual culture of childhood. In the last two decades, we have initiated social rituals around ultrasound imagery, which extend a baby's social life back months before its birth. New ceremonies have come into being, such as "gender-discovery parties," at which friends gather around a pregnant woman to celebrate good ultrasound surprises. We send copies of ultrasound pictures to friends and relatives, for instance. We frame prints of ultrasound images and display them in our homes. In the words of Idaho abortion opponent Brandi Swindell: "Who doesn't love an ultrasound image of a baby?"[1] We place prints of ultrasound images in baby albums to establish continuity between pregnancy, birth, and childhood. Photo albums create a visual narrative arc for a baby's life. That arc now begins with an ultrasound.

An initial desire to obtain medical and genetic information about a fetus has been overtaken by a much more general desire to start having pictures of children long before they are born. In our rush to see a Child as soon as we can, we assume we should avail ourselves of whatever is technologically possible. Our logic has hurtled us toward unintended political consequences. We are layering onto the original medical purposes of fetal ultrasounds our social interpretation of its representational signs. Once we have done that, we become able to close the gap between two fictions: between the fiction of the ultrasound picture and the fiction of ideal childhood.

When we look at fetal ultrasound pictures, we project cherished ideals onto them. Whatever an ultrasound may lack is easily supplied. For three centuries, our visual imaginations have been furnished with great images of Romantic Childhood.

The origins and chronology of a modern idea of childhood has been hotly debated. Did our modern ideas about childhood take shape in the seventeenth century or in the eighteenth? Was childhood at first a peculiarly western concept, or an even more peculiarly Anglo–Saxon one? Did it depend on a demographic revolution that allowed a majority of children to survive infancy for the first time in history, or was it a cultural construct? What is the relationship of visual representation to the realities of children's lives? Though the answers to these big questions, which obviously are highly relevant to pictures of children, may never be definitively resolved, the pictures themselves do have a reasonably clear, if maybe narrowly specific, history of their own.

Pictures of a childhood, categorically different than adulthood, first appeared in significant numbers in mid-eighteenth-century British portraits. In the domain of the visual, at least, evidence points to an eighteenth-century Anglo-Saxon invention of childhood which required exceptionally gifted artists to create new signs of the Child. British painters like Joshua Reynolds, Thomas Gainsborough, and Thomas Lawrence introduced the vision of a disembodied childhood, a cute childhood, a miniaturized childhood. In their paintings, children appeared almost as human parts of nature. Posed in compositional harmony with landscapes and harmless animals, with wide sparkling eyes and limpidly calm faces, they were painted as emblems of innocence. Indeed, Reynolds called one of his child portraits *The Age of Innocence*. Several of these British paintings, such as Gainsborough's *Blue Boy* (bright fresh blue) and Raeburn's *Boy with a Rabbit* (an archetypal pet) became icons of childhood. Mass reproduced throughout the nineteenth and early twentieth centuries, they hung on the walls of countless homes throughout the western world, and shaped ideas of childhood for generations.

By the end of the eighteenth century, the ideal of the innocent and cute child had acquired its negative reverse image: the unjustly exploited child, whose misery is measured by its distance from innocence. And again, Britain seems to have been in the lead. Artists like William Blake, especially in his *Songs of Innocence and Experience*, showed how the ideal of perfect childhood innocence required two sides to convince. The plight of a young chimney sweep, for instance, could only be compellingly condemned if the brutally long hours he worked in filthy conditions were implicitly contrasted with the lyrical vision of the new Romantic Child. These sorts of pictures reminded their audiences, as they should remind us, that the ideal of a protected and free childhood was, in practice, granted only to a tiny, affluent, white, and western fraction of all children. And while new images of childhood softened earlier distinctions between girls and boys, they maintained gender differences. Boys, especially at play, were represented learning to control the world around them, while girls were represented more passively, as the objects of admiring adult gazes.

Also by the end of the eighteenth century, a few artists had begun to make images predicated on the Romantic ideal of childhood, which nonetheless also challenged its optimism. Francisco de Goya in Spain, Ann-Louis Girodet de Roussy-Trioson and Théodore Géricault in France, and Philipp Otto Runge in Germany, all made troubling portraits of children. In these images, resistance to discipline, malicious overtones, cruelty to pets, or simply a forceful physical ugliness, hinted at a darker side of the Romantic Child. The boy in a Girodet portrait of his guardian's son Trioson, for example, turns away from his lessons toward a glowing light, while scrawled graffiti mar his notebooks, and broken violin strings coil. A dreamy boy in Goya's portrait of Manuel Osorio holds a bird on a ribbon leash, oblivious to the leering cats emerging from the shadows behind them. At their distance from the British center of Romantic imagery, these perturbing sorts of images may have been echoing older, Christian, ideas of children born into sin, but they nonetheless revealed tension inherent in new ideas.

Paradigms of childhood invented in the medium of painting sank deep into popular consciousness thanks to mass-reproduction. The images of iconic paintings became

Figure 16.1 "The Age of Innocence" by Sir Joshua Reynolds.

widely available through engravings and lithographs; increasingly mechanical and cheap image technologies exponentially increased the types and number of prints; illustrations of children's literature and advertisements provided outlets for yet more pictures of children, which appealed to mass audiences for books, magazines, and consumer goods.

Some illustrators added their own original interpretations of childhood, despite being deeply influenced by paintings, and obliged to visualize texts written by others, or to promote commercial products. Illustration was not constrained by the formality, the expense, or the realism of painting. Some children's literature texts had already opened up fantasy worlds when illustrators were assigned to them. Illustration was often, therefore, during the nineteenth and early twentieth centuries, the medium in which the imagination of the child was visually explored. Subordinate though they were to Lewis Carroll's profoundly witty texts, illustrations of *Alice's Adventures in Wonderland* and *Through the Looking Glass*, to cite the most important example, contributed memorably to the impact of those stories. From John Tenniel onward,

Figure 16.2 Alice Grows Too Tall for the Room by John Tenniel.

Figure 16.3 Alice in Wonderland 1951 Walt Disney cartoon.

illustrators and their cartoon-drawing descendants, including Arthur Rackham and Walt Disney, invented signs, like a particular shade and style of bright blue dress accompanied by white stockings and black strap shoes, which allowed audiences to access Carroll's scenes through visual cues. Many people now have never read Carroll's books, yet feel they know the stories because they know its pictures.

At the turn of the nineteenth to twentieth centuries, a dynamic generation of American illustrators – including N.C. Wyeth, Jessie Wilcox Smith, and Maud Humphrey – consolidated ideals of scrubbed boyish adventure, demure girlish virtue, and plump rosy infancy. Women entering the field of illustration were strongly encouraged to specialize in the subject of childhood, on the grounds that women naturally understood children. Their scrubbed and rosy children confirmed the health and happiness of their society. Their heir was Norman Rockwell, the perennially popular creator of *Saturday Evening Post* covers. Rockwell's children embodied the United States' favorite image of its children: free, folksy, generous, loyal, and innocuously mischievous.

It was in the medium of photography, however, that Romantic childhood found its fullest expression. By its very definition, "art" represented reality. It was commonly accepted that painting and illustration, being manifestly artistic media, interpreted their subjects. However persuasive their images of childhood, consequently, paintings and illustrations could not pretend to simply capture real childhood. Romantic Childhood needed a medium whose claims to natural innocence and spontaneity were as credible as its own. That medium was photography.

For decades, the seemingly transparent realism of photography prevented it from being considered an art at all. Many applications of photography consciously pursued absolute neutrality for the purposes of scientific documentation. Add to those qualifications instantaneity. Because cameras recorded a moment – ever more rapid as camera equipment was developed – photography seemed exactly the right medium to seize a childhood whose poignancy had been equated with its fleeting evanescence. The identification of childhood with photography became a self-fulfilling prophecy. Because photographers felt able to express childhood, they did.

Over time, the hold of photography over ideas about childhood only increased. Now we can barely distinguish between the medium of photography and the message of childhood. Do we look at children, or at photographs of children? Countless snapshots stream through our daily lives. Many, if not most, of them are produced by private individuals for personal consumption. Their number cannot be accurately calculated. We can be sure it runs annually somewhere into the billions.

Childhood is not the principal subject of photography intended to be perceived as art. It is, however, the favorite subject of commercial and domestic photography. Whether destined for framing at home, posting on Internet social sites like Facebook or YouTube, for casual circulation on cellphones, for advertisements, or charity appeals, photographs of children are everywhere. A charity brochure exclaims: "Look into her eyes," to trigger the effect of its photograph. A health magazine advocates prenatal care with a cover shot of a mother gazing at her infant. Our culture demands our attention to its childhood ideal.

Photographic images of children have saturated our consciousness. Do we remember our childhoods, or photographs of our childhood? Do we remember our children's earliest days, or photographs of them? We rely on photographs of childhood to trigger emotions of all sorts, to make sense of history, to denounce injustice, to propose futures. We look nostalgically at photographs of children, remembering through each child a collective childhood, a vision of hope and boundless possibility. Newspaper stories about adult illness, for instance, begin beneath photographs that contrast the sick adult with a healthy child, heightening the pathos of suffering by its difference from the pristine. Analyses of communities in crisis dramatize the severity of catastrophe with a photograph of adults gathered around the burial of a tiny body, or clutching a wasted child.

The image of the Romantic Child naturalizes and vindicates adult values by pretending to spring unbidden from innocence. Childhood is represented by adults who have the experience and finances to master image techniques and distribute media. Photographs that purport to see the world through a child's eyes are usually the most adult of all. Children's fashion editorials, for example, promote outfits designed for grown-up consumers. Electronic invitation and holiday card services make it easier than ever to put children's faces on messages whose real purpose is to consolidate adult social networks. All too often, the most common photographs of children mask adult agendas by avoiding the signs of everyday contemporary life. Ballet tutus, fairy gear, nostalgic out-of-date clothing styles, animal, insect or plant costumes allow adults to escape into dream worlds.

Despite the enduring appeal of idealizing photographs, we learn more about the history of childhood from difficult ones. Photographs that acknowledge the ideal of Romantic innocence, and also analyse its ambiguities, help us to understand its failures as well as its successes. Most, though not all, of those complexly instructive images were intended to be seen as art. For obvious reasons, commercial images could not risk alienating mass audiences, whereas artistic Modernism encouraged skeptical investigation into middle-class values. The label "art" is no guarantee of intellectual quality, let alone truth. Yet "art" is a rubric which, among other functions, has rallied photographers who investigate their subjects rather than accept them, and who are not afraid to upset their audience's expectations.

By the middle of the nineteenth century, within two decades of its official announcement, great photographs had been devoted to the subject of childhood. Some of the first were by none other than Lewis Carroll, who began his photographic career well before he wrote his famous *Alice* books. (Remarkably, both his artistic careers remained amateur. Professionally, under his real name, Charles Dodgson, he taught mathematics at Oxford.) Carroll used a glass plate negative, wet collodion technique, which enabled a high degree of precise detail and optical differentiation among represented surfaces. By pushing at the technical potential of his medium, Carroll created optically dense, busy zones of clothing and setting that retained a viewer's gaze and, by contrast, heightened the effect of luminous child skin and shining eyes. He also had a gift for recognizing photogenic children, including, notably, Alice Liddell, the girl who would later become the Alice who went down the rabbit hole into *Wonderland* as well as *Through the Looking-Glass*. Carroll's children are forever just beyond our reach. He consistently placed his camera at exactly the right distance to make children look tantalizingly close and yet apart, vividly present and yet in a world of their own. The small format of his prints compounded the effect of his compositions and framing. Carroll's image of childhood was on the other side of a mirror, seen through photography's looking-glass magic.

Figure 16.4 "Effie Millais" by Charles Dodgson.

By insisting that children are categorically different than adults, we create a sharp boundary around childhood. No one, in reality, goes from being a child to being an adult all of a sudden. There is no one irreversible instant of transformation. But by photographing young people as if there were such an instant, we create the Child. Photographs of children became a self-fulfilling prophecy. The adorable child enshrined in staged photographs became a cultural ideal to which children conformed, or were made to conform. Individuals internalized the prescriptions of photographs. Life imitated art.

Except when it didn't. Or except when art imitated the vagaries, ambiguities, and troubles of life. Carroll's photographs show us both the appeal of the perfectly innocent Child, and its dangers. The adorable Child was also a desirable Child, and desire

Figure 16.5 "Tenement Child Handicapped in Every Way" by Lewis W. Hine.

moves in uncontrollable ways. Consciously, Carroll adamantly believed in the angelic purity of children. Surviving records indicate his behavior toward his models, who he called his "child-friends," was irreproachable. His photographs, however, have seemed to many twentieth-century viewers to betray a sexually tainted attraction to children. For some interpreters, the issues of Carroll's photographs are not his alone, but rather symptoms of systemic tensions in Victorian culture.

Against the cultural grain, several great photographers after Carroll consciously called into question the Romantic ideal. Among them were social reformers who campaigned for the extension of Romantic childhood to all children, no matter what their social position. Other dissenters were individualists who delighted in showing exceptions to stereotypes. Most unusually, a few photographers flatly denied the Romantic Child, and persistently represented alternative visions of childhood.

Artists at the turn of the twentieth century, who worked in the mode of investigative journalism, notably Jacob Riis, indicted child poverty. His photographs revealed the squalid conditions in which many poor children lived, especially immigrant children, packed into filthy tenements and loitering in grimy back-alleys. When it suited his purposes, he was not above enlisting stereotypes of childhood, such as the Madonna and Child image, to make his points. Photographers campaigned against child labor, chief among them Lewis Hine. His photographs of child-laborers argued against their exploitation by revealing the dangerous and dehumanizing conditions in which they worked, and also by visualizing their dignity, courage, humor, or even defiance. Like many of the children in later depression-era Farm Security Administration (FSA) photographs by artists, among them Dorothea Lange, Hine's children were photographed to look like they deserved help.

Similarly, photographers who work the edge between art and investigative journalism have encapsulated the injustices of war by enlisting our visual ideals of childhood innocence. Just to cite one exceptionally influential example, Nick Ut, in his 1972 photograph *Trang Bang,* created an image in which screaming children seem to rush toward us. One naked girl reaches her arms out, as if imploring our aid. American soldiers march indifferently behind. For many people, Ut's image summarized the Vietnam War.

The line between artistic and documentary photography is not as sharp as it might seem. Many great documentary photographs are staged, not accidentally captured, which is precisely why their visual impact can be so powerful. Nonetheless, expectations of a rigid difference between documentary and artistic conventions have frequently sparked debates about the ethics of important photographs in the history of childhood. Dorothea Lange was reprimanded by the administration of the WPA for altering the negative of her iconic image of Depression maternity, *Migrant Mother,* because it impugned the truth of the photograph; Ut has been criticized for staying behind the camera instead of helping the suffering children in *Trang Bang.*

Some photographers specialized in exploring children's psyches. They found much more there to express that anticipated mainstream culture. The scenes they photographed existed in the material world, but they evoked mysterious affinities, encounters, and communications. In the middle of the twentieth century, Helen Levitt's photographs paid tribute to children's mastery over the sign, respectfully finding in their games, graffiti, and costumes echoes of her own representational endeavor. She photographed children playing seriously, often with each other, engaged in their own learning, rather than performing cuteness for the camera. The children in her photographs are not sophisticated in adult ways, but they are extremely intelligent and organized. Ralph Eugene Meatyard also made powerful images of children wearing masks or costumes. Unlike Levitt's work, which tended to set children in gritty contemporary urban scenes, Meatyard found or staged children in haunting places which evoked the subconscious and associated children with the ruin and the grotesque. Emmet Gowin allowed the distortions of the photographic lens to express children's imaginations; one classic 1969 image, *Nancy, Danville, Virginia* shows a girl's arms impossibly elongated and twisted, holding an egg in each hand. In fact, the image was produced by the normal optical effect of foreshortening, yet the effect was magic. Diane Arbus chose child subjects who allowed her to explore the margins of society, and find there a humanity that contradicted the premise of margins. She was among the first to make sympathetic images of children with Down's syndrome, opening up possibilities for the recognition of all children with disabilities. Although Arbus's photographs did rely on the shock of seeing what was considered deformity, they also emphasized laughter, creativity, and affection.

Such photographs make it impossible to draw any clear boundary between childhood and adulthood. They allow us to glimpse the passionate angers, frustrations, cruelties, and terrors of childhood. Occasionally, and unconsciously, they have even called into question an absolute distinction between innocence and erotics. They dared to represent flawed, quirky, even damaged children, children toiling, children suffering in hypocritical social systems that sheltered some children in the name of innocence while exploiting others.

In a different category belongs the work of mother-artists. Was it a coincidence that among the first truly great women artists was a photographer who took childhood as one of her subjects, or not? Working in the same Victorian period as Carroll, Julia Margaret Cameron proved that there could be more than one way to interpret childhood at any given moment. Unlike Carroll, Cameron championed haptic immediacy, as opposed to his optical distance: her soft focus and her intimate framing in dramatic zones of light and dark, as well as her many prints which rendered her subjects' heads almost life-size, made her subjects feel sensually close to their viewers. Emotionally, she was among the first photographers to express the tender communion of maternal love. Of course the bond between very young children and their mothers had been perpetually fascinating to artists in many cultures. But until photography lowered the barriers for entry into art careers, women did not usually have the chance to represent that hallowed subject from their own point of view. Cameron, for instance, was able to begin her photographic career only after fulfilling her social obligations by raising a large family; photography did not require training in exclusively male academies, nor gigantic studio space or uninterrupted time.

Photography unleashed the passions of maternity into the realm of art. Clementina, Viscountess Hawarden, who worked, like Carroll, in an amateur mode, left images of the sisterly love between her daughters so unconventional that they have often been mistaken for images of lesbian love. In a later generation, Gertrude Kasebier translated maternal love into the soft-focus idiom of Pictorialist photography. From Cameron, through Gertrude Kasebier, and onward, the history of photography includes images whose deep psychic investments masqueraded as dutiful femininity.

The single most important turning point in the history of photographs of children occurred at the convergence of the contrary and the maternal. After Sally Mann published a book of photographs titled *Immediate Family* in 1992, photographs of children would never be the same again. The book opened by invoking the history of photographs of childhood with a 1984 portrait of one of her three children, titled *Damaged Child*, named after a canonical 1936 photograph by Dorothea Lange. By referring to the history of photography, Mann positioned herself within it, aligned herself with the troubling lineage to which Lange belonged, and challenged the idealizing history of most photographs of children. Drawing attention to the limpid clarity of one child's eye with the swollen closure of the other, Mann announced she was going to both celebrate the beauty of children, and damage our vision of childhood.

In photograph after photograph, *Immediate Family* showed Mann's three gorgeous children at feral play in rural surroundings. Many people thought they were shocked by the sexual content of the photographs. More deeply shocking was their exposure of countless stereotypical images – clichés – of childhood. Inspired by Carroll, Cameron, Arbus, and Gowin, not to mention Lange, Mann immolated the cute. She created smoldering contrasts between the physical beauty of the children she photographed and the artificial signs by which we identify both childhood and adulthood. Even when the bodies of the children she pictured seemed to be completely "natural," or be in settings apart from civilization, Mann's scenes and their titles pivoted around ritual moments or sayings associated with childhood. Visually, she cited the stereotypical "Kodak Moments" promoted in commercial photography and consecrated in family photograph albums, but infused their trite platitudes with carnal force. In a Mann photograph, a child does not cuddle a fuzzy pet, but instead grips a flayed rodent by the neck. In a Mann photograph, a little girl in a ballet tutu doesn't just curtsy coyly, she curtsies coyly next to the cut throat of a hunted deer. In a Mann photograph, a child doesn't sniff a lovely bouquet, she wears drooping blooms slung on her chest. The photographs were controversial, but scandal only increased their impact.

Mann's work marks a crucial edge. It was at once visceral and artful, immediate and alienating. The Child she represented still inhabited the natural *Age of Innocence* invented by eighteenth-century British portrait painters, but her revelation of its dark side had ruined its credibility. Her lushly printed analogue photographs still produced a compelling reality effect, but their iconography was so socially loaded it could only have been contrived. A revolution in childhood and photography was about to occur. It was the last great moment of analogue photography, and the last great moment, as it were, of analogue Childhood.

Digital Childhood made pictures self-conscious. When the problems of Romantic Childhood had become fully apparent, both popular and artistic pictures of children became acutely aware of themselves and their history. In part this shift can be attributed to the sheer accumulation of visual imagery made possible by digital storage along with a seemingly limitless circulation of imagery on the Internet, coupled with the unprecedented ease with which pictures could be composed, altered, or re-mixed. Whether new image technology is a cause or an effect, however, can be debated. Technology certainly creates conditions of conceptual possibility. Yet it is also likely that changing perceptions of identity summoned digital technology to express new values, positive or negative.

Anxiety about the exploitation of children by mass media began to gain momentum in the late 1970s. What might have been seen earlier as the pure appeal of children's bodies began to be perceived as insidious sexualization. Scandals erupted over advertisement campaigns, over clothing styles, even over Victorian paintings. At their most acute, concerns about the commercial exploitation of children by photographs took the form of unprecedented legal action.

During the 1980s and 1990s, while other forms of government censorship were on the decline, the first child pornography laws were passed. In 1986, the United States Attorney General's Commission on Pornography began to define photographs of children by different standards than texts, or other images of children, or photographs of adults. Among cases or laws in the United States, the 1989 *Massachusetts v. Oakes*, the 1991–1994 *Knox v. the United States*, and the 1996 Child Pornography Prevention Act shifted the blame for child abuse from human perpetrators to photographs. Likewise in Britain, where the 1978 Protection of Children Act, the 1994 Criminal Justice and Public Order Act, c 33 & 84, and the 2000 Criminal Justice and Court Service Act, c.41 & 43 followed the same trend toward singling out the medium of photography. All of this legislation was predicated on the realism of photography. Lawmakers believed photographs were so transparent that they could see right through them to actual crimes against real children. Politicians, for whom the issue of child abuse could reliably rally support from left and right, fanned the flames of scandal and demanded child pornography legislation, regardless of its internal logic or the precedents it set.

Digital image technology has made us aware that all photographs can be fabricated. Any computer user can combine, recolor, retouch, erase parts of, or add elements to photographs. No one even needs to make the photographs they work with. Photographs can just be downloaded from anywhere on the Internet. To some extent, recognition of this technological revolution has prompted the revocation or limitation of child pornography law. Conservative courts have been especially unwilling to impose government restraints on the commercial Internet. In 2002, *Ashcroft v. the Free Speech Coalition* overturned the 1996 Child Pornography Prevention Act. The United States Supreme Court ruled that digitally artificial images could not be prosecuted as pornography because they did not document any actual child abuse. The legislative branch of the government fought back with the Protect Act of 2003. In another round of struggle between branches of government, a US federal court ruled in 2008 that the Child Online Protection Act violated the freedom of speech rights, and the Supreme Court refused in 2009 to hear an appeal on the ban.

Meanwhile, judicial efforts to control pictures of children continued. By 1994, English law had invented what it called "pseudo-photographs." In Australia in 2008, in *McEwen v. Simmons & Anor*, a court in New South Wales ruled that altered cartoons of a Simpson cartoon character, which had been posted on the Internet, were illegally pornographic. Manifestly, a cartoon character is not a real person. The judge ruled, however, that if a picture was "about a person," it was a person. Whatever may have been its logical absurdity, the ruling paid backhanded tribute to the power of the visual.

In the fall of 2010, western definitions of pornography reached around the world. Western and Japanese artistic traditions have influenced each other vigorously since the 1860s. Japanese art has turned many western visual signs of childhood into an esthetic so pervasive it has a name: *kawai*. In the past, however, western and Japanese ideas about the signs of childhood were quite different. In Japanese *manga*, signs like big round starry eyes and school-girl plaid skirts were as often used in association with extreme violence and erotics as with innocence. Magazines of a type called Junior Idol are based on the sexual appeal of *kawai*. Colors and shapes, thought of as child-like in the West – bright pink and purple, fuzzy stuffed animals, short puffy skirts, round plastic toys, gingham checks, hearts etc. – constitute an entire esthetic in Japan which is practiced by women as much as by girls. By the 1980s, the phenomenon was widespread enough for the singer Kuniko Yamada to coin a word for women's performance of the kawai esthethic: *burikko* (鰤子). Yet in the fall of 2010, the Japanese Government proposed a ban on manga cartoons that featured underage girls in sexual acts.

Perhaps the most fundamental challenge to absolute visual boundaries between adult and child is the increasing production and use of photographs by children themselves. The prevalence of cameras built into cellphones, and the ease with which they can be altered and sent, thanks to innovative applications, has allowed children to make and distribute photographs more than ever before. Much to adults' chagrin, children make and send each other sexually explicit photographs of themselves (called sexting). By prevailing legal standards, adolescents who are not yet legally adults routinely invade each other's privacy by producing and receiving obscene photographs. How then are we to define what is "natural" or "unnatural," "private" or "public"? How will we differentiate what is exploitive from what is expressive?

Meanwhile, the same medium on which some people rely to enforce the ideals of the Romantic Child is also being used to create new ideals. Artistically ambitious photographers have turned the medium of photography against itself, or, at the very least, folded it in on itself. Since the 1990s, many photographers have sought to match the monumental scale, expressive color, narrative duration, and layered referencing of the Old Master and Modernist painting. The effect on images of the Child has been profound. The change is too deep to be merely a matter of technology. Much of the best new work on the subject of childhood is not technically digital, and yet displays an attitude to both its subject and to the photographic world that could be called digital.

In 1999, a New York gallery exhibition titled "Another Girl, Another Planet" marked a coming of age. Thirteen young photographers – including Justine Kurland, Katy Grannan, Malerie Marder, Jitka Hanzlova, and Dayanita Singh – some of them barely out of graduate school, achieved critical acclaim and financial success for photographs whose ambitious artifice was manifest: "It doesn't have to be real to be true."[2] Six of the photographers had studied under the same teacher, Gregory Crewdson, well-known for his staged narratives (and co-curator of the exhibition). The exhibition's success was all the more remarkable because it was concertedly and unrepentantly feminine and child-like: Another *Girl*. Twelve out of the thirteen exhibitors were female. By aggressively embracing the subjects of women and children, these young artists staked a claim to public significance for what had previously been marginal. By visually "covering" a song called "Another Girl, Another Planet," which had first been sung by *The Only Ones* in 1978, the exhibition implied a time span. Its artists had in fact been born around 1978, and so was the mood on which their work would eventually be based.

Since then, photographers have been dismantling the visual signs of the Romantic Child, and replacing them with a new vision of childhood. No single artist tackles every visual habit, though some artists deal with several. The most persuasive photographs, as always, work on the levels of both form and content, often pitting form against content. Though each artist may enlist a different formal aspect of the medium, or a different configuration of aspects, what they have in common is a use of the medium itself to make their arguments.

Take, to start, the basic issue of size. The sheer surface area of new photographs alters our perception of children. As *Another Girl, Another Planet* announced in 1991, photographic monumentality redefines the reality of childhood. When it comes to the subject of children, life-size or near-life-size scale and densely saturated color printing lend children a physical presence we are not accustomed to. When we actually stand in front of photographs in a gallery or museum (rather than looking at them in small reproductions) we occupy the same terrain as the children represented. By itself, this begins to counteract the old tendency to miniaturize children, which, though charming, tended to objectify children by reducing them to toys.

Miniaturization, can also, ironically, be counter-acted by the contraction of scale. Loretta Lux's photographs, for instance, are as small as work by artists like Anna Gaskell or Justine Kurland is large. At both extremes of size, the manipulation of the photograph to alter perception is manifest. Lux forces us optically to peer at little prints, at which point we can start to notice her Photoshop alterations. The heads of children, which are larger in proportion to their bodies than adult heads, are just one size too large. The clothing is just one style outdated. The colors are just one shade too pale, too eerie, and too coordinated. We thought Lux's children were cute, but as we linger, her distortions, with their almost mortuary overtones, disturb our first impressions. Lux pictures seem tiny and cute, at first. After a while, they look tiny and deadly.

Young documentary photographers have renewed the tradition of the investigative series. Importantly, photographers have begun to include children of all races and ethnicities on an equal basis in their work, even as they acknowledge differences. In a 2004–2009 series on school groups, for example, Julian Germain uses the seriality of photographs and their documentary aura to express a balance between individual and collective identities among children from around the world. Far from lapsing into sentimental stereotypes of a common humanity, let alone of a natural universal human origin, Germain taps into the grand painting tradition of the social group portrait to represent the civics of learning. Within Germain's photographs, each child is individuated by pose, placement, glance, and small variations in costume, yet each one clearly belongs to a schoolroom and to a geographic location, both of which Germain emphasizes with his titles. When Germain's photographs are seen together, each group has it own distinctive identity, yet each group has been represented as parts of a global community of learning. Attentively focused on the photographer who occupies the spatial position of the teacher, these are dynamic variations on the inert tradition of the "class picture." The children in Germain's photographs are caught in the process of education, and in that process they educate us.

Another tendency among younger photographers is the investigation of adolescence. Over the last fifteen years or so, a significantly large number of photographers have dedicated themselves to representing a porous zone of ambiguity and diffidence, experimentation and role-playing, rather than any edge or boundary. Some photographers, like Helen Meene, rely primarily on a discerning choice of subjects, pose, props, and costume, set off by calm, even light. Others rely on expressive depth of field, angle, viewpoint, foreshortening, light, shade, or color in their re-interpretations of adolescence. Their work refuses all sharp distinctions between Child and Adult. Are their subjects boys or men, girls or women? If we cannot be sure, then they have made their point. When the codes based on binary opposites fails us – Child means not Adult, innocence means not experience, boy means not girl – they lose their prescriptive authority. The best artists who summon those codes now do so in order for the codes to fail us.

Rineke Dijkstra has made a career out of extremely subtle alternatives to binary opposites. Like other photographers, Dijkstra relies on differences between what her photographs superficially offer, and what sustained attention delivers. She has produced extensive series of photographs about children, or adolescents who are legally children. The children seem, at first, to be posed in natural settings, notably beaches and parks. Her compositions seem, at first, to be simple, almost neutral: children standing in the middle ground of a space, at the center of a frame. Yet Dijkstra has an uncanny ability to select people, clothing, poses and settings that inflect nature with exquisitely delicate signs of culture. The bathing suit is neither timeless nor universal; the park is cultivated. The children veer ever so slightly away from conventional ideals of beauty, but never so much that we could dismiss them as freaks or inferiors. With uncanny consistency, their postures hover between the casual and the formal, the relaxed and the posed.

For some photographers, challenges to traditional boundaries between nature and culture have allowed challenges to gender roles. Alessandra Sanguinetti, for example, in her 1999–2002 *Adventures of Guille and Belinda and the Enigmatic Meaning of Their Dreams*, charted the play-acting of two Argentinian cousins, one noticeably plump and the other noticeably slender. Contrary to many expectations, Guille and Belinda staged an astonishing variety of personae and relationships for the camera, including a double Ophelia scene, a heterosexual wedding, and a movingly simple embrace in bathing suits. Catherine Opie is also among those for whom childhood offers the possibility to create finely textured zones of photographic sedition. Like her peers, she creates an unsuspected in-between realm, in which adult sexuality is fluidly acquired, rather than dogmatically imposed. We assume, when we first look at her child subjects, that we recognize whether they are girls or boys. But if we look long enough, which the commanding format and regal composition of Opie's photographs urge us to do, we begin to doubt what we assumed. With strategic subtlety, she has presented portraits that could, on further examination, be of either girls or boys. She enlists our belief in the veracity of photography to search for visible clues that could tip identification toward one side or the other, but leaves us uncertain. Opie's portraits demand that we come to conclusions only after considering evidence carefully.

What does innocence mean today? Photographers like Simen Johen associate childhood not so much with innocence, but with an uninhibited and fertile unconscious. Children, they suggest, are not blank slates on which adult experience leaves its traces. Instead, they stage scenes of self-invention, intimations of mysterious narratives or epic games, opaque hints at teeming psychic ferment. A bare-chested little boy, looming hugely in the image foreground hunches over a mound of dirt, poking it with a stick, intently concentrating on his task while unearthly insects come teeming out, crawling toward the boundary between the image's space and ours. In such images, photographic realism gives access to the vividly felt reality of children's inner lives. Today's best photographs of children ask adults to stop constructing a childhood that satisfies adult narcissism with fantasies of a pure and perfect origin. It asks us to accept murky, riven, coagulated miseries, doubts, and erotic turbulence, alongside crystalline, shining bliss, and open wonder. The silvered mirror of our youth, which photography now offers us, is no longer entirely bright, or empty.

Photography has matured. Its mirror is marked by age. All ambitious photographs now are self-conscious. They know their past. Today's photographs of childhood refer with wit and ease to a richly layered visual history. Artistic inspirations from classics like Carroll, Cameron, Hine, Lange, Meatyard, or Gowin mix with sly citations of popular sources like commercial advertisements, television programs, or rock songs. Enough time has passed for today's photographs to cite citations. Disney's images of *Alice* are as influential as Carroll's original books. Photography history icons are refracted through Mann's photographs from the 1990s.

To each age its beauty. The challenge for photography now, and for childhood, is to find its own, new, ideals. The first ages of modern childhood and photography could not be prolonged. In some ways, they had to be corrected. But could they be corrected, even contradicted, while we inherit from them what is marvelous and hopeful? The miracles of youth and light might still be visible.

Notes

1 www.msnnbc.msn.com/id/46820426.
2 "Hot Shots," *Harper's Bazaar*, February 2000.

Suggestions for further reading

Brown, Marilyn, ed. *Picturing Children; Constructions of Childhood Between Rousseau and Freud*. Farnham, UK: Ashgate, 2002. This academic collection of essays considers in fine detail many of the crucial ideological issues governing nineteenth-century pictures of children. Paintings, prints, and photographs are all considered, in the context of literature, psychoanalysis, and social history.

Family Pictures; Contemporary Photography and Video from the Collection of the Guggenheim Museum. New York, NY: Guggenheim Museum, 2005. *Family Pictures* provides a strong selection of photographs made in the very late twentieth century on the subject of childhood. It also includes a few important photographic predecessors from earlier years. The emphasis is on work that has questioned ideals of childhood, and complements the *Presumed Innocence* selection.

Higonnet, Anne. *Pictures of Innocence; the History and Crisis of Ideal Childhood*. London, UK: Thames & Hudson, 1998. A general history of the image of childhood from the eighteenth to the very late twentieth century. Paintings, prints, illustrations, and photographs are all considered, as well as legal issues.

Lafo, Rachel Rosenfield. *Presumed Innocence; Photographic Perspectives of Children*. Lincoln, MA: DeCordova Museum and Park, 2008. This exhibition catalogue presents a strong, balanced, and representative selection of photographs of children, taken throughout the twentieth century. It complements the selection in *Family Pictures*.

Mavor, Carol. *Pleasures Taken; Performances of Sexuality and Loss in Victorian Photographs*. Durham, NC: Duke University Press, 1995. A lushly written and deep investigation into many of the most powerful and troubling nineteenth-century photographs of children.

Nickel, Douglas. *Dreaming in Pictures; the Photography of Lewis Carroll*. New Haven, CT: San Francisco Museum of Modern Art and Yale University Press, 2002. An excellent choice among Carroll's historically important photographs, accompanied by both a sensitive essay and much useful information.

17

CHILDREN'S LITERATURE

Maria Nikolajeva

Literature written, published, and marketed for the benefit of the young audience has throughout centuries been employed as an instrument of power for socialization of a particular social group. Similarly to histories and literatures featuring disempowered groups, such as women, working classes, sexual minorities, ethnic minorities, and indigenous people of colonized territories, children's literature is produced by those in power and thus reflects the empowered view of the disempowered. However, unlike other disempowered groups that have recently resisted oppression through writing their own histories and literatures – feminist, queer, postcolonial – children still occupy an inferior socio-economic position, and children's literature is therefore written, marketed, and consumed within the unequal power hierarchies. The interrogation of this asymmetrical power structure can only come from the empowered, which arguably makes the dilemma of children's literature more complex than that of any other marginalized category. Every book addressing a young audience inevitably has its shadow text that reflects the beliefs and opinions of the adults behind it. In most children's books, these are overt, but even books that seemingly take the child's part cannot fully deny adult authority. Heteronormativity has been strongly interrogated in queer studies. Children's literature, on the other hand, with very few exceptions, inevitably creates and maintains aetonormativity, that is, adulthood as norm. This fact is the most important premise for any consideration of children's literature and its connection with childhood.

Origins and history

Oral and written storytelling began as a means to establish a set of behavior codes that regulated early societies, including the hierarchies of elders and young members. Adults' incentive to instruct and educate the young through stories is therefore natural. Today's evolutionary literary criticism claims that storytelling played a significant role in our ancestors' survival strategies. Whether we subscribe to this stance or not, storytelling is a powerful factor in ideology and education. Children's literature can potentially convey knowledge of the perceptible world, of societal norms and behavior, and of ethical values. In this regard, it is no different from mainstream literature. The difference lies in the cognitive level and limited life experience of children, which makes children's literature more educational, instructive, and intentional than the mainstream; however, another function of arts and literature, the aesthetic one, was until recently denied in children's literature. The educational project was considered more important than the aesthetic qualities. This is not unique for children's literature either because preference for ideology is also characteristic of religions and totalitarian regimes. Yet while religious and political dissenters use arts and literature to subvert oppression, children's socio-economic status allows them limited resistance toward imposed ideology. Nevertheless, the aesthetic aspect of children's literature, although emerging later than the educational, has been prominent and is manifested primarily in the urge to entertain. In this, children's literature had initially the same role as did Elizabethan drama or eighteenth-century chapbooks: as stories that appealed to "simple" tastes.

Yet another aspect of children's literature, that many children's writers have openly admitted, is nostalgia, the writers' indulgence in their embellished memories of childhood and the irretrievable loss of innocence. This feature, strongly criticized in the seminal study by Jacqueline Rose, *The Case of Peter Pan, or The Impossibility of Children's Fiction* (1984), has resulted in a number of works referred to as indisputable masterpieces, including *The Secret Garden* (1911) by Frances Hodgson Burnett, *Peter Pan* (1911) by J.M. Barrie, and *Winnie-the-Pooh* (1926) by A.A. Milne. Such texts arguably speak volumes about the adult authors' attitudes, but little about childhood as it was or is.

There is no consensus among scholars of children's literature as to when this phenomenon emerges because it depends heavily on the definition of childhood and its separateness from adulthood. The general understanding of children's literature is based on the constructivist rather than essentialist view of childhood. Contemporary studies in psychology and neuroscience have disputed the rigid constructivist views of childhood emphasised in the 1990s; yet the premises for the emergence and evolution of children's literature are determined by the status of childhood in any given society at any given time. Clay tablets, scrolls, codices, hornbooks, and eventually printed books were used as literacy tools; yet this does not justify describing any text that may have been read by a young person as a children's book. (It is also a matter of social definition how old such a young person should be to count as a child). As long as children participate in reading on equal terms with adults, we can hardly speak of children's literature.

Those scholars who find children's literature in Sumer in the third millennium BCE do not acknowledge that in order to identify a text as distinctly addressing a young audience, it has to be defined against something else. The Sumerian texts were doubtless used to spread literacy; yet there were no other texts to oppose them. Likewise, the texts used in teaching literacy and societal norms to a small proportion of young men in Ancient Egypt, Babylon, Greece and Rome, medieval Europe, or the Middle East, did not specifically address this category of readers, but were used because they were available; most had the status of sacred texts. The emergence of books specifically addressing young readers became possible after the invention of printing, when books became less expensive, thus encouraging literacy. However, even during the Renaissance and the Enlightenment, reading matter was perused by readers of all ages. Moreover, as books marketed for children finally became a lucrative business for printers, they were equally popular with adult readers. Children's literature is thus primarily the phenomenon of the modern and post-modern era. Some further conditions for the emergence of children's literature include consolidation of the middle class with economic potential for buying books and sufficient leisure for perusing them;

the general rise of literacy and the establishment of mandatory schooling; and the development of printing, which made books accessible for a wider range of readers. Yet the educational views were of primary importance.

An attempt to sketch the historical development of children's literature with conventional tools meets substantial difficulties. Histories of Western literature start in the Ancient World and go through overlapping epochs with their characteristic features, such as Middle Ages, Renaissance, Enlightenment, Romanticism, Naturalism, Modernism, and Postmodernism. Children's literature, with its considerably shorter history, has not gone through similar transformations and lacks clearly delineated historical periods, especially in an international perspective. Its history is instead related to pedagogical views and has oscillated between two extremes: education and pleasure. What we intuitively recognize as the best children's books try to reconcile these extremes. The tension between the incompatible desires to instruct and to entertain young readers results in a broad variety of genres and themes, and the range of styles from bland simplicity to elaborate complexity.

Another significant trait in the historical development of children's literature is its divergence from and convergence with the mainstream. Children's literature became a distinct category in Western culture by the beginning of the nineteenth century and was primarily fiction, at that time considered a low genre. Two separate trends in early children's literature were books of high literary quality by major, predominantly, male authors, and didactic books by third-rate, predominantly female writers (occasionally male writers hiding behind female pseudonyms). The male authors were often representatives of highly regarded parts of society, including academia, the church, the economy, and politics. Most of them wrote prose, poetry, and drama for the general audience and did not regard themselves as children's writers, even though this is how they are remembered by posterity. Few of these writers had any substantial knowledge of real children. Hans Christian Andersen, doubtless one of the epitomes of children's literature, considered himself a novelist and playwright, his fairy tales a mere trifle. In contrast, female writers frequently either wrote to support themselves and their families – children's literature being a profitable enterprise in great demand – or to express strong educational views, such as Maria Edgeworth. The integration of these trends led to the full-scale emergence of children's literature in the twentieth century, segregated from the mainstream, for better or worse.

In terms of its aesthetic origins, children's literature did not appear in a vacuum. It is hardly fruitful to point at the "very first ever" book for children in a given culture. *Orbis Sensualium Pictus* (1658), by Johannes Comenius, can be treated either as a children's book or a textbook. Written in Latin and German, it was widely used in the Western world, and is doubtless addressed to learners, as are the numerous exempla, "mirrors for princes" and other books of instruction. Today, non-fiction, such as encyclopedias, popular history and geography, biography, and hagiography, is typically included in accounts of children's literature, while primers and school books are not. *Orbis* is a prototype of a contemporary picture dictionary, in which illustration has an essential educational role.

The first genuine children's books were influenced by oral narratives, such as myths and folktales; not, as is sometimes casually claimed, because "children like fairy tales" or "fairy tales are suitable for children," but because traditional stories provided narrative and thematic models for children's literature, including such patterns as quest, trials, struggle for survival, coming of age, and child–parent conflict. There is a tangible similarity between the typical folklore hero and the typical protagonist of a children's book: an underprivileged young person, frequently an orphan who has to seek their fortune away from home. There are also obvious similarities in plots and character constellations. Romanticism, with its interest both in the folk tradition and in childhood as a period of innocence and natural goodness, contributed significant momentum to children's literature.

Several genres borrowed or derived from the mainstream catered for the initial need in young people's reading matter, such as nursery rhymes, fables, folktales and adaptations. The source of nursery rhymes is folklore, often with lost sacral meaning and transformed into "nonsense." Based on rhyme and rhythm it is devoid of rational content. Some rhymes had pragmatic purposes, such as lullabies, yet most were purely entertaining and eventually developed into modern poetry for children.

Fables, by La Fontaine in France, by the Greek Aesop in most other European countries, were considered suitable for children, presumably due to two misconceptions. First, they offer a clear and unambiguous moral, exemplifying human virtues and vices in a disguised form. Second, children ostensibly enjoy stories about animals because animals are similarly disempowered; a view that has survived to the present day. The idea of cuteness, projected onto children and animals, reflects contempt toward both as inferior to adult, predominantly male, humans. With their open mockery and punishment of vice, fables lead into the genre of cautionary tales for children, of which Heinrich Hoffmann's *Slovenly Peter* (1845) is the foremost example. Corporal punishment and untimely death were recurrent outcomes of these tales.

Retold folktales was another dubious inclusion in children's reading. Folktales reflect archaic social practices that primarily regulated marriage, but also child–parent relationships. Today, folktales have lost their direct socialization function, but they still depict the fundamental human relationships, including prohibited relationships such as incest. Most folktales feature heroes and heroines of marriageable age, whose final goal is beyond a child's experience. The widely known folktales portraying child characters are no exceptions. The original versions of "Little Red Riding Hood" reflected sexual norms; "Goldilocks" was a late adaptation of a tale featuring a disgusting old woman. "Hansel and Gretel," focused on oral gratification, might seem more pertinent for young readers than procreation, yet food in myth is commonly a circumscription of sex. The popularity of folktales in children's reading lies in their empowerment of the underdog which originally reflected the social and juridical practice of inheritance. However, these heroes represent highly dubious morals, achieving their goals through cheating, stealing and killing.

Folktales were believed to appeal to young readers because of their happy endings, a trait that children's literature has appropriated. Unlike fables and cautionary tales, in which vice is punished, the demand of happy endings in fairy tales and subsequent children's fiction reflects the changed view of childhood. Three major sources of folk and fairy tales incorporated into children's literature were Charles Perrault's volume from 1697, the Oriental collection *Arabian Nights* brought to Europe through French and English translations in the early eighteenth century, and the brothers Grimm collection from 1812, the latter the only of the three explicitly addressed to a young, middle-class audience. These collections, with their radically different purposes, were incorporated into Western children's reading and are still today the most widely known narratives, developed, borrowed, parodied, and transmediated. (Notably, the stories commonly believed to originate from the collection of the *Arabian Nights*, "Aladdin," "Ali Baba" and "Sindbad," come from other sources). Of Andersen's volumes that contain retold folktales and original stories, only the early ones were intended for children; his later stories are dark and cryptic; yet some of Andersen's tales appear among the universally famous stories for children.

Eighteenth- and nineteenth-century children's books were frequently adaptations of existing texts for general readership, including Shakespeare's plays in Britain and *Don Quixote* in Spain, that were normally bowdlerised, that is, purified of anything that a particular culture regarded as inappropriate or offensive. Adaptations reveal the beliefs of what was suitable for children and what children were capable of understanding. Daniel Defoe's *Robinson Crusoe* (1719) can serve as an example of a novel appropriated by educators and incorporated into Western children's literature. One of the foremost representatives of literary Enlightenment, it was recommended by Rousseau in his famous treatise *Émile, or On Education* (1762) as the only suitable reading matter for young minds. It was spread in Europe through an adaptation by the German pedagogue Joachim Heinrich Campe, which was not only abridged but profoundly altered to match ideas of children's abilities and needs. Yet with all the indignation one might feel toward the perfunctory corruption of the original, it is worth contemplating what qualities of the novel were considered appropriate enough to be adapted for the young audience: rebellion against paternal authority, survival without parental supervision, rationality and curiosity about the world, exploration and the search for knowledge.

With innumerable adaptations and imitations, *Robinson Crusoe* became the cornerstone for children's literature in most Western countries. It set a model not only for the vast genre of Robinsonnade, or survival story, but a broader category of adventure stories, which, likewise, were not necessarily meant for children, but became an indispensable part of young people's reading: Alexander Dumas, Walter Scott, Robert Louis Stevenson, R.M. Ballantyne, James Fenimore Cooper, Jules Verne, Karl May, Emilio Salgari, and more. The characters of these stories are young men, whose concerns are beyond the scope of children's concerns, such as social status, economic stability, choice of a partner, and procreation; yet these characters were supposed to inspire young boys because of their virtues of courage, honesty, and justice.

Paralleling adventure stories, stories of virtuous children, or children converted from vice to virtue, such as *Jessica's First Prayer* (1867), by Hesba Stretton, appealed to middle-class readers of both genders. Thus, perhaps not unexpectedly, child characters in children's literature first became prominent in two radically different genres: the cautionary tale and the educative tale. The fact that children's literature was from its very start highly gendered reflects the difference in education of boys and girls. By the time the adventure novel became a fully developed genre, novel reading was no longer considered a feminine pastime, and adventure heroes were viewed as role models, for instance in the works by Horatio Alger and G.A. Henry. The ostensible prototype for boys' books, *The Adventures of Tom Sawyer* (1876), by Mark Twain, is a parody of the conventional adventure novel. Conversely, *The Adventures of Huckleberry Finn* 1884), seemingly a sequel to *Tom Sawyer*, is a forerunner of the novel of adolescence that takes characters beyond childhood and yet both books emphasize character traits believed to be indispensable for socialization of young men.

Young girls, if taught to read at all, were, through reading, socialized into conventional gender roles of obedient daughters, wives, and mothers. *The Governess, or The Little Female Academy* (1749), by Sarah Fielding, is a typical, but by far not the only example of instructional reading for young ladies in which feminine virtues are rewarded and deviation from these punished. Characteristically, early girls' novels are hardly read by today's children because of their extreme didacticism and out-dated value system. By mid-nineteenth century, a new girls' novel emerged, perhaps not accidentally in the United States, parallel with the development of democracy and the anti-slavery movement. *Little Women* (1868) by Louisa M. Alcott, propagated progressive views on women's education and social status, and although it could not portray fully emancipated women, it was sufficiently challenging for its time. Still didactic, it allows its heroines some room for independence, not least through writing and art. The tomboy girl of *Little Women* paved the way for the radical girls' novel, such as *Anne of Green Gables* (1908) and especially *Emily of the New Moon* (1923), both by L. M. Montgomery, in which education and creativity are presented as women's way to emancipation. Yet the Sarah Fielding tradition continued in books such as *What Katy Did* (1872), by Susan Coolidge, in which the protagonist is pun-ished for misbehavior by physical immobility; or *Daddy Long Legs* (1912), by Jean Webster, in which an arrogant man anonymously pays for a female orphan's education in order to bring her up according to his taste to become his wife. Characteristically, both early boys' books and girls' books suggest growing up as a desirable goal, which later children's literature avoided because of the typical twentieth-century idealization of childhood.

The Western canon of children's literature

Early Western children's books knew no cultural or language borders. French and German books were translated, or retold, into English; *Robinson Crusoe*, adapted in Germany, returned to England in new versions. The role of translators was also that of educators. From the late eighteenth century onwards, national traits can be dis-cerned. The English-language children's literature canon tends to be Anglo-American, while taking the Western European and North American cultures as a whole, there are few common denominators. The British canon includes William Blake's *Songs of Innocence* (1789); the German typically starts with E.T.A. Hoffmann's *The Nutcracker* (1816), Wilhelm Hauff's fairy tales (1826), and Wilhelm Busch's proto-comic strip *Max and Moritz* (1865); French children's literature features François Fénelon's *Telemachus* (1699), and Hector Malot's *The Foundling* (1878); Italian, Carlo Collodi's *Pinocchio* (1881) and Edmondo De Amicis' *The Heart* (1886); and Swedish, *The Wonderful Adventures of Nils* (1906–1907) by Selma Lagerlöf. For many European countries, including Germany and Italy, the emergence of children's literature coincided with the building of nationhood. While Collodi's *Pinocchio*, *Heidi* (1880) by the Swiss Johanna Spyri, and Andersen's stories have become universally known, many national classics are considerably less recognized outside their own cul-ture, even though they may have affected the development of a national children's literature.

Further, there is a distinction between milestones, inevitably mentioned in histori-cal overviews, such as John Newbery's *A Little Pretty Pocket-book* (1744), and books that have survived and are still read and enjoyed today, such as Lewis Carroll's *Alice in Wonderland* (1865) and Kenneth Grahame's *The Wind in the Willows* (1908). However, the selection of books to enter the canon is performed by adults, based on their view of the suitability of these texts for children and thus, once again, on their view of childhood. Books that appeal to adults, either for nostalgic or educational reasons, remain in circulation for generations without being subjected to critical scrutiny. In contrast, an ahistorical approach may lead to rejection of certain texts on the basis of their obsolete and, in the eyes of later generations, offensive ideology, including racism and sexism. Such intervention by adult gatekeepers is based on the assessment of young readers as incapable of understanding the historical and cultural context. Finally, there is a distinct gap between "adult" children's literature canon, that is, books that adults judge to be important and influential, that are included in scholarly overviews, encyclopedias, academic courses, and school curricula, and children's canon – books, such as those by Enid Blyton and Roald Dahl, that have been read and enjoyed by children, although disapproved of by adults.

The genre system of children's literature is firmly rooted in education. While children's literature has a lower status than "literature" at large, its internal hierarchies are remarkably different. The most radical distinction is the role of imaginative fiction, especially fantasy, which in the mainstream is labeled trivial. Within children's literature, fantasy is one of the most respectable genres enjoying both critics' attention and readers' engagement. Some works of fantasy, for instance by L. Frank Baum, C.S. Lewis, Lloyd Alexander, Diana Wynne Jones, and Michael Ende are recognized among the best children's books ever (and read by adults). Purportedly, children like stories about imaginary worlds and are more likely than adults to engage in them because of their natural inclination toward play as well as their incapability of distinguishing between reality and imagination. While both views need further consideration, the high status of fantasy in the system of children's literature results from its origin in Romantic literature with supernatural elements, but it is also based on the Romantic belief about the innocent child who can deliver the world from evil by the mere fact of being innocent. The motif of the chosen child is central in fantasy, which allows for the introduction of ethical and philosophical dimensions. Finally, fantasy is an educational device, presenting social and psychological dilemmas for young readers in a distanced and disguised form.

Historically, children's literature has oscillated between the imaginative and realist extremes, connected with views of childhood that either emphasize the importance of imagination or focus on instruction. The definition of realism within children's literature is broad and imprecise as compared to the mainstream; it is an educational rather than aesthetic category. That realist representation should, in itself, be more educational is debatable; however, opponents of imaginative literature for children, from Rousseau to radical pedagogues of the 1970s, object to the distorted picture of the "real world" in non-realist modes. For many educators and critics, even today, realism has higher educational, social, and epistemic value than fantasy. Fantasy is recurrently accused of escapism, while realism is presented as authentic and credible. Numerous adventure and mystery stories, boarding-school stories, naughty-child stories, and horse and pony stories have credible settings and somewhat credible characters, but less credible events that largely depend on serendipity: characters happen to be in the right place at the right time to find treasure or reveal criminals. Characters in plot-driven adventure stories are frequently too flat to be credible. In "issue novels," also referred to as social realism, settings, characters, and events are plausible, yet events and ideology are given priority, and frequently overemphasized. Paradoxically, non-realistic modes can convey more reliable knowledge of the world, society, and other people than realism, and it offers, just as fairy tales can, an excellent training field for introducing morals and ethics. Both realism and fantasy can contain substantial psychological dimensions. Therefore, fantasy within children's literature is a narrative mode rather than a genre, and there is no radical difference between realism and non-realism in terms of character development. All children's literature is generically a Bildungsroman.

Supposedly, young readers prefer action-oriented stories to character-oriented, hence a vast variety of adventure stories, including runaway and survival stories, high seas adventure, treasure seeking, detective stories, and domestic adventures. Similarly to fantasy, these genres do not necessarily have a derogatory status within the children's literature system. Series fiction includes a good deal of these genres, and sequels and series are more common in children's literature than in the mainstream, for commercial as well as educational and aesthetic reasons. The phenomenon of series fiction is based on the belief that unsophisticated readers, including children, want "more of the same." An all-time phenomenon, including Nancy Drew, Hardy Boys, Bobbsey Twins, Just William, and The Famous Five, it has reached gigantic proportions in the twenty-first century, accompanied by a wide practice of new sequels and prequels to classic children's books.

The prominent role of illustrations in children's books is yet another characteristic feature. Illustrations began to appear in early editions and were woodcuts or copper-plate engravings, both expensive to produce. The development of printing technology, especially color printing, opened possibilities for picturebooks, a distinct subcategory hardly existing within the mainstream. Picturebooks are unique in their ability to create meaning in the tension between the verbal and the visual; they appeal to readers in a more immediate manner than purely verbal texts. Although elaborately illustrated books existed in the late nineteenth and early twentieth century, such as those by Kate Greenaway and Beatrix Potter, sophisticated, multi-layered picturebooks emerged in mid-twentieth century, with Maurice Sendak's *Where the Wild Things Are* (1963) a foremost example. A common misconception about richly illustrated books and picturebooks is that they target very young children, which reflects the priority given by Western education to verbal literacy. In actual fact, picturebooks offer excellent options to deal with themes and issues that prove too challenging to present verbally. Parallel to picturebooks, comics and subsequently graphic novels developed their own techniques for word/image interplay, appealing to a wide range of readership.

Themes

Contrary to common beliefs, there are no themes that cannot appear in children's literature; rather it is a question of how they are presented. Themes believed to be taboo, such as death, are on the contrary ubiquitous. Death is the most pervasive theme in children's literature and the most sensitive indicator of the particular historical period's, culture's, or individual author's views about childhood. Historically, children were exposed to the death of their grandparents, parents, and siblings, which is duly reflected and deliberately exaggerated in fiction. Moreover, the view of childhood as the period of innocence led to the idea of child death as beneficial because the child was removed from the sinful world and united with its Creator. Many nineteenth-century children's books, such as Charles Kingsley's *The Water Babies* (1863) or George Macdonald's *At the Back of the North Wind* (1871), portray the protagonists' death as desirable. Twentieth-century children might be familiar with death as the aftermath of the two World Wars; yet for a modern Western child, death is alien and therefore frightening. Numerous books deal with the child coping with death, often in the form of a parable, such as Antoine de Saint-Exupery's *The Little Prince* (1943) or E.B. White's *Charlotte's Web* (1952). The awareness of one's own mortality is a traumatic, but inevitable human experience, and children's writers address it with a variety of strategies, from total omission, which creates a false sense of stability, through the promise of reversibility and rebirth, to acceptance and reconciliation. Death is the immediate consequence of growing up, and books that deny growing up as desirable, such as *Peter Pan*, circumvent the idea of death.

The motifs of growing up, aging, and death dictate the dominant setting of children's literature as the innocent Arcadia, Paradise before the Fall. Conventional children's literature is utopian by nature. Childhood is represented not as it is, but as adult authors remember it, as they wish it were or has been and might be in the future, and not least what they wish, consciously or subconsciously, that young readers should believe it is. Society, as depicted in utopian children's literature, has little to do with reality, whether a realist or non-realist mode is employed. By definition, some prominent elements of societal order are absent from utopia: government or any form of social power, law, money, and, especially pertinent to childhood, education. Even such an essential social structure as family is circumvented in various manners. As a result, children's literature creates a sense of harmony and security that transmit a highly distorted, not to say false picture of the actual society. Books such as *The Wind in Willows*, *The Secret Garden*, or *Winnie-the-Pooh* maintain that childhood is a safe and happy place.

Children's literature that goes beyond utopia, either in a realist or imaginative mode, represents society in the form of carnival, that is, a temporary and sanctioned reversal of power, the purpose of which is to interrogate, but not necessarily overthrow the existing order. In children's literature, child–adult power hierarchies are of special interest because adult authority can be temporarily suspended and the child character empowered in a way impossible within the existing societal norms. This empowerment can be achieved through a number of strategies; yet, with extremely few exceptions, such as *Pippi Longstocking*, children's literature, written by adults, resolutely confirms adult normativity. Portraying young characters with physical, cognitive, political, or pecuniary superiority to adults is a distortion, whether deliberate or not, of the actual situation.

The fictional child's social networks, including family and school, are subjected to the narrative design. Orphans are archetypal figures in world literature, which reflects archaic rites of passage when young people were removed from the family and placed in unfamiliar situations. An actual or symbolically abandoned child is the most prominent protagonist in children's literature, and the removal of parental authority is an indispensable trait. Young protagonists must have freedom to explore the world on their own, without parental supervision, which is best demonstrated in adventure and fantasy stories based on temporary carnivalesque empowerment, such as *The Wonderful Wizard of Oz* (1900) by L. Frank Baum or *The Lion, the Witch and the Wardrobe* (1950) by C.S. Lewis. Thus the function of parental figures is to be absent, physically or emotionally, allowing the protagonists to test their independence in a safe mode and the readers to have a vicarious experience of freedom. In early realist stories, it was plausible that an absent father returned home from war, a prolonged business journey or mission, and the family reunion offered a satisfactory ending. It is less likely that divorced parents reunite; therefore, in a contemporary novel, such an ending is habitually precluded. The role of parental figures in stories does not reflect the actual role of adults in a child's life at any given historical moment. A happy, harmonious family does not provide a good plot. If family is the focus of a narrative it must be dysfunctional in some way.

An evil stepmother is a stock figure in conventional children's literature, which goes back to folktales, told from the perspective of the oppressed child who must fight for his or her rights to the birth parent's inheritance. The abundance of step-parents in older children's literature reflects the actual structure of family due to high mortality, not least childbirth mortality; yet it is also a narrative device enabling writers to explore the child–parent conflict while circumventing its most offensive dimensions, including incest and patricide. In fact, the original versions of folktales portray biological parents. Thus literary step-parents are both symbolic figures and reflections of relevant social order. In a contemporary children's novel, step-parents and step-siblings are likely to result from a divorce rather than death, which creates a variety of additional problems with tangled loyalties. The structure of the contemporary Western family is different from the conventional family and includes single parents, divorced and remarried parents, and more recently same-sex parents. This undermines the traditional stability of the family in utopian children's literature. The portrayal of mothers as homemakers and fathers as bread winners is culturally dependent, but children's literature tends to be conservative in gender representation. Likewise, the depiction of grandparents does not match the prolonged activity of elderly people in contemporary Western society: most children's books present grandparents as feeble and passive. Thus grandparents, or substitute grandparents, are also symbolic figures employed to provide support and guidance when parents fail.

Sibling structure in children's novels is another narrative device. A group of siblings of both genders and various ages, for instance in Edith Nesbit's *The Treasure Seekers* (1899), *Five Children and It* (1901), and *The Railway Children* (1906), provides a multiple protagonist in which every constituent represents a particular trait. In series fiction, a large family is convenient to give each sibling a separate narrative. On the other hand, a single child, or a child separated from siblings, allows the symbolic orphan status that supports the maturation plot. The portrayal of the family in children's literature does not reflect actual demographic facts, but is a deliberate construction for educational and aesthetic purposes.

School is another social institution of overall importance for a Western child misrepresented in children's literature. In many children's books, school is absent or circumvented, for instance through setting the story during summer holidays or in an imaginary world. In the overwhelming majority of children's books, from *Tom Sawyer* to *Pippi Longstocking* and beyond, school is depicted as a place of imprisonment and purposeless, mind-numbing learning, and teachers as wicked or stupid, which seemingly impedes the educational thrust of children's literature. This satirical depiction and contempt toward school is an adult's attempt to win the reader's attention, to be on the child's side; yet it is remarkable that education is consistently presented in an unfavorable light. Even in school stories, a prominent genre, school is merely a convenient setting for the plot. The subgenre of wizard school stories, that existed long before it was employed in the *Harry Potter* series, is a humorous intertextual device. In contemporary children's literature, school is a backdrop against which a variety of social relationships is played out.

The differentiation between children's literature and literature about children and childhood is a matter of narrative perspective rather than content. Childhood narratives are a prominent part of world literature, and in some cultures they compensate for the lack of children's literature. What makes children's literature distinctive is the purported child perspective. The recurrent feature of children's literature, and its foremost dilemma, is the contradiction between the (adult) narrative voice and the (child) point of view, the asymmetrical position of the implied author and the implied reader. The inevitable discrepancy between the narrating and the experiencing agency, even though they can merge in the same fictional character, creates substantial problems. While in literature aimed at the mature audience, narrative irony may be a deliberate artistic device, children's literature presents a delicate balance between the authority of the (adult) narrative agency and the desire to convey a genuine child perspective. Historically, children's literature tended to employ either a didactic omniscient perspective or retrospective narration. In both cases, an adult agency was used to manipulate readers' interpretation. Developing a specific voice has been the central effort of children's writers for the past centuries. Children's literature emerged when the mainstream had shifted from the subjective truth of (pseudo)autobiography and the purported authenticity of narratives based on fact toward the purportedly objective truth of an omniscient and omnipresent narrator. Such deceptive objectivity served the educational project of children's literature well because it allowed an authoritative (adult) voice to comment on young protagonists and guide young readers.

Contemporary children's literature attempts to reflect modern views of childhood and create authenticity, either through first-person perspective or through various forms of blended narration, including interior monolog and free indirect speech. Multi-voiced, multi-strand, occasionally multi-medial, narratives have become common even in literature for very young readers. While adding to complexity, such narrative forms do not eliminate the issue of adult writers addressing an audience with a dissimilar social and cognitive competence. An adult voice always has more authority than a child's voice, and this covert oppression against the child character as well as the young reader is a distinctive feature of children's literature, even when – or perhaps especially when – it is employed for educational purposes. Although the didactic, omniscient adult voice may seem to belong to the past, there is inescapably an adult narrative agency behind a child focalizer or a personal child narrator. On closer consideration, children's literature tends to be more conservative than the mainstream in its ideology because it is created by the previous generation as compared with the intended audience.

Toward new definitions of childhood and literature

The twentieth century produced the idea of the emancipated and competent child, best epitomized by Astrid Lindgren's *Pippi Longstocking* (1945). Freud's ideas of child sexuality made childhood less alienated from adulthood, which in some cases paradoxically amplified the writers' striving to keep children in the state of innocence. In contrast, many writers started exploring the possibility of allowing fictional children more agency, not only through carnivalesque devices, but also by acknowledging their cognitive and psychological integrity. These endeavors led to growing complexity in narrative structures employed to express the complexity of the child's inner life.

The rapid social changes in Western society of the twentieth century, including urbanization, the impact of two World Wars, the fall of colonialism and massive immigration from Africa, Asia, and Latin America, and youth revolts of the 1960s were inevitably reflected in children's literature. The post-Second World War era brought in new social patterns and issues, new family configurations, new personal concerns. With the development of modern media, children were exposed to extensive information about the world, other cultures, other social groups, and other individuals. Western children's literature became more democratic, going beyond portrayals of middle-class children.

A distinctly new phenomenon of post-war Western society was the idea of adolescence, the prominence of youth culture, and subsequently the emergence of separate young adult fiction in the border zone between children's and mainstream literature; with these came inevitable intersections and fluctuations. The protagonists of young-adult fiction perform in the liminal space between childhood and adulthood; their dilemmas and their behavior reflect the confusions of puberty and feature risk-taking typical of adolescence, including drugs and alcohol, violence and crime, generational conflicts, exploration of sexuality, and identity crises leading to self-harm, including attempted or accomplished suicide. Writers such as Aidan Chambers in the United Kingdom, Judy Blume and Robert Cormier in the United States, and Gunnel Beckman and Peter Pohl in Sweden ventured into the most intimate aspects of adolescent life. Young-adult novels also allow wide exploration of gender issues. Today, young-adult fiction is typically considered a category separate from children's literature; yet it is widely read by pre-teens and is one of the strongest socialization implements for young people.

The 1990s and the first decade of the twenty-first century witnessed the old/new phenomenon of crossover, books shared by two different audiences, children and adults, although clearly and purposefully marketed separately. This is not necessarily the result of children's literature becoming more sophisticated and thus approaching the mainstream; rather the border zone is created within genres that are considered "low" in the mainstream, such as fantasy and horror. At the same time, novels and picturebooks of highest quality have appeared within this specific cultural space. This trend can be understood both in terms of content and form. Contemporary children's and young-adult literature explores a wide range of issues that, while not completely neglected by previous writers, have not been addressed with substantial candor. These include sexuality, tolerance, social injustice, and psychological issues such as depression. Literature reflects a contemporary child's complex relationships with adults and peers. Today's children's social networks are considerably wider than those of their counterparts at an earlier time, which could have been limited to family and school. They have almost unrestricted access through various media to information, which includes violence, terrorism, and natural catastrophes. These facts compel children's writers to consider the experiences of modern childhood in their writing. Thus, rather than claiming that writers have become bolder or gatekeepers more lenient, it is accurate to observe that a child's or young person's life experience in the twenty-first century has become more diverse and complex. This, however, does not necessarily lead to the emancipatory role of children's literature in today's society. Many scholars, notably Alison Lurie, claim that subversiveness is an inherent feature of children's literature; yet while children's literature can potentially be subversive, questioning adult authority and social institutions, this potential is not often realized. On the contrary, the overwhelming majority of children's literature still confirms the existing order.

The experimental, "post-modern" nature of children's literature of the twenty-first century, especially prominent in picturebooks and young-adult novels, has several reasons and implications. At least some part of children's literature has caught up with the mainstream in terms of its aesthetic qualities, including genre eclecticism, intertextuality, and metafictional elements, that can be viewed as artistic devices employed to treat complex issues in a playful manner. Yet, the sheer volume of Western children's literature market makes the phenomenon so diverse that it precludes generalizations. A vast number of children's books are still didactic and instructive, using an authoritative voice and propagating views and beliefs that suit a particular group of adults for the moment. A still larger proportion of children's books are commercial products without any artistic merit.

Nevertheless, scholars are inevitably re-defining children's literature from the vantage point of the twenty-first century. With today's conspicuous crossover literature, the evolution has gone full cycle, back to the situation when adults and children share their reading matter. The distinct boundary between children's literature and the mainstream is once again hard to define. The *Harry Potter* series (1997–2007) by J.K. Rowling punctured several myths about children's literature. It shows that young readers can easily manage books of well over five hundred pages if these are engaging enough; that children's books can be popular without losing complexity and artistic quality; that children's books can be enjoyed by readers of all ages and transcend cultural borders. The series is probably the first example of literature ever to receive substantial scholarly attention long before the last volume was published. It also started the trend of aggressive marketing that, with young readers' access to media, targets them directly, irrespective of adult tastes and norms. In short, *Harry Potter* changed the world of literature and reading. Yet, revolutionary in size and public appeal, the novels epitomize children's literature with all its conventions, not least the confirmation of adult normativity. The *Harry Potter* series is not the first, but the most prominent expression of crossover literature that signals the blurring of boundaries between children's and adult markets. *Harry Potter*, as well as Philip Pullman's *His Dark Materials* (1995–2000) and many other books, are today published in parallel editions, with different covers. This implies that children's literature can no longer be distinguished from the mainstream through its content, but exclusively through marketing. The growing phenomenon of complex, artistic picturebooks aimed at multiple audiences – young children, older children, teenagers, adults – is another indicator of the ambivalent status of certain types of books, while the graphic novel is a crossover genre that bridges the gap between reader categories. Western children's literature is once again becoming transnational and transgenerational.

As depicted in children's literature, the twenty-first century appears to reflect a renewed idealization of childhood, but by adopting an image of the child as competent rather than innocent. Today's childhood is portrayed as dark, complex, and highly problematic, while children's literature itself becomes substantially more sophisticated and demanding, both in terms of ethics and of aesthetics. It can be questioned, and has been questioned, whether contemporary literature marketed for children is aimed at young readers at all, or whether it is literature in disguise, employed by authors for a variety of purposes, from nostalgia and self-indulgence to social criticism. The widespread tendency toward dystopian ideas from the late 1990s to the present brings children's literature to the opposite of its conventional utopian features. On the one hand, this reflects the actual conditions of modern childhood, and on the other hand, it expresses the adult writers' beliefs in the competence of their readers to deal with dark issues. At the same time, dystopian visions, dark fantasy, and horror continue to propagate adult norms. Novels such as *Twilight*, for example, seemingly daring in content, are extremely conservative in ideology.

Another urgent issue is redefining children's literature with the emergence of digital media, including narrative games, enhanced e-books, and picturebook applications. Through fan fiction and blogs, young people are able to address their peers directly, avoiding adult gatekeepers. Although anxious voices predict the demise of children's literature (and literature at large) under the threat of digital media, Western children's literature has never been as vital and diverse as it is today. It is, for better or worse, a huge and highly profitable global industry. The recent expansion of children's literature research, its tangible presence in academia, and its visibility in press and media, testify to its growing significance in the Western world. And contemporary research in neuroscience emphasizes the role of literacy and reading for any kind of human knowledge and activity. Children's literature is facing new challenges in the rapidly changing world.

Suggestions for further reading

For the first brief overview, start with Kimberley Reynolds's *Children's Literature: A Very Short Introduction* (Oxford, UK: Oxford University Press, 2011). For further historical and thematic orientation, see Peter Hunt's *An Introduction to Children's Literature* (Oxford, UK: Oxford University Press, 1994) and *Children's Literature: An Illustrated History* (Oxford, UK: Oxford University Press, 1995); Matthew Grenby's *Children's Literature* (Edinburgh, UK: Edinburgh University Press, 2008); and *The Child Reader 1700–1840* (Cambridge, UK: Cambridge University Press, 2011). Various aspects of children's literature, including its social and historical context, genres, themes, and critical approaches to the subject, are treated in handbooks and companions, such as *The Cambridge Companion to Children's Literature* (Cambridge, UK: Cambridge University Press, 2009), *The Routledge Companion to Children's Literature* (London, UK: Routledge, 2010), *Routledge Handbook of Research on Children's and Young Adult Literature* (London, UK: Routledge, 2010), and *The Oxford Handbook of Children's Literature* (New York, NY: Oxford University Press, 2011). Peter Hunt in *Criticism, Theory and Children's Literature* (London, UK: Blackwell, 1991) and John Stephens in *Language and Ideology in Children's Fiction* (London, UK: Longman, 1992) were among the first scholars to theorize children's literature from different critical perspectives.

The debates on the definitions of and approaches to children's literature are summarized in Perry Nodelman's *The Hidden Adult. Defining Children's Literature* (Baltimore, MD: The Johns Hopkins University Press, 2008), which also suggests that children's literature can never be free from adult ideology. A similar idea is developed in Maria Nikolajeva's *Power, Voice and Subjectivity in Literature for Young People* (New York, NY: Routledge, 2009). Both studies respond to the seminal and controversial book by Jacqueline Rose, *The Case of Peter Pan, or The Impossibility of Children's Fiction* (London, UK: Macmillan, 1984) that described children's literature as the expression of adult writers' nostalgia and self-indulgence. Conversely, Alison Lurie treats children's literature as subversive by nature in *Don't Tell the Grownups. Subversive Children's Literature* (Boston, MA: Little, Brown, 1990). Barbara Wall was the pioneer in examining narrative perspective and multiple address in children's literature in *The Narrator's Voice. The Dilemma of Children's Fiction* (London, UK: Macmillan, 1991). The idyllic nature of children's literature is discussed in Fred Inglis's *The Promise of Happiness. The Value and Meaning in Children's Fiction.* (Cambridge, UK: Cambridge University Press, 1981), Humphrey Carpenter's *Secret Gardens. The Golden Age of Children's Literature* (London, UK: Unwin Hyman, 1985), and Maria Nikolajeva's *From Mythic to Linear: Time in Children's Literature* (Lanham, MD: Scarecrow, 2000).

Karín Lesnik-Oberstein was early to emphasize the cultural constructedness of the child in *Children's Literature. Criticism and the Fictional Child* (Oxford, UK: Clarendon, 1994). Further connections between children's literature and childhood are explored in John Zornado's *Inventing the Child. Culture, Ideology, and the Rise of Childhood* (New York, NY: Garland, 2000), Roni Natov's *The Poetics of Childhood* (New York, NY: Routledge, 2003), and Beverly Lyon Clark's *Kiddie Lit. The Cultural Construction of Children's Literature in America* (Baltimore, MD: The Johns Hopkins University Press, 2003).

Some profound readings of classical and modern children's books are offered in Jack Zipes's *Sticks and Stones. The Troublesome Success of Children's Literature from Slovenly Peter to Harry Potter* (New York, NY: Routledge, 2001), Alison Lurie's *Boys and Girls Forever: Children's Classics from Cinderella to Harry Potter* (London, UK: Vintage, 2004), and Maria Tatar's *Enchanted Hunters. The Power of Stories in Childhood* (New York, NY: Norton, 2009). *Introducing Children's Literature. From Romanticism to Poststructuralism* by Debora Cogan Thacker and Jean Webb (London, UK: Routledge, 2002) combines a historical overview with discussions of key texts. Kimberley Reynolds's *Radical Children's Literature: Future Visions and Aesthetic Transformations in Juvenile Fiction* (Basingstoke, UK: Palgrave, 2007) is focused on contemporary children's literature and its experiments in form and content. Sandra Beckett's *Crossover Fiction: Global and Historical Perspectives* (London, UK: Routledge, 2008) examines various aspects of this phenomenon.

For an introduction to feminist approaches to children's literature, Roberta Seelinger Trites's *Waking Sleeping Beauty. Feminist Voices in Children's Novels* (Iowa City, IA: University of Iowa Press, 1997) can be recommended. Victor Watson's *Reading Series Fiction: From Arthur Ransome to Gene Kemp* (London, UK: Routledge, 2000) is the only book-length study of the genre.

Children's literature scholarship is a rapidly expanding area, with scores of books on particular historical periods, individual authors, and specific genres and modes, such as fantasy, adventure, school stories, and picturebooks. There is a vast number of academic journals devoted to the subject, and major publishers such as Routledge and Palgrave have series in children's literature studies.

Part III

SPECIAL CHILDREN AT SPECIAL TIMES OR PLACES

18

CHILDREN IN NORTH AMERICAN SLAVERY

Steven Mintz

Childhood is central to an understanding of slavery. Children, across a wide range of countries and historical eras, occupied a pivotal demographic and economic role within slavery. For masters, slave children were an important source of wealth and labor. For slave parents, children assisted in a variety of work tasks and supplemented family diets. By focusing on the lives of slave children, much can be learned about the master–slave relationship. Slavery's horrors cannot be fully grasped unless one recognizes its effects on its youngest and most vulnerable victims. In children's lives, we can see the human meaning of exploitation, punishment, and family separation in high relief.

Slave owners in disparate societies described slaves as child-like. In fact, in many societies a substantial proportion of the slave population consisted of children. In classical antiquity, abandoned newborns were a major source of slaves.[1] In the non-Western world, a number of societies took children away from their parents in order to create a class of soldiers or administrators loyal only to a ruler or the state. Some Islamic societies created a class of soldiers, like the Mamluks or Janissaries, by separating boys from Christian families. In China, some parents surrendered their sons to the service of the Emperor.[2] These boys would serve in an administrative cadre of eunuchs.

Children made up a substantial and increasing number of those caught up in the Atlantic slave trade starting in the seventeenth century. In the decades before the Civil War, two-fifths of all slaves in the US South were under the age of sixteen, and a third were under ten.[3] For many slaveholders, slavery's profitability and productivity depended on the birth rate.

Today, young people constitute a significant number of those held in slave-like conditions: as domestic or migrant workers, forced laborers, and sex slaves. Still others are held captive in "servile marriages": an arrangement in which a girl or young woman is involuntarily married in exchange for a payment to her family, and who can be sold to another person or inherited after her husband's death.[4] The story of children in slavery is not yet over.

Recent directions in the study of slavery

Over the past quarter century, historical understandings of slavery have undergone a sea change. Slavery today is viewed from a global perspective. Although only a handful of polities – including the city states of Ancient Greece, the Roman Republic

331

and Empire, and the American South – became true slave societies, relying largely upon slaves as their primary source of labor power, the institution of slavery could be found worldwide, in societies as disparate as Babylon, Ancient India, and China, and among the Indians of the Pacific Northwest. In the New World, slavery thrived, nearly to the end of the eighteenth century, from Quebec to the tip of South America.[5]

Scholars have also learned a great deal about continuities and discontinuities in slavery over time and space. Although slavery dates to prehistoric times (apparently modeled on the domestication of animals), slavery in the ancient and non-Western worlds took radically different forms than the New World slavery that began in the sixteenth century. For one thing, ancient and non-Western slavery were not based on race. Indeed, it was not until the mid-fifteenth century that slavery in Christian and Islamic societies was associated primarily with sub-Saharan Africans. For another, in many societies slavery did not constitute the most menial form of labor. Although many slaves were used in construction and agriculture, substantial numbers were household servants whose numbers signified their owner's wealth and status. Further, in many societies, slaves or their children achieved freedom during their lifetime. Finally, it was only beginning in the fifteenth century, initially in a series of islands in the Mediterranean or off the coast of Africa, that slavery became the combustion engine that powered a capitalist system of production of agricultural commodities geared toward maximum productivity.[6]

It has become clear that slavery was a key to the making of the modern world. Not only was slavery found in the most economically advanced societies of their time, but it played an instrumental role in the development of modern notions of race, of multinational systems of banking, and of international trading networks. In the United States, where slaveholders held the presidency for fifty of the nation's first seventy-two years, slave-grown cotton constituted three-quarters of the value of American exports, helping to attract the capital that financed the nation's railroads. It supported brokerages, insurance companies, and shippers, not to mention textile mills.[7]

Historians today see slavery less as a system of domination in which masters exercised a monopoly of force than as a system involving negotiation, resistance, and conflict. Indeed, slavery's efficiency as a labor system depended on a master's ability to achieve accommodation with enslaved African–Americans.[8] Scholars have found that in this process, African cultural traditions were not obliterated during the Middle Passage (the forced transport from Africa to the Americas), and that an intricate process of cultural borrowing, blending, and adaptation took place in the New World, one that created not only new Afro–American cultures but also transformed European cultures.[9]

Children and the slave trade

Although most sub-Saharan Africans forced into slavery were in their teens and twenties, the proportion of captives consisting of children grew considerably between the fifteenth and the nineteenth centuries. This reflected the fact that it was easier to enslave children than those who were older. Enslavement of children took a variety of forms. Most were captured in wars and raids. But many others were taken as tribute by African chiefs or were sold by their relatives, especially in times of famine. Still others served as pawns, who were enslaved to repay a parent's debt. In multiple societies, children served as a form of "capital," useful as collateral for credit or in settling debts. These children were commodities with exchange value, whose value appreciated as the children grew. Some children were taken captive by themselves, apart from other family members. But many others were transported along with a parent or siblings. A large number were left orphaned following a parent's death either in Africa, following capture, or during the Middle Passage.[10]

Scholars of US slavery only recently became aware of the size and scale of a "second middle passage," the movement of a million slaves from the Atlantic coast and upper South into the Old Southwest, the territory that now includes Alabama, Mississippi, Louisiana, and Texas, during the first half of the nineteenth century. Many more slaves were moved shorter distances, a process that preyed particularly hard on children who were frequently separated from other family members. Children and youths were viewed as especially desirable for "manning" plantations in frontier areas because they were considered less likely to run away.[11]

Fertility and childbirth

In the United States, in contrast to Brazil or the Caribbean, the slave system's viability, profitability, and productivity depended largely on natural reproduction. Thomas Jefferson claimed that "a child raised every 2 years is of more profit than the crop of the best laboring man."[12] Not only could children contribute labor from an early age, but in their teens, they could be leased out or sold for a profit. Especially in the pre-Civil War American South (after the cessation of the slave trade in 1808), the sale of excess domestic slaves was a major source of income for slaveholders along the Atlantic seaboard and in the border states.

The American South was unique in the ability of the slave population to naturally increase its numbers; in the Caribbean, by contrast, the slave population would have dropped by as much as 5 percent a year in the absence of fresh imports.[13] A number of factors contributed to differences in fertility rates, including dissimilarities in work regimens, climate, and diet. Raising sugar cane was more physically demanding than raising cotton or tobacco, and malnutrition was more widespread in the Caribbean than in the South. But disparities in birth rates also involved different breast-feeding practices. Lactation can reduce women's fertility, and mothers in the Caribbean nursed their children far longer than their US counterparts – for as many as five years compared to just one or two in the American South.

Although there is little evidence to suggest that masters in the American South deliberately bred slaves, they did pursue a variety of strategies to maximize births.[14] Even in the colonial period (1607–1776), the slave population in Britain's mainland colonies had a more equal sex ratio. By the nineteenth century, young women at auctions were evaluated based on their capacity as "breeders." Many slaveholders gave bounties in the form of cash or household goods to mothers who bore healthy children. They increased rations and lightened the workload of pregnant and nursing women.

In the American South, childbirth proved to be an important arena of conflict between masters and slaves. Masters frequently sought to oversee the birth process. White plantation mistresses frequently supervised births or, in especially difficult circumstances, hired white physicians, while slave women, for the most part, preferred to be assisted by black midwives and lay healers.[15]

It is noteworthy that despite planters' efforts to encourage early childbearing among slaves, there was a several year gap between the age of menarche and first birth in the

American South. Typically, slave women in the American South gave birth around the age of twenty or twenty-one, about a year earlier than their white Southern counterparts. The interval between births – about two or two-and-a-half years – was somewhat longer than among Southern white women.[16]

Enslaved parents looked forward to their children's births with bittersweet emotions. A fugitive slave named Lunsford Lane reprinted a slave mother's address to her infant child, which read: "And much I grieve and mourn/That to so dark a destiny/My lovely babe I've borne." Harriet Jacobs, who was sexually exploited under slavery, wrote that "My heart was heavier than it had ever been before when they told me my new-born babe was a girl," because she could expect the same treatment for her daughter. Slave fathers, too, gave voice to this ambivalence. Thomas Jones felt "unspeakable anguish as I looked upon my precious babes, and have thought of the ignorance, degradation, and woe which they must endure as slaves."[17]

Children's experience of slavery

Children's experience in bondage varied widely. In a small number of cases, young male slaves assumed relatively privileged positions in their society. In some places, including in Egypt, they were inducted into the military; in China, a number became eunuchs; and in the Ottoman empire, slaves assumed important administrative roles. In many places, a few young female slaves were adopted into their owner's household as servants and, at times, taken as concubines or wives. In the New World, in contrast, most child slaves were destined to become field workers. Yet even in the Americas, significant numbers of male slaves became skilled artisans, coachmen, river pilots, or drivers, responsible for managing other slaves.[18] Females were sometimes concubines or "fancy women."

Nevertheless, deprivation and physical hardship were the hallmarks of childhood under slavery. In the American South, slave children were much more likely than southern or northern whites to die prematurely, suffer malnutrition or dietary deficiencies, and a slave child was more likely to die in infancy. At birth, over half of all slave children weighed less than five pounds, or what today is considered to be seriously underweight. Slave newborns weighed significantly less than their white Southern counterparts. Plantation records reveal that over half of all slave babies died during their first year of life, a rate twice that of white babies. Although slave children's death rate declined after the first year of life, it remained twice the white rate.[19]

The average child slave's small size indicates a deficient diet. On a few plantations in the antebellum American South, "sucklings were allowed to come to [their mothers in the fields] three times a day, for the purpose of nursing." But it was more common for mothers to suckle their babies just once during the day, usually around ten in the morning. At other times, infants were fed cow's milk, thin porridge, "potlicker" (the broth left in a pot after the greens were cooked), a mixture of mush and skimmed milk, or bread mashed into gravy. Not only were these foods unsanitary and unhygienic, but because many African–American infants were lactose intolerant, they were unable to digest them.[20]

Throughout their childhoods, slaves were smaller than white children of the same age. The average slave children did not reach three feet in height until their fourth birthdays. At that age they were five inches shorter than a typical child today and about the same height as a child in present-day Bangladesh. At seventeen, slave men were shorter than 96 percent of present-day American men, and slave women were smaller than 80 percent of American women. Many Southern white children were also badly fed and quite small, indicating that many children, white as well as black, suffered from the slave system.[21]

Slave children's diet was monotonous and unvaried, consisting largely of corn meal, salt pork, and bacon. Only rarely did these children eat fresh meat or vegetables. As a result of this diet, many slave children suffered from vitamin and protein deficiencies, and were victims of such ailments as beriberi, kwashiorkor, and pellagra. Poor nutrition and high rates of infant and child mortality contributed to a short average life expectancy – just twenty-one or twenty-two years compared to forty to forty-three years for whites. Those children who lived into adolescence, however, would likely live well into their prime adult years.[22]

The physical conditions in which slave children grew up were appalling. Lacking privies, these children had to urinate and defecate in the cover of nearby bushes. Lacking any sanitary disposal of garbage, they were surrounded by decaying food. Chickens, dogs, and pigs lived next to the slave quarters, and in consequence, animal feces contaminated the area. Such squalor contributed to high rates of dysentery, typhus, diarrhea, hepatitis, typhoid fever, and intestinal worms.[23]

Slave quarters were cramped and crowded. The typical cabin was a single, windowless room with a chimney constructed of clay and twigs and a floor made up of dirt or planks resting on the ground. It ranged in size from 10×10 to 21×21 feet. These small cabins were often quite crowded, containing five, six, or more occupants. On some plantations, slaves lived in single-family cabins; on others, two or more family groups shared the same room. On the largest plantations, unmarried men and women were sometimes lodged together in barrack-like structures. Josiah Henson, the Kentucky slave who served as the model for Harriet Beecher Stowe's Uncle Tom, described his plantation's cabins this way:

> We lodged in log huts ... Wooden floors were an unknown luxury. In a single room were huddled, like cattle, ten or a dozen persons, men, women, and children ... There were neither bedsteads nor furniture ... Our beds were collections of straw and old rags ... The wind whistled and the rain and snow blew in through the cracks, and the damp earth soaked in the moisture till the floor was muddy as a pig sty.[24]

In the pre-Civil War American South, slave children were much less likely to grow up in a two-parent household than any other children. About a quarter of enslaved children grew up in a single-parent household (nearly always with their mothers). Another tenth grew up apart from both parents; 5 percent of young slaves lived in their owners' homes. Even in two-parent families, children frequently reported that they spent little time with their parents. In the South Carolina low country, wealthy slaveholders took young slaves for weeks or even months at a time into the upcountry during malaria epidemics in order to protect their health and future labor. On these occasions, parents were only able to visit their children on Sundays, if at all.[25]

Temporary or permanent family separation was an almost universal experience for slave children by the time they reached their late teens. Nevertheless, through distinctive patterns of co-parenting, godparenting, and naming patterns that reinforced kin connections throughout an extended community, parents provided their children with a network of support. The fragility of nuclear families gave heightened significance to the larger community of extended kin and non-kin. From a very early age, children were taught to refer to older slaves on their plantation as aunt or uncle and to young slaves as cousins, regardless of their actual biological relationship.[26]

Slave children's clothing was minimal and it was common to see boys "of about Fourteen and Fifteen years Old" with "their whole nakedness exposed." Few owners distributed shoes to children who did not work in the field, and slave children usually wore shoes only during the coldest months. Most youngsters had to make do with moccasins their fathers fashioned from animal hides or rags wrapped around their feet. Slave owners typically issued children two sets of clothing a year, one for the winter, and one for the summer. No underclothes were provided, although leggings might be worn in winter. Young children usually wore a shapeless garment of rough cloth that was called a shirt when worn by boys and a shift, a shimmy, or a dress when worn by girls. Made of plainly woven, coarse cotton cloth, these one-piece garments, seamed at the shoulders, fell from the shoulders to below the knees. Booker T. Washington wrote that his shirt felt like "a dozen or more chestnut burrs" rubbing on his skin. But however inexpensive their clothing might be, enslaved African–Americans sought to individualize their clothing. Girls' clothing, in particular, was often patterned and colorful. Enslaved girls might embellish their clothes with shards of cloth thrown away by the master's family.[27]

As early as five or six years of age, or even younger, slave children were put to work. Very young slave children swatted flies at their master's dining table, polished furniture, and served as nursemaids or companions for white children. Some served as human scarecrows, frightening crows away from corn stalks; they toiled on trash gangs; hauled water and wood, or pulled weeds. They were also used for sweeping yards, driving cows to pasture, and cutting tree limbs for firewood. They fed chickens, gathered eggs, milked cows, churned butter, shelled, peeled, and washed vegetables. They plucked grubs off tobacco plants, and sometimes were forced to swallow those that they missed. Between the ages of seven and ten, children began to perform field work, and between ten and twelve they were inducted into the full work routines of adults.[28]

In addition to providing their masters with labor, slave children were active members of their family economy. Children might gather wood for the fireplace, help their mothers card cotton or spin thread, and supplement the family diet by fishing, trapping animals, and collecting fruits, vegetables, and nuts. Enslaved children also assisted in cooking, cleaning, and caring for younger children.

Like their parents, slave children were subjected to harsh physical discipline. A white Southern physician acknowledged that anyone who heard "the loud sharp crack of the whip upon the naked skin, would almost tremble for the life of the poor sufferer." But this apologist for slavery insisted that the whip's end was so soft that one "could scarcely hurt a child with it." Frederick Douglass observed that "a mere look, word, or motion" could provoke a lashing. Elizabeth Keckley, a Virginia slave who later become Mary Todd Lincoln's closest confidante, described a whipping she received at the age of fourteen: "It cut the skin, raised great welts, and the warm blood tickled down my back. Oh God! I can feel the torture now – the terrible, excruciating agony of those moments."[29]

For slave children, play was much more than an innocent pastime. Through their play, these children tested their wits, and dealt with a host of anxieties stemming from slave status. Through their games and songs, children steeled themselves for the insecurities and pangs of life in bondage. Games such as "Hide the Switch," which concluded with the loser being flogged, and mock auctions offered a way to prepare psychologically for slavery's cruelties. Children's songs – with lyrics like "Mammy, is Ole' Massa gwin'er sell us tomorrow?" – also provided a way to deal with their fears.[30]

Even on model plantations, children between the ages of seven and ten were taken from their parents and sent to live in separate cabins. By their mid-teens, however, the young were especially vulnerable to sale or separation from other family members. The threat of sale was greatest during the teenage years, when a majority of slaves could expect to be separated from other members of their family. Adolescent females were also especially vulnerable to sexual exploitation.

Autobiographical accounts of slave childhoods

Even worse perhaps than slavery's physical severities were its psychological cruelties. There was the danger that children would internalize a sense of dependence, inferiority, and subordinate status. Some children suffered from a sense of inferiority and shame. Thomas Jones, who spent his childhood in slavery in North Carolina, described his memory of growing up under slavery:

> My recollections of early life are associated with poverty, suffering and shame. I was made to feel, in my boyhood's first experience, that I was inferior and degraded, and that I must pass through life in a dependent and suffering condition.[31]

Play could buttress a sense of subordination. Thomas Jefferson believed that "the whole commerce between master and slave is a perpetual exercise of the most boisterous passions ... Our children see this, and learn to imitate it."[32] In fact, many interracial games among children re-enacted the relationship between masters and slaves, reinforcing the plantation hierarchy and accentuating the divide between white and black. When the game was wagon, slave children served as mules.[33]

For Frederick Douglass, the fugitive slave who became one of the United States's best-known abolitionists, slavery's greatest evil was the systematic deprivation of knowledge about one's ancestry, about reading, writing, and even one's birth date. Slavery, he later wrote, "made my brothers and sisters strangers to me; it converted the mother that bore me into a myth; it shrouded my father in mystery, and left me without an intelligible beginning in the world."[34] Slavery, in his view, had not merely robbed him of the attributes of childhood, but of certain defining elements of a human identity.

Several key incidents run through many first-hand accounts of childhood in bondage. Many slave narratives, describe the shocking moment when children first recognized that they were slaves. Despite the daily reminders of their subordinate status, many former slaves recalled a moment before or around puberty when they first confronted the harsh reality of lifelong servitude. A whipping, an abusive epithet, a sudden change in how one was treated by white playmates, revealed the full meaning of enslavement. For others, the harshest memory from their childhood was seeing their parents being whipped and discovering that they were impotent to do anything about this. For still others, the most severe trauma was learning that their parents were helpless to protect them from an abusive master or overseer.[35]

For slave children, there were repeated reminders of their subordinate status and dependence on their master's will. They were expected to display deference and undergo verbal and physical harassment without responding. Many suffered from fears of family separation. Many slave songs give poignant expression to these anxieties, with lyrics like "Mother, don't grieve after me" or "Sometimes I feel like a Motherless Child."

Yet the narratives also reveal that many slave children successfully carved out spaces where they could achieve a degree of autonomy. Resilience coexisted with victimization. For all of slavery's horrors, many enslaved children and youths were able to "steal a childhood." Children were not simply slavery's victims, they were also active agents who managed to resist slavery's dehumanizing pressures.

Play offered a way to learn adult skills and deal with the insecurities of life in bondage. Many games prepared children for adult roles, such as cooking or caring for babies, or taught values that would be useful in the adult world. Role-playing games were especially popular, as children acted out baptisms, funerals, and weddings, and dressed up like adults. Magic appeals to all children, but had a special significance for those who were enslaved. The children on one plantation liked to play conjure man in a game called hoodoo doctor, which gave them a sense of power and agency. Play helped forge a sense of solidarity among enslaved children and allowed them to create a semi-autonomous realm, beyond the direct control of their masters. Whether enslaved children on smaller and more isolated farms were able to create a space of relative freedom remains an unanswered question.[36]

Through religion, enslaved African–Americans were able to nurture an autonomous culture and community, beyond the direct control of their masters. Slave owners were quite open in their belief that religion could serve as a valuable mechanism of social control, instilling submissiveness and obedience. But Christianity had another face, emphasizing judgment, equality, and liberation. During the late eighteenth and early nineteenth centuries, slaves embraced Christianity, but molded and transformed it to meet their own needs. In Protestant Christianity, slaves found an emphasis on love and the spiritual equality of all people that strengthened their ties to others. Many slaves fused the figures of Moses, who led his people to freedom, and Jesus, who suffered on behalf of all humankind, into a promise of deliverance in this world.

A surprising proportion – between 5 and 10 percent of US slaves – succeeded in learning how to read and write. Learning to read and write under slavery was an arduous process that took tenacity and determination and often extended over several years. For many children, literacy was an act of resistance, which instilled a sense of self-worth and offered psychological freedom. It allowed them to read the Bible for themselves and not depend on the interpretations of white Southerners. Also, a slave who could write could forge a pass.[37]

Slave childhood as an arena of conflict

In the pre-Civil War American South, where plantations were far smaller and interactions between masters and slaves were much more frequent than in Brazil or the Caribbean, childhood was an arena in which masters and slaves struggled, as masters sought to instill loyalty and dependence within slave children, while parents and other adults sought to instill loyalty to the slave community. Conflict began even before a child's birth, as pregnant mothers sought to convince owners to increase their rations and lighten their workload. Conflict continued as masters sought to dictate the frequency of mothers' nursing and the timing of weaning.[38]

Struggle sometimes took place over the selection of a child's name. During the seventeenth and eighteenth centuries, some masters had imposed classical names, such as Hercules, or place names, such as London, on slaves, a naming pattern rarely found among white colonists. But most slaves were named by their parents, who often followed the West or Central African practice of "day-naming"– assigning names based on the day of their birth. Name-saking, naming children after grandparents or other kin, was a common practice. Name exchanges, in which brothers named sons for one another, were also common, underscoring the significance attached to kinship ties.[39]

Conflict persisted as children grew older. The treatment of children was central to planters' self-image as benevolent paternalists. Some masters and mistresses provided young slave children with gifts and other small tokens of affection that threatened to undercut the authority of parents. On larger plantations, many owners instituted forms of collective childcare that removed mothers from direct supervision of their children during the workday.[40]

Slave parents, in turn, strove against all odds to instill a sense of pride in their offspring and to educate them to maneuver through the complexities of slavery. Through folktales, parents sought to transmit important cultural values. Slave folktales were much more than amusing stories; slaves used them to comment on the whites around them and to convey everyday lessons for living. Among the most popular slave folktales were animal trickster stories, like the Brer Rabbit tales, derived from similar African stories, which told of powerless creatures who achieve their will through wit and guile rather than power and authority. These tales taught slave children how they had to function in a white-dominated world and held out the promise that the powerless would eventually triumph over the strong.[41]

Parents also had to train their children in the etiquette of race relations. They taught their children to show deference to whites and to be sensitive about the information they revealed. Children were also reminded they could never appear "uppity" or impudent or disrespectful. Above all, they had to learn to flatter the egos of whites by behaving in an obsequious manner or feigning stupidity or gratitude without internalizing a sense of inferiority or losing a sense of self-worth.[42]

Slave children and the valorization of childhood

At a time when the white urban middle class was freeing its children from work responsibilities, prolonging and intensifying their family ties, and devoting an increasing number of their years to formal schooling, a slave childhood was a world apart. It was a world of poverty, privation, harsh physical punishment, and early physical labor. In the United States, the travails of slave children contributed to the rise of a middle-class ideal of a "protected" childhood, an ideal that emphasized intense parent–child bonds and insulation from the realities of the adult world.[43]

Much as the early nineteenth-century abolitionist struggle and the mid-twentieth century civil rights and anti-colonialist struggles reinvigorated global ideals of liberty and equality, so, too, the mistreatment of slave children played a critical role in the ever escalating valuation of childhood among the emerging early nineteenth-century urban middle class. Precisely because a slave childhood represented the antithesis of an emerging ideal, it gave a visceral meaning to the notion that childhood should be a stage of life devoted to schooling and to play, and a time of prolonged residence and protection within the family home.

Slavery's aftermath

The outbreak of the Civil War brought new uncertainties to the lives of enslaved children. According to Booker T. Washington, who was nine when the war began, slaves – parents and children alike – followed the progress of the war closely. The war penetrated into every aspect of enslaved children's lives, including their play. Candis Goodwin, a Virginian slave, recalled that black and white children on her plantation would "play Yankee and 'Federates,' course de whites was always the 'Federates. They'd make us black boys prisoners an' make b'lieve dey was gonna cut our necks off...."[44]

As the war dragged on, tens of thousands of slave women and children fled to northern lines. By November 1863, aid workers estimated that at least 50,000 slaves, mainly women and children, had fled to refugee camps, where they had no shelter except crude tents fashioned out of leaves and branches. Meanwhile, those who remained on plantations had to make up for the labor of those who had escaped. Elizabeth Scantling, who was fifteen years old in 1865, said that she was required to plow with "a mule an' a wild un at dat. Sometimes my hands get so cold I jes' cry."[45]

Slavery's abolition as a legal institution was followed by a protracted struggle to define the meaning of freedom. Childhood quickly became a central battleground in this struggle. Former slave owners viewed black children as a potential source of labor and used apprenticeship laws to force them to work without wages. In a number of Southern states, any fatherless children or any whose fathers "do not habitually employ their time in some honest industrious occupation" could be bound out as orphans to their former master. In addition, children whose mothers were not legally married might be classified as bastards who could be legally indentured. Children of parents deemed "unfit" could also be indentured without their parents' consent.[46]

Although many white Southerners defended apprenticeship as a way to care for orphans, it was essentially a system of labor exploitation. Most apprentices were of working age, mainly between the ages of ten and thirteen. Most were bound without their parents' consent, received no training, and were held beyond the legal age. Although legal slavery had been abolished, the exploitation of African–American children remained.

Notes

1 Keith Bradley and Paul Cartledge, eds., *The Cambridge World History of Slavery: Vol. I, The Ancient Mediterranean World* (Cambridge, UK: Cambridge University Press, 2011).

On children in ancient Egypt, see 208, 298; in ancient Greece, refer to 93, 127, 147; among early Jews, see, 442; in Rome, see 297–299, 358, 496.

2 Gwyn Campbell, Suzanne Miers, and Joseph C. Miller, eds., *Children in Slavery Through the Ages* (Athens, OH: Ohio University Press, 2009).

3 Wilma King, *Stolen Childhood: Slave Youth in Nineteenth-Century America* (Bloomington, IN: Indiana University Press, 1995); Marie Jenkins Schwartz, *Born in Bondage: Growing Up Enslaved in the Antebellum South* (Cambridge, MA: Harvard University Press, 2000).

4 C. Nana Derby, *Contemporary Slavery: Researching Child Domestic Servitude* (Lanham, MD: University Press of America, 2009); Kevin Bales, *Disposable People: New Slavery in the Global Economy* (Berkeley, CA: University of California Press, 2004); Joel Quirk, *Unfinished Business: A Comparative Survey of Historical and Contemporary Slavery* (Unesco, 2008).

5 David Brion Davis, *Inhuman Bondage: The Rise and Fall of Slavery in the New World* (New York, NY: Oxford University Press, 2006).

6 David Brion Davis, *Slavery and Human Progress* (New York, NY: Oxford University Press, 1984).

7 Don E. Fehrenbacher, *The Slaveholding Republic: An Account of the United States Government's Relation to Slavery* (New York, NY: Oxford University Press, 2001); Leonard L. Richards, *Slave Power: The Free North and Southern Domination, 1780–1860* (Baton Rouge, LA: Louisiana State University Press, 2000).

8 Ira Berlin, *Generations of Captivity: A History of African–American Slaves* (Cambridge, MA: Belknap Press of Harvard University Press, 2003).

9 Michael A. Gomez, *Exchanging Our Country Marks: The Transformation of African Identities in the Colonial and Antebellum South* (Chapel Hill, NC: University of North Carolina Press, 1998); James Sweet, *Recreating Africa: Culture, Kinship, and Religion in the African–Portuguese World, 1441–1770* (Chapel Hill, NC: University of North Carolina Press, 2003); John K. Thornton, *Africa and Africans in the Making of the Modern World* (Cambridge, UK: Cambridge University Press, 1998); Sheila S. Walker, *Africa Roots/American Cultures: Africa in the Creation of the Americas* (London, UK: Rowman & Littlefield, 2001).

10 Campbell, Miers, and Miller, *Children in Slavery Through the Ages*, 4–8.

11 Susan Eva O'Donovan, "Traded Babies: Enslaved Children in America's Domestic Migration, 1820–60," in Campbell, Miers, and Miller, *Children in Slavery Through the Ages*, 88–102.

12 Thomas Jefferson to John W. Eppes, June 30, 1820 (Farm Book 45–46).

13 Richard H. Steckel, "The African American Population of the United States, 1790–1920," in *A Population History of North America*, eds. Michael R. Haines and Richard H. Steckel (Cambridge, UK: Cambridge University Press ,1999), 433–482.

14 Marie Jenkins Schwartz, *Birthing a Slave: Motherhood and Medicine in the Antebellum South* (Cambridge: MA: Harvard University Press, 2006), 9–31.

15 Ibid., 143–187.

16 Steckel, "African American Population of the United States," 433–482.

17 King, *Stolen Childhood*, xxi, 1, 90; Thomas H. Jones, *The Experience of Thomas H. Jones, who was a Slave for Forty-Three Years* (Boston, MA: Bazin & Chandler, 1862), 6.

18 Campbell, Miers, and Miller, *Children in Slavery Through the Ages*, 8–11.

19 Michael P. Johnson, "Upward in Slavery," *New York Review of Books*, December 21, 1989.

20 King, *Stolen Childhood*, 9–11. Schwartz, *Born in Bondage*, 64, 68; Steven Mintz and Susan Kellogg, *Domestic Revolutions: A Social History of American Family Life* (New York, NY: Free Press, 1988), 73.

21 Johnson, "Upward in Slavery," http://www.nybooks.com/articles/3792.

22 Stephen Mintz, *Huck's Raft: A History of American Childhood* (Cambridge, MA: Belknap Press of Harvard University Press, 2004), 101.

23 Mintz and Kellogg, *Domestic Revolutions*, 73.

24 Josiah Henson quoted in Steven Mintz, ed., *African American Voices* (Malden, MA: Wiley–Blackwell, 2009), 92.

25 Schwartz, *Born In Bondage*, 85, 87–88, 126; Peter Bardaglio, "The Children of Jubilee: African American Childhood in Wartime," in *Divided Houses: Gender and the Civil War*, eds. Catherine Clinton and Nina Silber, (New York, NY: Oxford University Press, 1992), 216; Mintz, *African American Voices*, 90–92.

26 Schwartz, *Born in Bondage*, 91, 102, 105; King, *Stolen Childhood*, 24, 105; David K. Wiggins, "The Play of Slave Children in the Plantation Communities of the Old South, 1820–60," in *Growing Up in America*, eds. N. Ray Hiner and Joseph M. Hawes, (Urbana, IL: University of Illinois, 1985), 175; King, *Stolen Childhood*, 45, 48; Webber, *Deep Like the Rivers*, 95; Albert J. Raboteau, *Slave Religion: The "Invisible Institution" in the Antebellum South* (New York, NY: Oxford University Press, 1978), 282; Stephen C. Crawford, "Quantified Memory" (Ph.D. diss., University of Chicago, 1980), 169–70.

27 Schwartz, *Born in Bondage*, 83, 140–41; King, *Stolen Childhood*, 15, 17, 30.

28 King, *Stolen Childhood*, 24, 29–30, 34–35; Schwartz, *Born in Bondage*, 108, 145.

29 Joseph Holt Ingraham, *The South-west* (New York, NY: Harper & Brothers, 1835), Vol. II, 287, 288; Frederick Douglass, *Narrative of the Life of Frederick Douglass, an American Slave* (Cambridge, MA: Harvard University Press, 2009), 83; Elizabeth Keckley, *Behind the Scenes* (New York. NY: G. W. Carleton & Co.,1868), 34.

30 King, *Stolen Childhood*, 45, 48, 53; Webber, *Deep Like the Rivers*, 20, 95; Wiggins, "Play of Slave Children," 175, 185; Raboteau, *Slave Religion*, 282.

31 Sylviane A. Diof, *Growing Up in Slavery* (Brookfield, CT: Millbrook Press,2001), 25.

32 Thomas Jefferson, *Notes on Virginia*, Query 18: Manners, quoted in *The Founders' Constitution*, eds. Philip B. Kurland and Ralph Lerner (Chicago, IL: University of Chicago Press, 1987), 1:536–37.

33 King, *Stolen Childhood*, 53; Webber, *Deep Like the Rivers*, 20; Wiggins, "Play of Slave Children in the Plantation Communities of the Old South," 185.

34 Frederick Douglass, *My Bondage and My Freedom* (New York, NY: Barnes & Noble Classics, 2005), 57.

35 Mintz, *Huck's Raft*, 104.

36 Ibid., 107–108.

37 Janet Duitsman Cornelius, *"When I Can Read My Title Clear:" Literacy, Slavery, and Religion in the Antebellum South* (Columbia, SC: University of South Carolina Press, 1991), 1, 61, 69; Diouf, *Growing Up in Slavery*, 70; Webber, *Deep Like the Rivers*, 66, 134.

38 Schwartz, *Birthing a Slave*, 107–186.

39 Cheryll Ann Cody, "Naming, Kinship, and Estate Dispersal: Notes on Slave Family Life on a South Carolina Plantation, 1786 to 1833," *William and Mary Quarterly*, 3d ser., 39 (1982): 192–211; and "There Was No 'Absalom' on the Ball Plantations: Slave-Naming Practices in the South Carolina Low Country, 1720–1865," *American Historical Review* 92 (1987): 563–96; John C. Inscoe, "Carolina Slave Names: An Index to Acculturation," *Journal of Southern History* 49 (1983): 527–54; John Thornton, "Central African Names and African–American Naming Patterns," *William and Mary Quarterly*, 3d ser., 50 (1993): 727–42.

40 Schwartz, *Born in Bondage*.

41 Mintz, *Huck's Raft*, 106–107.

42 Ibid., 105–106.

43 Ronald G. Walters, *The Antislavery Appeal: American Abolition After 1830* (New York, NY: W. W. Norton, 1984).

44 Quoted in Mintz, *Huck's Raft*, 112.

45 Ibid.

46 Ibid., 113.

Suggestions for further reading

Gwyn Campbell, Suzanne Miers, and Joseph C. Miller, eds. *Children in Slavery Through the Ages* (Athens, OH: Ohio University Press, 2009) examines children's experiences in the slave trade and the treatment and uses of children acquired for sexual, military, political, or domestic purposes in the British Caribbean, China, East Africa, France, the Muslim world, and the American South.

Two key books recover the realities of childhood in bondage in the pre-Civil War American South. Wilma King, *Stolen Childhood: Slave Youth in Nineteenth-Century America* (Bloomington, IN: Indiana University Press, 1995) and Marie Jenkins Schwartz, *Born in Bondage: Growing Up Enslaved in the Antebellum South* (Cambridge, MA: Harvard University Press, 2000) explore the experiences of slave children, looking closely at their work experiences, family lives, and play.

Schwartz's *Birthing a Slave: Motherhood and Medicine in the Antebellum South*, (Cambridge: MA: Harvard University Press, 2006), examines pregnancy and childbirth within the slave community, showing how struggles over reproduction, sexuality, and mothering are central to an understanding of slavery. Especially important studies of the education of slave children include Janet Duitsman Cornelius, *"When I Can Read My Title Clear": Literacy, Slavery, and Religion in the Antebellum South* (Columbia, SC: University of South Carolina Press, 1991); Thomas L. Webber, *Deep Like The Rivers: Education In The Slave Quarter Community, 1831–1865* (New York, NY: Norton, 1978); and Heather Andrea Williams, *Self-Taught: African American Education in Slavery and Freedom* (Chapel Hill, NC: University of North Carolina Press, 2007). For information about slave children's leisure activities, see David K. Wiggins, "The Play of Slave Children in the Plantation Communities of the Old South, 1820–60," *Journal of Sport History* 7(2) (1980): 21–39.

19

MIXED-RACE CHILDREN IN THE AMERICAN WEST

Conquest and its categories

Anne F. Hyde

When we imagine children who lived in the American West, popular culture immediately fills our heads. Tow-headed children bumping along in covered wagons, the Ingalls girls and other northern European immigrant children living in sod houses and creaky frame buildings in windy plains towns, or the playmates of Dustin Hoffman's *Little Big Man* running through Indian camps. The moment we drill down into any of these images, however, a different vision of the West and its children emerges. Indian camps, homesteads, wagon trails, and towns did not appear on empty landscapes; they evolved in places where other people once lived and still lived. If the American West can be understood best as a place that has a long, complex legacy of conquest, mixed-race children are that inheritance. Popular culture offers fewer images of these children; their presence as a legacy makes us uncomfortable by reminding us how Anglo-Americans came to settle this place. Two generations of theorists have uncovered the huge cultural work it took to make the American West empty and then white in our national imaginations, but a "veil of race," to use W.E.B Dubois's words, still covers this place. It wasn't empty. Trade, war, imperial adventure, and finally conquest by the United States were all demographic engines that brought peoples together. Together they created families with children who bore the burden of racialization as the nineteenth century progressed.

My essay aims to do three things. It explains how a particular category – mixed-race children – was created and used in the nineteenth-century West. Working through specific family examples, it then examines how this category made sense to both the institutions of the state that imposed it and to the people who inhabited it. How did these young Westerners experience being mixed-race children? Finally, the essay suggests how the category disappears at the end of the nineteenth century and what this meant for western children and their families. These aims, of course, turn out to be complicated. Mixed-race children, Indian, White, Hispanic are terms that exist only like sand paintings – their meanings blow away the moment the picture becomes clear. I'm compounding the trouble by including groups of mixed-race people who combined Anglo, Native, and Hispanic in different ways.

Operating at the edges of empire, the United States West offers us a fine opportunity to look at conquest at its most intimate level. The fur trade and imperial conquest performed the magic of demographic change on a vast landscape. People who perceived each other as culturally different (if not racially distinct until the mid-nineteenth century), met as part of business and war. As people do, they created families with children. These children, ubiquitous and unremarkable on eighteenth- and early-nineteenth-century frontiers, became noticeable and problematic in the middle of the nineteenth century.

So, how do we uncover these children and make sense of deeply suspect numbers? We don't have any idea how many people inhabited the trans-Mississippi West in the nineteenth century nor how many of them were children, much less how we might understand them racially. The US Census is designed *not* to see mixed-race people of Native or Hispanic ancestral backgrounds. Native people and mixed-race people weren't systematically counted until 1870, and then only Indians on reservations. People with Hispanic heritages weren't delineated in the census until after World War II, though they were certainly noticed in other places: church, mission, and military records, Native population counts, paintings and photographs, Indian Service and Bureau of Indian Affairs records, traders' licenses, and family stories.

Why should we care about illuminating this group of people? They are a numerous and complex group that worried the American state considerably. And, historians of colonial practices, Ann Laura Stoler in particular, have examined the intimate side of imperial behavior and have pointed out the centrality of marriage, child rearing, and education in making conquest work. Her critique of American historiography for having ignored these issues is enormously helpful, but her view may be too institutional. Stoler and her critics see these personal matters as far more state-controlled and determined by official policies than the decisions I watch unfold around mixed-race families in the nineteenth century. People have sex, get married, have children, and raise children and they do their best to "make sense" of whatever situation faces them. Their choices may look irrational or very circumscribed to our eyes, but they offered hope and possibilities for them. We can see this most clearly in the stories of families who mix ancestral heritages and how their calculations about what "makes sense" changed over the nineteenth century. Being mixed blood, or métis, or mestizo, or simply not white meant something very different by the end of that century.[1]

The most obvious place to start is with the fur trade, the economic engine of eighteenth- and nineteenth-century North America. The fur trade giant, the Hudson's Bay Company (HBC), and its employees created a society in the North American West that demonstrates the intimate nature of conquest. HBC policy and practice resembled colonial behavior in India and Africa. This global behemoth encouraged employees to "produce" mixed-race children in order to get crucial knowledge from Native people and to build lasting cultural bridges. Most importantly, the company needed a particular kind of colonial worker – not native and not British – to staff its workforce but never to threaten ideas of British-ness at home. Native people and their mixed-race children quickly challenged categories of British-ness and later some versions of American-ness as well. Living and making a living in the region required insider knowledge that could be acquired most easily though marriage and family. In these settings, mixed-race people made sense and parents could assume that their children would always have respectability and opportunity.

Despite what parents hoped, in the mid-nineteenth century many people in the West suddenly found their families labeled as "mixed blood" and their children became objects of attention and concern. Traders on the Northern Plains, farmers in New Mexico, hunters in the Rocky Mountains, elite families in St Louis and commoners in Santa Fe suddenly faced hard decisions about categorizing their children. Ethnicity and nationality marked children, just as borders between the United States and Canada and between the United States and Mexico newly mattered as well. Mixing blood could have remained a sensible choice, but it didn't. Warfare, execution, and extermination replaced trade and family building. This change had enormous personal implications: Euro-American men abandoned their mixed-race families, communities began to demand segregated education, and job and marriage opportunities – especially for young men – became limited. And this is the story we really need to untangle. Historians debate when the change in attitude about racial identification congealed – many locate it in the early nineteenth century; however, what people actually did in the West during the nineteenth century – marriage and birth patterns – indicates a different timing. Stubborn patterns of optimism and human behavior meant that inter-cultural relationships lasted much longer and were tolerated at the local level well after the Civil War.

Children and racialization: erased by nostalgia

The children of these families bear a lot of weight in exposing the tension between a fiercely held democratic ideology of a republic made up of citizens whose differences should not matter and equally powerful notions of the need for absolute racial purity. Mixed-race children stood in the crosshairs of these ideas. Sometimes they saw themselves as a racial vanguard of the future of the West, and certainly their parents hoped this would be the case. Too often, however, other people saw them as threatening mongrels who needed to be especially distinguished and noticed because they could become white, a dangerous threat. Looking at these children and the cultures that produced them involves several strands of historiography: histories of racialization, and race (and race that is not about the black/white divide, but still has everything to do with that divide), ethnicity, family history, and histories of particular cultures.

Given the fact that Europeans arrived in a place filled with millions of native people, the project of maintaining racial purity was a mighty work. What is amazing is not that ideologies were created to uphold racial difference in support of European superiority, but that these ideologies worked at all, given the demographics involved. Colonial societies in the New World, in order to remain respectable, refused to accept mixed bloods as equals no matter how much wealth or status they might attain. Instead they degraded them in law and in custom. Spanish, English, and French colonial administrators all kept careful records to ensure that mixed bloods were kept out of lineages and power. Popular culture did similar work as mixed-blood people came to have terrible and troubled reputations as racial traitors. Despite such an overpowering negative push, many people chose to cross the racial divide no matter what legal and cultural structures prohibited it. Partly, people responded to what Thomas Ingersoll calls the paradox of racial mixture in the Americas that "produced both suffering and a remarkable progressive opportunity for the human race."[2] And partly, these children made particular economic and cultural sense in the North American Wests of the eighteenth and nineteenth centuries.

Canadian historians, focused on the fur trade that had so much import there, have told the story of a colonial past with racial mixing with depth and sophistication. We know a lot about children there. Even though mixed blood people and the fur trade were similarly essential in the Great Lakes, Missouri, Mississippi, and Arkansas River worlds, this story has been told very differently south of the Canadian border. The ubiquity and longevity of the fur trade and other industries that produced mixed-race children flies in the face of Frederick Jackson Turner's view of a West that inevitably ended with Euro-American farmers and merchants running the show. In this tenacious rendering, Native people, the fur trade, and its cultural patterns were supposed to be a passing phase, a romantic stage in which white men and dusky maidens produced children with the faint hue of the savage stained on their cheeks. While these sojourners – traders, mountain men, army explorers and troops, and state officials who married Native women – might be treated as a cultural joke from such an evolutionary perspective, they left behind hundreds of thousands of actual children.

Journalist Matthew Field, who accompanied a Scottish nobleman on a pleasure trip through the American West in 1843, typifies the way most people "noticed" mixed-race children. As part of a crabby diatribe about his patron's poor management of the trip, his journal noted one evening that "the good looking squaw of Henry, the hunter, gave birth last night to a little female half-breed." Field complained bitterly that "His Omnipotence" had ordered the camp to *lay by* on this account." He insisted that this delay counted as "the first occasion ever known of a mountain journey being delayed by *one hour* for such a reason!" While he snarled about "the second day now lost by blind and bad management," he noted that he used the time to make "moccasins for my Indian dog, Skamokin [Flathead for dog] his [feet] being sore."[3] His remarks are stunning in their layered assumptions about hierarchies of value and power. The Indian canine clearly deserved more care than the "good looking squaw" and her half-breed child because these are people destined to disappear – only relics and reminders of an older world in the process of fading away for a more civilized world that values a particular kind of progress.

Two governors and their children

Our first two examples provide evidence for the importance of mixed-race people and the role their children played in various parts of the West. Neither story can simply be dismissed as a romantic vestige of an old and savage West, lost when the "real" founders arrived. They are drawn from the fact that the early governors of Michigan, Minnesota, New Mexico, Kansas, Missouri, Illinois, Arkansas, and Wisconsin, the first Anglo mayor of Los Angeles, the founders of Detroit, Chicago, Denver, St Louis, Kansas City, Santa Fe, and Austin, all had roots in the fur trade, and most had close family connections with Native and mixed-race people. I have chosen two examples from this list: Henry Sibley, the first governor of Minnesota, and Charles Bent, the first Anglo governor of New Mexico. For both men, personal family choices have been erased from the "official" histories of the region. None of the early histories of Minnesota or even the vast biography of Sibley, written immediately after his death, mention his mixed-race children, even though Sibley wrote about them in his never-completed autobiography. Charles Bent too has the details of his personal life stripped from his story. The *Annals of St. Louis* tells us: "Charles Bent, born in 1799, died single, Governor of Taos, New Mexico, murdered."[4] This entry has us picturing a lonely death, but in fact, Charles Bent died in the arms of his wife, Ignacia Jaramillo, and in the presence of three of his children, Teresina, Alfredo, and Rumalda. The erasure of intimate relationships happens everywhere: in accounts of founding families in Alta California, New Mexico, Missouri, and Minnesota, we find unmarried men and childless women. What a sad and barren past, if it were true. The work of many historians in the past twenty years reveals a messy inter-ethnic past of marriages, casual liaisons, and children among many groups of people that, to later observers, mixed people and nations in dangerously promiscuous ways. Sibley and Bent, similarly ambitious men born of the Western Frontier, made very different choices about how to live in the region and how to make sense of their mixed-race families.

Henry Hastings Sibley, who became the first governor of Minnesota, spent most of his life as a trader with the Ojibwe and Dakota nations. A native of Detroit, he was born in 1811 to Sarah and Solomon Sibley; his father was the first Anglo-American lawyer in Michigan. Like most young men living in the Great Lakes and the Upper Mississippi River region, he made his living in the fur trade, working at various forts, stores, and towns as he climbed the corporate ladder of the industry. Sibley's first employer was an Ojibwe woman named Susan Johnston, who had married an Irish trader and who ran a store on Lake Superior. Sibley then worked for the Upper Mississippi Division of the American Fur Company in 1835. He spent years running the business among the Dakota and Ojibwe near Fort Snelling. Like most traders, he needed relationships with Native people to make his work successful. He made these bonds in several ways, using his position sometimes to advocate on their behalf and sometimes to fill his own pocket. In 1837 Sibley got powers of attorney for twenty mixed-blood children named in treaties with Dakotas, Ojibwes, and Winnebagoes and went to Washington to make sure that debts to him were paid first, but also to make sure that the half-breed rights in the treaty were upheld.[5]

He also formed a sexual union with a Dakota woman named Red Blanket Woman; they had a child together in 1841. It is revealing that Sibley stopped writing his autobiography when he reached the point of having to describe this relationship. As his most recent biographer points out, perhaps Sibley had no way to explain these inter-racial mixings now that he was writing in the 1870s as a famous "pioneer." Red Blanket Woman's death left Sibley with the toddler girl. Reluctant to take on the challenge of single fatherhood with a mixed-race child, Sibley had her baptized as Helene and placed her with a mixed-race family of an old friend, William R. Brown. He paid for her upkeep but made little effort to integrate her into his white family after he married in 1843. Sibley, and his Anglo family, lived in a fine stone house just outside of Fort Snelling, a military post that also served as an Indian agency where Helene and her Dakota family visited regularly.[6]

Sibley did not make such choices about children and family in a vacuum. He surrounded himself with influential friends who built similar families. Not just fur traders, but merchants, farmers, carpenters, ministers, and army officers also had Native families. Many men abandoned these families because they became liabilities rather than advantages when the fur-trading community became small-town Minnesota. Beginning in 1830, Captain Seth Eastman served several stints as commander of Fort Snelling. Eastman, already a noted artist of Native America, had a relationship with a Dakota woman named Wakaninajin. A daughter, Nancy Eastman, was born in the summer of 1831. Eastman left his Native wife and child when he was transferred to a post in Florida in 1835. Seth did not see his daughter Nancy again until 1848, even though he was re-assigned to Fort Snelling in 1841 along with his Anglo wife Mary and their two children. Mary Eastman, avidly interested in Indian life and lore, developed friendships with a number of local Dakota women. She eventually wrote a book entitled *Dakotah; or Life and Legends of the Sioux around Fort Snelling* that was beautifully illustrated by Seth's drawings. When she published the book in 1849, Mary Eastman dedicated it to Henry Sibley.[7] If she knew that both Sibley and her own husband had Dakota daughters, the fact is not recorded.

Not all Anglo fathers abandoned their Native or mixed-blood families. Native women often left Anglo husbands and took their children with them when they decided to remain with their own kin. Many mixed-race families stayed intact. The range of family choices and the numbers of "half-breeds" and "mixed bloods" emerge in the records of the Indian Department. At the St Peters trading post and agency alone, where Helene Sibley and Nancy Eastman were born, several hundred "half-breeds" were recorded in agency records, noted there because these children had access to land and trust accounts often held by traders and Indian agents like Sibley. These children included Charles Eastman, son of Nancy Eastman and grandson of Seth Eastman, who grew up to be a successful medical doctor and Native activist.[8]

Sibley, with his long-time connections in the fur trade and the military, served as the sole Congressional representative from Minnesota and was then appointed first territorial governor in 1858. As Congressman and as Governor, he recommended that Minnesota deal with the issue of Indian land claims before white settlers flooded the region. He warned "Your pioneers are encircling the last home of the red man, as with a wall of fire," and that if Indians and their lands and needs were not considered "you must suffer the consequences of a bloody and remorseless Indian war." The Anglo-booster world of territorial politics ignored any suggestion about slowing white settlement or about the need for Indian policy. Inevitably, the result of rapid and uncontrolled settlement was Indian war. The violence in Minnesota between Indian residents and white squatters began with a widespread Dakota uprising. Hundreds of settlers were killed, derailing settlement in Minnesota for at least a decade. The fact that Henry Sibley, with his long years of experience as a trader and his intimate connections with Minnesota Natives, became the obvious choice to lead the expeditions against the Indians demonstrates how much frontier culture had shifted away from the strategy of using kin relationships as diplomacy. "General" Sibley defeated the Indians after several years of the "bloody and remorseless" war he had predicted, but he made sure that the mixed-race families of many of the traders and army officers were protected because these people had saved white families in the initial weeks of the uprising.[9]

As the war spread, many people fled to Canada, where mixed-race families felt safer. For those who remained, the question of how to provide for Minnesota's mixed-race children in treaties, reservations, and schools set up after the war became a morass of legal and cultural confusion. Both Native and Anglo-Minnesotans tried to define who was an Indian and who was not. "Mixed blood" and "half-breed" as opposed to "full blood" became official descriptors of children as they entered school or inherited land. Helene Sibley, educated in St Paul and in an eastern school for two years, remained in Minneapolis as part of its growing mixed-race population. She married a Cree and French trader and they disappear in the record after her marriage. Helene received payments as part of Dakota half-breed treaty settlements in 1858 and funds from railroad speculation that her father had invested in her name; traces of Helene's existence can be tracked through her father's business records.[10] Though Governor Sibley wouldn't win any fatherhood awards in the twenty-first century, his actions reflect the shifts in racial thinking around children in the nineteenth century. He needed Helene and her Dakota mother in the industry that built his fortunes, but he needed a different family in the mercantile world of Anglo-America that arrived in the upper Midwest in the 1840s. He provided for Helene with money, but erased her from his official story.

Charles Bent, another fur trader, successful merchant, governor, and father, was a product of an elite St Louis family. Like Henry Sibley, Charles, born in 1799, spent his early life in the fur trade but tired of its economic risk and violence. He watched the development of the new trading network between Santa Fe and St Louis, and by the late 1820s had concluded that the diversified Santa Fe trade looked promising. In 1829, Charles and his younger brother William outfitted a caravan filled with trade goods and rumbled along the busy Santa Fe Trail into Mexico. In Santa Fe they traded their goods for furs, buffalo hides, blankets, and Mexican silver, which they carried back to St Louis and sold at a handsome profit. The Bent brothers and their partners ended up in St Louis with merchandise worth perhaps $200,000, an enormous fortune in 1820s Missouri that would be equivalent to several million today.[11]

Given this success, Charles decided to become a permanent resident of New Mexico. He centered his operations in Taos, an old trading town on the Rio Grande River in what is now northern New Mexico. To trade legally in a foreign country, Charles had to become a citizen of Mexico and develop trading relationships with local merchants. As thousands of American men had discovered while living in the Mexican north of New Mexico, California, and Texas, the path to this set of relationships was marriage and children. Charles married Ignacia Jaramillo, a young widow from a prominent Taos family, in 1835. They raised five children in a complicated household that included orphaned relatives and adopted Indian children as servants.

Like Henry Sibley, Charles Bent found intimate personal relationships across ethnic boundaries essential, but Bent's choice had different consequences. When Charles and Ignacia chose to get married, they expected their children to benefit from this decision. They had the strong support of the Jaramillo family and the entire surrounding community. Charles Bent's position as an Anglo-American trader married into an elite Taoseño family gave him important benefits. He served in local political office, amassed land grants from the Mexican Government for himself and his friends, and negotiated trade agreements with both the Mexican and United States Governments. After the New Mexico part of the Mexican War ended in 1846, Charles was appointed as the new American Governor. As an old New Mexico resident, Charles Bent should have known that this appointment would brand him as a traitor in the Taos region, still boiling with anger over American occupation. Early in the morning of January 19, 1847 a group of angry Taos residents ignited a revolt. A large group of local men – Mexican, Native, and Anglo – marched to Charles Bent's house. Even though he had children that connected him to all of these communities, he had become a man with whom nearly every Taoseño could find fault, now that he served the occupying Americans.[12]

Bent's choices had enormous impact on his family. On that winter dawn, the mob shouted, fired shots into the house, and began to tear the roof off. The family dug desperately through the adobe walls of the house using fire pokers and spoons. As three of his five children, Teresina, Alfredo, and Rumalda watched, the angry men scalped Bent, shot arrows and bullets into his body, and completed the task by stripping the body and mutilating it. They tacked Bent's bloody scalp to a board and paraded it through the streets as the Bent family huddled on the floor next to what remained of their father's body, wondering what fate their American connections would bring them. In the context of American occupation, these children had become famously mixed-race, a status that had become dangerous.[13]

After watching their father's brutal murder in 1847, Charles Bent's children stayed in New Mexico with their mother's family. A dense web of family, who could now be labeled as Mexican–American, still linked Taos and Santa Fe to ranches and trading communities further east and north in what is now Colorado, and protected the Bent children as they began their adult lives. Ignacia stayed in Taos with Teresina, who married a German man and remained in Taos. Estafina married an American trader named Alexander Hicklen, and in 1860 she lived next door to her mother with her husband and infant son. Alfredo Bent, who attended Catholic schools in Santa Fe and St Louis, first set up business in Taos where he had family support. The 1860 census finds him at the age of twenty-three a successful merchant married to Guadalupe Long, another child of an Anglo father and a New Mexican mother. The young family had a nine-year-old Indian servant living with them to help care for their baby son, Donacio Charles, surely named in part for his dead grandfather.[14] These children, with connections to an important Anglo St Louis family and to a respected Hispanic family in Taos, managed reasonably well after their father's death. Unlike Henry Sibley's efforts to forget his intimate connections to native Minnesota, Charles Bent's connections to Hispanic New Mexicans allowed his children to continue to benefit from their mixed cultural status, an asset in tolerant and isolated New Mexico. However, even the Bent name didn't protect his sons and grandsons when Anglo-American courts divided up land in late nineteenth-century legal battles; like all Hispanic New Mexicans, they lost most of their land.

The Drips: race and family choice on another frontier

Kansas and Missouri, in the crosshairs of American expansion, would prove to be even more challenging than New Mexico. The experiences of the Drips family provide a useful example of the ubiquity of the mixed-race world in the West during the 1830s through the 1860s – what would become Missouri, Kansas, Iowa, and Nebraska, but in the 1830s was Indian Country. I capitalize "Indian Country" because it is a real place, labeled on maps, that policy makers, Indian agents, military officials, and all manner of local folks understood as being controlled by Native nations. The debate focused on its borders and its future, not its reality. The Missouri River, where it turns north along what is now the Kansas–Missouri border, formed the heart of this Indian Country. It was a very complex place, created by the fur trade and by the human miseries of Indian removal that took Native peoples from several nations in the Upper Midwest and placed them in Kansas. Plains Indians, Missouri River Indians, and what came to be known as emigrant nations, all met in Kansas, and so did the Euro-Americans who operated on the edge of this world. With long practice at using intermixing as a cultural strategy, a huge mixed-race population grew up here. By 1846, when the region became a staging area for overland migration, some ten thousand Indians lived in what is now Kansas. Among them were thousands of mixed-raced people who gathered in towns like Westport, St Joseph, and Shawnee Mission.[15]

Many worlds came together: Plains and Missouri River Indian nations came here to trade with French, Spanish, British, and American traders and armies. Because of its significant location, in 1808 the US government granted this land to the Osage and built a fur-trading factory and store to serve plains tribes. Hundreds of traders set up business nearby or retired there with their families after careers in the fur industry. Thus the region has a long tradition of mixed-race communities. One important family, the Chouteaus, settled here and followed family diplomatic traditions by having two families – one in Creole French St Louis and one among the Osage, Kaw, and Otoe people. Several Chouteaus made the choice to marry Shawnee and Osage women exclusively, a pattern of serial monogamy where men (both European and Native) married into the tribe in which they were trading, but left these families (years or decades) later if they needed to form new relationships with a different tribe, a choice common among even the most elite members of the trading world.[16]

We can see legal recognition of this cultural style in an 1818 treaty made by the state of Missouri to begin wresting this rich river country away from local Native nations. The treaty specially allowed land and status for people labeled as mixed-blood and half-breed Osage, Otoe, Shawnee, and Kansas who made up part of the mixed-blood community at Kawsmouth, where traders, natives, and removed Indians had built a community over two generations. They built it on the backs of children, the people designated in treaties to inherit land because white fathers couldn't get Native land and Native people, especially women, couldn't own land in white areas. The Kawsmouth region grew even more cosmopolitan as removed Indians from East of the Mississippi and from Missouri arrived in Kansas. The local Kansas or Kaw Indians refused to give up their lands or to accept newly removed Indians without large annuities, a significant land base north and west of the Missouri River, and a settlement for their mixed-race members. These mixed-race children, largely the product of French trappers and Kansas and Kansas/Osage women, in particular from the wealthy Chouteau family and other important St Louisans, were ceded land in what became known as "half-breed tracts" that were sprinkled all over Indian country in these years.[17]

The Drips family fit right in. Far more ordinary than the gubernatorial Sibleys or Bents, the Drips were part of fur trade middle management. The patriarch, Andrew Drips, was born in Ireland in 1789 and came to the United States as a small child. Like many young immigrant men, he moved steadily West, serving in the War of 1812 in the Ohio militia, but finally settling in the fur trade. He led trading expeditions among the Pawnee, Osage, and Otoe and worked at several different forts as a trader for a couple of the large operations. He married an Otoe woman named Macompemay in 1828 and settled into the routines of the Missouri River trade. Like most traders working in this region, Drips had developed close personal ties with Otoe people and when he wanted a more intimate connection, building a family seemed sensible. Most men in his world made similar choices and Native groups in the region encouraged young women to use marriage and family to connect their peoples to the Euro-American world.

As a young trader, Drips often brought his wife and children along on extended trading trips. They spent some winters entirely in Native villages. Native women traveling with fur brigades served as cultural mediators; helped to make and repair traps; processed furs for storage; and cared for the children. In 1832, Drips and Macompemay headed north into Blackfoot country at the specific instruction of his employer Pierre Chouteau. This turned out to be a particularly bloody season with the upper Missouri tribes (as reported in grisly detail in the St Louis newspapers), which devolved into all-out war with the Blackfoot and Gros Ventre. In fur-trade families, however, life went on and Macompemay gave birth to her second daughter Katherine during a famous battle at Pierre's Hole in October of 1832.[18]

Through Drips' letters and his meticulous accounts, we can see how the fur trade changed in these years and how this mixed-race family negotiated these changes. By the end of the 1830s, Drips and Macompemay had four children: Charley, Jane, Katherine, and Willie. As the children got older, he and Macompemay decided to sacrifice family intimacy for stability and education. Many fur-trade families, particularly those at the upper echelons of the business who had the economic support to make choices, began to worry that the fur trade might not provide opportunities for their offspring. St Louis Catholic boarding schools became second homes for these children, and more than half of the students at the biggest schools were mixed-race children from fur-trade families. Entirely unlike the reservation boarding schools where Native children would be warehoused in the late nineteenth and early twentieth centuries, these schools served the St Louis elite of all ethnicities. Students learned classical languages, advanced mathematics, drawing, music, and the etiquette necessary to move in sophisticated circles.[19]

When Drips served as a trader at Fort Pierre, Fort John, and also at Fort Laramie, the older children stayed in St Louis in order to attend school. Drips paid their boarding school bills and provided them with the silk hats and umbrellas, and tortoiseshell and ivory combs they required to join the aspiring elite. To help pay for such expenses, Drips took on the position of a special Indian Agent for the United States Government. He also bought land in 1841 among the mixed-race families of retired traders living in Kawsmouth, just north of today's Kansas City. Drips and Macompemay married in the Catholic Church at Westport in 1841 and Macompemay became Margaret Jackson as they entered the local merchant elite.

When Macompemay died in 1846, Drips married a younger French and Sioux woman named Louise Geroux, who had lived in Kawsmouth her entire life. Drips and Louise had five children and adopted several others, including the mixed-race daughters of Lucien Fontanelle, Drips' former partner. Faced with supporting a large family, the Drips used varied strategies to educate these children and to find places for them on the changing Missouri frontier. Drips and Louise remained in Kawsmouth, where a large number of retired traders brought their families, making it a small-scale version of the Red River settlements in Canada. Drips worried about what would happen to his children once the fur trade no longer dominated the western economy. He set up his eldest son Charley with an interest in a Missouri riverboat, hoping the boy could succeed in that endeavor. In 1847, a family friend wrote Drips that Charley had a good head for figures, "not usual for a half-breed," indicating the category into which Charley had been placed.[20]

The Drips were not alone in these efforts. As Westport, Independence, and Kansas City grew, so did this mingled population. Most of the early founders made their living in the fur trade and had at least one "fur-trade marriage" and some had made several. We see numerous educational institutions, job market niches, and marriage patterns supporting these families. In Westport, children from trader families attended Mr Huffaker's Classical Academy, and in Independence, Love's Academy served these children. Some parents chose to send their children to the mission schools at Fort Osage or at Shawnee Mission for their basic education. For the most privileged and ambitious, Catholic colleges in St Louis, like Sisters of St Joseph Convent that Jane and Katherine Drips attended or the Christian Brothers College or St Louis University, provided educations for mixed-race and Native children to prepare them for life among the merchant and professional classes.[21]

Even with such educations, mixed-race children had fewer choices about how to conduct their lives as the nineteenth century progressed. Few moved into the merchant elite circles in which their parents had lived. Many became important in tribal politics as the United States Government struggled to reduce Native land ownership, and mixed-race people were often at the forefront of treaty arrangements and land-claim negotiations – and were often accused of being two-faced and complicit as a result. The term "half-breed" comes into official use here as a descriptor in treaty language and as a pejorative term with the same cultural sense as the "tragic mulatto" – a person caught between two worlds and comfortable in neither. We don't know how the Drips children experienced this transition, but we do know that all nine received land along the Missouri River as a result of the treaty negotiations with Otoe and Sioux people in the 1830s. Traders, often with mixed-race children, and Native negotiators, often mixed-race themselves, insisted that the "half-breed" children be specially recognized in each treaty. The Drips children and grandchildren received title to thousands of acres of land in the 1850s when the land was allotted, but only one 400-acre piece remained in the family by 1870, suggesting something about their experience in the enormous dispossession of land enacted on all Native people, mixed-race or not, in these years.[22]

The Drips children were flesh and blood reminders of an important culture that still operated on the Missouri River frontier. Their parents worked hard to carve out secure lives for them and to integrate them into the agricultural and merchant economies that were replacing trade. Despite such efforts, they mostly failed to protect their children's class status. They did, however, protect them from being removed to Indian Territory, the fate of nearly all "full-blooded" Indians in Kansas. Andrew Drips continued to work in the fur trade and to employ his sons and sons-in-law well into the 1860s. He applied for trading licenses for himself and served as bondholder for his son William's license. When he hired his sons as hunters and translators, Drips was careful to list them as "half-breed" rather than "Indian" because he could justify a higher wage scale that way. He made trips to trade for furs along the Platte and Upper Missouri, working with them until his death at the age of seventy.[23]

When it stops making sense: mixed-race children and the state

The Drips were too optimistic about their children's chances in the racially obsessed culture of the mid-nineteenth century. The US Government and its agents do not spend money or invent policy unless there is a political or cultural need. So, we have to examine a couple of large, expensive programs that involved children of mixed cultural heritage. One category was organized to determine and manage the vast project of extinguishing Indian land claims as the last step of conquest, and involved hundreds of millions of acres, complex accounting procedures, and volumes of demographic information. Another expensive government program was the set of commissions, courts, inspectors, and surveyors that worked to ascertain the legality of Spanish and Mexican land grants in the part of the United States won in the Mexican War. Finally, at great expense, the United States sent in agents and soldiers to remove the illegal Mexican "squatters" who had been there for generations. These programs directly affected mixed-race children. Such elaborate administration was required to figure out who deserved land and title, and much of that determination was driven by race and culture. In both situations, mixed-race people caused difficulties because they weren't clearly Indian or Mexican. These special arrangements for "half-breeds" appeared in treaties between Indian nations and the US Government until the 1880s.[24]

The story of the Nemaha Half-Breed Reservation illustrates the complexity of such bureaucratic efforts. This set of agreements, only one example among scores of treaties, set aside tracts of land in what is now Wisconsin and Illinois for the mixed-race descendants of French-Canadian trappers and women of the Otoe, Iowa, and Omaha, as well as the Yankton and Santee Sioux tribes. The "half-breeds," interwoven into these communities, moved along with their Native families from Wisconsin, Minnesota, Illinois, and Iowa as part of the removal process and its treaty agreements. They all finally found themselves located in part of the Indian Territory just west of the Missouri River in what is now Kansas and Nebraska. Once settled, they demanded reservations and individual land allotments for the half-breeds, a group that included people like the Drips children but also children with much stronger connections to their Native families. Before Nebraska Territory and then the state of Nebraska could be created, these old treaties had to be upheld. So treaty commissioners, eager to open up all of Nebraska for white settlement, designated a special piece of land for half-breed children, 1,125 of them, in the 1856 division of land. The tract's eastern border was the Missouri River, where the Drips family took up land in 1856. Never required to live on the properties they had been allocated, and held in trust by local white bankers and real estate speculators, many of the underage "owners" immediately turned over their lands to white settlers.[25]

Treaties involving the Sac and Fox in Iowa and Illinois; the Osage in Missouri and Kansas; the Dakota, Lakota, and Sioux in Wisconsin, Minnesota and the Dakotas; Cree and Ojibwa in Minnesota; and Cheyenne and Arapaho in Colorado all had extensive provisions for half-breeds, with special "half-breed scrip" being printed to indicate exact locations and sizes of claims. William Clark – explorer, Missouri Governor, father and guardian of mixed-race children, and superintendent of Indian affairs for the Louisiana Territory between 1812 and 1837 – justified these special claims for children. He wrote that only in these children could "an attachment for fixed residence and an idea of separate property be imparted without which it is in vain to think of improving the minds and morals of the Indians."[26] These children (and their white fathers) could be trusted to manage land, while adult full-blooded Indians could not. Despite Clark's obviously self-interested and flawed thinking, his words do reflect malleable ideas about race and the significance of mixed-race children.

We see similarly shifting ideas about race and landownership in the Southwest. Charles Bent and thousands of Anglo-American men like him married Mexican women, received land grants from the Spanish Crown or the Mexican Government and passed them on to their children, fully expecting that their wealth would be protected by the state and preserved for their mixed-race children. However, these ideas no longer meshed with American notions of property, citizenship, or family in the years after the Mexican War. Children who inherited land that had once been part of New Spain or Mexico found that their land had been made part of the United States public domain after conquest, even though such confiscation had been expressly forbidden in the Treaty of Guadalupe Hidalgo. These children, many Spanish speakers and increasingly labeled racially as Mexican, found themselves defined as squatters on their own land. Millions of acres, seen by American policy makers as wasted in the hands of unproductive Mexicans who held land in common ranches rather than working small family farms, were taken from their owners. Special Land Claims Courts, state courts, and the US Supreme Court consistently ruled against these children and their land claims in cases that rivaled *Bleak House*'s case of Jarndyce and Jarndyce for their length and complexity. Alfredo Bent, his two sisters, Estafina and Teresina, and their children remained mired in court for two generations until their claim was finally and completely denied.[27]

The children we have just followed through the nineteenth-century American West can tell us much about cultural shifts around racial ideology and demonstrate how much ideas matter. In the 1830s and 1840s, mixed-race children were made visible all over the West in surprising numbers. Into the 1850s, the industries and colonial practices that encouraged their parents to make these choices continued to demand their presence, even as American conquest and Indian War made their lives more challenging. Charley Drips and Alfredo Bent had very different experiences than their sisters – race seemed to matter more for young men in these years. Lives and choices narrowed considerably in the 1860s and 1870s as Mary Bent or Katherine Drips would discover, when concerns about racial passing of any kind began to erase the already insecure place mixed-race children had created in the West. The Homestead Act, enacted in 1862 to support wide ownership of land for white families, could only offer up its largesse at the expense of other families whose claims to land were ignored by the new American state. The Ingalls family and its wagons rolled over land given to Helene Sibley and owned by Thomas Drips.

We don't know the ending of this story because so many mixed-race children disappeared between the cracks of racial distinctions, but the places that may have protected them steadily disappeared. Mixed-race disappears as a category as rigid definitions of race replaced an earlier flexibility that western conquest had required. The census and western American culture demanded that people be White or Indian. Children re-categorized in this way could not claim land from the government, nor could they count on protecting land they had inherited because they had no firm status in court. Without land, these children lost cultural status as well. In formerly French and Indian St Louis or Mexican and Anglo California for example, where mixed-race children were educated in Catholic schools as an entree into the world of the elite, new institutions like Washington University or Occidental College positioned themselves to educate young Anglo Protestants as an exclusive elite. The loss became final when American culture rewrote the pioneer story to erase these mixed-race children whose presence and claim to land in the West interrupted the heroic story of white settlers claiming virgin land.

Notes

1 Ann Laura Stoler, "Tense and Tender Ties: The Politics of Comparison in North American History and (Post)-Colonial Studies" *Journal of American History* 88 (Dec. 2001), 829–865; Theresa Schenck "Border Identities: Métis, Halfbreed, Mixed-Blood" in *Gathering Places: Aboriginal and Fur Trade Histories,* ed. Podruchny and Peers (Vancouver: University of British Columbia Press, 2010).

2 Thomas N. Ingersoll, *To Intermix With our White Brothers: Indian Mixed Bloods in the United States from Earliest Times to the Indian Removals* (Albuquerque: University of New Mexico Press, 2005), 7.

3 Matthew C. Field, *Mountain and Prairie Sketches*, Gregg and McDermott, eds. (Norman: University of Oklahoma Press, 1957), 163.

4 Frederick A. Billon, *Annals of St. Louis in its Territorial Days From 1804–1821* (St. Louis: n.p, 1881), 200.

5 Rhoda R. Gilman, *Henry Hastings Sibley: Divided Heart* (St. Paul: Minnesota Historical Society Press, 2004), 1–8, 22–3.

6 Theodore C. Blegen, "The Unfinished Autobiography of Henry Hastings Sibley" *Minnesota History*, 8, no. 4 (Dec. 1927), 329–62; Gilman, *Divided Heart*, 66–8.

7 Gilman, *Divided Heart*, 66–68; 74–76; Sarah Boehme, Christian Feest, and Patricia Condon Johnston, *Seth Eastman: A Portfolio of North American Indians* (Afton, MN: Afton Historical Society Press, 1995), 4, 8–10; Charles Eastman, *Indian Boyhood* (New York: McClure, Phillips, and Co, 1902), 6–11.

8 Cathleen D. Cahill, *Federal Fathers and Mothers: A Social History of the United States Indian Service, 1869–1933* (Chapel Hill: University of North Carolina Press, 2011), 156–58; National Archives, BIA General Records, Letters Received 1824–1907, St. Peters Agency, (1848–1855), Northern Superintendency.

9 Wilson P. Shortridge, "Henry Hastings Sibley and the Minnesota Frontier" *Minnesota History Bulletin*, 3 (Aug. 1919), 123–25; Gary Clayton Anderson, *Kinsmen of Another Kind: Dakota-White Relations in the Upper Mississippi Valley, 1650–1862* (Lincoln: University of Nebraska Press, 1985), 267–73.

10 Eastman, *Indian Boyhood*, 48, 61; Melissa L. Meyer, *The White Earth Tragedy: Ethnicity and Dispossession at a Minnesota Anishinaabe Reservation* (Lincoln: University of Nebraska Press, 1994), 29–41; Gilman, *Divided Heart*, 135–137; William Watts Folwell, *History of Minnesota* (St. Paul: Minnesota Historical Society), 2: 103, 149.

11 Harold H. Dunham, "Charles Bent," in Hafen, *The Mountain Men*, v.2, 30–34.

12 David J. Weber, *On the Edge of Empire: The Taos Hacienda of Los Martinez* (Santa Fe: Museum of New Mexico Press, 1996), 52–55, 64–65; Colonel Sterling Price, "Report to Adjutant General," Feb. 15, 1847, U.S. Congress, *Insurrection Against the United States Government in New Mexico and California, 1847–1848*, Senate Doc. 442, 56th Congress, 1st Sess, 1900.

13 Anne Hyde, *Empires, Nations and Families: A History of the North American West, 1800–1860* (Lincoln, NB: University of Nebraska Press, 2011), 385–388, Teresina Bent, "Account of Her Father's Death," *New Mexico Historical Review* 8 (1933), 121–122.

14 Ralph Emerson Twitchell, *Leading Facts of New Mexico History, v.2* (Cedar Rapids, Iowa, 1911–1917), 235; 8th Census of the United States, New Mexico Territory, Precinct of San Fernando, County of Taos, 23, 103: Morris F. Taylor, "A New Look at an Old Case: The Bent Heir's Claim in the Maxwell Grant" *New Mexico Historical Review* 43 (July 1968), 215–17.

15 H. Craig Miner, *Indian Kansas The End of Indian Kansas* (Lawrence, KS: Regents Press of Kansas, 1978), 4–14; Thorne, *Many Hands*, 149–59; Charles Kappler, ed. *Indian Affairs: Laws and Treaties, v.2* (Washington, D.C: 1904).

16 Hyde, *Empires, Nations and Families*, 31–50.

17 William Unrau, *Mixed Bloods and Tribal Dissolution: Charles Curtis and the Quest for Indian Identity* (Lawrence: University Press of Kansas, 1989), 22–6; Thorne, *Many Hands,*135–38; Prairie du Chien Treaty of 1825, Article 6, Article 8, in Kappler, comp. *Indian Treaties, v.2.*

18 Harvey Carter, "Andrew Drips," in *Mountain Men and the Fur Trade, v.8*, ed. LeRoy Hafen, 143–45; *St. Louis Times*, March 23, 1833; Thomas Ermatinger to Andrew Drips, Oct. 14, 1832, Andrew Drips Papers, Missouri Historical Society (MHS).

19 Carter, "Andrew Drips," 150–153; Thorne, *Many Hands*, 169–73.

20 Carter, "Andrew Drips," 152–156; Thorne, *Many Hands*, 171; Charles E. Hoffhaus, *Chez Les Canses: Three Centuries at Kawsmouth* (Kansas City: Lowell Press, 1984) 150–61; John Sarpy to Drips, June 18, 1847, Drips Papers, MHS.

21 David Halaas and Andrew Masich, *Halfbreed: The Remarkable Story of George Bent* (Cambridge, MA: Da Capo, 2004), 76–80; Adam Arenson, *The Great Heart of the Republic: St. Louis and the Cultural Civil War* (Cambridge: Harvard University Press, 2011), 52–53.

22 National Archives, RG75 E-401, Nemaha Half-Breed Reserve, Register Log of Individual Allotments According to The Treaty of Prairie du Chien, July 1830 and July 31, 1854.

23 National Archives, Washington, DC, RG 75 Records of the Miscellaneous Division, Register of Traders Licenses, 1847–1873 PI – 163 E941; Miner and Unrau, *End of Indian Kansas*, 139–41.

24 Maria E. Montoya, *Translating Property: The Maxwell Land Grant and the Conflict Over Land in the United States, 1840–1900* (Berkeley: University of California Press, 2002), 8–14.

25 Miner and Unrau, *Indian Kansas*, 12–20; National Archives, RG75 E-401, Nemaha Half-Breed Reserve, Register Log of Individual Allotments; Berlin B. Chapman, "The Nemaha Half-Breed Reservation" *Nebraska History* 38 (March 1957), 1–23.

26 Clark quoted in Thorne, *Many Hands*, 141.

27 Montoya, *Translating Property*, 46–51; Taylor, "A New Look," 213–28.

Suggestions for further reading

Children, families, and fur trade

A generation of Canadian and American scholars, beginning with Sylvia Van Kirk, *Many Tender Ties* (Norman, OK: University of Oklahoma Press, 1980); Jennifer Brown, *Strangers in Blood* (Vancouver, Canada: UBC Press, 1980); followed by Susan Sleeper-Smith, *Indian Women and French Men* (Amherst, MA: University of Massachusetts Press, 2001); and Tanis Thorne, *The Many Hands of My Relations* (Columbia, MO: University of Missouri Press, 1996) have investigated family formation in the fur trade.

Marriage and children in Canada have been examined in Sarah Carter's *The Importance of Being Monogamous: Marriage and Nation-Building in Western Canada to 1915* (Edmonton, Canada: The University of Alberta Press, 2008).

For the United States, see John Mack Faragher's "The Custom of the Country: Cross-Cultural Marriage in the Far Western Fur Trade," in *Western Women: Their Lives, Their Land* edited by Lillian Schlissel, Vicki L. Ruiz, and Janice Monk (Albuquerque, NM: University of New Mexico Press, 1988); Margaret Jacobs's "The Eastmans and the Luhans: Interracial Marriage between White Women and Native American Men, 1875–1935," *Frontiers* 23(3) (2002); Carol Devens's *Countering Civilization: Native American Women and Great Lakes Missions, 1830–1900* (Berkeley, CA: University of California Press, 2005); Sylvia Van Kirk's "A Transborder Family in the Pacific North West," in *One Step Over the Line: Toward a History of Women in the North American Wests*, edited by Elizabeth Jameson and Sheila McManus (Edmonton, Canada: University of Alberta Press, 2008), and most recently in Cathleen Cahill's *Federal Fathers and Mothers: A Social History of the U.S. Indian Service* (Chapel Hill, NC: University of North Carolina Press, 2011).

Race and ethnicity

The literature on mixed-race people is vast, but begin with Jacqueline Peterson and Jennifer Brown, eds. *The New Peoples: Being and Becoming Métis in North America* (St Paul, MN: Minnesota Historical Society Press, 1985); Theda Purdue, *Mixed Blood Indians: Racial Construction in the Early South* (Athens, GA: University of Georgia Press 2003); and Thomas Ingersoll, *To Intermix With our White Brothers* (Albuquerque, NM: University of New Mexico Press 2005).

Ariela Gross's *What Blood Won't Tell*, (Cambridge, MA: Harvard University Press, 2008) and Peggy Pascoe's *What Comes Naturally* (New York, NY: Oxford University Press, USA, 2009) take the story into the twentieth century and consider legal definitions around mixing race.

20

INFANTICIDE, ABORTION, CHILDREN, AND CHILDHOOD IN SWEDEN, 1000–1980

Bengt Sandin

The life course of women and men in most societies simply does not allow for childbirth and rearing during the entire period women are able to reproduce. Choices have always been made not to have children. Child bearing and the choices it involves have also been a source of social, cultural, and political conflict as the historiography of women, family, and fertility makes very clear. Yet it is also evident that revealing a society's attitudes towards infanticide and abortion, the subjects dealt with here, exposes the parameters of what is sanctioned or accepted as ways to limit reproduction in any particular society at any particular moment in time. Determining these restrictions has been central to policies on the regulation of populations practiced by the church, the state, government agencies, and civil society organizations such as medical societies and philanthropic organizations. Boundaries were also set by the norms developed in families and kinship networks.[1] The negotiations related to these limitations reflect not only the position of women and concepts of family, but they are also integrated into the understanding of children and childhood during different periods of time.

Critical issues such as these have been addressed through legal changes, the development and use of church registers, the establishment of midwives, the refinement of statistical surveys, the spread of education, and the conscious development of family and population policy. In a wider context, the understanding of population change and analyses of sexual behavior also had a bearing on and interacted with the techniques and technology of governance as early as the introduction of Christianity, during the debates on the high rates of infanticide of the seventeenth century, during the eighteenth- and nineteenth-century discussions about the predicament of unwed mothers, and in the discussions on the rise of the welfare system during the early to mid-twentieth century. The alternatives that emerged over the course of the centuries – criminalization, moral sanctions, more lenient legislation, the use of welfare schemes, and information campaigns – all had relevance, but the development of new surveillance techniques and knowledge systems also formed and transformed the understandings of the identity of the fetus and the newly born.[2] The conflicts during the introduction of the Christian church form the backdrop for this article, beginning with the early modern era. It continues through the pivotal legislative action of the seventeenth and nineteenth centuries, and then discusses the political and scientific premises on which the Swedish welfare system was created in the late nineteenth and twentieth centuries.

Negotiating meaning – infanticide – between popular culture, state, and the church

The introduction of Christianity in Sweden prompted conflicts between cultural traditions and political power in questions of infanticide and the "putting out of children," that also involved a contest over the control of family formation. In pre-Christian society burial in communal cemeteries or mounds was most likely reserved for a specific group of people – preferably those born as free landowners.

Children are occasionally found in such places but in numbers nowhere near their proportion in the population, indicating that such placement was connected to special cases. With the acceptance of the Christian faith, child burials became more extensive and, in the case of infants, this burial was closer to the churches, a development that parallels a broader acceptance of burials for the whole flock of parishioners. At the same time, early medieval Norwegian laws indicate an acceptance of certain kinds of infanticide that had pre-Christian roots. The practice was clearly bound to culturally defined arrangements. A child that was to be "put out" must not be offered its mother's breast or fed as a symbol of inclusion in the family. The conditions under which the child was made a part of the society were defined by the family/kin network system. The consequence of accepting the Christian faith involved the transfer of authority to the church, a political institution with the ambition of abolishing heathen practices. The development of the legal system indicates how traditional customs were gradually negotiated and accommodated to church guidelines. For example, the "putting out" of children was accepted if done at the churchyard, but by removing such decisions from the private sphere of the household, such practices were clearly discouraged. With the establishment of secular governments, the ambitions of the church became the responsibility of the crown and a government that aimed to control the local courts. The church aspired to save souls, not only the one threatened with being "put out," but all children.[3] The fact that children were pointed out as part of the congregation meant that children also became objects of the disciplining and civilizing ambitions of the church. Sins and evil needed to be cleansed from children's bodies, at times with harsh disciplinary measures, to make them full members of the congregation.

In reality the church may not have had much influence on the everyday life of children or, indeed, practices of infanticide. The church struggled to have its interpretations of culture gain precedence over the social institutions of popular culture. The life of most children was most likely not influenced much by the transformation from the pre-Christian to the Christian periods. It is therefore not surprising that infanticide emerges as a political issue during the period of nation building and involved a similar interaction between the state, the church, and the local population.

During the seventeenth century it became obvious that the law was inadequate to deal with secret childbirths that resulted in the death of the child. Unmarried women sometimes concealed their pregnancy and gave birth in hiding, at the same time denying complicity in the death of the child. Lack of evidence made it difficult to take legal action even in obvious cases. The Royal Law Commission that was established in 1642 addressed the matter. The *Edict om Barnemord* (Edict on Infanticide) proclaimed that if women had conceived an illegitimate child that was delivered in solitude and the child died, the presumption would be made that the child had been killed.[4] The legal procedure did not have to rely on witnesses or other proof if a newborn was found dead or had disappeared. Guilt could be presumed. By distinguishing infanticide as a separate category of crime perpetrated by illegitimate mothers and by changing the burden of proof, the legislators had a chance to convict suspected offenders. The deaths of infants, smothered in married mothers' beds, were defined under a different legal framework.

In seventeenth-century Sweden, the ecclesiastical control of the population's morals was strongly enforced by the state. The system for control and surveillance of the population involved registration in church records, and this registration system was used to normalize and regulate behavior. In this process, acts of individuals became visible for the state and the church, and thereby punishable. It is significant that the rate of illegitimacy declined from 10 percent in 1600 to a mere 1 percent a century later. The church's grip on the population made moral offences more visible and the need to act against infanticide an important issue. The church also acted against expressions of popular culture and of youth culture, which could sometimes lead to more intimate relationships and the birth of children outside marriage. Up to the mid-eighteenth century, according to the civil agreements common in peasant society, children conceived under promise of marriage were not considered illegitimate. Local clergy repeatedly warned young people that, for promises of marriage to be valid, they had to be certified by witnesses if young women were to claim that a child was conceived under such a promise. This was a way to promote the church ceremony of marriage. If parishioners knew a woman was pregnant with an illegitimate child, they were expected to inform the authorities and take steps to prevent infanticide. Otherwise they also risked being held accountable for the crime. This was a clear expression of the increased control by central authorities over the local church proceedings, popular culture, and youth culture. The ambition was to root out different aspects of popular culture, but it also made the cohorts of young people visible in the registers of the authorities for the first time. All citizens, but particularly children, had to show proof of proficiency in reading and the ability to explain the meaning of the catechism. Reading skills gave access to the religious community at a certain age, became an important signifier of citizenship for young people, and established the bounds of the moral order.[5]

In the late seventeenth and early eighteenth centuries the penalties became the objects of criticism because they did not seem to have the desired effect. Such arguments were articulated in Parliament and by the presiding judges of the major courts. The system of religious shame imposed by the church for adultery and illegitimate childbirth added to the pressure to commit infanticide as a way of avoiding added penalties such as public shaming. In 1734, the public shaming ceremony was replaced with a private ceremony that only involved the sinning mother and the parish clergyman. Concern about population size and its possible decline influenced Gustav III (1772–1792), the monarch who took power in 1772. The nation needed a larger population, and the early years of Gustav III's reign saw a focus on legal reform to fight the ostensibly high level of infanticide. According to the Royal Decree of 1 November 1778 all capital sentences had to be confirmed by the king, who could then exercise his right to pardon the offender and create a uniform and more lenient application of the penalties.

The narrative of the unmarried mother was now cast in a different mode. She was a victim of prejudice and slander, to which his Majesty objected according to the Royal Proposition:

> The primary genesis of this act so shameful to humanity is to be sought in the shame and dishonor a pregnant woman has to suffer... a result of the prejudice and incorrect conceptions of vileness and its consequences... [It is] a crime committed to protect one's honor against others' distrust and harsh judgments....[6]

In 1779, the king declared void the presumption of guilt established in 1655. Intent to kill had to be proven in cases in which capital punishment could be applied. Cases of infanticide were to be tried and scrutinized with greater care, as the presumption of guilt was no longer applicable. Gustav III issued a Royal Decree, *Barnamordsplakat* (the Infanticide Ordinance) that, in essence, made it possible to give birth to a child without publicity or public disgrace. The solution was to make it possible for unmarried mothers to give birth to their children without stating the name of the father and to remain anonymous themselves. The decree's narrative told of the vulnerability of unmarried mothers and their need for support. Neither mother nor child should be ostracized by the clergy, be it in ceremonies or procedures, or by the congregation. Instead of reporting a possible infanticide in the making, neighbors and relatives should support and care for the mother, so she would not be forced to take desperate measures. Money should be spent financing orphanages. At the same time the clergy was ordered once again to remind their flock from the pulpit about the punishments for infanticide.

The control of childbirth drifted as a consequence in a more secular direction. A system of midwives was to be established across the country that would be responsible for helping in all deliveries. Among their duties was to help women who chose to keep their identity undisclosed without risking the health of the illegitimate child. The establishment of the institution of midwives ran parallel to a merging of the legal discourse with a medical-based discourse on the issue of infanticide, as is evident from instructions for judges, medical doctors, and midwives that were published in 1776. These instructions were intended to be used by legal and medical personnel to recognize when crimes had been committed, and contained detailed information on the signs of pregnancy as well as the development of a fetus. It also contained a description of the characteristics of a child that had been born prematurely, as well as information on how to detect whether a child had been born alive and later killed. The instructions were intended to facilitate the detection of infanticide when these officials were confronted with supposedly stillborn fetuses and to help detect illegitimate pregnancies that risked becoming cases of infanticide. The text also dealt with abortion, as an obvious variant on infanticide, its procedures, and detection.[7] In this process, however, the mode of expression was slightly altered when compared to the actual wording of the law.[8] This shows a shift in the use of the term fetus, which had earlier described both the period before and immediately after birth to a distinction between fetus and child, the latter being associated with the moment of birth. Quickening was important in terms of medical development, but in legal terms the distinctions between the fetus before and after quickening was of no consequence. It may also reflect reigning popular norms about the development of the fetus. The newborn's ability to breathe was an important legal signifier; that the deceased infant had been born alive defined the methods of testing of lung tissue.

The scheme of governance in the making had consequences for the conceptual distinctions; fewer spectacles were associated with the punishment of women who broke the system of norms, and it involved a different system of control based on a new profession. It produced a distinction between "child" as an overarching concept, albeit one primarily associated with the period immediately after birth, and "fetus" as confined to the period before birth. It is interesting to note, however, that the ordinance was in force parallel to the draconian consequences for infanticide in the ordinary law.

The church protested that the legislation undermined its ability to keep control of the most volatile and itinerant parts of the population, which would lead to an increasing proportion of children born out of wedlock. The clergy returned to this point repeatedly in the years to come, arguing for a revision of the Royal Decree on the basis that the number of illegitimate children was evidence of its failure, an expression of a dissolving system of governance and inadequate supervision of public morals. The transformation of the system of surveillance was contested by the same church representatives who had enforced it and whose positions were now in question. Penalties that aimed more at reaching the souls and less at stating examples of horror undermined, in the clergy's eyes, the institutions that upheld a control of public morals. The ambitious control of the population focused also on the larger cohorts of children that were a result of the demographic transition and whose morals might be a threat to the society. The education of girls – their moral redemption and reading ability – was at the center of attention, stimulated by the rising number of illegitimate births. The morals of girls as future mothers, responsible for the religious reading instruction in the home, seemed, to some, to illustrate the very core of the social problem. An intense debate about the use of education as a system of surveillance in urban and rural environments led to the development of institutions of mass schooling during the early nineteenth century to complement the reading associated with religious instruction. This went hand-in-hand with a transformation of the notion of childhood as, ideally, a period of education and gradual moral maturity, to be achieved not by public threats, punishments, and intimidations but by systems of rewards that could stimulate political and social maturity in the future adult individual.[9]

Prolonging the fetal period and child saving – conflicting terms

In the years that followed, the clergy returned to this issue, and the different estates of Parliament collaborated and tried to come to grips with the consequences of the Royal ordinance. The suggested alterations to the ordinance demonstrate clearly that the use of the terms fetus or child was changing, but at the same time that it was politically laden. The *coup d'état* against Gustav III's successor, Gustav IV, in 1809, led to a number of proposals to change not only the constitution but also the legal codes. Parliament established a commission in 1810 to review all alterations to the legal framework made since 1734. The proposal published in 1832 stated that infanticide should no longer be a capital offense; however, as before, an unmarried mother could not seek to give birth in secrecy without facing severe punishment if the child was found to be dead afterwards. The change in the law was based on a re-evaluation of the difficult situation facing the unmarried mother.[10]

The problem for unmarried mothers contemplating public disgrace was now given a psychological meaning. Unmarried women could not be held fully accountable immediately after childbirth; however, anyone helping her would be tried for murder because they did not share the confused state of the mother. The exemption was to be applied only if the crime took place less than twenty-four hours after delivery, after which time it was to be considered murder. By that time, a woman was supposed to have come to her senses. In the case of a stillborn or a not fully developed fetus, the punishment was waived. The primary objective was not only the acknowledgment of shame for illegitimate births that was the basis for the *Barnamordsplakat*, but primarily to recognize women's precarious physical and mental state just after delivery.[11]

The concept used in the proposal of just how long a mother's temporary mental instability could excuse infanticide was "child." The paragraph surrounding this concept would cause intense discussion when the law was debated. Should an unmarried mother be excused for twenty-four hours for as long as the child was "small," or was the correct phrase "shortly?" Was it the size of the child or was it the period of time that mattered? The legislators solved the problem by using the word "fetus" instead of the word "child" in all the appropriate paragraphs.[12] This ensured it would be clear to all that it was until the period immediately after childbirth that the infanticide code was applicable, and the penalty for infanticide was made less stern than for murder. While fetus obviously had the connotation of applying to the period before birth, the legislators chose to use the word "fetus" with its prenatal connotations to demarcate the preferred mode of treatment of women. Thus, legally, the fetal period did not end with childbirth, but had a somewhat longer duration. Capital punishment for infanticide was abolished in the new legal code of 1864.[13] It was also critical that the new laws no longer strictly defined abortion as infanticide. Instead it became subject to a lesser punishment.

The public disgrace which unmarried mothers faced was aggravated by the psychological consequences of the strain of childbirth according to the parliamentary debates. For the first time, the discourse began to also include married women, and the new distinction between abortion and infanticide helped to pave the way for a discussion of abortion as an issue for the medical profession. The public statistics continued to lump the two together, but debates about abortion in medical journals during the latter part of the nineteenth century expressed new concerns.[14] Starting in 1909, midwives were compelled not only to report suspected infanticide, as they always had been, but also to report successful or attempted abortions. Attitudes were changing and the laws regulating the penalties for infanticide and abortion were modified as regards the length of sentences in 1890 and in the early twentieth century.[15]

The discussion took place against a backdrop of a dramatic social situation. The number of children born out of wedlock was large, having begun to rise as early as the latter part of the eighteenth century. By the early nineteenth century, the number of illegitimate children born was around 30 percent for the nation's capital, Stockholm; in 1850 the figure was almost 50 percent. This also meant that the number of children in orphanages and foster care showed a constant increase. By the early twentieth century, the number of children in different kinds of care systems was quite significant.[16]

During the late nineteenth century, the protection of children and women became the focus of a wide political discussion, as did the political rights of women. The number of children in orphanages and foster care was seen as a social problem in a society that was increasingly wedded to the bourgeois nuclear family. The role of the father was to be that of a provider; that of the mother was building the family as an emotional entity. Shirking the responsibility for an illegitimate child by fathers was also unacceptable as it put a large burden on the local poor relief system.

Arguments by reformers for greater leniency for married and unmarried women seeking to terminate their pregnancies gathered momentum at the turn of the twentieth century. Revulsion over infanticide was tempered by an understanding that an unmarried mother was not fully accountable, that the penalty had no deterrent function, and that men bore some responsibility for the predicament of the women. In 1911, the politician Verner Ryden petitioned Parliament with a claim that the legislation penalized women who gave birth in maternity clinics and committed their crime after their release from hospital. The law was unfair to abandoned mothers and to the judges who had to sentence them for murder. If the law was rephrased, by replacing the word "fetus" with the word "child," a mother could be sentenced under the lenient infanticide law, which was in effect when a somewhat older child was killed.[17] The basis for calling the newly born child a fetus in the infanticide legislation had been that it was experienced and understood by women as being not quite distinct from their own bodies, and made possible the use of lesser penalties. The committee agreed that was unreasonable because this concept obviously limited the time span to the immediate period after birth. Popular sentiment held the punishment for the crime to be unfair, and respect for the law could be damaged because all these women were eventually pardoned. But, unlike the petitioner, the Parliamentary Law Committee did see a problem in the usage of the word "child"; such a statute would allow women to kill their children of any age. They proposed that a government commission be established to look into the possibility of a new law. And they added an important rider for Parliament to consider: the possibility that the new law should include married women.[18]

The Parliamentary debate did not add much to this discussion but the voice of a Mr Stendal stood out. He claimed to have witnessed cases that might motivate an even more rigorous legal code given the behavior of some mothers.[19] He disputed the definition of the postnatal fetus, arguing that the use of that concept arose in empathy for women who killed their offspring, and argued for the use of the word "child," but contrary to the original proposal, signifying a right to protection.

The shifting focus to the protection of all women is also demonstrated in another proposal to Parliament in the same year. Verner Ryden also asked that Parliament support unmarried mothers by making sure that the fathers of illegitimate children could not avoid their duties.[20] These proposals led to a revocation of the 1789 *Barnamordsplakat* in 1917. Women could no longer give birth without stating their own names and the name of the father. Fathers were to be sought out and made to pay for their offspring. Starting in 1918, a guardian was appointed for the child if the mother was unmarried, which increased the control but also the system of support for unwed mothers.[21] The fetus was understood in the discourse as an embodied part of the woman, and the fetal period extended legally past the moment of birth. The fact that more women were giving birth in hospitals created a problem in terms of such a concept and called for a change. The extension of the period during which unmarried mothers could expect empathetic treatment seemed feasible to a majority of the debaters. But opposition was also mobilized against giving preferential treatment to single mothers, when other political and social reforms aimed at creating two-parent families – a wage-earning husband and a dependent wife. According to some, the fetus and the newborn could also demand protection by the state. The debate indicates a shift from the unequivocal support of the unmarried mother to support for both unmarried and married mothers.

At the same time, the lack of effective birth control alternatives was an aggravating problem. The debates and the questioning of the illegality of contraception indicated a growing conflict around reproductive issues that had a close relationship to the political discussion about abortion and sexual hygiene, as well as the positions for women on the labor market and their civil rights.[22] The turn of the twentieth century was signified by a growing interest in the social and legal position of children and families, as well as parental gender roles, which actualized children's social rights and protection, but also the welfare and protection of women. A number of so-called Child Laws was passed that included regulation of adoption and fostering practices, and established boards dealing with juvenile delinquency. Family law and educational acts, as well as statutes about spare time activities and cultural consumption of children (censorship of movies), also demarcated notions of normalcy in childhood as a period of education and play.

The medical profession and parliamentary discussions – conflicting views

The proposal to change the law led to no action by the government, but re-emerged in the Swedish abortion debates in the early 1920s, when Parliament discussed yet another new proposal for more liberal legislation on infanticide.[23] The initiative to change the law came from the cabinet that was now in the hands of the Social Democrats. The purpose of the proposal was to argue for a more lenient punishment, in regard to both infanticide and abortion.

The Parliamentary Law Committee's discussion was illustrative of the changing sentiments. It considered the social pressure that might cause a woman to hide the fact she was carrying a child conceived out of wedlock, and the depression and the economic problems facing women deserted by the fathers of their children. Just as important was the inability of women to separate the newborn child from the experience of pregnancy itself.[24]

The exclusive latitude for unwed women was questioned, both on the grounds that unwed women could be notoriously sexually unrestrained and thus less deserving of sympathy, and also on the grounds that wed women might have even stronger causes to be distressed by a problematic life situation. Furthermore, the improvement of the social positions of unmarried women and the public ambition to protect the child made such women's neglect of children less tolerable.

> As the position, economically and socially, of the unwed mother, of late, has improved this unconditional latitude is less motivated . . . in regard to the protection of the newly born children in their utmost helpless stage and what kind of retribution ought to be exercised on women that push their neglect of children past the extreme limit.[25]

The central issue in the proposal was infanticide but it also had to deal with the penalty for abortion. The minimum consequences of abortions were the same as for infanticide, which to the committee seemed unreasonable. The moral grounds of the legislation and the right to protection by the law were based on the idea that life begins from the moment of conception. However, an important distinction appears in relation to the difference between protecting the fetus or a child. The terminology of the text here phrased this as the difference "between a fetus and an independent human." If a woman harmed the fetus, it was not as serious an offence as hurting an independent individual, and consequently attempts to induce abortion should not be punished if not successful.[26]

The point was thus made that it was time to question the unwed mother's privileged position and extend the legislation to all women because the mental and physical depression after childbirth might have the same problematic consequences. Given the social importance of the issue, a new investigation was called for that would critically study the legality of abortion, the prime target of investigation. The proposed changes in the legislation passed Parliament and resulted in a reduction of the penalties for infanticide and abortion. An important precondition for the discussion in Parliament was that both were declining and therefore the stern punishments were unwarranted, and indeed of no consequence for the number of crimes committed.

At the same time, however, the Swedish Medical Association noted a worrying increase in the number of abortions – contrary to the observations made by the members of Parliament. The fact that many abortions were conducted by members of the medical profession at medical clinics and not at back street offices was also a source of anxiety. Their position on the status of the fetus was the opposite of the one taken in the Parliamentary discussion. Association members declared that the role of doctors was to protect all life, including the fetus. The fetus was to be regarded as a separate individual from the mother, even if the mother's social circumstances, single or married, sometimes justified terminating the pregnancy. The doctors at the meeting were concerned about the fact that the medical profession did not agree on this matter. They feared that some physicians performed abortions on less than clearly justifiable medical grounds.[27]

The discussions that took place at the medical school at Lund in southern Sweden in October 1920 dealt with so called humanitarian and eugenic motivations for abortion and situations in which abortions might be motivated by social needs. They unanimously agreed that life began at the moment of conception and that the doctor had the obligation to protect the life of the child/fetus. However, the introductory speaker emphasized that information by doctors on how to avoid pregnancies must be made legal. Sex education and access to contraceptives were central to redress the problem with the rising numbers of abortions.

It was acknowledged that in some cases it was legitimate to protect the health of women through induced abortion. Abortions might be motivated by social causes, at least one speaker argued, when related to the health of women. But the absence of government regulations on the right to terminate pregnancies was problematic. A huge increase in abortions between 1902 and 1919 by both married and single women was documented at hospitals and maternity wards in Stockholm. The increase was alarming. It was clearly not only a problem for unmarried women but also an indication of family planning within marriage: abortion was simply a form of unregulated family planning. This actualized the health risks associated with illegal abortions and the need for distinct bylaws from the central medical authorities. The practice of medical doctors had to be overseen more closely by the authorities because some doctors were performing abortions that might be questionable on medical grounds: "the freedom protecting the professionally privileged profession to perform such procedures is to be reduced by normative regulations."[28]

The discussion amongst the physicians clearly marked the emergence of abortion as a problem during the first decades of the twentieth century, but also the beginning of a change in the discourse. No longer was infanticide central to the discussion.[29] Abortion mobilized politics in a different way than infanticide. In the positions taken by the medical doctors and those taken by the Parliament, a potential conflict can be discerned, but also between a medical/biological definition of the fetal identity and socially motivated causes for abortion, conditions that apply to all women, not only the unwed mother.

In spite of these differences, the choice of what to do was clear to the doctors and Parliament alike: by accepting socially motivated abortions, women's circumstances could be treated individually or their situation could be improved though sex education and information on birth-control techniques. The medical association's discussion was a sign that medicine, as a profession, was beginning to stake a clearer claim to be heard in battles over the definition of abortion.[30] The debate was to take on a new direction again when proposals for women's right to abortion were negotiated in relation to professionals and the political interests of an evolving welfare state. The agenda for major abortion reform was beginning to be set but was not yet defined in terms that made it possible to fundamentally question the character of abortion as a crime.

Abortion – a crime or a social problem?

In the 1920s, the Social Democratic Party rose to prominence in Swedish political life as a consequence of the establishment of universal suffrage in 1917. This also gave a voice to other leftists, from the Communist Party to Progressive Liberals, but propelled political life into a series of unstable minority governments. During the parliamentary discussions in the late 1920s, social debates drifted from the plight of mothers of illegitimate children to matters concerning all pregnancies and abortion, as the left wing political program called for a more equal society. The discussion of birth control and sex education paralleled this new focus on abortion. Moreover, for the first time, the debate included children's potential quality of life, as well as elaborations on the unborn child's right to protection. The mental state of women during and after delivery was no longer a focus. Instead, it was the general predicament of the working woman with a job, a home, and a husband to look after that became central concerns, as were class inequalities in general. Access to abortion, however, formed a primary focal point. The proposals to legalize abortion in 1927, 1928, and 1929 referred to the increase in numbers of abortions, the ineffectiveness of the law, and a definite class bias in its application, as well as the control of medical practices in administering abortions.

Official government inquiries documented rising numbers of abortions at medical clinics. Many were a consequence of attempted abortions or induced miscarriages, where the health of women motivated the medical procedures. Abortion was available to middle- and upper-class women from doctors acting under freedoms granted them under the Hippocratic Oath or in illegal clinics that charged money and endangered the health of women. These abortions were not available to the worn-out working-class women. The discussions in Parliament, exemplified by the Parliamentary Law Committee's report and recommendations, evolved from a relatively narrow focus on access to abortion, to a broader approach to issues such as the general decline of the nation's morals or calls for a general reform of the legislation on abortion, sex education, and health information campaigns.[31]

Two different positions emerged. One deplored the growing immorality and lack of self-control and looked to moral redemption for its answers. It also argued that the unborn should be protected by the state, and that life began at the moment of conception. Abortion for eugenic or health reasons was acceptable, but the emphasis was meant to be on improving morals by education and better living conditions for poor or unfortunate women. The other argued that the ban on abortion was class biased because it penalized lower-class women, while those who could afford it resorted to illegal abortions. Women should not be forced to give birth to children they could not care for properly; it was an act of compassion to spare children a life of misery. Some claimed that it should be the woman's individual choice to decide which children she should bear, while others downplayed this argument, pointing to the broader issues of population health and welfare, the need for sex education, and the legalization of contraceptives, not to mention the importance of establishing child-care institutions and the like. Ultimately, the political situation in the 1920s left the question of abortion irresolvable, although it was almost included as a topic for a public parliamentary inquiry in 1927 after moves by the Liberals, Social Democrats, and Communists.

Together, the references to medical abortion practices, legal discussions, and the public documentation of abortion frequencies show that abortion was obviously a frequent procedure in hospitals and at the discretion of the doctors, but the sheer volume could not be accounted for. This was a matter of debate at the Swedish Medical Society meetings for it indicated that doctors had different ways of interpreting needs, not to mention the leeway taken under the Hippocratic Oath. Abortion may have been prohibited by law, but it was very much a social reality and only a proportion were performed in back street clinics.[32] The arguments presented by the medical profession referred to their impressions garnered in practice. The consideration of women's and children's social circumstances acknowledged the impressions of the parliamentarians, but was also supported by reference to public statistics produced by the government and public medical institutions. The proposals for more liberal abortion legislation, however, were echoed in an increase in the numbers of women taken to court for criminal abortion, thus bearing up the accusation of class bias. It seems as if the debate about abortion practices and the apparent lack of practical control took place simultaneously, with an increase in attempts to enforce the law. These figures reappeared in later government inquiries when the debate took a new turn in the 1930s, as the Social Democrats began to re-evaluate their political program. The parliamentary attention during the 1920s had altered the nature of the debate as new information about the social conditions of women and families was mobilized, but it was yet to be formed into systems of knowledge and understanding of fertility, reproduction, and population change. That could only happen when abortion was set in relation to a wide array of social reforms benefitting women and children, as well as the fact of population decline, and then presented as normal behavior with roots in a pre-modern society.

Bio-politics – the politics of abortion law

In the 1930s, Parliament was faced with the challenge of resolving the conflicting positions in the debate against the background of a changing political landscape, as the Social Democrats grew and then formed an alliance with the Farmer's Party in 1936, thus ending a long series of minority rule governments. At the same time, they launched the idea of the "people's home," a welfare system for the whole nation, a concept initially based on a conservative frame of reference that was taken over and used by the Social Democrats. It became the cornerstone in their reformist ambitions and cooperation with other political parties.[33]

A large number of public inquiries were initiated with the intention of shaping a political consensus on the challenges facing society. The implementation of welfare measures was, to a large degree, defined by fear of a dramatic population decline that would endanger the sustainability of the nation. Government programs designed to engineer social change, housing programs, and population growth were created to influence gender relations, marriage patterns, and the situation of children. The importance of the abortion issue in the political proposals for free prenatal care and child-care clinics should not be underestimated, nor the biting criticism of the illegality of birth-control regulations. The "population crisis," as Gunnar and Alva Myrdal chose to label the discovery of Sweden's declining birth rate, gave the welfare project a particular urgency, and it also helped to redefine the nature of abortion. The government inquiries formed a political arena where medical, legal, and social sciences negotiated the nature of abortions in the light of the developing welfare system.[34]

Gunnar Myrdal focused on the need for an extensive and state-supported system of "rational" sex education. He claimed that socially motivated abortions should not be permitted, a clear stand against earlier positions taken by Social Democrats and also by the governmental Abortion Inquiry that had supported legalizing abortions motivated by the social situation of women. He stressed that the circumstances that created the need for socially motivated abortions must change. The Population Inquiry's proposed social reforms would have to be realized in order to improve the dilemma facing women. Moreover, there was a crying need for a change of the prevention policy. The government had to insure that abortion was not used as a form of birth control, particularly among the poor; the rational alternative was sex education. He issued a warning when addressing the parliament. If neither social reforms nor sex information campaigns were implemented:

> The time will be ripe for the lifting of restrictions on the right of every woman to an abortion, irrespective of her reasons for the same. Perhaps that time is not very far off when such a demand can no longer be resisted.[35]

This was not just a casual remark. It was obviously important to Myrdal. He chose to quote the important Population Inquiry, which he had chaired. His petition clearly presented an assurance, and a threat, that if that the abortion law was not supported by other kinds of social legislation, the Social Democrats would be forced to support more unrestricted abortion legislation for women. Conversely, he tried to make it clear to women's organizations, some liberals and Social Democrats, that social reforms – child and health care, the right to keep one's job if pregnant – would not be possible if they continued to claim the right to abortion at will. By noting that one of the accepted criteria could include some cases of socially motivated abortion, he tried to appease critics in the Social Democratic camp who were inclined to support such ideas. Abortion for medical, eugenic, and humanitarian reasons should be legalized under strict government control.[36] Myrdal's was also a very statist position: women's bodies in a developed welfare system came under the control of the state. The development of women's individual reproductive rights was presented as a threat to comprehensive welfare reform. But another interesting point was made. The low and declining Swedish birth rate not only propelled social reform benefitting population growth and the quality of life for children; it also re-conceptualized abortion. Abortion was presented as the product of a pre-modern Swedish popular culture that condoned premarital sex and the use of abortions as a check on fertility, which subsequently ran amok in a modernizing society. As such, abortion was a reasonable and normal behavior in a pre-modern social milieu. In modern society, with contraceptives available and an emerging welfare system, women should not need to resort to abortions. That logic, though, also encouraged certain tolerance towards unmarried mothers: the important point for society was motherhood and more children of better quality – not marriage – at the same time as a progressive family policy became a key object of social reform. The Conservative politician Karl Magnusson, one of the Chamber's Deputy Speakers and former member of the Population Inquiry, supported the Social Democratic government position. He echoed the argument put forward by Gunnar Myrdal of the negative relationship between social reform and women's right to choose. Social welfare measures would have to be regarded as failures if they had to be supplemented by legislation that permitted abortion:

> When the state seeks in every way possible to improve the position of women and families, society also has the right to demand of its citizens that they shoulder their societal duties and responsibilities associated with child-bearing, or else the social reforms are pointless.[37]

Myrdal's position was, however, not left uncontested. Arguments against accepting all abortions for medical, eugenic, or humanitarian reasons were made, while others argued that women should have the right to choose because children were a luxury that poor women could not afford. A radical position was taken by Anders Vilhelm Lundstedt, the Social Democratic professor of law in Uppsala, who rejected the idea that the fetus would have metaphysical rights which might come into conflict with the rights of women. He also questioned whether a woman had a special kind of moral responsibility based on her involvement in the conception.[38] He claimed that it was a "totally false notion, that the child has a right to live and thus demand that the society has an obligation to protect it."[39]

The Minister of Justice, a Social Democrat, made a similar point. For him, it was not obvious that the conflict of interest between mother and society should be resolved in favor of the mother. The need for new, able citizens should tip the balance between the risk to mothers from child bearing and society's wishes for more children. The law was duly passed by the Second Chamber on 8 May 1938. This meant a reformist position had gained precedence over an emancipatory stance on abortion. A difficult aspect of the legislation was the close link between the justifications for abortion, which meant that an application for abortion on social grounds or on mixed social and medical grounds involved a discussion of eugenics that castigated working-class women living in problematic social circumstances. More children of better quality were seen as a political instrument for those arguing for changes in the different aspects of the welfare policy, which involved the development of institutions to care for mothers and children. The quality of the population also allowed for a sterilization policy curbing unwanted reproduction as well as sex-information. In this process the freedom of the medical profession to perform abortions was subsumed under the close surveillance of the medical authorities. Doctors performing abortions not properly motivated were in danger of losing their authorization.[40]

There were relatively few legal abortions performed between 1939 and 1944, while analysts reported that illegal abortions were on the increase. Doctors were unable to accommodate socially motivated abortions as part of mixed social and medical legal motivations for conducting an abortion, and the social motivations were still being argued by women's organizations. After careful sociological analyses of applications for abortion relative to the family support system, the renewed Population Inquiry in the 1940s concluded that it was not possible to accept socially motivated abortions because that would imply an acceptance of the society's inability to create acceptable living conditions for its population.[41] The law was changed in 1946, to include specific social motivations such as a serious risk to the mother's health, described colloquially as "weakness" and basically defined as a medical condition. The new rules also called for the establishment of a Social Psychiatry Committee by The National Medical Board to consider applications for abortions that previously had been assigned to the Forensic Psychiatry Committee. The change signified the fact that abortion was not a criminal problem but a health issue with psychiatric connotations. As a result of the new law, abortion could be obtained either through a local procedure administered by two doctors or an application to this central board after a local screening by a doctor and a social worker.[42] As a result, legal abortions increased from 500 in 1942 to 2,378 in 1946 and 5,889 in 1950. An increasing proportion of these were based on women's claims of weakness (from 5.9 percent in 1945 to 50.7 percent 1950) at the same time as abortions justified by illnesses fell (from 65.9 to 30.2 percent), as did those justified on eugenic grounds (from 27.3 to 9.2 percent).[43] The significance of these changes was not only the increase in socially motivated abortions accepted by the Social Psychiatry Committee, but also in the nomenclature being used to make these decisions. "Weakness" was redefined as a psychiatric condition brought on by the prospect of giving birth. This was obvious from the results of an official inquiry set up in the early 1950s to scrutinize the reasons for the increase in accepted abortions. It concluded that local communities should have a board to handle abortion applications, staffed by social workers, psychiatrists, and counselors, who could advise and convince women to seek alternatives to abortion, and to convince them to give birth. The problem was defined in psychiatric terms, relative to a notion of normality and normal womanhood. Weakness and women's problematic situations were defined in plain medical terminology as an aspect of normal–abnormal reactions to pregnancy.

The new post-war social welfare measures that had greatly improved the situation of most Swedish women were presented as a background. Legitimate social and familial reasons not to have a child had been much reduced, and thus considered evidence of a potential imbalance in the psyche of women.[44] Given the support offered by various state measures, the reluctance of women to consider giving birth was defined as a medical condition that should be dealt with by psychiatric help and social counseling. The ambitions of the welfare state after World War II were deeply associated with supporting a housewife–breadwinner family model and child support through comprehensive welfare schemes; child and mother health centers, hospital and dental care, and child allowances. Subsidy was geared towards the "normal family model." Childhood and the life of children were, as a consequence, intimately associated with the nuclear family and its gendered social system, which also characterized, for example, policies on adoption and social care.[45] For women the duty to give birth was only terminated if she could convince the authorities of her inability to be a good mother; even then she should be persuaded to give birth and to put the child up for adoption.

The ambitions to control abortion rates were partly successful during the 1950s as the numbers sank dramatically. During the 1960s, the possibilities to obtain abortions in neighboring countries, for example, Poland, and a more vocal argumentation from feminist organizations undermined the restrictions of abortion rights. The processing of abortion applications became more liberal, and during the 1960s, the number accepted increased many times from the level during the 1950s. However, the administration around such applications delayed decisions, which was extremely humiliating for the applicants, and conflicted with the understanding of female citizenship rights. In 1974, women were given the right to abort until week eighteen of the pregnancy. Politically, this was based on the need for female participation in the labor market and on a questioning of traditional gender roles with demands for a more equal society. The expansion of the female labor market was in growing sectors such as child and hospital care, and resulted in an extremely gendered labor market. A comprehensive day-care system made women's participation in the labor market a reality, in spite of a slow transformation of gendered division of labor within families. Day care made it also possible for single women to care for children, and the number of children given up for adoption, as well as those entering foster care, declined, creating the basis for an increase in foreign adoptions. The importance of the relationship between family and childrearing was supported by development of public childcare. Investments in medical care also resulted in one of the lowest infant mortality rates in the world. Path-breaking pictures of the fetus by the photographer Lennart Nilsson during the mid-1960s changed the imagery of fetal development. His images anticipated the consequences of the use of ultrasound during pregnancies, providing alternative understanding of the fetus to the sequencing shaped by legal criteria and the experience of the quickening.[46] His book, however, also underwrote the close association of the care of children, as well as the fetus, and the welfare of mothers and fathers that signified other aspects of the development of the welfare society. It was also a period when the development of children's rights reflected such investments in the welfare of children. The causal relationships are complex but the abortion rights granted women during the 1970s were closely associated with the transformation of childhood.

Conclusion

The histories of infanticide and abortion as they have evolved over the centuries are associated with the relationship between the organization of political and religious power, the traditions entrenched in popular culture and in forms of family/kin reproduction. Social and cultural practices were questioned in different ways depending on forms of government and how the problems were defined. These problems might be regarded as authority over family reproduction; the morals or problems of unmarried mothers; the social and political situation of mothers and women generally; or the size of the population. The discussions reflected which political issues occupied the foreground: the authority of the church over marriage and family formation; the control over the population during a period of imperial nation building; the conflicts between religious traditions and secularizing governments; the evolution of new mechanisms of governing through medical and educational institutions; the creation of a democratic political landscape; perceptions of crises in population, the welfare system and politics; changes in the regulation and policy of sexuality; the political mobilization of women; and women's participation in the labor force. These factors involved, at times, tough conflicts between representatives of different political interests and professional groups and were indeed part of reshaping professional and political authority and political legitimacy.

Such discussions had consequences for how the identity of the fetus was expressed in social and cultural terms, and the debate mobilized, at certain instances, conflicting understandings of the rights of the fetus and concepts of the child and/or fetus. The duration of the fetal period proved to be negotiable in specific historical contexts. Changes such as these also influenced, shaped, and transformed notions of childhood and youth, which were related to the very same issues: changes in the understanding of family and household; control of the population through the church or education; and the development of the labor market and the educational system. These relationships are complex and sometimes contradictory. Significantly, arguments for socially justified abortion went hand-in-hand with demands for social reform during the 1920s, but evolved from being a complementary aspect of such ambitions to being a challenge to the building of a social welfare state in the 1930s. The Swedish Parliament was asked to choose between expanded abortion rights for women or social reform. Consequently, the high incidence of illegal abortions and their ineffectual regulation became an argument not only in favor of increased control, but also for reforms of the women's labor market, maternity benefits, and child-care. At the same time, sex education, birth control, and medical practice were also instrumental in shaping a new understanding of children and childhood.

Notes

1 Donald T. Critchlow, ed., *The Politics of Abortion and Birth Control in Historical Perspective* (University Park, PA: Pennsylvania State University Press, 1996); Lena Lennerhed, *Historier om ett brott: illegala aborter i Sverige på 1900-talet* (Stockholm, Sweden: Atlas, 2008); Linda Gordon, *Woman's Body, Woman's Right: a Social History of Birth Control in America* (Harmondsworth, UK: Penguin Books, 1977); Elisabeth Elgán, "Genus och politik: en jämförelse mellan svensk och fransk abort-och preventivmedelspolitik från sekelskiftet till andra världskriget." (PhD diss., Acta Universitatis Upsaliensis. Studia Historica

Upsaliensia 176. Uppsala, Sweden: Uppsala Universitet, 1994); Lionel Rose, *The Massacre of the Innocents: Infanticide in Britain 1800–1939* (London, UK: Routledge & Kegan Paul, 1986); Otto Ulbricht, *Kindsmord und Aufklärung in Deutschland* (München, Germany: Oldenbourg, 1990); Ida Blom, *Barnebegrensning - synd eller sunn fornuft* (Bergen, Norway: Universitetsforlag, 1980).

2 Eva Bergenlöv, "Skuld och oskuld: barnamord och barnkvävning i rättslig diskurs och praxis omkring 1680-1800." (PhD diss., Lund University. Studia Historica Lundensia 13. Lund, Sweden: Nordic Academic Press, 2004): Yvonne Hirdman, *Att lägga livet tillrätta: studier i svensk folkhemspolitik*. 2. uppl. (Stockholm, Sweden: Carlsson förlag, 2000).

3 Lotta Mejsholm, *Gränsland: konstruktion av tidig barndom och begravningsritual vid tiden för kristnandet i Skandinavien* (Uppsala, Sweden: Uppsala universitet, 2009) http://urn.kb.se/resolve?urn=urn:nbn:se:uu:diva-98163.

4 Inger Lövkrona, *Annika Larsdotter, barnamörderska: kön, makt och sexualitet i 1700– talets Sverige* (Lund, Sweden: Historiska media, 1999), 176–218.

5 Sandin Bengt, "Hemmet, gatan, fabriken eller skolan: folkundervisning och barnuppfostran i svenska städer 1600–1850." (PhD diss., Lund University. Lund, Sweden: Arkiv, 1986), 59–83; David Gaunt, *Familjeliv i Norden* (Stockholm, Sweden: Gidlund, 1983).

6 *Sveriges Riddarskapets och Adelns protokoll 1778–1779*. Allegator 1. Kongl [AQ19] Maj:ts proposition om dödstraff för barnamord, (Stockholm, Sweden, 1982) 72–73.

7 J. A. Kiernander, *Utkast til medicinal-lagfarenheten: domare til uplysning, läkare til hjelpreda och barnmorskor til underwisning i ämnen som röra människo-kroppen*, (Stockholm, Sweden, 1776); Nordenheim Johannes, *Oförgripelig underrättelse huru angifne Barnamörderskor samt Wittnen, som deraf någon kunskap hafwa kunna examineras at utröna den rätta sanningen om saksens sammanhang och beskaffenhet*, (Stockholm, Sweden, 1726); Bergenlöv, *Skuld och oskuld*, 359–386.

8 Bengt Sandin, "Foetal identity redefined – notes on the changing identity of the fetus in the nineteenth and early twentieth centuries," in *Barn, barndom och föräldraskap*, eds. Ann-Marie Markström, Maria Simonsson, Ingrid Söderlind, and Eva Änggård (Stockholm, Sweden: Carlsson, 2009), 32–55.

9 Sandin, *Hemmet, gatan,* 227–261.

10 Sandin, "Foetal identity redefined."

11 Parliamentary minutes, *Sveriges Presteståndets protokoll 24 mars 1860*, 51–54.

12 Parliamentary minutes, *Bihang till riksståndens protokoll vid 1859–60 års riksdag*, saml. 7 avd . 1 utl 20, 39, 8, 21–22.

13 Sandin, "Foetal identity redefined."

14 Svante Jakobsson and Sten W. Jakobsson. *"Orons och förtviflans gerningar": ogifta kvinnors vånda för havandeskaps och barnsbörds skull: Stockholmsförhållanden 1887–1901*. 1. uppl. (Stockholm, Sweden: Allmänna förl., 1987).

15 Sandin, "Foetal identity redefined"; Lisa Öberg, "Barnmorskan och läkaren: kompetens och konflikt i svensk förlossningsvård 1870–1920." (PhD diss., Stockholm University. Stockholm, Sweden: Ordfront, 1996), 40–77, 338; Parliamentary minutes. *Lagutskottets Utlåtande N:o 15, Bih. Till Riks. Prot. 1907. 7 Saml. 13 Häf (N:is 15,16)*, *Riksdagens skrivelse N:o 29*, 1–8.

16 Sandin, *Hemmet, gatan,* 141–179; Johanna Sköld, "Fosterbarnsindustri eller människokärlek: barn, familjer och utackorderingsbyrån i Stockholm 1890–1925." (PhD diss., Acta Universitatis Stockholmiensis. Stockholm Studies in Economic History 49. Stockholm, Sweden: Stockholm University, 2006). http://urn.kb.se/resolve?urn=urn:nbn:se:su:diva-1026.

17 Parliamentary minutes, *Andra kammaren (AK) Motioner i*, Nr 213, 5–6; *Lagutskottets Utlåtande N:o 19, Bih. till Riks. Prot. 1911*, 7 Saml. 1 Afd. 18 Häft. (Nr 19).

18 Parliamentary minutes, *Lagutskottets Utlåtande N:o 19, Bih. till Riks. Prot. 1911*, 7 Saml. 1 Afd. 18 Häft. (Nr 19) 7–8; *Riksdagens skrifvelse till Konungen. Nr 48 1911*, 8–13.

19 Parliamentary minutes, *Riksdagens protokoll Andra Kammaren Nr 14.* Lördagen den 18 mars., 35–36.

20 Parliamentary minutes, *Motioner i Andra kammaren*, 214, 7–9; *Lagutskottets Utlåtande N:o 20, Bih. till Riks. Prot. 1911*, 7 Saml. 1 Afd. 19 Häft (Nr 20), 1–3.

21 Helena Bergman, "Att fostra till föräldraskap: barnavårdsmän, genuspolitik och välfärdsstat 1900-1950," (PhD diss., Acta Universitatis Stockholmiensis. Stockholm, Sweden: Stockholm University, 2003).

22 Sandin, "Foetal identity redefined,"; Öberg, *Barnmorskan och läkaren*, 40–77; Carlsson Wetterberg Christina, "Kvinnosyn och kvinnopolitik: en studie av svensk socialdemokrati 1880–1910." (PhD diss., Lund University. Lund, Sweden: Arkiv, 1986).

23 Parliamentary minutes, Proposition, Nr 71. Bihang till riksdagens protokoll 1921. 1 saml. 61 häft. 1921 Samt Utdrag av protokollet över justitiedepartementsärenden, hållet inför Hans [AQ19]Maj:t Konungen i statsrådet å Stockholms slott fredagen den 14 januari 1921, Stockholm: Riksdagstrycket; Första lagutskottets utlåtande nr 38 Bihang till riksdagens protokoll 1921, 9 saml. 1 avd. 29 häft., Stockholm: Riksdagstrycket.

24 Parliamentary minutes, *Första lagutskottets utlåtande Nr 38*, 4–5.

25 Ibid., 7.

26 Ibid., 10–13.

27 *Svenska läkartidningen. Organ för Sveriges läkarförening* (28 January 1921): 49–58.

28 Ibid., 52.

29 In public statistics child murder and abortion were listed separately from the 1890s. Tabell, "Barnamord och fosterfördrivning i svensk rättstatistik 1878–1973." *BiSOS. Fångvården 1887–90; SOS Rättsväsende – Brottsligheteten. Kriminalstatistik Del 2.*

30 Maud Eduards, *Kroppspolitik: om moder Svea och andra kvinnor* (Stockholm, Sweden: Atlas, 2007); Eva Palmblad, *Den disciplinerade reproduktionen: abort-och steriliseringspolitikens dolda dagordning* (Stockholm, Sweden: Carlsson, 2000); Lennerhed, *Historier om ett brott*; Bengt Sandin, "Infanticide and Abortion, the social engineering of sexuality, and welfare policy in Sweden 1900–1950," submitted 2012.

31 Ann-KatrinHatje, "Befolkningsfrågan och välfärden: debatten om familjepolitikoch nativitetsökning under 1930- och 1940-talen." (PhD diss., Stockholm, Sweden: Stockholm University, 1974); Elgán, *Genus och politik*; Sandin, "Infanticide and Abortion, the social engineering."

32 Lennerhed, *Historier om ett brott*, 97–10; Sandin, "Infanticide and Abortion, the social engineering."

33 Henrik Berggren and Lars Trägårdh, *Är svensken människa: gemenskap och oberoende i det moderna Sverige.* (Stockholm, Sweden: Norstedts, 2006)

34 Yvonne Hirdman, *Att lägga livet tillrätta. Studier i svensk folkhemspolitik* (Stockholm, Sweden: Carlsson, 1989); Elgán, *Genus och politik*; Hatje, *Befolkningsfrågan och välfärden*; Ann-Sofie Kälvemark (Ohlander), *More Children of Better Quality? Aspects on Swedish Population Policy in the 1930's* (Uppsala, Sweden: Uppsala University, 1980); Bengt Sandin and Kriste Lindenmeyer, "National Citizenship and Early Policies Shaping 'The Century of the Child' in Sweden and the United States," *Journal for the History of Children and Youth* 1(1) (2008); Sandin, "Infanticide and Abortion, the social engineering."

35 Parliamentary minutes, *FK (Första Kammaren)Motioner 1936* Nr 254, 3.

36 Parliamentary minutes, *FK Motioner 1936* Nr 254.

37 Parliamentary minutes, *AK (Andra Kammaren)*, 1938, 33.

38 Parliamentary minutes, *AK (Andra Kammaren)*, 1939, 7–11.

39 Parliamentary minutes, *AK (Andra Kammaren)*, 1939, 11.

40 Palmblad, *Den disciplinerade reproduktionen: abort- och steriliseringspolitikens dolda dagordning* (Stockholm, Sweden: Carlsson, 2000); Maija Runcis, "Steriliseringar i folkhemmet." (PhD diss., Stockholm University. Stockholm, Sweden: Ordfront, 1998); Gunnar

Broberg and Mattias Tydén, *Oönskade i folkhemmet: rashygien och sterilisering i Sverige*, (Stockholm, Sweden: Gidlund, 1991). Lennerhed, *Historier om ett brott*, 149–163; Sandin, "Infanticide and Abortion, the social engineering."

41 *SOU 1944:51.*

42 Palmblad, *Den disciplinerade*, 29–30, 61–4.

43 *SOU 1953:29* 1950 års abortutredning (1953), *Abortfrågan: betänkande* (Stockholm, Sweden), 40.

44 SOU 1953:29. See also, Lennerhed, *Historier om ett brott*, 149–163 on RSFU's advice activities and the normative evaluation of applicants, 149–167; see also Palmblad, *Den disciplinerade*; Sandin, "Infanticide and Abortion, the social engineering."

45 Cecilia Lindgren, "En riktig familj: adoption, föräldraskap och barnets bästa 1917–1975." (PhD diss., Linköping University. Stockholm, Sweden: Carlsson, 2006); Bengt Sandin, "Children and the Swedish welfare state: from different to similar," in *Reinventing Childhood after World War II*, eds. Paula Fass and Michael Grossberg (Philadelphia, PA: University of Pennsylvania Press, 2012), 110–138.

46 Barbara Duden, *Disembodying women: perspectives on pregnancy and the unborn*, (Cambridge, MA: Harvard University Press, 1993); Lennart Nilsson, Mirjam Furuhjelm, Axel Ingelman-Sundberg and Claes, red., *Ett barn blir till: en bildskildring av barnets tillblivelse före födelsen och praktiska råd när man väntar barn. 7., helt omarb. uppl.* (Stockholm, Sweden: Bonnier, 1989 [1976]); Roger Klinth, "Göra pappa med barn: den svenska pappapolitiken 1960–95," 1. uppl. PhD diss. Linköping University (Umeå, Sweden: Boréa, 2002).

Suggestions for further reading

Identity of the fetus

Dubow, Sara. *Ourselves Unborn: a History of the Fetus in Modern America*. New York, NY: Oxford University Press, 2011.

Duden, Barbara. *Disembodying Women: Perspectives on Pregnancy and the Unborn*. Cambridge, MA: Harvard University Press, 1993.

Nilsson, Lennart, and Lars Hamberger. *A Child is Born*. London, UK: Doubleday, 1990.

Infanticide

Badinter, Elisabeth. *L'amour en plus: histoire de l'amour maternel (XVIIe-XXe siècle)*. Nouv. ed. Paris, France: Flammarion, 1981.

Critchlow, Donald T., ed. *The Politics of Abortion and Birth Control in Historical Perspective*. University Park, PA: Pennsylvania State University Press, 1996.

Hoffer, Peter Charles, and N.E.H. Hull. *Murdering Mothers: Infanticide in England and New England 1558–1803*. New York, NY: New York University Press, 1981.

Kramar, Kirsten Johnson. *Unwilling Mothers, Unwanted Babies: Infanticide in Canada*. Vancouver, Canada: UBC Press, 2005.

Rose, Lionel. *The Massacre of the Innocents: Infanticide in Britain 1800–1939*. London, UK: Routledge & Kegan Paul, 1986.

O'Connor, Anne. *Child Murderess and Dead Child Traditions: a Comparative Study*. Helsinki, Finland: Suomalainen Tiedeakatemia, Academia Scientiarum Fennica, 1991.

Peters, Kirsten. *Der Kindsmord als schöne Kunst betrachtet: eine motivgeschichtliche Untersuchung der Literatur des 18. Jahrhunderts*. Würzburg, Germany: Königshausen & Neumann, 2001.

Abortion and the law

Bergenlöv, Eva. "Skuld och oskuld: barnamord och barnkvävning i rättslig diskurs och praxis omkring 1680–1800." PhD diss., Lund University. Studia Historica Lundensia 13. Lund, Sweden: Nordic Academic Press, 2004.

Grothe Nielsen, Beth. *"Letfærdige qvindfolk:" fosterdrab og fødsel i dølgsmål retshistorisk belysning.* Copenhagen, Denmark: Institute of Criminal Science, Copenhagen University, 1980.

Guarnieri, Patrizia. "Men Committing Female Crime: Infanticide, Family and Honor in Italy 1890–1981." *Crime, History & Societies* 13(2) (2009): 41–54.

Guarnieri, Patrizia. *A Case of Child Murder: Law and Science in Nineteenth-century Tuscany.* Cambridge, UK: Polity Press, 1993.

Reagan, Leslie J. *When Abortion was a Crime: Women, Medicine, and Law in the United States, 1867–1973.* Berkeley, CA: University of California Press, 1997.

Abortion, politics and welfare

Blom, Ida. *Barnebegrensning – synd eller sunn fornuft.* Bergen, Norway: Universitetsforlag, 1980.

Brooke, Stephen. *Sexual Politics: Sexuality, Family Planning, and the British Left from the 1880s to the Present Day.* Oxford, UK: Oxford University Press, 2011.

Elgán, Elisabeth. "Genus och politik: en jämförelse mellan svensk och fransk abort – och preventivmedelspolitik från sekelskiftet till andra världskriget = Genre et politique: une comparaison entre les politiques d'avortement et de contraception suédoise et française de la Belle époque à la deuxième guerre mondiale." PhD diss., Acta Universitatis Upsaliensis. Studia Historica Upsaliensia 176. Uppsala, Sweden: Uppsala Universitet, 1994.

Gordon, Linda. *Woman's Body, Woman's Right: A Social History of Birth Control in America.* New York, NY: Grossman, 1976.

Kälvemark (Ohlander), Ann-Sofie. *More Children of Better Quality? Aspects on Swedish Population Policy in the 1930s.* Acta Universitatis Upsaliensis. Studia Historica Upsaliensia 115. Uppsala, Sweden: Uppsala University, 1980.

Mohr, James C. *Abortion in America: the Origins and Evolution of National Policy, 1800–1900.* Oxford, UK: Oxford University Press, 1979.

Pollack Petchesky, Rosalind. *Abortion and Woman's Choice. The State, Sexuality and Reproductive Freedom.* Boston, MA: Northeastern University Press, 1990.

21

SOCIAL WELFARE IN THE WESTERN WORLD AND THE RIGHTS OF CHILDREN

Ivan Jablonka

"The Christianity and the civilization of a people may both be measured by their treatment of childhood," Benjamin Waugh, chairman of the London Society for the Prevention of Cruelty to Children, wrote in 1886.[1] Of the eight Millennium Development Goals that the United Nations has set for 2015, half are directly or indirectly related to children. Between the end of the eighteenth century and the beginning of the nineteenth, child welfare became not only an objective that featured prominently in the range of state (and supra-state) missions worldwide, but also a yardstick of civilization – the criterion by which one could measure a country's development. In that sense, child welfare is a fundamental element of our modernity.

However, this kind of general presentation is liable to conceal several important facts. First, Western societies were at the forefront of theorizing about and implementing policies regarding child welfare. The Frenchman Joseph Raulin in *De la conservation des enfants* (1768), the Britons Florence Davenport Hill in *Children of the State* (1868) and John Eldon Gorst in *Children of the Nation* (1907), the Swede Ellen Key in *The Century of the Child* (1902), and the American Grace Abbott in *The Child and the State* (1938) in their own ways all defined the community's responsibilities with regard to children. This leads us to highlight the role of cultural, social, and political factors in the encounter between children and social welfare – the "sense of childhood," to use Philippe Ariès's term – but also the construction of the nation, the development of the state of law and the welfare state, as well as the rise of the middle classes molded by individualism and Christian values.

Second, child welfare did not develop in a continuous manner. It was first and foremost a response to the upheaval caused by the Industrial Revolutions, the social and economic crises, and the wars that affected Europe and the United States since the outset of the nineteenth century. In this respect, the period between 1870 and 1914 was vital. The scope of state intervention increased, encompassing the family and children, and dozens of social laws were passed around the Western world. Children – from a working-class background, unhappy, forced into labor, delinquent, or abandoned – became a matter of national interest under the influence of charitable and philanthropic organizations (known as "Child Savers" in the United States).

There is a very rich historiography of the different aspects of child welfare (reducing infant mortality, banning child labor, protecting orphans, educating delinquent

children, fighting child abuse, etc.). On the other hand, the way in which it was universalized has not been studied to the same extent, given that the history of childhood is
often structured around a national framework. However, it is essential to understand
the way in which states, philanthropic organizations, scholars, and jurists helped to
bring about a common conception of children and child welfare in Europe, Canada,
and the United States, while themselves being rooted in a particular national context,
with its own legislative framework, social set-up, and political agenda.

This essay will try to analyze, based on the European and North American experience, both the globalization of child protection understood as the spread and
unification of practices and standards worldwide, and its internationalization, which
combines the exchange of knowledge with the sharing of experiences and cross-border
trends in method and imitation. Both of these are closely linked.

Transnational perspectives on juvenile delinquency

Taking young vagrants and delinquents into care was emblematic of child welfare,
because neglected children were considered culprits as well as victims (even thought to
be culprits on account of being victims), as well as constituting a threat on account of
being poor. This kind of analysis was common from the nineteenth century onwards.
From then on, they had a specific status which, on a criminal level, lessened their
responsibility and, on an institutional level, gave permission to take children away
from their family in order to fully nurture them and try to get them back on the right
path.

Throughout the nineteenth century, a large number of reformatories and "houses
of correction" (the term used in the French penal code of 1791) appeared in Europe.
This proliferation owed a great deal to American experiences. During his exile in the
United States in the 1790s, the Duke de La Rochefoucauld discovered the prisons
of Philadelphia and developed a passion for Quaker philanthropy, which sought to
improve people by dint of work and kindness. Once back in France, after the fall of
Napoleon, he entertained the idea of opening a "trial prison" for young offenders
following that model.[2] Under the July Monarchy (1830–1848), all the prison specialists were required to visit the United States; Charles Lucas did so in 1828, as did
Alexis de Tocqueville in 1833. In *On the Penitentiary System in the United States
and Its Application to France*, Tocqueville praised the Philadelphia system of solitary
confinement and the houses of refuge on the East coast, created in the 1820s; these
half-schools/half-prisons received young delinquents, as well as abandoned children,
young vagrants, and beggars, who were sent there as a precautionary measure.

In the 1820s and 1830s, the Netherlands was another source of inspiration for
criminal lawyers and philanthropists. The Rotterdam "prison for young offenders,"
founded in 1833, was one of the first in Europe to combine solitary confinement with
pedagogical ambition. In particular, General Johannes van den Bosch's charity established several farming colonies intended to take the strain off almshouses by sending
thousands of destitute children into the countryside. From the enthusiasm shown by
Huerne de Pommeuse to the serious condemnations of French and Belgian inspectors
in the middle of the century,[3] all the studies mention the colonies of Frederick's-
Oord, Ommerschans, and Veenhuizen (with the latter being reserved for orphans and
foundlings). Quickly, houses of correction and colonies turned out to be riddled with

flaws: terrible conditions of living and hygiene, overcrowding, endemic violence, etc. Therefore an increasing number of pedagogues and philanthropists denounced them as "dungeons" and "labor camps." At the end of the 1830s, while these institutions were coming increasingly under fire, a third model emerged, whose aim was to remove children from the prisons.

The success of Mettray, a penitentiary farming colony established near Tours (France) in 1839, shows the extent to which the appropriation of foreign experiences led to the creation of a "national model" and its subsequent export. Frédéric-Auguste Demetz, the founder of Mettray, combined three major influences: first, the pedagogy of Swiss farming refuges which, like those of Neuhof and Hofwyl, brought together several dozen abandoned children in order to raise them with respect for family, religion, and work; second, the paternalism of the *Rauhe Haus* ("Rough House"), founded by Johann Hinrich Wichern near Hamburg in 1832, a residential home without bars or walls, where young delinquents worked the land in small groups; third, the discipline of the English settlement of Parkhurst, which trained young people (forced to emigrate to Canada, South Africa, and Australia as farmers) and subjected them to a strict regime.

While the establishment of Mettray demonstrated a certain cosmopolitanism, it was carried out with patriotic overtones: family environment, the development of moral standards through work, and the farming solution were soon presented as the expression of French genius. Conversely, solitary confinement, cherished by Protestant nations and "self-help" societies, did not suit what was believed to be "the charitable nation par excellence," whose Latin and Catholic warmth alone could properly prepare young people for their return to society.[4] Several dozen colonies were established in France based on the Mettray model, and parliamentarians claimed to adhere to it, passing the law of May 5, 1850 on the education of young offenders. The Touraine institution also enjoyed considerable prestige abroad – the farming colony of Ruysselède, in Belgium, was based on it. The Dutch philanthropist Suringar visited Mettray in 1847; he admired Wichern's "Rough House," but the institution he established five years later was named "Nederlandsch Mettray." Taking the French colony they had visited as a model, in 1849 members of the Royal Philanthropic Society, based in London, created the Farm School at Redhill, Surrey. According to Joshua Jebb, Surveyor-General of prisons, those two institutions were "admirably adapted" to offer children a new start.[5]

In the same way, the Americans undertook "continental tours" – Calvin Stowe in 1832, Horace Mann in 1846, Charles Loring Brace in 1853, and Henry Barnard in 1854. The ritual visit to Mettray and the "Rough House" made them realize the obsolescence of the houses of refuge, prison-like, gloomy, and impersonal – a relic of the Jacksonian era. When they returned, they stated in their travel reports that young offenders should receive individual treatment based on affection, a family environment, and human relationships, which would be more likely to bring about a sincere reform. In 1880, the philanthropist Enoch Wines wrote, "Holland boasts one of the model reformatories of Europe, founded some twenty-five years ago under the name of the Netherlands Mettray."[6] In the 1850s and 1860s, as a result of these transatlantic exchanges, several "family reform schools" were established in Ohio, Wisconsin, Illinois, and Indiana. In 1854, the Massachusetts Industrial School for

Girls housed around 30 boarders in a family atmosphere. From then on, it was the Americans who found inspiration in Europe.

In the second half of the nineteenth century, industrialization, urban growth, the rise of the working classes and the increase in pauperism made child poverty more visible and justified intervention earlier in life. Aimed at minors under the age of fourteen who had been left to fend for themselves, the British "industrial schools" enabled help to be given to those who had not yet fallen into crime. A large number of these establishments were set up in London, Manchester, and Birmingham, as well as in the United States and, after 1869, Quebec. While the farming colonies at Mettray were criticized for their violent atmosphere and inability to reform young offenders, French philanthropists turned once again to English and American institutions. The Elmira reformatory, created in the state of New York in 1876, attracted a great deal of interest. Based on the Australian "mark system," which awarded credits to the most deserving, it subjected young offenders to a comprehensive, individualized treatment that would turn them into good citizens.[7]

Similarly, in the 1880s, French members of parliament examined foreign legislation that guaranteed protection for homeless or mistreated minors. The health of children was as much of a concern to them as national pride. A report noted that, "France, the first nation to have resolutely taken steps towards the effective protection of children, was then overtaken in that task by Belgium, Holland, England, Germany, and the United States."[8] These unfavorable comparisons illustrated the urgent need for legislation: on July 24, 1889, the French Parliament passed a law allowing mistreated and "morally abandoned" children to be taken away from their parents (that same year, the United Kingdom made its own provision in the Act for the Prevention of Cruelty to Children). Scholarly reviewing and extended bibliographies in journals also provided evidence of an international open-mindedness, although this had its fair share of jealousy: this curiosity for the neighbors' achievements fueled national contention and competition. Paul Strauss's *La Revue philanthropique* gave monthly digests of recent foreign-language publications, and experiments carried out in Europe and worldwide. In 1897, the year in which it was established, it reported on the activities of the Royal Caledonian Asylum for orphans in London and the protection of newborn babies in Nuremberg. Before praising the English "College Settlements," in which young people from around the world devoted themselves to working-class children in order to save them from idleness and pilfering, a reformer wrote, "One of our gravest failings, indeed, is to ignore what is said and done abroad, while other countries are so quick to take on our ideas and assimilate them!"[9]

The increase in international congresses that were being held was another factor making for convergence in ideas and policies. Philanthropists and magistrates from all over Europe – from Sweden to Italy and from Paris to Warsaw – met in Brussels in 1847 to exchange views on the issue of poor, delinquent children. Eight other International Prison Reform Congresses were held before World War I, mostly in Europe, with the French and Belgians featuring prominently on the programs, which included a section devoted to "questions concerning children and minors."[10] Other international meetings tackled the issue of deviant or poor children indirectly (with congresses being held on penal law, school hygiene, public and private welfare, etc.). National legislation and experiences were presented, the virtues of a particular system were debated, and sometimes there were arguments, but those congresses helped to strengthen the common *doxa*.

It was partly through this international academic sociability that innovation spread, as shown by the example of the juvenile courts. The idea of distinguishing between minors and adults during legal proceedings is by no means recent. Since 1791, the French penal code had authorized the acquittal of young delinquents acting "without discernment," and, in the event that they were convicted, allowed their sentence to be lessened. In 1874, Massachusetts introduced special proceedings for children; in 1892, the Canadian penal code authorized closed hearings for the benefit of children. It was in Illinois in 1899, however, that the first court specialized in trying children was established. The law, thanks to the actions of the reformer Julia Lathrop, provided for the establishment of release on parole and the extension of the judge's supervisory powers, with all delinquent, poor, abandoned, homeless, or mistreated minors becoming "wards of the court." Not only did this measure serve as a prototype for other American states (Wisconsin and New York copied it in 1901, Ohio in 1902, Maryland in 1902, Colorado in 1903, and almost all states by the end of the 1920s), but most countries also came around to it within a few decades.

In Great Britain, the Children Act of 1908 established special courts for minors between seven and sixteen, introduced closed hearings, and separated young people from adults before and after the hearing. Portugal adopted the measure in 1911. A few months later, Belgium did so, and France passed a law on July 12, 1912 establishing courts for children and teenagers, and instituting release on parole. That year, a jurist wrote that:

> From the United States – where twenty-six states, to this date, have adopted this new legislation – children's courts have spread throughout the world: to Canada, Australia, New Zealand, and then to England and Germany. Austria, Belgium, Italy, Hungary, Sweden, Switzerland, Russia and France are preparing to organize them from scratch or to harmonize them with their own institutions.[11]

In 1934, an international inquiry led by the League of Nations studied the way in which around twenty countries had implemented the reform: the United States, Spain, Denmark, Belgium, Canada, Norway, the USSR, Sweden, and Switzerland had special juvenile courts; in Germany, Greece, Great Britain, France, Hungary, Italy, the Netherlands, Poland, and Czechoslovakia, minors were tried in ordinary courts that were turned into juvenile courts for the occasion; only a few countries, such as Bulgaria and Romania, tried minors in ordinary courts.

All of this transnational movement – which was brought about through private reading and travel, academic debates, and exchanges within professional organizations – united child welfare by harmonizing the ways in which poor children and juvenile delinquents were taken into care around the world. However, although this internationalization evened out any disparities, it did not lead to the abolition of national "models" because the spread of standards and practices took place through traditions and national institutions.

Do child welfare models exist?

The two main authorities which guaranteed that a child would be cared for, educated, and socialized were family and (public and private) institutions. The latter came into play when the former failed. In Europe and the United States, between the end of the eighteenth century and the middle of the twentieth century, the existence of a large number of establishments for minors was evidence of the recognition of a collective responsibility.

The complementarity, which was never refuted, between the state, the local authorities, the churches, and the private sector showed that the coordination between social welfare and children took place on several levels. In France, the law of August 5, 1850 on the education of young offenders gave priority to private associations during a five-year period; at the high point of the anti-church campaign at the beginning of the twentieth century, the republican welfare system relied on the Catholic church, the figure of the priest, and the rite of first communion. In Great Britain, from 1834 onwards, public institutions in London worked to take in homeless children, and the Poor Law Commission oversaw the policy at a national level (it was replaced in 1847 by the Poor Law Board). However, this very loose framework did not stop charitable organizations from proliferating, including the East End Juvenile Mission, created in 1868, and the whole network of homes set up by the philanthropist Thomas Barnardo. In the interwar period in Italy, the National Organization for the Protection of Motherhood and Infancy was financed by a tax on unmarried people; in turn, it subsidized associations and institutions.

Nevertheless, it would seem that the state was a driving force within this coalition of stakeholders and interested groups, on both a legislative and a moral level (through the law, ministerial supervision, inspections), and a financial one (through subsidies). At the start of the 1870s, several laws passed in Great Britain and France were aimed at protecting babies and child workers: the 1872 Infant Life Protection Acts and the 1874 Roussel Law protected newborn babies by sending inspectors to the wet-nurses' homes,[12] and the 1874 Tallon Law punished parents who handed their child over to traveling performers or beggars. Locally, child welfare was organized by government services. Between 1870 and 1880 in France, the welfare system implemented the ideas of the new republican regime by sending wards of the state into rural areas and avoiding foster parents with industrial occupations.

It is difficult to assess the dimensions of child suffering in the Western world and to draw international comparisons because the statistics, apart from being incomplete and heterogeneous, reflect more bureaucratic procedures than "actual" situations: it is much easier to reckon juvenile offenders tried by local courts or orphans admitted to institutions than "kids wandering in the streets." In the United States, in 1909, according to the White House Conference, 92,000 orphaned and abandoned children lived in institutions, and 50,000 in foster families. During the New Deal, 29,000 boys and girls under 21 were housed in institutions for young offenders.[13] Between 1853 and the 1890s, 91,000 children from the East Coast were sent to New England, the South, and the Midwest by the Children's Aid Society. Compared to France, a much smaller country, those figures seem quite low. There, the number of foundlings and abandoned children under 13 amounted to 40,000 in the 1780s, peaked at 131,000 in 1833, fluctuated between 50,000 and 90,000 in the second half of the century, reached a second maximum of 120,000 at the eve of World War I, and eventually decreased to 50,000 in the 1960s.[14] In the meantime, other categories of children in need of care had been created: at the end of the nineteenth century, French philanthropists were concerned that 40,000 "morally abandoned" children (i.e. neglected children, young vagrants, and prostitutes) were left to themselves, and in the 1920s there were 1.1 million war orphans (called "wards of the Nation" by the French law).

Within this general framework, it would be useful to highlight the different types of child welfare that existed in the Western world, particularly in Europe. In 1889, Loys Brueyre, former head of service for children in care in the Seine area, wrote, "The sentimental side of Latin people has driven them to take pity on children of a young age," whereas "the practical and positive spirit of nations of Germanic origin has shown them the usefulness for society of setting older children on the right path, who, because of their parents, wander the city."[15] Orphans and foundlings for some, young vagrants and delinquents for others? As Jean-Pierre Bardet and Olivier Faron show, the Old Continent was divided along confessional lines, which had an effect at the institutional level. Latin, Catholic southern Europe represented "the vast area of foundlings." Abandonment was a major problem there, particularly after the start of birth control from the 1750s onwards, and the existence of a large number of archives reveals a truth: the burden of unwanted babies was transferred to the institutions.[16] In the fifteenth century, Italy set up a home for foundlings; in France, in the 1630s, Vincent de Paul took pity on the newborns who were being brought to him as fragile as baby Jesus. In Mediterranean countries, priority was given to saving and fostering foundlings, to the detriment of the young vagrants whose parents were known. In 1823 in France, a directive from the Minister for the Interior, Corbière, prevented poor orphans and abandoned children over the age of twelve from receiving welfare. In the 1830s–1860s, approximately 100,000 babies were abandoned each year in Southern Europe (33,000 in Italy; 31,000 in France; 15,000 in Spain; and 15,000 in Portugal).[17]

Conversely, in Northern Europe, which included Germany, Great Britain, the Netherlands, and Scandinavia, abandoning children to institutions was rare. In England, abandonment was not controlled by the state. Instead, individuals made private arrangements with what were known as "baby-farmers," where the child was brought up (or, more often, neglected until he or she died) by a wet-nurse after the parents had paid her a fixed fee. On the other hand, Protestant philanthropy gave rise to a great many institutions for children who were homeless, begging, neglected, etc. The Swiss and German experiences of the first half of the nineteenth century have already been mentioned. Following in the tradition of the Poor Laws, Great Britain and the United States had a whole range of houses of refuge, homes for destitute lads and girls, juvenile asylums, training ships and reformatories. For a number of months or years, the children were given a semi-repressive education, dividing their time between study, training and work, after which they were returned to their families or placed with a new family. In Massachusetts, the Boston House of Reformation for Juvenile Offenders (founded in 1826), the Boston Society for the Prevention of Pauperism (created in 1833 by the Reverend Joseph Tuckerman), the Children's Mission to the Children of the Destitute (established in 1849 by the Reverend George Merrill), and the Boston Children's Aid Society (1864) took in children who were delinquent, homeless, or unruly, taken there by their parents, school teachers, churchmen, or "overseers of the poor."[18]

In fact this division along confessional lines was more nuanced and complex. The first reformatories were opened in Italy by churchmen, for example, in Florence in the second half of the seventeenth century. The French laws of 1889 and 1898 established that children who were homeless or neglected by their parents would be taken into care. Conversely, orphanages were a vital part of social welfare in the United States, although they appeared much later there than in Mediterranean Europe. There were 33 before 1830; almost 200 in 1860; 600 in 1890; 970 in 1910; and 1,300 in 1933. After the Civil War, four "foundling asylums" opened in New York for abandoned children; one of these was the Infant's Home, created in 1865 based on the model of the Foundling Hospital in London.

While the dividing line between these two main models blurred somewhat towards the end of the nineteenth century, it then seems to have resurfaced in a new form. Julie Miller notes that, in Catholic Europe, the foundling hospitals were at the heart of an extensive network of wet-nurses, charity workers, doctors, churchmen, and bureaucrats; in Protestant countries, on the other hand, the system was completely decentralized, based on parishes and almshouses, and the lack of a national network prevented connections from being formed between cities and rural areas. Like the English system from which it was derived, the American system did not enmesh its foundlings in bureaucratic procedures; like the immigrants and outlaws, they could set off for the West and blend into the population while hiding their origins.[19] From the 1850s and 1860s onwards, Charles Loring Brace's Children's Aid Society in New York and Henry Watson's Children's Aid Society in Baltimore sent thousands of children to rural areas in the East coast states, as well as to the Midwest. In the 1870s, Michigan withdrew children from public institutions and established the "placing-out" system, which was later copied by Wisconsin, Minnesota, and other states.[20]

However, national models tended to converge again in the last third of the nineteenth century because institutions fell into disfavor all over Europe and in the United States, while family placements became increasingly popular. There was concomitance between the idealized glorification of the countryside, entirely Jeffersonian, by pediatricians and American reformers such as Abraham Jacobi and Charles Loring Brace (who, himself, was influenced by the practices carried out by services for abandoned children in France and by German family education), and the way in which the Third Republic, in France, made rural family placement its official policy, on the grounds that family education was universal, and that the child needed affection and did not find it in the "collectivist systems." It was no coincidence that Abraham Jacobi condemned the nursery system (institutional forms) at a time when, in Europe, foundling wheels (wooden cylinders installed in nurseries in which people could abandon newborn babies) were being criticized: a nursery should no longer be a place of transit before the baby was sent off to the countryside. In 1889, at the first international congress of welfare held in Paris, with 405 members from 24 countries, speakers praised "French traditions," among which rural family placement featured prominently.

The same phenomenon of deinstitutionalization could be observed at the end of the twentieth century, after the collapse of the dictatorial regimes in Europe. Such was the case in Romania in the 1990s when it broke with the policy of state orphanages established under Nicolae Ceausescu.[21] In Spain, the Franco regime favored the internment of deviant children, with their troubles being attributed – as with the nineteenth-century model – to their family's immorality or their supposed vices. The return to democracy at the end of the 1970s turned child welfare upside down. For the first time in Spain, a 1987 law introduced the notion of placement in a foster family, which was different from adoption or placement in an institution. But public supervision only occurred in cases when parents were unable to assume their responsibilities and the minor suffered from a blatant lack of care.[22]

While institutions were in general decline, the biological family returned to favor during the twentieth century, and was considered to be the most legitimate authority for socialization. In the United States, at the White House Conference of 1909, social assistance was proposed for single mothers and their children, in order to guarantee the latter the right to a home life. Unlike the credo of nineteenth-century reformers, the conference focused on prevention and family assistance, with the child only being taken away as a last resort (in which case a foster family was preferable to placement in an institution). Like the Illinois Funds to Parents Act of 1911, several laws gave support to mothers whose only failing was to be widowed or poor, with young unmarried mothers being excluded from the measure in Massachusetts and other states. For Matthew Crenson, who compares the systems of four states (New York, Massachusetts, Ohio, and Minnesota), this series of measures resembled an "invisible orphanage." The mothers' pensions movement (which, under the New Deal, gave rise to the Aid to Dependent Children, or ADC), developed alongside the practice of probation, which allowed young offenders to be supervised within their family rather than placed in closed institutions.[23]

Help for single mothers, established in France in the 1870s (the principle had been envisaged during the Revolution), had the aim of preventing abandonment, with the child's presence expected to instill moral values in the unmarried mother; the 1892 law allowed single women to give birth free of charge in hospitals. Foreshadowed by the 1912 law on juvenile courts, the "educational action in an open environment" (*action éducative en milieu ouvert* or AEMO) came into force in the 1960s: it consisted in sending a social worker to the parents' place in order to oversee the education of the child deemed "in danger." The Bianco–Lamy report of 1979, extended by two laws passed in 1984 and 1986, urged social services to work with families, with the child only being taken away as a last resort.

While northern and southern Europe have different traditions with regard to social welfare, it is nevertheless true that care became more harmonized from the end of the nineteenth century onwards, with the decline of closed institutions, the rise of rural family placements, and the belief that the biological family was a sanctuary. It is therefore possible to identify child welfare models at national levels; but their gradual convergence tended to blur their underlying rationale. Does that mean that all the countries of Europe, as well as the United States, took children into care in the same way?

Authority over the child and national legal measures

If we restrict ourselves to the North-Atlantic area, two major patterns of state intervention can be observed, depending on whether it was the legislators or the judge who were first to rescue the child. These models of protection regulated relations between families and the state, providing evidence of a deep-rooted continuity over centuries.

The French model, which can be categorized as "Latin-Republican," defined the protected child in terms of the law. At the beginning of the nineteenth century in France, neither the civil code nor the penal code could prevent a father's abuse or violence – which was a way for Napoleon to make the family the ark of society. In order for the state to take away the father's prerogatives, the child had to have broken the law: article 66 of the penal code provided that the young offender who had acted "without discernment" could be taken to a reformatory in order to be "raised and held" until his twentieth birthday. In the event that children became orphaned, the state classified them – found, abandoned, orphaned – and the law determined what would happen to them. The decree of March 20, 1797 (30 ventôse an V in the republican calendar) placed them with a wet-nurse until the age of twelve, after which they went to work for farmers, artisans, or manufacturers. The law of February 4, 1805 (15 pluviôse an XIII) did away with the sovereignty of parents by giving almshouses guardianship over the children who arrived there "for whatever reason."

This legislation remained in place throughout the nineteenth century. The law of July 24, 1889 was the crowning achievement of this movement; it linked the protection of mistreated children to the total deprivation of their parents, who completely forfeited their rights with regard to all their children, whether minor, of legal age, legitimate, natural, or even unborn. In France, the salvation of "children of the law" was carried out by and for the state.[24] The paradox was that this legal omnipotence went hand in hand with very real neglect. In the Ain region, "supervision is not carried out…; it is not known what becomes of children over the age of twelve." In Brittany, Burgundy, and the Pyrenees, the ward was simply "abandoned" to himself or herself. Overall, in three-quarters of the departments of France, children grew up unsupervised.[25]

The system was different in England, where it was the judge (and not legislators supported by the administration) who led child welfare. There, from the sixteenth century onwards, the principle of *parens patriae* ("father of the homeland") allowed the Crown to take care of those subjects who were incapable of leading their own lives, such as "lunatics," "idiots," and abandoned children, with whom the monarch must behave like "a father." Widows appealed to the chancellor when orphans were likely to suffer in matters of inheritance, accounts, or marriage. Increasingly, *parens patriae* was applied to children's upbringing itself, and to the moral aptitude of the living father or mother: in 1817, the courts refused to grant the poet Shelley custody of his children (whose mother had died), after he was accused of publishing blasphemous and immoral writings, and the 1839 Custody of Infants Act enabled custody or visiting rights to be transferred from the father to the mother.[26] Considered in the wider sense, the principle of *parens patriae* therefore enabled the protection of minors, whose health and morality were endangered by inadequate parents.

The United States inherited the English tradition. In 1817, a Pennsylvania court ruled that the public protection given to young delinquents required neither the father's approval nor the child's cooperation. The *parens patriae* entered into American case law thanks to the *Ex Parte Crouse* ruling, delivered in 1838 by the Supreme Court of Pennsylvania (the young Mary Ann Crouse remained in a Philadelphia home where she had been taken at her mother's request, but against her father's will). The creation of juvenile courts at the end of the century further strengthened this trend.[27] This judicial, decentralized process of removing parental rights and protecting children could be found in many countries. In Sweden, at the end of the nineteenth century, preventing juvenile delinquency was the responsibility of local school councils. In the 1920s, specialized services became autonomous and had the power to take a child away from his or her parents if thought to be in danger. The *barnavårdsnämnd*, found in each village, supervised children's well-being, investigated cases of abuse, and so on.[28]

Two models of state intervention can therefore be identified: a legal patriarchy, which was dominant in countries with Roman law, and a judicial patriarchy, found in common law countries. Traditionally, it could be found that interpreting common law left the judge with some room for maneuver (and, no doubt, for arbitrariness) of which his French counterpart was deprived, as he was solely supposed to apply the law in the same way in all cases. What is more, the diversity of legislation and local jurisdiction in the United States, and the absence of a centralized government (particularly in the area of family and education), was in sharp contrast with the uniformity of the French nation-state, strengthened by its laws and directives within a single territory. English legislators did, nonetheless, intervene actively in child welfare: in Great Britain, 79 laws relating to education and protection were passed between 1870 and 1908. Conversely, in France it was the courts that applied the 1889 law on parental deprivation. In reality, the law did not have the same function everywhere.

The "Latin-Republican" system, which was deeply integrating, first had to identify children at risk before removing them and then, once rehabilitated, reinserting them into the national community. Assistance from the French state presupposed the prior definition of the legal beneficiary – "foundling," "poor orphan," "morally abandoned," "temporarily taken in," etc. Conversely, the English and the Americans were concerned little with differentiating between the different beneficiaries of their institutions. According to the law passed on April 12, 1853 in New York State, a minor aged between five and fourteen found wandering, idling, or begging could be sent to a charitable institution by the courts, regardless of his or her parents' wishes (or existence). In Great Britain, the justice of the peace could send a child considered at risk to an institution in order to undergo training. Symptomatically, English reformers combined all these categories using idiomatic expressions (such as "gutter snipes," "waifs and strays," or "street Arabs") to indicate gangs of marauding young vagrants. This lack of a legal definition had important consequences: in order to come to a child's rescue, an English magistrate could simply identify pre-delinquent behavior, whereas a French lawmaker, before the 1889 law, had to wait until he or she committed an offence.[29]

These two models also differed in their relationship with the families (in this case, poor, single-parent, or delinquent families). It is not a paradox to observe that the laws stemming from the Roman tradition, in which the father was like the king of the family, were also those that stripped him of his powers most fully when he failed in his children's upbringing. The father, a delegate of the sovereign, owned a fragment of the *imperium*, and this passed back into public ownership if he failed. This "all or nothing" rationale, which shifted between the father's omnipotence and that of the state, went hand-in-hand with the utopia of the newborn child, so characteristic of Republican France, which consisted of saving the child by taking him or her away from the family in order to start from scratch. Regeneration took place without the "unworthy" parents, and, as far as possible, away from the place of origin. The foundling wheel, an Italian invention dating back to the sixteenth century (known as *torno* or *ruota*), became a requirement in France in accordance with the decree issued by Napoleon on January 19, 1811. It made it possible for a newborn baby to be taken in anonymously and for the child's civil status to be rebuilt out of nothing. This distrust of lower working-class families led to parents being challenged *a priori*, and to the expected break-up of family ties. The republican welfare system tried to undermine wards' "backgrounds" by moving them far from the place where they grew up, by forbidding parents to visit or exchange letters with the child, by preventing the child from being returned and refusing the child access to his or her personal file.[30]

Between the 1860s and the late 1950s, Great Britain sent around 150,000 children, without their families, out to the colonies. The English welfare system did not resist the temptation to wipe the slate clean, and the *parens patriae*, like in France, sanctioned an educational failure due to unfit parents; even so, the English system was more sensitive to family rights. In the mid-nineteenth century, while the Industrial Revolution was impoverishing the working class, destabilizing families, keeping fathers away from home, and leaving isolated single mothers and children, the British reformer Mary Carpenter described what the supreme principle meant to her:

> Where a parent, through his culpable neglect, or actual criminality, proves that he cannot retain the guardianship of his child without injury to society, and therefore is deprived of it, he is not thereby freed from the duty imposed by nature of maintaining his child, and must be compelled to do so.

And when the judge leaned towards a reformatory, the parents should be allowed to have their rights restored at any time.[31] In the 1880s and 1890s, the Society for the Prevention of Cruelty to Children embodied the principle of public interventionism; however, it gave priority to warnings, advice and incentives as a way of encouraging families to assume their responsibilities. In 1889, the Prevention of Cruelty to Children Act entrusted the abused child to a charitable organization or to the state, but the parents' responsibility did not end with the child's removal because they could be sentenced to pay up to five shillings a week as maintenance.

In the United States, even if magistrates and philanthropists recognized the need for intervention in the private sphere in order to protect the child's interests, they showed a certain reticence, which showed through in the case law of several states. In 1867, Illinois passed a law authorizing the apprehension of any child found homeless, abandoned, neglected, or begging, aged between six and sixteen, as well as his or her internment in a Chicago reformatory, against the parents' wishes if necessary. Three years later, however, the Supreme Court of Illinois declared this to be unconstitutional in its *People v. Turner* decree, on the grounds that the taking away of a child by the state came close to despotism. The support that Isaac Redfield, judge of the

Supreme Court of Vermont, lent to this decision in an article from 1872 reflected the mistrust of the judiciary towards reformers, of the principle of coercion contained in the law, and of the use that could be made of it against the children of immigrants or Catholic parents. In the 1880s, several states adopted laws protecting mistreated children (Michigan in 1881, Indiana in 1889), but, unlike France, those laws did not do away with parental authority. Likewise, American states authorized the adoption of minors in the second half of the nineteenth century (1851 in Massachusetts), whereas the French Government, unyielding of the authority it had over the abandoned children, only authorized this after the World War I, and even then in a very restrictive form.[32]

At the end of the nineteenth century, the reformers of the Progressive Era, such as Florence Kelley and Lilian Wald, wanted priority to be given to the law and the federal government. The US Children's Bureau, a federal agency created in 1912, aimed at reducing infant and maternal mortality, protecting children's health, preventing their exploitation, etc; however, its director, Julia Lathrop, and her successors had difficulty convincing Americans that the child's interests should be taken care of by a federal agency at the national level. The most important texts voted on at the instigation of the Children's Bureau were, in the end, rejected: the Keating–Owen law of 1916 on the employment of children was declared unconstitutional by the Supreme Court two years later, and the Sheppard–Towner law of 1921 promoting the health of mothers and children, although highly decentralized, fell victim to the detractors of "socialized medicine." In the first third of the twentieth century, the well-being of American children depended largely on family initiative, and many states gave prominence to the right of parents compared to the children's interest. This explains the reason why, in the United States, there was no federal law making school compulsory, unlike those established by more centralized, structured legislation in France or Sweden.[33] Instead, each state independently passed compulsory schooling laws by the early twentieth century (but after the 1960s, the federal government began to establish rules regarding schooling of a variety of kinds). The pre-eminence of judges, the strength of the private sector, respect for the family and the weakness of the federal state explain why the initiatives of the Progressive Era (what we might call the "Latin-Republican period" of American child welfare) ended in failure.

The Latin and Anglo-American systems both aimed to save the child who had been placed in danger by his or her environment and upbringing; however, while the former tended to identify the lonely child with the state whose aims it was serving, the latter maintained a certain level of local autonomy and pragmatism regarding familial situations.

Beyond those juridical differences, a common concern has emerged in many Western countries: the whole system of child welfare seems to be breaking down and the juvenile justice system is also seen as deeply flawed. Those anxieties precisely explain why so many historians and sociologists have been focusing on child welfare since the late 1960s. The first sentence of Eric C. Schneider's famous *In the Web of Class* (1992) reads:

> We have never dealt successfully with our troubled children. We lock them
> up, put them on probation, place them in foster care, or keep them at home

and utilize home visitors and social services – the limited possibilities have all been tried before and failed.[34]

Many other scholars have dwelt upon the failure of all the "systems" invented to fight idleness, vagrancy, poverty, and crime among youths.

Conclusion

In 1922, Eglantyne Jebb, a founder of Save the Children Fund UK, wrote a memorandum in order to promote a Children's Code, while, in the same period, the Socialist Youth International and the International Council of Women wrote a Children's Charter and a Declaration of the Rights of the Adolescent. On September 26, 1924, taking up this initiative, the League of Nations proclaimed the first Declaration of the Rights of the Child. It stated in article 2: "The child that is hungry must be fed, the child that is sick must be nursed, the child that is backward must be helped, the delinquent child must be reclaimed, and the orphan and the waif must be sheltered and succored." After the United Nations Declaration of 1959 and the celebration of an International Day of the Child in 1979, on November 20, 1989, the United Nations adopted the Convention on the Rights of the Child, signed and ratified by 191 countries. Recognition was given of the child's right to be cared for by one of his or her parents (art. 7), the right to freedom of expression (art. 13), freedom of thought and religion (art. 14), and the right to benefit from the highest possible standard of health (art. 24), an adequate standard of living (art. 27), education and equal opportunities (art. 28).

Any reflection on child welfare leads to a questioning of the way in which European and American philanthropists in the nineteenth century helped to make children the permanent subject of rights that we know today. This connection, encouraged by this chapter's comparative and long-term perspective, may come as a surprise to some readers. Should one not draw a distinction between paternalistic, Victorian "child saving," and the rights of children as the fruit of a progressive twentieth century? Is there no difference in nature between the moral aims of rescuing a child, and freeing the child as an autonomous subject? When an analysis is made of the links between social welfare and childhood, it may be necessary to identify two types of action: on the one hand, the protection of all minors in general, through school, the healthcare system, the right to work, and the monitoring of certain publications; and, on the other hand, taking care of specific categories such as children who are abandoned, delinquent, abused, or with special needs.

In fact, children's rights, in their most general sense and their purest abstraction, have been established within institutions that were specifically designed to protect children in need of special care, abandoned children, or children at risk, whose health, safety, and morality needed to be guaranteed. The great declarations of 1924, 1959, and 1989 incorporated the fruits of the major struggles of the nineteenth and twentieth into international law: the protection of life and physical well-being, the right to live in a family, the right to education, the banning of economic and sexual exploitation, etc. In short, European and American philanthropists, in their ambitions and convictions, helped to forge children's rights as they are understood today. The phasing-out of the institutions such as houses of refuse and orphanages, which had dominated child welfare in the nineteenth century, and the restoration of the family (biological, foster, or adoptive), illustrate the convergence of child welfare on a global scale.

But we must be careful not to draw a too rosy picture. In the twentieth century many problems resulted from relying increasingly on foster care: "round trips" between the parents' unfit home and the foster one, impediment to adoption, child abuse, etc. Besides, if the asylum has lost its name, it has not been discarded. The United States still has many juvenile detention centers (JDC) and group homes, though few are called "orphanages" as they were before the 1970s. Sweden in 1999 and Spain in 2000 have outlawed prison for children under age, but juvenile delinquents are still committed to "closed centers" under the supervision of social workers. In Britain, where the percentage of incarcerated children is the highest in Europe, detention centers and separated areas in prisons do coexist. The problems of child poverty, abandonment, and neglect seem not to have actually been solved by Western societies despite several experiments since the eighteenth century.

Outside the Western world, child welfare is somewhat limited. In 2004, more than 200 million children were exploited: 14 percent of all children were working, even if the proportion has decreased since 2000 (16 percent). As for child soldiers, they grew from 250,000 in 1998 to more than 300,000 in 2005, both boys and girls being used as warriors, saboteurs, spies, "wives," etc.[35] Though criminalized, the exploitation of children for economical, sexual, or military purposes is far from having disappeared.

How do Western societies tackle the paradox of the ambiguous success of child welfare at home and the perpetuation of endemic problems in Asia or in Africa? This paradox, which relates to national/international perspectives, leads to two opposite attitudes. For more and more Western bourgeois families, international adoption is a way to fill the "empty cradle,"[36] while saving a needy child. But instead of "importing" the non-Western child, it is possible to "export" the values of Western child welfare. Indeed, children's rights, with their universal scope, and international aid as implemented by the UN and hundreds of non-governmental organizations around the world, descend from an earlier globalization of legislation and practices, as well as a collaboration between stakeholders at state, para-state and private level, as was established starting from the end of the eighteenth century. In the space of two centuries, in Europe and North America, but also in the Middle East, the Far East and Latin America, the circulation of ideas, knowledge, and experience, the activation of professional networks, and the spread of methods and models – accelerated by a certain emulation between nations – presided over the birth of an international sensitivity and a common language that transcends different cultures.

All things considered, it seems that the protection of minors first developed in industrialized Western nations, that child welfare and the "child's interests" are linked to the construction of the nation-state, and that these have sometimes crystallized into striking national traditions, whether religious or legal. Nevertheless, the fact remains that, following a chronology shared by a great many countries, the convergence of legal and institutional structures enabled children's rights to flourish in the second half of the twentieth century. These crossings-over and fusions did not challenge national traditions any more than children's rights, at the end of the twentieth century, overcame cultural, political, or legal reservations in certain countries: the United States did not ratify the Convention on the Rights of the Child as a way to avoid abolishing the death penalty for minors, and France, attached to a woman's right to relinquish a child at birth, found itself at odds with the right of the abandoned child to know his or her origins. Despite everything, an international culture was forged starting from the end of the eighteenth century, developing in a state of continual tension between globalization of practices, absorption of foreign experiences, and preservation of national models.

Notes

1 Henry E. Manning, and Benjamin Waugh, "The Child of the English Savage," *Contemporary Review* 49 (1886), 687–700.

2 François-Alexandre-Frédéric de la Rochefoucauld-Liancourt, *Des prisons de Philadelphie, par un Européen* (Paris, France: Du Pont, an IV, 1795).

3 Michel-Louis-François Huerne de Pommeuse, *Des colonies agricoles et de leurs avantages* (Paris, France: Huzard, 1832); Gabriel de Lurieu, Hippolyte Romand, *Études sur les colonies agricoles de mendiants, jeunes détenus, orphelins et enfants trouvés. Hollande, Suisse, Belgique, France* (Paris, France: Librairie agricole de la Maison rustique, Dusacq, 1851).

4 Léon Faucher, "Du projet de loi sur la réforme des prisons," *La Revue des Deux Mondes* V, 1 (1844), 373–408.

5 Joshua Jebb, *Report on the Discipline and Management of the Convict Prisons* (London, UK: Clowes and Sons, 1851), 26.

6 Enoch Cobb Wines, *The State of Prisons and of Child Saving Institutions in the Civilized World* (Cambridge, UK: Wilson and Son, 1880), 400.

7 *Bulletin de la Société générale des prisons* (Paris, Chaix, 1878–1879), in particular session of June 12, 1879.

8 *Annales du Sénat et de la Chambre des députés (nouvelle série). Documents parlementaires*, XIII, 2nd part, session of May 26, 1884 (Paris, France: Imprimerie du Journal Officiel, 1884), 13.

9 "Chronique étrangère," and Marguerite Cremnitz, "Les *College Settlements*," *La Revue philanthropique* 1(1) (1897), 605, 868.

10 The congresses were held in London (1872), Stockholm (1878), Rome (1885), Saint-Petersburg (1890), Paris (1895), Brussels (1900), Budapest (1905), Washington (1910), London (1925), Prague (1930), and Berlin (1935). See Thorsten Sellin, Valy Degoumois (eds.), *Proceedings of the 12 International Penitentiary Congresses, 1872–1950. Analytical and Name Index* (Bern, Staempfli, d.u., roughly 1952).

11 Pierre de Casabianca, *Tribunaux pour enfants. Premier congrès international de tribunaux pour enfants* (Paris, France: Davy, 1912), 6.

12 By the end of the century, nearly 200,000 children under two were protected by the Roussel law.

13 Kriste Lindenmeyer, *"A Right to Childhood": The U.S. Children's Bureau and Child Welfare, 1912–1946* (Urbana, IL: University of Illinois Press, 1997), 19–20, 152.

14 Adolphe de Watteville, *Rapport à M. le ministre de l'Intérieur sur la situation administrative, morale et financière du service des enfants trouvés et abandonnés en France* (Paris, France: Imprimerie nationale, Guillaumin, 1849), 6, 22; and Alfred Nizard, Monique Maksud, "Enfants trouvés, reconnus, légitimés. Les statistiques de la filiation en France aux XIXe et XXe siècles," *Population* 6 (1977): 1164.

15 Loys Brueyre, *De l'éducation des enfants assistés et des enfants moralement abandonnés en France* (Paris, France: Mémoires et documents scolaires publiés par le musée pédagogique, 2/46, Imprimerie nationale, 1889), 23.

16 Jean-Pierre Bardet, Olivier Faron, "Des enfants sans enfance: sur les abandonnés de l'époque moderne," in *Histoire de l'enfance en Occident* II, eds. Egle Becchi, and Dominique Julia (Paris, France: Seuil, 1998), 112–146.

17 Volker Hunecke, "Intensità e fluttuazioni degli abbandoni dal XV al XIX secolo," in *Enfance abandonnée et société en Europe, XIVe–XXe siècle. Actes du colloque international tenu à Rome les 30 et 31 janvier 1987* (Rome, Italy: EFR, 140, 1991), 37.

18 Peter C. Holloran, *Boston's Wayward Children. Social Services for Homeless Children, 1830–1930* (London, UK: Toronto, Associated University Presses, 1989), 24 and following.

19 Julie Miller, *Abandoned. Foundlings in Nineteenth-Century New York City* (New York, NY: New York University Press, 2008), 6–8 and chapter 4.

20 Grace Abbott (ed.), *The Child and the State*, 2, *The Dependent and the Delinquent Child, the Child of Unmarried Parents* (Chicago, IL: The University of Chicago Press, 1938), 5–13.

21 Fern Greenwell, "The Impact of Child Welfare Reform on Child Abandonment and Deinstitutionalization, Romania, 1990–2000," *Annales de démographie historique* 111/1 (2006), 133–157.

22 Cecilia Valiente, "The Value of an Educational Emphasis: Child Care and Restructuring in Spain since 1975," in *Child Care Policy at the Crossroads: Gender and Welfare State Restructuring*, eds. Sonya Michel and Rianne Mahon, (New York, NY: Routledge, 2002), 57–70; María Ángeles García Llorente, Laura Martínez-Mora, "The Process of Deinstitutionalization in Spain," in *Children in Institutions: The Beginning of the End? The Cases of Italy, Spain, Argentina, Chile, and Uruguay*, eds. Miguel Cillero et al., (Florence, Italy: Tipografia Giuntina, 2003), 25–48.

23 Matthew A. Crenson, *Building the Invisible Orphanage. A Prehistory of the American Welfare System* (Cambridge, MA: Harvard University Press, 1998).

24 Ivan Jablonka, *Les Enfants de la République. L'intégration des jeunes de 1789 à nos jours* (Paris, France: Seuil, 2010), chapter 1–3.

25 Adolphe de Watteville, *Statistiques des établissements et services de bienfaisance* (Paris, France: Imprimerie nationale, Guillaumin, 1849), 26, 127–132.

26 Neil H. Cogan, "Juvenile Law, Before and After the Entrance of 'Parens Patriae'," *South Carolina Law Review* 22 (1970), 147–181; Sarah Abramowicz, "English Child Custody Law, 1660–1839: The Origins of Judicial Intervention in Paternal Custody," *Columbia Law Review* 99(5) (1999) 1344–1392.

27 Alexander W. Pisciotta, "Saving the Children: The Promise and Practice of Parens Patriae, 1838–1898," *Crime and Delinquency* 28(3) (1982), 410–425; Michael Grossberg, *Governing the Hearth: Law and the Family in Nineteenth-Century America* (Chapel Hill, NC: University of North Carolina Press, 1985), chapter 7.

28 Maria Sundkvist, *De vanartade barnen. Mötet mellan barn, föräldrar och Norrköpings barnavårdsnämnd, 1903–1925* (Uppsala, Sweden: Hjelms förlag, 1994).

29 Interestingly, in their 1912 study, Breckinridge and Abbott broke down the "customers" of juvenile courts into sociological problems, instead of taking official categories for granted: the adjustment of immigrant children, the poverty of homeless children, the misfortune of orphans, the degeneration of children living in slums, the school dropout, the disobedience in wealthy families, etc. See Sophonisba P. Breckinridge, Edith Abbott, *The Delinquent Child and the Home* (New York, NY: Arno Press, 1970) [1912].

30 Sylvia Schafer, *Children in Moral Danger and the Problem of Government in Third Republic France* (Princeton, NJ: Princeton University Press, 1997); Ivan Jablonka, *Ni père ni mère. Histoire des enfants de l'Assistance publique (1874–1939)* (Paris, France: Seuil, 2006).

31 Mary Carpenter, *Juvenile Delinquents, Their Condition and Treatment* (London, UK: Cash, 1853), 377–379.

32 Julie Berebitsky, *Like Our Very Own: Adoption and the Changing Culture of Motherhood, 1851–1950* (Lawrence, KS: University Press of Kansas, 2000), chapter 1; Ivan Jablonka,

"L'adoption aux États-Unis et en France (*XIXᵉ–XXᵉ siècles*)," *Histoire et sociétés* 15 (2005), 56–65.

33 Kriste Lindenmeyer and Bengt Sandin, "National Citizenship and Early Policies Shaping 'The Century of the Child' in Sweden and the United States," *The Journal of the History of Childhood and Youth* 1(1) (2008) 50–62.

34 Eric C. Schneider, *In the Web of Class: Delinquents and Reformers in Boston, 1810s–1930s* (New York, NY: New York University Press, 1992), 1.

35 Tom W. Bennett, *Using Children in Armed Conflict: A Legitimate African Tradition?* (Pretoria, South Africa: Monograph 32, Institute for Security Studies, 1998).

36 Margaret S. Marsh, and Wanda Ronner, *The Empty Cradle: Infertility in America from Colonial Times to the Present* (Baltimore, MD: Johns Hopkins University Press, 1996).

Suggestions for further reading

Child abandonment and institutions

Bellingham, Bruce. "Waifs and Strays: Child Abandonment, Foster Care, and Families in Mid-Nineteenth-Century New York." In *The Uses of Charity: The Poor on Relief in the Nineteenth-Century Metropolis*, edited by Peter Mandler. Philadelphia, PA: University of Pennsylvania Press, 1990.

Boswell, John. *The Kindness of Strangers: The Abandonment of Children in Western Europe from Late Antiquity to the Renaissance*. New York, NY: Pantheon, 1988.

Carp, E. Wayne. "Orphanages vs. Adoption: The Triumph of Biological Kinship, 1800–1933." In *With Us Always: A History of Private Charity and Public Welfare*, edited by Donald T. Critchlow, and Charles H. Parker. Lanham, MD: Rowman and Littlefield, 1999.

Davin, Anna. *Growing Up Poor: Home, School and Street in London, 1870–1914*. London, UK: Rivers Oram Press, 1996.

Dupoux, Albert. *Sur les pas de Monsieur Vincent. Trois cents ans d'histoire parisienne de l'enfance abandonnée*. Paris, France: Revue de l'Assistance publique, 1958.

Hacsi, Timothy A. *Second Home. Orphan Asylums and Poor Families in America*. Cambridge, MA: Harvard University Press, 1997.

Hendrick, Harry. *Child Welfare: England, 1872–1989*. London, UK: Routledge, 1994.

Jablonka, Ivan. "Fictive Kinship: Wards and Foster Parents in Nineteenth-Century France." In *Emotions in the Household, 1200–1900*, edited by Susan Broomhall. New York, NY: Palgrave Macmillan, 2008.

Murdoch, Lydia. *Imagined Orphans: Poor Families, Child Welfare, and Contested Citizenship in London*. New Brunswick, NJ: Rutgers University Press, 2006.

Rose, June. *For the Sake of the Children: Inside Dr Barnardo's. 120 Years of Caring for Children*. London, UK: Hodder & Stoughton, 1987.

Società italiana di demografia storica. *Enfance abandonnée et société en Europe, XIVᵉ–XXᵉ siècle. Actes du colloque international tenu à Rome les 30 et 31 janvier 1987*. Rome, Italy: EFR, 140, 1991.

Tiffin, Susan. *In Whose Best Interest? Child Welfare Reform in the Progressive Era*. Westport, CT: Greenwood Press, 1982.

Juvenile offenders and juvenile justice

Bennett, Paul W. "Taming the 'Bad Boys' of the 'Dangerous Class': Child Rescue and Restraint at the Victoria Industrial School, 1887–1935." *Histoire Sociale* 21(41) (1988): 71–96.

Berlanstein, Leonard. "Vagrants, Beggars, and Thieves: Delinquent Boys in Mid-Nineteenth Century Paris." *Journal of Social History* 12 (1979): 531–552.

Cox, Pamela. *Gender, Justice and Welfare. Bad Girls in Britain, 1900–1950.* New York, NY: Pelgrave MacMillan, 2003.

Duckworth, Jeannie. *Fagin's Children. Criminal Children in Victorian England.* London, UK: Hambledon & London, 2002.

Dupont-Bouchat, Marie-Sylvie and Éric Pierre, eds. *Enfance et justice au XIXᵉ siècle. Essais d'histoire comparée de la protection de l'enfance, 1820–1914. France, Belgique, Pays-Bas, Canada.* Paris, France: PUF, 2001.

Fisher, Jaimey. *Disciplining Germany: Youth, Reeducation, and Reconstruction After the Second World War.* Detroit, MI: Wayne State University Press, 2007.

Gaillac, Henri. *Les Maisons de correction (1830–1945).* Paris, France: Éditions Cujas, 1991 [1971].

Hawes, Joseph M. *Children in Urban Society. Juvenile Delinquency in Nineteenth-Century America.* New York, NY: Oxford University Press, 1971.

Maynes, Mary Jo, Birgitte Søland, and Christina Benninghaus, eds. *Secret Gardens, Satanic Mills: Placing Girls in European History, 1750–1960.* Bloomington, IN: Indiana University Press, 2005.

Ménard, Sylvie. "L'Institut Saint-Antoine et la problématique de réforme des garçons délinquants au Québec (1873–1909)." PhD diss., University of Quebec, Montreal, 1998.

Myers, Tamara. *Caught: Montreal's Modern Girls and the Law, 1869–1945.* Toronto, Canada: University of Toronto Press, 2006.

Oberwittler, Dietrich. "The Decline of Correctional Education, ca. 1900–1920. England and Germany Compared." *European Journal of Crime, Criminal Law and Criminal Justice* 7(1) (1999): 23–40.

Perdriolle, Sylvie. "Centres fermés pour mineurs délinquants. Les ambiguïtés d'un projet." *Études* 11 (2003): 463–473.

Platt, Anthony M. *The Child Savers. The Invention of Delinquency.* Chicago, IL: University of Chicago Press, 1969.

Ryerson, Ellen. *The Best-Laid Plans: America's Juvenile Court Experiment.* New York, NY: Hill and Wang, 1978.

Schlossman, Steven. *Love and the American Delinquent: The Theory and Practice of "Progressive" Juvenile Justice, 1825–1929.* Chicago, IL: Chicago University Press, 1977.

Sutton, John R. *Stubborn Children: Controlling Delinquency in the United States, 1640–1981.* Berkeley, CA: University of California Press, 1988.

Trépanier, Jean, and Françoise Tulkens. "Juvenile Justice in Belgium and Canada at the Beginning of the Century: Two Models or One?" *International Journal of Children's Rights* 1 (1993): 189–211.

Protecting/controlling the child

Behlmer, George K. *Child Abuse and Moral Reform in England, 1870–1908.* Stanford, CA: Stanford University Press, 1982.

Chauvière, Michel, Pierre Lenoël, and Éric Pierre, eds. *Protéger l'enfant. Raison juridique et pratiques socio-judiciaires (XIXᵉ–XXᵉ siècles).* Rennes, France: PUR, 1996.

Coninck-Smith, Ning de, Bengt Sandin, and Ellen Schrumpf, eds. *Industrious Children: Work and Childhood in the Nordic Countries, 1850–1990.* Odense, Denmark: Odense University Press, 1997.

Cooter, Roger. *In the Name of the Child: Health and Welfare, 1880–1940.* London, UK, New York: Routledge, 1992.

Dekker, Jeroen. *The Will to Change the Child. Re-education Homes for Children at Risk in Nineteenth Century Western Europe*. Frankfurt, Germany: Peter Lang, 2001.

Jablonka, Ivan. "Paths Toward Autonomy: The Living Conditions of Fostered Children in Western France in the Early twentieth Century." *History of the Family* 6 (2001): 401–421.

Jablonka, Ivan. "Children and the State." In *The French Republic. History, Values, Debates*, edited by Edward Berenson, Vincent Duclert, and Christophe Prochasson. Ithaca, NY: Cornell University Press, 2011.

Katz, Michael B. "Saving Children." *In the Shadow of the Poorhouse: A Social History of Welfare in America*. New York, NY: Basic Books, 1996 [1986].

Lawrence, Jon, and Pat Starkey, eds. *Child Welfare and Social Action in the Nineteenth and Twentieth Centuries: International Perspectives*. Liverpool, UK: Liverpool University Press, 2001.

Lindsey, Duncan, and Aron Shlonsky, eds. *Child Welfare Research: Advances for Practice and Policy*. New York, NY: Oxford University Press, 2008.

Mason, Mary Ann. *From Father's Property to Children's Rights: The History of Child Custody in the United States*. New York, NY: Columbia University Press, 1994.

Michel, Sonya. *Children's Interests/Mothers' Rights: The Shaping of America's Child Care Policy*. New Haven, CT: Yale University Press, 1999.

Mnookin, Robert H., and D. Kelly Weisberg. *Child, Family, and State: Problems and Materials on Children and the Law, 5th edition*. New York, NY: Aspen Publishers, 2005.

Perrier, Sylvie. *Des enfances protégées. La tutelle des mineurs en France (XVIIe–XVIIIe siècles)*. Saint-Denis, France: Presses universitaires de Vincennes, 1998.

Rollet, Catherine. *La Politique à l'égard de la petite enfance sous la Troisième République (1865–1939)*. Paris, France: INED, 1990.

Schiratzki, Johanna. *Vårdnad och vårdnadstvister* [*Custody and Custody Disputes*]. PhD diss., University of Stockholm, Sweden, 1997.

Sealander, Judith. *The Failed Century of the Child: Governing America's Young in the Twentieth Century*. New York, NY: Cambridge University Press, 2003.

The rights of the child

Breen, Claire. *The Standard of the Best Interests of the Child: A Western Tradition in International and Comparative Law*. The Hague, The Netherlands: Nijhoff, 2002.

Coons, John E., and Robert H. Mnookin, "Toward a Theory of Children's Rights." *Harvard Law Bulletin* 28(3) (1977).

Earls, Felton, ed. "The Child As Citizen," special volume of the *Annals of the American Academy of Political and Social Science* 633 (2011).

Eekelaar, John. "The Emergence of Children's Rights." *Oxford Journal of Legal Studies* 6(2) (1986): 161–182.

Hawes, Joseph M. *The Children's Rights Movement: A History of Advocacy and Protection*. Boston, MA: Twayne, 1991.

Neirinck, Claire. *Le Droit de l'enfance après la convention des Nations Unies*. Paris, France: Delmas, 1992.

Veerman, Philip E. *The Rights of the Child and the Changing Image of Childhood*. Dordrecht, The Netherlands: Nijhoff, 1992.

Youf, Dominique. *Penser les droits de l'enfant*. Paris, France: PUF, 2002.

22

CHILDREN AS VAGRANTS, VAGABONDS, AND THIEVES IN NINETEENTH-CENTURY AMERICA

Timothy J. Gilfoyle

The street child was an inescapable fixture of the nineteenth-century North American city. Lacking formal education, adult supervision, and sometimes even a home, such youths were commonly identified as vagrants and vagabonds. More often, they were vilified as "rats," "gamins," "Arabs," "waifs," "urchins," and "gutter-snipes." "Street-rats" in New York City, concluded one Children's Aid Society report, "gnawed away at the foundations of society undisturbed." In a country that identified geographic mobility and individual economic independence as freedom, the street kid represented a logical nightmare – the replacement of community, familial, and even spiritual bonds with the rootless individualism of the nomad.[1]

Many bemoaned this new urban reality. In 1851, the New York City attorney George Templeton Strong deplored "the hordes of ... children who live in the streets and by them." In cities across the United States, unsupervised children – some as young as six years of age – labored at casual, unskilled "street-jobs" – blackening boots, selling flowers, sweeping side-walks, hauling goods, scavenging, or hawking newspapers. By the end of the century, at least 6,000 youths worked as newsboys in Chicago. Street children labored, lived, slept, and ate in streets, alleyways, and hallways. Surrounded by "the vilest passions by the vilest portion of humanity," reported the *New York Times*, such children became "in turn themselves vagabonds, outcasts, and criminals, and form the plague-spots of the community – 'the ulcers of society.'"[2]

The Connecticut Yankee, Protestant minister, and social reformer Charles Loring Brace epitomized the popular, yet contradictory views regarding street children. Just as street children in the rapidly developing cities in contemporary Latin America and Asia are viewed with a mixture of pity and fear, Brace openly admired their autonomy, describing them as "sharp, ready, light-hearted, quick to understand and quick to act, generous and impulsive." Yet, that same independence terrified Brace. Street children represented a nascent, turbulent threat to the property, morals, and political life of civil society. Brace's binary vision and conflicted conclusions embodied the incongruous and paradoxical stereotypes held by many Americans regarding street children. On one hand, they were cute, fastidious urchins filled with energy, entrepreneurial values, and pragmatic wits; on the other, they were irredeemable devils, a terrifying pathology, a frightening contagion to public health, a threat to domestic or familial tranquility. The street child was emblematic of the "dangerous class."[3]

City children adapted to harsh economic and familial conditions by resorting to independent street behavior, self-employment, and innovative usage of public spaces. The result was a separate world for children with its own distinct milieu. The street often proved more formative than many of the interventionist, educational, municipal, and sometimes familial institutions, ultimately compelling youths to place their primary loyalty and identity with their peers.[4] Recent anthropological and ethnographic studies confirm that many of these childhood patterns and distinctive subcultures persist today in Latin America and parts of the developing world.[5]

Street children were an unanticipated product of the new urban, industrial economy powered by immigrant and low-wage laborers working twelve- and fourteen-hour days, six days per week, with high accident rates and short life spans. After 1840, apprentices virtually disappeared from artisan workshops as factories and sweatshops rapidly replaced craft and artisanal households across the United States. In American agricultural communities and European peasant households, children started working at domestic and field tasks at early ages, sometimes as young as five or six years of age. Consequently, as American society transitioned to an urban and industrial economy during the nineteenth century, few regulations governed the employment of children. Most were engaged in wage labor by the age of fourteen, many much earlier. Despite numerous attempts by municipal and state governments in the late nineteenth and early twentieth centuries, the US Supreme Court did not uphold any law prohibiting child labor until 1937.

The decline of urban craft production and the supervisory obligations of adult masters over young apprentices corresponded with the unprecedented flood of European immigrants to the United States. By 1860, more than 40 percent of the populations of New York, Chicago, Milwaukee, St Louis, Cincinnati, and San Francisco were foreign-born. At the turn of the twentieth century, at least one-third of the population of cities like New York, Boston, Chicago, Cleveland, Detroit, and San Francisco were immigrants.[6] Increasingly, certain parts of the working class, especially those confined to the casual labor market, were pushed into street trades and the informal, underground economy.

Street children were one visible reminder of the grim reality of the new industrial metropolis. These were youths who literally slept with rodents, who rarely found an adult shoulder on which to cry, who lacked any family to console them. Theirs was a world which few adults cared to understand and many hoped would vanish. Street children struggled to carve out a place for themselves, to find a space between personal autonomy and adult authority, or between self-sufficiency and economic dependence. For much of their childhoods, street kids fertilized and cultivated their own independent subculture.

The precise number of street children was a subject of debate in every city. Few, however, doubted it was a significant problem. By the 1850s, New York police chief George Matsell and the Reverend Samuel B. Halliday separately estimated that 5,000 to 10,000 boys lived on Gotham's streets. Another minister, while criticizing exaggerated figures of 50,000, nonetheless believed between 10,000 and 30,000 unsupervised children roamed the streets. In 1870, New York's Children's Aid Society provided various services to more than 24,000 different children, including nearly 6,000 orphans and 15,000 homeless youths. In 1876 alone, Gotham's police force "recovered" 5,593 "stray" children found wandering the streets (roughly fifteen per day). One report in 1886 claimed 12,000 homeless youths could be found nightly "wandering in the street." These figures were comparable to nineteenth-century London with a population between three and four million and the estimated 50,000 to 100,000 "vagrant" children on the streets.[7]

Demographically, this was hardly surprising. By the mid-nineteenth century, children were a significant proportion of America's burgeoning urban populations. Between 1860 and 1880, five- to seventeen-year-old children in New York City numbered between 230,000 and 305,000 children, more than a quarter (27 percent) of the city's total population. This demographic pattern was repeated in Brooklyn, Philadelphia, Chicago, Boston, and most large and growing American cities as the proportion of children between the ages of five and eighteen ranged between 23 and 28 percent.[8] Large numbers of these children were without one or both parents: approximately 50 percent of all American children between 1860 and 1880 lost a parent by the age of twenty; and as late as 1900, 20–30 percent of all children in the United States had lost a parent by the age of fifteen.[9]

Most of these youths experienced a swift, early and sometimes brutal introduction into the market economy. The basis of urban working-class life was the family wage, which required both parents and children to work and pool their resources. Consequently, children – especially those from impoverished families – were expected to work for wages as early as five or six years of age. Most labored in "street trades." For boys, selling newspapers, blackening boots, and "scavenging" for coal, wood, metal, glass, or anything that could be sold as "junk" were the most common occupations; for girls, selling flowers, "hot corn" or other food items, and street sweeping offered the most common employment opportunities.[10] Some resorted to prostitution. Just as contemporary teenage street girls are attracted to certain forms of sex work – pornographic acting, striptease performances, escorting tourists – so their nineteenth-century predecessors sometimes viewed prostitution as means for economic or social mobility.[11] While American cities experienced unprecedented economic expansion during the nineteenth century, that growth was uneven and punctuated by major depressions in 1837, 1857, 1873, and 1893, all of which lasted several years. Such conditions diminished job prospects for inner-city immigrant and low-income youths. "Strictly speaking, they have neither childhood nor boyhood," lamented the writer Junius Browne. "They pass from neglected infancy, almost by a bound, to an immature and unnatural manhood, compelled by a sense of self-protection to a rugged and semi-savage independence."[12]

Formal education had little impact. Because school registration requirements were weakly enforced before 1900, numerous children in cities everywhere avoided school. Indeed, for most of the nineteenth century, fewer than half the children residing in US cities regularly attended school, a pattern replicated in rapidly growing European cities such as London. The street child and later pickpocket George Appo, for example, never spent a single day in a classroom. He was not alone. In 1860, the average daily attendance in New York City public schools was only 58,000 (out of 153,000 registered school-age children in public and private schools). In 1870, the figure rose to 103,679 out of 270,000. On average, males left school at age fourteen after irregular attendance.[13]

Truancy was easy to explain: children were not required to attend school, although most states required that they be registered. Massachusetts enacted the first compulsory attendance law in 1852, but only one other state (Vermont) passed a similar statute before 1870. Thirteen others states followed suit during the 1870s. But in general, most United States municipalities and states were slow to require school attendance. As late as 1880, five of the ten largest US cities – Philadelphia, Chicago, Baltimore, St Louis, and New Orleans – lacked any statewide compulsory school attendance law. Even in municipalities with such statutes, public officials lacked both the resources and resolve to search for, find, and bring to school the thousands of truant youths. "Our compulsory-education law remains a dead letter," complained the New York reformer and writer Jacob Riis in 1894.[14]

Weak enforcement of compulsory education and other child-protecting statutes was a reflection of weak municipal authority. The principal local institutions of law enforcement – specifically the jail and the police – simply proved inadequate. As a teenager, Larry Caulfield vividly remembered how older youths taught him how to "bang a super" (pickpocketing a watch by breaking it off the chain) as a fifteen-year-old inmate in jail. Other incarcerated youths reported similar experiences. Nineteenth-century city jails, argued some, were little more than "seminaries of crime."[15]

Municipal authority was equally weak on the street. Throughout the nineteenth century, urban police forces were small in size and undermanned. For most years between 1855 and 1900, for example, New York City had one police officer for every 400 residents; some years the figure exceeded 500 residents. By contrast, in 2010, the city employed approximately one officer for every 240 residents. In general, nineteenth-century municipal police forces were small in number of officers, poorly funded, and had little control over state-controlled punishment systems or local courts. Such conditions did little to discourage teenage boys from engaging in multiple forms of street crime, much less regulate the behavior of children.[16]

The street was sometimes the only recourse for youths in abusive households. Recent anthropological studies demonstrate that youths in African, Latin American, and other less economically developed cities elsewhere openly prefer the risks of the street to a family life characterized by physical punishments, forced labor, or coerced prostitution.[17] The same was true in nineteenth-century American cities. The newsboy Johnny Morrow explained that after the death of his mother, migration to New York, and his father's remarriage, his domestic life deteriorated. He and his siblings were required to peddle goods to supplement the family income and, increasingly, to compensate for his father and stepmother's drinking habits. Frequent floggings and beatings – "till the blood came trickling down" – typified Morrow's daily, domestic life. Peddling and other forms of street employment constituted a vehicle of freedom for youths like Morrow. Thousands of children and teenagers – neglected, abandoned, abused, or orphaned by parents or caregivers – consciously sought employment and other opportunities available only on the street.[18]

Most nineteenth-century Americans and municipal authorities were oblivious to the daily trials and tribulations of street children. And they failed to recognize the distinctive, complex, and sometimes invisible (to adult mainstream society) communities of nineteenth-century urban youths. Astute observers, however, recognized that certain street children – notably newsboys – were part of distinct subcultures. Every day, thousands of young males showed up outside the offices of specific daily newspapers eager to hawk their penny publications. Pedestrians confronted small infantries of children eager to "bargain and swap and giggle and sell," observed one contemporary. Another concluded that newsboys informally divided themselves into two groups – "speculators" and "working bees." Older, entrepreneurial youths were "speculators" because they worked directly with editors and newspaper executives, sometimes even hiring younger counterparts. "Working bees" were lower in status, usually the offspring of impoverished parents. Once they received their newspapers, they scattered throughout the central business districts, the busiest ferry wharves, crowded transit centers and blocks with the most popular hotels. The streets adjoining the "newspaper rows" of New York (Park Row), Boston (Washington Street), Washington, DC (Pennsylvania Avenue), Minneapolis (Fourth Street), and other cities became the haunts of newsboys for decades.[19]

In the second half of the nineteenth century, the newsboy was a national icon. Settlement house worker Ernest Poole estimated that at least 5,000 labored on the streets of New York. Thousands more could be found in Chicago, San Francisco, New Orleans, and other US cities. Some even migrated from city to city – "wandering newsboys" in the words of Poole, who believed they were little more than "tramps in the making." Newsboys even became fixtures in popular urban culture: *Harper's Weekly* portrayed newsboys in feature articles. Songs such as Chapman's "Newsboy" (1844), D.W. Boardman's "The News Boy" (1868), W.C. Parker's "Jimmy the Newsboy" (1893), and Alfred T. Smith's "The Orphan Newsboy" (1910) reflected the transformation of the newsboy into a nineteenth-century cultural stereotype.[20]

The world of the street child was heavily, but not entirely, masculine. Newsgirls were to be found, but young females generally enjoyed fewer opportunities within the rough-and-tumble street culture. Simply put, more opportunities existed for boys. "Girls can only sell papers, flowers or themselves," lamented criminal attorneys William Howe and Abraham Hummell, "but boys can black boots, sell papers, run errands, carry bundles, sweep out saloons, steal what is left around loose everywhere, and gradually perfect themselves for a more advanced stage and higher grade of crimes." Young girls played and worked in the same spaces as boys such as City Hall Park, the Battery, Union Square and Madison Square in New York, the South Street corridor in Philadelphia, and the "newsboy alleys" in Denver, Chicago, and other cities. Sophie Lyons remembered working as a child pickpocket and using sharp, little knives "to slit open the bags so that I could get my fingers in." One male pickpocket remembered a teenage female friend so talented at pickpocketing "that older guns of both sexes were eager to take her under their tuition and finish her education."[21]

The combination of declining apprenticeships, the increasing proletarianization of industrial occupations, and poorly enforced school attendance provided fertile conditions for street children to engage in "mischief," theft, and "criminal" forms of commerce. For them, the boundary between the licit and illicit street trades was fluid, even non-existent. In some cases, it was a means of survival. Most juvenile crime was spontaneous and unplanned, focusing primarily on merchants or less organized forms of thievery in semipublic areas such as dumps, junkyards, and railroad grounds. The more astute and adventurous, however, became pickpockets. "A remarkable number of the Chicago pickpockets," concluded the writer Josiah Flynt in 1901, "are youngsters still in their teens." As New York City teenagers, George Appo and Larry

Caulfield bragged that they had teamed up with other newsboys and picked the pockets of unwitting pedestrians on Manhattan streets with impunity and without interruption for years before their first arrests. Sometimes they accumulated hundreds of dollars for a day's work. New York's Larry Caulfield not only believed that most of his fellow pickpockets were teenage males, but that such youths enjoyed distinct advantages over older counterparts. "[A] boy can get next to a woman in a car or on the street [for the purpose of pocketpicking] more easily than a man can," he reminisced. Appearances were important, insisted Caulfield. "[I]f he is a handsome, innocent-looking boy, and clever, he can go far in this line of graft."[22]

Boys held no monopoly over such forms of criminal commerce. Sophie Lyons, for example, testified that when her father went to fight in the Civil War, her stepmother, instead of sending her to school, taught her how to steal. Lyons reminisced that she pilfered people's pockets on a daily basis, frequently returning home with loot in excess of $100. When apprehended, it mattered little. "[M]y stepmother knew how to bring influence to bear in my favor," Lyons explained. "I did not know it was wrong to steal; nobody ever taught me that."[23]

Juvenile pickpocketing was, in certain respects, an invisible crime. Few pedestrians ever witnessed such activities; young pickpockets claimed they worked for years at a time before any arrest. New York's Children's Aid Society and others concurred, reporting that child pickpockets were so "quick and cunning" that they usually avoided detection, much less apprehension by law enforcement. In 1875, the *Times* declared newsboy "pocket-pickers" so adroit "that the real offender is scarcely ever captured, and the accomplice, if arrested is generally acquitted for lack of proof." In time, portions of certain cities – lower Broadway and Fulton, Nassau, and Wall Streets in New York, the "Loop" in Chicago – were reputed havens for child pickpockets. Some specific spaces – corners, blocks, even particular boats in the case of ferries – were considered to be their private property by particular boys. "Let a strange boy make his appearance on any of these consecrated grounds," noted one observer, "and he fares worse than a wounded porpoise in the midst of a school."[24]

Pickpocketing emerged as an underground alternative to the traditional but vanishing forms of apprenticeship in the new urban market economy. Ironically, participants sometimes adopted the language of the old craft economy: older teenage pickpockets taught the secrets of the trade to young "apprentices," police detectives concluded that pickpockets underwent "a course of instruction," and older pickpockets, "incapacitated for work on their own hook," instructed the younger charges and reduced the subject "to a science." Others insisted that in saloons and pool rooms, street youths were "instructed by New York Fagins in the arts of petty pilfering, of pocket-picking, sneak-thieving, circulating counterfeit coin," and other kinds of crime. Police chief George Matsell believed that as early as 1854 "crime among boys and girls has become organized, as it never was previously."[25] Such informal and fluid instruction was part of the clandestine activity of child street culture.

These complaints were not simply middle-class paranoia. References to "Fagins" and young "Oliver Twists" were common because of the similarities in juvenile crime and their subcultures in nineteenth-century London and New York. Fourteen-year-old Edward Logenstein, after being arrested for pickpocketing, admitted that he was part of a "thieves' school" run by an older man on New York's Ludlow Street. Every afternoon, boys were sent to different parts of the city accompanied by older teenagers who instructed and watched them work. Stories of street boys being trained by older teenagers or "professional criminals" were commonplace in the second half of the nineteenth century. Abe Solomon, for example, operated a "pickpocket school" on Suffolk Street. Larry Caulfield remembered being approached by an adult counterpart after his first successful pilfer. "He had heard of our achievement and kindly 'staked' us, and gave us a few private lessons in picking pockets," Caulfield explained. "We were proud enough, to be taken notice of by this great man." Others simply obeyed their parents: Sophie Lyons was taught to steal by her different stepmothers. The picture of Fagin in Dickens's *Oliver Twist* was, said one former child pickpocket, "true to life."[26]

Such adult "supervision" was common but not typical. Criminal commerce tended toward the informal part of the fluid movement between legal and legitimate forms of street work and illegal and illegitimate temptation. Child "vagabonds" such as pickpockets, petty thieves, small burglars, "cotton-baggers," "copper-stealers," and young prostitutes were little different from the "peddlers, street-sweepers, and boot-blacks that swarm in various parts of the city," recognized some observers from the Children's Aid Society. Simply put, wrote reformer Helen Campbell, bootblacks were "practiced [sic] pickpockets." She acknowledged that children engaged in legal commerce differed little from their criminal counterparts. The newsboy's view of life, Campbell concluded, originated "from association with 'flash-men' of every order, with pugilists, pickpockets, cockfighters, and all the habitues of pot-houses or bucket-shops."[27]

The "newspaper dodge" typified the fluidity of legal and illegal street commerce. Newsboys routinely waved a newspaper in the face of a potential customer; if the opportunity presented itself, they simultaneously reached into the customer's pocket and took what they found. Larry Caulfield remembered how he boarded New York streetcars, approached male passengers, and shoved a newspaper in their face, yelling "News, boss?" The diversion allowed him to pick their watch and chain. Caulfield bragged: "If you will stand for a newspaper under your chin I can get even your socks."[28] For such youths, selling newspapers and picking pockets were overlapping entrepreneurial enterprises.

The rise of child pickpocketing and other forms of illegal behavior was rooted in the changing social ecology of the city. For most children, the street was a workplace, a social center, a place of amusement, indeed a playground. The large parks created in the nineteenth century – Central Park in New York, Prospect Park in Brooklyn, Fairmont Park in Philadelphia, Golden Gate Park in San Francisco, Jackson and Washington Parks in Chicago, to name a few – were initially located on the physical edge of most cities. They were, consequently, inaccessible to the vast majority of city children. Smaller parks and squares – City Hall Park and Union Square in New York, Rittenhouse Square in Philadelphia, Boston Common, Lakefront Park in Chicago – were overcrowded, on the edge of business districts, or poorly located. Playgrounds were almost half a century away (the first ones were built in the 1880s and 1890s). Consequently, streets served multiple functions in a child's life. By the 1860s, parts of Park Row and the Bowery in New York – not to mention numerous post offices, hotels, elevated railroad stations, and ferries – were filled with youthful panhandlers. In the vicinity of the Western Union Building, child pickpockets ranging from ten to sixteen in age preyed on messengers, customers, and even company executives. The most congested pathways of metropolitan commerce became the workplaces of child pickpockets. Appropriately, lower Broadway was soon identified as "pickpockets' paradise."[29]

Arrest records confirmed popular charges that petty larceny was "a boy's crime." This phenomenon was particularly acute in New York. One grand jury concluded in 1854 that 80 percent of the city's felony indictments and 50 percent of the city's petty offenses were committed by teenagers. Between 1859 and 1876, the number of pickpockets alone brought to trial by the city's district attorney nearly quintupled, increasing to almost 250. While indictments represent an imprecise measure of pick-pocketing (because the most successful were rarely arrested), they nevertheless open one of the few windows into this hidden, secretive child universe. The overwhelming majority was between the ages of 14 and 17, native-born, and male. Most of these larcenies occurred in the street, and only a small percentage (less than 20 percent) were physically aggressive assaults where the perpetrator violently snatched an object and ran away.[30]

By the children's own admission, the term "child pickpocket" was an oxymoron. Arrested youths rarely considered themselves children or even teenagers. Rather, they were adult wage earners, although they ranged in age from 10 to 17. A greater number claimed to be "unemployed" than students attending school. Most arrested youths were employed in part-time positions or in downwardly mobile crafts. In New York, newsboys and bootblacks accounted for roughly a quarter of all arrested. Those in service jobs such as clerks, errand boys, messengers, and telegraph operators represented less than 10 percent. A very small number (less than 5 percent) were engaged in manufacturing. Particularly striking was the breakdown of the craft system: among more than 200 arrested in New York, only two claimed they were apprentices.

Street children were not "homeless" in most cases. The majority had at least one parent living, but their home life suffered from economic, domestic, emotional, and frequently violent trauma. Like street children in contemporary Brazilian, Colombian, and American cities, their begging, scavenging, or illegal behavior was motivated in part to help support their impoverished domestic households.[31] Nineteenth-century observers continually commented in hyperbolic language on the "broken homes" of such youths because domestic life for many was indeed fraught with difficulty. In one informal survey of Gotham's street children in 1871, the Children's Aid Society found that 34 percent were orphans or without known parents, while another 23 percent were victims of abandonment, abuse, or desertion. Most children arrested for pick-pocketing in New York were not homeless. Rather, 85 percent of those brought to trial provided specific addresses when interrogated about their residence. Yet, traditional or secure family structures for such youths were at best weak, at worst non-existent.

In the absence of familial support structures, a childhood and teenage fraternity emerged among young pickpockets and other street children. Larceny especially had its own division of labor, an informal apprenticeship system and a community of colleagues with patterns of support and exclusion of outsiders. Youth crime was characterized by small, intimate groups of youths working in collaboration. George Appo, for example, described working with George Dolan for several years. Picking pockets, like other forms of street life, produced a subculture with arcane, intricate, and complex forms of communication, which described all the salient roles and procedures of the craft. "Those who have been to the business [of thievery] use this *argot* to such an extent," pronounced one reporter, "that a stranger finds it as impossible to understand them as he would if they were speaking in a foreign tongue." He was right. Pickpockets working in groups of two to four referred to their accomplices as "mobs." The trolleys, streets, or parks where they labored were "beats." The "touch" or larceny was performed by a "tool, "bugger," "wire," or "pick," while the victim was jostled or distracted by a "stall." Pocketbooks were "leathers" and money was a "roll." The novelist Herman Melville labeled the underworld vocabulary as "the foulest of all human lingoes, that dialect of sin and death, known as the Cant language, or the Flash."[32]

Street children – unsupervised by parental, church, or municipal authority, underemployed by the industrial economy, and uneducated by municipal or private institutions – sought each other out in various leisure institutions. In numerous cities, street kids were regular *habitues* of theaters, dime museums, concert halls, and similar entertainments by the 1850s. New York's Bowery Theater, in particular, was described as "a common ground for the gamins." Saturday evenings in the 1870s were "a night on which all the *elite* of the bootblacks and newsboy world make a point of going to the play," recognized one observer. Most juveniles crowded into the pit in front of the stage, "packed like sheep," in the words of one horrified adult. In the pit of the Chatham and Olympic theaters, the writer George Foster noted that newsboys inscribed their names on the benches with knives, thereby "securing them against invasion, and occupying them by as good a right, and with more regularity nightly, than the rich frequenters of Grace Church and St Patrick's, their pews." The theater for young boys proved so magnetic that newsboy lodging houses in New York deliberately scheduled dinner during the hours of theatrical performances.[33]

The Bowery, in particular, served as a surrogate home for New York's street children. Into the 1880s, reformers complained how young boys "infest the Bowery at all hours of the day and night." The attractions of the Bowery were allegedly so powerful that juveniles often remained away from their real homes for days and even weeks. After a daily regimen of selling papers, begging, stealing from stores, or "going through" drunken men to pilfer money, street children spent their earnings at the theater and "thus they live till arrested or picked up," concluded one Society for the Prevention of Cruelty to Children report. Investigator George McDermott, after visiting a Bowery theater in 1882, was "most astonished" by the many unsupervised children, including more than 200 between seven and ten years of age, 500 under fourteen. "For the purpose of corrupting the minds of children," concluded McDermott, "this place affords better advantage than any other resort I know."[34]

Street children even indulged in thespian creations of their own, or "low theatre and obscene plays," in the words of one critic. At the Newsboy's Lodging House, Johnny Morrow remembered youths performing productions of Shakespeare's *Macbeth.* Another writer observed children "producing" their own theatrical drama with a makeshift stage and seating in a Chicago alley in the 1880s. Perhaps the most organized example of street culture production was their self-created theater. In 1871, newsboys, bootblacks, and other youths founded the Grand Duke's Opera House in New York. Located in a Baxter Street cellar and sometimes called the "newsboys theater," the establishment had a manager, actors, musicians, and stage hands. They, like the audience, were composed entirely of young boys. For years, the Grand Duke's

Opera House was the only theater that reportedly defied municipal efforts to collect the license fee with any success.[35]

Some youths banded together in groups identified as "gangs." Little is known about the internal structure of such groups. Most tended to be informal gatherings that persisted for only a few years. "I began as what they call a river thief," reminisced one. "A push o' us kids used to own a rowboat on the East River, an' at night, ... we'd prowl around the wharves, hold up somebody, an' then make a get-away in the boat." Contemporaries offered confused, conflicting, and contradictory definitions of gangs, often lumping informal street-corner groups with organized bands of murderers. Some gangs were little more than homeless youths with no place to go, illustrated by the numerous so-called "shanty gangs" in New York. For male youths with little education and adult supervision, these informal bodies addressed the psychological needs of outcast teenage males, offering companionship, protection, and respect. Some neighborhoods in working-class and immigrant neighborhoods reportedly had gangs on almost every block. Others, such as the Schuykill Rangers and Buffers in Philadelphia reportedly existed for more than a decade.[36]

In most cases, shared poverty and social marginalization bound street children together. The newsboy John Morrow claimed that boys were sometimes divided into Protestant and Catholic groups in the Newsboys Lodging House. But often the common, everyday experiences of youths on city streets broke down adult forms of collective identity. "As a rule," concluded social reformer and writer Helen Campbell in 1893, street boys "are known by nicknames and nothing else." She observed that they rarely identified each other with names or categories based on race, ethnicity, or religion. Rather, Campbell noted, "these names indicate some personal peculiarity or characteristic." Commentators and criminals alike infrequently focused on the ethnic or immigrant origins of New York's street children, much less any notion of self-described ethnic or national identity. Contemporaries described such youths by a street occupation or activity: newsboys, copper pickers, wood-stealers, ragpickers, swill-gatherers, bootblacks. Perhaps the native-born origins of the majority of Gotham's child pickpockets muted any shared ethnic, racial, or religious bond, for undoubtedly a large percentage of these children had immigrant parents. More often than not, street life leveled or minimized such forms of identity.[37]

As adults reminiscing on their childhood, former street children infrequently mentioned ethnic identity. Larry Caulfield, after growing up in a Roman Catholic household in New York's Lower East Side in the 1860s, teamed up with a Jewish female partner when he became a pickpocket. Similarly, George Appo never identified himself by a single, ethnic category, even though he was Irish, Chinese, and Roman Catholic by birth. Adult recollections by former street children confirmed observations by some child reformers that ethnic identity was incidental among their charges; instead street children were part of "an unconscious society for vagrancy and idleness."[38]

In these multiple ways, in their attitudes toward work, family, education, and property, street children followed an alternative and sometimes competing value system, especially compared to that of the evangelical middle class. The absence of parental authority, the rejection of formal schooling and legitimate employment, and the disregard for law and order simply horrified adults. Critics failed to acknowledge, however, that this was adaptive and functional for children. Paradoxically, the street child's behavior often imitated the middle-class values of consumption and accumulation. George Appo, for example, admitted that as a child he admired older pickpocketing peers because they "always were well dressed and had plenty of money." Similarly, one burglar and safe robber who grew up in New York admitted that he became a river thief because he believed he made ten times the income of a machine shop apprentice. "I wanted a lot o' dough, an' the only way 't I know how to get it was to steal it." On another occasion, the reformer Charles Loring Brace asked a group of street children what would make them happy. Their blunt retort: "When we'd plenty of hard cash, sir!"[39]

The petty crimes and commonplace mischief of street children also challenged the vague boundaries of urban commerce. The increase in pickpocket crime was partly the product of an expanding market economy with fashionable and expensive consumer goods. The diamond-studded stickpins, gold pocketwatches, and hard cash conspicuously advertised by pedestrians walking the streets were the symbolic and concrete evidence of these new patterns of affluence. These advertisements of conspicuous consumption and personal prosperity not only invited their secret removal, but also generated resentment by many a child turned thief. Some articulated an alternative morality. Asked to explain the difference between right and wrong during one court appearance, George Appo replied, "I know that I ain't doing wrong in picking pockets." When the judge inquired if he had a right to steal, he retorted, "To a certain extent, yes, I do."[40]

Such responses, however, more accurately reflected anger, not class consciousness among such children. Even for young pickpockets like Appo, who envisaged stealing as an ongoing, daily strategy, the overwhelming majority of his thefts presented no overt or even symbolic protest to authority or to property arrangements. Pickpocketing and other forms of theft were more often acts of personal maintenance or economic sustenance for impoverished youths; to others they were playful rebellion. Stealing property was integrated into the daily street life of many children, at times irrespective of class. Even well-off youths sometimes engaged in petty theft. Such boys treated the pilferings not as a crime, but rather as a contest, a youthful display of personal courage, a form of mischief, a product of peer pressure.[41]

In general, street children created an alternative subculture with social institutions that functioned as networks of resistance, propagating sentiments of exasperation, disaffection, and indignation. They developed their own standards regarding public space, family domesticity, and respect for personal property. Coffeehouses, saloons, theaters, museums, even prisons, were an extension of this street milieu. Such spaces and institutions allowed for indulgence in what some defined as adult activity and socialization with like-minded friends, while catering to those with a penchant for risk-taking and danger. Youths thereby shared common experiences with their friends, defended themselves against adult outsiders like the police, truant officers, school authorities, even parents and their surrogates. This alternative community of children embodied a new struggle, played out on the streets of America's exploding urban centers, between adults with money, consumer goods and power, and unsupervised children with few such benefits.

Adults reacted to this increasingly visible, underground, informal child economy by creating new institutions. Before 1800, impoverished and delinquent children were placed in household environments as apprentices, servants, or laborers of some sort.

But with larger numbers of displaced, orphaned, or abandoned children, city officials were compelled to find new solutions. Truant, vagrant, and delinquent children were initially placed in local almshouses, a practice that remained commonplace in many cities until late in the nineteenth century. As late as the 1870s, more than 5,000 children annually spent time in New York's Workhouse on Blackwell's Island or the Tombs, the city's jail. In 1875, New York State passed the "Children's Act" decreeing the removal of all healthy children ages two to sixteen from the state's poorhouses in order to remove them from "pauper influences." Others states (Indiana in 1881, Pennsylvania in 1883) soon followed.[42]

In order to help street children, or youths with long-term or permanent domestic problems, reformers developed congregate institutions during the first half of the nineteenth century: "houses of reform," "houses of reformation," "houses of refuge," "protectories," "reform schools," and orphanages, all of which were designed to separate youths from older offenders, remedy problems related to poverty, provide some education, and instill values of discipline, frugality, and hard work. These institutions originated with utopian, remedial, and idealistic goals that children could be reshaped when placed in the proper environment, and expanded throughout the century. All too often, however, the institutions suffered from inadequate funding, overcrowding, strict regimentation, and violent punishments.

The most common child-care congregate institution was the orphanage. In 1800, only six such asylums existed in the United States; by 1900, approximately 1,200 orphanages housed more than 100,000 children nationwide. Ironically, the majority of children in orphanages had one or both parents still alive; they were simply unable or unwilling to support them. In some cities, reformers and religious leaders created competing and supplementary reformatory institutions, partly in response to the problems associated with state- and municipally-operated institutions. Roman Catholic authorities, fearing Protestant evangelization, established "protectories" to care for orphaned, abandoned, and neglected Catholic children.[43]

Some private, charitable organizations resisted institutionalized and congregate solutions to juvenile delinquency. The leader in this approach was Charles Loring Brace, founder of New York's Children's Aid Society. Brace feared that juvenile institutionalization resulted in repression, coercion, and other forms of mistreatment, and inevitably did more harm than good. Influenced by the ideas of Charles Darwin as well as the moderate Christianity of Horace Bushnell, Brace created institutions that combined religious charity with social environmentalism. Groups such as the Children's Aid Society actively sought to change the behavior and social conditions of street children. They employed persuasion, rhetoric, symbolism, and tangible rewards to solve child criminality.

Most controversial was the "placing out" system sponsored by the Children's Aid Society. From 1854 to 1929, the organization and similar groups sent approximately 200,000 urban youths to rural and small-town communities in western states, in an effort to remove city children from urban temptations and local jails on one hand and address the labor shortage in the West on the other. Initially, Brace rejected indenturing or adopting these children (in part because some still had a living parent); by the end of the nineteenth century, however, most were removed from orphanages or charitable institutions and formally adopted by new families. In New York, the Five Points Mission, the Five Points House of Industry, the Juvenile Asylum, and the Home for the Friendless adopted variants of this placement system during the course of the nineteenth century, as did the Children's Mission and the New England Home for Little Wanderers in Boston, the Women's Industrial Aid Association in Philadelphia, and the Children's Home Society of Chicago. Because the children traveled West via the railroad, the cars carrying them were known as "orphan trains."[44] The program remained controversial for decades.

Placing out, however, never eliminated the problem of unsupervised street children. By 1869, Brace and the Children's Aid Society advocated the creation of specialized children's courts, compulsory education, and the licensing of child street-sellers. In 1874, Elbridge Gerry founded the New York Society for the Prevention of Cruelty to Children (SPCC), which enjoyed certain forms of policing power and acted as a conduit between municipal courts, private institutions, and impoverished children. Judges routinely followed the SPCC's recommendations regarding the treatment of street children and thereby bestowed unparalleled influence on the institution. Similar organizations appeared in Boston, Philadelphia, Rochester, San Francisco, and other American and European cities. Municipal governments in the United States, unable to adequately police families and children, resorted to private agencies to address the problem of unsupervised street children or "juvenile delinquency." In 1876, Gerry and the SPCC successfully lobbied on behalf of another "Children's Act," which prohibited theatrical, concert, and musical performances by children under 16 without the written consent of the mayor. The campaign grew into a nationwide movement to remove child performers from professional stages. Despite these efforts, over 25 percent of the more than 900 cases in the SPCC first ten annual reports involved families and children occupied in some form of street life.[45]

More influential were private ameliorative institutions like the Newsboy's Lodging Houses in New York, also administered by the Children's Aid Society. For five to eight cents per night, young boys were provided with a bed, meals, bathing facilities, and an environment noted for promoting formal learning, order, and cleanliness. Many more street children passed through these doors than were placed in western homes; in fact, newsboys were only a small percentage of the youths in these establishments. Between 1854 and 1885, over 150,000 different youths entered the six lodging houses operated by the Children's Aid Society (five for boys, one for girls). By 1872, nearly 12,000 individual youths (roughly 400 per night) annually sought refuge in the lodging houses. The Children's Aid Society also created 22 industrial schools to supplement the growing public school system and, in Brace's words, to "refine and purify the wild children of the street, and to *teach them to work*."[46]

The autonomy juveniles enjoyed in lodging houses, however, did little to discourage most forms of street life culture. The average stay lasted only one week, hardly enough time to counteract criminal and other delinquent behaviors. One newspaper reporter complained that such institutions were counterproductive, little more than "training schools for vice." Lodging houses, admitted a former resident, included youths who became "respectable citizens," others "the swellest of crooks."[47]

By some measures, municipal authorities responded with more coercive solutions. After 1875, New York City's municipal courts annually *convicted* over 1,500 (sometimes more than 2,000) children age 14 years or younger of some infraction. In 1876 alone, New York's police justices convicted more than 9,500 teenagers; over 2,600 of them were under 14, a figure that exceeded the number of convicted

African–American adults. Child pickpockets in particular were severely punished. Before 1870, only the rare teenager was sent to prison – never more than six in a single year. But in both 1874 and 1876, judges sentenced 25 such youthful offenders to Sing Sing. By the time a teenage pickpocket reached 15 years of age, he was just as likely to end up in the penitentiary as the House of Refuge, the Juvenile Asylum, or the Catholic Protectory. For sixteen and seventeen-year-old males, the odds were worse – 85 percent ended up in Sing Sing – and some punishments were draconian: youths convicted of stealing one dollar or less were sentenced to prison for at least one year, in one case five years.[48]

Nineteenth-century American street youths lived and worked in a world barely comprehended and largely misunderstood by adults. Such children were little influenced by the demands and values associated with evangelical faith or middle-class domesticity. Few enjoyed the traditional familial protections or the "civilizing" social structures of the bourgeois Victorian household. Instead, they flourished in a world shaped by the material conditions of poverty and an alternative subculture of immediate or older associates, friends, and like-minded peers. Forced to "grow up" early, street children had no childhood.

Street children were a paradox. On one hand, they lived on the margins of urban society, immersing themselves in underground and informal economies, which propagated a confrontational subculture resistant to and challenging adult authority. Yet they simultaneously adopted consumerist and entrepreneurial values emblematic of that same adult world. In this ironic way, they presaged the "cocaine kids" and teenage gangs in late twentieth-century American cities.[49] In order to survive, these "vagrants," "vagabonds," and "thieves" resorted to individualistic values, which aped elements of the dominant society. They labored at a pace, place, and time of their choosing like independent contractors. Reciprocal obligations, fundamental to group solidarity or collective cohesion, were fleeting and often non-existent. Street children never professed a larger conception of mutual obligation or shared suffering; their moral economy was immediate and defined by their personal struggles to survive on city streets. Personal gain and individual accumulation was their goal, not political revolution or economic redistribution. Rather than seeking a broad, collective, or communal solution to their lot in life, they simply sought a different avenue of upward mobility. The goal was not to turn the world upside down, but rather inside out.

Notes

1 Children's Aid Society (hereafter CAS), *Sixteenth Annual Report* (New York, NY: Children's Aid Society, 1869), 6 (gnawed away). "Annual Report" is abbreviated as "AR" hereafter. Pejorative terms appear in Charles Loring Brace, *The Dangerous Classes of New York, and Twenty Years' Work Among Them* (New York, NY: Wynkoop and Hallenbeck, 1872), 41, 79 (Arabs); George C. Needham, *Street Arabs and Gutter Snipes* (Boston, MA: D.L. Guernsey, 1884); Horatio Alger, Jr., *Tattered Tom; or, The Story of a Street Arab* (Boston, MA: Loring, 1871); Jacob Riis, *How the Other Half Lives*, edited by David Leviatin, (New York, NY: Bedford/St Martin's, 2011; orig. 1890), chapter XVII, "The Street Arab."

2 Allan Nevins and Milton Halsey Thomas, eds. *The Diary of George Templeton Strong* (New York, NY: Macmillan, 1952), II:57; *New York Times*, 5 March 1859.

3 Brace, *Dangerous Classes*, ii, 26–27, 344; CAS, *Nineteenth AR for 1871* (New York, NY: Children's Aid Society, 1872), 5; Tobias Hecht, "Children and Contemporary Latin America," in *Minor Omissions: Children in Latin American History and Society*, ed. Tobias

Hecht (Madison, WI: University of Wisconsin Press, 2002), 242; Lewis Apteker, *The Street Children of Cali* (Durham, NC: Duke University Press, 1988).

4 For the literature on "child saving" and street child subcultures, see Timothy J. Gilfoyle, "Street-Rats and Gutter-Snipes: Child Pickpockets and Street Culture in New York City, 1850–1900," *Journal of Social History*, 37 (2004), 872, n3–4 and Suggestions for Further Readings.

5 Tobias Hecht, *At Home in the Street: Street Children of Northeast Brazil* (Cambridge, UK: Cambridge University Press, 1998); idem, *Minor Omissions*; Apteker, *The Street Children of Cali*.

6 For 1860, see US Census Bureau, "Nativity of the Population for the 25 Largest Urban Places and for Selected Counties: 1860," released 1999, at http://www.census.gov/population/www/documentation/twps0029/tab20.html; for 1900 see US Census Bureau, "Nativity of the Population for the 50 Largest Urban Places: 1870 to 1990," released 1999, at http://www.census.gov/population/ www/documentation/twps0029/tab19.html, both accessed 31 March 2011.

7 Samuel B. Halliday, *Little Street Sweeper* (New York, NY: Phinney, Blakeman & Mason, 1861) 142–43; CAS, *First AR* (New York, NY: Children's Aid Society, 1854), 3–4; idem, *Sixteenth AR*, 6, 51; idem, *Seventeenth AR* (New York, NY: Children's Aid Society, 1869), 47–48; Brace, *Dangerous Classes*, 31 (20,000–30,000), 132–33; John H. Warren Jr., *Thirty Years' Battle With Crime, or the Crying Shame of New York, as Seen Under the Broad Glare of an Old Detective's Lantern* (Poughkeepsie, NY: AJ White, 1875), 218 (6,000); Helen Campbell, Thomas W. Knox and Thomas Byrnes, *Darkness and Daylight: or, Lights and Shadows of New York Life* (Hartford, CT: A.D. Worthington & Co., 1891), 112, 153, 213 (15,000 homeless children); David Dudley Field, "The Child and the State" *Forum*, April 1886, reprinted in *Speeches, Arguments, and Miscellaneous Papers of David Dudley Field*, ed. Titus Munson Coan, (New York, NY: D. Appleton & Co., 1884), III:343 (12,000); *Tribune*, 17 Jan. 1877 (5,593 stray children); Linda Gordon, *The Great Arizona Orphan Abduction* (Cambridge, MA: Harvard University Press, 1999), 8 (150/month); Seth Koven, *Slumming: Sexual and Social Politics in Victorian London* (Princeton, NJ: Princeton University Press, 2004), 90; Ellen Ross, *Love and Toil: Motherhood in Outcast London, 1870–1918* (Oxford, UK: Oxford University Press, 1993), 13.

8 New York Secretary of State, *Census for 1855* (Albany: Weed, Parsons & Co., 1857), 8, 38–39; idem, *Census for 1865* (Albany, NY: C. Van Benthuysen & Sons, 1867), 39–45; United States Department of the Interior, Census Bureau, *Population of the United States in 1860; Compiled from the Original Returns of the Eighth Census* (Washington, DC: Government Printing Office, 1864), 322–23; United States Department of the Interior, Census Bureau, *The Statistics of the Population of the United States . . . From the Original Returns of the Ninth Census* (Washington, DC: Government Printing Office, 1872), I:633, 626, 629, 633, 634; United States Department of the Interior, Census Office, *Statistics of the Population of the United States at the Tenth Census* (Washington, DC: Government Printing Office, 1883), I:422, 660, 649, 652, 655, 660, 662.

9 Steven Mintz, *Huck's Raft: A History of American Childhood* (Cambridge, MA: Harvard University Press, 2004), 157.

10 Tyler Anbinder, *Five Points* (New York, NY: Free Press, 2001), 129–33; Christine Stansell, *City of Women: Sex and Class in New York, 1790–1860* (New York, NY: Alfred Knopf, 1986), 52–54.

11 Laura Maria Agustin, "Introduction to the Cultural Study of Commercial Sex," *Sexualities*, 10 (2007) 403, 406; Kamala Kempadoo and Joe Doezema, eds., *Global Sex Workers: Rights, Resistance, and Redefinition* (New York, NY: Routledge, 1998); Joyce Outshoorn, ed., *The Politics of Prostitution: Women's Movements, Democratic States and*

the Globalisation of Sex Commerce (Cambridge, UK: Cambridge University Press, 2004); Jill Nagle, ed., *Whores and Other Feminists* (New York, NY: Routledge, 1997).

12 Junius Henri Browne, *The Great Metropolis: A Mirror of New York* (Hartford, CT: American Publishing Co., 1869), 425; David M. Gordon, Richard Edwards, and Michael Reich, *Segmented Work, Divided Workers: The Historical Transformation of Labor in the United States* (New York: Cambridge University Press, 1982); Alexander Keyssar, *Out of Work: The First Century of Unemployment in Massachusetts* (New York: Cambridge University Press, 1986), 1–4, 340–44.

13 Josiah Flynt, *The World of Graft* (New York, NY: McClure, Phillips & Co., 1901), 92 (no schooling); *National Police Gazette*, 18 Feb. 1880; Gilfoyle, "Street-Rats and Gutter-Snipes," 877, n23. On urban school attendance, see Carl F. Kaestle, *The Evolution of an Urban School System: New York City, 1750–1850* (Cambridge, MA: Harvard University Press, 1973), 96; Diane Ravitch, *The Great School Wars: New York City, 1805–1973* (New York, NY: Basic Books, 1974), 405–06.

14 Jacob Riis, *The Battle with the Slum* (New York, NY: Macmillan, 1902), 231 (dead law); idem, "The Making of Thieves in New York," 49 (1894), 114 (dead letter). On compulsory school attendance laws by state and date, see *http://www.infoplease.com/ipa/A0112617.html*, accessed March 2011.

15 *Harper's Weekly*, 29 March 1873; Hutchins Hapgood, ed., *The Autobiography of a Thief* (New York, NY: Fox, Duffield, 1903), 45–46; Brace, *Dangerous Classes*, 399; John Josiah Munro, *New York Tombs: Inside and Out!* (Brooklyn, NY: The Author, 1909), 12–13, 120–25, 241.

16 Edward T. O'Donnell, "Number of Police Officers in New York City;" and O'Donnell and James Bradley, "The Growth of the Budget of New York City, 1830–1990," both in Kenneth T. Jackson, ed., *The Encyclopedia of New York City* (New Haven, CT: Yale University Press, 1995), 166, 911; *Herald*, 9 March 1855.

17 Gilberto Dimenstein, *Brazil: War on Children* (London, UK: Latin American Bureau, 1991), 2–6; Hecht, *At Home in the Street*, 26–40; Joe L.P. Luggalla and Colleta G. Kibassa, eds., *Poverty AIDS and Street Children in East Africa* (Lewiston, NY: Edwin Mellen Press, 2002).

18 John Morrow, *A Voice from the Newsboys* (New York, NY: Published for the Benefit of the Author, 1860), 15–92, 49 (blood), 128; *Evangelical Magazine and Missionary Chronicle*, August 1861, 589–90.

19 CAS, *First AR*, 3; idem, *Eighteenth AR* (New York, NY: Children's Aid Society, 1870), 51; idem, *Nineteenth AR*, 8; idem, *Sixteenth AR*, 6; *New York Times*, 6 April 1875; Hapgood, *Autobiography*, 32–35; The Autobiography of George Appo (typewritten manuscript), 3, 29, Box 32, Society for the Prevention of Crime Papers, Rare Book and Manuscript Library, Columbia University, New York, NY (hereafter Appo), 2–3.

20 Vincent DiGirolamo, "'Tramps in the Making': The Troubling Itinerancy of America's News Peddlers," in *Cast Out: Vagrancy and Homelessness in Global and Historical Perspective*, eds. A.L. Beier and Paul Ocobock, (Athens, OH: Ohio University Center for International Studies, 2008), 232–49; *Harper's Weekly*, 19 Sept. 1868; Box 524, DeVincent Sheet Music Collection, Archives Center, National Museum of American History, Smithsonian Institution, Washington, DC.

21 Hapgood, *Autobiography*, 55; William F. Howe and Abraham H. Hummel, *In Danger; or, Life in New York. A True History of a Great City's Wiles and Temptations* (New York, NY: J.S. Ogilvie, 1888), 20–22; Sophie Lyons, *Why Crime Does Not Pay* (New York, NY: Ogilvie, 1913), 12–14; Sherri Broder, *Tramps, Unfit Mothers, and Neglected Children: Negotiating the Family in Nineteenth-Century Philadelphia* (Philadelphia, PA: University of Pennsylvania Press, 2002), 6, 60, 61, 252 (South Street corridor); Nasaw, *Children of the City*, 72–73 (newsboy alleys).

22 Flynt, *World of Graft*, 26; Hapgood, *Autobiography*, 34.

23 Lyons, *Why Crime Does Not Pay*, 11–14.

24 CAS, *Sixteenth AR*, 6; *New York Times*, 6 April 1875; Hapgood, *Autobiography*, 32–35, 51; *Harper's Weekly*, 19 Sept. 1868.

25 CAS, *Seventeenth AR*, 48; Howe and Hummell, *In Danger*, 20; unmarked clipping, 2 Feb. 1884, in New York City District Attorney Scrapbooks, New York City Municipal Archives and Records Center (hereafter DAS).

26 *Tribune* and other clippings, 15 May 1894, vol. 127; unmarked clipping, 10 Sept. 1894, vol. 132, both in DAS; Lyons, *Why Crime Does Not Pay*, 11–14; *New York Sun*, quoted in Minneapolis *Evening Journal*, 18 March 1881; Hapgood, *Autobiography*, 33, 149–50. On London, see Stephen Inwood, *A History of London* (New York, NY: Carroll & Graf Publishers, 1998), 595–96.

27 Hapgood, *Autobiography*, 35; Campbell, *Darkness*, 117, 152; Gilfoyle, "Street-Rats and Gutter-Snipes," 875, n15–16.

28 Gilfoyle, "Street-Rats and Gutter-Snipes," 875, n17.

29 CAS, *Seventeenth AR*, 48; Howe and Hummell, *In Danger*, 20; unmarked clipping, 2 Feb. 1884, DAS; Nasaw, *Children of the City*, 17–38.

30 Sources for this and information in the ensuing paragraphs is in Gilfoyle, "Street-Rats and Gutter-Snipes," 875–77.

31 Hecht, "Children and Contemporary Latin America," in *Minor Omissions*, ed. Hecht, 242; idem, *At Home in the Street*, 25, 188–214; Apteker, *Street Children of Cali*; Terry Williams, *The Cocaine Kids: The Inside Story of a Teenage Drug Ring* (New York, NY: Da Capo Press, 1989); Philippe Bourgeois, "Families and Children in Pain in the US Inner City;" and Donna M. Goldstein, "Nothing Bad Intended: Child Discipline, Punishment, and Survival in a Shantytown in Rio de Janeiro, Brazil," in *Small Wars: The Cultural Politics of Childhood*, eds. Nancy Scheper-Hughes, and Carolyn Sargent, (Berkeley, CA: University of California Press, 1998), 331–51, 389–414.

32 Hapgood, *Autobiography*, 34; Allan Pinkerton, *Thirty Years a Detective* (Chicago, IL: A.G. Nettleton & Co., 1884), 37; *Sun*, 4 March 1861; Herman Melville, *Pierre, or The Ambiguities* (New York, NY: Library of America, 1984), 281; James D. McCabe, Jr. [Edward Winslow Martin], *The Secrets of the Great City* (Philadelphia, PA: Jones Brothers & Co., 1868), 358–59, 369; Jonathan Slick, *Snares of New York; or, Tricks and Traps of the Great Metropolis* (New York: n.p., 1879), 37–38; A.E. Costello, *Our Police Protectors: History of the New York Police* (New York, NY: C.F. Roper & Co., 1885), 417; *Tribune*, 2 July 1883, 25 Dec. 1887.

33 McCabe, *Secrets*, 262, 265, 442; Foster, *New York in Slices*, 105–06; Eric Monkkonen, "Nineteenth-Century Institutions: Dealing with the Urban 'Underclass'," in *The "Underclass" Debate: Views From History*, ed. Michael B. Katz, (Princeton, NJ: Princeton University Press, 1993), 358–59.

34 Society for the Prevention of Cruelty to Children, *AR* (New York, NY: Society for the Prevention of Cruelty to Children, 1884), 23; George McDermott to Mayor William R. Grace, 2 May 1882, Box 84-GWR-14, Mayors' Papers, New York City Municipal Archives and Records Center, New York, NY (hereafter MP).

35 Morrow, *A Voice from the Newsboys*, 120; Needham, *Street Arabs and Gutter Snipes*, 61–69 (low theatre); *Frank Leslie's Illustrated Newspaper*, 17 Jan. 1874, 30 June 1877; *Herald*, 20 Feb. 1874.

36 Flynt, *World of Graft*, 92; *Truth* clipping, 24 Aug. 1884; *World* clipping, 25 Aug. 1884, both in vol. 8; *Sun* clipping, 8, 15, 20 Sept. 1884, vol. 9, all in DAS; David R. Johnson, "Crime Patterns in Philadelphia," in *The Peoples of Philadelphia: A History of Ethnic groups and Lower-Class Life, 1790–1940* (Philadelphia, PA: Temple University Press, 1973), 97–100.

37 Morrow, *A Voice from the Newsboys*, 68; Campbell, *Darkness*, 124, 151–54.

38 CAS, *Sixteenth AR*, 6, 27–33, 65–66; Hapgood, *Autobiography*, 10–61.
39 Brace, *Dangerous Classes*, 81; Howe and Hummell, *In Danger*, 27; Appo, 3; Flynt, *World of Graft*, 91–93; Pember, *Mysteries*, 191.
40 George Appo statement to the Commissioners of Public Charities and Corrections, 6 Oct. 1896, 17–18, in People v. George Appo, 24 July 1896, New York City District Attorney Records, New York Supreme Court, New York City Municipal Archives and Records Center, New York, NY.
41 Gilfoyle, "Street-Rats and Gutter-Snipes," 879, n41.
42 Mintz, *Huck's Raft*, 155–84; Resolution of Commissioners of Department of Public Charities and Correction, 10 Nov. 1875, Box 83-CE-3, MP; *World*, 13 Jan. 1879.
43 Michael B. Katz, *In the Shadow of the Poorhouse: A Social History of Welfare in America* (New York, NY: Basic Books, 1986), 104–08, 123.
44 Marilyn Irvin Holt, *The Orphan Trains: Placing Out in America* (Lincoln, NE: University of Nebraska Press, 1992), 4, 42, (Darwin), 65–66, 69 (150,000), 81, 88–89, 94, 103, 116, 141; idem, "The Orphan Trains as an Alternative to Orphanages," in *Home Away from Home: The Forgotten History of Orphanages*, ed. Richard B. McKenzie, (New York, NY: Encounter Books, 2009), 218 (200,000); Anbinder, *Five Points*, 235–65.
45 Katz, *In the Shadow of the Poorhouse*, 117–50; Timothy J. Gilfoyle, *City of Eros: New York City, Prostitution, and the Commercialization of Sex 179–1920* (New York, NY: W.W. Norton, 1992), 181–96; Shauna Vey, "Good Intentions and Fearsome Prejudice: New York's 1876 Act to Prevent and Punish Wrongs to Children," *Theater Survey* 42 (2001): 53–68; White House Conference on Child Health and Protection, *Dependent and Neglected Children* (New York, NY: D. Appleton-Century Co., 1933), 381–82.
46 CAS, *Twelfth AR*, 61; idem, *Sixteenth AR*, 19–22, 27–33, 63–68; idem, *Twentieth AR* (New York, NY: Children's Aid Society, 1872), 5; idem; *Thirty-third AR* (New York, NY: Children's Aid Society, 1885), 5; idem, *Forty-fifth AR* (New York, NY: Children's Aid Society, 1897), 13; Brace, *Dangerous Classes*, 97–113; Morrow, *A Voice from the Newsboys*, 61–78; Holt, *The Orphan Trains*, 43.
47 Hapgood, *Autobiography*, 89; *National Police Gazette*, 27 May 1882; CAS, *Sixteenth AR*, 20–21, 27–33, 65–67.
48 Gilfoyle, "Street-Rats and Gutter-Snipes," 881–82, n44–51; *National Police Gazette*, 18 Feb. 1880.
49 Williams, *Cocaine Kids*; Goldstein, "Nothing Bad Intended," 389–91.

Suggestions for further reading

The most recent overview of nineteenth-century childhood is Steven Mintz, *Huck's Raft: A History of American Childhood* (Cambridge, MA: Harvard University Press, 2004). Influential contemporary accounts of nineteenth-century street children include: John Morrow, *A Voice from the Newsboys* (New York, NY: Published for the Benefit of the Author, 1860); Charles Loring Brace, *The Dangerous Classes of New York, and Twenty Years' Work Among Them* (New York, NY: Wynkoop and Hallenbeck, 1872); George C. Needham, *Street Arabs and Gutter Snipes* (Boston, MD: D.L. Guernsey, 1884); Jacob Riis, *How the Other Half Lives: Studies Among the Tenements of New York* (New York, NY: Charles Scribner's Sons, 1890); and Jacob Riis, *The Battle with the Slum* (New York, NY: Macmillan, 1902).

The earliest historical studies of urban children and street life in the United States focused on the interventionist programs of reformers, "the invention of juvenile delinquency," and the emergence of new systems of penology. Much of this literature demonstrates how communities responded with a combination of public and private measures. See Robert S. Pickett, *House of Refuge: Origins of Juvenile Reform in New York State, 1815–1857* (Syracuse,

NY: Syracuse University Press, 1969); Anthony Platt, *The Child Savers: The Invention of Delinquency* (Chicago, IL: University of Chicago Press, 1969); Joseph M. Hawes, *Children in Urban Society: Juvenile Delinquency in Nineteenth-Century America* (New York, NY: Oxford University Press, 1971); LeRoy Ashby, *Saving the Waifs: Reformers and Dependent Children* (Philadelphia, PA: Temple University Press, 1984); Michael B. Katz, *In the Shadow of the Poorhouse: A Social History of Welfare in America* (New York, NY: Basic Books, 1986); Bruce Bellingham, "The 'Unspeakable Blessing': Street Children, Reform Rhetoric, and Misery in Early Industrial Capitalism," *Politics and Society* 12 (1983): 303–30; Peter C. Holloran, *Boston's Wayward Children: Social Services for Homeless Children, 1830–1930* (Rutherford, NJ: Fairleigh Dickinson University Press, 1989).

Later and more recent examinations of urban childhood de-emphasize adult and institutional responses to childhood abandonment and imbue street children with greater agency, while identifying multiple subcultures of street children. See David Nasaw, *Children of the City: At Work and at Play* (Garden City, NY: Anchor/Doubleday, 1985); John E. Zucchi, *The Little Slaves of the Harp: Italian Child Street Musicians in Nineteenth-Century Paris, London, and New York* (Montreal, Canada: McGill-Queen's University Press, 1992); Vincent DiGirolamo, "Newsboy Funerals: Tales of Sorrow and Solidarity in Urban America," *Journal of Social History* 36 (2002): 5–30; DiGirolamo, " 'Tramps in the Making': The Troubling Itinerancy of America's News Peddlers," in *Cast Out: Vagrancy and Homelessness in Global and Historical Perspective*, eds. A.L. Beier and Paul Ocobock, (Athens, OH: Ohio University Center for International Studies, 2008), 232–49; and Timothy J. Gilfoyle, "Street-Rats and Gutter-Snipes: Child Pickpockets and Street Culture in New York City, 1850–1900," *Journal of Social History* 37 (2004): 853–82.

Influential examinations of Charles Loring Brace and the "orphan trains" include: Thomas Bender, *Toward an Urban Vision: Ideas and Institutions in Nineteenth Century America* (Lexington, KY: University of Kentucky Press, 1975); Miriam Z. Langsam, *Children West: A History of the Placing-Out System of the New York Children's Aid Society, 1853–1890* (Madison, WI: State Historical Society of Wisconsin, 1964); Marilyn Irvin Holt, *The Orphan Trains: Placing Out in America* (Lincoln, NE: University of Nebraska Press, 1992); idem, "The Orphan Trains as an Alternative to Orphanages," in *Home Away from Home: The Forgotten History of Orphanages*, ed. Richard B. McKenzie, (New York, NY: Encounter Books, 2009); and Linda Gordon, *The Great Arizona Orphan Abduction* (Cambridge, MA: Harvard University Press, 1999).

23

CHILDREN IN SCOUTING AND OTHER ORGANIZATIONS

Jay Mechling

Children and youths tend to be very social animals. They easily form playgroups and friendship groups, from "best friend" dyads to larger groups. If sustained over time, these groups develop rich folk cultures, replete with nicknames, taunts, jokes, stories, playfighting, fantasy play, and other traditional folk genres. The folk culture of a children's group is an informal culture created, sustained, and repaired by the participants themselves, often away from surveillance by adults. These folk groups have the autonomy, spontaneity, creativity, and general playfulness western adults have come to expect from children and youths since the Enlightenment's romanticizing of childhood.

The adults in some societies create more formal organizations for children and youths. The history of such organizations reflect the history of those societies, including the history of ideas about children and the political, economic, and cultural history of each society. Formal organizations for children had to wait for the conditions of the nineteenth century to converge, conditions such as the rise of the concept of childhood as a separate stage of the lifecycle, the invention of public schooling, and worries about the psychic and social costs of modernity.

Children experience their everyday lives as relatively powerless. Some societies give children more independence than others, but children know that they are under the control of adults. Children live with a dilemma; they aspire to be adults, but at the same time children understand that the informal, folk cultures that sustain and give meaning to their everyday lives often differ from adult cultures. Those societies that create organizations for children tend to value closer surveillance of children; the adults typically want to organize and control the lives of children away from home and school. At the same time, children in those societies bring to the formal organizations their own informal folk cultures, and the customs and values of those folk cultures may not match those of the adults. Thus, children develop an informal folk "culture of resistance" in schools and in the other organizations adults create for the socialization of children.

What all this means is that the culture of a formal organization for children and youths is a *tertium quid*, a third thing, a syncretic culture that is neither the formal culture created by the adults nor the informal culture borne by the children. The culture of an organization for children and youths is the product of the interaction between the adults' goals and the children's goals. It is a site for the emergence of a dynamic border culture where adults and children meet.

The historian who wants to reconstruct the variations of this border culture in organizations for children and youths must study both the formal and informal cultures of the organizations. It is easy enough to write the histories of organizations like the Boy Scouts. More difficult, as every historian of childhood and youth knows, is writing the history of these formal organizations from the point of view of the children. The evidence of their everyday lives that children leave behind are scant and often ephemeral, but there are theoretical and methodological strategies historians have adopted to write this history. So first I shall survey briefly what we know of the formal organizations for children and youths, and then I consider the far more interesting and difficult questions about writing the history of children's informal cultures in organizations.

The formal cultures of youth organizations

Youth organizational cultures have a history documented by the usual sorts of evidence, some of it verbal – such as institutional records, correspondence, autobiographies, newspaper and magazine stories – and some of it material, including buildings, uniforms, equipment, photographs, and moving pictures on film and video. The adult point of view dominates this history, of course, because it is the adults who create and preserve this evidence.

We can think about the history of these organizations in terms of the changing history of ideas about children and youths, ideas that are themselves grounded in the history of a society. And, although the aim of this chapter and of the entire work is to write a comparative history of childhood and youth in the western world, my emphasis will be on the United States and the United Kingdom, where we find the fullest realization of the use of formal organizations to socialize children and youths.

The history of formal organizations for children and youths is largely a history of "moral panics" experienced and expressed by the adults. Historians use "moral panics" as symptoms of a society or cultural system or institution in stress, such as the moral panic about witchcraft in Europe and the American colonies, the moral panic about the evil effects of comic books in Cold War America, the moral panic about child abduction in the 1980s and 1990s, and the more recent moral panic about the effects of violent video games on young players. Historians assume that a moral panic reflects the projection, to use the psychoanalytic term, of adult anxieties onto the children. The subjects of these moral panics should not be taken as evidence of real threats to children and youth. It is important to see these as "moral" panics because that word reminds us of the central role religion has played in the history of the organizations, especially in the Unites States.

The moral panics in the United States and United Kingdom and in some European countries like Germany and France that led to the formation of formal organizations for youths in the last half of the nineteenth century were responding to the perceived threats to children by the transformation of economies, by the rise of cities, and by the modernization of consciousness. The Industrial Revolution and accompanying urbanization created an underclass of children working in factories and roaming cities, children who often committed crimes. Increasingly in the United States the children in the streets were immigrants from abroad or migrants from rural areas of the country. Economic cycles of boom and bust created further uncertainty, as did the perception that women had too much control over the socialization of boys in homes and schools.

One response to these conditions was the emergence of a class of reformers known as "child-savers," who embraced the mission (with all the religious meanings of that word) of saving children from poverty, neglect, and danger.[1]

George Williams founded the YMCA in London in 1844, for example, in response to the appalling working and living conditions of young men employed in England's factories that were threatening their health and morals. Williams and other boy-workers helped initiate the ideology and practices that have been called "muscular Christianity," the idea that physical activity, from sports to camping, was good for the boys' body, mind, and morals. The idea appealed to Christian reformers in Canada and the United States, who also worried about the increasing urbanization and indus-trialization of those countries. In 1851, the first Young Men's Christian Associations (YMCA) were established in Boston and Montreal, and in 1854, the first Young Men's Hebrew Association (YMHA) was formed in Baltimore. Soon reformers in the United Kingdom and the United States saw a need for the same sort of attention to the minds, bodies, and morals of young women. The Young Women's Christian Association (YWCA) was founded in 1855 in the United Kingdom and soon spread throughout the British Empire. The YWCA in the United States was founded in 1858 in New York City. In 1888, The YWHA (Young Women's Hebrew Association) began as an adjunct to the YMHA in New York, and by 1902 independent YWHAs were appearing in American cities. In most cities, the YMHA and YWHA combined in 1917 to become Jewish Community Centers.

More secular organizations founded in this period also saw the connection posited by the ideology of muscular Christianity between a healthy body, an agile mind, and sound morals. Lord Robert Baden-Powell (1857–1941) founded the Boy Scouts in 1908 in England in response to the weak bodies and minds of soldiers he commanded during the Boer War (1899–1902), and when a group of youth workers and business-men founded the Boy Scouts of America (BSA) in 1910, the Scout Oath they adopted enshrined the goals of muscular Christianity:

> On my honor, I will do my best
> To do my duty to God and my country
> And to obey the Scout Law;
> To keep myself physically strong, mentally awake, and morally straight.

Similarly, the 4-H organization, founded in rural communities beginning in 1902, stressed "head, heart, hands, and health."

The moral panic over girls' character in the late nineteenth and early twentieth century most often focused on the perceived loosening of female morality, especially regarding sexuality. The initial reforming impulse was to protect girls as victims of the city and of modernity, but soon the reformers began defining the "wayward" girls as the problem, inventing the notion of the "female delinquent" to match the image of the male delinquent.[2] Worries about female delinquency and changing morals in girls led reformers to create institutions like Jane Addams's Hull House in Chicago. Baden-Powell decidedly did not want girls in the Boy Scouts, so his wife and sister cre-ated the Girl Guides in 1910. There was similar resistance in the Boy Scouts America (BSA) to including girls, so Juliette Gordon Low (1960–1927) created the Girl Scouts of America in 1912. Luther Gulick worked with his wife, Charlotte, to create the Camp Fire Girls of America in 1910.

The movement for women's rights in the late nineteenth and early twentieth century had a great impact on these organizations. The 19th Amendment to the United States Constitution, finally ratified in 1920, gave women the vote, so the 1920s opened a whole new world of what it would mean to train young women to be "new women." While the Boy Scouts were learning domestic skills like cooking, their female counterparts were learning to be self-reliant, competent citizens. The Girl Scouts and Girl Guides reinforced the duties and skills of girls in the domestic sphere to be sure, but the handbooks and fiction aimed at girls in the early years of scouting pursued a goal of empowering girls with skills normally considered masculine, skills such as camping, tracking, signaling, rescue work, and even shooting. Activities and badges connected with "citizenship" acknowledged a new, active role of women in politics and governance.

Scientific psychology provided a set of ideas guiding youth workers. G. Stanley Hall (1844–1924), the founder of the *American Journal of Psychology* in 1892 and the American Psychological Association's first president, created a scientific, Darwinian "child-study" movement and produced the two-volume work, *Adolescence*, in 1904.[3] Hall argued that children recapitulate the evolution of the human race, so it was important for parents, teachers, and youth workers to understand that the unruly, "savage" behavior of preadolescent boys, for example, was natural because they were experiencing a tribal, hunting stage of human evolution. Hall entertained a romantic view of male adolescence, seeing that stage as ripe for religious conversion and for developing altruism. Hall addressed the physical, mental, and emotional development of both boys and girls, but clearly his interest was in males. Hall's ideas appeared everywhere in the writing of youth workers in the early twentieth century.

The youth workers who created these formal organizations from the 1850s through to the Great War constituted what anthropologist Anthony F.C. Wallace would call a "revitalization movement," a social movement meant to bring a wayward society in crisis back to its central values, in this case from materialism back to idealism, from selfish and competitive individualism to a renewed sense of duty to the group.[4]

By the 1920s, then, the youthwork landscape in the United States, United Kingdom, and some European countries, like France, contained all of the important formal organizations for children and youths, many of them in existence today. One track of organizations (the YMCA, Boys' Clubs, City Clubs) worked mainly with poorer and more urban kids, while the other track (the Boy Scouts, Girl Scouts, and Camp Fire Girls) worked primarily with middle-class kids. All of these movements shared a basic set of goals and strategies. They wanted to build physically fit, mentally agile, patriotic, and moral citizens.

The organizations' programs

When the adults who developed these organizations for children and youths turned to the task of creating activity programs aimed at improving the bodies, minds, and morals of young people, they arrived at a remarkably similar set of practices, which was based on the new science of understanding children. The gymnasium and the physical fitness programs of local chapters of the YMCA and related urban organizations became the best-known aspects of the YMCA's mission. Scouting and Camp Fire encouraged physical fitness through hiking and camping in the outdoors, away from cities. Rural and wilderness summer camps, organized by all sorts of youth organizations (discussed below), became a favored site for creating healthy bodies, minds, and hearts in children and youths.

Many formal organizations for youths aimed to foster selflessness by creating organizational structures emphasizing leadership of the young by older youths. In the BSA, this principle is known as "the patrol method," which meant that the boys in a "troop" belonged to "patrols" (no more than eight boys) led by slightly older boys ("patrol leaders"). The troop, in turn, was led by a teen "Senior Patrol Leader." Scoutmaster handbooks and other training materials emphasize that the adult leaders should be mentors but let the boys design and deliver the scouting program themselves as much as possible. Certainly organizations varied in the degree to which they relied on leadership by youths, but in western democratic societies the adults seemed to want to create these organizations as small democracies and to establish a balance between adult and youth leadership.

A strong element in the anti-modern impulse and ideology of youth organizations like Scouting and Camp Fire was the rejection of machine-made objects in favor of the handmade. What Ernest Thompson Seton (1860–1946) called "Woodcraft," both in a chapter in the first BSA Handbook (1911) and throughout his program for the Woodcraft Indians, was a set of skills for living in the wild, skills first mastered by Native Americans. Thus, self-reliance was an important goal of Woodcraft for the boy who could find directions from nature, who could build a fire without matches, who could fashion a lean-to for shelter in the wilderness, and so on. "Campcraft" expanded the boys' self-reliant skills to include outdoor cooking, making and erecting tents, paddling canoes, rowing and sailing boats, and building camp structures with a variety of knots and lashings. The Girl Scouts, Girl Guides, and Camp Fire Girls also wanted girls to acquire outdoor skills toward self-reliance in all situations.

Native American cultures provided skills, symbols, and ideas that served well the anti-modernist impulses of the youth organizations.[5] "Indian Lore" in scouting and in other programs provided white children and youths with romanticized views of Native Americans. Making Indian costumes, learning Indian outdoor skills, hearing and telling traditional Indian stories, and inventing "Indian rituals" for a camp's "council fires" all became part of the anti-modernist effort to revitalize white civilization with practices and ideas thought to be more "authentic" and closer to nature.

Formal organizations for children and youths also built programs attending to political socialization, with the goals of making youths suitably patriotic and knowledgeable about the workings of government. Democratic societies fostered the first formal organizations in the nineteenth and early twentieth centuries, but even youth organizations created by totalitarian regimes – the *Hitlerjugend*, Hitler Youth, is the most infamous example (see Dirk Schumann's chapter, this volume) – made a show of "democratic process" within the organization, controlled strictly by the adult political organizations and government.

The initial term used by the BSA to describe an understanding of the workings of a democratic society was "civics," but eventually the BSA settled on "citizenship" and all the rights and responsibilities that term implied. Some of this instruction was book-learning about American history and American government, but the real civics and citizenship training in the BSA and in the girls' organizations was the living experience of democratic procedures within the organizations, as youths elected their peers for leadership and as the groups enacted patriotism through flag ceremonies, parades, and public service projects during national emergencies. The American Legion, a war veterans association founded in 1919, created "Boys State" (1935) and then "Boys Nation" (1946) programs to foster patriotic citizenship and political leadership through simulated legislative practices, and the women's American Legion Auxiliary created a "Girls State" program in 1937.

As nationalistic as the BSA and similar organizations were in the United States and United Kingdom, WWI brought a greater sense of urgency to the nascent efforts of scouting to create an international movement. Baden-Powell organized the first international Boy Scout Jamboree at London's Olympia in 1920. Eight thousand Scouts from 34 countries participated, and there has been an international Jamboree every four years (though not during WWII). Out of this came the World Organization of the Scout Movement, founded in 1920. Baden-Powell's wife, Olive, who was the Girl Guides UK Chief Guide in 1918, formed the International Council of the Guides in 1919; this organization became the World Association of Girl Guides and Girl Scouts in 1928.

In part, the successful spread of scouting around the world was due to the reach of the British Empire. In these colonial places, scouting had the paradoxical possibilities of both reinforcing and resisting western cultures and western brands of nationalism and internationalism. The middle-class origins and aspirations of scouting in the United Kingdom and United States provided a model for the burgeoning middle classes as colonial states moved into the modern world. In most cases, the origins of scouting in non-western countries had little to do with a masculinity crisis and everything to do with other identities – racial, class, and national.

The decades between the two World Wars also witnessed a different sort of internationalism of youth work. The Socialist Party in the United States created a Young Peoples Socialist League in 1915. The Palmer Raids of 1920 in the United States drove such organizations underground. The Young Communist League USA, the youth organization of the Communist Party USA, was organized in 1920 but struggled as an underground, illegal organization. In 1922, the members created an above-ground, legal organization called the Young Workers League of America, which became the Young Workers (Communist) League in 1926, and back to the Young Communist League, USA, in 1929.

Meanwhile, fascist youth organizations countered the socialist and communist ones. In Germany, a thriving Boy Scout organization became absorbed into the Hitler Youth. In the 1930s in the United States, a Nazi-friendly organization named the Friends of the New Germany (FOTNG) became the German American Bund in 1936, and the youth movement of the Bund included three summer camps – Camp Nordland in Sussex County, New Jersey, Camp Siegfried in Yaphank, New York, and Camp Hindenberg in Grafton, Wisconsin.[6]

Summer camps

Many organizations counted on a new invention – the residential summer camp – for an intensified version of the programs aimed at outdoor experiences, physical fitness, and training in cooperative community. The history of summer camps parallels the history of organizations for youth. The summer camp deserves separate attention, however, because overnight camps have the characteristics of what Erving Goffman calls a "total institution," an institutional setting with control over the whole range of children's lives, including eating, sleeping, and bathing.[7] While the adult surveillance of children and adolescents in summer camps is not without its cracks, the summer camp offers intensive socialization, reproducing somewhat the conditions of the family.

The YMCA recognized as early as the 1880s that camps away from the city were a good setting for the muscular Christianity they practiced. The earliest camps were for boys alone, but by WWI the Girl Scouts of America and Camp Fire Girls had created camps promising "traditional feminine gentility as well as female physicality."[8] Urban organizations like Boys' Clubs, settlement houses (e.g. Chicago's Hull House), city newspapers (e.g. the *Detroit News*), charitable organizations (e.g. Lend-a-Hand) created summer camps for poorer and working-class youths. On the rural side, the 4-H Clubs (begun in Ohio in 1902) created summer camps for the members to develop the values embodied in the four H's – Head, Heart, Hands, and Health. Church camps have practiced "muscular Christianity" into the present, and Jewish camps arose as a response to the exclusion of Jews from many private camps. Other western societies created summer camps, usually with the same motives and programs as the American model. Beginning in the late nineteenth century in France, for example, the *colonies de vacances* movement provided summer camp experiences for urban, working-class children, and the movement spread to serving the middle-class French youth by the late 1940s.[9]

Summer camps tap into several strains of adult thinking about children and their recreation, including character development. Camps typically occupied picturesque landscapes, preferably alongside rivers and lakes. The rural camps offered pure air and aesthetic surroundings in contrast with dirty, ugly cities. Campers learned the campcraft and handicrafts consonant with the anti-modern ideology of the early twentieth century, but camps also sought to help children and youths acquire social skills (teamwork, good sportsmanship, etc.) and even citizenship skills. Paradoxically, summer camps sometimes gave young people a sense of greater agency than they experienced at home, in school, and in the meetings of the youth organizations. Adolescent counselors usually delivered the camp program of activities to the younger campers, and adolescent counselors usually led the smaller, sleeping units at an overnight camp. Summer camps in general were fairly tolerant of some elements of children's and adolescent folk cultures, such as hazing, pranking, and taunting. Resistance to camp authority even could be routinized in "traditions," such as games of capture-the-flag or "color wars," campers against staff.

Summer camp directors and professional staff members paid close attention to developmental theories in psychology and education, incorporating into their programs the latest ideas; in a few cases, social scientists even used camps as natural setting laboratories for their inquiries and experiments. Summer camps were born when the Darwinian instinct psychology of Hall and William James was in vogue, but as psychologists moved toward the behaviorism of Edward L. Thorndike (1874–1949) and the pragmatic psychology and philosophy of John Dewey (1859–1952), camp programs moved away from the view of the instinct-driven child to the view that children learn through direct experience and positive reinforcement. Dewey, especially, provided the intellectual basis for experiential-based learning outside of the classroom, and it was also Dewey who argued for practical education for living in a democratic society. By the 1940s, camps were organizing their activities around the idea of "child-centered recreation," loosening the adult control and letting campers choose their own experiences.

Youth sports

Organized youth sports outside of schools were born in the same era of muscular Christianity as the YMCA and urban Boys' Clubs. Reformers thought that poor urban youths could be "saved" through sports, especially sports created for or adapted to urban environments. James Naismith invented basketball in 1891 while teaching at the School for Christian Workers (YMCA) in Springfield, Massachusetts, and indoor gyms provided safe urban spaces for gymnastics, boxing, wrestling, and swimming. Sports were valued for the physical fitness they brought boys, but even more valuable for Progressive Era reformers were the life lessons learned in team sports, lessons in teamwork, good sportsmanship, leadership, and selflessness. Pop Warner Football was founded in 1929, Little League Baseball in 1939, and the American Youth Soccer Association in 1964. The National Alliance for Youth Sports was founded in 1981.

The phenomenal rise and popularity of youth sports in the United States reveals the same sorts of adult anxieties that prompted the creation of youth organizations more than a century ago. In the nineteenth century, the adult worry was about the physical fitness, mental acuity, and morality of boys, all of which could be aided by participation in team sports. After WWII, adults again worried about the physical fitness of children. In 1953, President Eisenhower created the President's Council on Physical Fitness and Sports, a response to a report that America's children were less physically fit than their European counterparts. In the Cold War atmosphere of the 1950s, anxieties about current affairs and political tensions were displaced easily upon the young. American adults were in a moral panic about various "threats" to their children and youth, from comic books to juvenile delinquency, from rock 'n roll music to provocative dance styles. Parents saw organized sports and organizations such as the Boy Scouts and Girl Scouts as "clean" alternatives to the "contamination" of the white middle class by lower-class and "Negro" influences in the teens' music and dancing.

Organized team sports for youths in the United States were predominantly male until the 1970s. In 1972, Congress amended Title IX of the Civil Rights Act of 1964 to forbid exclusion of girls from educational programs or activities, including athletics. Title IX eventually brought large numbers of girls and young women into organized sports, creating a true gender revolution in the United States.[10] Title IX, controversial as it has been, accelerated a twentieth-century trend in girls' play, which has become more like boys' play. Coaches of girls' sports talk about the "lessons learned" in language very close to those used by coaches of boys' sports – lessons in teamwork, in leadership, in good sportsmanship, and in learning from losses. Girls and young women may be acquiring, through participation in organized team sports, some of the characteristics thought to define boys and men in American culture, characteristics such as mastery of emotions like anger, physical toughness ("playing through the pain"), and aggressiveness. Though it is beyond the scope of the present essay to explore this point, it is likely that Title IX and the changing traits young women have acquired through participation in organized team sports have helped to create the new woman comfortable in the previously all-male military setting, including combat service in Iraq and Afghanistan.

The culture wars, 1980s–present

By the 1980s, Americans were using the phrase "the culture wars" to describe the fault lines they saw in American politics and culture. One sociologist sees the warring parties as divided on a key epistemological issue – whether there is an absolute, knowable source of truth and moral guidance, or whether our knowledge is always partial, imperfect, and largely constructed socially through consensus.[11] These culture wars have saturated every corner of American life, affecting debates in politics, in schools, and in communities.

A signal of the resemblance between the 1890s debates and the culture wars of the 1990s was the return of concerns regarding "character." The "character education" movement began in the 1980s outside of the schools, led by developmental psychologists like Dr Thomas Linkona, a Professor of Education at the State University of New York at Cortland. Linkona created the Center for the Fourth and Fifth Rs (Respect and Responsibility) at Cortland, and he is connected with other organizations established in the 1990s to provide resources and programs in support of character education in the schools and in the co-curriculum, among organizations such as the Boy Scouts and the Girl Scouts. Another organization prominent in this landscape is the Josephson Institute of Ethics, based in Marina del Ray, California. The character education program created by the institute proclaims six "pillars of character" – trustworthiness, respect, responsibility, fairness, caring, and citizenship – which sound very much like the avowed values of Scouting and Camp Fire. The Institute created the "Character Counts!" Coalition, a network of organizations (e.g. the BSA, Camp Fire USA, Boys and Girls Clubs of America) and educators building character education programs.[12]

All of these people are stoking a moral panic about children at the century's end. The claims-makers muster an array of "facts" – ranging from macro-social indicators, like juvenile crime statistics, to anecdotes – which they say characterizes American society in the present. The claimants see the present state of moral thinking as an unhappy inheritance from nineteenth century philosophy, sociology, psychology, and anthropology, which colluded to argue for moral relativism. More immediately, the claimants blame the rise of "personalism" in the 1960s, with its therapeutic sensibility about the individual's rights, its views about liberty versus freedom, its attack on authority (often with the modifiers white, patriarchal, sexist, and heterosexist), its elevation of the "real self" or the "authentic self" apart from constructing social roles and norms, its equating sexual freedom with political freedom, and its moral relativism.

The BSA was sucked into the culture wars in the 1990s when atheists and gay young men began suing the organization for excluding them from membership. In 2000, the Supreme Court of the United States finally settled conflicting rulings by the California and New Jersey State Supreme Courts. In a 5–4 decision, the Supreme Court of the United States sided with the BSA and concluded that the BSA was a private organization exempt from civil rights guarantees of free access to public accommodations regardless of sex, race, or gender orientation. The Girl Scouts, faced with a parallel challenge, easily accommodated atheists with a small change in the Girl Scout promise. But the Girl Scouts could be more flexible on atheism (and on the issues of sexual orientation, for that matter) because, unlike Boy Scout troops, Girl Scout troops do not have sponsoring organizations, like churches.

The informal cultures of youth organizations

I have surveyed here the conditions that gave birth to formal organizations for the socialization of children and youths in the United States, United Kingdom, and other western societies from the mid-nineteenth century to the present. These organizations have clear, well-documented histories. We know from those histories that adult moral panics about children and youths led to an agenda of "saving" children from unsafe and unhealthy environments, and of providing for the healthy socialization of young bodies, minds, and morals. Very often the workers in these organizations saw their movements as initiatives to "revitalize" their societies.

I began this chapter with the warning that we should not take the adult intentions in these formal organizations as evidence of the actual, everyday cultures of the organizations, that the informal cultures children and youths bring to these organizations create a syncretic border culture that is the product of the interaction – some might say struggle – between the adult intentions and the youth's desire to exercise as much autonomy and agency as possible. Now I turn to the informal cultures of these organizations. Whereas the formal cultures of these organizations leave plentiful evidence for the historian, the informal cultures are far more ephemeral. Still, there are ways for the historian to approach the reconstruction of the informal cultures of children and youths.

Fieldwork studying the informal cultures of children and youths provides the best direct evidence of the verbal, customary, and material cultures of young people. The scientific study of children's cultures began in the late nineteenth century, when psychologists like G. Stanley Hall began the "child study movement." Some of this research was conducted in child development laboratories and other controlled settings, but for our purposes the best work has studied children in their "natural settings," places like street corners, playgrounds, and parks, where there is less adult surveillance. At first, the late-nineteenth-century collection of children's folklore followed the same "salvage ethnography" paradigm found in the new disciplines of anthropology and sociology. By the mid-twentieth century, the ethnography of children's cultures in natural settings, while not common, yielded new insight into the continuities of these cultures and their relative independence from adult intentions. Some ethnographies have studied the informal folk cultures of children within formal organizations, such as schools, scout troops, group homes, and summer camps. All of this work by folklorists, sociologists, and other ethnographers of children's lives (primarily in the United States and the United Kingdom) provides insight for historians, who in most cases are attempting to write history from scant evidence. What are these insights?

The ethnographic work demonstrates surprising continuity in western children's cultures across time and space. This suggests that adult cultures must layer onto some basic human developmental dynamics the cultural particulars that distinguish adult cultures in a society. Given the relatively short history of formal organizations for youths in western and westernized cultures (e.g. Japan), this evidence of continuity across time and space makes it reasonable to assume that the way we see children use their folklore as resources in the power struggle with adults in contemporary settings would be much the same as a century ago.

The ethnographic work also alerts us to particular zones in the "border culture" where adults and youths negotiate their power relationships in organizations. The scholarship on children's informal folk cultures identifies several genres that youths tap as resources in these border cultures. Some of the strategies are found in both male and female cultures, while others are particular to one gender or the other. The following discussion is meant merely to suggest to historians some of the features of children's folk cultures that help determine their actual experiences in the formal organizations adults create for them. More comprehensive discussions of the folk cultures of children and youths can be found in the work cited in the "Folk cultures of children and adolescents" and "Ethnography of youth cultures in organizations" sections of the annotated bibliography for this essay.

First, children and youths tend to adopt strategies for *disorderliness*, which has the potential to disrupt the orderliness enforced by the adults in the formal organizations. Sometimes the disorderliness is oral; noise has the potential of capturing attention in the formal organization, and the use of profanity or obscenity asserts some independence in the violation of adult norms for children's speech. Sometimes the disorderliness is physical. Playfighting is common in both male and female folk cultures, though the female versions tend to be less physical (e.g. throwing food or other soft items) than male versions (e.g. wrestling, pushing). Scholars who have studied campers' behavior note the prevalence of "raids" on other campers' cabins, campsites, and other "home" zones (precursors to the "panty raid" tradition on college campuses), raids which often result in stolen belongings and trashed living spaces.

Second, children and youths often invent informal *initiation rituals* apart from the formal initiation rituals created and controlled by the adults. Some of these rituals are benign, such as the well-known "Snipe Hunt" and its variants, where a "newbie" (new member) is sent on an impossible mission. Older campers socialize newbies with local ghost legends meant to scare the campers; sometimes the older campers enact the legend to further the fright. Episode 109, "Notes on Camp," of the radio documentary series *This American Life* includes a participant-observation report on a group of campers enacting the "Bloody Mary" legend.[13]

Other initiation rituals resemble the hazing found in adolescent cultures. Hazing rituals as initiations into the group usually create a play frame for building trust and loyalty to the group. In male groups, especially, the hazing ritual usually involves a "test" of masculinity and loyalty, and sometimes involves dangerous activity. Female groups, notably young women's sports teams, appear to be adopting male-style hazing in their informal initiation rituals. Formal organizations usually forbid the informal initiation rituals and informal hazing, hoping instead that the safer formal initiations will serve the same psychological and social functions as the informal rituals.

Related to initiation rituals is the folk genre of *pranks* (sometimes known as practical jokes). Summer camps, where youths live together for weeks at a time, are the site of many traditional pranks, from placing materials in a camper's bedding to moving large objects (e.g. a canoe) into a campers' cabin. Pranking can be a test of relationships; to take a prank or joke "well" and to deliver a clever prank in retaliation is seen as positive bonding with the group. But pranks can also be mean-spirited, a form of harassment or bullying. On one Boy Scout hike, I observed older boys secretly putting rocks in the backpack of a boy thought to be "too bossy." Some formal organizations will tolerate a small amount of pranking of the friendly sort.

Young people in organizations often engage in *parody* as a form of resistance to the adult norms of the organization. Campfire skits, obscene versions of camp songs, and open mimicry of counselors are examples of parodies campers use to invert the institution's sacred symbols and usual structures of authority.

These few examples of the informal strategies children and youths use to assert their agency and autonomy in formal organizations created and largely controlled by adults stand for a much larger body of evidence gathered in ethnographic work with young people in their natural settings. The historian needs to be familiar with this work on children's vernacular cultures as a corrective to the temptation to take the adult-centered history of the organizations as evidence of the experiences of children and youths in the organizations. Armed with this familiarity, historians bring new eyes to the photographs and material culture that is the far more abundant evidence of youth cultures than the written evidence we use to write the histories of the formal organizations.[14]

Conclusion

The history of formal organizations for the socialization of children and youths in the West is the history of the intersection of adult ideas about the nature of children and adult "moral panics" about the societal threats to children. We can read into these moral panics specific crises in thinking about national identity, race, gender, and social class. These are all tensions between order and disorder, between clean and dirty, and throughout this history the adults seem to have focused upon the child as a dense symbol of the society. Boys and their bodies serve as especially potent symbols in this history, though an important element of the narrative of the history is the ways girls have become more like boys.

Lurking in this adult-centered history of formal organizations for children and youths are glimpses of the agency children are able to grasp and assert as they work to shape the formal organizations toward their own goals and desires. Being able to write the history of childhood and youth from the kids' point of view is the brass ring historians aspire to grasp. Formal organizations – their written records, but even more their visual records – paradoxically might be the most fertile ground for attempting to write this history from the young actors' point of view, for it was the youth workers who realized in their day-to-day experiences with kids that the adult goals were best met by creating some free, safe space for the kids to give expression to their folk cultures.

Notes

1 Anthony M. Platt, *The Child Savers: The Invention of Delinquency* Chicago, IL: University of Chicago Press, 1969.

2 Mary E. Odem, *Delinquent Daughters: Protecting and Policing Adolescent Female Sexuality in the United States, 1885–1920* (Chapel Hill, NC: University of North Carolina Press, 1991).

3 Dorothy Ross, *G. Stanley Hall: The Psychologist as Prophet* (Chicago, IL: University of Chicago Press, 1972).

4 Anthony F.C. Wallace, "Revitalization Movements," *American Anthropologist 58* (1956): 264–281.

5 Philip J. Deloria, *Playing Indian* (New Haven, CT: Yale University Press, 1999).

6 Marvin D. Miller, *Wunderlich's Salute* (Smithtown, NY: Malamud-Rose, Publishers, 1983).

7 Erving Goffman, *Asylums: Essays on the Social Situations of Mental Patients and Other Inmates* (New York, NY: Doubleday Anchor, 1961).

8 Leslie Paris, *Children's Nature: The Rise of the American Summer Camp* (New York, NY: New York University Press, 2008), 49.

9 Laura Lee Downs, *Childhood in the Promised Land: Working Class Movements and the Colonies de Vacances in France, 1880–1960* (Durham, NC: Duke University Press, 2002).

10 D.L. Brake, *Getting in the Game: Title IX and the Women's Sports Revolution* (New York, NY: New York University Press, 2010).

11 James Davison Hunter, *Culture Wars: The Struggle to Define America* (New York, NY: Basic Books, 1991).

12 http://www.charactercounts.org.

13 http://www.thisamericanlife.org/radio-archives/episode/109/notes-on-camp.

14 The use of photographs as historical evidence of children's lives is far too large a topic to consider here, but see Jay Mechling, "Found Photographs and Children's Folklore," *Children's Folklore Review* 27 (2005): 7–31.

Suggestions for further reading

Histories of Boy Scouts, Girls Scouts, and other organizations

Block, Nelson R., and Tammy M. Proctor, eds. *Scouting Frontiers; Youth and the Scout Movement's First Century*. Newcastle Upon Tyne, UK: Cambridge Scholars Publishing, 2009. This collection of essays, many begun as papers read at the 2008 conference celebrating the Centennial of the founding of scouting (Baden-Powell's initial camp on Brownsea Island in 1908), includes scholarly examinations of the history of scouting in several countries, including the United States, United Kingdom, and countries originally part of the British Empire.

Gustav-Wrathall, John D. *Take the Young Stranger by the Hand: Same-Sex Relations and the YMCA*. Chicago, IL: University of Chicago Press, 1998. Although the subtitle of this book announces a central theme of the book, the author provides a quite good and comprehensive history of the YMCA and the YWCA.

Jeal, Tim. *The Boy–Man: The Life of Lord Baden-Powell*. New York, NY: Morrow, 1990. This is the definitive, comprehensive biography of the founder of scouting. Jeal's book is somewhat controversial in scouting circles because of his argument that Baden-Powell was a latent homosexual.

MacDonald, Robert H. *Sons of the Empire: The Frontier and the Boy Scout Movement, 1890–1918*. Toronto, Canada: University of Toronto Press, 1993. MacDonald shows the cultural conditions that gave rise to Baden-Powell as a military hero and the invention of the Boy Scouts. British colonial discourse established a model of white masculinity reproduced in scouting's ideas and programs.

Macleod, David I. *Building Character in the American Boy: The Boy Scouts, YMCA, and Their Forerunners, 1870–1920*. Madison, WI: University of Wisconsin Press, 1983. Macleod's carefully researched history is the best account of the social and cultural contexts that gave rise to the YMCA, Boy Scouts, and other organizations.

Murray, William D. *The History of the Boy Scouts of America*. New York, NY: Boy Scouts of America, 1937. This was the first official, detailed institutional history of the Boy Scouts of America. Not an interpretive history, but full of facts and information.

Parsons, Timothy H. *Race, Resistance, and the Boy Scout Movement in British Colonial Africa*. Athens, OH: Ohio University Press, 2004. Parsons shows the tension between British imperial intentions in the internationalization of scouting and the efforts by the colonized Africans to construct a new definition of their citizenship and nationality.

Proctor, Tammy M. *Scouting for Girls: A Century of Girl Guides and Girl Scouts*. New York, NY: Praeger, 2009. Proctor traces the history of these girls' organizations, with attention to the internationalization of the movement. Proctor is alert to the tensions experienced in these organizations as they struggle over what sort of women the founders and volunteers wanted the organizations to create.

Rosenthal, Michael. *The Character Factory: Baden-Powell and the Origins of the Boy Scout Movement*. New York, NY: Pantheon Books, 1986. Rosenthal recounts the life of Baden-Powell as centered on the founding of scouting. The author summarizes the ideological foundations of scouting, especially as issues of masculinity, race, and character were foundational to the understanding of the British Empire in the first half of the twentieth century.

Tedesco, Laureen. "Making a Girl into a Scout: Americanizing Scouting for Girls." In *Delinquents and Debutantes: Twentieth-Century American Girls' Cultures*, edited by Sherrie A. Innes, 19–39. New York, NY: New York University Press, 1998. The author uses Girl Scout manuals of 1913 and 1916 to show how the authors wanted girls to acquire some of the physical skills and self-reliance the boys acquired in scouting. Tedesco discovers some ambivalence in the manuals as the authors struggled with what qualities they wanted in the adult woman.

Wills, Chuck. *Boy Scouts of America: A Centennial History*. New York, NY: D.K. Adult, 2009. An official history of the BSA commissioned for its Centennial. Not an interpretive history, but rich in coverage and illustrations.

History of summer camps

Bennett, Roger, and Jules Shell. *Camp Camp: Where Fantasy Island Meets Lord of the Flies*. New York, NY: Crown Publishers, 2008. Not a scholarly book, but valuable to historians and folklorists for the vast array of interviews, memoirs, letters, and photographs the authors collected from people relating their summer camp experiences from the 1970s to the present.

Dimock, Hedley S., and Charles E. Hendry. *Camping and Character: A Camp Experiment in Character Education*. New York, NY: YMCA Association Press, 1931. An early study of a summer camp by a scholar and a youth worker interested in the educational values of summer camps. While the authors have social scientific goals, they describe in enough detail camp experiences that their book comes close to being an ethnography of everyday life at camp.

Downs, Laura Lee. *Childhood in the Promised Land: Working Class Movements and the Colonies de Vacances in France, 1880–1960*. Durham, NC: Duke University Press, 2002. Downs uses a number of written sources and interviews to write this history of the French summer camps, which began in the nineteenth century to restore the vitality and morals of working-class children and which by the late 1940s were serving middle-class youth.

Paris, Leslie. *Children's Nature: The Rise of the American Summer Camp*. New York, NY: New York University Press, 2008. Paris uses the history of summer camps (most on the Northeast

United States) to the 1940s to examine the ways the categories "children" and "nature" were constructed by adults. She makes good use of her sources to construct, as far as possible, the ways campers exercised some agency through their folk customs.

Van Slyck, Abigail A. *A Manufactured Wilderness: Summer Camps and the Shaping of American Youth, 1890–1960*. Minneapolis, MN: University of Minnesota Press, 2006. Van Slyck has a primary interest in the way summer camps created built landscapes out of wilderness and created ways for youths to interact with the built and natural landscapes, but she also provides a history of summer camps and of the adult ideologies that led to certain sorts of programming, such as Indian Lore.

Folk cultures of children and adolescents

Bronner, Simon J. *American Children's Folklore*. Little Rock, AR: August House, 1988. Scholars should consult the longer edition with the extended footnotes, including long interpretive footnotes. Bronner organizes his survey by genre (e.g. games, material culture).

Mechling, Jay. "Children's Folklore." In *Folk Groups and Folklore Genres*, edited by Elliott Oring, 91–120. Logan, UT: Utah State University Press, 1986. This succinct essay summarizes the character of children's folklore and points to certain themes, such as resistance and the child's body, to guide the interpretation of the meanings of the folklore.

Sutton-Smith, Brian, Jay Mechling, Thomas W. Johnson, and Felicia R. McMahon, eds. *Children's Folklore: A Source Book*. Logan, UT: Utah State University Press, 1999. A project of the Children's Folklore Section of the American Folklore Society, this volume collects nineteen essays on children's folklore, some essays on genres (e.g. games, riddles, teases and pranks) and some on settings (e.g. playgrounds, camps, schools).

Ethnographies of youth cultures in organizations

Fine, Gary Alan. *With the Boys: Little League Baseball and Preadolescent Culture*. Chicago, IL: University of Chicago Press, 1987. Based on three years of participant observation with Little League teams in five communities, Fine's book describes the small group cultures that arose in these organizations.

Horan, Robert. "The Semiotics of Play Fighting at a Residential Treatment Center." In *Adolescent Psychiatry: Developmental and Clinical Studies*, vol. 15, edited by Sherman C. Feinstein, 367–381. Chicago, IL: University of Chicago Press, 1988. Horan's essay, based on his fieldwork in a Residential Boy's Home in the early 1980s, shows in detail how the play, especially the verbal and physical playfighting, of the 30-odd boys, ages 13–18, was a resource for the boys' handling of interpersonal relationships at the home.

Mechling, Jay. *On My Honor: Boy Scouts and the Making of American Youth*. Chicago, IL: University of Chicago Press, 2001. Based on nearly 25 years of fieldwork with a troop in Northern California, Mechling constructs a representative two-week annual summer encampment in the mountains, giving detailed description and analysis of the folk cultures of both the adult staff and the adolescent boys and of the negotiations between the two cultures.

Sherif, Muzafer, O.J. Harvey, B. Jack White, William R. Hood, and Carolyn W. Sherif. *The Robber Cave Experiment: Intergroup Conflict and Cooperation*. Middleton, CT: Wesleyan University Press, 1988. (Originally published 1961.) A famous classic in the field of social psychology, this study created an "experiment" in group formation, intragroup relations, and intergroup relations by bringing 22 boys to a summer camp, splitting them into two groups, and then closely observing the group dynamics as the boys engaged in both formal and informal camp activities.

24

NEW OPPORTUNITIES FOR CHILDREN IN THE GREAT DEPRESSION IN THE UNITED STATES

Kriste Lindenmeyer

The Wall Street stock market crash in October 1929 was the symbolic beginning of the Great Depression in the United States. Part of an international financial crisis with distinct histories in industrialized nations throughout the world, the Great Depression in the United States continued through the 1930s and did not end until the massive wartime mobilization launched at full speed after the Japanese attack on Pearl Harbor, December 7, 1941. Of course the experiences of individual children and their families varied as the Great Depression dragged on in the 1930s for more than a decade. Race, class, ethnicity, and region were important factors. Some children were barely touched by the era's hard times. Others suffered terribly with hunger and homelessness as the nation's economic activity fell to its lowest levels in US history. For those already living in poverty before the Great Depression, the New Deal helped to ease their circumstances. Overall, most children and families found that the Great Depression meant making do with less, while facing a very uncertain future. Nevertheless, Robert McElvaine cautions that anyone who views the 1930s as *only* grim misses much of its flavor and significance. The era is also important for its political and social innovations as well as cultural changes more often attributed to the post-war period.

Examining the history of childhood and the experiences of young Americans highlights the dramatic changes in politics, society, and popular culture that shaped the complex history of the Great Depression in the United States. Most important for the nation's youngest citizens, the decade solidified in public policy, law, and popular culture a modern American childhood defined as a protected and dependent period of life from birth through at least age seventeen. This prescription was not a new idea, nor was it a reality for the majority of young people growing up in the 1930s. However, during the Great Depression the public embraced this ideal and young Americans accepted it as a right for all children in normal times.

The onset of the Great Depression and America's children

The 1930s was an unusual decade in American history. For children, the onset of the Great Depression threatened the social welfare reforms accomplished in the Progressive Era designed to better the lives of the nation's youngest citizens. Each day, the worsening depression-era economy left a growing number of parents unable to provide even basic necessities for their children. The US Children's Bureau estimated that by 1932, one-fifth of preschool and school children were showing the effects of poor nutrition, inadequate housing, and the lack of medical care. The agency's chief, Grace Abbott, argued that providing economic security for children was one of the most important responsibilities of government because it would help to secure the nation's future. A 1933 Congressional report on relief payments showed that while individuals under sixteen years of age made up only 31 percent of the country's population, they composed 42 percent of Americans living in households that received relief.

Using such data is one way to gain insights about the depth of the economic crisis for American children. From 1929 through 1932, the US Gross National Product fell from $104.4 billion to $74.2 billion. Farm income dropped by 61 percent. Unemployment peaked at 25 percent in 1932 and never fell below 14 percent until the United States' entry into the Second World War. Families lost their savings as thousands of banks closed. Many families were forced from their homes by mortgage foreclosures, and evictions rose to astronomical rates. At the same time, some municipal and county governments simply ran out of money. Racism and ethnic prejudice often made the situation even worse. For example, on average, the unemployment rate among blacks was twice as high as the rate for whites. Government could also make things worse. Under Herbert Hoover's National Repatriation program, more than 300,000 Mexican-Americans were forcibly deported, some illegally because they were actually US citizens. Over half of all Native American Indian families living on reservations had incomes of less than $200 per year. Among older adolescents and youths who had historically worked by age sixteen, overall unemployment was double that of Americans over thirty.[1]

Science and medicine had made significant advances by the 1930s, but medical care was expensive and health insurance rare. Malnutrition, disease, and death especially hurt families unable to pay for even minimal medical care. Teas, herbal medicines, Epsom salts, cod liver oil, and a variety of alcohol-based potions served as common medicines in most families. Besides the high cost, many Americans lived far from good medical facilities. Robert Hastings remembers that his brother, LaVerne, fell ill at the family's rural Illinois home. The nearest hospital was ten miles away, but most people viewed the facility as a place where people went "to die." A better hospital was seventeen miles away in Carbondale, but the Hastings family had given up their car due to hard times. Without access to a hospital, twenty-one-year old LaVerne died two days after falling ill. The Great Depression did not cause LaVerne Hastings's death, but the family's poverty and isolation contributed to the sad outcome.[2]

Other families told similar stories of loss. Contagious children's diseases like whooping cough and measles presented serious problems. A headline like the one in the *Milwaukee Sentinel* on May 16, 1936 was typical after a measles outbreak, "Students Suspended As Health Measure." US Census Bureau records show that epidemics in the United States in 1934, 1935, and 1938 doubled the incidence of measles from an average of approximately 300 cases per 100,000 population to 600 cases. Diphtheria was another scary threat to children.

Despite visible evidence of suffering among many children and their families, from 1929 to 1932, President Herbert Hoover and officials in his administration seemed oblivious to the worsening circumstances. Secretary of the Interior, Ray Lyman Wilbur remarked in a speech before the National Conference on Social Work, "unless we descend to a level far beyond anything we at present have known, our children are apt to profit, rather than suffer, from what is going on." In a December 9, 1931 address to Congress, President Hoover stated that figures from "Public Health Service show an actual decrease of sickness and infant and general mortality below normal years." He argued that no "greater proof could be adduced that our people have been protected from hunger and cold." Environmental catastrophes – drought in the Midwest, flooding in the central South – added to the dire situation for many children and their families. When disastrous floods struck parts of Arkansas, Kentucky, and Tennessee in 1931, Hoover announced that the Army Corps of Engineers found relief services in the area "adequately meeting the existing need." US Children's Bureau reports that same year came to a very different conclusion. In a summary read in Congress on February 2, 1932, the bureau noted that malnutrition was a serious problem among the nation's children. Republican Senator Robert LaFollette of Wisconsin warned that failure to institute a federal relief program for unemployed parents would mean "we would be paying the toll in malnutrition and its effects upon adults and children for 50 years to come."[3]

On the edges of the nation's cities, displaced and homeless adults, children, and teens built makeshift shelters out of cardboard and scrap metal in squatter communities labeled Hoovervilles. Long lines for free soup and bread, distributed by charities and local governments, were testaments to the growing needs of children and adults. The commissioner of relief in Salt Lake City proclaimed that hundreds of children in his city were slowly starving to death and being kept home from school because they had nothing to wear. As evidence of Americans trying to cope with the bad situation, families "doubled up," and marriage and birth rates declined to the lowest levels up to that point in US history. The divorce rate also declined, but instead of an indicator of increased marital harmony, rising unemployment, underemployment, lost wages, and psychological stress led many men, and some women, to simply abandon their families. Reports of domestic violence and child abuse increased. In 1933, the US Children's Bureau counted an estimated 120,000 children in foster care and an additional 144,000 in orphanages. The situation at the State Home for Dependent and Neglected Children in Waco, Texas was typical. The facility housed 42 children in 1923 and 307 by 1933.[4]

In November 1932, American voters showed their desire to try something new by overwhelmingly electing Franklin D. Roosevelt over the incumbent, Herbert Hoover. Roosevelt quickly went into action by implementing a variety of federal programs under the New Deal umbrella. In his second inaugural address, Roosevelt lamented that he still saw "one third of the nation ill-housed, ill-clad, ill-nourished" and "millions denied education, recreation, and the opportunity to better their lot and the lot of their children." The New Deal did not end the Great Depression, but it changed expectations for Americans about what government could and should do.

The building blocks of modern American childhood

While child welfare reformers had long advocated for a protected and dependent childhood, communities lacked the physical infrastructure and economic safety net necessary to make the ideal a reality for most young Americans. Amenities such as electricity, good public sanitation, public schools and recreational facilities, and funding to care for neglected and abused children were fundamental building blocks to secure the modern childhood ideal as the normative experience for all American children.

Alan King was part of the generation of Americans growing up during the Great Depression. As an adult, King appeared in 29 Hollywood films and was a well-known television and nightclub entertainer. Praised as someone "in touch with what was happening in the world," King's persona made him seem like an average guy to many Americans. Born Irwin Alan Kniberg on December 26, 1927, the youngest of eight children, King's Russian-Jewish immigrant parents, Minnie and Bernard Kniberg, lived in a working-class neighborhood in Brooklyn, New York. The Knibergs struggled to provide for their large family and, like others, things got worse after the 1929 stock market crash. King remembered being aware of his parents' struggles and understood that he lived in a "tough" neighborhood hit hard by the Great Depression. Nevertheless, like many Americans who grew up during the 1930s, King also had fond memories of his childhood.

At age eight, King started doing impersonations on street corners to earn money after school. He liked performing and also had fun playing street games like stickball with his buddies. Some of his fondest memories were the times spent at the McCarran Park Pool. Mayor Fiorello LaGuardia proudly dedicated the enormous facility before a crowd of 75,000 people gathered on July 31, 1936, a warm Friday evening. The highpoint came at sunset when the mayor flipped on the pool's underwater lights and declared, "Okay, kids, it's all yours!" More than hyperbole, the pool was for everyone, but most important, it was a very visible and safe space for the neighborhood's children and teens.

The massive Romanesque-style McCarren Park Pool was touted as able to hold up to 6,800 swimmers at once. Bigger than a football field, McCarren was the eighth of eleven giant swimming pools opened in the summer of 1936 in New York City's five boroughs. With daily temperatures climbing to over 100 degrees, the pools were welcome relief from the heat. But they provided much more than just a place to get cool, especially for the area's young people. Comparing the facility to an exclusive East Coast resort, King recalled, "It was our Hamptons."[5] The Works Progress Administration (WPA), one of the New Deal's premier agencies, constructed New York's eleven pools, and spent more than $750 million on similar projects in communities throughout the United States.[6] Beginning in 1933, the New Deal included an alphabet soup of agencies designed to help ease unemployment and level the playing field of opportunity for Americans of all ages, as well as offer new services for Americans. Besides providing the physical facilities, the WPA employed adults to guide the recreation of young Americans. Children and teens learned to swim, ski, dance, act, draw, and play sports in a variety of WPA programs. After 1934, the number of cities with public recreational programs doubled to over 2,100, and public expenditures for recreation increased from $27 million to $57 million in 1940. Thousands of public works projects and recreation programs provided jobs for adults and also built the twentieth century's modern infrastructure that were the essential building blocks of modern childhood.

Government programs also helped to make life safer for children and teens. For example, thousands of youngsters drowned each summer in the nation's lakes, ponds, streams, and rivers. In 1934 in New York City alone, an estimated 450 children and adolescents lost their lives in the area's waterways. In the mid-1930s, the New York City Board of Education appealed for volunteers to assist recreational programs designed to "compete with the thrill and excitement of so many forbidden pleasures – playing along the waterfront, hitching onto trucks, [and] scrambling into vacant buildings."[7] WPA jobs are often portrayed as little more than busywork, but it is also important to recognize that programs centered on children's recreation brightened the lives of millions of young Americans and helped to keep many safe during the Great Depression.

Jeff Wiltse argues that New Deal swimming pools had a special meaning for many Americans. They were visible reminders that the federal government was helping them and their communities deal with the economic and social hardships of the depression.[8] Such public facilities, however, reinforced racial segregation practices at the same time as they eroded other forms of social stratification. Although racially segregated, public recreational facilities were generally accessible on some level to all children. Although far from perfect, this shift planted the seeds for more significant advances in civil rights in the decades after the Second World War.

Public schools were another area where the public embraced the idea that the government had a responsibility to equalize opportunities among young Americans. Even before Roosevelt became president, the 1930 White House Conference on Child Health and Protection's "Children's Charter" included a declaration that every child in America had the right to attend "a school which is safe from hazards, sanitary, properly equipped, lighted and ventilated." The charter also stated that younger children had the right to attend "nursery schools and kindergartens." Local school districts were urged to provide health programs for students as part of school curriculums. Above all, the participants in the White House Conference concluded,

> equalization of opportunity [should be] sought in all schools, by all possible means, for all school children ... this applied to all schools whether urban or rural, to Negro Schools, Indian Schools, and all other types of schools in the United States and ... territories.[9]

The 1930 White House Conference set high standards, but as communities faced reduced revenues it was nearly impossible to meet such goals. School districts across the United States had a hard time just keeping their doors open. In May 1932, the US Senate held hearings investigating the school funding crisis in Chicago, Illinois, where the district had not paid teachers for two months. Consistent with the Hoover Administration's general approach to such problems, senators expressed sympathy, but offered no financial aid. Almost a year later, on April 16, 1933, more than 20,000 students, teachers, and parents took part in a march through Chicago protesting the lack of pay for teachers. Part of a national crisis, the previous spring, 20,000 schools across the United States ended their terms when they ran out of money. Entering the White House in 1933, Roosevelt brought some relief in the form of grants and loans to needy school districts. The New Deal also provided 70 percent of the cost of school construction in the United States in the 1930s. This translated to more than 40,000 schools. The influx of federal money rapidly spread the modern model of age-based and grade-based consolidated schools across the nation.

Hiroko Kamikawa grew up in Fresno, California. She went to elementary school in her local neighborhood, but then attended larger, consolidated schools for the upper grades. Samuel Prince grew up in New York's Hebrew National Orphan Home on the other side of the United States. Although on the surface the lives of these two young Americans' might seem very different, both went to their local elementary school and then on to large consolidated high schools where each studied virtually the same curriculum.

The growing emphasis on a standard school-based education as the key to a successful future encouraged demands for greater equality in the nation's schools. One successful challenge involved Chicano and Chicana students living in Lemon Grove, California, a small multi-ethnic community located approximately ten miles outside San Diego. There was little social interaction among Lemon Grove's Anglo- and Mexican-American adults. This social division, however, did not transfer as readily to the town's children because every child in the first through eighth grades attended the Lemon Grove Grammar School. David Ruiz, a Chicano student, recalled that the children got along well. However, a few influential Anglo parents caused a rift in the community in 1930 and 1931 known as the "Lemon Grove Incident."

During the late summer of 1930 the Anglo-controlled Parent Teacher Association and members of the Chamber of Commerce proposed the establishment of a separate school for Mexican-American children. The idea was not unusual because a number of communities in California and other parts of the West already segregated black, Asian, and American Indian children in public schools.

On January 5, 1931, 169 students returned to start the new year's classes at the Lemon Grove Grammar School. The school's principal, Jerome T. Green, met the returning students, but refused to let the 75 Mexican-Americans enter the building. The students and their parents protested and filed a suit against the school board. Twelve-year-old Roberto Alvarez represented the community's Chicano and Chicana children. Alvarez and 95 percent of the excluded students were American citizens, "entitled to all the rights and privileges common to all citizens of the United States."[10] On March 30, 1932, San Diego's Judge Claude Chambers decided the case in favor of the students. The plaintifs successfully used an argument later incorporated in the famous 1954 *Brown v. Board of Education* decision. The Lemon Grove case was not typical of the 1930s, but the case points to the growing importance many students and parents placed on access to quality school-based education.

Fourteen-year-old Margaret Williams became the center of another significant civil rights case originating in Maryland in the 1930s. The Williams case is further evidence of the increasing demand for access to quality education during the Depression. Born September 28, 1921 and growing up in Cowdensville, Maryland, a small black community located in the southwestern section of Baltimore County, Margaret Williams attended Colored School #21, a racially segregated one-room schoolhouse. At the end of the 1934–1935 school year, her teacher recommended Williams for promotion to the eighth grade, along with the only other seventh graders in the school, Lucille Scott and Edward Fletcher. Baltimore County's superintendent rejected the recommendation, arguing that only the boy, Edward Fletcher, should move on to the eighth grade. In his mind there was "no reason to pass the girls, because by the time [they] were fifteen or sixteen years old, [they] would be having babies." Williams thought the superintendent's words were "unfair to say to a person," and her "parents were tremendously upset."[11]

National Association for the Advancement of Colored People (NAACP) attorney and future US Supreme Court Justice, Thurgood Marshall, took Williams' case to court. Marshall fed information about the case to a sympathetic Baltimore newspaper reporter, explaining that the suit's goal was to force Baltimore County to build a "Negro" high school, not integrate its all-white schools. Unlike the judge that heard Roberto Alvarez's lawsuit, Baltimore Circuit Court Judge Frank I. Duncan seemed uninterested in sorting out the details of the Williams case. Williams lost, but fearing another expensive lawsuit, the Baltimore County School Board opened three "separate but equal" secondary school facilities for black students at the start of the 1938–1939 academic year. Williams had not achieved her own goal, but her challenge opened the door to a high school education for other black students living in Baltimore County.[12]

The history of American Indians involved another kind of problem that often limited access to quality schools. Notorious for their blatant Americanization programs designed to erase Indian traditions and culture, the government's policies for Indian schools improved somewhat in 1934 with passage of the Indian Reorganization Act and the Johnson–O'Malley Act. The new laws included important and positive alterations in the operation of day and boarding schools. John Collier, Commissioner of Indian Affairs in the US Department of the Interior from 1933 to 1945, oversaw these reforms, but it should be noted that the new policies never fully reached the lofty goals of fair treatment and equality Collier advocated.

At the start of the 1930s, 95 percent of children six through thirteen years of age in the United States attended school full time. Every state had enacted some form of a compulsory school attendance law for children aged six through fourteen, and a majority extended the requirement to sixteen-year-olds. These facts, however, do not give a full picture of the status of American education at the time. There was a wide variance in quality and accessibility. Southern states struggled to pay for two unequal systems under the Jim Crow regime of segregation. A few states required schools to remain open less than three months a year. The one-room schoolhouse was still standard in many rural communities. Above all, state officials and educators found it very difficult to keep a majority of adolescents in school beyond the elementary grades. In 1920, only 35 percent of fourteen through seventeen-year-olds were in school. Things changed during the 1920s, expanding to 51 percent in 1929. Still, in 1930, almost half of the nation's adolescents left school before earning a high school diploma. Somewhat ironically, the onset of the Great Depression increased attendance. Unemployment among adolescents and youths was twice that of adults. Many decided, instead of staying home, to remain in school. Among fourteen-through seventeen-year-olds, attendance jumped 25 percent in just the first four years following the stock market crash (64 percent in 1933). By 1940, 73 percent of American fourteen- through seventeen-year-olds were attending school; a 43 percent increase over the decade. The number of high school graduates in the total population climbed from 667,000 to 1,221,000.[13]

The Roosevelt Administration also expanded education by introducing WPA Emergency Day Nurseries. WPA nurseries were essentially established to provide jobs for unemployed teachers, but they also brought cutting edge pedagogy to pre-schoolers across the United States. By the end of the 1930s, the prescription for focusing on school as a child's work extended from pre-school through high school graduation.

Still, it was not easy for all young Americans to stay in school. Sixteen-year-old Lusette Smith finished high school in North Carolina, but it was not an experience she liked to remember. She told an interviewer with the Federal Writers Project, "Most people look back on their Senior year as a pleasant time in their lives, but I won't." With no money for bus fare, Lusette walked six miles on school days. "The walking wouldn't have been so bad if I hadn't been afraid each day that my ragged shoes would fall apart before I could possibly get to school." Smith recalled, "walking in the early morning can make you awfully weary when you haven't had any breakfast and not much supper the night before." Students like Lusette Smith tried to stay invisible. "Without decent clothes and without enough food I went every day and heard my classmates discuss their plans for the future. I didn't talk any because I was afraid to even think what my future might be."[14]

For other students who also felt discouraged by their economic circumstance, dropping out of school seemed like a reasonable solution. In 1934, Thomas Patrick Minehan published *Boy and Girl Tramps of America*. The book highlights the lack of opportunities and poverty that influenced many young Americans in the midst of the Great Depression to quit school. Minehan conducted interviews with almost 1,500 young transients from 1931 to 1933 for his master's thesis in sociology at the University of Minnesota. Often dubbed as "the youth problem," the rising unemployment and lack of opportunities for young people worried many Americans who feared the situation might fuel civil unrest and anti-social behavior. Hard times was the most common reason young transients gave for leaving school and their family homes. Others dropped out and hit the road because they found school boring or useless. "Nothing I ever did ever satisfied anybody in school," one girl told Minehan. "I hated them all," she continued. A boy nicknamed Omaha Red explained that he ran away because, "All my life I hated school."[15] The problem of young transients looking for work and not attending school was identified as part of "the youth problem" of the 1930s. By the early 1930s, an estimated 250,000 young transients hitchhiked, walked, and hopped freight trains across the United States. Most were male (90 percent) and many Americans worried that this was a lost generation headed for a life of crime and adult dependency.

When Franklin Roosevelt entered the White House in 1933, he established the Civilian Conservation Corps (CCC), primarily to employ out-of-work First World War veterans, but also to give seventeen- through twenty-three-year-old males from families on relief a job and a purpose. In 1934, the CCC lowered the age of eligibility to sixteen. Recruits lived in residential camps where they worked on conservation projects by day, and learned middle-class standards of behavior each evening. Some also earned a high school diploma. The government and the American public believed that younger teens should be in school, and not seeking work.

In 1935, the New Deal added another program specifically directed at older adolescents and youths in their early twenties. The National Youth Administration (NYA) supported the idea that young people should remain dependent on their parents and stay in school. Somewhat different from the CCC, the NYA was not a residential program and it also included girls. NYA recruits were paid stipends as long as they remained in high school or college and continued to live with their parents or a guardian. During its existence from 1935 to 1943, the NYA enrolled 1.5 million high school students and 600,000 college youths. Another 2.6 million unemployed young Americans registered for the agency's training programs. Mary McCloud Bethune, head of the NYA's Colored Division, maintained that the agency "tunneled its way into the rural and urban conditions of our country, awakening and inspiring thousands and thousands of youths, opening doors of opportunity ... I have worked and fought with my sleeves rolled up day and night."[16]

None of these education programs alone provided equality of opportunity for all American children, but they did signal important shifts in public attitudes about the necessity of a quality school-based education to secure a bright future. For the first time in American history, staying in school long enough to earn a high school diploma became the expected norm, not the exception. By the end of the 1930s, high school, not the workplace or home, was the prescribed training ground for all adolescents.

The 1938 Fair Labor Standards Act (FLSA) was another important building block in this transformation from wage work to school as the prescribed realm for children and adolescents. This seminal legislation successfully set forth federal child labor regulations for the first time in US history. The FLSA prohibited the employment of individuals under age sixteen in industries engaged in interstate commerce or work deemed hazardous by the Department of Labor. The law also limited working hours and prohibited employment past 10 pm on school nights for anyone under eighteen. It also limited the number of hours sixteen and seventeen-year-olds could work at all, something that many states did not do at the time. Despite its progressive policies, the law included important exemptions that left some young Americans outside government protection, for example, most agricultural labor was left out of the law. Fourteen- and fifteen-year-olds could still engage in wage work (other than mining and manufacturing) that "did not interfere with their schooling, health, or well being." The law did not "end child labor" as President Roosevelt claimed, but it underscored the model of modern childhood, emphasizing school over wage work through age seventeen.

Economic security for all American children, those who came from families with limited resources as well as those who were orphaned, abused, or abandoned, was another feature of the modern childhood ideal that established a new role for government during the Great Depression. In 1935, President Franklin Roosevelt signed the Social Security Act (SSA). The SSA is best known for its old age pension program, but the law also defined the parameters of American childhood protection and dependency in federal law for the first time as birth through age seventeen. In other words, under the SSA, the federal government took on the ultimate responsiblity for the care and protection of individuals under eighteen. Title IV, Aid to Dependent Children; Title V, Maternal and Child Health for needy children living with their mothers; and Title VII, Aid for Children with Special Needs were seminal programs directed at the nation's young people. The SSA clearly recognized that politicians and the American public now acknowledged and approved the idea of childhood dependency from birth through adolescence. Advocates had worked since the late nineteenth century to make this possible. The economic interests of adults and developments in popular culture helped to change people's mindsets about the proper nature of modern childhood for all young Americans.

Modern childhood and popular culture

In the 1930s, American popular culture reinforced public policy prescriptions for a protected and dependent childhood. The rapid spread of radio broadcasting and improved technology in movies made the image a part of the everyday lives of Americans. From 1929 to 1932, as advertising revenues fell by half, toy sales plummeted, and one-third of America's movie theaters closed their doors, advertisers looked for new markets. One solution was to focus on children and adolescents as a distinct groups of consumers. America's mass consumer culture developed in the late nineteenth and early twentieth century, but advertisers and manufacturers did not distinguish among children and adults. In the 1930s, this changed as marketers increasingly saw young Americans as independent consumers. And, for the first time in US history, teens were identified as a discrete market, distinct from adults and young children. Young consumers, however, were not merely blank slates manipulated by commercial interests.

It is difficult to overstate the importance of radio in the commodification and universalization of American popular culture for children and teens in the Depression decade. In 1930, only 50 percent of all US households had a radio. Ten years later, the rate had risen to 83 percent. Ownership among urban families was nearly universal. Rural households were less likely than urban households to have a radio, but it is noteworthy that even in the countryside, 70 percent of residents joined the national radio trend. Some Americans built their own crystal sets (radios). Others bought commerical radios that cost about $30 for a simple table unit to hundreds of dollars for fancy console models. Even in hard times, most Americans considered owning a radio a necessity. Nevertheless, while over 90 percent of urban households had access to commercially produced electrical power in 1930, under 10 percent of rural families did. The New Deal's Rural Electrification Administration and the Tennessee Valley Authority helped to spread radio's influence and universalize American culture.

John Smith Barney and his playmates grew up in tiny Wheelersburg Village, Ohio. Most families in the community did not have much money, but kids still found ways to have fun. Listening to the radio was a favorite pastime. The first children's adventure program on radio, *The Little Orphan Annie Show*, began broadcasting from Chicago's WGN. The NBC network picked up the show in 1931, sending it to affiliates across the United States. Run as a weekly serial adventure program from 1931 to 1950, *The Little Orphan Annie Show* had its roots in the famous newspaper comic strip of the same name. Unlike the newspaper version that attracted fans of all ages, the radio show targeted elementary and middle-school-aged youngsters. Other producers quickly copied the format. These 15-minute adventure programs for young listeners aired each weekday afternoon, during what broadcasters called the "children's hour."

In many ways the decision by radio executives to add programming for the nation's young audience was built on a marketing model created in the late-nineteenth century by book publishers selling dime novels. Radio turned out to be an even more effective distributor and it also offered new opportunities for linking children's entertainment, consumerism, and the modern childhood ideal. John Barney's recollection of a cold winter morning during the mid-1930s shows the clever way advertisers used radio to take advantage of the commodification of children's entertainment.

> I was ready by eight o'clock," Barney recalled. "I had eaten two big bowls of WHEATIES and drunk some Ovaltine, but had to finish up one jar before Mom would buy me a new jar; no new jar meant no protective inner-seal to send in to Little Orphan Annie.

Proofs-of-purchase, like the Ovaltine protective seals or box tops from cereals like Wheaties, could be exchanged for gadgets touted by children's radio serial heroes. Barney liked chocolate-flavored Ovaltine, but some children such as Minneapolis's Ralph Luedtke hated the stuff. Still, even Luedtke could not resist participating in the special offers presented to young radio fans. Despite his distaste for the powdered chocolate-flavored drink, Luedtke asked his mother to buy Ovaltine so that he could get the premiums promoted on his favorite program.[17]

Some adults worried that the purveyors of radio, movies, and commercial products put profits before the best interests of young Americans. Such complaints about popular culture were not new, but examining the rising wave of criticism that arose during the 1930s underscores the pervasiveness of popular culture directed at children and teens in the Great Depression years. Critics seemed to understand that commercial culture had become an unavoidable part of modern childhood. Instead of calls to shut down movie theaters, radio stations, and other for-profit businesses, reformers focused on shaping the content of such entertainment. They called for a celebration of what many identified as the all-American values of loyalty, patriotism, obedience to authority, community service, perseverance, clean living, democracy, freedom, and good sportsmanship. Advocates demanded that Hollywood and radio broadcasters portray the idyllic middle-class American childhood that had been touted by child welfare reformers for several decades. Critics also demanded the elimination of what they identified as excessive images of violence, criminal behavior, rebellion, and sexuality in films, radio, and other aspects of popular culture.

In 1933, *Parents Magazine* featured articles condemning the violent content in radio's children's hour serial adventure programs. One cartoon in the magazine depicted a frightened young girl listening to a radio blaring "Scram! Don't Shoot! Kidnapped! They're Going To Kill Me! Help! Murder! Bang! Bang! Kill Him! Police!" Critics maintained that the American capitalist business model was the problem. In 1934, responding to such criticism, radio executives defended their medium through a campaign entitled "Radio as a Means of Public Enlightenment." In May 1935, Franklin Roosevelt asked the Federal Communications Commission (FCC) to put pressure on broadcasters to clean up their programming or face increased government control. Hoping to avoid government dictates, CBS and NBC responded by announcing self-censorship policies. Perhaps to the surprise of many filmmakers and broadcasting executives, the choice to focus on assumed all-American values and eliminate much of the violence and sexuality in films was a boon for business.

For kids, radio and the movies were simply fun. *The Little Orphan Annie Show*'s success quickly encouraged the creation of similar programs. Evil doers existed in the world of radio adventurers, but the good guys always won in the end. *Jack Armstrong,*

The All American Boy (1933–1950) was another successful radio show that preached traditional American values and adventure stories directed at young listeners.

Hollywood helped to attract children and teens to the movies by putting more young faces on America's screens than ever before. Movies gave the generation coming of age during the Great Depression a collection of shared images that they carried with them for the rest of their lives. Movies also portrayed a world of possibilities that many young people would not have seen without the increasingly popular medium. Jean Lobe grew up in Milwaukee, Wisconsin during the Great Depression and was a huge film fan. She remembered that going to the movies "was a great thrill," and always left her coming "out of the theater completely dazed to be back in my own life."[18]

Despite their popularity, movies also caused controversy with some adults. By the mid-1930s, the Motion Picture Producers and Directors Association of America (MPPDA) began to enforce a self-censorship code (the Hayes Production Code). The MPPDA refused to put the organization's stamp of approval on films that did not follow its guidelines. This was a significant threat because the studios owned or had very close business relationships with most of the major movie theaters in the United States. *Tarzan and His Mate* became the first movie censored under the newly enforced code. Like the radio industry's guidelines, the film studios' Hayes Production Code sanitized the industry's products. Walt Disney's *Snow White and the Seven Dwarfs* (1937) was a good example of the Hayes' Code's prescription for films directed at children and families. Disney's emphasis on traditional American stereotypes and morality tales made it a very popular purveyor of mainstream children's entertainment in the 1930s and beyond.

Besides romance and fairytale endings, filmmakers also used new technologies and marketing strategies to draw audiences to theaters. By the 1930s, children, teens, and adults escaped the summer heat in movie theaters cooled by air conditioners where they could also sit in warm comfort during the winter. "The talkies," movies with sound, had entered theaters during the 1920s, but during the 1930s studios improved audio quality and added color. New animation techniques developed by Disney and Warner Brothers popularized cartoons among children and adults. Extravagantly expensive color movies like *The Wizard of Oz* and *Gone With the Wind* (both released in 1939) paid off big at the box office and also drew children and teens to the nation's theaters.

Shirley Temple is arguably the best known child film star of all time. During the 1930s, her image became an icon of American childhood. In addition, no film or stage star's likeness was more marketable. A singing, dancing, and acting phenomenon, the precocious Temple began making film shorts in 1932 when she was only three years old. The dimple-cheeked curly-topped girl's film persona seemed to offer just the right combination of sentiment and spunk that defined childhood and appealed to children and adults hungering for happy endings and the promise of a brighter future. At the height of her popularity, Temple received 60,000 fan letters a month. In 1933 alone, toy manufactures sold 1.5 million Shirley Temple dolls. The Academy of Motion Picture Arts and Sciences recognized the young actor's contribution to the film industry's remarkable turnaround by awarding her a special miniature Oscar statuette in 1935. The thirties decade was filled with images of sweet-faced young film stars who emphasized that childhood and adolescence should be a carefree time, free from adult worries and responsibilities.

The *Little Rascals* film shorts supported this viewpoint by putting the series' pre-adolescent actors in various adult situations where they inevitably behaved in comedic and childish ways. Their antics were funny because the effort to imitate grown-ups looked so out of place, therefore reinforcing the modern childhood ideal that the lives of children should be distinct from that of adults. Hal Roach began filming the first *Little Rascals* shorts in 1922. During the 1920s, some communities sponsored *Little Rascals* look-alike contests,, and a few even made their own copy-cat films. By the 1930s MGM (Metro Goldwyn Mayer) distributed the *Little Rascals* films, bringing them to an even wider audience. Roach sold the series to the studio in 1938, which released the last films in the series in 1944. Over the years, Roach and MGM produced 221 individual episodes, each lasting approximately 10 to 20 minutes. The original cast grew too old for the series' storylines, so the individual child actors changed, but the basic characters continued to fit the predictable social and cultural stereotypes outlined in the first *Little Rascals'* episodes: the fat kid, the freckled-face redhead, the skinny kid with the bow tie and cowlick, the black boy with big eyes and a toothy grin, and several cute girls complete with curls, dimples, and frilly dresses. The *Little Rascals'* shorts portrayed childhood as a time of mini-adventures, largely separate from the world of adults, where no one was ever seriously hurt or emotionally harmed.

The Dead End Kids series offered a slightly darker depiction of American childhood that centered on the lives of troubled adolescents in a poor New York City neighborhood. The original 1938 film was popular with audiences so Warner Brothers quickly signed the ensemble of young actors for six more movies, released from 1938 to 1939. In such films even juvenile delinquents could be saved if given the chance to have a more protected and idealized childhood spent in school, protected from abuse, and supported by a loving family. A young Mickey Rooney contributed further to the proliferation of this idyllic image of adolescence through the very successful *Andy Hardy* film series that started in 1937. Andy Hardy and his high school friends lived in happy and stable middle-class families in small town America. The teens spent their time going to school and enjoying social lives overseen, but not controlled, by parents and teachers. The series' storylines followed Andy and his pals, both boys and girls, as they interacted with their families, went to school, and spent time in the local soda shop. The young people experienced joy and sadness as they struggled to mature into adults, but their lives were limited to dress rehearsals for adult realities.

Comic books were another popular form of commercial entertainment in the 1930s that attracted young Americans. In 1933, M.C. Gaines and two associates asked and received permission to reprint newspaper comic strips in book form. Entitled *Funnies on Parade*, Gaines and his associates distributed 10,000 copies to Procter and Gamble Company customers. Gaines next sold the comic books on newsstands for 10 cents a piece. Major Malcolm Wheeler-Nicholson established the first distinct comic book publication in 1935 with *New Fun Comics* and formed D.C. Comics in 1937. In June 1938, D.C. Comics released *Superman*, the first major comic book character with superhuman powers. The next year, D.C. Comics sold over one million copies per issue of *Superman*. From 1940 to 1945, comic book publishers released more than 400 different superhero characters.

By the 1930s, radio, movies, and current events influenced children to slightly alter the rules of some traditional games. Board games were also popular. Philadelphia's Wanamaker Department Store and New York's F.A.O. Schwartz began selling *Monopoly* in 1934, and the next year, the toy manufacturer Parker Brothers signed the agreement with the game's designer that launched it as the most successful board game in history. Jigsaw puzzles were also a popular pastime. Franklin Roosevelt helped to spur an interest in stamp collecting that could be shared by children and adults. But even the cheapest forms of commercial entertainment were out of reach for some American children during the Great Depression. Robert Hastings put it this way in his memoir, *A Nickel's Worth of Skim Milk*: "The Depression may have denied me some of the frills of growing up, but it didn't rob me of the fun of just being a boy with my friends." Some games could be played with no special equipment or toys. Many had been passed down by generations of American children.[19]

As more American adolescents remained in school longer than ever before, their leisure time activities became progressively distinct from that of children and adults. The image of American adolescence portrayed in *Andy Hardy* films was far from reality for many teens. The expansion of high school attendance, however, reinforced an image in popular culture of late adolescence and early youth as a unique period of life that centered on socializing with peers. The sound that came to be known as Swing served as the background music for a generation coming of age during the 1930s.

The combination of radio and teens created a synergy that fueled the phenomenal popularity of Swing. Radio listeners had a wide range of musical choices during the 1930s, but nothing attracted teens and youths more than Swing. Popular memory tends to associate Swing music with the Second World War years, but the genre was first widely heard during the Great Depression. Swing music had its roots in a combination of New Orleans' style jazz, southern blues, and the Charleston sound, popularized during the 1920s by black musicians like Louis Armstrong and Eubie Blake. In 1932, the elegant African–American band leader Duke Ellington coined one of his most popular tunes, "It Don't Mean a Thing" (If It Ain't Got That Swing). Ellington did not invent Swing, but his song named a genre.

The clarinetist and band leader Benny Goodman is often given the credit for turning the Swing sound into a national phenomenon. In 1934, Goodman was the twenty-five-year-old leader of a 12-piece band working in New York City, when the group joined NBC's Saturday night 10.30 pm to 1.30 am broadcast *Let's Dance*. Dance crazes such as the Lindy Hop, Suzy Q, and the Big Peach were part of a style popularly known as Jitterbug. Dancers could improvise moves, but many spent hours practicing Jitterbug's fast steps, body throws, and spins. As couples became more proficient at the new style, Swing dance contests spread across the country. In 1936, Benny Goodman made several recordings with black musician Lionel Hampton. In 1938, he performed in concerts at New York City's Carnegie Hall with both black and white musicians. Such steps did not end racial segregation or the refusal by most radio stations to play "race records" (recordings made by black musicians), but they marked an important shift toward the racial integration of commercial music that would become more commonly associated with rock 'n' roll.

The Great Depression and American children

Scholars writing about the history of the Great Depression generally focus on politics and the lives of adults; however, it is a mistake to overlook the experiences and contributions of the generation that grew up and came of age in this important era of American history. Including the perspectives of the era's children and youths highlights the important political, social, and cultural changes that took place in the Great Depression decade. Following demands to do something about the growing economic crisis, the federal government's reach lengthened, especially after Franklin D. Roosevelt's election in 1932. New technologies also contributed to the increased role of the federal government in the lives of average Americans, including children and youths. Young Americans heard the president's voice over the radio and saw his image at the movies. With Roosevelt's election, the majority of American voters signaled that they wanted a more active federal government and young Americans were also part of this shift from tradition.

Jim Mitchell grew up during the Great Depression. Mitchell's attitude about the role of government was shaped by his experience as part of the Depression generation. He credits Franklin Roosevelt with preventing the social unrest and political turmoil that happened in many other countries at the time. "Despite all the horrors of the Depression, we didn't live in terror but looked ahead. We knew that down the road things were going to get better."[20] For young Americans coming of age in the 1930s, life was not always easy, but federal policies helped equalize the playing field for access to education and the promise of basic economic security. Popular culture gave them a model of American childhood, which they expected to become reality "in normal times," and for the young Americans who became the children of the Depression generation after the Second World War.

Notes

1 Data for this essay was collected from a variety of sources including Robert S. McElvaine, *Encyclopedia of the Great Depression* (New York, NY: Macmillan Reference, Thomas Gale, 2004), vol. 1; Grace Abbott, "How Have Children Fared as a Whole? The Chief of the Children's Bureau Deals with These Questions," *New York Times*, December, 1932; US Children's Bureau, "Effects of the Great Depression Child Health and Child Services, *Congressional Record*, 72nd Cong. 1st sess., 3095–3099; Robert Cohen, "Great Depression and New Deal," in *Encyclopedia of Children and Childhood: In History and Society*, ed. Paula Fass (New York, NY: Macmillan Reference, 2004), 397; T.H. Watkins, *The Hungry Years: A Narrative History of the Great Depression in America* (New York, NY: Owl Books, 2000).
2 Robert J. Hastings, *A Nickle's Worth of Skim Milk: A Boy's View of the Great Depression* (Carbondale, IL: Southern Illinois University Press, 1972), 46–47.
3 Ray Lyman Wilbur, "Children in National Emergencies," *Proceedings of the National Conference of Social Work*, (Chicago, IL: National Conference on Social Work, 1932).
4 Leroy Ashby, *Endangered Children: Dependency, Neglect, and Abuse in American History* (New York, NY: Twayne Publishers, 1997), 108–112.
5 "Everything About a Pool: The McCarren Park Pool," *The New Big Thing*, radio broadcast aired July 4, 2003, http://www.wnyc.org/shows/tnbt/2002/aug/25/, accessed April 18, 2011.

6 D. Laszlo Conhaim, "Alan King," *Encyclopedia of World Biography*, http://www.notable biographies.com/newsmakers2/2005-Fo-La/King-Alan.html, accessed April 18, 2011; and "Alan King," *Washington Post*, May 10, 2004.

7 Jeff Wiltse, *Contested Waters: A Social History of Swimming Pools in America* (Chapel Hill, NC: University of North Carolina Press, 2007), 206.

8 Ibid., pp.121–122, 206; "Everything About a Pool: The McCarren Park Pool," *The New Big Thing*, radio broadcast aired July 4, 2003. http://www.wnyc.org/shows/tnbt/2002/aug/25/, accessed April 18, 2011.

9 "The Children's Charter," President Herbert Hoover's White Conference on Child Welfare and Protection, November 19–21, 1930, (Washington, DC: Government Printing Office, 1930).

10 Superior Court of the State of California, San Diego County, Writ of Mandate, February 13, 1931, cited in Robert R. Alvarez, Jr., "The Lemon Grove Incident: The Nation's First Successful Desegregation Court Case," *Journal of San Diego History* 32 (1986): 116–135, available online without page numbers at http://www.sandiegohistory.org/journal/86spring/lemongrove.htm, accessed May 2, 2004.

11 W. Edward Orser, "Neither Separate Nor Equal: Foreshadowing *Brown* in Baltimore County, 1935–1937," *Maryland Historical Magazine* 92 (1997): 5–35; Louis Diggs, *In Our Voices* (Baltimore, MD: Uptown Press, 1998), 61–63.

12 Ibid.

13 Data gathered from a variety of sources such as US Census Bureau, "Educational Summary – Enrollment, Graduates, and Degrees: 1900–1998, and Projections 1999 and 2000, No. 1425" in *Statistical Abstracts of the United States, 1999, Section 31, 20th Century Statistics*, (Washington, DC: Government Printing Office, 1999), 876; and US Census Bureau, "High School Graduates by Sex, 1870–1970," *Historical Statistics of the United States, Bicentennial Edition*, (Washington, DC: Government Printing Office, 1976), 379.

14 Interview with Lusette Smith, Federal Writers Project, 1936–1940, August 23, 1938, included in "American Life Histories," Library of Congress American Memory Project, Washington, DC, http://memory.loc.gov/wpaintro/wpahome.html, accessed May 16, 2011.

15 Thomas Minehan, *Boy and Girl Tramps of America* (Seattle, WA: University of Washington Press, reprint of 1934 edition, 1976), 35, 49, 51.

16 Paula S. Fass, *Outside In: Minorities and the Transformation of American Education* (New York, NY: Oxford University Press, 1991), 128–134.

17 John Smith Barney, *Porter Township* (Urbana, OH: Rotabar, 1988), 34.

18 Jean Lobe, "Simple as Child's Play: Memories of 1930s Pastimes," May 1, 2001, "Children in Urban America," http://www.marquette.edu/cuap/, accessed April 7, 2012.

19 Robert J. Hastings, *A Nickel's Worth of Skim Milk: A Boy's View of the Great Depression*, (Carbondale, IL: University of Illinois Press, Shawnee Books, 1986), 83.

20 Erroll Lincoln Uys, *Riding the Rails: Teenagers on the Move During the Great Depression* (New York, NY: TV Books, 1999), 255–263.

Suggestions for further reading

Balderrama, Francisco E. and Raymond Rodriguez. *Decade of Betrayal: Mexican Repatriation in the 1930s*. Albuquerque, NM: University of New Mexico Press, 1995.

Bremner, Robert H., John Barnard, Tamara Hareven, and Robert Mennel. *Children and Youth in America: A Documentary History*. Cambridge, MA: Harvard University Press, 1974.

Clausen, John A. *American Lives: Looking Back at the Children of the Great Depression*. New York, NY: The Free Press, 1993.

Cohen, Robert. *Dear Mrs. Roosevelt: Letters From Children of the Great Depression*. Chapel Hill, NC: University of North Carolina Press, 2007.

Cravens, Hamilton. *Great Depression: People and Perspectives*. Santa Barbara, CA: ABC Clio, 2009.

DeWitt, Larry W., Daniel Beland, and Edward Berkowitz. *Social Security: A Documentary History*. Washington, DC: Congressional Quarterly Press, 2008.

Fass, Paula S. *Outside In: Minorities and the Tranformation of American Education*. New York, NY: Oxford University Press, 1987.

Lindenmeyer, Kriste. *The Greatest Generation Grows Up: American Childhood in the 1930s*. Chicago, IL: Ivan R. Dee Publisher, 2005.

McElvaine, Robert S. *Encyclopedia of the Great Depression*. New York, NY: Macmillan Reference, Thomas Gale, 2004.

Minehan, Thomas. *Boy and Girl Tramps of America*. Seattle, WA: University of Washington Press, reprint of 1934 edition, 1976.

Reiman, Richard A. *The New Deal and American Youth: Ideas and Ideals in a Depression Decade*. Athens, GA: University of Georgia Press, 1992.

Sealander, Judith. *The Failed Century of the Child: Government America's Young in the Twentieth Century*. New York, NY: Cambridge University Press, 2003.

Watkins, T.H. *The Hungry Years: A Narrative History of the Great Depression in America*. New York, NY: Owl Books, 2000.

Young, William H., and Nancy K. Young. *The 1930s*. Westport, CT: Greenwood Press, 2002.

25

CHILDHOOD AND YOUTH IN NAZI GERMANY

Dirk Schumann

In his book *Father Land*, published in 1948, American psychiatrist Bertram Schaffner offered an influential interpretation of the root causes of the catastrophe brought about by the Nazi regime. Echoing the concept of the "authoritarian personality," developed by Theodor W. Adorno, Erich Fromm, and other members of the "Frankfurt School" in exile, it centered on the "authoritarianism" of the German family. A towering and emotionally rather distant father, expecting strict obedience from all family members, inculcated a strong sense of discipline and subordination toward the greater nation in his offspring. Children thus did not learn to become independent-minded personalities but were raised with a pronounced "fear of failure." While an emphasis on order and cleanliness reinforced this authoritarianism, a cult of manliness prepared young boys to become future soldiers. This "enforced obedience" in childhood came at a price. Aggressiveness and brutality in adulthood, directed not at previous family authorities but against people deemed of inferior rank or outsiders, would serve as its compensation. From this – primarily male-oriented – perspective, childhood in Nazi Germany had not been radically different from previous childhoods in Germany but essentially a continuation, with its dangerous traits enhanced further.[1]

Subsequent research, however, has primarily stressed how the Nazi regime sought to shape children and youths by diminishing the power of traditional institutions of education – family and school – in favor of newly established organizations – Hitler Youth (Hitler Jugend, HJ) and League of German Girls (Bund Deutscher Mädel, BDM) – that combined an emphasis on military-like discipline with attractive offers of leadership positions and leisure activities. While most recent research has found less tension between family and state, this was obviously one of two features that made childhood in Nazi Germany special: the attempt by a totalitarian regime to control the education of the young as completely as possible from infancy to adulthood; by guidelines for parents; curricula at school as well as by the new youth organizations, including those for adolescents and young adults; the Labor Service; and a mandatory military. While the implementation of this policy was tempered in many ways, by parents and teachers and by the young themselves, on balance young Germans would adopt a *habitus* of self-discipline and sense of duty that helped sustain the regime until its downfall, and carried over, with different connotations, into the two post-war Germanys. The second key feature that made childhood in Nazi Germany special was a rigorous separation between those children and youths who were defined as "Aryan," healthy, and willing to fit in, on the one hand, and those who were believed to be lacking in these criteria on the other – a small number of African-Germans, Sinti and Roma, and, most notably, Jews (as defined by the regime). While this distinction began to be translated into exclusionary measures right after the regime came to power, it subsequently became stricter and took on a new deadly quality after the beginning of the war, when deviant youths were sent to special Schutzstaffel (SS) camps, handicapped children killed, and Sinti, Roma and Jewish children deported to and murdered in the extermination camps.

Nazi policy towards children and youths did not come out of the blue. Since the turn of the twentieth century, conservatives had deplored the fall of the German birthrate and demanded measures to reverse the decline, denouncing liberal world views and the modern big city as forces of decay. The German youth movement, which harbored vague but overall rather rightist political views, called for a renewal of sclerotic bourgeois society and claimed to take the lead, with increased vigor after the devastating First World War, which had left Germany defeated and in political turmoil. Reform pedagogy had devised a new child-centered approach to family and school education prior to the war and successfully implemented some of its proposal in German schools as the war began to foster children's patriotism.[2] While most reform pedagogues opted for the left in the Weimar Republic, their concept proved adaptable to the demands of the Nazi regime.

For the Nazi regime, the continuing drop of the German birthrate was to be reversed and families with many children were to be created by returning to the traditional definition of gender roles and by providing financial support to young families. Nazi family policy was not unequivocally pro-natalist, however, but was coupled with a deliberate anti-natalism that targeted those men and women deemed unworthy for procreation, as the family was subordinate to the *Volk*, and this *Volk* was to be "racially pure" and healthy. Implementing this somewhat paradoxical policy that aimed at raising the birthrate on the one hand while preventing certain parts of the population from having children at all on the other, proved less easy than anticipated, however. To ensure that marriages resulted in "Aryan" and healthy offspring, couples ready to marry were supposed to obtain a marriage certificate from a physician prior to their wedding. While this had been recommended already in the Weimar Republic, the Nazi regime emphasized its importance after taking power. Given the number of physicians in Germany, who were likely to become overwhelmed by the sheer number of applicants, and the prospect of unrest as a result of protracted procedures and unclear criteria, however, the regime, while denying Jewish-Gentile couples the permission to marry right away, even prior to the infamous "Nuremberg Laws" of 1935, made marriage certificates mandatory only for those "Aryans" who wanted to be granted a marriage loan. This form of financial support, introduced in 1935, came up to a maximum of two-thirds of an average worker's annual wage and made it easier for young couples to raise a family. By 1938, 51 percent of all couples received a loan, and other measures to boost the creation of large families, such as the introduction of the "mother's cross" for women who had given birth to four and more children, were now also in place, but Nazi family policy was only partly successful. While the birthrate returned to its 1925 level in 1939, the number of large families, i.e. those with four children and more, decreased from 25 percent of all families in 1933 to 21 percent in 1939. Nazi pro-natalism apparently did not induce couples to change their habits of procreation or to stop practicing birth control.[3]

When a newborn child was officially registered, parents (or the single mother, whose status the regime sought to improve with limited success in the face of entrenched popular attitudes)[4] were given the *Book of Childhood*, which was a combination of advice book and parents' diary. Quoting Hitler, it reminded couples that the child was not their property but belonged to the greater whole of the German *Volk*. Raising the infant meant subjecting him/her to a strict regime to ensure that he/she would become a well-functioning member of the *Volksgemeinschaft*.[5] This regime has been described by previous research as specific for Nazi Germany and as aiming at preventing close emotional bonds between mother and child in order to create a void that was later to be filled by bonds with the community provided by the Nazi youth organizations.[6] The two leading child-rearing experts, psychologist Hildegard Hetzer and physician Johanna Haarer, emphasized that parents lacked expertise and, in slightly different terms, demanded unwavering adherence to the rules they prescribed. While their behaviorist approach to childcare was not in itself specifically German, its intensity and the monopoly it enjoyed made it peculiar. Growing up in Hetzer's and Haarer's view, in essence, was to learn the "mastering of life" ("Lebensbemeisterung"): life was a dangerous and potentially overpowering force, and only by learning regular habits would the child be able to get along and become a productive member of the *Volksgemeinschaft*.[7]

When Bertram Schaffner noted in 1948 that "early habit-training, and the inculcation of strict obedience and sense of duty in infancy and childhood" were likely to explain the Germans' "obsessive" character,[8] he referred to this focus on control. Mothers were warned not to overindulge their love, but to emerge victorious from the inevitable battles of will with their child. For this purpose, a recalcitrant and screaming child was to be "kaltgestellt," i.e. placed in a separate room and deprived of attention, as Johanna Haarer recommended.[9] In a recent study that draws in particular on a close reading of parents' diaries from the Nazi period, Miriam Gebhardt has rejected the argument that this practice precluded close emotional bonds between mother and child. These diaries showed deep affection for the children: as one father put it in the summer of 1941, he and his wife felt "unrestrained joy" when waiting for the return of their son, who had stayed for a while with his grandparents.[10] But these emotional bonds were grounded in praise for the children's physical fitness and vitality. To prevent this vitality from devolving into "tyranny," control regimes, noted in the diaries, became tighter than in the previous generation of parents, which in turn triggered increased resistance on the part of the children. While parents became closer to them, this closeness was meant to keep them on the right track.[11] Parents may have had their own reasons not to heed the Nazi call to produce a large number of children. But they seemed to be receptive to the experts' demands for strict control and a focus on the corporeal. If these infants later were to become well-functioning Hitler Youth, it was not due to a lack of emotional bonds to their families but to this combined emphasis on discipline and physical fitness.

While very young children were influenced by Nazi ideology indirectly, via the behavior of their parents and other family members, once children began attending school and became members of the new organizations set up for children and youths, the regime targeted them directly. When the Nazis came to power in 1933, however, they had not devised a comprehensive program for its educational policy. In his *Mein Kampf*, Hitler had only stated its basic aims. As the well-being of the "race" was paramount, education had to turn a young person into a "valuable element for future procreation."[12] Its main priority therefore was the corporeal. Education had to produce, first and foremost, healthy and strong bodies. Character formation was its second priority, while the teaching of academic subjects, quite contrary to traditional concepts of (school) education, was only of tertiary importance. This hierarchy of goals applied to both boys and girls, albeit in different form: while the former had to be shaped as future soldiers, the latter had to be prepared for their role as mothers. Even though the Nazis did not have a blueprint for the reshaping of German education in 1933, they were poised to break with one core element of the traditional understanding of education. Instead of allowing adolescence to function as a moratorium during which a young person had the opportunity to develop her/his own personality, they would aim for completely controlling this process of growing up. A network of organizations would guarantee that young people would "no longer be free for the rest of their lives," as Hitler put it in a speech in 1938.[13]

This totalitarian approach to education did not mean a complete break with the past, however, as there were continuities between academic pedagogy in the Weimar Republic and the Nazi regime. By positioning their discipline above politics, leading Weimar educationists had implicitly rejected the pluralism of parliamentary democracy and expressed their longing for a state that defined itself as educator of a unified nation that would draw upon their expertise and service. Hence, the Nazi takeover in 1933 met with widespread approval in the profession. Reform pedagogy also proved malleable enough to be a resource, given the crucial role it ascribed to communitarian experiences. Furthermore, as the "nature" of the child had been increasingly defined in biological terms by Weimar educationists, Nazi pedagogy could follow suit, adding an emphasis on "race." Serving as a tool of inclusion and of exclusion, the category of "race" also represented a utopian condition because being an "Aryan" was not necessarily given but had to be diagnosed, and all "Aryans" had to be formed to become more valuable members of the *Volksgemeinschaft*. Thus, the Nazi state was to be an "educational state" ("Erziehungsstaat"), aimed at perfecting the coherence and efficiency of a present *völkisch* community.[14]

As for the traditional three-tier German school system, this approach translated into attempts from different angles to bring Nazi ideology to bear, and produced mixed results. Structural changes remained limited. Given the absence of a comprehensive plan for change, the inertia of well-established structures made itself felt, along with the fact that the majority of teachers and ministerial bureaucrats had been trained prior to 1933. In addition, a basic tension of Nazi education policy militated against major structural changes. While its ideological priorities devalued intellectual training, the German labor market, once the depression was over in 1936, needed, not least for the purposes of rearmament, qualified graduates that only a competitive and intellectually challenging high school system could produce.[15] Nazi ideological claims were felt more broadly and effectively in other ways. In the first months after coming to power, the regime dismissed 3,000 teachers for political reasons or because they were Jewish, including a third of all female head teachers and directors. Moreover, all teachers had to fill out detailed questionnaires on their former political and social activities and affiliations. While measures, such as these, created pressure from above, many teachers welcomed the new regime and a considerable number of directors were already eager in the first months after January 1933 to exclude Jewish students from their schools beyond what the initial decrees of the regime demanded. This was "opportunism from below," as the education ministry noted. Teachers did not turn overnight into ardent Nazis but they were not likely to put up much resistance against the regime's education policy. At best, they might be willing to temper its implementation.[16]

This policy affected the practice of schooling in two ways. For one, the introduction of new symbols and rituals, such as the "German greeting" and an elaborate calendar of festivities that included new as well as traditional holidays and that was supported by the use of the new media of radio and film, were to create deep emotional bonds between students and teachers and the Nazi regime. Then, curricula were redefined to "develop and harness all physical and mental powers of youth for the service of the people and the state," as a directive of 1940 put it. One result was an increased importance of physical education, differentiated by gender, and of national sports activities that, for boys, took on a partly paramilitary character. It also meant that industrial applications for military purposes were emphasized in the teaching of physics and chemistry, or the costs of caring for the hereditary ill calculated in mathematics assignments. German became more "Germanic," as increased emphasis was placed in the curriculum on folklore and Nordic myths, just as it now included stories of the benevolent "Führer," of Nazi heroes such as the murdered Horst Wessel, and of mothers sacrificing themselves for their many children.[17] Most importantly, the new subject of "racial studies" was introduced, not to be taught separately, but to provide a guideline for all subjects and to permeate instruction on all levels in all types of schools. Hence, "Aryan" superiority was not only to be pointed out by teaching the laws of heredity and the alleged danger of "miscegenation" in biology; it was also to be given broad coverage in history, for example, and began in elementary school. Its curriculum contrasted the geographically and culturally rooted Nordic people and the wandering Jew by starting in sixth grade with the farming cultures of Nordic peoples in the Stone Age and then presenting Germans who heroically fought the Romans with their retenue of Jewish traders in the German lands. Most intense attention was given to the conflict between Germans and Jews in eighth grade, when the domestic problems of the Second Reich after 1871 were attributed to a lack of racial consciousness among German citizens and the grave mistake of granting Jews full citizenship. German renewal and a determined fight against the Jews came with the Third Reich and the Nuremberg laws of 1935.[18] This is but one example of a plethora of materials and textbooks for teachers that sought to imbue children at school with a deep-seated anti-Semitism and prepare the ground for radical measures to "solve" the "Jewish question." While most new textbooks were not available before the end of the 1930s, and while it is far from clear how teachers actually used the materials and how students responded, there is no doubt that anti-Semitism in school instruction was not limited to citing some phrases from Hitler's *Mein Kampf* in the classroom. As Gregory Paul Wegner has pointed out, what was new about anti-Semitism in German schooling during the Nazi era was not its content – a combination of traditional and more recent, "scientific" anti-Semitism – but the fact that the state now officially made it a prime goal of school instruction. Thus, school in Nazi Germany became "one of the most important instruments for the spreading of racism."[19]

This was even more true for the two new school institutions that the Nazi regime established for secondary education, the Nationalpolitische Erziehungsanstalten (NAPOLA) and the Adolf Hitler Schools (AHS). Combining paramilitary training as a boarding school experience with high school instruction, they were meant to train the future elite of Nazi Germany. While the NAPOLAs, founded by the Reich Ministry of Education and from 1936 directly controlled by the SS, had a more traditional profile as they kept an emphasis on academic achievement, the AHS, founded under the auspices of the German Labor Front and the HJ as a rival to the NAPOLAs (a typical case of competition among Nazi organizations), gave clear priority to the training of leadership qualities. By not charging any fees in contrast to its rival, the AHS also conveyed the promise of upward social mobility and had less of a middle-class profile than the NAPOLAs. Both institutions required passing a tough entrance exam and a probation period of six months. Political and ideological training was even more important than at regular schools. Physical prowess and stamina were key, students were put under enormous pressure and kicked out when they showed signs of weakness. However, NAPOLAs in particular also offered an attractive range of outdoor activities such as outings to the Alps, skiing, and gliding, as well as travelling, as students were sent abroad on exchange programs to the United States and Britain. Hence, students later remembered both the enormous physical and mental stress and the adventurous aspects of their stay at the NAPOLAs.[20] However, NAPOLAs and AHS failed to provide a real alternative to existing institutions of higher education because they did not obtain the resources to expand as planned and never comprised more than a fraction of German students completing their high school exam (*Abitur*).[21]

The core institutions for the attempt to turn young Germans into ardent followers of the regime were the HJ and its affiliate BDM, with their suborganizations. Taking up traditions of the German youth movements but gaining the monopoly to organize the young, they sought to exert decisive influence on children and youths, in competition and sometimes in conflict with family and school. This far-reaching intention stands in stark contrast to many post-war recollections of former HJ and BDM members who describe their (pre-war) years in the organizations as a time of adventure and communal experiences with no specific political character. Research in the past two decades has contributed to a more nuanced picture of the relationship between intention and reception.

Founded in 1925, the HJ remained a fairly insignificant organization until the breakthrough of the National Socialist German Workers Party (National Sozialistische Deutsche Arbeiter Partei, NSDAP) at the national election of 1930. One year later, while now comprising a membership of 35,000, it was still clearly behind the Bündische Jugend, the leading middle-class youth organization, and far behind the youth organizations of the two Christian churches and the labor movement with their hundreds of thousands of members. Led since 1931 by Baldur von Schirach (b. 1907), a would-be poet from an educated middle-class family with American ancestors, the HJ grew massively after the Nazi takeover to more than 2 million members at the end of 1933 and to 5.4 million three years later. This enormous growth was due more to massive pressure on rival organizations than to a voluntary option for the HJ. While social democratic and communist youth organizations were banned soon after the regime took power and attempts to continue them in a clandestine way were stifled by the Gestapo, the Bündische Jugend was allowed to exist until 1936, but became the target of discrimination and sometimes even murderous violence by HJ groups. Protestant youth groups had joined the HJ already in 1933 in exchange for the permission to continue their own bible lectures, but were eventually not able to preserve this remnant of their independence. Catholic youth groups, trusting in vain that they were protected by the concordat that Hitler had concluded with the Vatican, were dissolved from 1935 to 1939. In December of 1936, a law stipulated that the HJ "comprised" the whole of German youth, but only in March of 1939 did membership become compulsory for all children and youths between age ten and eighteen. In late 1933, 30.5 percent of this age group had been members of the HJ, and this figure had risen to 64 percent four years later and reached almost 100 percent in mid-1939. As the police would now enforce membership and in 1942 was even given the right to send youths refusing to join directly to special concentration camps, chances to dodge membership responsibilities were now slim, even though they did exist to some degree in big cities and in some Catholic rural areas.[22]

On the eve of the war, the HJ, along with the BDM, which was de facto under its control, had become a big organization with two faces. On the one hand, it provided leadership positions to 765,000 young males and females who were only slightly older than the members of their groups. It helped enforce protective regulations at the workplaces through their representatives in the firms, and it offered a variety of leisure activities, most notably an annual summer vacation. On the other hand, it was strictly hierarchical because all leaders were appointed from above, and it sought to shape and discipline German youths for the purposes of the regime, eventually even providing from its ranks a patrol force that was to confront deviant and rebellious youths during the war. Regular meetings every week, as well as on weekends and during school vacations, combined ideological indoctrination with a variety of activities.[23]

For male youths, physical training that was meant as a preparation for military service played a pivotal role. This was not a completely novel idea: Prussian authorities had instituted pre-military education for boys in the last years before the First World War and Weimar youth groups, in particular the Bündische Jugend, had integrated elements of military training in the activities, not least because a military draft had been banned in Germany by the Versailles Treaty. The HJ now had its members engage in small-bore shooting, marches, and other pre-military exercises such as bending knees or crawling through mud. In addition to hiking and mountain climbing, a variety of sports were practiced, such as swimming, gymnastics, soccer, and fencing, with a particular emphasis on boxing. In contrast to its precursors in Weimar Germany, however, these activities now deliberately included elements of cruelty and sadism to put the resilience of the boys to a test. HJ members also had to serve as money collectors for the "winter-help" program, which supported various social services, and, from 1934 on, were sent to farms to help bring in the harvest. A modern element of HJ instruction was the use of film. Regular screenings featured movies about heroes of the past like Frederick the Great and Bismarck and, during the war, stories of self-sacrifice and heroism. HJ members were also taught to produce documentary films about their activities.[24]

BDM training was somewhat "softer" than that of the HJ. Physical education did play an important role, but it placed its emphasis on the healthy body of the future mother. Gymnastics and exercises that centered on creating harmony between the individual and the group took precedence over fostering a spirit of competitiveness, even though this element was not absent, for example, in running and swimming activities and in national sports festivities for girls. While the latter set the BDM apart from the female youth movement of the Weimar period, its outings with campfires, theater performances, singing, dancing, and folklore undertakings were more of a continuation of Weimar traditions than HJ activities. Sports activities and outings together were to help BDM girls develop a sense of comradeship that would later allow them to be real partners and not simply child bearers for their husbands.[25] In keeping with their role as future German mothers, BDM girls were not supposed to present themselves as frivolous "vamps" and therefore not allowed to use make-up, among other things; however, the uniforms they had to wear were devised to make them appear attractive, featuring a dark blue skirt, a white blouse with a black kerchief and a leather knot. Arranging one's hair in different ways provided some limited room for individuality. To create a specific German femininity, the regime even went one step further, and in 1938 established a new organization, Glaube und Schönheit (Faith and Beauty) for young unmarried women between age seventeen and twenty-one, who had to prove "Aryan" descent, were not gainfully employed, and had to volunteer for four years. In contrast to ordinary BDM girls, they had access to more exclusive sports, such as riding and fencing, designed their own fashions, and practiced interior decoration. Both groups had to undergo ideological instruction. In addition to household work training, health education was paramount. This included being taught the alleged laws of heredity and the racist worldview of the regime.[26]

How children and youths reacted to the offers and demands of HJ and BDM is not easy to assess. Based on the findings of a number of oral history projects, Alexander von Plato has distinguished three categories of HJ and BDM members: a large group of "pragmatists and opportunists," a small group of "opponents," and a medium-sized group of "enthusiasts." The opportunity to see new regions and places through hiking trips and sports competitions and, even more so, the leveling of social barriers and chances for upward social mobility connected with good performance in the HJ were regarded as positive experiences in retrospect. Furthermore, wearing a uniform helped one to be recognized as not just a child. HJ and BDM activities were also seen as having provided opportunities for meeting members of the opposite sex in an unsupervised environment. For girls and young women in particular, the experience of assuming positions of leadership and engaging in activities no longer supervised by their families was a novel and – in part – liberating experience. It did not fully conform to the expectation of the regime, which wanted a rather passive German female, but it remained within the bounds of a polarized gender order. Social activities, such as helping on farms, in retrospect, received mixed reviews as meaningful but also as exploitative, but the main criticism focused on the constraints on one's life produced by HJ activities. Leisure time, but also time for schoolwork or an apprenticeship, was seen as partly taken up by the HJ. What oral history accounts generally fail to convey, however, is the degree of ideological influence exerted by HJ and BDM. When German writer Erich Loest, during the Nazi era a lower-level HJ leader, remembers himself as having been "enticed" and then "enticing others" without ever thinking of resistance, this may be an accurate description of how many HJ and BDM members acted and reacted.[27]

Since the Nazi regime sought comprehensively to shape the bodies and minds of German children and youths, this meant rigorous repression for some. It also implied the exclusion of those not deemed valuable for the *Volksgemeinschaft* but regarded as a burden because of mental and corporeal deficiencies or because of their "race." One major group of young people who were particularly affected by the new forms of repression and discrimination generated by this distinction were the inmates of correctional institutions. When the regime took power, authorities used this instrument of control more widely than before. It raised the number of children and youths committed to reformatories and foster care for a variety of reasons, now including male homosexuality with greater emphasis than prior to 1933, the number rising from 6,000 in 1933 to 10,000 by 1937.[28] Reformatories, traditionally run in many cases by Catholic or Protestant organizations, also had to introduce ideological instruction, along with Nazi rituals and HJ and BDM groups, and emphasize harsher discipline than prior to 1933 as corporal punishment was officially reintroduced. Under the impact of the Great Depression, welfare authorities had already begun in the final years of the Weimar Republic to exclude those inmates defined as "ineducable" from the institutions to save costs. Following the Nazi takeover, this group grew, now also including children of school age, as heads of reformatories were eager to get rid of "hopeless" cases, and the biologistic ideology of the regime seemed to provide clear criteria for exclusion. The "ineducable" were sent to workhouse-like institutions that provided only a bare minimum of education and material resources for the inmates. Those considered mentally retarded were particularly affected, and they were also the group most likely to become the target of forced sterilizations, following the Nazi law of December 1933 that was to prevent the "hereditary ill" (defined by a murky mix of moral and medical criteria) from procreating. In the Prussian province of Rhineland alone, after comprehensive examinations, more than 1,200 inmates of correctional institutions (i.e. almost 6 percent of all inmates) became victims of this brutal procedure.[29]

Nazi racism created or increased discrimination against those children and youths not considered "Aryan." Children born to African-French occupation soldiers and German mothers in the 1920s, the so-called "Rhenish bastards," were registered by the authorities, 145 in Prussia, and in 1937, after being examined by a committee of physicians, sterilized.[30] The main target group of discrimination and persecution were Jews. As early as February 1933, Prussian (and, a year later, German) minister of education Bernhard Rust publicly declared his intention to remove all Jewish children from German state schools. Given that attending elementary school was mandatory for all children, and also for fear of foreign policy repercussions, the regime leadership hesitated to immediately take such a radical step at this level of the school system. Removing Jewish students from high schools began early because these were not mandatory. A law against the "overcrowding" of high schools and universities in April 1933 stipulated a ceiling of 1.5 percent for newly accepted Jewish high school students in relation to all students for one individual school. This came also in reaction to pressure from below, e.g. from the city council of Brunswick, which had called for limiting the share of Jewish students even further ten days before the law was promulgated. The complete exclusion of all Jewish children from state schools came in the wake of the pogrom of November 1938, and in line with general radicalization of the persecution of the Jews. Many other legal measures, in dry bureaucratic language that could hardly conceal their vicious intentions, had earlier aimed at making conditions at school miserable and humiliating for Jewish children. A decree for the high schools of the city of Berlin, already promulgated as early as May 1933 prohibited the reduction of fees for (talented) Jewish students; Bavaria excluded them from participating in summer camps in 1935; the state of Baden no longer allowed Jewish students to earn special recognitions for good grades in the same year. In addition, teachers contributed their part in the discrimination against Jewish students, by placing them on special seats, overlooking their raised hands, or describing their allegedly inferior features in front of their classmates in order to humiliate them. Many students left under the pressure – by the end of 1937, only 40 percent of Jewish school students were in state schools, as opposed to 75 percent in 1933[31] – and attended the schools of a growing but underfunded Jewish school system, which against all odds tried to maintain a decent academic level. True, teachers might also temper the prescribed racism by only reading from the book phrases about "Aryan" superiority, and other classmates might not break off contact.[32] Still, no non-Jewish German child who attended school with Jewish classmates at the time could escape the notion that school had become a different place, a place of officially sanctioned meanness and ostracism against a group of children singled out by the regime.

After the beginning of the war in 1939, the Nazi regime radicalized its policy towards children and youths. It placed even more emphasis on ideological indoctrination, attempted to eliminate any form of opposition, and drew an even more rigorous line between mainstream and marginal children and youths, with murderous consequences for the latter. The killings of the "euthanasia" program included not only many children who were inmates of psychiatric institutions along with adults there, but also targeted newborn children anywhere with severe mental and corporeal handicaps. Medical personnel all over the country had to report them and mislead the parents by pretending their children were transferred to special clinics for care.[33] Children of Sinti and Roma, who had already been subject to various forms of discrimination prior to the war and were excluded from attending German schools in 1941, were deported with their families to the Lodz ghetto and labor camps in Poland in 1940, and starting in 1942 sent to Auschwitz.[34] The deportations of German Jews to the East and its extermination camps began in October 1941, one month after all Jews over the age of six had been forced to wear the "yellow star," and children and youths were not spared. Only 2,583 students at Jewish schools were left in June 1942 (out of 6,742 eight months earlier), when all remaining schools were closed down by the regime.[35]

Mainstream state schools came under heightened ideological pressure. Remaining institutional challenges to Nazi ideology were removed in 1941, when the regime, against parents' protests, closed down private Catholic high schools and made elementary schools non-denominational.[36] While the quality of schooling deteriorated because teachers were drafted and extra-curricular activities, such as helping farmers with their harvest, took up time, militaristic and anti-Semitic propaganda was stepped up, the latter in particular after Stalingrad, when a new curriculum included manifold "evidence" for a Jewish conspiracy against Germany.[37]

Hitler Youth leader von Schirach attempted to gain decisive influence on schooling, with limited success, by establishing the program of Kinderlandverschickung (child evacuation to the countryside) in the fall of 1940. Meant as temporary relief (as was its counterpart in Britain where children were removed to safer locations), but also as an instrument to weaken the influence of parents and teachers, children from age six to fourteen who lived in the cities targeted by Allied bombing were to be sent to camps in the countryside where they would continue to be taught by teachers, but also undergo HJ and BDM training. Parents, however, on whose voluntary consent Hitler insisted for fear of unrest, often declined to send their children, even as the bombing war became worse, not least because the officially stated limit of the stay of six months was extended by local authorities at their discretion. All in all, close to two million children participated, a third or less of those eligible, and after 1945 reported primarily negative experiences of military-like camps with a much degraded education.[38]

Increased regime pressure, not least the now mandatory character of the Hitler Youth, as well as the war and the persecution of the Jews, resulted in various forms of resistance by young people against the regime. Small groups that had attempted to continue the tradition of the banned youth organizations in clandestine form had been discovered and destroyed by the Gestapo prior to the war. Now, explicit political resistance by young people was rare. Its most prominent example was the "White Rose" group in Munich (1942–1943), whose members came from middle-class families and were already students when they began their activities. Their key figures were Hans (b. 1918) and Sophie Scholl (b. 1921), who had risen to junior leadership positions in the Hitler Youth and the BDM before their initial enthusiasm waned under the impact of the militarism and racism of the regime and by what they learned about the conduct of the war. Driven to resistance by Christian motives and liberal traditions of the banned Bündische Jugend, the group produced and secretly distributed six subsequent leaflets calling for a new Germany built on humanistic traditions and placed in a new democratic Europe. Caught by accident, several members, including Hans and Sophie Scholl, were executed in the spring of 1943. The "Swing Youth" in Hamburg and in other big German cities such as Berlin and Frankfurt, also middle class and getting into trouble not for explicit political views but for their lifestyle, came into conflict with the regime because they openly displayed their rejection of the role models provided by HJ and BDM. Male members wore their hair long and sported English blazers, while females used make-up and nail polish and dressed like the American film stars who, until the end of 1941, could still be seen on screen. Meeting in particular bars or in private homes, they listened to American swing music and were sexually promiscuous, even with Jewish partners. Authorities began moving against the "Swing Youth" in early 1940 and destroyed its groups by 1942–1943. While these middle-class youths tried their best to simply ignore the HJ, groups of proletarian youths, who loathed the conformity imposed by the now compulsory organization, did not shy away from violent confrontations with the HJ. Continuing a tradition of resistance against attempts by authorities to intervene in proletarian subcultures, male members of these "wild cliques," as many of them were called, wore their own outfits, often including elements and insignia of the banned Bündische Jugend but also resembling American "zoot suits." They carried knives as symbols of their masculinity, which came in handy when HJ patrols entered their home turfs. Some "wild cliques" had contacts with communist cells, most notably in Cologne, where a small group of "edelweiss pirates" supported communist resistance fighters in acts of sabotage such as derailing train cars and the killing of a Nazi official. Most of their members, however, were not totally opposed to the regime but shared its ideology in part, emphasizing male superiority and, in some cases, even volunteering for the *Waffen-SS*.[39]

The Nazi regime reacted to all forms of deviant behavior and outright resistance with increased repression. Criminals between age sixteen and eighteen from 1939 onwards could be treated like adults and even sentenced to death, and the age for being liable to criminal prosecution was lowered to twelve. Having obtained the right to target deviant youths between age sixteen and twenty-one directly, the SS in August 1940 opened a special internment camp for boys in Moringen near Göttingen and two years later another one for girls close to the Ravensbrück concentration camp. Resembling ordinary concentration camps more than traditional reformatories, these camps subjected their inmates, about 1,400 young males and 1,000 females, to brutal and exploitative slave labor. At least 56 died, many were later transferred to psychiatric institutions and regular concentration camps.[40]

For mainstream children and youths, the HJ turned ever more strongly into an institution preparing young males for fighting in war, and having quite a few of them actually serve in auxiliary military functions and, finally, in actual combat. Large numbers of BDM members also left their homes to support the war effort in various capacities. From the summer of 1942, Hitler Youth between age sixteen and eighteen had to take part in military training camps during the summer – more than half a million in 1943 – and in 1944, those over age fifteen also had to join them. This additional service, interfering with other summer activities or an apprenticeship, rather decreased regime loyalty. But another new service for young males, introduced as the defeat at Stalingrad and an increasingly devastating Allied bombing campaign caused the need to tap any manpower available for military purposes, had ambivalent effects. Male high school students between age fifteen and seventeen, (and from the end of 1944 also including apprentices), altogether 200,000 by 1945, were deployed as "Flakhelfer" (auxiliary anti-aircraft gunners) to anti-aircraft batteries around the big cities, where they were supposed to continue receiving school instruction. This soon proved to be largely illusionary because Flakhelfer had to perform strenuous work and suffered from exhaustion and fear, given the dangers they were facing, which left hundreds dead and thousands wounded. And yet, being a Flakhelfer meant wearing a uniform similar to that of an air-force soldier, except for the HJ insignia. As those could be hidden with some dexterity, however, this allowed a Flakhelfer to pass for a real soldier and attend movies reserved for adults, go to bars late in the evening, and smoke and drink in public. Flakhelfer thus, in a sense, shortened their adolescence, even though their status vis-à-vis HJ leaders and their parents remained somewhat ambiguous.

While training in the military education camps and as Flakhelfer (along with ideological instruction at school and activities in the HJ) instilled and maintained a sense of duty, it only turned a fairly limited number of Hitler Youth into ardent fanatics. Recruitment efforts by the *Waffen-SS*, undertaken with increased pressure starting in 1942, also met with limited success due to the rough behavior of SS recruitment officers and the fear of being sent to particularly dangerous places of combat. Its main result was the formation of the tank division HJ that comprised 20,000 HJ members and saw action soon after the Allied invasion close to Caen. While its members fought hard, also committing war crimes such as shooting British and Canadian

POWs, losses were horrendous. Only 600 were able to leave the Falaise pocket and escape the destruction of the division.[41]

For BDM members, the beginning of the war now meant being drafted to the Labor Service once they turned seventeen. While for male Germans this had been a familiar experience since 1935, placed as they were between HJ and military service, for girls this was a break with BDM routines because they were now forced to wear blue collar clothing and get used to long working hours. Starting in October 1941, a Kriegshilfsdienst (war auxiliary service) of six months was added, typically meaning work in an armament factory. In addition, over 10,000 BDM members were sent to occupied areas in Poland, where they were to support ethnic Germans, take on attitudes of colonizers, and participate in violence against Poles. Moreover, beginning in 1940 a total of half a million BDM members volunteered as Wehrmachtshelferinnen (military auxiliaries) in a variety of functions, some serving eventually even as Flakhelfer and others being directly confronted with violence and death especially on the Eastern front. This was a very ambivalent experience for these girls and young women between age sixteen and twenty-six. On the one hand, they were performing work important for sustaining the German war effort at places far away from home, and they gained self-confidence and had unprecedented opportunities for sexual encounters. On the other hand, they could also become easy prey of male soldiers and superiors and were to suffer under military violence and as victims of rape in the final phase of the war.[42] As Franka Maubach has recently argued, on balance this cannot be considered an emancipatory experience but rather a temporary enhancement of the female self that was intricately linked to brutal German expansion policy.[43] Directly linked to the apparatus of repression and persecution were the 3,000 BDM members who were hired by the SS, quite a few of whom became guards in the concentration and extermination camps and showed that sadistic violence was not a male monopoly.[44]

Individual life stories from the final phase of the war demonstrate how contrary the fates of "Aryan" and "non-Aryan" German children and youths had become, even though they were now all possibly facing death. By the time fifteen-year-old Anne Frank, at the end of a long odyssey from Frankfurt to Amsterdam to Auschwitz and back to Germany, died of typhus in the living hell of the Bergen-Belsen concentration camp, hundreds of HJ boys of the same age, who had been drafted into the makeshift military formation of Volkssturm, were killed in battles with Russian troops in Königsberg, Prague, or Berlin.[45] Thirteen-year-old Ruth Klüger survived the deportation from Vienna to Theresienstadt, Auschwitz and Groß Rosen and, having escaped from a death march, met American soldiers in Bavaria where she finally knew that she was now safe. At the same time, future journalist Lothar Loewe, just turned sixteen, having tenaciously fought in his hometown Berlin against the Russian onslaught, was taken prisoner and, to his utmost astonishment, was lent a mess gear by a Russian soldier, an incident that thoroughly shattered the stereotype of Slavish brutality Loewe had once held.[46] The chances of survival for so-called "Aryan" and Jewish children and youths were hardly even, however. While there are no exact figures available for each group, the basic difference is obvious. One hundred and sixty thousand Jews, i.e. about a third of those who had been living in Germany in 1933, died as victims of the persecution by the regime. Only about 15,000 survived the deportations and the death camps. The share of children and youths among those Jews who were still living in Germany when deportations began was already lower than in 1933. Between 1933 and 1939, it had already been reduced by more than a third,[47] as about 18,000 children and youths had been rescued by being sent abroad unaccompanied – up to 8,000 of them to Britain, another 4,800 to Palestine, and about 600 to the United States. Children were much less likely to survive the death camps than adults.[48] In contrast, 5.3 million German soldiers and, in the course of Allied bombardments and the Russian advance in the East, about one million German civilians lost their lives during the war, i.e. about 9 percent of the country's pre-war population. Most likely to die were not children and youths of "Aryan" Germans, but somewhat older males serving as soldiers, primarily those born between 1920 and 1925, of whom 40 percent lost their lives.[49]

Death and violence were ubiquitous at the end of the war and hardly any of the surviving children and youths remained unscathed. But describing them as collectively traumatized would be going too far and would gloss over crucial differences between the causes of their losses and wounds.[50] While all children and youths who survived the war and the Holocaust may have matured faster, those who had been drilled and indoctrinated in the HJ and BDM did not eventually stand out for their fanaticism (there was only a small number of "werewolves," who heeded the regime's call for acts of sabotage and terror against the Allied occupiers) but for their pronounced sense of duty, which kept many of them fighting till the very end.[51] Total defeat brought thorough disillusionment with Hitler and basic tenets of Nazi ideology, but it did not destroy the self-reliance the young had acquired in the preceding years. While the hardships of the immediate post-war years strengthened the family, fathers – if they were present at all – did not wield unquestioned authority but had to prove that they were able to accommodate the needs of all family members, including the young.[52] As children and youths made vital contributions to post-war family survival, the *habitus* of self-discipline and sense of duty they had internalized during the Nazi years was now, under very different circumstances redefined and oriented in different ideological directions, to build up the West German "achievement society" after the late 1940s as well as the new Socialist paradise on the other side of the Iron Curtain. It also did not prevent a cultural Americanization from taking hold among the young over the course of the 1950s in West and, to some extent, also in East Germany. German children and youths – those who were not excluded from the *Volksgemeinschaft* and interned or killed – became more complex personalities under the Nazi regime than Schaffner suggested in 1948. While they did follow orders, they did so not simply as obedient subjects, but also as assertive youngsters who, on account of the new opportunities the regime had provided for them, had gained a very ambivalent and insecure self-confidence that combined liberating elements with chauvinism and racism.

I would like to thank Franka Maubach for her critical comments and Lena Freitag and Anja Thuns for their help in completing this essay.

Notes

1 Bertram Schaffner, *Father Land. A Study of Authoritarianism in the German Family* (New York, NY: Columbia University Press, 1948), 5–66, the quotes 5, 43, 48; cf. Max

Horkheimer, ed., *Studien über Autorität und Familie. Forschungsberichte aus dem Institut für Sozialforschung* (Paris, France: Félix Alcan, 1936); Theodor W. Adorno et al., *The Authoritarian Personality, Studies in Prejudice Series, Vol. I.* (New York, NY: Harper & Row, 1950).

2 On this latter point, see Andrew Donson, *Youth in the Fatherless Land. War Pedagogy, Nationalism, and Authority in Germany, 1914–1918* (Cambridge, MA: Harvard University Press, 2010).

3 Michelle Mouton, *From Nurturing the Nation to Purifying the Volk. Weimar and Nazi Family Policy* (Cambridge, MA: Cambridge University Press, 2007), 48–68, 124–139, 151f.; Lisa Pine, *Nazi Family Policy, 1933–1945* (Oxford, UK: Berg, 1997), 95–116, the figure on the four-children families 116. On birthrates: Dietmar Petzina, Werner Abelshause, and Anselm Faust, *Sozialgeschichtliches Arbeitsbuch. Vol. III: Materialien zur Statistik des Deutschen Reiches, 1914–1945* (Munich, Germany: Beck, 1979), 32.

4 Mouton, *Nurturing*, 212–235.

5 Miriam Gebhardt, *Die Angst vor dem kindlichen Tyrannen. Eine Geschichte der Erziehung im 20. Jahrhundert* (Munich, Germany: Deutsche Verlagsanstalt, 2009), 79–81. When this book was introduced and how many copies of it were distributed is not clear.

6 Gregor Dill, *Nationalsozialistische Säuglingspflege. Eine frühe Erziehung zum Massenmenschen* (Stuttgart, Germany: Enke, 1999); Sigrid Chamberlain, *Adolf Hitler, die deutsche Mutter und ihr erstes Kind. Über zwei NS-Erziehungsbücher* 4th ed. (Gießen, Germany: Psychosozial-Verlag, 2003).

7 Gebhardt, *Angst*, 76–94.

8 Schaffner, *Father Land*, 45f.

9 Johanna Haarer, *Die deutsche Mutter und ihr erstes Kind* (Munich, Germany: J.F. Lehmanns, 1941 [1934]), 271.

10 Gebhardt, *Angst*, 109 ("freuten sich unbändig," translation by author).

11 Ibid., 106–118. The more rigid approach to childrearing seems to have triggered conflicts with grandparents.

12 Adolf Hitler, *Mein Kampf* 780–784th ed. (Munich, Germany: Franz Eher, 1942), 451 ("ein wertvolles Glied für die spätere Weitervermehrung," translation by author).

13 Wolfgang Keim, *Erziehung unter der Nazi-Diktatur. vol. 1: Antidemokratische Potentiale, Machtantritt und Machtdurchsetzung* (Darmstadt, Germany: Wissenschaftliche Buchgesellschaft, 1995), 15–18; Harald Scholtz, *Erziehung und Unterricht unterm Hakenkreuz* (Göttingen, Germany: Vandenhoeck & Ruprecht, 1985), 15.

14 Dieter Langewiesche and Heinz-Elmar Tenorth, "Einleitung," in *Handbuch der deutschen Bildungsgeschichte, vol. V: 1918–1945. Die Weimarer Republik und die nationalsozialistische Diktatur*, ibid., eds. (Munich, Germany: C.H. Beck,1989), 1–24, here 13f.; Heinz-Elmar Tenorth, "Pädagogisches Denken," in: ibid., 111–153, here 140–147; Heinz-Elmar Tenorth, "Erziehungsutopien zwischen Weimarer Republik und Drittem Reich," in *Utopie und politische Herrschaft im Europa der Zwischenkriegszeit*, ed. Wolfgang Hardtwig (Munich, Germany: Oldenbourg, 2003), 175–198, here 180–198.

15 Bernd Zymek, "Schulen," in *Handbuch*, vol. V, eds. Langewiesche/Tenorth, 155–208, here 190–197; Wolfgang Keim, *Erziehung unter der Nazi-Diktatur. vol. 2: Kriegsvorbereitung, Krieg und Holocaust* (Darmstad, Germany: Wissenschaftliche Buchgesellschaft, 1997), 34–40.

16 Keim, *Erziehung*, vol.1, 97–110, the quote 84; vol. 2, 48–52; Zymek, *Schule*, 192.

17 Lisa Pine, *Education in Nazi Germany* (Oxford, UK: Berg, 2010), 41–56, 61–65, the quote 41.

18 Gregory Paul Wegner, *Anti-Semitism and Schooling under the Third Reich* (New York, NY: Routledge Falmer, 2002), 29–156, the curriculum example 138; cf. Pine, *Education*, 57–58.

19 Wegner, *Anti-Semitism*, 182–187 and passim; Keim, *Erziehung*, vol. 2, 95–104, the quote 104 (translation by author).
20 Harald Scholtz, *Nationalsozialistische Ausleseschulen. Internatsschulen als Herrschaftsmittel des Führerstaates* (Göttingen, Germany: Vandenhoeck & Ruprecht, 1975); Keim, *Erziehung*, vol. 2, 105–113; Pine, *Education*, 71–83. Three NAPOLAs for girls, established after the Austrian *Anschluss* of 1938, never really took off the ground because it was not clear to what extent they were to train future qualified personnel or elite mothers.
21 According to Christian Schneider, Cordelia Stillke, and Bernd Leineweber, *Das Erbe der NAPOLA. Versuch einer Generationengeschichte des Nationalsozialismus* (Hamburg, Germany: Hamburger Edition, 1996), 45; NAPOLA graduates comprised only 1.5 percent of all German high school graduates. For the AHS, the figure was even lower (cf. Michael H. Kater, *Hitler Youth* (Cambridge, MA: Harvard University Press, 2006), 48).
22 Kater, *Hitler Youth*, 15–28; cf. Keim, *Erziehung*, vol. 1, 126.
23 Winfried Speitkamp, *Jugend in der Neuzeit. Deutschland vom 16. bis 20. Jahrhundert* (Göttingen, Germany: Vandenhoeck & Ruprecht, 1998), 222f.
24 Kater, *Hitler Youth*, 30–34; Pine, *Education*, 104–107.
25 Dagmar Reese, "Kamerad unter Kameraden. Weiblichkeitskonstruktionen im Bund Deutscher Mädel während des Krieges," in *Die BDM-Generation. Weibliche Jugendliche in Deutschland und Österreich während des Nationalsozialismus*, ibid., ed., (Berlin, Germany: Verlag für Berlin–Brandenburg, 2007), 215–253.
26 Kater, *Hitler Youth*, 73–84; Pine, *Education*, 119–129; Dagmar Reese, *Straff, aber nicht stramm – herb, aber nicht derb. Zur Vergesellschaftung von Mädchen durch den Bund Deutscher Mädel im sozialkulturellen Vergleich zweier Milieus* (Weinheim, Germany: Beltz, 1989).
27 Alexander von Plato, "The Hitler Youth Generation and Its Role in the Two Post-War German States," in *Generations in Conflict. Youth Revolt and Generation Formation in Germany 1770–1968*, ed. Mark Roseman, (Cambridge, UK: Cambridge University Press, 2003), 210–226; Dagmar Reese, "The BDM Generation. A Female Generation in Transition from Dictatorship to Democracy," in ibid., 227–246; Pine, *Education*, 107.
28 Edward Ross Dickinson, *The Politics of German Child Welfare from the Empire to the Federal Republic* (Cambridge, MA: Harvard University Press, 1996), 213; Sven Steinacker, *Der Staat als Erzieher. Jugendpolitik und Jugendfürsorge im Rheinland vom Kaiserreich bis zum Ende des Nazismus* (Stuttgart, Germany: Ibid., 2007), 700–829, in particular 704; cf. Gerhard Rempel, *Hitler's Children: the Hitler Youth and the SS* (Chapel Hill, NC: University of North Carolina Press, 1989), 50–53.
29 Steinacker, *Staat*, 640–643, 781–797.
30 Reiner Pommerin, *"Sterilisierung der Rheinlandbastarde." Das Schicksal einer farbigen deutschen Minderheit 1918–1937* (Düsseldorf, Germany: Droste, 1979), in particular 44–84. The actual number of those sterilized is not known.
31 Wolf Gruner, *Die Verfolgung und Ermordung der europäischen Juden durch das nationalsozialistische Deutschland 1933–1945. Vol. 1: Deutsches Reich, 1933–1937* (Munich, Germany: Oldenbourg, 2008), 41.
32 Ruth Röcher, *Die jüdische Schule im nationalsozialistischen Deutschland, 1933–1942* (Frankfurt, Germany: Dipa, 1992), in particular 33–70; Keim, *Erziehung*, vol. 1, 103f.; vol. 2, 48–52; cf. Pine, *Education*, 30.
33 Hans-Walter Schmuhl, *Rassenhygiene, Nationalsozialismus, Euthanasie. Von der Verhütung zur Vernichtung "lebensunwerten Lebens", 1890–1945* (Göttingen, Germany: Vandenhoeck & Ruprecht, 1987), 182–189.
34 Michael Zimmermann, *Rassenutopie und Genozid. Die nationalsozialistische "Lösung der Zigeunerfrage"* (Hamburg, Germany: Christians, 1996). More than 13,000 Sinti and Roma

perished in Auschwitz-Birkenau, the exact number of children among them is not known (ibid., 343); Pine, *Education*, 30.

35 Röcher, *Jüdische Schule*, 51; Moshe Zimmermann, *Deutsche gegen Deutsche. Das Schicksal der Juden 1938–1945* (Berlin, Germany: Aufbau, 2008), 92–125, in particular 124f.

36 Zymek, *Schule*, 200f.; Wilhelm Damberg, *Der Kampf um die Schulen in Westfalen, 1933–1945* (Mainz, Germany: Matthias-Grünewald, 1986), 232–253.

37 Keim, *Erziehung*, vol. 2, 137–142; Nicholas Stargardt, *Witnesses of War. Children's Lives under the Nazis* (London, UK: Cape, 2005), 253f.

38 Kock, *Kinderlandverschickung*, the figures 11, 141f.; Keim, *Erziehung*, vol. 2, 153–160.

39 Kater, *Hitler Youth*, 115–148; Stargardt, *Witnesses*, 245f., 265, 73f.; Wolfgang Ayaß, *"Asoziale" im Nationalsozialismus* (Stuttgart, Germany: Klett-Cotta, 1995), 180–184; Arno Klönne, *Jugend im Dritten Reich* (Cologne, Germany: Diederichs, 1982), 228–282; Alfons Kenkmann, *Wilde Jugend. Lebenswelt großstädtischer Jugendlicher zwischen Weltwirtschaftskrise, Nationalsozialismus und Währungsreform* (Essen, Germany: Klartext, 1996), especially 255–259.

40 Kater, *Hitler Youth*, 151–166; Patrick Wagner, *Volksgemeinschaft ohne Verbrecher. Konzeptionen und Praxis der Kriminalpolizei in der Zeit der Weimarer Republik und des Nationalsozialismus* (Hamburg, Germany: Christians, 1996), 376–379.

41 Kater, *Hitler Youth*, 196–215; Stargardt, *Witnesses*, 231–234; Rempel, *Hitler's Children*, 188f., 200–203.

42 Kater, *Hitler Youth*, 231–246; Jill Stephenson, "Der Arbeitsdienst für die weibliche Jugend," in Reese, ed., *BDM-Generation*, 255–288; Elizabeth Harvey, *Women and the Nazi East. Agents and Witnesses of Germanization* (New Haven, CT: Yale University Press, 2003), in particular 93–99; Franka Maubach, *Die Stellung halten. Kriegserfahrungen und Lebensgeschichten von Wehrmachthelferinnen* (Göttingen, Germany: Vandenhoeck & Ruprecht, 2009).

43 Maubach, *Stellung*, 311f.

44 Kater, *Hitler Youth*, 246.

45 Eberhard Kolb, *Bergen-Belsen. Geschichte des "Aufenthaltslagers" 1943–1945*, 6th ed. (Göttingen, Germany: Vandenhoeck & Ruprecht, 2002), 40; Kater, *Hitler Youth*, 219–223; Rempel, *Hitler's Children*, 235–243.

46 Ruth Klüger, *Weiter Leben. Eine Jugend* (Munich, Germany: dtv, 1994), 170–191; Stargardt, *Witnesses*, 315f.

47 According to Wolfgang Benz, ed., *Die Juden in Deutschland 1933–1934. Leben unter nationalsozialistischer Herrschaft* (Munich, Germany: Beck, 1988), Appendix, 734, the share of Jews (defined by faith) between age 0 and 20 was 21.5 percent in 1933 and had fallen to 13.5 percent by 1939.

48 Ino Arndt and Heinz Boberach, "Deutsches Reich," in *Dimension des Völkermords. Die Zahl der jüdischen Opfer des Nationalsozialismus*, ed. Wolfgang Benz, (Munich, Germany: Oldenbourg, 1991), 52, 64; Inge Hansen-Schaberg, "Kindheit und Jugend," in *Handbuch der deutschsprachigen Emigration, 1933–1945*, eds. Claus-Dieter Krohn et al., (Darmstadt, Germany: Wissenschaftliche Buchgesellschaft, 1998), 81f.; Gerhard Sonnert and Gerard Holton, *What Happened to the Children Who Fled Nazi Persecution* (New York, NY: Palgrave Macmillan, 2006), 55–57; Zeev W. Mankowitz, *Life between Memory and Hope: The Survivors of the Holocaust in Occupied Germany* (Cambridge, UK: Cambridge University Press, 2002), 19.

49 Ian Kershaw, *The End. Hitler's Germany 1944–45 (London, UK: Allan Lane, 2011)*, 279f; cf. Hans-Ulrich Wehler, *Deutsche Gesellschaftsgeschichte. Vol. 4: Vom Beginn des Ersten Weltkriegs bis zur Gründung der beiden deutschen Staaten 1914–1949* (Munich, Germany: Beck, 2003), 942–944.

50 Emphasized by Stargardt, *Witnesses*, 9f., 371f.

51 Ibid., 12–15.
52 Barbara Willenbacher, "Zerrüttung und Bewährung der Nachkriegs-Familie," in *Von Stalin-grad zur Währungsreform. Zur Sozialgeschichte des Umbruchs in Deutschland, 3rd ed.*, eds. Martin Broszat, Klaus-Dietmar Henke, and Hans Woller (Munich, Germany: Oldenbourg, 1990), 595–618, in particular 612–614; Rolf Schörken, *Jugend 1945. Politisches Denken und Lebensgeschichte* (Opladen, Germany: Leske & Budrich, 1990), 145–147.

Suggestions for further reading

While the experience of German youths under the Nazi regime has been covered fairly well, that of young children has received much less attention. Michelle Mouton, *From Nurtur-ing the Nation to Purifying the Volk: Weimar and Nazi Family Policy* (Cambridge, MA: Cambridge University Press, 2007) emphasizes the agency of mainstream families in dealing with Nazi family policy against the older focus on the all-powerful state. Miriam Gebhardt, *Die Angst vor dem kindlichen Tyrannen. Eine Geschichte der Erziehung im 20. Jahrhundert* (Munich, Germany: Deutsche Verlagsanstalt, 2009) shows, against older accounts, how the interplay of control and affection in the early childhood education contributed to the mak-ing of Nazi subjects. Lisa Pine, *Education in Nazi Germany* (Oxford, UK: Berg, 2010) is a solid overview of Nazi education policy and also covers HJ and BDM. Wolfgang Keim, *Erziehung unter der Nazi-Diktatur, 2 vols.* (Darmstadt, Germany: Wissenschaftliche Buchgesellschaft, 1995/1997) provides a more comprehensive, if in part oddly structured, dis-cussion of the German education system under the Nazi regime, and also includes the Jewish school system, which is examined in greater detail by Ruth Röcher, *Die jüdische Schule im nationalsozialistischen Deutschland, 1933–1942* (Frankfurt, Germany: Dipa, 1992).

Children and youths in correctional institutions have found greater interest only in recent years. A good introduction is provided in Edward Ross Dickinson, *The Politics of German Child Welfare from the Empire to the Federal Republic* (Cambridge, MA: Harvard University Press, 1996). The best, if lengthy, recent study is Sven Steinacker, *Der Staat als Erzieher. Jugendpoli-tik und Jugendfürsorge im Rheinland vom Kaiserreich bis zum Ende des Nazismus* (Stuttgart, Germany: Ibidem, 2007). Michael Kater, *Hitler Youth* (Cambridge, MA: Harvard Univer-sity Press, 2006) is the best introduction to the history of HJ and BDM and the wartime experience of mainstream German youth as well as to the various forms of dissent and resistance.

Thoughtful assessments of the effects of membership in HJ and BDM are provided by the essays of Dagmar Reese and Alexander von Plato in Mark Roseman, ed., *Generations in Con-flict. Youth Revolt and Generation Formation in Germany 1770–1968* (Cambridge, MA: Cambridge University Press, 2003). Gerhard Rempel, *Hitler's Children: the Hitler Youth and the SS* (Chapel Hill, NC: University of North Carolina Press, 1989) explores (and somewhat overemphasizes) the various forms of contact and cooperation between SS and HJ. Nicholas Stargardt, *Witnesses of War: Children's Lives under the Nazis* (London, UK: Cape, 2005) provides a well-documented and moving account of the wide variety of children's experi-ences during the war, discussing both mainstream children and those who became victims of repression, persecution, and murder.

26

INTERNATIONAL CHILD SAVING

Dominique Marshall

Introduction

Why do children become an object of international concern? How has the sense of responsibility felt by societies from one part of the globe for "saving" the children of another evolved? The history of international child saving needs to be placed in many contexts, and told along many themes. Children in the abstract have often been the symbols of international campaigns of rescue. In particular, the idea of childhood often represents a powerful means of persuasion to gather public support and legitimacy. It does so in ways that often obscure the history of the actions and beliefs of the actual children involved. In other cases, where specific groups of children have become a cause for international protection, we need to examine the principles and motivations that underlie sympathy across borders, as well as the methods employed and the people involved. Children themselves have frequently played a role in shaping campaigns, institutions, and outcomes of international child saving.

This essay will address all these variations. It will examine the changing division of responsibilities between private and public institutions and the moving scales of actions of child saving, especially the mutual influence between domestic and international movements. Finally, the essay looks at the changing and unstable nature of the humanitarian public to explain the central place of children, and at the transformative role international child saving has exerted on other institutions. I will follow traditions of practices and beliefs from the nineteenth-century evangelical movements, through international intergovernmental organizations, the birth of major child relief agencies and international children's rights, to the humanitarian dilemmas of the present day.

Child saving before the First World War

Christian churches and charities of all denominations have collected money among their believers to save children in foreign lands since the beginning of colonial encounters. Missions devoted to religious conversion, a goal that is often assumed in the very use of the word "saving," have aimed much of their work and resources at children's education, welfare, and spiritual initiation. This attention came from the belief that children were especially vulnerable and less attached to the traditions of their surroundings, and from the fact that it was easier to underline the personal relations between donor and recipient, when the recipient was a child.

In early modern times, the Jesuits established that working with the adults of the future in a systematic fashion could have far-reaching consequences for the

Christianization of a people. The methods they brought back first from China, then from America and India, were potent enough to inform domestic campaigns of rechristianization of European countrysides, the "other India," in a way that inaugurated a recurrent flow of methods between home and away. Schools, hospitals, and orphanages catered to the isolated child, a symbol of poverty and backwardness. Children's identity with the figure of the child Jesus helped charitable campaigns, and it was easier to raise money among Christian parishioners when the souls of children were at stake, because it was harder to accuse them of being responsible for their own misfortune. Missionaries paid particular attention to children at home in their capacity as good contributors and fundraisers. The greater chance of convincing children of the importance of charitable work during their frequent stays in schools and churches, the strength and simplicity of their beliefs less hampered by responsibilities, and the availability of their time all militated in favor of children as collectors of money.

If the possibility of converting those who were seen as less civilized was always an object of debate, the familiar figure of foreign children often helped convince Europeans that members of indigenous populations had souls, and that they were equal to the proselytes before God. The work of missionaries abroad often served as a service to commercial and colonial enterprises. From the 1870s to the 1960s, for instance, the Canadian Government counted on Catholic and Protestant missionaries to give aboriginal children compulsory education and work training in a network of up to 80 "residential schools" that assimilated them to white society at a cheap price, away from aboriginal parents and communities who were not seen to be fit to raise proper citizens. Native political leaders' critiques, the protest of children and parents against the degradation of their culture, the exhausting physical demands, the poor quality of instruction, and western authorities' acknowledgement of the cost of such enterprise in child saving, forced the institutions to close, starting at the end of the 1960s. Similarly, during the movements for decolonization of the second half of the twentieth century, religious institutions and their staffs have often been treated as the emblems and agents of capitalism and cultural domination: after its foundation in 1949, for instance, the People's Republic of China witnessed a campaign to expel the nuns who controlled Catholic orphanages, which were depicted as the agents of American cultural imperialism.[1]

But this was more than a matter of superior missionaries helping lacking people. The picture becomes complicated when the large number of native missionaries is considered, as well as the large part local revenues occupied in the budget of missions abroad. Moreover, the stereotype, then as now, tended to underestimate what Henrietta Harrison, a historian of French missions in China, calls "the unspoken similarities" between the failings of the missionaries' own societies and those of the societies they helped, and to overestimate the "imagined differences."[2] Such was the case of the Catholic campaigns of the Holy Childhood Association, under the guidance of which, from 1843 and for a century after, thousands of European and North American children under 12 contributed monthly towards the baptism and rescue of Chinese children, as well as toward orphanages for them.

Finally, the very constitution of scientific disciplines devoted to the study of childhood bears the mark of these early missionary child-saving efforts. Several ethnological works, conducted by missionaries, fostered a critical look at European practices of child rearing. The Jesuits' depictions of the trust and love American aboriginals gave to their children, published in Europe during the seventeenth century, might have played a crucial role in the transformation of ideas about childhood.[3] By 1931, several missionaries, gathered in Geneva for the Conference on the African Child, underlined the positive aspects of native cultures of parenting and criticized the deleterious effect of European systems of acculturation and economic exploitation on child raising.

International child saving was also directly marked during the nineteenth century by the increase of public responsibility for health, welfare, and education as part of the changing history of state responsibilities. The movement, which can be traced to the Enlightenment, is understood as a product of enlarged ideas of citizenship, with the accompanying rights and responsibilities of individuals, and as the product of the concomitant changes in the nature of political rule, from the strict defense of sovereignty to the administration of national populations. As a result of such transformations, the perceived immaturity of aboriginal people became a mainstay of colonial rhetoric. The trusteeship of the British Empire and the civilizing mission of the French colonial enterprise spoke of natives, young and adults alike, as children. It is as if, within empires and denominations, the language of family responsibility offered the best way to talk about people at once equal before God or state and incapable of having public authority. It was also likely that in imperial countries that were becoming more democratic, saving children became a means to justify foreign possessions to the voting public.[4]

In this same colonial context, the movements to protect aboriginal children and to abolish slavery bear much responsibility for shaping the form, discourses, and techniques of international child saving, and providing its early personnel: such was the case of the British philanthropists Henry, Victoria, and Charles Roden Buxton, who helped found the Lord Mayor's Armenian Relief Fund and the Save the Children Fund in 1916 and 1919, respectively. They were members of the family of the prominent anti-slavery campaigner of the first half of the nineteenth century, Sir Thomas Buxton. The indictment of bondage intersected with the question of childhood in many ways. The cruelty and blindness of the institution of slavery was nowhere more visible than when associated with childhood, and the very vulnerability and innocence that had made children targets of colonial endeavors could turn against the legitimacy of the same enterprises. When in the 1900s the Congo Reform Association denounced the forced labor imposed in rubber plantations by the Belgian monarch, images of atrocities committed against children figured prominently.[5] Historians of such movements now insist on the role of native communities themselves in the abolition of institutions of subjection. For a history of childhood, it becomes important, then, to underline the significant role slave and native children played in the abolition of slavery and trusteeship, as well as the importance of aboriginal parents' concern for their children amongst their motivations for freedom.[6] With the exception of ecumenical movements and the Quakers, the anti-slavery movement and the missionary endeavors represented hierarchical forms of international child saving, largely informed by imperial prejudices. Universal commitments to all children were still a fact of the future.

Philanthropy and imperialism also decided the fate of some 130,000 children who were sent from the homes of the urban poor in Britain to rural families in the

Dominions of the British Empire. An important chapter in the movement of assisted emigration of the poor, which began in 1618 and culminated at the turn of the twentieth century, it often concerned children who, like the inmates of orphanages everywhere, had families who cared for them without having the means to support them close by. The history of their later fate varies, from utter deprivation to success stories, and the rightfulness of such charitable method was debated from the start. By the mid-twentieth century, new standards of welfare, added to the demands of British workers and returning soldiers for the rights of the children of their class to remain with their families and be at school, succeeded in putting an end to the movement of what was known as the "Home Children." Many of their descendants have struggled to remember this history, underline the abuse of many, and obtain public apologies. They have joined historians to show the cost and the dangers of such disruptions in countries of origins and destinations.[7]

From the mid-nineteenth century, the rise of professions devoted to children, including jurists and doctors, and later social workers, social scientists, psychologists, and public health nurses, occurred together with these political changes. Campaigns to save children in countries of Europe and North America were soon influencing each other, thanks not only to an array of means of exchange, from international congresses and associations to professional journals, international legal libraries, internships abroad, and tours,[8] but also to the increasing problem of the welfare of foreign children, in an uneven and contentious process of "internationalization of social policies" studied by Joelle Droux. Dangerous classes alarmed the richer members of urban communities; besides, their plight, in their extreme manifestations, contradicted uncomfortably the promises of liberal economic developments, and jarred with the romantic sensibilities of the second half of the nineteenth century.

Women activists figured prominently beside and among reformers and professionals, invested as they were in their identity as public guardians of the fate of children, an extension of their domestic roles, and a basis from which to demand leverage in diplomatic encounters. Their claims to responsibility for the children of other countries varied, as they did for their charitable work at home, from the frequent condescension of mothers to the occasional sisterhood of equal citizens. Such was the case of the Maori and western members of the New Zealand delegations at the Pan Pacific Women's Association meetings from its foundation in 1928;[9] and, still in 1974, it was the UN Commission on the Status of Women that piloted the Declaration on the Protection of Women and Children in Emergency and Armed Conflict. In international work of welfare, as well as in work within borders, the notion of "saving" is often gendered: a masculine version concerning rapid and drastic operations of removal and rescue cohabits with a feminine version associated with longer term and less spectacular activities of care.[10] Young peoples' organizations also joined the international child savers, chiefly under the aegis of the Young Men's Christian Association (YMCA), an ecumenical and lay project which spread across the western world, and which was aimed at the recreation, welfare, and safety of young people. The work of the YMCA across borders was recognized by an international alliance starting in 1855, and it is of note that the future founder of the Red Cross, the Swiss Henry Dunant, started his humanitarian activities under these auspices.

Jurists pioneered in the building of transnational techniques, and the concurrent elaboration of a universalistic idiom of children's rights was inspired by their respective national traditions.[11] In their wake, doctors and public hygienists founded a variety of networks, alliances partly based on the transnational nature of diseases and natural disasters and encouraged by the advances of medical knowledge necessary to save young lives. The term child "saving" is also imbued with this notion of rescuing children from lethal diseases. Based in Brussels, where the ambition to become the humanitarian capital of the world thrived before the First World War, early movements of child welfare federated doctors and reformists, gathered knowledge from the world, and sent advice to interested states and organizations. Motivating these exchanges were the autonomous wishes of legal and medical experts to solidify their expertise and legitimacy by adopting neutral and international claims. The universalism of their respective knowledge and practices was related to the growing belief in a language of universal entitlements. Their stance helped understand better the actual problems of children left outside national jurisdiction. In addition, the very migrations of doctors and reformists, especially from Germany, helped such transnational exchanges.[12]

A similar movement occurred concerning the uses of child labor, carried at once by middle-class reformists, by the labor movement and, at times, by poor peoples' movements for whom the control of the work of the young was often a premier demand. The internationalization of child saving in this context occurred not only for the strength it provided to its protagonists, but also because international regulations would counter the argument of international competition coming from employers. As early as in 1901, the predecessors of the International Labor Office made the regulation of child labor a priority.

The most publicized campaigns of child saving of the nineteenth century concerned what was called, in its time, "white slavery" or the sexual trafficking of white children.[13] The traffic of women and children was the object of a convention in the early years of the twentieth century and of international congresses. It received a permanent headquarters in Paris. Added to this concern was that of the international standards for age of consent to marriage of girls. Less visible, but devoted to a larger contingent of young people, were movements to regulate the nationality of children born of parents from different countries, orphaned by war, born in states which ceased to exist in the large redrawing of the political map of Europe at the turn of the twentieth century, or those displaced by conflict, migration, or poverty.

As a result, on the eve of the First World War, there were treaties between nations concerning child labor, child migrations, and the trafficking of children. Children had thus entered the world of official diplomacy, a phenomenon that would increase over the subsequent decades.

International child saving during the First World War

The situation of children in times of war acted as a catalyst for many internationalist ventures in the years to come. At a time of high patriotism, when charity was better left for one's own community, humanitarian sentiments expressed themselves most acutely in the sympathy toward wounded soldiers, of the kind that had been at the core of Red Cross activities since 1863. The fate of child victims of the war occupied the center of patriotic rhetoric, for example when French girls were raped by German soldiers or when children were born of these rapes.

In this polarized context, and for long after, sympathy towards enemy children would often serve as a way to oppose the war. Pioneering in this realm was the work Emily Hobhouse had started, during the Boer War of 1900–1903. Inspired by religious and liberal conviction, as well as the belief in the betterment of the status of women, she launched a campaign to support Boer women and child victims of British imprisonment in concentration camps. She urged supporters to send funds, volunteer in the theater of war, and mount a political campaign against the "cruel system." As her actions unfolded, a movement, born to maintain the morality of the British Empire, led many of its founders to become critics of the whole colonial enterprise. What distinguished such activities of international child saving from its predecessors and contemporaries was the idea that international collaboration towards child saving would encourage peace, and the rights of the children, rather than their belonging to a faith or an empire, offered the moral basis for relief.

Hobhouse would devote the same energy to help women and children of Austria and Germany during the First World War and in Central Europe in the immediate aftermath of the conflict. Her ambition converged with that of many humanitarians during the conflict, who often found themselves writing, traveling, and working together. The British Quakers, who had supported Hobhouse's work in South Africa, for instance, also became involved in the relief of civilians and soldiers on European battlefields, often in collaboration with the French and the British Red Cross. The non-violence of their creed explains the moral nature of Quakers' motivations. Their history of exclusion from mainstream professions and their subsequent involvement in business also underlie the organizational skills they would bring, time and again, to the conduct of child saving.

Founded in 1915, the Women's International League for Peace and Freedom (WILPF) worked in the same direction, identifying women's activism not only with children's advocacy but also with pacifism. The relief activities undertaken during the Boer War continued during the First World War in the form of a Rubber Teats Fund for Austrian and German Babies. The group's decision to divide such humanitarian activities from their political work would become an important element in the creation of the Save the Children Fund.

While the United States was still neutral, the relief of children of occupied countries of Europe became its largest point of mobilization for the home front. Led by Herbert Hoover, the "Great Humanitarian," the Committee for Belgian Relief distributed unprecedented quantities of food. The American mining engineer and future President, who came from a Quaker background, had originally been asked to help American nationals evacuate Belgium, but after the occupation of the country by Germany, his operation extended to all civilians. It came to involve a large number of local Belgian charities, as well as young American men, many of them Hoover's fellow students, and it is interesting how, in such cases, child saving could easily be understood as a masculine and muscular effort. There were also large numbers of civilians helping from their homes in North America; recent immigrants and political leaders in exile from occupied European countries eager to help their own; charitable women and children; or organized workers' sympathetic to the fate of a country that, like the United States, had proclaimed its neutrality. Aimed initially at all civilians, Hoover's initiatives quickly focused on children, a way to convince the German occupier and the American public of the neutrality of the relief.

With the entry of the United States into the conflict in 1917, the work of child saving ceased to be neutral. Hoover's endeavors became a branch of the American Government, and extended to other populations caught in theaters of war. They became undistinguishable from the mainstream of international child saving of other populations at war, which had already become a matter of patriotism. The ideal of non-alignment present in many humanitarian histories, and the image of children often associated with it, all receded considerably. Even the Quakers could no longer help in areas beyond allied control. Soldiers on all sides were fighting in the name of their own children and those of their allies, national Red Cross Societies became auxiliaries of the armies of their respective countries, and civilian populations were enrolled in charitable work destined only to war-stricken peoples in friendly countries. Children, once again, figured prominently, not only amongst recipients, but also as a substantial proportion of the volunteer staff of war charities: they raised money, recycled and economized goods, and replaced adults in the production of food. Pictures of children holding tins and singing songs are found in many archives of wartime; amongst them, one portrait of black children in French Africa collecting money for the soldiers of Europe stands as a reminder of the overwhelming power of patriotism, even in the colonialized world.

The immediate aftermath of the First World War

The war over, those committed to child welfare abroad saw their public support dwindle, despite the extraordinary need for resources to rebuild institutions and ensure a minimum of well-being to civilian populations – a measure of how much international child saving had been motivated by patriotism. True to this state of affairs, when it came to help the costly work of reconstruction in the theaters of war, fundraisers continued to use the language of war, invoking the humanity of their soldiers and the eternal gratitude of allied civilians. Impressed by the strength of home fronts, and still under the shock of the extent of ill health uncovered by military recruiters, public authorities turned to domestic institutions. In Canada, for example, the government founded the Canadian Council of Child Welfare to federate the efforts of private charities and social work across the country.

Nevertheless, the immediate aftermath of the war era represents a high point in the history of international child saving. On June 28, 1919, a week after the signing of the treaty of peace, the first group of foreign civilians to enter Germany was a gathering of British and American Quakers, together with Jane Addams, the American pioneer of social work and delegate to the WILPF; they had the blessing and assistance of Herbert Hoover, who had himself been central to the peace negotiations over food allocations. All wanted to assess the need of the vanquished population and organize relief operations. The Quakers were now eager to prove their lack of partisanship. To the newer humanitarians, the Friends' presence and their long tradition acted as a guarantee of neutrality, and their special appeal on behalf of children pointed at a future without hatred: at the back of the cards issued to children eligible to their meals, a message described the charitable offering as "a greeting of Friendship from America" distributed by the Quakers "who have, for 250 years, and during the several years of war just ended, maintained that only service and love, and not war and hatred, can bring peace and happiness to mankind."[14] Once again, children belied their image as victims: in famine-stricken Vienna, American and European relief workers counted to a large extent on the work of local children in order to manage their vast operations of feeding and clothing the population.[15]

From the date of its creation in 1919, the Save the Children Fund (SCF) based its techniques on those of the half-a-century-old International Committee of the Red Cross, wishing to do for children, as its founder Eglantyne Jebb wrote, what the Red Cross had accomplished for wounded and captive soldiers. A branch of the Fight the Famine Council, intent on ending the blockade imposed on the vanquished populations of Europe in the month between the armistice and peace, the SCF took over the relief activities of the WILPF. Two sisters, Dorothy and Eglantyne Jebb, had been translating dispatches from the enemies during the war for the *Cambridge Magazine* to foster understanding between civilians of nations at war. Amongst them were reports on the plight of starving children in Vienna, written by doctors affiliated with the Red Cross. In order to avoid being associated with one religion and one nationality, Eglantyne inaugurated an international organization in Geneva in 1920, the Save the Children International Union (SCIU), to draw upon existing private networks and encourage new ones. Within a few months, they were joined by *Rada Barnen* (RB), as Save the Children was called in Sweden, where their pacifist feminist friends of the earliest hour found an outlet for their activism. RB also benefitted from the support of Swedish politicians willing to establish a legitimate presence in the post-war world, despite their absence from the conflict.

In an effort to keep up with the rising leverage of the league of all national Red Cross Societies, the ICRC redirected the resources and personnel of its highly praised International Prisoners-of-War Agency into peacetime work with children. The popularity of the cause of children, first within the British working class and then amongst the Catholics of Europe invited by the Pope to assist the SCIU (in an effort to restore a reputation of neutrality blemished by the war), confirmed many war relief workers' belief that collaboration to save the young could become the main vector of international work for peace.

At the end of 1919, Hoover himself embarked on a solely private venture – an activity first centered in Poland, then in Russia – the European Children Fund (ECF). With demobilization and the return to private energies and donors, came a tighter focus on children, not only because their fate could better move donors abroad, but also because the cruelty of withdrawal, at a time when European populations were in dire need, appeared at its most scandalous when children were concerned. The ECF took over the remaining equipment of the American Government's war food agency and raised $30 million from private American donors. By 1919, films, newspaper advertisements, and public meetings showed how epidemics and disease added to the problems of reconstructing war-torn places; among the donors, once again, was a large contingent of recent immigrants to the United States from these very lands. Historians estimate the number of children helped was more than ten million, and the qualitative impact on the shape of institutions of public and private systems of child welfare of Eastern Europe was long lasting. In Poland for instance, the impoverishment and dispersal of the Jewish people due to the war rendered the care of orphans, previously based on the charity of local and wealthy elites, impossible; the intervention of German and US donors made for the adoption of practices of social medicine and organized bureaucracies.[16]

The motivations of this unprecedented humanitarian movement of goods and volunteers have been the object of many studies. Beside the convenience of an outlet for American surpluses of cereals, which would create changes in European diets, was the fear that vulnerable populations would become enemies of the West. SCF joined in, contributing a fifth of the effort, in war-devastated Poland and in Russia, where the consequences of the recent revolution and famines perpetuated hardship long into the 1920s. They were joined in Poland by a number of religious and lay charities, the Red Cross among them, and by local volunteers, whose actions are less often remembered, as is still the case with local actions in humanitarian crises. The varied operation was marked by the presence of American military personnel and manners, by the jealousies of different organizations, and by the inability, and often unwillingness, of those who came to help to make sense of the larger implications of their intervention on local needs.

As for the SCF, the large flow of donations from Britain and its dominions was sustained by the publicists of the organization, who downplayed the fact that contributions might help feed former enemies. As Emily Baughan has shown, they managed to reconcile national pride with international child saving, at the cost of the radical internationalism of many if its founders. Inspired by the missionary and anti-slavery propaganda of the nineteenth century, humanitarian images of neutral and suffering children protected by one's nation comforted the popular idea of the superior morality of a civilized empire, this time in a secular context. In 1919, in the midst of the Russian Civil War, American Red Cross officials imbued not only with a sense of urgency but also with the idea that they could teach Russians the ways of progress, guided hundreds of children away from Moscow and Petrograd, where food was scarce, to Western Siberia, with the consent of their parents. Some of these "Children of the Urals" were trapped by war and winter despite the help of teachers, local officials, and nurses. Others followed their American benefactors, and the vicissitudes of the conflict brought some as far as California and New York; some of these later returned home three years after their departure, a story of heroism which has resurfaced in a post-Soviet world hungry for tales of collaboration with the West.[17] In the meantime, relief workers observed how Russian children subverted humanitarians' strict policies of child feeding by smuggling food outside of the large kitchens in order to sustain other members of their respective families.

Child saving in the interwar years and the League of Nations

From the inception of the League of Nations in 1921, humanitarians in charge of large mass feeding and rescue operations asked the new intergovernmental organization for resources in order to coordinate relief efforts in post-war Europe. The Red Cross, Hoover, and the SCF all received praise for their work of relief, which added a universal legitimacy to their work. But the League provided no insurance of material and institutional support for future campaigns of international assistance. Member states refused to commit resources away from national sovereign bodies; the same powers had denied a membership in the League to defeated countries, to the Soviet Union, and to territories under colonial rule.

Not surprisingly, the League's direct humanitarian actions would take place in mandated territories, where the absence of sovereignty allowed a freer hand. It is in this context that the rescue of thousands of Armenian and Greek children from Turkey to Syria and Greece took place. In addition, the League of Nations and humanitarian agencies cooperated in saving children who were made refugees by the war. In the face of the new size of the population of refugees, international solutions to save children became more systematic and comprehensive. The Scandinavian explorer and humanitarian Fridjoff Nansen lent his name and resources not only to large operations of mass feeding through the Red Cross and the International Russian Relief Executive, but also to relief and political representation in favor of displaced civilians. Appointed High Commissioner for Refugees by the League of Nations, he planned vast operations of return or, for those who had no safe home to go back to, uneasy schemes of resettlement. The respective virtues of each of these strategies for the well-being of unaccompanied children and of families are still debated today. Children figured noticeably in the priorities of this variety of international rescue, by their number, and because those amongst them who had no parents presented an obvious case for international responsibility. Despite these successes, the campaigns of the Save the Children movement toward a convention for the protection of foreign minors failed. This was partly because of the lack of public funds during the Great Depression of the 1930s, and partly because statesmen feared that policies for the welfare of foreign children would inevitably lead to policies for the welfare of their relatives, who were foreign adults and did not receive enough sympathy in the signatory countries.

Hoover's efforts in Eastern Europe were short lived, and his operations folded by 1924. Aware of the incompleteness of his contribution abroad, he chose to redirect the resources and energies of a decade of child saving toward the young of the United States. With his support, existing national movements for children's health were rejuvenated, and the American Public Health Association embarked on an extraordinary decade of voluntary campaigns. The Save the Children movement faced a similar fall in its popular support: the Canadian chapter closed down after the campaign toward refugee children in Greece ended, and in Britain its domestic activities increased in the face of mounting criticism for its lack of concern for children at home. Similarly, once post-war efforts to muster public support for children of the devastated countries of Europe dwindled, the League of Red Cross Societies opted officially in 1921 for a program of public health, aimed at the children of the country of each national society. The international mission of the movement remained in the form of articles and films about children abroad, or pen friendship programs between young members. In such programs conducted in the name of children and internationalism, the difficult questions of neutrality, of the workings of international peace, and of the democratization of diplomatic relations were avoided; moreover, children were enlisted in international activities of child saving upon which they exerted little control.[18]

In this context, the fact that the League of Nations accepted formal responsibility for child saving came from another direction – a resurgence of the pre-war efforts to gather existing knowledge across borders, share practices, and standardize existing institutions. The Covenant of the new intergovernmental organization offered an umbrella to existing international agencies devoted to social problems, with the belief that cooperation in times of peace would help overcome or heal animosities that led to wars. The history of its employees and international correspondence shows that the work of international child saving was becoming increasingly professionalized.

The scientific and democratic ideal was that experts, in child welfare as in other domains, would use the very objectivity of their knowledge to better the lives of young people. The question of the welfare of all children proved harder to finance than that of traffic, and much more difficult to coordinate than it had been in times of war. The Child Welfare Committee, which met every year for a month, was composed of national delegates of selected countries acquainted with the subject, together with private "assessors," a motley collection of advocates of child welfare widely dissimilar in their motivations and traditions. The French Léonie Chaptal, a conservative pioneer of public nursing and member of a prominent Catholic family, and the British Katharine Furse, the head of the international movement of Girl Guides and former nurse in the British Ambulance Service, sat beside the pacifist and feminist American social worker Jane Addams, her compatriot and champion of juvenile delinquents Julia Lathrop, and the co-founder of the SCF, Eglantyne Jebb. Among the new permanent staff were women who found in Geneva a way out of the impasses of the public job market in their respective countries, as well as people trained in youth politics, such as the Canadian Mary McGeachy, a pivotal member of the Information Section.[19]

Convincing people and politicians to give resources and institutional support in favor of children of other lands in times of peace proved hard. In such context, the language of universal children's rights seemed to offer hope for cooperation. The WILPF and the SCIU drafted their respective declarations in the early 1920s, which established the moral foundations of international child saving: social, economic, and civic entitlements for children regardless of their nationality, creed, or race. The General Assembly of the League of Nations of 1924 adopted unanimously the resulting draft, a Declaration of the Rights of the Child; one of the five articles further affirmed the primacy of child saving: "The child must be the first to receive relief in times of distress." In addition, the fifth article of the Declaration concerned young people's participation in public life, which the authors mainly understood in the limited sense of work collecting money and learning about other countries.

From then on, the main work of the Child Welfare Committee consisted of the establishment of standards of childcare, the legal status of "home children," cinema for children, juvenile delinquency, the treatment of illegitimate children, and placement in foster families. The League made significant inroads into internationalizing child welfare concerns, and several aspects of its machinery continued under the UN, especially in the constitution of UNICEF as we will see later. But in general, as Droux has demonstrated, the Committee's recommendations, such as the adoption of juvenile courts by all member states, exerted little influence on member states' legislation.

Those, like Eglantyne Jebb, who yearned for practical advances, were frustrated by the slow rhythm of this new order of international exchanges. However, the reports on children as well as the large inventories of the League, by their universal wish to include all territories, imposed a measure of visibility and accountability to colonial powers; they also offered a way for new states to establish their international presence and, at times, made for better institutions at home.[20] Similarly, the Declaration of the Rights of the Child acted in several instances as a trigger to reform domestic and international institutions of child saving. In Canada, one schoolteacher took upon herself to tour her rural district in Alberta to measure the extent to which each of the five articles had been implemented. Her paper describing the results was widely published and shamed Canadian authorities.

In Geneva, the Declaration served as the launching pad of an international Conference on the African Child in 1931, which gathered hundreds of participants, including a dozen young Black African leaders. Among those who came to Geneva were critics of empire from North and South, several of whom were soon to fight for the independence of their countries, and saw in this idiom a way to speak against the dislocating impact of European enterprises on the continent. At the same time, they learned much about the establishment of universal institutions of welfare and education and a path to full citizenship. Too many universal promises to Africans remained unfulfilled, and the attention to children a device to delay the future entitlements for adult citizens. To be sure, SCF officials had not abandoned ideas of western superiority altogether because they still considered the achievements of norms of child welfare as the very sign of what they called the progress of civilization.

In the meantime, private philanthropic organizations provided the main means to conduct work of relief abroad, and the SCIU helped new central European states to build public institutions of child welfare. Together with women's groups, they also militated against extremes of child subjugation, such as the Mui-Tsai in the East, a form of bonded labor.[21] During that period, the Save the Children movement continued to pioneer techniques of gathering support and funds from the public: with the use of photo cards, first for Russian refugee children and for Ethiopian children, a system of virtual adoption was born. This strategy represents the strength of private organizations and their ability to foster a sense of personal relation between donors and recipients. The SCIU attempted to turn its energies to field work in Africa. It took an international conflict for the fundraisers to muster enough resources. The first, short-lived, lay humanitarian experience on the continent was launched in 1935: a child welfare center in Addis Ababa for the children of the soldiers of the Italian–Ethiopian war.

Interest in Ethiopia soon took a back seat in western publics behind the fate of Spanish children after the start of the Civil War in 1936. In this polarized world, those relief workers for children in Spain, who were committed to neutrality, found it impossible to help the Nationalists and Republicans at the same time. The Quakers withdrew, and the SCF remained, despite this infringement on their doctrine of non-partisanship. A large evacuation scheme of the children living in the areas of civilian mass bombardment from both sides was launched, involving France, Britain, the Soviet Union, Italy, Germany and Portugal. Only with the promise of a short stay away from Spain, of siblings being kept together, and children being accompanied by teachers and priests, did the parents agree to the separation. In Britain, the sponsors of the 4,000 young evacuees were an amalgam of private concerns, from the SCF to trade unions, who were surprised by how politicized the youngsters were who replayed battles on the beaches near their encampments because this contradicted the image of neutrality promised by humanitarian propaganda. The children were left with mixed feelings, as their memoirs attest, between a devoted gratitude to rich benefactors, the pain of a long separation from their families, and resentment towards the Spanish Government for those who returned to a hostile country. The evacuees who stayed long enough in Britain, or forever, played an active part in the struggle to be accepted away from home, either by participating enthusiastically in the fundraising exhibitions of Basque singing and dancing organized by adults, or by taking seriously their responsibility for their younger siblings and, for some, by squarely beating richer English boys in friendly football matches.[22] These mixed results led the Save the Children movement to question the very idea of evacuation, and their 1938 guidelines for the protection of children in times of war argued for the maintenance of families as a whole or, in case of blanket bombings, shelters to which families could move together. International child savers of the Spanish Civil War also became pioneers in the psychological treatment of traumatized children. They noted, for instance, how difficult and important it was for distressed victims of civilian bombings to recapture some trust in the country from which they came. Their lessons would later serve to help young victims of the Holocaust and of the nuclear bombardments of Japan, and, more lastingly, autistic children.

In the USSR, 3,000 Spanish children endangered by the Civil War were welcomed by the State, surrounded by ideals of international brotherhood, and treated like local orphans, in disregard of promises of respect for their culture made to their parents. They were trapped in the host society by the victory of Franco and the indifference of the Soviet public during the late 1930s.[23] The Workers International Relief (Red Aid) also established schools and helped orphanages in Spain. In general, as political philosophers Michael Hardt and Antonio Negri write, the history of communist ventures in international child saving is of a different nature, the internationalism of socialist and communist parties being a matter of solidarity rather than charity, related as it is to national fights for workers' liberation.[24] In 1931, an international campaign on behalf of the eight black "Scottsboro boys" wrongly convicted for the rape of two white girls in Alabama showed how European communists could successfully muster humanitarian interest for children in foreign lands, in the name of such international brotherhood. However, they did so at the cost of having to downplay the radical nature of their egalitarianism, not unlike the pacifists of the Save the Children movement.[25]

International child saving, national socialism, the Second World War and its aftermath

A history of international child saving should not obscure the millions of children killed and wounded in the events leading up to the Second World War and during the conflict itself – 300,000 for Yugoslavia alone. Nor should it hide the fact that the main efforts to rescue children, as in most cases documented in this article, were by local populations largely bereft of the means to do so. As early as 1933, Jewish organizations planned for the transfer to Palestine of German Jewish young people aged fifteen to seventeen, victims of Nazi policies, where a scheme of training and work awaited them. Most subsequent efforts to save Jewish children from the exterminations of the Holocaust were the fruit of Jewish efforts. From November 1938 to September 1939, led by the Central British Fund for German Jewry, now World Jewish Relief, the "Kindertransports" also relied on non-Jewish foster families, hostels, and farms run by Jewish youths. A change in British immigration laws, and British funds, allowed the sending of 10,000 children from Nazi areas to the United Kingdom. The object of much commemoration today, and of the Oscar-winning documentary "Into the Arms of Strangers" (2000), the movement to rescue Jewish children is also remembered for its failures: the end of public resources after the outbreak of the war; the refusal of the Canadian Government to answer the appeal of British authorities despite their emphasis on the despair of Jewish parents; and the United States' reluctant welcome of "one thousand children" from 1934 to 1945, including the opposition of a majority of Congress to the 1939 bill to admit 20,000 Jewish refugee children. The effectiveness of such international mobilization of Jewish solidarity can be traced to the Damascus Affair of 1840, when modern means were put to work to save eight Jewish men falsely accused of killing a Christian monk. Of equal importance is the history of the *Alliance Israélite Universelle* based in France, which, from 1860, established a network of schools for Jewish children of Muslim lands in order to "civilize" them, and that of the modernizing Jewish welfare societies for orphans in the Russian Empire, which received funds from western Jewish relief institutions such as the Paris and London-based Jewish Colonization Association (1891–1978).[26]

Also during the Second World War, more than 16,000 British children were sent by their parents overseas to be protected from German aerial attacks and an eventual invasion – 2,664 of them by the government's Children's Overseas Reception Board (CORB), and the rest through private organizations. That 200,000 parents applied to the CORB shows the extent of the popularity of this international form of child saving. Most of those 1,500 who went to Canada were hosted by parents or sympathetic families, a testimony to the strength of commonwealth and family solidarity.[27]

Starting in 1939, efforts to succor children in conflict areas proved even more arduous than a quarter century earlier. When Herbert Hoover attempted to renew his program of feeding children in occupied territories, he was denied permission by the Allied leaders, Churchill and Roosevelt. The imperatives of a "total war" commanded that civilians under enemy rule be left unaided until the country fell. Then, however, the apparatus of relief that awaited the freed population had gained in organization and state support, fueled by the work of many employees determined not to repeat the disarray of 1918. From November 1943 until the end of 1946, the United Nations Relief and Rehabilitation Administration (UNRRA) prepared for the relief of seven million displaced persons by overseeing the management of camps, organizing the return or the relocation of refugees, and contributing to the reorganization of public health and farming in devastated areas. This included China, where UNRRA estimated that more than half of the school children had suffered from malnutrition during the Japanese occupation. At its peak, the agency employed 25,000 workers, mainly financed by the United States; one of its six special branches was devoted to children. In 1946, its documentary film, "Seed of Destiny" warned Western audiences that the starved children of today could become the Hitlers of tomorrow; it raised $200,000,000 for relief and won an Oscar.[28] Beginning in September 1945, the "German Red Cross refugee relief organization – investigation service – central tracing file" recorded children without families and missing civilians in order to reunite displaced persons.[29]

The closing of UNRRA's operation mirrors that of the American Relief Agency at the end of the Great War: popular support in the West helped humanitarians to convince reluctant UN member states to transfer the remaining resources and personnel of UNRRA to a permanent agency, UNICEF. At its head was Maurice Pate, one of

Hoover's oldest companions, and it remains to this day the UN agency that receives the most donations from the public. The Universal Declaration of Human Rights of 1948 bears the mark of this activity, guaranteeing childhood "special care and assistance" (art. 25) and establishing the family as "the natural and fundamental group unit of society ... entitled to protection by society and the State" (art. 16, 3). In 1959, the UN Declaration of the Rights of the Child of 1959 affirmed more explicitly the commitment of states towards the welfare of the young. Besides, in 1949, the Geneva Convention relative to the Protection of Civilian Persons in Time of War, which consecrated international child savers' efforts to condemn total wars, was a document monitored by the International Committee of the Red Cross, and strengthened 25 years later by the UN "Declaration on the Protection of Women and Children in Emergency and Armed Conflict."

Under the aegis of the early institutions of the United Nations and of an increasing number of non-governmental organizations (NGOs) of a humanitarian nature, much of international child saving turned to the developing world. The history of Oxfam, at first a British organization devoted, like the SCF of 1919, to overcoming blockades in order to "Fight the Famine," is exemplary of this shift, first to the reconstruction of war-torn Europe, then, from the end of the 1950s, to areas of famine in the whole world. In 1946, Herbert Hoover, himself on return from an international mission to assess the post-war world's need for food, emphasized the need to think about Africa and Asia. Child savers moved easily from public to private ventures, and after independences, many dismissed employees of colonial institutions found in the new international humanitarianism a place where their knowledge and skills would be of use. The first operations of reconnaissance of UNICEF in Africa frequently counted on missionary knowledge and infrastructure.

The UN launched ad hoc campaigns, which were highly popular: World Refugee Year in 1959–60, the Freedom from Hunger Movement in 1963, and the Decade of Development from 1961. Diplomats and relief workers from South Asia and Africa were pivotal in effecting the shift to the South. In the meantime, the large organizations of women and humanitarians that had laid the foundations of international child saving half a century earlier, opened their structures to members from the South. In the context of these transformations, many NGOs reviewed the dominating nature of their practices critically. One prime target of such criticism was the practice of isolating children from their local, family, and cultural contexts, as well as the lack of knowledge about the South amongst northern populations.

The operations of UNRRA and of the International Refugee Organization in its wake, on behalf of the "lost children" of the Second World War, had already shown how international hopes for child saving could weaken when children were taken as "national patrimony": children fathered abroad by servicemen and their mothers were treated harshly, and recovering countries competed for orphans to bolster their demography and economy.[30] The Cold War presented further difficulties of the same nature. International commitments to human rights were halted, and the adoption of the conventions, which were intended to give strength to the Universal Declaration, jeopardized. The SCG followed the British Government uncritically in its work of relief during the Korean War, and the neutrality of Oxfam's impact in occupied Cambodia at the turn of the 1980s was under question. Moreover, from the early 1960s, the new governmental agencies of technical aid to developing countries, US

Aid above all, subjected humanitarian energies to political projects, along the lines of Cold War alliances. In the new Communist China, saving the children of Christian orphanages became one major symbol of national unity against imperialism. Stories of child-eating nuns, testimonies of orphans and of their cheated families, expositions of hundreds of bones, and mass protests combined to vilify this long-lived institution, especially during the Korean War, at a time when the communist government needed to bolster national spirit against the United States.

Recent problems in historical perspective

After the Second World War, the sheer magnitude of the loss of child life informed the gathering of diplomats who, in 1949, adopted an international convention to protect civilians in wartime, under the aegis of the ICRC. However, the international form of this agreement made for problems that culminated during the Nigerian Civil War of 1967–1968. The image of starving Biafran children, held hostage by the Nigerian Government's armed violence, and the withholding of relief became the symbol of this impasse, and the beginning of a humanitarianism ready to ignore the will of national governments. The question of the protection of civilians reached new heights in the wake of the Rwanda Genocide of 1994. The large number of orphans now acts as a potent reminder of the atrocity. The UN doctrine of the "Responsibility to Protect" has further questioned the respect for borders in time of humanitarian crisis by supporting the "humanitarian intervention" of armies.

Protracted conflicts, frequently within borders, and in the poorer regions of the world, have made for situations of endemic brutality for large concentrations of displaced persons in camps, which last much longer today than their mid-twentieth century predecessors. The fate of children brought up in such environments is one of the main concerns of recent humanitarian international child saving, especially questions regarding their sexual safety, and the problems raised by child soldiers. Again, the powerful images of children in arms and cases of sexual exploitation of the young have mobilized international child saviors and donors. They highlight the problematic nature of the enshrinement, according to the UN Convention of the Rights of the Child of 1989, of the age of eighteen as the end of childhood; at the tension (in the same convention) between the new and heralded promotion of children's agency and the protection of children's innocence; and of childhood as a discrete, and longer time in the lifecycle. The professionalization of international child saving has led to the construction of bureaucracies whose pace and self-interest, at times, impede the flexibility and innovation often necessary for humanitarian tasks, problems far larger today than those which had already made Eglantyne Jebb impatient in 1924.[31]

It is not easy to make sense of the multiplication of NGOs devoted to international child saving in historical perspective. The fact that many of these new agencies are founded on religious affiliation goes against any simple idea of the secularization of charity. To a certain extent, this growth is also a mark of the disengagement of state resources from social policies and international relations. In this light, and in view of the difficult question of the public accountability of NGOs, the general idea of a democratization of international relations, which has often taken the welfare of children as its goal, also needs to be qualified.

Most new faith-based NGOs, like their predecessors, have learned to deal with children as a specific segment of population to be saved, and as an object of discourse to legitimize their activity and frame their fundraising drives. Many non-Christian religions, Islamic or Hindu, have increasingly based their proselytizing activities on the Christian precedent. This is the case of Muslim relief organizations that thrived in the wake of the Afghanistan War, and of older cross-border charities from the Muslim world, especially those of the Aga Khan foundation network (founded in 1967, and based in Geneva), which all rely on the Islamic tradition of care for orphans. In 2009, Islamic Relief, located in Britain and founded in 1984, cared for 4,000 orphans in more than ten countries. Orphans figure prominently amongst most Muslim charities, which answer precise calls from the Prophet on behalf of children dispossessed by displacement, conflict or poverty, and ensure that other adults educate them in the faith. This is also the case of Buddhist organizations, amongst which the Taiwanese based Tzu Chi ("Compassionate Relief") Foundation, created in 1966 initially for domestic charitable, medical and humanistic purposes, figures prominently. Originating mainly from Asia and directed towards 70 countries, its current volunteers and doctors work on behalf of thousands of South African AIDS orphans, and its scholarships for poor children of mainland China exemplify the goals of helping all, regardless of religion or politics.[32]

Another prominent contemporary issue concerns international commitments to child "saving" within rich countries. The problem of aboriginal children is not new: in the early 1960s, Oxfam Canada had upset domestic donors and public authorities by directing some funds to northern communities inside the country. But the reliance of aboriginal communities on international organizations to attract the attention of donors and citizens beyond borders to the plight of their young has become more systematic. The other group is that of ill-treated children of rich families, to the well-being of whom UNICEF now devotes regular reports.

Half a century after the end of colonial empires, the asymmetric nature of international child saving is still debated. More disturbingly, a focus on child saving can contribute to perpetuate inequalities. The programs of child-sponsorship of the evangelical venture World Vision reached 30,000 children in Zimbabwe alone in 1996. Using the unifying power of religion, family belonging, and money remittances, it raises varied, and often conflicting, expectations from parents (whose authority they often undermined), children (who are honored by being selected but isolated from their communities as a result), sponsors (who welcome the chance to act away from the frustrating rigidity of economic and political institution), and humanitarian employees. The total of 526,694 children sponsored around the world via World Vision in 1996 attests to a vast success; but the distance away from politics and inequality is only achieved by censuring letters by children to their sponsors of all passages pertaining to public life, curtailing the very rights to active political participation affirmed since 1989 by the UN Convention on the Rights of the Child. On the other hand, World Vision is particularly adept at convincing children of donors' countries in a way that recalls missionaries and Junior Red Cross Societies: in the early 1990s, "30 hour famines" involved more than 485,000 young Americans yearly, who raised millions of dollars, some of them on their way to be the adult sponsors of years to come.

In the 1980s, the main humanitarian organizations undertook a critical review of their own discriminatory depictions of children and proposed guidelines that would make for an equal and fairer treatment of societies and of recipients of aid. The UN Convention on the Rights of the Child now obliges states to save children within their own borders. In addition, they have to help international institutions, public and private, to promote child welfare: the preamble states "the importance of international co-operation for improving the living conditions of children in every country, in particular in the developing countries." In such co-operative work, states have to take "due account of the importance of the traditions and cultural values of each people for the protection and harmonious development of the child." Nevertheless, the weaker participation of countries in the South in drafting of the document, as well as the prevalence of an idiom forged in countries of the North, and the questionable neutrality of many scientific methods of social work, have led some to charge that children's rights is a new form of imperialism.[33]

At the center of this debate is the fairness of the increasing number of international adoptions from poor to rich countries, some 500,000 since 1945. This subject raises thorny questions, among them the availability of emotional and material support in communities of origin, and the ways by which these conditions are affected by adoptions. The commercialization of adoptions and the methods for the determination of the child's best interest all recall the history of the Holy Childhood Association of almost two centuries ago.[34] Mirroring these debates, recent associations of adoptees, led by Koreans, with the most numerous adoptees since 1945, are at the forefront of demands for reform of this "one way traffic." In Sweden, the country with the largest proportion of adoptions given the size of the population, the movement to adopt started as a way to save the orphans of the Korean War, in line with earlier operations for children of occupied Finland during the Second World War.[35] In this case, as in the case of the German orphans of the First World War, populationist and national economic motivations complicated humanitarian intentions.

The United Nations Convention on the Rights of the Child can be seen as the inheritor of unequal economic, cultural, and political relations. It represents an important moment in the difficult process of internationalization of child protection. Crafted in universal language, informed by experts, guaranteed by the authority of the vast majority of national governments, it is maintained and debated by a diverse group of humanitarian organizations and publics, and by the citizens, young and old, to whom the Convention is directed.

Acknowledgements

Many colleagues have contributed to the writing of this article, and I thank them warmly: Emily Baughan; Jonathan Benthall; Joelle Droux; Marie-Luise Ermisch; Sarah Glassford; Jaclyn Granick; C. Julia Huang; Paul Nelles; Pierre-Yves Saunier; Will Tait; and John Walsh.

Notes

1 Fang Qin, "'Revenge for our Children!!' The Stigmatization of Christian-controlled Orphanages in the Early 1950s in China" (paper presented at the AAS Annual conference, 2008).

2 Henrietta Harrison, "A penny for the little Chinese: The French Holy Childhood Association in China, 1843–1951," *American Historical Review* 113(1) (2008): 72–92.

3 Denise Lemieux, *Les petits innocents: L'enfance en Nouvelle-France* (Québec, Canada: IQRC, 1985), 162.

4 Alice L. Conklin, "Colonialism and Human Rights, A Contradiction in Terms? The Case of France and West Africa, 1895–1914," *American Historical Review* 103(2) (1998), 419–442.

5 Kevin Grant, "Christian critics of empire: Missionaries, lantern lectures, and the Congo reform campaign in Britain," *The Journal of Imperial and Commonwealth History* 29(2) (2001), 27–58.

6 Barbara Bennett Woodhouse, *Hidden in Plain Sight. The Tragedy of Children's Rights from Ben Franklin, to Lionel Tate* (Princeton, NJ: Princeton University Press, 2008).

7 Joy Parr, *Labouring Children: British Immigrant Apprentices to Canada, 1869–1924* (Toronto, Canada: University of Toronto Press, 1994).

8 D. Rodogno, B. Struck, J. Vogel, eds. *Shaping the Transnational Sphere. Transnational networks of experts and organizations C. 1850–1930* (New York, Berghahn Books).

9 Fiona Paisley. *Glamour in the Pacific: Cultural Internationalism and Race Politics in the Women's Pan-Pacific. (Perspectives on the Global Past)* (Honolulu, University of Hawai'i Press, 2009).

10 Michael Reid, "Understanding Children's Aid: Meaning and Practice in Ontario's Children's Aid, 1893–1912" (MA thesis, Canadian Studies, Trent University, 2008).

11 Marie-Sylvie Dupont-Bouchat and Éric Pierre, eds. *Enfance et justice au XIXe siècle. Essais d'histoire comparée de la protection de l'enfance 1820–1914. France, Belgique, Pays-Bas, Canada* (Paris, France: PUF, 2001).

12 Catherine Rollet, "La santé et la protection de l'enfant vues à travers les congrès internationaux (1880–1920)" *Annales démographie historique* 1 (2001): 97–116.

13 D. Gorman, "Empire Internationalism and the Campaign against the Traffic in Women and Children in the 1920s," *20th Century British History* 19(2) (2008): 186–216.

14 Cited by Lester M. Jones, *Quakers in Action. Recent Humanitarian Reform Activities of the American Quakers* (New York, NY: MacMillan, 1929), 69.

15 Francesca M. Wilson, *In the Margins of Chaos: Recollections of Relief Work in and between Three Wars* (London, UK: John Murray, 1944).

16 Natan Meir, "From communal charity to national welfare: Jewish orphanages in Eastern Europe before and after World War I," *East European Jewish Affairs* 39(1) (2009): 119–34.

17 Everett M. Ressler, *Evacuation of Children from Conflict Areas. Considerations and Guidelines.* UNHCR and UNICEF, Geneva, 1992.

18 Sarah Glassford, "'The Greatest Mother in the World': Carework and the Discourse of Mothering in the Canadian Red Cross Society during the First World War," *Journal of the Association for Research on Mothering* 10(1) (2008): 219–232; John Hutchinson, "The Junior Red Cross Goes to Healthland," *American Journal of Public Health* 87 (1997); 1816–1823.

19 Mary Kinnear, *Woman of the World: Mary McGeachy and International Cooperation* (Toronto, Canada: University of Toronto Press, 2004).

20 Iris Borowy, "World Health in a Book – The International Health Yearbooks," in *Facing Illness in Troubled Times. Health in Europe in the Interwar Years. 1918–1939*, eds. Iris Borowy and Wolf D. Grune (Frankfurt and Main, Germany: Peter Lang, 2005), 85–128; J.P.

Laughton, "Documenting Colonial Violence: The International Campaign against Forced Labor during the Interwar Years," *Revue de l'Histoire de la Shoah* 189 (2008).

21 Susan Pederson, "The Maternalist Moment in British Colonial Policy: The Controversy over 'Child Slavery' in Hong Kong 1917–1941," *Past & Present* (171) (2001): 161–202.

22 Tom Buchanan, "The Role of the British Labour Movement in the Origins and Work of the Basque Children's Committee, 1937–9," *European History Quarterly* 18 (1988); Natalia Benjamin, ed., *Recuerdos: Basque Children Refugees in Great Britain. Niños wascos refugiados en Gren Bretana.* (Oxford, UK: Mousehold Press, 2007). Alfred Brauner and Françoise Brauner, *J'ai dessiné la guerre. Le dessin de l'enfant dans la guerre* (Paris, France: Expansion scientifique française, 1991).

23 Daniel Kowalski, *Stalin and the Spanish Civil War* (New York, NY: Columbia University Press, 2004), chapter V.

24 Michael Hardt and Antonio Negri, *Empire* (Cambridge: Harvard University Press, 2000), pp. 49–50.

25 Miller, Pennybacker, and Rosenhaft, "Mother Ada Wright and the International Campaign to Free the Scottsboro Boys, 1931–1934," *The American Historical Review* (2001) http://www.historycooperative.org/journals/ahr/106.2/ah000387.html (28 Nov. 2011), 64.

26 Aron Rodrigue, *French Jews, Turkish Jews: The Alliance Israelite Universelle and the Politics of Jewish Schooling in Turkey 1860–1925* (Bloomington, IN: Indiana University Press, 1990); Meir, 2009.

27 "Children's Overseas Reception Board," The National Archives, http://yourarchives. nationalarchives.gov.uk/index.php?title=Children's_Overseas_Reception_Board, consulted 29 November 2011.

28 I.K. Atkins, "Seeds of Destiny: a Case History," *Film and History* 2 (1981): 25–33.

29 Deutsches Rotes Kreutz, Central Name Files, History, https://www.drk-suchdienst.de/en/ node/1199. See also their film, German children are searching for their parents, siblings and acquaintances, 1945, 3.35 min, http://www.archive.org/details/1945-xx-xx-Die-Deutsche-Wochenschau-DRK-Suchdienst_983. I thank Jennifer Evans for this information.

30 Tara Zahra, " 'A Human Treasure': Europe's Displaced Children between Nationalism and Internationalism," *Past and Present* (2011): 332–350.

31 David Rosen, "Child Soldiers, International Humanitarian Law, and the Globalization of Childhood," *American Anthropologist* 109(2) (2007): 296–306. Additional protections for child soldiers have entered the Geneva Conventions in the 1970s.

32 Mark O'Neill, *Tzu Chi: Serving With Compassion* (Singapore, John Wiley, 2010). I thank Pierre-Yves Saunier for the bulk of this paragraph.

33 Vanessa Pupavac, "Misanthropy without borders: The international children's rights regime," *Disasters* 25(2) (2001): 95–112.

34 Elizabeth Bartholet, "International Adoption: The Child's Story," *Georgia State University Law Review* 24(2) (2007); Harvard Public Law Working Paper No. 07–21. Available at SSRN: http://ssrn.com/abstract=1025472

35 Tobias Hübinette, "The adopted Koreans of Sweden and the Korean adoption issue," *The Review of Korean Studies* 6(1) (2003): (251–266).

Suggestions for further reading

Overviews

Barnett, Michael. *Empire of Humanity: A History of Humanitarianism.* Ithaca, NY: Cornell University Press, 2011. A good history of the humanitarian movements, well informed by the recent literature, and the best introduction to the main debates in the field.

Benthall, Jeremy. *The Charitable Crescent: Politics of Aid in the Muslim World*. London, UK: I.B. Taurus, 2009. A comprehensive introduction to the principles and actions of Muslim humanitarianism based on original case studies.

Droux, Joëlle. "L'internationalisation de la protection de l'enfance : acteurs, concurrences et projets transnationaux (1900–1925)," *Critique Internationale* 52 (2011): 17–33 and "Les projects de conventions sur l'assistance aux mineurs étrangers (1890–1939): enjeux et impasses sur l'internationalisation des politiques sociales (1890–1939)." Paper presented at the Conference "Towards a New History of the League of Nations," Geneva, 2011. An important reflection on the themes and vectors of the internationalization of child saving.

Iriye, Akira, and Pierre-Yves Saunier, eds. *The Palgrave Dictionary of Transnational History* Basingstoke, UK and New York, NY: Palgrave Macmillan, 2009. A very useful collection of articles that explored many of the themes in this article.

Porter, A. "Trusteeship, Anti-Slavery, and Humanitarianism." In *Oxford History of the British Empire, Vol 3: The Nineteenth Century*, ed. A. Porter. Oxford, UK: Oxford University Press, 1999. A subtle and very well-documented assessment of the role of missions in international relations of aid.

Veerman, Philip. *The Rights of the Child and the Changing image of Childhood*. Dordrecht, The Netherlands, Nijhoff, 1992. Still the best compendium of the changing history of international standards for the young.

Weindling, Paul. ed. *International Health Organizations and Movements 1918–1939*. Cambridge UK and New York, NY: Cambridge University Press, 1995. A good collection on the variety of endeavors in the realm of international health.

Cases of international child saving

Baughan, Emily. "Building a 'True League of Nations' Collaboration between the League of Nations and the British Save the Children Fund in Relief for Russian refugees and Famine Victims, c. 1920–1930." Paper presented at the Conference "Towards a New History of the League of Nations," Geneva, 2011. "'Every Citizen of Empire Implored to Save the Children!' Empire, Internationalism and the Save the Children Fund in Interwar Britain," *Historical Research* (forthcoming, 2012).

Black, Maggie. *A Cause for Our Time: Oxfam: the first Fifty Years*. Oxford, UK: Oxford University Press, 1992. This well documented official history is a good start for the history of Oxfam.

Black, Maggie. *The Children and the Nations: the Story of Unicef*. New York, NY: UNICEF, 1986. This well-documented official history is good for exploring the history of Unicef.

Hutchinson, John F. *Champions of Charity: War and the Rise of the Red Cross*. Boulder, CO: Westview Press, 1996. A pioneering study, critical of the official image of the Red Cross, which presents experiences in many countries.

Bornstein, Erica. *The Spirit of Development. Protestant NGOs, Morality and Economics in Zimbabwe*. New York, NY: Routledge, 2003. On World Vision, founded in 1953 by an American, which was first to help the children victims of the Korean War.

Mahood, Linda. *Feminism and Voluntary Action: Eglantyne Jebb and Save the Children, 1876–1928*. New York, NY: Palgrave Macmillan, 2009. This biography discusses the possibilities and problems of women's involvement in international child saving.

Nehlin, Ann. *Exporting visions and saving children: the Swedish Save the Children Fund*. Linköping, Sweden: Department of Child Studies, Linköping University, 2009.

Patenaude, Bertrand M. *The Big Show in Bololand: The American Relief Expedition to Soviet Russia in the Famine of 1921*. Stanford, CA: Stanford University Press, 2002. A vast and varied analysis of a venture in international child saving of unprecedented scale.

Polks, Jennifer. "Constructive Efforts: The American Red Cross and YMCA in Revolutionary and Civil War Russia, 1917–24." PhD thesis, University of Toronto, 2012.

Sellick, Patricia. "Responding to Children Affected by Armed conflicts: A Case Study of the Save the Children Fund (1919–1999)," PhD thesis, Bradford University, 2001.

In these following articles I have tried to discuss the actors and ideas of NGOs and intergovernmental organization (IGO), and the changing nature of children's rights:

Marshall, Dominique. "The Formation of Childhood as an Object of International Relations: the Child Welfare Committee and the Declaration of Children's Rights of the League of Nations," *International Journal of Children's Rights* 7(2) (1999): 103–147; "Children's Right and Imperial Political Cultures: missionary and humanitarian Contributions to the Conference on the African Child of 1931," *International Journal of Children's Rights* 12 (2004): 273–318; "Children's Rights and Children's Actions in International Relief and Domestic Welfare: The Work of Herbert Hoover between 1914 and 1950," *Journal of the History of Children and Youth* 1(3) (2008): 351–388; Dominique Marshall, "The Rise of Coordinated Action for Children in War and Peace: Experts at the League of Nations, 1924–1945." In *Shaping the Transnational Sphere. Transnational networks of experts and organizations c. 1850–1930*, edited by D. Rodogno, B. Struck, J. Vogel. New York, NY: Berghahn Books, 2012.

Marshall, Dominique. "The Rights of African Children, the Save the Children Fund and Public Opinion in Europe and Ethiopia: The Centre of Child Welfare of Addis Ababa, Spring 1936." In *Proceedings of the International Conference of Ethiopian Studies, Hamburg, July 20–25, 2003*, edited by Siegbert Uhlig, 296–306. Wiesbaden, Germany: Harrassowitz Verlag, 2006; and "Canada and Children's Rights at the United Nations, 1945–1959." In *Canada and the Early Cold War, 1943–1957*, edited by Greg Donaghy, 183–214. Ottawa, Canada: Department of Foreign Affairs and International Trade, 1998.

27

LATIN AMERICAN CHILDHOODS AND THE CONCEPT OF MODERNITY

Nara Milanich

Readers may ask what an essay on Latin America is doing in a book that takes the West, defined culturally and historically, as its focus. Certainly Latin America's conceptual relationship to the West has long been a complex and contradictory one. The region is often seen as part of the West and yet as one of "the rest," or to invoke another famous formulation, as simultaneously "in" but not "of" the West.[1] But precisely because of this ambiguous relationship, Latin America provides a useful lens for scrutinizing western children's history and the analytic paradigms that frame it.

Perhaps the field's most enduring paradigm concerns the rise of modern childhood. Since Philippe Ariès's *Centuries of Childhood* laid the groundwork for the history of childhood, modernity has served as one of the field's central analytic categories. Much of the scholarship in the succeeding half century has addressed questions that Ariès first posed about the birth of modern childhood: when and why it emerged, how and where it spread, with what consequences, and whether the distinction between traditional and modern childhoods has been overstated. Historians of varying schools and conceptual persuasions – sentimentalists and demographers, sociologists, and those dedicated to recent social–cultural approaches – evince a surprising degree of consensus regarding the basic contours of modern childhood. Emerging in a context of declining infant mortality and birth rates, it is the idea, simultaneously descriptive and prescriptive, of childhood as a distinct stage of life distinguished by dependence, vulnerability, consumption rather than production, sentimentalization, and intensive emotional investment. It is characterized by heightened differentiation from the stage of life deemed adulthood and a concomitant segregation of activities and institutions by age, most obviously in the displacement of work by schooling. The rise of modern childhood not only affects children but also creates new roles and responsibilities for women and men, families, states, and societies. Finally, it implies a transformation in which older, more differentiated childhood forms are gradually subsumed into "a common experience of childhood for all children" regardless of gender, race, or class.[2]

Of course until very recently, the vast majority of historical scholarship on children has focused on European and North American societies. The West is posited as the staging ground for the emergence of modern childhood, such that "modern" childhood and "western" childhood are essentially synonymous. But this geo-cultural focus is quickly changing, as scholars of western childhood turn to themes of globalization and colonialism, and historians of societies beyond Europe and North America turn to childhood as a new lens to illuminate historical questions specific to these places.[3]

What happens when paradigms of childhood rooted in the concept of modernity, and histories of children structured as narratives of modernization, meet up with "non-modern" areas of the world? This interpretive essay explores the relationship of childhood to modernity through the lens of Latin America's historical experience, asking not only what children and childhood tell us about modern Latin America but also what Latin America tells us about the concept of "modern childhood."

As Bianca Premo has observed, "the history of childhood and youth in Latin America fits uneasily into the teleology that ends with 'modern' [and] 'Western.'"[4] The problem is historical – many of the key processes associated with modern childhood in the West (industrialization, urbanization, the rise of the middle class) occurred tardily or unevenly across the region – but also interpretive. For the field's largely unexamined use of the concept of modernity evokes the specter of modernization theory. Emerging in the post-war era to explain differences between advanced western nations and the rest of the world, modernization theory posited that all societies pass through a broadly uniform, unidirectional path from political, economic, and cultural "tradition" to "modernity." Such signifiers were of course normatively laden: traditional values, practices, and institutions were identified as irrational and inhibitive of progress.[5] While modernization theory was once a dominant paradigm for understanding the "Third World" (particularly in scholarship produced in North America), today most social/cultural historians and anthropologists are skeptical of it as an explanation of cross-cultural difference and as an account of social change.

The recent historiography of childhood tends to avoid modernization theory's normative judgments and to reject simplistic models of transmission in which western modernity diffuses outward to the non-West. But the concepts of modern and pre-modern childhood nevertheless echo modernization theory's polarities, assume them to be mutually exclusive and historically sequential, and subsume within them a range of values, practices, and patterns.

And yet if modernity is a problematic concept, historians of Latin American childhoods will likely find it difficult to banish from their conceptual lexicon altogether. For the relationship of childhood to modernity has a history that long pre-dates either Ariès or modernization theory. Since the nineteenth century, and arguably since the colonial period, childhood has been central to discourses of modernity produced in and about Latin America. The subordination of the child to the adult is of course one of the most ubiquitous metaphors of colonial domination, and even after the end of formal colonialism, childhood served as a recurring referent for expressing and naturalizing the place of Latin America in the global political–economic order. In the twentieth century, childhood has served as a powerful measure of modernity the world over. Key social-science indicators of relative development – rates of primary schooling, for example, and demographic indicators such as birth rates and infant mortality – involve children, such that the achievement of a modern childhood becomes a widely used metric of a society's modernity itself. Modernization may be an inadequate narrative to describe patterns of historical change in Latin America, yet conversations about childhood in the region have evinced an acute and persistent preoccupation with the problem of modernity.

While an analysis of childhood as a metaphor of (non)-modernity in Latin America is beyond the scope of this essay, it does treat the reverse relationship, namely, how the idea of modernity has been central to Latin American discourses about childhood. I argue that Latin America has actively engaged in global conversations about childhood, not just as an enthusiastic recipient of knowledge, ideology, or policy originating elsewhere but as a generator and exporter of its own ideas of modern childhood.

But ideological enthusiasm for modern childhood did not necessarily bring about its achievement. The second part of the analysis seeks to decouple certain political, economic, or ideological processes often lumped together as "modernity" or "modernization." In Latin America, "modern" ideologies of childhood have sometimes been mobilized in the service of what the scholarship would characterize as "non-modern" practices, and "modern" institutions have been actively productive of "non-modern" childhoods.

Moreover, as I argue in the third section, the history of childhood in Latin America challenges the temporality of modern childhood by showing that distinct childhoods do not necessarily follow as successive historical "stages." Radically divergent childhoods can and have coexisted, simultaneously and in stark contrast to one another. If many children in Latin America today experience a childhood the literature would characterize as "non-modern," it is not because of the survival of "traditional" ideologies or colonial practices or the uneven introduction of modern ones. Rather, modernization often perpetuates new childhood forms that bear little relation to the sentimentalized, nurtured condition denominated modern. Indeed, fundamentally distinct notions of childhood mutually define one another and help structure the broader social orders of which they are a part. Divergent and differentiated childhoods do not simply *persist* in the face of a universalizing modern ideal; they are continuously reproduced and reinvented as part of the very condition of modernity in Latin America. Finally, while the region's vexed relationship with modernity may highlight such patterns with particular clarity, the broader implication is that modernity may prove an inadequate framework for understanding childhood in western societies as well.

Global discourses of modern childhood

In a seminal essay that sketched an agenda for an anthropology of childhood, Sharon Stephens suggested the need to attend to how "once localized western constructions have been exported around the world" in order to "grasp the specificity of childhood and children's experiences" in particular locales, and "to illuminate the historical processes" that have linked and transformed them.[6] Ideas about childhood in twentieth-century Latin America reflect such patterns of specificity and, perhaps especially clearly, those of global linkage. Indeed, the region has been so tightly engaged with European and North American conversations about modern childhood that it is often difficult to determine where local, "Latin American" discourses leave off and "imported" ones begin. Beginning in the late nineteenth century, the region's policy makers, philanthropists, pediatricians, and child welfare advocates closely followed the activities of their European and North American counterparts. Foreign texts, from declarations by scientific conferences to the League of Nations' Geneva declaration of 1924, circulated widely in Latin America. Ellen Key's *The Century of the Child* was published in Spanish in 1906 and became a reference for some Latin American reformers. French influences were particularly strong, with French pediatric texts routinely used and the French "administrative and juridico-institutional approach to children's welfare" serving as a model. An elite coterie of doctors studied and regularly attended health and child welfare conferences in Europe.[7]

Latin America also actively produced its own knowledge about childhood. One key venue was the Pan-American Child Congresses, which brought together pediatricians, jurists, social workers, and other advocates from across the hemisphere. Initiated in 1916, over the next century the conference would convene some twenty times, in more or less regular intervals, in cities around the hemisphere (most recently in 2009), although its influence and prestige waned in the second half of the century. The purpose of the gathering was to " '[Latin-] Americanize' the study of childhood," accounting for differences with other parts of the world while at the same time serving to communicate Latin America-based policies, knowledge, and experiences to an international arena. The Congresses influenced national legislation among member countries, and some South American delegates later contributed to the League of Nations' child welfare initiatives.[8]

Some issues on which child welfare advocates focused were specific to the region. At the turn of the twentieth century, Latin America had the highest rates of out-of-wedlock birth anywhere in the world, and the socio-medical and legal issues that surrounded illegitimacy were an enduring preoccupation. Other issues – infant mortality, juvenile delinquency, abandoned and vagrant children, child labor – were familiar to European and US contexts. Regardless of the issue, a language of comparative modernity framed much of the discourse on childhood in Latin America: "In the most civilized countries of Europe more than 90 percent of births are legitimate," declared a Chilean congressman in 1928, and "where illegitimacy reins ... backwardness prevails."[9] Infant mortality was discussed in similar terms, with national Latin American statistics often appearing in tables alongside European data. Chilean reformers claimed that their country had the highest rates of infant mortality anywhere in the "civilized" world, which they defined as Latin America, North America, and (most of) Europe. Regardless of the veracity of that claim, this definition of "civilization," of course, reflected their self-perception as members of a common western community that shared a modern ideal (if not yet the generalized reality) of a low mortality childhood.

In stark contrast to Chile around 1900, Uruguay achieved some of the lowest recorded infant mortality rates in the world (only Norway and Sweden had lower ones), thanks to the public health and social provisions of its precocious welfare state. Besides reflecting the difficulty of generalizing about childhood across Latin American societies, the Uruguayan example suggests how global circuits of knowledge operated in both directions. Uruguayan reformers borrowed enthusiastically from European policies, for example establishing a French-inspired system of clinics (*gouts de lait/gotas de leche*) that may have served more mothers and children per capita than in France. But Uruguay was also a "net exporter" of knowledge about child health – and hence of modern childhood – to the global arena. Home to the world's first permanent, international child welfare institute (the International American Institute for the Protection of Childhood, established in 1927), Montevideo shaped ideas of health as did Washington, Paris, or Geneva. In 1930, the best-known Uruguayan pediatrician, Luis Morquio, became president of Save the Children in Geneva. Subsequently, Uruguay established the world's first Ministry of Child Protection, and its 1934 Children's Code received attention in international fora – and would later serve as an important source for the 1989 Convention on the Rights of the Child.[10] Uruguay's experience suggests how Latin American societies elaborated and exported their own knowledge and policy about modern childhood. Indeed, given the density of such ties and exchanges, it becomes difficult to conceive of Latin America as a "social world" (to invoke Sharon Stephens' conception) linked to, but manifestly distinct from, the "western" societies where the ideal and practice of modern childhood originated.

By the end of the twentieth century (and perhaps well before, given the notorious difficulty of accessing children's own perspectives in the historical record), ideas of modern childhood were espoused not only by powerful professionals or elite reformers but also by the region's poorest and most marginal children. In other words, even in contexts of poverty, inequality, and violence, the ideal of a protected and carefree childhood has nevertheless become familiar and even hegemonic, even among young people who, by all accounts, including their own, have not enjoyed such a childhood. Witness one Nicaraguan adolescent's appraisal of his early experiences in the Sandinista liberation movement, recounted to a foreign journalist: "We had forgotten the things of childhood. Like play. We had attained such a high moral mission that we were no longer children." Another young Sandinista, who by age eleven was being dispatched to his poor neighborhood to engage adults in casual conversation in an effort to educate them politically, recounted the "most fundamental" lesson he received in his own political education: that "our ancestors had not conquered for us the right to grow up and have fun as young people. That the times we lived in were for struggle and to conquer the new fatherland for the new generation." Consider too the self-portraits of Brazilian street children featuring father-headed, nuclear families, although almost none of them experienced families of this type, or the nine-year-old whose mother had tried to give him away as a baby and later turned him out of the house, who, when asked if his mother loved him, replied without hesitating, "She's my mother, she *has* to love me!"[11]

Whether offered in a spirit of compensation or conviction, such comments suggest the speakers' close familiarity with a set of normative ideals: childhood as a time of carefree play and personal growth, cultivated in nurturing, "intact" families by loving mothers. That these children so readily invoked such norms (indeed, wielded them as a political indictment, in the case of the young Sandinistas) despite the glaring incongruity with their own lives, attests to the norms' ideological power and their wide dissemination.

Modernization and the production of "non-modern" childhoods

Yet despite this deep and abiding commitment to an idea of modern childhood, modern political and economic transformations in Latin America have often instantiated other childhood forms. The advent of modern, liberal law in the nineteenth century provides one example. Chile's widely influential, forward-looking civil code revolutionized many aspects of contract, property, and family law, including parent–child relations. According to older constructions of parenthood rooted in natural law, all parents shouldered inalienable responsibilities to their offspring regardless of their marital status. Drawing on liberal notions of free will, privacy, private property, and contract, the Civil Code rejected this idea, giving fathers (and in more limited cases, mothers) unfettered freedom to renounce all responsibility for their non-marital offspring. In a social context in which a quarter, and later some 40 percent, of children were born out of wedlock, the code effectively created a class of children without families, at the very moment that modern, liberal republics consecrated the idea of equality before the law, in other words, civil law inscribed new forms of inequality among children and undermined the notion of family as a universal entitlement of childhood.

The Chilean Code's empowerment of fathers at the expense of children was new, but the extra-kin networks and institutions for child rearing that the reform implicitly encouraged were not. One enduring historical characteristic of Latin American childhoods has been the diverse and fluid contexts within which children have been reared. Child circulation – the rearing of children beyond their natal progenitors – has taken many forms, from informal fosterage to apprenticeship. One common practice was the rearing of orphaned, supernumerary, illegitimate, poor, and often indigenous or Afro-descended children in private households where they received basic sustenance in exchange for their labor. Their status in these arrangements of tutelary servitude was distinctly vulnerable and stigmatized. In their most benign manifestation, such arrangements fed and clothed needy children, inserting them into the patronage networks necessary to subaltern survival. But they could also reinscribe patterns of extreme social and racial-ethnic subordination, reproducing an underclass of dependent, unskilled, nameless individuals.

Dating from the colonial period, tutelary servitude was systemic and widely accepted in the nineteenth century, and in many Latin American societies, well into the twentieth. Today a version of it lives on in the *reste-avec* system in Haiti and in the institution known as *criadazgo* in Paraguay. In recent years, the International Labor Organization and Anti-Slavery International have organized initiatives to abolish what they call "child domestic slavery." It is tempting to characterize the practice as a colonial anachronism that confirms the persistence of non-modern childhoods in modernizing Latin America. And yet it is associated with some of the very historical processes typically highlighted as formative of the "modern" history of Latin America. The abolition of slavery, expansion and consolidation of nation-states, and growth of capitalist export economies resulted in shifting demands for labor that fomented unfree forms of servitude and apprenticeship involving children, as well as the "pre-modern" childhoods they implied.

Meanwhile, the ideological underpinnings of tutelary servitude were ambiguous. On the one hand, it obviously reflected a "pre-modern" valuation of children's labor, and the conflicts that sometimes arose around these arrangements typically revolved around the question of which adult (parent, godparent, or master) enjoyed rights to that labor. Yet these adults often dwelled on the valuable time, effort, and resources they had invested in rearing the youngsters in their care. They argued that it was precisely the intensive nurture and education that children required (material, vocational, and moral in nature) that justified caretakers' right to recompense via labor. Thus the practice also drew on notions of intensive stewardship and child dependency usually associated with a modern, sentimentalized childhood.

Meanwhile, such modalities of servitude were actively appropriated and perpetuated by public institutions across Latin America. In the nineteenth century, and in many places through the first half of the twentieth, state-sponsored orphanages from Uruguay to Ecuador and Mexico to Puerto Rico trained and distributed wards of both sexes as domestic servants in private households. Such institutions were emblematic of the deeply ambiguous articulation of "modern" and "non-modern" childhoods in Latin America. On the one hand, the asylums embraced modern notions of childhood. Founded in the late eighteenth century, they reflected Enlightenment constructions of childhood and political authority in which the Father-King assumed responsibility for the empire's children. By the late nineteenth century, they embodied the state's growing responsibility for child welfare as well as newly emerging ideas about a nurtured childhood. The sprawling orphanage in Santiago, Chile, which received more than 51,000 children between 1853 and 1924, is a case in point. The asylum was an incubator of modern pediatric, psychological, and social work expertise, and its wards enjoyed a merry-go-round and movie theater on the premises, as well as toys and sweets at Christmas, thanks to an administrator's extraordinary 10,000-peso donation. Here was a vision of carefree amusement and happiness as a birthright of childhood. Yet the perennially overcrowded and underfunded orphanage also placed its wards as servants in local households. While the practice was sometimes criticized, it persisted, and in the 1920s, a School of Domestic Service was established for the orphans that lent a veneer of modern professionalization to the practice. Thus, public institutions steeped in the latest child science and ideological currents simultaneously relied on – indeed actively reinscribed – "pre-modern" arrangements of sustenance-for-labor.

A similarly ambiguous story may be told about the evolution of adoption in twentieth-century Latin America. In the United States, the legal institutionalization of adoption in the nineteenth century has been interpreted as reflecting "a new conception of parenthood emphasizing affection and stewardship" and the transition from instrumental to sentimental childhood.[12] In Latin America, modern adoption law reflected less a shift from one childhood to another so much as an institutionalization of the distinction. In some countries, a two-tiered system provided for "full" adoption, which created legal kin ties between adopter and adoptee modeled on the parent–child relation, as well as "simple" adoption, which gave the child rights only to basic support and education but created no kin tie and ended when s/he reached the age of majority. (In other countries, only one form of adoption existed, and it followed the simple model.) This limited form of adoption institutionalized inferior categories of children in the household (not unlike the Chilean Civil Code's posture toward extra-marital progeny in the previous century), and in practice was sometimes used to formalize tutelary servitude.

Thus, instances of what contemporaries understood as modernization in Latin America – whether in the realms of family law, institutional social provision, or economic and labor relations – did not necessarily serve to instantiate a hegemonic modern childhood, and indeed, sometimes had the opposite effect. Modern childhood may have been widely propounded as an ideal, as we saw earlier, but it has stood in stark contrast to quotidian practices that have not simply "persisted" but have been actively fomented by modern legal structures and public institutions.

The limits of diffusion

One of the central tenets of the narrative of modern, western childhood is that over time it progressively transformed the experience of all children in western societies, regardless of class, race, gender, or region. The early "sentimentalist" scholars of childhood and family – first Philippe Ariès and later Edward Shorter, Lloyd deMause, and Lawrence Stone – all espoused a diffusionist model in which changes first impacted the upper or middle classes of Europe, eventually to filter down the social spectrum. Written in a different interpretive vein and about a different time and place, Viviana Zelizer's work on the nineteenth-century United States nevertheless posited a parallel transformation of the child from "object of utility" to "object of sentiment," which began in the middle class but spread to the lower classes by the 1930s. More recently, synthetic treatments, such as Hugh Cunningham's survey of five centuries of western childhood, echo this assertion of change across "all social classes and both genders." So too does Steven Mintz's history of children in the United States, which, while placing greater emphasis on the diversity of childhoods than some other accounts particularly in the nineteenth century, discerns a process of convergence in the twentieth.[13]

Recent world historical perspectives on the history of childhood press the argument still farther, conceptually and geographically, by tracing diffusion not just across classes but also across global societies. Peter Stearns argues that from its birthplace in the West, modern childhood has filtered outward to shape childhood elsewhere in the globe.[14] Stearns's is not a simple or celebratory narrative of globalization, and he offers numerous caveats about a complex, uneven, and sometimes resisted process. Nor is its endpoint the homogenization of childhood cross-culturally because he allows for the existence of more than one modern childhood. Still, the progressive expansion of a "common childhood" is the fundamental dynamic. "With all essential qualifications," Stearns asserts, "the central point should not be lost: modernity generated a crucial new version of childhood" that spread outward from the West and continues to work its way across the globe. Late-twentieth-century globalization only "intensifies and further disseminates the basic transformations" to a childhood entailing less labor, more schooling, lower birthrates, and lower mortality.[15]

This last element – mortality – offers some of the most powerful evidence for the global diffusion of a modern childhood ideal. Infant mortality has declined in all countries of the globe during the last half of the twentieth century. Such evidence leads Stearns to argue that while it is "certainly appropriate to note the huge gaps between rich countries and poor, and the equally huge differences in childhood experience that these gaps reflected," this fact does not obscure the more fundamental point that "the directions of change were widely shared."[16]

The trend is also unmistakable in Latin America. Indeed in many countries, mortality decline began well before other parts of the developing world. As we saw, Uruguay achieved rates on par with those in Western Europe at the turn of the twentieth century. Today, Chile, Costa Rica, and Cuba enjoy that distinction (with Cuba's rate lower than that of the United States). To the extent that infant mortality is a key indicator of modern childhood, Latin America would seem to be well on its way to achieving it.

Yet even as the longitudinal trend is one of unmistakable decline, it is not one of convergence. Alongside the steep reduction in infant mortality rates for the region as a whole and for all individual Latin American nations in the second half of the twentieth century, cross-national variations persist. Indeed, the relative inequality of infant mortality rates between Latin American countries *remained almost unchanged* between 1955 and 1995, the period of sharpest mortality decline.[17] Even more important, national statistics obscure regional, rural–urban, ethno-racial, and class-specific heterogeneities that are often even starker. Thus, alongside the trend of an absolute decline in infant mortality is a trend of continued, and sometimes growing, differentiation between nations, regions, and social groups – a trend that complicates the narrative of modern childhood's advance.

Local ethnographic research elucidates this heterogeneity. Anthropologist Nancy Scheper-Hughes' work with mothers in a slum (favela) in northeast Brazil over the course of several decades, beginning in the mid-1960s, reveals the existence of two starkly contrasting, class-based, demographic–cultural regimes of infant mortality. Among the middle class, "child death is as shocking and aberrant as for affluent women anywhere else in the [contemporary] world." In the shantytowns, meanwhile, a mother can observe of her infants' deaths: "I think the first five had to die to make way for the next three who were more 'disposed' to live." Scheper-Hughes argues that in the 1980s and 1990s Brazil witnessed the "modernization" of child mortality. Whereas epidemic diseases once indiscriminately killed children across social classes, now poverty-specific maladies – namely, malnutrition and diarrhea – became the primary causes of mortality, and child death has thus been confined to the poorest sectors. Other studies in Brazil suggest divergent patterns of child mortality by race.[18]

Sharply divergent patterns of infant mortality are an attribute of childhood generally. In Latin America, the region that, by most measures, is characterized by the worst social inequalities in the world, a central theme of ethnographic and historical work on childhood has been the existence of multiple, often starkly contrasting childhood experiences, as well as the reproduction of social inequality through cultural, medical, legal, and institutional practices associated with children. Indeed, one might argue that the *defining characteristic* of modern Latin American childhood is the absence of a single experience or even an ideal that could meaningfully be said to apply to all or even most children. This is not simply a tale of the "persistence" of differentiated childhoods in the face of a universalizing modern ideal, but rather the continuous reproduction and reinvention of plural childhoods as part of the very condition of modernity in Latin America.

The historical production of divergent childhoods is exemplified in the early-twentieth-century child welfare movement. If Latin American child saving, as discussed earlier, shared many commonalities with parallel developments in Europe and North America, it also exhibited an important difference. As Hugh Cunningham notes, child saving in Europe and North America represented the moment at which "the [modern] ideology of childhood ... began to influence public action,"[19] which aimed to achieve a non-working, nurtured, and protected experience for children across the social spectrum. Indeed, it was the shocking deviation in childhoods among the poor that provided the moral fervor for these initiatives. What is more, while historians differ as to why, most agree that efforts to impose a common childhood ideal were largely successful.

In Latin America, by contrast, child saving was associated with the imposition of distinct childhoods on different groups of children. Indeed, reforms explicitly designed to enhance child welfare often exacerbated distinctions between them. In Ecuador, mid-twentieth-century child welfare initiatives were couched in universal language, but in practice tended to apply to poor urban mestizo children and not to rural indigenous ones (or affluent white ones). In Brazil, educational and welfare institutions had distinct aims for different populations of children, and universal education was conspicuously absent as a goal. For example, the bylaws of one school whose mission was the "rehabilitation" of minors declared that because "the institution is meant for social pariahs, the education imparted herein shall not go beyond that which is indispensable to the integration of the internees within society." Far from democratizing a particular childhood ideal, extending it to those unable to achieve it, or imposing it on those who resisted it, child saving encouraged, in the words of Irene Rizzini, "a dichotomization of childhood" according to class and race.[20]

In a society in which race-based chattel slavery was abolished only in 1888, it is of course not surprising to find sharply differentiated childhoods at the dawn of the twentieth century. What is noteworthy is the fact that modern state institutions and policies actively promoted them. Rizzini concludes that child welfare initiatives "contributed to the social exclusion of the poor," and, ultimately, constituted "an impediment to the extension of . . . citizenship in Brazil."[21] Such exclusions would prove persistent. In the late 1980s, anthropologist Nancy Scheper-Hughes visited a public reform school in northeast Brazil that instructed children aged eight to fifteen years old in a series of "professional pathways": weaving hammocks, cultivation with hoe and machete, sewing and embroidery, domestic skills, and broom making. Signs on the school's walls reminded its pupils, "All work is honorable." The persistence of such class-based pedagogies suggests how poor children continued to be seen first and foremost as workers, or as workers-in-formation.[22]

Adoption law is another, more recent, state policy that has inscribed divergent childhoods. In recent decades, Latin American countries have enthusiastically embraced global child rights norms, signing international conventions and reformulating national law in accordance with their principles. As part of this trend, Latin American law has moved towards "full" adoption, implying the child's unqualified inclusion in the adoptive family and a corresponding complete rupture from the natal one. By ameliorating the lesser rights and exploitive potential of "simple" adoption, the reform addresses one historic vector of legal discrimination and differentiation among children, yet it has in essence displaced, rather than eliminated, inequality. Where older, "simple" adoption norms could accommodate the additive logic of popular, informal modes of child circulation whereby youngsters maintained ties to multiple families, newer laws mandate the obliteration of natal ties by adoptive ones. From Ecuador to Peru to Brazil, these norms have had highly disruptive consequences, as popular circulation practices are interpreted as "child abandonment," and poor birth mothers are deprived of the informal power they once exercised to select caretakers and otherwise shape their children's future. In short, recent reforms, which in notable contrast to earlier public policies framed around egalitarian ideals of children's citizenship and rights, have exacerbated inequality between poor birth parents and better-off adoptive ones and widened the rift between legal and popular constructions of adoption.

Plural childhoods in the present evoke obvious analogies with the past, which anthropologists sometimes make explicit through their use of historical referents. Ethnographer Tobias Hecht draws on Viviana Zelizer's comparison of sentimentally priceless and economically valuable children in the late-nineteenth-century United

States to posit the existence of two childhoods, one nurtured and the other nurturing, in contemporary Brazil. Whereas the former "are loved by virtue of *being* children, the love received by [the latter] is to a great extent a function of what they *do*." Even more explicitly, Nancy Scheper-Hughes has referred to Brazilian shantytown childhoods as reminiscent of the "premodern version of the child as miniature adult" in contrast to the "middle-class notion that conforms to Ariès's model of the modern protected and innocent child."[23] Here historical signifiers are decoupled from their temporal associations and repurposed as class-based descriptors. But whereas Zelizer and Ariès posited these two childhoods as overlapping but essentially discrete and successive historical stages, Hecht and Scheper-Hughes suggest that in Brazil contrasting childhoods coexist and mutually define one another.

Indeed, ethnographic analysis makes clear that these childhoods are not just "premodern survivals," their persistence a temporary circumstance on the path to "a" common childhood. Rather, they are continuously produced in the present. Scheper-Hughes and Hoffman argue, for example, that "hypermodern" Brazilian cities are producing them actively. In northeast Brazil, rapid urbanization and the dissolution of peasant squatters as a result of the expansion of agribusiness fomented the presence and visibility of poor street children. While unaccompanied poor children have long inhabited city streets and "street urchins" figure in accounts of Latin American cities dating back to the colonial period, urban public spaces in Brazil have become increasingly marked by privatization and hyper-segregation, a trend that has criminalized the poor, usually dark-skinned young people who tend to occupy them. Urban "hypermodernity," in other words, produces a "deviant" childhood. In this context, "the 'two childhoods' of Brazil, already so distant, can only grow farther apart."[24]

As childhoods across classes grow apart, however, childhoods cross-culturally may grow closer together. As Tobias Hecht has observed, in terms of their experiences, aspirations, and consumption patterns, well-off Latin American children share more in common with their class counterparts in other parts of the West than with their poor compatriots. Emblematic of a shared, transnational culture of affluent childhood is the ubiquitous rite-of-passage of well-to-do Latin American, and especially Brazilian, youth: a pilgrimage to Disney World. Well before their country's recent economic boom, Brazilians ranked second only to Canadians among foreign tourists in central Florida. The Disney trip constitutes a symbol of modernity and serves as a "validation of class standing," writes Maureen O'Dougherty, who devotes a chapter of her ethnography of the Brazilian middle class to the Disney trip.[25]

If the convergence of affluent childhoods transnationally implies the "Disneyfication" of Latin American childhood, there is a concomitant "Latinization" of Disney. In 2007, the theme park began to offer the hemisphere's fifteen-year-old girls the possibility of celebrating their *quinceañera*, the debutante party traditional in many Latin American countries and among US Latinos, in the park itself (packages for "Disney Quinceañera" range from $1,800 to over $20,000). If the Disney trip reflects the transnational convergence of consumption practices among affluent young people, Disney Quinceañera reflects how Latin American societies not only participate in but also elaborate on these practices. More broadly, this example provides a twist on diffusionist arguments by showing how convergence among some groups (in this case, the hemisphere's affluent youth) may highlight persistent divergence among others (rich and poor children within Latin America).

Contemporary child rights as a metric of modernity

In the 1980s, just as Brazil's middle classes began to incorporate the Disney trip into their cultural repertoires, a very different image of Latin American childhood gripped the international press: young people living, and dying, on the streets of the hemisphere's cities. If the Disney trip symbolized Brazilian middle-class modernity, the street child, in the discourse of humanitarian and human rights organizations and the media, embodied precisely the opposite: retrograde urban poverty and underdevelopment.

Across Latin America, in the context of democratic transitions in the 1980s and especially 1990s, societies ravaged by Cold War-era state terrorism and civil violence gave renewed public attention to children's well-being – now configured as children's rights or citizenship. In Brazil, where street children provoked palpable national embarrassment, a remarkable non-governmental-organization-led social movement emerged that spurred major constitutional and legislative reforms on behalf of children's rights. The culmination was the 1990 Child Statute, which was widely seen as a test case of re-democratization five years after the end of military rule. Such initiatives reflected the discursive power of human rights and democratic principles generally, as well as the fact that children were some of the most potent symbols of past rights violations. Revelations of the systematic kidnapping of babies of political prisoners during the Argentine military dictatorship, for example, galvanized the political movement against impunity and became one of the only political crimes whose perpetrators did not enjoy amnesty. Child rights reforms overhauled penal systems' treatment of youthful offenders, rewrote adoption regulations, and abolished legal discrimination against "illegitimate" children (as in the long overdue reform of Chile's nineteenth-century Civil Code, which occurred only in 1998).

As in the past, public policies for children evinced an abiding preoccupation with modernity, and in this context, global rights norms exercised tremendous influence. Jessaca Leinaweaver's observation that the Peruvian state's enthusiastic embrace of global child rights reflected "a performance of modernity" in the wake of a brutal civil conflict perceived as "atavistic" could be extended to many countries. Time and again, conformity with international rights protocols served as a metric of the quality of national legislation. Thus, Brazil's 1990 Child Statute was touted as "worthy of the First World" and "even more advanced than" the UN's Convention on the Rights of the Child.[26]

But "legislating toward modernity" has produced a decidedly mixed bag[27] because in the past, the fervent embrace of modernity and the global norms associated with it do not necessarily lead to the instantiation of modern childhood as conventionally defined. This is so for various reasons. For all its symbolic power, legislation may in practice be ignored – a common critique of Brazilian legislation, for example – and as we saw previously, international norms sometimes mean assiduous disregard for local practices. In this context, modernizing legislation has tempered some inequalities but inadvertently created others. "Modern" principles do not always have "modern" outcomes in specific local contexts. As long as gross social inequalities persist in the region, we may expect the continued existence of radically divergent childhoods.

Indeed, ultimately we are presented with the limitations of the concept of "modernity" itself. Child circulation illustrates as much. Evaluated through the lens of western childhood, child circulation appears distinctly "pre-modern," a throwback to traditional survival strategies and practices of wet nursing, apprenticeship, or life-cycle service that in Europe pre-dated the emergence of modern childhood, family, mothering, social provision, and schooling. Yet practices of child circulation in Latin America, historically and in the present, exhibit tremendous variation in their forms, meanings, functions, and consequences for children, households, communities, and societies. Even leaving aside the normative valences that the terms modern and traditional often imply, to label child circulation "traditional" appears arbitrary and reductive, flattening cultural meaning and shoehorning practices into a historical timeline derived from other societies. The label does little, in short, to enhance our understanding of the practice.

This essay posed the initial question of what happens when paradigms of childhood rooted in modernity, and histories of children structured as modernization narratives, meet up with "non-modern" areas of the world? One response is that this encounter reveals just how deeply and historically meaningful, and yet how profoundly analytically insufficient, modernity is as a concept. This response emerges from a survey of Latin American childhoods, but this particular historical case, whatever its specificity, may be more emblematic than exceptional. Historians of western societies might ask whether some of the questions that Latin America raises about modernity as a basis for the historical analysis of childhood, might also apply to the societies seen as its historical and historiographic cradle.

Notes

1 This aphorism, attributed to C.L.R. James, was originally applied to the Caribbean but is often extended to Latin America.
2 Hugh Cunningham, "Histories of Childhood," *American Historical Review* 103(4) (1998): 1195–1208; 1206.
3 Paula Fass, *Children of a New World: Society, Culture, and Globalization* (New York: New York University Press, 2007); Peter Stearns, *Childhood in World History* (New York, NY: Routledge, 2006); *Journal of Social History*, special issue "Globalization and Childhood," 38(4), 2005; Heidi Morrison, *Global History of Childhood Reader* (New York, NY: Routledge, 2012).
4 Bianca Premo, "How Latin American's History of Childhood Came of Age," *Journal of the History of Childhood and Youth* 1(1) (2008): 63–76; 64.
5 A classic description and critique of modernization theory is Samuel Valenzuela and Arturo Valenzuela, "Modernization and Dependency: Alternative Perspectives in the Study of Latin American Underdevelopment," *Comparative Politics* 10(4) (1978): 535–552. Because children were seen as incubators of particular values or orientations, the modernization literature sometimes attempted to identify patterns of education or socialization conducive to or inhibitive of development.
6 Sharon Stephens, "Introduction," *Children and the Politics of Culture* (Princeton, NJ: Princeton University Press, 1995), 14.
7 Jorge Rojas, "Los derechos del niño en Chile: una aproximación histórica, 1910–1930," *Historia (Santiago, Chile)* 40(1) (2007): 129–164. It was apparently not published in Portuguese. Anne-Emanuelle Birn, "Historiography of Child and Infant Health in Latin America" in *Healing the World's Children: Interdisciplinary Perspectives on Child Health in the Twentieth Century* in Cynthia Comacchio, Janet Golden, and George Weisz, eds. (Montreal: McGill-Queen's Press, 2008), 834.

8 Anne-Emanuelle Birn, "The National-International Nexus in Public Health: Uruguay and the Circulation of Child Health and Welfare Policies, 1890–1940," *História, Ciências, Saúde-Manguinhos* 13(3) (2006): 675–708; 50; Birn, "Historiography."

9 Cited in Nara Milanich, "Historical Perspectives on Illegitimacy and Illegitimates in Latin America" in Tobias Hecht, ed. *Minor Omissions: Children in Latin American History and Society* (Madison, WI: University of Wisconsin Press, 2002).

10 Birn, "Nexus," 44, 35, 55; Birn, "Historiography," 88, 90.

11 María Gravina Telechea, *Que diga Quincho* (Managua: Editorial Nueva Nicaragua, 1982), 78, 30; Nancy Scheper-Hughes and Daniel Hoffman, "Brazilian Apartheid: Street Kids and the Struggle for Urban Space" in Nancy Scheper-Hughes and Carolyn Sargent, eds. *Small Wars: The Cultural Politics of Childhood* (Berkeley, CA: University of California Press, 1998), 362–363, 379.

12 Steven Mintz, *Huck's Raft: A History of American Childhood.* (Cambridge, MA: Harvard University Press, 2006), 164; Viviana Zelizer, *Pricing the Priceless Child: The Changing Social Value of Children* (New York: Basic Books, 1985), 180.

13 Zelizer, *Pricing the Priceless Child*, 6; Hugh Cunningham, *Children and Childhood in Western Society since 1500* (London, UK: Longman, 1995), 2; Mintz, *Huck's Raft.*

14 Stearns, "Conclusion: Change, Globalization, and Childhood," *Journal of Social History*, special issue on Globalization and Childhood 38(4), 2005, 1041–1046; Stearns, *Childhood in World History.*

15 Stearns, "Conclusion," 1042–1043.

16 Stearns, *Childhood in World History*, 166.

17 M.C. Schneider et al., "Trends in Infant Mortality Inequalities in the Americas, 1955–1995," *Journal of Epidemiology and Community Health* 56(7) (2002): 538–541; see also C. Castillo-Salgado et al., "Inequalities in Infant Mortality in the American Region: Basic Elements for Analysis," *Epidemiological Bulletin* 22(2) (2001): 4–7.

18 Nancy Scheper-Hughes, *Death Without Weeping: The Violence of Everyday Life in Brazil* (Berkeley, CA: University of California, 1992), 280, 328; Scheper-Hughes and Sargent, "Introduction," *Small Wars*, 3; Birn, "Historiography," 22.

19 Cunningham, *Children and Childhood*, 134.

20 Irene Rizzini, "The Child-Saving Movement in Brazil," in Hecht, *Minor Omissions*, 177.

21 Esben Leifsen, "Adoption and the Governing of Child Welfare in Twentieth-Century Quito," *Journal of Latin America and Caribbean Anthropology* 14(1) (2009): 68–91; Rizzini, "Child-Saving Movement," 176, 178.

22 Scheper-Hughes and Hoffman, "Brazilian Apartheid," 370–371.

23 Tobias Hecht, *At Home on the Street: Street Children of Northeast Brazil* (New York, NY: Cambridge University Press, 1998), 80; Scheper-Hughes and Sargent, "Introduction," in *Small Wars*, 26.

24 Scheper-Hughes and Hoffman, "Brazilian Apartheid," 356, 382.

25 Hecht, "Conclusion," in *Minor Omissions*, 245–46; L. Clark. "Visits from Overseas Rise 7%," *Orlando Sentinel Tribune*, 5/27/98, B4; Maureen O'Dougherty, *Consumption Intensified: The Politics of Middle-Class Daily Life in Brazil* (Durham, NC: Duke University Press, 2002), 101; Jessaca Leinaweaver, "Kinship into the Peruvian Adoption Office: Reproducing Families, Producing the State," *Journal of Latin America and Caribbean Anthropology* 14(1) (2009): 44–67; Fonseca, "Inequalities," 403.

26 Leinaweaver in *Journal of Latin America and Caribbean Anthropology* 14(1) (2009): 48; Claudia Fonseca, "Inequality Near and Far: Adoption as Seen from the Brazilian Favelas," *Law and Society Review* 36(2) (2002): 403.

27 This is Leinaweaver and Seligmann's characterization of adoption law, but it could extend to children's rights generally; Jessaca Leinaweaver and Linda Seligmann, "Introduction: Cultural and Political Economies of Adoption in Latin America," *Journal of Latin American and Caribbean Anthropology* 14(1) (2009): 1–19; 10.

Suggestions for further reading

The history of children and childhood in Latin America as an identifiable field of study is very new, although historians of gender, the family, slavery, labor, and other topics have certainly included children within their purview. Given the newness of the field, there are relatively few monographs that take children as the principal category of analysis, making edited collections especially important. Second, given that similar analytic concerns animate historical and anthropological work on Latin American childhoods, this bibliography, like this essay, draws amply on ethnographic work.

Historiographic/conceptual overviews

Birn, Anne-Emanuelle. "Historiography of Child and Infant Health in Latin America." In *Healing the World's Children: Interdisciplinary Perspectives on Child Health in the Twentieth Century*, edited by Cynthia Comacchio, Janet Golden, and George Weisz. Montreal, Canada: McGill–Queen's Press, 2008. A wide-ranging overview of childhood as seen through the lens of health.

Kuznesof, Elizabeth Anne. "The Home, the Street, Global Society: Latin American Families and Childhood in the Twenty-First Century." *Journal of Social History* 38(4) (2005): 859–872. Broad sketch of the role of "globalization" and its impact on children from 1492 to twenty-first-century neoliberalism.

Premo, Bianca. "How Latin America's History of Childhood Came of Age." *Journal of the History of Childhood and Youth* 1(1) (2008): 63–76. A thoughtful synthesis of the field observing that children have long been present in Latin American social historiography even if not as an explicit focus; grapples with the problem of modernity explored above.

Edited volumes/special journal issues

Special issue. "Children in the History of Latin America." *Journal of Family History* 23(3) (1998). Perhaps the earliest attempt to draw together work into a discernible sub-field, preceded by an introduction by Sonya Lipsett-Rivera.

Hecht, Tobias, ed. *Minor Omissions: Children in Latin American History and Society.* Madison, WI: University of Wisconsin Press, 2002. An interdisciplinary collection moving from colonial art history to the wars in Central America, with a thoughtful introduction that gives the early lay of the field.

Mannarelli, María Emma, and Pablo Rodríguez, eds. *Historia de la infancia en América Latina.* Bogotá, Colombia: Universidad Externado de Colombia, 2007. A voluminous edited collection of some 31 separate chapters on all aspects of childhood from colonial to contemporary Latin America.

Premo, Bianca, and Ondina González, eds. *Raising an Empire: Children in Early Modern Iberia and Colonial Latin America.* Albuquerque, NM: University of New Mexico Press, 2007. Spanning the Atlantic and including both Iberian Europe and colonial Latin America in its purview, this volume raises the question of what is specifically "colonial" about colonial Latin American childhoods.

del Priore, Mary. *História das crianças no Brasil*. São Paulo, Brazil: Contexto, 1999. An early collection of articles focused on Brazil, which continues to be the center of writing on childhood anthropology and history in Latin America.

Edited collections of broad analytic and geographical scope that explore childhood beyond "the West" include:

Morrison, Heidi. *Global History of Childhood Reader*. London, UK: Routledge, 2012. Collection of classic and new work on childhood globally.

Scheper-Hughes, Nancy, and Carolyn Sargent, eds. *Small Wars: The Cultural Politics of Childhood*. Berkeley, CA: University of California Press, 1998. Ethnographic collection that takes modernity as a central concept, provocatively arguing that "the modern conception of the child as vulnerable and needing protection is giving way to that of the child as miniature adult, a full-circle return to Philippe Ariès's notion of pre-modern childhood."

Stephens, Sharon, ed. *Children and the Politics of Culture*. Princeton, NY: Princeton University Press, 1995. Anthropological volume whose introductory essay explores "the role of the child in structures of modernity."

Children and social inequalities/state structures

One major organizing theme that emerges from the study of childhood in Latin America is the importance of unequal childhoods and the intersection of childhood and the production of inequality.

Fonseca, Claudia. "Inequality Near and Far: Adoption as Seen from the Brazilian Favelas." *Law and Society Review* 36(2) (2002): 397–432. An ethnographic study of child circulation in a Brazilian shantytown.

Milanich, Nara. *Children of Fate: Childhood, Class and the State in Chile, 1850–1930*. Durham, NC: Duke University Press, 2009. Explores the social–legal construction of family and its relationship to class structures and state formation.

Premo, Bianca. *Children of the Father King: Youth, Authority, and Legal Minority in Colonial Lima*. Chapel Hill, NC: University of North Carolina Press, 2005. One of first monographic treatments of childhood in Latin America, it explores the relevance of social practices and political ideologies surrounding childhood to the structures of colonial society.

Children and labor

Not surprisingly, given the uneven and comparatively belated onset of industrial development in much of Latin America, children's factory work is not a major topic as it is in the North American and European historiography. A comparatively greater literature has grown up around children's domestic or household labor.

Blum, Ann. *Domestic Economies: Family, Work, and Welfare in Mexico City, 1884–1943*. Lincoln, NE: University of Nebraska Press, 2009. Pioneering work linking women and children's labor and welfare to changing state structures in pre- and post-revolutionary Mexico.

Milanich, Nara. "Degrees of Bondage: Children's Tutelary Servitude in Modern Latin America." In *Child Slaves in the Modern World*, edited by Gwynn Campbell, Suzanne Miers, and Joseph C. Miller. Athens, OH: Ohio State University Press, 2011. Argues that children's tutelary servitude helped bridge the transition from slavery to emancipation and that it is a specifically *modern* form of unfree labor.

Many works on slavery, abolition, and servitude that do not take childhood as an analytic focus nevertheless shed important light on children and labor:

Aguirre, Carlos. "Patrones, esclavos y sirvientes domésticos en Lima (1800–1860)." In *Familia y vida privada en la historia de Iberoamérica*, edited by Pilar Gonzalbo, and Cecilia Rabell. Mexico City: El Colegio de México, 1996.

Garcia Alaniz, Anna Gicelle. *Ingênuos e libertos: estratégias de sobrevivência familiar em épocas de transição, 1871–1895*, Campinas, Brazil: CMU/UNICAMP, 1997.

Gomes da Cunha, Olívia Maria. "Learning to Serve: Intimacy, Morality, and Violence," *Hispanic American Historical Review* 88(3) (2008): 455–491.

Matos Rodríguez, Félix V. "Quién trabajará: Domestic Workers, Urban Slaves, and the Abolition of Slavery in Puerto Rico." In *Puerto Rican Women's History: New Perspectives*, edited by Félix V. Matos Rodríguez and Linda Delgado, 62–82. Armonk, NY: M.E. Sharpe Publishers, 1998.

Meznar, Joan. "Orphans and the Transition to Free Labor in Northeast Brazil: The Case of Campina Grande, 1850–1888." *Journal of Social History* 27(3) (1994): 499–515.

Child circulation

Another major theme that distinguishes the historical-ethnographic literature on Latin American childhoods is child circulation.

Blum, Ann. "Public Welfare and Child Circulation, Mexico City, 1877–1925." *Journal of Family History* 23(3) (1998): 240–271.

Leinaweaver, Jessaca. *The Circulation of Children: Adoption, Kinship, and Morality in Andean Peru*. Durham, NC: Duke University Press, 2008. Ethnography of child circulation in post-civil conflict Peru.

Milanich, Nara. "Casa de Huérfanos and Child Circulation." *Journal of Social History* 38(2) (2004): 311–340.

Special issue. "Cultural and Political Economies of Adoption in Latin America." *Journal of Latin America and Caribbean Anthropology* 14(1) (2009). Includes important contributions by Leifsen, Leinaweaver, Seligman, Fonseca, etc.

Child saving

The pan-hemispheric and transnational context of child welfare initiatives in the first half of the twentieth century are brought into relief by:

Birn, Anne-Emanuelle. "The National–International Nexus in Public Health: Uruguay and the Circulation of Child Health and Welfare Policies, 1890–1940." *História, Ciências, Saúde – Manguinhos* 13(3) (2006): 675–708.

Guy, Donna. "The Pan American Child Congresses, 1916 to 1942: Pan Americanism, Child Reform, and the Welfare State in Latin America." *Journal of Family History* 23 (1998): 272–91.

Rojas, Jorge. "Los derechos del niño en Chile: una aproximación histórica, 1910–1930." *Historia* (Santiago, Chile) 40(1) (2007): 129–164.

Poverty, street children, infant mortality

Hecht, Tobias. *At Home on the Street: Street Children of Northeast Brazil*. Cambridge, UK: Cambridge University Press, 1998. An ethnography that critically scrutinizes public responses to street children as much as the children themselves. See also, Nancy Scheper-Hughes and Daniel Hoffman. "Brazilian Apartheid: Street Kids and the Struggle for Urban Space" In

Small Wars: The Cultural Politics of Childhood, edited by Nancy Scheper-Hughes, and Carolyn Sargent. Berkeley, CA: University of California Press, 1998.

Scheper-Hughes, Nancy. *Death Without Weeping: The Violence of Everyday Life in Brazil*. Berkeley, CA: University of California, 1992. A now classic, controversial ethnography about motherhood and infant mortality in a Brazilian favela; while the mothers are a more explicit focus than their children, the analysis nevertheless contains valuable insight into many aspects of childhood.

INDEX